PRAISE FOR

RUSH

"Entertaining . . . Benjamin Rush has been undeservedly forgotten. In medicine . . . [and] as a political thinker, he was brilliant."

—*The New Yorker*

"A perceptive analysis . . . reveal[s] a dedicated humanitarian with an enduring influence. . . . What Benjamin Rush characterized as 'the distant and more enlightened generations' are now better placed to judge him."

—*The Wall Street Journal*

"Reminds us eloquently, abundantly, what a brilliant, original man Benjamin Rush was, and how his contributions to Philadelphia and the United States continue to bless us all."

—*The Philadelphia Inquirer*

"An amazing life and a fascinating book."

—*CBS This Morning*

"Comprehensive and fascinating . . . Fried portrays Rush as a complex, flawed person and not just a list of accomplishments; . . . a testament to the authorial thoroughness and insight that will keep readers engaged until the last page."

—*Publishers Weekly* (starred review)

"[An] extraordinary and underappreciated man is reinstated to his rightful place in the canon of civilizational advancement in *Rush*. . . . [A] superb biography."

—*Brain Pickings*

"Fried, a talented story teller . . . has brought Declaration of Independence signer Benjamin Rush back to life for modern readers. . . . a most worthy addition to major biographies about the founding fathers."

—*Journal of the American Revolution*

"A biography with the color, detail and pace of a compelling historical novel. From the first page, Fried conjures up Rush as a flesh-and-blood human being rather than a steel-point engraving."

—*Jewish Journal*

"Dr. Benjamin Rush may not be a household name, but the young signatory of the Declaration of Independence led a remarkable life. . . . Historian Stephen Fried has brought this lesser-known revolutionary figure to life."

—WHYY

"Well crafted . . . a biography of a Founding Father, physician, and founder of psychiatric medicine. Quite a literary undertaking, and done with skill and grace."

—*The Lancet Psychiatry*

"Fried is able to bring a bygone era into focus. . . . a sweeping look at a complicated life."

—*Santa Fe New Mexican*

"A welcome biography of a Founding Father . . . renowned in the annals of American medicine as a pioneer of medical education and the treatment of the mentally ill . . . A complete portrait of a complex man . . . who excited attention and controversy in his day but then fell into the shadows. Fried does well to restore him to history."

—*Kirkus Reviews*

"An invaluable addition to American history collections and a solid recommendation to biography fans."

—*Booklist*

"The best books are full of surprises. *Rush* has more of them than any historical biography I have read in ages. It is vast and sumptuous and brings to life Founding Father Benjamin Rush in full Technicolor. Too long ignored, Rush's varied and mercurial brilliance puts him smack in the company of such figures as Adams and Jefferson and Washington and Hamilton with one exception: he is more interesting than any of them. He revolutionized *medicine*. He revolutionized *health care*. He revolutionized *life*. Fried draws it all out with his usual perfect pitch of reportage and writing. What a grand feast and feat."

—Buzz Bissinger, author of *Friday Night Lights* and *A Prayer for the City*

"Benjamin Rush is best known as the Founding Father the more famous founders wrote to. Stephen Fried, in this fascinating biography, shows us why we need to reconsider and pay more attention to a man whose talents rivaled Franklin's, opinions equaled Adams's, and facility with language approached Jefferson's."

—H. W. Brands, author of *The First American* and *Heirs of the Founders*

"Stephen Fried has written a gem of a book—the riveting story of a Founding Father who is too often forgotten. In this magnificent work, Benjamin Rush gets the biography he deserves, and readers get an expertly researched, splendidly written account of a brilliant, influential man."

—Jonathan Eig, author of *Ali: A Life*

"Anyone who cares about our past and future—politically, medically, spiritually—should read this masterful biography."

—Congressman Patrick J. Kennedy, coauthor of *A Common Struggle*

"An important and fascinating account of a relatively neglected yet critical Founding Father . . . Stephen Fried brings to life Rush's extraordinary political and medical contributions, as well as the times in which he lived."

—Kay Redfield Jamison, author of *An Unquiet Mind* and *Robert Lowell: Setting the River on Fire*

RUSH

ALSO BY STEPHEN FRIED

Appetite for America

A Common Struggle (with Patrick Kennedy)

Thing of Beauty

The New Rabbi

Bitter Pills

Husbandry

RUSH

REVOLUTION, MADNESS, AND THE VISIONARY DOCTOR WHO BECAME A FOUNDING FATHER

STEPHEN FRIED

B\D\W\Y
BROADWAY BOOKS
NEW YORK

Published in the United States by Broadway Books, an imprint of
Random House, a division of Penguin Random House LLC, New York.
crownpublishing.com

Broadway Books and its logo, B \ D \ W \ Y,
are trademarks of Penguin Random House LLC.

Originally published in hardcover in the United States by Crown,
an imprint of Random House,
a division of Penguin Random House LLC, New York, in 2018.

Library of Congress Cataloging-in-Publication Data
Names: Fried, Stephen, author.
Title: Rush : Revolution, madness, and the visionary doctor who became a
founding father / by Stephen Fried.
Description: First Edition. | New York : Crown Publishing, [2018] | Includes
bibliographical references.
Identifiers: LCCN 2018016147| ISBN 9780804140065 (Hardcover) | ISBN
9780804140089 (Trade Paperback) | ISBN 9780804140072 (eBook)
Subjects: LCSH: Rush, Benjamin, 1746–1813. | United States. Declaration of
Independence—Signers—Biography.
Classification: LCC E302.6.R85 F75 2018| DDC 973.3092 B LC record
available at https://lccn.loc.gov/2018016147

ISBN 978-0-8041-4008-9
Ebook ISBN 978-0-8041-4007-2

Printed in the United States of America

Book design by Elina D. Nudelman
Map by David Lindroth Inc.

10 9 8 7 6 5 4 3

TO MY DEAREST DIANE

CONTENTS

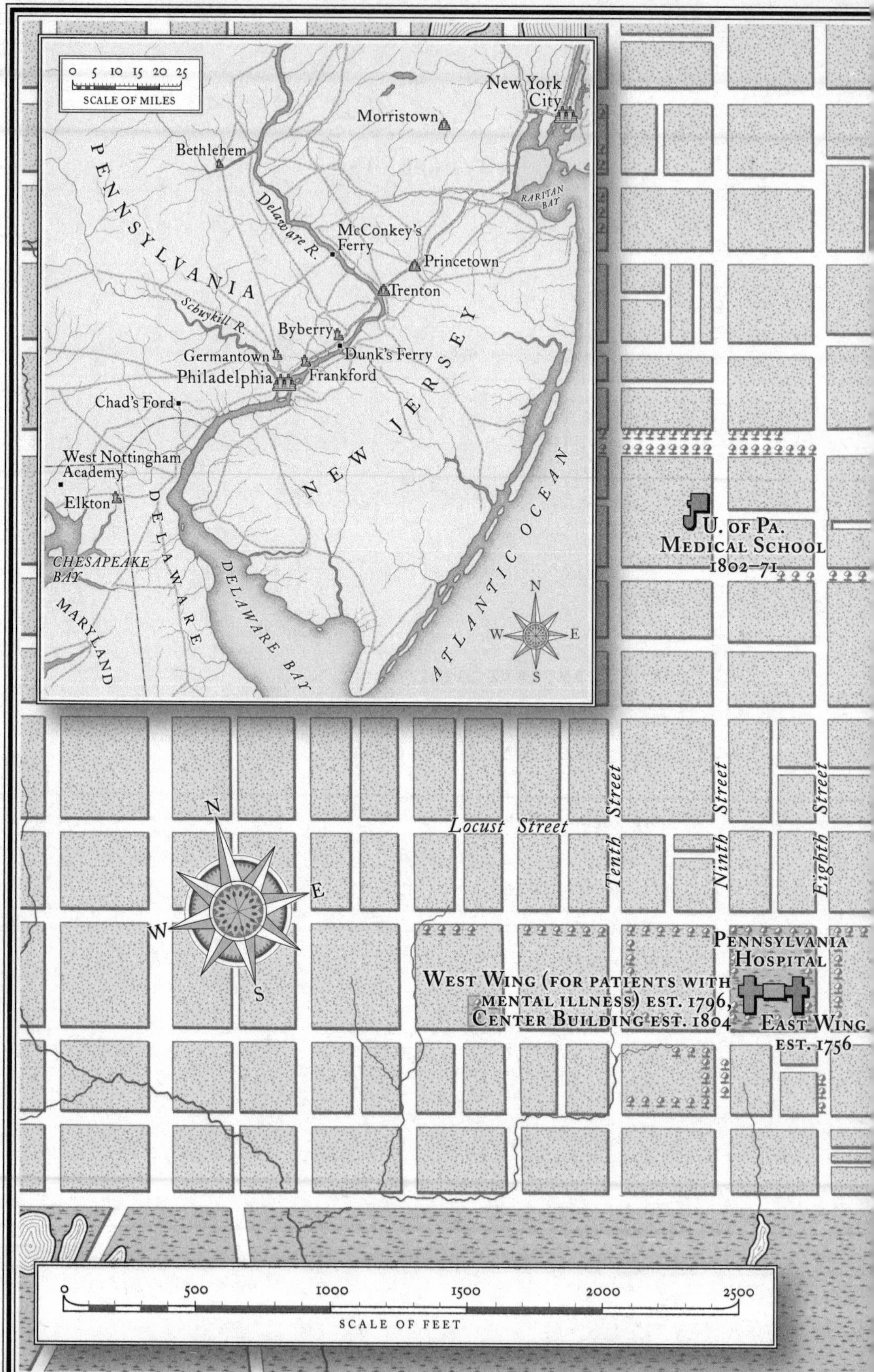
0 5 10 15 20 25
SCALE OF MILES
New York City
Morristown
Bethlehem
PENNSYLVANIA
RARITAN BAY
Delaware R.
McConkey's Ferry
Princetown
Trenton
Schuylkill R.
Byberry
Germantown
Dunk's Ferry
Philadelphia
Frankford
NEW JERSEY
Chad's Ford
West Nottingham Academy
Elkton
DELAWARE
CHESAPEAKE BAY
MARYLAND
DELAWARE BAY
ATLANTIC OCEAN
N
W
E
S
U. of Pa. Medical School 1802–71
Locust Street
Tenth Street
Ninth Street
Eighth Street
Pennsylvania Hospital
West Wing (for patients with mental illness) est. 1796,
Center Building est. 1804
East Wing est. 1756
0 500 1000 1500 2000 2500
SCALE OF FEET

Race Street
Medical School:
College of Philadelphia/
U. of State of Pa./U. of PA
1749–1802
Original
Rush Home
Front Street
Arch Street
Christ Church
Burial Ground
Seventh Street
Fifth Street
Fourth Street
Christ
Church
London
Coffee House
Market
Street
Third Street
President's House
1790–1800
Aitken
Bookshop
Rush Home
1786–89
Congress Hall
1790–1800
Pa. State House
(Independence Hall)
Chestnut Street
Rush Home
1780–86
Water Street
American
Philosophical
Society
Carpenters'
Hall
Surgeons'
Hall
Rush Home
1770s
Delaware River
Walnut Street
Rush Home
1796–1806
Rush Home
1789–91
African
Episcopal
Church of
St. Thomas
Dock St.
Rush Home 1791–93
Yellow Fever
Epidemic
Rush Home
1794–96 & 1806–13
Second Street
Spruce Street
Sixth Street
Pine Street
Mother Bethel
AME Church
Lombard Street
Front Street
South Street

PROLOGUE

In the late morning of August 29, 1774, a well-worn carriage made its way down dusty King's Highway, along the Pennsylvania side of the Delaware River just below Trenton.

In the carriage were the four members of the Massachusetts delegation to the first Continental Congress—including John Adams, a scruffy, gregarious thirty-eight-year-old lawyer, who was extremely anxious about the future of his country. He had written to his wife, Abigail, the evening before about how it would feel to finally arrive in Philadelphia at the "Theatre of Action," where he hoped that "God Almighty" would grant him and his colleagues "Wisdom and Virtue sufficient for the high Trust that is devolved upon Us."

But Adams also had some less lofty concerns. After more than two weeks on the road during the sultriest time of the year, he was sweaty and stinky and in desperate need of clean clothes. He had six shirts, five pairs of stockings, two caps, a pair of worsted stockings, and one silk handkerchief awaiting a laundress the moment they got to town.

Their carriage soon arrived in the farm town of Frankford, five miles north of the city, where Adams and his group were to be met by a local delegation. They presumed these would be like-minded

Pennsylvanians who believed in the cause of freedom from England and would laud their bravery; Massachusetts was, so far, the primary place where colonists and British troops had clashed. The delegation also included John's older cousin Samuel, a leader of the Sons of Liberty, who had instigated the recent Boston Tea Party.

Instead, the Philadelphians, after exchanging pleasantries and bringing the New Englanders to a nearby apartment for drinks in a private room, proceeded to tell their guests the last thing they expected to hear.

"You must not utter the word 'Independence,' nor give the least hint or insinuation of the idea, neither in Congress or any private conversation," Adams would later recall being warned. "If you do, you are undone." If they wanted this historic meeting of colonies to make any progress, the Philadelphians insisted, they needed to shut up with all their open talk about liberty.

Their hosts also lectured Adams and his colleagues about strategy. While they were "the representatives of the suffering state" and might reasonably expect to speak loudest, the Philadelphians advised that "you must not pretend to take the lead." Virginia, the largest colony, would be the key actor in bringing the southern and middle colonies into a union, and the Virginians would need to feel they were in charge. Adams and his colleagues had to suck it up and defer to them.

Perhaps more unexpected than the bold advice was that one of its loudest and most energetic proponents was the youngest and least known member of the welcome party: a twenty-eight-year-old physician named Benjamin Rush. He was one of the only people in the room who hadn't been selected as a delegate to the historic Continental Congress. And the closest he was going to get to that historic meeting in Carpenters' Hall was that every Tuesday at ten a.m. he and another young doctor gave free smallpox inoculations at the nearby State House.

But Benjamin Rush made quite a first impression. He was tall, lean, and handsome with active blue-gray eyes and an aquiline nose. His long blond-brown hair, tied back in a loose ponytail, accentuated his most prominent feature: an uncommonly large head. To some, the size of his skull bespoke "strength and activity of in-

Unpublished earliest image of Dr. Benjamin Rush

tellect," while others viewed him as having a head overfull of ideas he couldn't keep to himself.

Unlike the pedigreed doctors who had trained him in America, Scotland, England, and France, Dr. Rush was a medical and political prodigy from a middle-class family on the humbler side of Philadelphia. He had lost his father, a gunsmith, at the age of five, leaving him and his five siblings to be raised by their mother, who opened a package goods store and tavern just down the street from Benjamin Franklin's print shop and post office. But because of young Rush's astonishing mind—besides total recall, he had what he referred to as the "peculiar happiness" of being able to synthesize and humanize disparate ideas into searing rhetoric—he had finished school at thirteen, graduated from the College of New Jersey (now known as Princeton) at fourteen, finished medical training in Edinburgh and London at twenty-two, and begun practicing and teaching medicine at twenty-three. He was still single in his late twenties because his family had convinced him it would be bad for his career to marry before thirty.

All John Adams knew about Rush at that moment was that the lanky doctor was spellbindingly sure of himself. He talked *a lot.* Yet it wasn't quite clear where this promiscuously opinionated young fellow fit into this group of established lawyers and business leaders.

As they left the tavern, Rush managed to switch carriages so he could ride back to town with Adams and another Massachusetts delegate. Without his fellow Philadelphians around, he proceeded to fill in Adams on the local political gossip, warning him about citizens he would meet who might seem friendly enough to his cause but would, ultimately, remain committed to the Crown—because they were loyalists, pacifists, or haters of change. Rush seemed to understand people unusually well for a man so young, and his analysis moved easily from politics to religion to medicine to the calculus of liberty.

Adams listened and carefully asked questions. He did not completely engage with Rush, and the young doctor could sense it. Rush later described their first conversation as "cold and reserved." And when Adams mentioned Rush for the first time in his journal, it was several weeks later, and only to comment about how good the food was when the doctor had him and other congressmen over for dinner. The melons especially were "fine beyond description."

WHEN THEY MET that August day in 1774, Adams could not have imagined how important Benjamin Rush would become to him, to the revolution, and to the new nation—how this headstrong young man would become a Founding Father; a transformative writer and lecturer; and the nation's most famous, powerful, and controversial physician, who knew his fellow patriots as intimate friends, rivals, and patients. But Rush would surprise Adams, as he did so many others.

Before the Continental Congress met, Rush was already a protégé of Benjamin Franklin—who provided introductions, once Rush finished medical school in Scotland, for the young doctor to dine with Enlightenment luminaries, including Samuel Johnson and David Hume. Rush returned to America as one of four professors at the first medical school in the colonies. As a young writer and inconvenient truth teller, he had already made his mark on some of the social and political causes he would wrestle with throughout his life. Between medical publications, he had penned one of the boldest abolitionist pamphlets ever published, and had quietly coauthored the Philadelphia anti-tax proclamation the Sons of Liberty had adopted to justify the Boston Tea Party.

Energized by the contagious spirit of the congress, Rush went on to serve the revolution as a doctor, a politician, a social reformer, an educational visionary, and even an activist editor—when, in 1775, he convinced an unknown writer named Thomas Paine to write

"Common Sense," which Rush then edited, titled, and brought to a publisher. The doctor went from gleaning political gossip from dinner guests in 1774 to, after being elected to the Second Continental Congress in 1776 at the age of thirty, signing the Declaration of Independence. (He also married, after falling in love with seventeen-year-old Julia Stockton, the daughter of a fellow signer.)

He treated patients throughout the war, taking time off from Congress to triage troops. He crossed the Delaware that cold December night along with General George Washington's forces, patched up shot and bayonetted soldiers on the bloody battlefields of Trenton and Princeton, and survived being briefly captured during the Battle of Brandywine. He went on to serve as a surgeon general and adviser to Washington, but he would eventually leave the war—and the government—over a political showdown that led to the court martial of a former mentor.

Before leaving, he penned a pamphlet that would transform military medicine in America and become a standard guide for soldiers and officers in too many wars, its opening line still resonant today: "Fatal experience has taught the people of America the truth . . . that a greater proportion of men perish with sickness in all armies than fall by the sword."

At the age of thirty-two, Rush retreated to Philadelphia to navigate the limbo years after British occupation and the successful end of the war. There, as he and Julia raised a growing family, he came to understand that the American Revolution was not over at all—that in fact it had barely begun. His new nation would need more than a Constitution to thrive: it would have to define and encourage a new form of active, responsible citizenship. While building his medical career at America's first hospital and first medical school, Rush also recommitted to politics and made it his mission to identify and champion the causes the American people would have to embrace to become what he called "republican machines"—upholders of the new democracy.

In a landmark speech delivered at the American Philosophical Society on February 27, 1786, Rush diagnosed the challenge of the newly united states. The struggle, he said, would be to balance "science, religion, liberty and good government." He would spend the rest of his life trying to embody that balance, through writing, teaching, and the building of associations and institutions, amassing several careers' worth of accomplishments.

Over the next three decades Rush became the most prominent physician and public health advocate in America, and one of the few American public intellectuals whose writings were read in Europe. His 1786 speech also provided the groundwork for his most lasting contribution to medicine: fusing his ideas about equality and republicanism with clinical work, he declared that mental illness and addiction were medical conditions and deserved to be treated as such. At Pennsylvania Hospital he enacted this philosophy, laying the foundation for the development of psychiatry, clinical psychology, and addiction medicine.

Outside the hospital, Rush became the nation's loudest advocate for public schooling, helping open education to women, to African Americans, and to non-English-speaking immigrants. He founded the nation's first rural college, Dickinson, in far-off central Pennsylvania. He also rejoined the abolition movement and the battle against racial prejudice. Defying public opinion and Philadelphia's religious establishment, he helped young African American clergymen found and fund two of the nation's first churches led by and for black worshippers.

Rush played a key role in the ratification of the U.S. Constitution; though a man of deep faith himself, he was one of the nation's first resonant voices to argue for the separation of church and state, and for the protection of religious liberty.

As the U.S. Capitol returned to Philadelphia in 1790, just after the death of its most beloved native son, Franklin, Rush did his best to become the nation's next Benjamin.

In the following years he grew closer to Presidents Adams and Jefferson, along with other founders in the new government, who came to rely on Rush for medical care, intellectual stimulation, and the best local gossip. In private and public he wrote with expanding breadth and sometimes humor. Adams loved Rush's rants on issues such as American materialism ("We are indeed a bebanked, and a bewhiskied & a bedollared nation") but also knew the doctor had been keeping notes for years about revolutionary personalities and intrigues, including spot-on sketches of every signer and important military leader. (Rush's three-word assessment of himself in his Founding Father burn book: "He aimed well.")

Jefferson would declare, "I read with delight every thing that comes from your pen."

Yet, after years in the new American spotlight, both Rush and Philadelphia were nearly destroyed by the most horrific medical crisis in the history of the new world: the 1793 yellow fever epidemic. Rush, among a handful of prominent doctors who didn't flee the city, became a public health hero to many, though also a villain to those who considered his high-dose purges and bloodletting to be less heroic than extreme. While his wife and children were sent away for their safety, his sister, Rebecca, stayed to take care of him. She died of yellow fever, as did several of his apprentices and many of his friends. He narrowly escaped death himself.

In just three months, almost 10 percent of the capital's population was lost. Neither the country nor Dr. Rush would be quite the same.

He held his life together, just barely, with the help of his wife and children, his colleagues and students, and the friendship of John and Abigail Adams. While Rush and President Adams developed political disagreements as the nation split into Federalists and Republicans, they had much in common personally. They were both married to strong, bright women they relied upon as reality checks. And among their broods of children, each had a son who was a rising star: Rush's son Richard would become a cabinet member for three presidents, including Adams's son John Quincy, whom he also served as a vice presidential running mate. Each also had an equally promising son overwhelmed by private struggles. Adams's son Charles died from alcoholism at the age of thirty, just as Adams lost the presidential election of 1800 to Thomas Jefferson. Several years later, Rush's eldest child, Lt. John Rush, a navy surgeon he had hoped would take over his practice, descended into mental illness, triggered in part by a tragic duel. He would spend the rest of his life in his father's care, and his situation would inspire Rush's last and most influential book, the first American volume on "diseases of the mind."

ADAMS CUT OFF all contact with Rush after his bitter defeat in the election of 1800. Rush remained in touch with Jefferson, who made him medical adviser to the Lewis & Clark expedition. But he didn't hear from Adams for nearly five years, until the aging president decided to reach out, with one of the great first lines in American letters: "it seemeth unto me that you and I ought not to die without saying good-bye."

His letter reignited an impassioned correspondence that stretched over their remaining years and allowed two old founding friends to retell their own stories and the story of their nation with unique perspective, humor, and candor. Rush eventually used the correspondence to try and heal the broken friendship between Adams and Jefferson, which he considered his duty as a friend and a patriot. He worked on each of them for years, in what would be his final act as a Founding Father. Not long before his death, they reconnected.

Adams wrote that Rush had contributed more to the American Revolution than Franklin—beginning with what the doctor and his fellow Philadelphia Sons of Liberty told him the day they met in 1774. Adams once told a cabinet member that without that surprising advice, "Mr. Washington would never have commanded our armies, nor Mr. Jefferson have been the Author of the declaration of Independence. . . . This conversation and the principles facts and motives suggested in it . . . [gave] a colour complection and character to the whole policy of the United States."

THROUGH IT ALL, Benjamin Rush contended openly and engagingly with the same challenge he had put to the new nation: how to be a man of science, a man of liberty, and a man of faith—all while striving to be a good friend, husband, and father of nine children. Rush was a medical pioneer and a political pathfinder, donating his time, his money, even, at times, his sanity for the causes he worried were beyond the reach of laws. His life and writings provide a guided tour through the most public and private moments of the Revolution and the creation of America, seen through the eyes—

first awestruck, then frustrated, and finally worldly wise—of a physician and reformer who was, in every sense, revolutionary.

And yet, after Rush died in 1813 at the age of sixty-eight, those who loved him most, and best understood his achievements, took steps that prevented his full story from being told.

Rush had been controversial in many ways. He was referred to as "the American Hippocrates," sometimes as a compliment but other times as an insult to his outsized ego. He openly criticized powerful slave owners—even during the ten years after the war when he owned an enslaved person himself. He had questioned George Washington's leadership when the war was at its bleakest, for which the general, once his friend, never forgave him.

The recriminations over the 1793 yellow fever epidemic never really ended—including a fight between Rush and his neighbor, Alexander Hamilton, who claimed to have been cured by another doctor with a milder treatment (leading Jefferson to claim Hamilton had never been sick in the first place). As each summer ended, fear and loathing of yellow fever and its treatments returned in major American port cities. While this made Rush even more famous, his popular books and public persona made him an even riper target. He even got caught up in—and won—one of the nation's first major libel trials to defend his reputation and treatments.

All his life, his capacious mind was paired with a fast, glib tongue, and he was sometimes caught rushing ideas into print before he had thought them through. Yet, in the end, it wasn't so much what he had said and done that made his most powerful friends worry. It was what they had told him. Adams and Jefferson especially had shared years of confidences about their feelings, their politics, their religion—even their bathroom habits—with Dr. Rush: the kind of information men mindful of their legacies might not want entering the historical record. Rush was the founder who knew too much.

Only weeks after Rush's death, Jefferson urged his family to return the most revealing letters he had sent the doctor. He feared how "bigots in religion, in politics, or in medicine" might react if they were ever allowed to read them. And when a writer approached Adams about publishing a collection of the great doctor's correspondence with him, the former president admitted, "I shudder at the thought. A complete collection of Dr. Rushes letters never will be published, or if they should, they would excite as much surprise and as much learned controversy and more factious Fury, than if a collection of Hypocrates had been dug out of the Ruins of Herculaneium."

Newspapers at the time compared the death of Benjamin Rush to the loss of Washington and Franklin, and he was mourned across the country. But beginning with Adams and Jefferson, and helped along by his own family—especially his politically ascendant son, Richard, who had his own reasons for suppressing his father's writing—his legacy dimmed. He became a footnoted founder, a second-tier signer.

As a result, many Americans know very little about Benjamin Rush.

I THINK ABOUT this a lot while sitting on the small bench near his grave at Christ Church Burial Ground in Philadelphia's historic district. The original six-foot-high redbrick wall still surrounds the cemetery, guarding it from the present and separating it from the large buildings now nearby: the National Constitution Center and the U.S. Mint. The bench is near the oak tree under which Rush and his family are buried. His grave is the most prominent in the family plot, a large but simple sarcophagus. He is flanked by his wife and his mother. And nearby, marked by a headstone eerily eroded so only the tops of the letters are slightly visible, are two John Rushes who haunted him: his father, who died too soon, and his son, who was felled by mental illness.

The doctor spends eternity here with Benjamin Franklin and three other signers of the Declaration; with Dr. Thomas Bond, who started America's first hospital with Franklin and helped mentor Rush; with Dr. Philip Syng Physick, one of Rush's protégés who later became known as the "Father of American Surgery"; with Matthew Clarkson, who was mayor of Philadelphia during the three months that made and unmade Rush, the 1793 yellow fever epidemic; with John Dunlap, one of Rush's publishers and the first printer of the Declaration; and with others of Rush's friends and patients.

The bench is a peaceful place, a perfect spot to ponder the questions about life in America that Benjamin Rush was one of the first to ask—of himself and of his towering contemporaries, whose intentions we debate to this day. What all this questioning about liberty, morality, and equality came down to, for Rush, was *health*, in the broadest definition of the word. Physical health, mental health, spiritual health, economic health, political health, public and private health. He saw the American experiment through the prism of diagnosis; he saw everything that was wrong as something that could be treated; and he saw every lost patient as an opportunity to save the next.

He also understood, as a physician and scientist, how many things he knew for certain would later be proved wrong; how many diseases, medical and social, could appear to be cured but later recur. In this was the "peculiar happiness" of cautious optimism, the comfort and discomfort of the truly long view.

History would one day rediscover and appreciate Rush, he was certain of it. As he once wrote: "The most acceptable men in practical society, have been those who have never shocked their contemporaries, by opposing popular or common opinions. Men of opposite characters, like objects placed too near the eye, are seldom seen distinctly by the age in which they live. They must content themselves with the prospect of being useful to the distant and more enlightened generations which are to follow them."*

---

* All quotations in this book, unless otherwise attributed, come directly from the writings of Dr. Benjamin Rush: from the autobiography, *Travels through Life*, that he wrote for his children in 1800; his commonplace books; his voluminous private and professional correspondence (which is still being discovered); his travel journals; or his many published books, essays, and lectures. I have done my best to let the doctor and his contemporaries write and talk as they did, retaining whenever possible the original spelling, capitalization, and punctuation, no matter how counterintuitive, and offering correct spellings in brackets only when absolutely necessary. I'd like to think that, as a man of medicine, Rush would have appreciated that I didn't use "sic" even once.

part one

TURBULENT SPIRIT

1

Benjamin Rush's "first *unwelcome* noise in the world" rang out from a second-floor bedroom of the stone farmhouse in Byberry, northeast of Philadelphia, on Christmas Eve, 1745.

His cries were heard downstairs in the first-floor common room, where the Rush family had been gathering at the hearth for three generations. The room had gone from a place for "conversations about wolves and bears and snakes in the first settlement of the farm" to a place for discussions "about cows, and calves and colts and lambs, and the comparative exploits of reapers and mowers and threshers," as Rush's grandfather had shifted from simple farming to metalwork, and Rush's father, John, developed as a talented blacksmith and gunsmith.

The news of Benjamin's birth was greeted with thanks to God. The Rush family were "pious people," their conversations infused "at all times with prayers and praises, and chapters read audibly from the Bible."

The Rushes were also quietly defiant people. An old sword hung in the farmhouse—and in every subsequent place Benjamin Rush lived—that had been carried into battle by his great-grandfather, John, a horse trooper in Oliver Cromwell's army during its fight against the Crown in the English Civil War. The family had left the Church of England to become Quakers, then fled England for

America with William Penn in 1683. There they split off from their original Quaker group of Byberry Friends in 1691, before departing Quakerism altogether to become Baptists, and eventually circling back around to the Church of England.

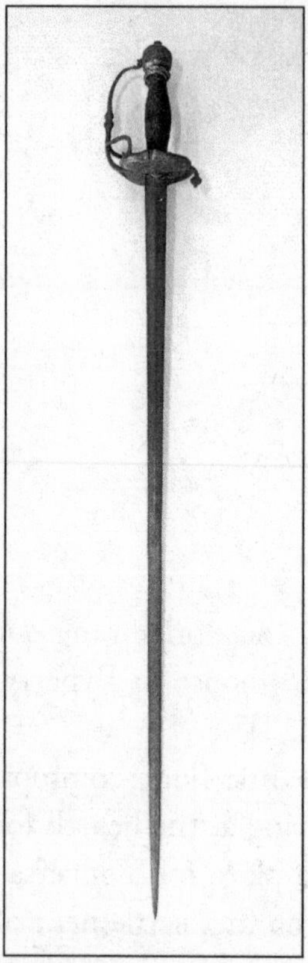

Rush's great-grandfather's sword

Benjamin Rush was the fourth of seven children and the second-eldest son. His father, John, was quiet and stolid, and what he lacked in formal education he made up for with hard work and "a talent for observation and combination"—an ability to understand people and connect dots that others didn't even see. While he didn't talk a lot, what he said was often notable; Rush's mother remembered that when their children began to speak, her husband said, "The first words of a child, and the last words of a saint, are the sweetest music in the world." Rush's mother, Susanna Hall Rush, was five years older than John and came from a more affluent family in nearby Tacony. She had attended boarding school in Philadelphia and was considered "a woman of a very extraordinary mind," full of energy and insight. She had been married once before, a pairing recalled as "unfortunate" and "full of misery," ending with her husband dying young of "extravagance and intemperance."

Rush spent the first several years of his life on the family farm, with his older brother James, his sisters Rachel and Rebecca, and a younger brother, Jacob: five children born over seven years. Susanna raised them with help from her daughter from her previous marriage, a cook, and several farmhands. Rush's strongest memories of the farm were of the apple orchard his father cultivated, and a "small but deep creek abounding with pan fish." The boys fished, shot and hunted, learning respect for the guns their father made and repaired—flintlock pistols, muskets, and the new American long rifle.

Rush was a thin, sturdy boy, with light-colored hair, expressive blue-gray eyes, a long nose, and a thin-lipped mouth that he almost never shut. He was aggressively curious about facts, opinions, Scripture, and people, to the point of seeming intellectually and personally nosy. He was clearly precocious but was not as serious-minded as his parents would have liked. "Those who knew me at that time," he recalled, "would remember me only as an idle, playful, and I am sorry to add, sometimes a mischievous boy."

Besides the farm in Byberry, John Rush's family owned property in Philadelphia, thirteen miles southwest down the Delaware River. There was more demand there for his talents, so he began working in the city, setting up shop in a building his mother's family owned. Eventually he decided to leave the farm and move his family from the serene countryside into what was becoming the largest city in the American colonies—where life was percolating, screeching, and reeking of whichever way the wind was blowing.

Philadelphia had just overtaken Boston as the most populated city in America, with over fifteen thousand of its 1.2 million inhabitants, and Pennsylvania was becoming the most powerful American colony. The city was in the midst of an American-style Enlightenment, much of it instigated, or at least personified, by the celebrated Benjamin Franklin. Tall and solidly built, with long, light brown hair and a wide, easy smile, Franklin was now in his early forties. As a teenager, he had moved to Philadelphia from Boston, gotten involved in the printing business, and founded the famed Junto, a combination salon and debating society that became a cornerstone of free thinking and the propagation of what he called "useful knowledge." He then helped create a successful newspaper, the *Pennsylvania Gazette*, wrote and published the contagiously quotable *Poor Richard's Almanac*, and began using his powers of civic persuasion to convince fellow citizens to help him build new institutions, including the first volunteer fire company, the first fire insurance company, and the first public library. In 1748, with change still coming too slowly for him, he retired from his printing business to dedicate his life to scientific study, politics, and civic entrepreneurship.

The Rush family arrived in town in the late 1740s, just as some of Franklin's most ambitious and transformative projects were coming to fruition. Thanks to his efforts herding rich and smart people, Philadelphia suddenly had the nation's first secular college and its first public hospital; in his spare time, Franklin had just published a paper proposing to prove lightning was electricity by experimenting with a kite in a storm.

John Rush settled his family in a house at number 82 N. Front Street, just a block north of the city's main commercial thoroughfare, its spinal cord. The wide avenue had originally been named High Street, like the main street in most English cities. But because William Penn had designed a large outdoor market to run up its center, with stalls that were busy year round, everyone referred to the street as "Market." (The produce sellers were often called the "Jersey Market," because so many of them brought produce and animals across from New Jersey on barges.) On either side of Market Street were many of the city's main stores and business offices, including, on the 300 block, Franklin's print shop and home.

Just north of Market on Second Street was Christ Church—the city's largest and most prestigious, at that time affiliated with the Church of England. Franklin worshipped there on Sundays in his family's reserved pew. While Rush's mother was Presbyterian, and had been raising the children in her faith on the farm, when they moved into town John had the family join Christ Church in part because it was the right thing to do for business; Benjamin Rush was baptized there and it was the first place he ever "heard divine worship."

Just south of Market on Chestnut at Fifth was the Pennsylvania State House, the seat of government for the commonwealth. Because political business was booming, too, the colonial assembly had decided to expand the building, with an addition topped off by the city's tallest structure: its first major clock tower with a new bell, the largest in the colonies, which would be used to mark time, sound for official meetings, and ring out for fires and other emergencies.

Just across the way from the Rushes' front door was the vast port of Philadelphia itself, the most active and profitable in America. It was crowded with boats from around the colonies and the world, which arrived there by sailing south, below the southern tip of New Jersey, and then up through Delaware Bay to the river. Philadelphia was bounded by another, smaller river to the West, the Schuylkill—but that was thirty blocks from the Delaware, almost in the countryside, and therefore much less of a thoroughfare. A tributary of the Delaware, the Dock Creek, flowed into the city around Spruce Street and served mostly as an open sewer and a place for local tanneries and other businesses to dump their waste.

Port of Philadelphia, as seen from New Jersey, drawn about five years after the Rush family moved into town; Pennsylvania State House is the tallest building

John Rush's blacksmith shop was on the first floor of a three-story redbrick building, and the family lived upstairs. Benjamin enjoyed the sounds and tactile pleasures of his father's heavy iron tools and the flintlock rifles and pistols he built and repaired. It didn't take John long to build up his business; more and more men were carrying guns instead of swords, so demand was good, and he developed a dependable reputation. As a child, Benjamin Rush often heard that one of the highest compliments you could receive in the neighborhood was to be told you were "as honest as John Rush."

John and Susanna Rush had two more children in Philadelphia: a daughter, Stephenson, who died within a year, followed by a son, whom they named John. But not long after the birth of his namesake, in the summer of 1751, John Rush unexpectedly died. He was only thirty-nine years old, and his mischievous son Ben (as he was called then) was only five and a half. Almost nothing is known about John Rush's death, and his son never speculated on what illness took him. He only related that "his death was peaceful and happy" and "the last words he uttered were 'Lord! Lord! Lord! Lord!'"

Weeks after her husband's death, Susanna Rush also lost her new baby. Father and son were buried together, on August 19, 1751, at the Christ Church burial ground. And Susanna Rush, then forty-four, was left to raise three boys and two girls ranging in age from four to twelve. Her situation became more grim when it became clear her husband had not left her enough money to support the family and school the children.

That fall, while settling his estate, she was forced to rent out his shop space and sell off his blacksmithing tools. She also offered for sale several people she could no longer afford, beginning with a "likely negroe woman [who] has had the small-pox and measles," as she advertised in the *Pennsylvania Gazette*. In an expanded version of the advertisement, two months later, she offered "to be sold two Negro women, one of which has two children, can do all manner of house-work and is fit for both town or country business."

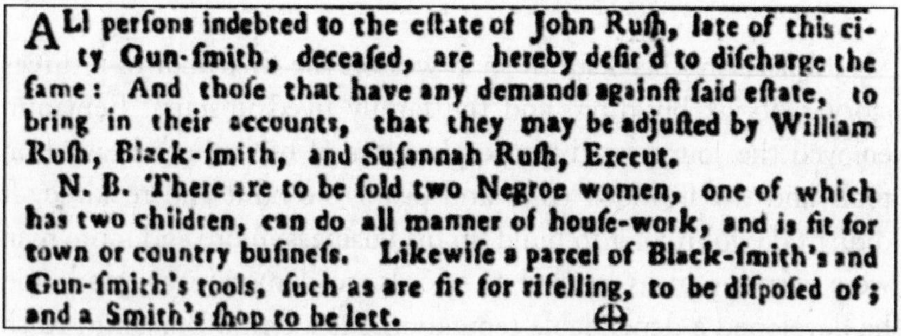
ALl perſons indebted to the eſtate of John Ruſh, late of this city Gun-ſmith, deceaſed, are hereby deſir'd to diſcharge the ſame: And thoſe that have any demands againſt ſaid eſtate, to bring in their accounts, that they may be adjuſted by William Ruſh, Black-ſmith, and Suſannah Ruſh, Execut.

N. B. There are to be ſold two Negroe women, one of which has two children, can do all manner of houſe-work, and is fit for town or country buſineſs. Likewiſe a parcel of Black-ſmith's and Gun-ſmith's tools, ſuch as are fit for rifelling, to be diſpoſed of; and a Smith's ſhop to be lett.

Pennsylvania Gazette *ad December 31, 1751, taken out by Rush's mother*

These ads suggest that, at some point, either Susanna or her husband had inherited or bought slaves, at least one of whom might have been with them back on the farm. An ad several years later (when Rush was nine) shows her selling two more servants. One of them is described as "a white lad" who "has upwards of three years to serve"—which means he was probably an "indentured" servant, his exclusive employment paid and contracted for over a set period of time. The other, a twenty-seven-year-old "Negroe woman . . . an excellent cook, understands a dairy very well, and is fit for a gentleman's country house," was likely a slave.

Benjamin Rush never mentioned that his family owned slaves when he later started writing passionately against the practice. But these women were likely the first slaves he knew as a child, and they helped raise him. They certainly informed his earliest ideas about slavery and race—as did living a block and a half from the main slave auction stand for Philadelphia's port, located in front of the Indian King Tavern, on Market just past Second. It wasn't far from Rush's house, and he may very well have been able to hear the auctions from his bedroom window.

With the proceeds from the estate sale, Susanna Rush opened a store around the corner on the south side of Market Street, four doors below Second. Her shop didn't have a name, just a sign painted with what appeared to be a comet, so its location was "at the Sign of the Blazing Star." (Numbered addresses were uncommon; most stores oriented themselves by proximity to landmarks and street corners.) The store at the Blazing Star sold food and liquors, both wholesale and retail, and became fairly successful.

Susanna quit Christ Church and began worshipping instead at the Presbyterian meeting house two blocks away on Fourth Street. It was led by forty-nine-year-old Rev. Gilbert Tennent, a rousing Irish-born evangelical orator who, like his father before him, was considered part of the spiritual "Great Awakening" in the colonies. Besides her preference for Tennent's fiery sermons, the switch probably had something to do with the fact that her younger sister, Sarah Hall, had married a close friend of Tennent's, the Rev. Samuel Finley. After a period on the pulpit, Reverend Finley had left to start a boarding school in Maryland, the West Nottingham Academy, which was a favorite of well-to-do Philadelphia families.

Tennent seemed like a good father figure and role model for her boys. And Reverend Finley's boarding school, if she could save up the money to pay for it, would offer them a chance for a prestigious religious and secular education, under the watchful eye of family.

This was especially important for Benjamin, who even at age six was demonstrating what some called a "genius for learning." He had an astonishing memory—not only amazing recall but an ability to make subtle connections that was even more pronounced than his father's. Susanna felt certain that Benjamin would benefit from boarding school, imagining that he might be inspired to join the clergy himself someday and spread the gospel. She expected her youngest son, Jacob, to go to boarding school as well. However, she apparently did not have similar optimism for her eldest son, James. Six years older than Benjamin, he was, Rush recalled, "a young man of promising character" who was "much afflicted with a nervous disease" after his father's death; his physicians "advised a sea-life," so he left home as a teen to work on ships.

Susanna Rush worked hard to keep her household going and scrape together the money to send Benjamin and Jacob to school, building up her business and eventually buying another building on the other side of Market Street to open a china shop. She raised her family without a husband for nearly four years—along with a cook and a servant and her daughter from a previous marriage. And she prospered, as one of colonial Philadelphia's few female entrepreneurs.

She was not, however, as fortunate in love as in business. In 1755 she married a local distiller, Richard Morris, who Rush recalled as "rough, unkind and often abusive" to her. Luckily, by the time the new husband arrived—or perhaps because of his arrival—Benjamin and Jacob were away at school.

The West Nottingham Academy was sixty miles from Philadelphia, near where the Susquehanna River crosses from Pennsylvania into Maryland—a bucolic setting far from city life. The school building was a simple log structure, near the large stone mansion house where the headmaster, Finley, lived with his wife, Rush's Aunt Sarah, and their children. Over the next five years Benjamin and Jacob lived in the mansion as well, along with all the other boys studying at the academy. Between family, students, and employees, there were generally about thirty people on the West Nottingham grounds, all committed to the moral education of young men.

Rev. Samuel Finley was demanding of his students and extremely attentive to detail. Every morning and evening meal was begun not only with prayers but with the reading and analyzing of a scriptural extract. He was clear on what he believed and what he expected his students to believe, and almost anything could be a lesson. While later in his life Rush would explore different denominations of Christianity—and was tolerant of, and interested in, many different religious beliefs—he was certain that the core of his faith was rooted in Finley's instruction that he never entertain "a doubt of the divine origin of the Bible."

Rev. Samuel Finley

Finley had strict, detailed rules for everything, and Rush recalled that "the slightest act of incivility was reproved." Admonishment sometimes came in the form of humor; Finley had invented characters such as "Bill Slovenly," who was messy, and "Ned Short," who was temperamental. Every student at Nottingham knew he was supposed to aspire to be "Johnny Courtley," who embodied "all that was proper and amiable in the conduct of a young man." Other times Finley brought the entire school together to discuss what punishment a classmate deserved. "The instrument with which he corrected," Rush recalled vividly, "was a small switch which he broke from a tree. The part he struck was the palm of the hand, and that never more than three times."

It was the buildup to the punishment that made the biggest impact. Rush recalled Finley once talking for half an hour "exposing the folly and wickedness of an offense with the rod in his hand" as the student stood "trembling and weeping before him." Finally Finley raised the switch as high as his arm could reach, brought it down until just above the boy's palm, and barely tapped.

"There, go about your business," he said to the quivering young man. "I mean shame, and not pain [to] be your punishment."

Rush might have had such powerful memories of Finley's discipline because he was often in trouble himself. "The early part of my life," he admitted, "was spent in dissipation, folly, and in the practice of some of the vices to which young men are prone." The one bad thing about a boarding school in the country, especially for "city boys," was "the facility with which the amusements of hunting, gunning and the like are to be obtained is so great as to overpower the relish for study."

Still, Rush found Finley warm and welcoming, even when his reverend and schoolmaster—who was, after all, also his uncle—was displeased with his conduct. He felt less close to his aunt, whose occasionally explosive temper unnerved him. At the same time, Aunt Sarah was one of the first people whose challenging actions he viewed as out of her control and "occasioned by bad health."

Since the school was also part of a farm, Rush learned not only how to read and write in Latin and Greek but also how to cut and bale hay during harvest. Reaping took him a little longer to master, and he proudly wore a severe scar on one of his fingers from the sharp blade. But perhaps the most important lesson Rush learned at West Nottingham Academy concerned the merits of memorization. Finley was interested in not only what students learned but how they learned, even by rote until truer understanding was possible. He taught "habits of attention and recollection," grilling students at the table after church services for details of the day's sermon. For a student with a normal memory, Finley's methods might have been helpful. For Rush, they were tools to control and extend what was already becoming a superpower.

IN 1759 REVEREND Finley decided that young Benjamin Rush had learned everything he could at West Nottingham and that it was time he moved on to an institution of higher learning. Both Finley and Rush's family clergyman, Gilbert Tennent, were on the board of trustees of the College of New Jersey, or what is now Princeton University; many of the best students from Finley's academy ended up there. Most of them, however, didn't begin as young as Rush, who was only thirteen and a half when admitted. Applicants were given a passage from the New Testament in Greek to translate into Latin; Rush must have done pretty well, because despite his age he was admitted not as a freshman but as a junior.

The school had only fifty-eight students then; Nassau Hall, the center of the college's academic and religious life, was one of its only large buildings. As Rush began, the school was adjusting to a new president, Samuel Davies, a charismatic Presbyterian minister from Virginia in his mid-thirties. A friend of Finley and a fellow college trustee, Davies had been appointed when the previous president died from smallpox after several months in office.

Davies immediately took to Rush. "It was my happy lot," Rush recalled, "to attract a good deal of his attention." But the young man didn't feel particularly challenged at the college. He believed Davies gave him too much credit for knowledge and thinking: "the facility with which I committed his lessons to memory" caused Davies to give "me credit for much more capacity than I possessed." Still, Rush felt Davies inspired in him "a love of knowledge . . . and if I derived but little from his instructions, I was taught by him how to acquire" knowledge—which turned out to be more useful.

Rev. Samuel Davies

Under Davies's instruction, Rush came to love taking notes: while he read, while he listened, sometimes even while he talked, a pen and inkwell were always handy. Other teachers discouraged this practice, believing that memorandum books caused "the destruction of memories." But Rush felt strongly that recording facts, and even rewriting entire passages, was a creative process; instead of "producing an oblivion" of facts, "it imprints them more deeply in the memory." So while he studied the philosophy of John Locke, he did it using Locke's own preferred format for note-taking and knowledge-gathering, the "common place book" (or memorandum book). In the late 1600s, Locke had written an entire book just on his own methods of writing and organizing commonplace books.

While at college, Rush practiced listening while taking down what was being said as dictation. As he would later teach his own students, the recording of facts and thoughts "should be done directly or even indirectly, at all times, and in all places," since one "should always, like a plant, be in an absorbing state." If he had no pencil handy, he would knot a handkerchief as a reminder for later note-taking.

Rush habitually wrote only on the right-hand page of his commonplace books, so he would always have room to reread and add additional ideas. And then when he filled many left-hand pages, he would sometimes rewrite the commonplace books all over again, leaving new blank pages.

DURING HIS TWO years in Princeton, Rush befriended a local family that would influence his life profoundly. At the age of thirty, Richard Stockton was one of the most powerful lawyers in New Jersey; he was also an important trustee of the College of New Jersey, as his father had donated the land the school occupied and much of the money that built it. Stockton likely reached out to Rush because he too was an alumnus of West Nottingham Academy. Reverend Finley probably asked him to keep an eye on the young man and perhaps occasionally feed him.

The Stockton family lived in the Stony Brook neighborhood of Princeton, on land granted to the family by William Penn in the early 1700s. Richard Stockton had inherited his father's mansion, parts of which were being rebuilt after a recent fire. Stockton's wife, Annis Boudinot Stockton, had redesigned the house and its extensive new gardens.

A striking woman in her early twenties—petite with strong dark eyes and eyebrows—Annis was an equally devoted wife, mother, and poet. She had grown up in Philadelphia, not far from the Rush family. Her father had a shop next door to Ben Franklin's post office on Market Street, where he worked as a silversmith and repaired clocks, and the Franklins and the Boudinots were friendly. They had moved to New Jersey when her father set up a company there to drill for copper ore. When that didn't work out, they settled in a house near Nassau Hall, and her father became postmaster of Princeton.

Annis Boudinot Stockton, and her husband, Richard Stockton

Annis was mostly interested in writing, spinning out intense poetry and lyrical letters. By the time Rush met her, she was already one of the first published female authors in America. She had placed a poem in the *New-York Mercury*, where the editor described her as having "so fruitful and uncommon a Genius" that he was certain her poem would be "acceptable to all, but more especially to . . . female readers." She was also a member of a small, active group of intellectuals in Philadelphia.

Rush had never met a woman like Annis Stockton. He hadn't even known there *were* women like her. She had just recently given birth—to a daughter named Julia—yet she remained immersed in the world of writing and literature.

Rush and the Stockton family developed a great fondness for one another while he was in Princeton, and he was a repeat guest in their home as they rebuilt it, christening it Morven. He would spend many important moments of his life there.

On September 21, 1760, Benjamin Rush attended the valedictory address to his graduating class at the College of New Jersey; at fourteen, he was one of eleven students receiving a bachelor's degree that year. The commencement exercises were held in the prayer room in Nassau Hall, with many of Rush's mentors in attendance: Reverend Finley came from Maryland for the event, and Richard Stockton from Morven down the street. While Rev. Gilbert Tennent could not make it, his brother, the Rev. William Tennent, Jr., did. As was traditional, most of the commencement was performed in Latin. The students sang two songs composed by Davies, after which he delivered a stirring address on "Religion and Public Spirit."

Invoking the story of David, Davies implored his students to "imbibe and cherish a public spirit. Serve your generation. Live not for your selves, but the public. Be the servants of the Church; the servants of your Country; the servants of all." He exhorted them to "esteem yourselves" not by how much "more happy, honourable and important" you can become but by how much "more *useful* you are!"

Three days later, Rush delivered the student speech at the commencement. The *Pennsylvania Gazette* in Philadelphia later described it as "an ingenious . . . Harangue in Praise of Oratory," delivered "in a very sprightly entertaining Manner." Most notable was the boldly modern choice Rush had made: he gave his address in English.

2

Benjamin Rush was sure of one thing when he finished college: he had no interest in the clergy career for which his mother had worked so hard. Considering the young man's amazing memory, and his growing passion for public speaking and debating, the Reverend Davies was certain that he should study the law. Richard Stockton no doubt concurred, and by the time Rush left college, he too was convinced.

Upon returning home, Rush's mother helped him arrange to work in the office of a Philadelphia attorney. Before he began his legal apprenticeship, however, a boarding school friend convinced him to come visit his family in Maryland, and on the way they stopped for a few days to visit Reverend Finley at West Nottingham.

As the visit was ending and Rush was about to leave, Finley took him aside and asked whether he had decided on a profession. When Rush told him he would be training for the law, Finley said that was out of the question, as the law was "full of temptations." Finley had no doubt there was only one proper course for him: to "study physic," the contemporary term both for "physician" and for "medicine."

Finley wouldn't let Rush leave until he agreed to reconsider his career decision. "Set aside a day for fasting and prayer," he advised, to "ask God to direct you in your choice." Like any teenager, Rush ignored the order to fast and pray, but he began to consider medicine, even though he knew almost nothing about physic, except that he couldn't stand the sight of blood and generally had "an uncommon aversion from seeing such sights as are connected with its practice."

Every one of his friends said he was making a mistake. Law in colonial Philadelphia was a well-developed and prestigious career, offering access to every institution that mattered. Medicine itself was only recently becoming more professional, with training and treatments more standardized; it was shifting from a largely philosophical pursuit to a more medical one. But physic was also more of a calling than the law—it was a chance to serve. Ultimately, Rush trusted the advice of Finley, who had been a surrogate father over the past decade. Reverend Davies finally came around and wrote Rush a recommendation for medical training. By February 1761, Rush had begun an apprenticeship with the leading physician in Philadelphia, Dr. John Redman.

Britain had a number of established medical schools, but in the colonies apprenticeship was the only way to train to be a physician. After serving as an apprentice, some simply began practicing—there was no licensure—while others went abroad for a formal medical degree. As with other professional apprenticeships, aspiring doctors like Rush lived with their masters, paying them for room and board.

They often signed elaborate contracts laying out how long they would serve and what they would do—and *not* do—during their service. The contract Benjamin Franklin used with his apprentices in the printing business was considered typical. It required that the apprentice "do no Damage to his said Master, nor see it to be done by others without lettting or giving Notice thereof to his said Master. He shall not waste his said Master's Goods, nor lend them unlawfully to any. He shall not commit Fornication, nor contract Matrimony within the said Term. At Cards, Dice, or any other unlawful Game, he shall not play. . . . He shall not absent himself Day nor Night from his said Master's Service, without his Leave: Nor haunt Ale-houses, Taverns, or Play-houses."

Dr. John Redman, who was known for making his house calls

riding a small black filly—rather than on foot or by carriage—had one of the largest practices in Philadelphia. He was thirty-nine when Rush started working with him, but he appeared older because his own health was compromised. He had recurring lung problems, and to stave off any more illness from his patients, he always chewed tobacco. When he visited a sickroom, his assistant had a bowl of vinegar placed near the bed, into which he would periodically plunge a red-hot iron from the fireplace to fill the room with its cleansing aroma. (Since diseases were believed to be spread by "toxic air," "miasmas," and other poisonous vapors, they were to be combated by diffusing strong smells: vinegar, garlic, tobacco smoke, even exploded gunpowder.)

Dr. John Redman

Most medical care was done in people's homes. Physicians were paid to make house calls. Once they made a diagnosis, if the treatment wasn't available in the cupboard, they would sell a prepared medicine or write a prescription for an apothecary to fill. Procedures, including surgery, would be performed by the doctor or his apprentices, all in the comfort, or discomfort, of a patient's parlor.

Popular medicines included vinegar, various wines and brandies, substances that emptied the bowels (purgatives) or caused vomiting (emetics, or "pukes") to rid the body of toxins, and opium derivatives for pain. Common procedures included bloodletting, blistering, and cupping, as well as an early version of the inoculation for smallpox.

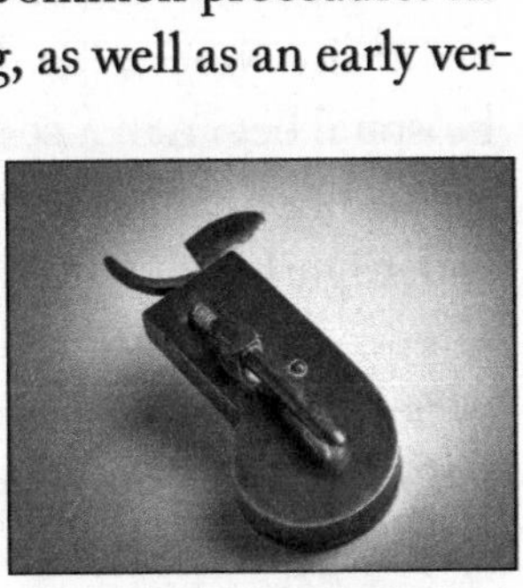

One of Rush's lancets

For bloodletting, a cut was generally made in the median cubital vein, either in the crook of the elbow or in the forearm. The vein was punctured with a sharp knife or a small, spring-loaded spike—called a lancet—after which the blood was allowed to drip or pour out into a bowl, so its volume could be measured. Leeches were also used to draw blood, where it had pooled beneath the skin or wherever the patient was in pain.

Blistering involved applying intense heat to areas of pain—or to areas believed to have general treatment value. The resulting blisters were sometimes rubbed open by hand or with cloths soaked in turpentine. Cupping meant attaching a heated glass cup to the skin and sometimes pumping the air out of it by hand, causing the skin to swell so that, supposedly, toxins could rise to the surface. Less dramatic treatments were also common, such as hot and cold baths and compresses.

Surgery was performed without much in the way of local numbing and with no general anesthesia. At this time, most surgical procedures involved cutting off diseased limbs and removing growths that could be seen on the skin or felt just below it. These procedures were usually carried out by a general physician, although surgery was slowly growing as a medical specialty. There were also several nonphysician specialties. Babies were generally delivered by female midwives, but physicians knew how to deliver them if necessary. And a "bleeder" could be called in to do a prescribed bloodletting, so the physician could move on to the next patient's home.

Only if a patient was indigent and couldn't afford to have a doctor come to the house, or was so floridly mentally ill that the family couldn't care for them at home, were these treatments administered in a hospital. And the colonies had very few of them. The first hospital in America was Pennsylvania Hospital, founded ten years earlier, in 1751, under the leadership of Benjamin Franklin and a leading physician, Dr. Thomas Bond. A largely Quaker charitable institution where the doctors volunteered their time, Pennsylvania Hospital began in a converted home on Market Street and was now a growing facility on the southern outskirts of town, at Pine Street and Eighth. Most of the indigent patients were cared for in beds in open wards. Those deemed "insane" were locked in cells in the unheated basement and chained to the floor, where they slept on straw. There were no treatments for them, only confinement.

Between his formal education and his voracious reading, Rush had studied almost everything *but* science and medicine; now he was trying to learn everything from scratch. Besides taking in the principles of "modern" medicine, he learned at Dr. Redman's side how to compound treatments, how to perform bloodletting, cupping, and blistering, and how to deliver a baby. He also learned how to keep the accounting books for Redman's huge practice. In all his other waking hours, Rush read—the medical books he was discovering and the literature he loved. And he took voluminous notes on both in his commonplace books.

It was a challenge to compare and contrast the various systems that had been put forward to explain the processes of the human body and to determine what should be done when something went wrong. Though medicine was slowly trending toward a more empirical, evidence-based ethos, the limitations of actual knowledge meant that decision making still often relied more on philosophy than on science. Rush was becoming a physician at the very beginning of a breakthrough period, when knowledge of the body, and of ways to test and monitor it, were just starting to eke forward. He would be part of the first generation of doctors who truly appreciated how much they didn't know.

Rush first dove deeply into the writings of Herman Boerhaave, because Dr. Redman had trained at the University of Leiden in the Netherlands, where Boerhaave had taught in the early 1700s and where his ideas dominated. Boerhaave (pronounced *BUR-have*) was a chemist and a botanist as well as a physician, and he tried to add more focus on the body's chemical and mechanical processes. He claimed to reject the ancient Greek humoral system of Hippocrates and Galen, which postulated that all bodily functions could be understood through the balance, or imbalance, of the four liquid "humors" in the system: blood, black bile, yellow bile, and phlegm. But in his focus on blood and the vascular system, Boerhaave still viewed many medical problems through the prism of fluid balance, which Rush came to view as hopelessly outdated, too "humoral." Boerhaave's treatments were generally mild—rudimentary medicines and changes in diet—and he encouraged bedside training, since medical education shouldn't consist only of lectures on theory.

He had made one discovery of his own, becoming the first to isolate and identify urea by purifying a residue from urine. While Rush admired some of Boerhaave's practical advice about building a career—he always remembered the great doctor's contention that the poor were his best patients "because God was their paymaster"—he came to consider his medical system to be the enemy of progress.

Rush was more taken by the works of seventeenth-century English physician Thomas Sydenham, who was credited with the idea of "fighting" disease and had pioneered new uses for basic medicines commonly used in the battle. These included the enormously popular opium derivative "laudanum," used for pain relief and sedation, and "Peruvian bark" from the cinchona plant of South America, which contained quinine and was used to combat fevers. Sydenham also strongly believed in bloodletting—the sicker the patient, the more blood let.

Sydenham, who had long, light-colored hair parted in the middle and steely eyes, also wrote dramatically about being a physician: "A murderous array of disease has to be fought against," he wrote, "and the battle is not a battle for the sluggard . . . I steadily investigate the disease, I comprehend its character, and I proceed straight ahead, and in full confidence, towards its annihilation." He told stories of being professionally criticized and even persecuted for his strong treatments and medical war metaphors. This all carried dramatic appeal for an idealistic medical trainee. Sydenham became Rush's hero from the older literature.

But Rush was also looking for new heroes and new ideas. Modern "systems" were mostly theories for medical students and their teachers to discuss. Rather than proposing new treatments, they were conceptual frameworks to explain why the same old treatments did or didn't work and how they should be employed. While physicians were taught about the various systems, it was mostly so they could learn to trust their own intuition, what they actually saw in their own practices, and whatever seemed useful in old and new books.

For the first year and a half, Rush toiled under Dr. Redman, doing more hands-on care than he had expected and rising in the ranks of his apprentices. Before long, he found himself overseeing the entire business side of Redman's practice and compounding all his medicines. Instead of just holding the bowl for bloodletting, he was often doing the messy venisection work himself.

OUTSIDE THE PRACTICE, Rush was also confronting illness and death. In early February of 1761, less than five months after Rush graduated from the College of New Jersey, his mentor there, Rev. Samuel Davies, died of pneumonia, at the age of thirty-seven. Eerily, only weeks before he became ill, Davies had preached a New Year's Day sermon at the college based on Jeremiah 28, entitled "This Year You Shall Die!"

As Rush wrote to a friend whom Davies had also taught, "When the silver locks of old age and unusefulness are taken away, then indeed it's vain to grieve. But when the charms of beauty, vigor, health, and youth, and all the united splendors of utility are snatched away, the blow is heavy and portends something important."

The college community was devastated by the loss, and the trustees implored Reverend Finley to leave his boarding school in Maryland and replace Davies as president. Finley had recently suffered his own loss—his wife, Rush's aunt Sarah, had died at thirty-two, leaving him to raise their five children. Deciding to accept the opportunity to start over, Finley took the job and remarried.

Later in 1761, Rush received word that his older brother, James, had died at sea at the age of twenty-one. From what the family was told, James's "nervous disease" had been "perfectly cured" by sea life. Unfortunately, while sailing to Jamaica, James contracted what was diagnosed as yellow fever—one of the most feared and deadly illnesses imaginable, with no reliable cure. He died a few days before his boat landed on the island. Upon hearing the news, Rush was overwhelmed by powerful grief. "It was the first time," he said, "I ever felt that species of distress."

A year later, the city of Philadelphia experienced an outbreak of yellow fever. Rush and Dr. Redman saw their first infected patient on August 28, 1762, and within a week they were seeing four such patients a day. Two weeks later they were seeing twenty a day.

These patients, Redman recalled, were "seized with a sudden

and severe pain in the head and eyeballs . . . depression of spirits, pain in the back and bones [and] a sick stomach . . . with frequent vomiting, more or less of green or yellow bile." When the illness resisted "the power of the medicines," patients often "grew comatose, which was a bad symptom, and generally continued until death"—unless they were awakened by black projectile vomiting. Only then did their eyes, and then their skin, begin to turn yellow. They generally died after four to six days, and in many cases, Redman noted, their skin grew more yellow after they succumbed.

For more than a month, Philadelphia lost twenty people a day—in a city of only fifteen thousand—to yellow fever. The deluge of illness was beyond anything Rush had imagined, much less seen. It was also during this epidemic that Rush first saw physicians performing, out of sheer desperation, more extreme care—so-called "heroic medicine," of the kind he had read about in Sydenham. They doubled or tripled doses to see what would work; they bled patients more profusely and gave them medicines to make them purge more quickly and fully, from every orifice, because there was no time to wait. Physicians and bleeders were run ragged making house calls.

In many of the medical texts Rush was reading, there was a basic debate about the role of a physician. Was it primarily to help nature take its course, or was the purpose of physic for the doctor to try to wrestle nature to the ground, to be its master, not its servant? Watching the epidemic with Sydenham's calls to medical arms ringing in his head, Rush could see there were "cases where the efforts of nature are too feeble to do service."

The yellow fever epidemic waned only in November, when the weather turned colder. Luckily, neither Rush nor Redman contracted the illness; nor did their families. But Rush did develop a harsh cough that fall, which sometimes brought up blood. He treated it with a light bloodletting, Peruvian bark, "malt liquors and wine," and a "low diet," cutting back on protein and trying, as much as possible, to live "chiefly upon vegetables, tea, coffee, and a small quantity of animal food [meat]." The cough went away, but later came back—and periodically recurred throughout his life. He came to believe that this lifelong "pulmonary complaint," as he called it, could be some form of tuberculosis. He remained on the "low diet" preventively, which certainly helped maintain his health. But his "recurring cough" also gave him the feeling of "being old when I was young."

Not long after yellow fever abated, William Shippen, Jr., the twenty-six-year-old son of one of Philadelphia's most successful physicians, returned to Philadelphia from a glorious medical education in London and Scotland—followed by the grand tour of Europe—to take his rightful place in the city's medical community.

Shippen had attended the same boarding school and college Rush had, but he traveled in more rarified company. His father was a prominent Philadelphia doctor and socialite, and a founder of the College of New Jersey. Dr. Shippen Jr.—known in Philadelphia as "Billy"—had studied surgery and anatomy. He was considered bright, overbearing, and far too sure of himself. Though he returned from Europe with a bride, he was known for his inability to keep his hands off the ladies.

"What a pity it is that the doctor is so fond of kissing," one young woman in Shippen's social circle lamented. "He really would be much more agreeable if he were less so fond. One hates to be always kissed, especially as it is attended with so many inconveniences; it decomposes the economy of one's handkerchief, it disorders one's high Roll, and it ruffles the serenity of one's countenance."

In addition to his pedigreed training, Shippen arrived with gifts for the hospital from London: none other than Dr. John Fothergill, the most important authority on surgery and anatomy in England, had sent seven large cases by ship. When the hospital staff opened them, they were stunned to see eighteen detailed anatomical drawings done during human dissection—a controversial procedure that had never been seen publicly in America—as well as four astonishing real-life castings of human bodies. One of them featured the fully visible skeleton of a mother and her fetus.

These items were, by their very existence, the most amazing anatomy lesson available in the new world. But Shippen had plans to take things further. Two days after the cases were opened, he announced he would offer the first anatomy class in America to include the real-time dissection of a human corpse. The introductory lecture would be given at the Pennsylvania State House, with subsequent sessions to be held in a large room in the Shippen family mansion on the southwest corner of Fourth and Locust Street (or, as it was known then, "Prune Street").

Dr. William Shippen, Jr.

Seventeen-year-old Benjamin Rush immediately signed up, agreeing to pay the substantial fee of five pistoles (over $5,000 today)* for the sixty-lecture course, a sum he likely got from his mother. He was there when the first class was called to order at six p.m. on November 16, 1762, by the bell in the State House clock tower. (The tower, the tallest structure in town, actually had two bells each tuned to the same note, E-flat, which were the city's main form of communication and time-keeping. One was rung by pulling a rope, as an alarm or call to action; the other was attached to the clock and marked the city's standard time.) Rush was one of ten or twelve students who took Shippen's entire anatomy course; as was true for most medical lectures, the public was able to buy single tickets for individual sessions. To improve walk-in business after a few weeks, Shippen advertised that he had finished with "the most dry, though the most necessary part of anatomy," and now that he was getting to the good stuff, he would "admit gentlemen who want to gratify their curiosity to any particular lecture" for a five-shilling ($35.80) ticket.

---

* All currency amounts in the book are followed by their approximate value today. These figures are based on pound-to-dollar conversions and consumer price index comparisons using the "Measuring Worth calculator" developed by economists at the University of Illinois at Chicago and Miami University, but considering the fluidity of currency values at the time, these conversions are very approximate.

Some classes knew in advance not only what Shippen would be dissecting that day but *whom*. Several weeks after the course began, a local newspaper reported that a coroner's jury had handed over to Shippen the body of a young black man who had committed suicide by cutting his throat with a glass bottle. Soon local authorities were regularly handing over bodies of suicides and deceased criminals; the chief justice of Gloucester County, New Jersey, had the body of an executed prisoner sent directly to "Dr. Shippen's anatomical theater for dissection."

This newspaper coverage backfired on Shippen and his students. Many people still considered dissecting a human body to be a sin, and Rush sometimes found himself weaving through angry protesters to get to class. Stones were thrown through Shippen's windows, and he once had to escape through a back alley after a dissection because the carriage waiting for him at the front door was being pelted with rocks and even musket fire. Every new insight into the body's workings electrified Rush.

For the next three years, he was immersed in his apprenticeship and medical studies. But he was also a teenager, growing into a young man of strong emotions that he constantly had to keep in check. He was considered quite attractive—tall and lanky, wearing his light hair long and pulled back—and was an effortlessly engaging conversationalist, able to make quick personal connections and share gossip that only a doctor could supply.

He found himself prone to crushes, falling in love early and often with young women who were both bright and beautiful; he always needed to be with someone he could talk to. This may have been one reason his mother and younger siblings insisted that he not marry until he was well into his career, preferably not before age thirty. There were also clear economic reasons for their insistence. His older brother James, along with his earning power, was now gone; his mother's marriage was unstable, as was the marriage of one of his sisters; and Rush still had a younger brother who would require financial support. The family needed him to maximize his income before he settled down.

Rush felt deeply conflicted by this situation. During his apprenticeship, he considered marrying several women, most of them Philadelphians, although there was also a "Miss Livingston of New York." While none of these relationships ended in wedlock, some may have been consummated. In his autobiography (parts of which he wrote to convince his children not to stray and sin in their youth the way he had), he admitted that during this time he had sought "the favor of God in his Son . . . [just as] the woman of Samaria was brought to a repentance of all her sins by the Son of God reminding her of but one of them . . . living criminally with a man who was not her husband." He appears to have gone through several cycles of sinning, recommitting to purity, and then shrugging off "a great deal" of his "spiritual sensibility."

While Rush took Dr. Shippen Jr.'s anatomy course, he decided not to sign up the next year for his classes on obstetrics and midwifery—which were also considered scandalous, because for the first time in America, Shippen was teaching the art of delivering babies to men training as surgeons as well as to female midwives. Yet Rush maintained great admiration for Shippen, referring to him as "my . . . friend and master."

But Shippen soon had competition for Rush's tutorial affections. In the spring of 1765, young Dr. John Morgan swept back into town, after earning his medical degree in Edinburgh, and immediately caused a commotion. Instead of starting a lecture series in his area of expertise as his friend Dr. Shippen had, he announced that he would start his own medical school.

Rush knew about Dr. Morgan—for a long time he had been following in many of his footsteps. Morgan was ten years older than Rush, but they were from the same middle-class neighborhood, where they had both lost their fathers prematurely. Morgan's father, Evan, had owned a shop at Second and Market at the Sign of the Two Sugar Loaves, and he had been a friend of Franklin (as well as an occasional advertiser in his newspaper) until his death at forty-eight. Young John Morgan had been sent to West Nottingham Academy, and after graduating, he joined the very first class at the new College of Philadelphia, which had grown out of the secondary school, the Academy that Franklin and others had founded. At age fifteen, Morgan was in the college's first graduating class while filling a job Rush would later have: the favorite apprentice of Dr. John Redman.

Dr. John Morgan

After several years of bleeding Redman's patients and compounding medicines, Morgan became the first apothecary at Pennsylvania Hospital, which he hoped would qualify him as an expert in medications, or what was referred to in physician training as *materia medica*. He served as a surgeon with the Pennsylvania provincial troops for several years, then left America to pursue a degree at the University of Edinburgh, where he was a great success.

Between his studies Morgan traveled to Europe—moving in circles opened up to him by Franklin, who had been living in London since the late 1750s as Pennsylvania's representative and had become the intellectual and social travel agent for clever Americans abroad. Morgan's adventures added to his reputation and prestige. The shopkeeper's son from Market Street had an audience at the Vatican with the pope (who was "affable and courteous," according to Morgan) and paid a visit to Voltaire in Geneva (who entertained him and his friends "with most singular politeness"). In Paris, he was named a corresponding member of the Royal Academy of Surgery.

Before returning to Philadelphia in 1765, Morgan reached out to trustees of the College of Philadelphia, proposing to create America's first medical school. Morgan had bold, even controversial ideas for the institution. One was his proposal that the professors shouldn't have to both teach and maintain a full traditional practice. Medicine, he believed, should be elevated above the "low drudgery" of pharmacy (which he knew from experience) and surgery. Therefore his professors should only teach, diagnose, prescribe, and offer bedside manner. This was a radically new way of thinking about what it meant to be a physician: separating procedures and pharmacy from the dispensation of medical expertise.

Morgan's second controversial proposal was to hire Dr. William Shippen, Jr., as a professor, to continue his lectures on anatomy under the college's auspices. The controversy here was personal: Shippen insisted that he and Morgan had come up with the idea of the medical school *together* while both were studying abroad. He was deeply offended by the notion that he should teach *at Morgan's school* rather than at a school they started and ran together.

When Morgan invited him to join the faculty of the new school, Shippen was openly angry—even as he took the position. In his September 17, 1765, acceptance letter, he pointedly explained that three years earlier, he had proposed creating a new medical school to Morgan, but had waited to seek the patronage of the trustees of the college until the return of his colleague, "who promised to unite with me in every scheme we might think necessary in the execution of the plan."

In fact, the story might have been a little more complicated: some evidence suggests that when Shippen first got home, he privately queried the managers of Pennsylvania Hospital to let him start a medical school there (rather than at the College of Philadelphia). But the hospital apparently turned him down. The managers had no interest in, or money for, broadening their mission beyond the care of indigent patients; and Shippen, a fine young surgeon but not a big medical thinker, did not inspire them to change their minds.

None of these behind-the-scenes maneuvers would have mattered once the school was up and running, except that even as Dr. Shippen, Jr., began as America's first professor of anatomy, he refused to accept that Morgan was his superior—and insisted on obsessively retelling the story, in medical and social settings, of how he had cofounded the medical school. While ego squabbles among professionals were hardly unknown, their degree of friction was unusual: two of the most promising young physicians in America had chosen to build their careers as open rivals, medical frenemies, leaving their friends, colleagues, and students caught in the middle.

And when twenty-year-old Benjamin Rush signed up for John Morgan's *materia medica* class in the fall of 1765, he put himself right between the two men. As a keen reader of newspapers and people—who had developed a fascination for institutional gossip—he surely knew of the friction between the two professors and perhaps wondered how it might impact his career. In fact, when he elected to take Shippen's anatomy class for a second time that year, he may have done it just to appear he wasn't choosing sides.

Their feud may have also helped Rush decide it was time to finish his apprenticeship with Redman and go abroad for his medical degree. He wanted to study at the University of Edinburgh, which was considered the most prestigious program in the world and was where both Shippen and Morgan had received their degrees.

But Rush dragged his feet about leaving, largely because of romance. He had fallen so deeply and inconveniently in love with a woman named Mary Fisher—"Polly" to her friends—that he was debating giving up his dream of being educated in Scotland for her. He considered her "the only woman whom I ever loved and, I may add, ever shall." And he felt tortured by the fear that "my knowledge of physic" would be "too dearly purchased" if he sacrificed for it the "opportunity of making myself happy" by marrying her.

Rush went so far as to write Polly Fisher a letter of proposal, but dutifully burned it when he received "unwelcome orders" from his mother "not to think of a wife for eight or ten years to come." He would not marry without his mother's consent—she was paying for his education—so he continued to see Polly until he was ready to go abroad.

JUST AS RUSH was falling for Polly, he also developed a passion for politics. In 1763, while he was in boarding school, the long French and Indian War had ended, dramatically expanding the British holdings to the north, west, and south of the thirteen colonies—and creating a huge British war debt. When Rush came of political age in spring of 1765, news arrived from across the Atlantic that as part of its efforts to be paid back that debt, Parliament had passed the Stamp Act—a new form of taxation for the colonies, which required most printed materials to carry a special revenue stamp purchased with British currency.

Like many in Philadelphia, Rush was immediately politicized by the new law. He was incensed that Benjamin Franklin, after first speaking out against the proposed tax from his post in London, had acquiesced to its passage. "O *Franklin, Franklin*, thou curse to Pennsylvania and America," Rush wrote to a New York friend, "may the most accumulated vengeance burst speedily on thy guilty head!" He fumed that even as some citizens in Philadelphia were hanging effigies of stamp officers from makeshift gallows, many Quakers seemed conciliatory toward the Crown: they "seem resolved to counteract all our efforts against the Stamp Act, and are daily endeavoring to suppress the spirit of liberty among us. You know I mean the Quakers."

Franklin did finally oppose the Stamp Act, and Rush joined with many other Philadelphians in protesting it. He waited with "anxious impatience" for word that the act might be repealed, as it finally was on March 18, 1766. Afterward he even memorized part of the speech that William Pitt, the first Earl of Chatham, gave in Parliament in favor of the Stamp Act's repeal.

He especially liked Pitt's line, "Americans are the sons, not the bastards of England!"

Unfortunately, on the same day Parliament repealed the Stamp Act, it passed the far more overbearing Declaratory Act, which established that British laws applied equally in England and in all its colonies. This opened the door to more British financial meddling in American life.

RUSH WAS FINISHING his courses with Morgan and Shippen, winding down his long apprenticeship to Dr. Redman, and preparing to leave for medical school in Edinburgh, when he learned that Reverend Finley was seriously ill. Having recently finished his fourth year as president of the College of New Jersey, fifty-one-year-old Finley was coming to Philadelphia for medical treatment. The nature of his illness was never disclosed, but his doctors told him it was terminal (likely cancer). As Finley's health declined, Rush "sat up with him every other night for several weeks." It was both a medical and a spiritual challenge to treat his old mentor and uncle, the man who had convinced him that his calling should be for healing. Rush still saw "the hand of heaven clearly" in Dr. Finley's advice.

Rush played host to all the people who came to pay Finley their last respects. Even in dying, he remained a charismatic preacher. He took each visitor "by the hand and, with his eyes swelled with tears, said to them, 'Fairwell, my dear children, I am not so much concerned at parting with you here as about meeting you in Heaven.'" Rush was frequently moved to tears himself—which he did his best to conceal.

On the morning of July 17, 1766, Reverend Finley grew so weak that he could no longer speak. When a visiting friend asked if Finley was still triumphing over his illness, the reverend slowly lifted his hand and nodded yes. He lived for four more hours and died at one p.m. without a groan or a sigh. Rush was with him until the end, and when it was over, it was the twenty-one-year-old medical trainee's responsibility to perform "the distressing office of closing his eyes."

And with that, Benjamin Rush's youth came to an end.

3

At noon on Sunday, August 31, 1766, Rush set sail from Philadelphia to Liverpool on the ship *Friendship*. He was accompanied by a fellow Philadelphia medical apprentice, a Quaker named Jonathan Potts, and they both had two immediate goals: getting to Liverpool alive, given that the sea was often rough, and presuming they did, reaching out to Benjamin Franklin for letters of introduction to the proper medical authorities in Edinburgh. They already had letters from their mentors who had studied there, but a letter from Franklin would open more doors.

They barely achieved the first goal. On September 2, Rush wrote to a friend that the "billows swell considerably but have as yet produced no seasickness." But once they reached open sea, according to the journal Rush kept of the trip, he was "seized with vomiting and sea sickness which continued on without intermission for . . . 12 days." He spent the entire time in bed, suffering "as much pain & Anxiety as ever I had done in my life before from any Cause whatever." Two weeks in, however, he realized he had severely underestimated just how horrible a person could feel when the sea was "dreadful & dangerous," and how close someone could come to death without actually dying. As the young doctor was in bed clinging to life, water flowing back and forth on the floor of his cabin, he prayed to live but also condemned "that Thirst for Knowledge which induced me to leave my native country." For three full days, he lay in "this painful suspence between Life & Death" until finally the storm cleared. The only thing that helped the seasickness at all was laudanum, the bitter, reddish-brown opium tincture that he sipped from the bottle when the harsh sea made pouring it into a spoon impossible.

Yet even though he had been deathly ill, Rush still felt slightly better than his friend Potts, who later wrote in his own diary that Rush had taken care of him "with the greatest compassion and tenderness." After seven weeks and two days at sea—much of it spent vomiting or trying not to—the passengers of *Friendship* arrived safely in Liverpool. Or so they believed.

During the trip, Rush and Potts became friendly with a Scottish merchant named James Cummins. When their ship finally reached calm seas and they were two nights from Liverpool, Cummins shrieked in his sleep, awakening his friends and bringing the captain running. Cummins admitted to being terrified by a dream but refused to say what it was about. The next morning at breakfast, he waited until Rush finished and left the table before telling the others the details of his nightmare. He had dreamed that Rush fell from a horse, fractured his skull, and died—then reappeared as a spirit saying Cummins would soon be joining him.

Nobody spoke of the dream again for their first few days in Liverpool, where they dined with friends of friends from Philadelphia, visited the local churches, and worked on their fawning letters to Franklin in London, hoping he would introduce them to his influential friends. Cummins left dinner early one night, saying he didn't feel well. When they got back to their lodgings—the three of them were staying together in one room—he was asleep. At midnight he awoke with what Rush called "convulsion fitts," evidently some form of seizure. Rush and Potts quickly bled him, which knocked him out, then called in more experienced local physicians for help. Rush hoped he and Potts had saved their friend, but Cummins lived less than twenty-four hours and died "in the utmost agony."

Rush was greatly troubled by the death, in part because the young merchant had spoken often during the boat trip of his desire to see his aging parents and his siblings again. Instead, Cummins died among people he had just recently met. "By foreign hands his Eyes were closed," Rush lamented. "Strangers followed him to his Grave & Strangers alone performed his last sad funeral Obsequies." Those strangers, Rush and Potts, also found themselves forced to pay off several of Cummins's debts and to cover his burial expenses at the graveyard of a local church. They wrote to Cummins's father in Aberdeenshire to let him know what had happened, and he later repaid them.

Their first Sunday in Liverpool, Rush availed himself of the opportunity to see how others worshipped. He went to St. Thomas Church in the morning, where he was interested not only in the preaching but also in learning what clergy got paid in England. In the afternoon he went to the Octagon, a church run by a "sect of Dissenters" who were a "Medium between the Church of England & the Church of Scotland." Rush was especially impressed by an "ingenuous moral discourse upon Gratitude by One Mr. Clayton." But he was rather astonished to hear that the minister "openly denies the Divinity of Jesus-Christ."

So ended Rush's first week in the mother country, where he was amazed by how much of a new world the old world could be.

After ten days in Liverpool, Rush and Potts had received no response from Benjamin Franklin, so they departed for Scotland on a post chaise, a two-horse carriage that seated three (or two with a lot of luggage). It took four days to get to Edinburgh, and in the evenings they lodged wherever they could. One night swollen creeks prevented them from proceeding any farther and forced them to stay in a cottage where they "supped upon a Bowl of milk," using spoons made of horn. The cottage was so filthy they slept in their clothes hoping to "avoid Catching the Itch," but to no avail. The next day poor Mr. Potts "enjoyed much of the Royal pleasure of scratching himself."

They arrived in Edinburgh the first week in November, presented their letters of introduction from Dr. Morgan, a favorite son among graduates, and purchased tickets for their first lectures by the school's legendary professors. To earn a degree, students paid for lectures—and either passed or failed for attending—then paid to be personally examined by the faculty on their accumulated knowledge, and to defend a thesis.

Most important to Rush was the eminent Dr. William Cullen, the fifty-six-year-old chair of the institutes of medicine (which referred to the teaching of the "science of medicine," or applied physiology). An engaging and challenging lecturer, he was a cornerstone of the Scottish Enlightenment (both as a thinker and as private physician to other major figures) and was emerging as an influential medical mind. A close second was Cullen's former student and protégé Dr. Joseph Black, who had discovered magnesium and carbon dioxide early in his research career in Glasgow and now, at thirty-eight, had recently returned to his alma mater to run the department of chemistry. It was the subject in which Rush knew he must excel. Before he left home, Morgan had told him that if he did well in Edinburgh, he would be the leading candidate for a chair at the College of Philadelphia's new medical school—and chemistry was the only open subject.

Dr. William Cullen

But it was Cullen who had drawn Rush to Edinburgh, which was the "first school of physic at present in the world," he believed, "chiefly owing to the extraordinary abilities & learning of Dr. William Cullen, a gentleman whose name & merit will be better known & more acknowledged a 100 years hence than it is at present." Dr. Cullen had bold features—dark eyes, full lips, and an immense coif of wavy hair, parted in the middle and puffed out like two cascading earmuffs. Along with his expressive hands, which he used to draw listeners into his lectures and conversations, he altogether exuded "a kind of wildness," Rush felt, "which denotes the perpetual agitation & thoughtfulness of his mind."

Cullen was not yet, when Rush studied with him, the very top professor at Edinburgh—he had taught chemistry and *materia medica* and was just beginning to lecture and write more broadly. But he was making a larger impact, and vying for the top job, because of his insights into how the different medical systems alternately cohered with and competed against each other. With a limited number of treatments, and an ever-growing world of theories on the different, sometimes mutually exclusive ways to apply them, Cullen's approach was invaluable. He was developing his own system, based on the primacy of the nerves. But, mostly, what he taught training physicians was how to understand the various systems without becoming beholden to any of them when it came to assessing actual patients.

Cullen also was interested in teaching life lessons. He told his students, for example, that they should never be late for anything—and not only because it was unprofessional. Rush never forgot the first time he was "warmly reproved by him on this account & no wonder" since being late was like treating those equal to "ourselves like our servants, & Often Obliges the Persons we Disappoint to disappoint Others in their Turn."

There was only one thing Rush found "wanting" with Cullen: "a regard to religion." Cullen "professes himself to be a sceptic, although he never [is] heard to say anything disrespectful against it in a public manner." He mentioned in lectures that he believed in the "immateriality and immortality of the soul," but he didn't seem to have formed any "regular system for himself" when it came to religion.

Rush struggled with this separation of church and science. He understood that "a man who has long been in the habit of thinking for himself & of doubting the truth of every principle of science until it is proved to him by the usual laws of demonstration is very apt to carry the same spirit of free inquiry with him to religious matters." But, he held, "many of the truths of religion are objects of faith & not of reason. We ought to believe them although we cannot comprehend them. . . . We are all sure that the sun is the principle cause of vegetation, but no one has been able to tell in what manner it operates in producing its effects upon plants and trees. nor should it in the least invalidate the truths of Christianity that we are not able to comprehend them. A proper notion of the infinite grandeur and wisdom of the Deity & and our own finite contracted minds would soon reconcile us to all ye seeming difficulties in the Christian religion."

Despite this firm statement of faith, Rush was going through a kind of religious crisis himself during this time. Years later, in his autobiography, he mentioned that during his first year at Edinburgh his "deep and affecting sense" of a certain "vice," left unnamed, "first led me to seek the favor of God in his Son." He made it clear that this moment of insight left him "far from . . . a complete union to God"—he was less reborn than reminded of the challenge of being Christian, and a scientist, and a single man. But the situation made "my mind more tender to sin of every kind, and begat in me constant desires for a new heart."

Rush dove into the religious life of Edinburgh. "I delighted in public worship and particularly in hearing evangelical ministers of all denominations," and he added "secret prayer" to his daily routines. He did not become an absolutist or a zealot; he was more interested in discussing why others did or did not hold their beliefs than in evangelizing his own. He was also candid that his own religious practice was sometimes lacking: "I am sorry to add my devotion was often a mere form, and carelessly and irreverently performed."

Rush was thoroughly occupied with his studies and his new city when his letters of introduction from Benjamin Franklin arrived, bearing a cover note brimming with advice. It was apparently the first time Rush had had any direct interaction with Franklin. As a child, he had seen him on the streets and in church, and more recently he had followed his life in the newspapers, but he never reported having met him.

"Letters of Recommendation may serve a Stranger for a Day or two," Franklin wrote to Rush, "but where he is to reside for Years, he must depend on his own Conduct, which will either increase or totally destroy the Effect of such Letters." Edinburgh, "where the people are very shrewd and observing," would be an important proving ground for the young doctor's character, Franklin said. Besides studying medicine, Rush should endeavor to obtain a "thorough Knowledge of Natural Philosophy in general. . . . I mention this, because I have observed that a number of Physicians, here as well as in America, are miserably deficient in it."

Franklin's introductions led to a dinner invitation that Rush could only have dreamed of as a student in America: an evening with David Hume, who was at the height of his fame after the publication of the sixth volume of his best-selling history of England (although the young doctor was partial to the "ingenous moral essays" Hume had written earlier). Rush dined with Hume at the home of Franklin's friend Sir Alexander Dick, a prominent physician.

Rush found the great philosopher less engaging in person than on the page; in general he seemed "rather ungenteel & clumsy." He didn't speak much, and when Sir Alexander tried unsuccessfully to draw him out on a point of English history mentioned in his book, Hume refused to play along, noting there were many things in the volume "which I have forgotten as well as yourself."

Even with his profile in Edinburgh society rising, Rush was still pining for Polly Fisher in Philadelphia. But he was soon reminded of why his mother and sisters begged him to contain his passions for the opposite sex and put off romantic entanglements.

Sometime in late January, his friend Potts received letters from friends back home concerning his fiancée, Gracey Richardson, the niece of a well-known Quaker goldsmith. Before Potts left for his studies abroad, she had agreed to wait for him to finish before they married, but apparently during their last moments together before Potts set sail, the couple had given in to carnal impatience. Now the unwed Gracey was carrying his child.

Potts abruptly left school and headed to London to arrange passage home. He narrowly missed the first boat and was stuck in London for three weeks before he could sail. While there he interacted with Franklin, who loaned him money for the trip home.

Potts failed to reach Philadelphia in time for the birth of his daughter, but he and Gracey were soon married; his family attended the wedding, hers did not. Once he got over the shock of how quickly life could change, he decided to continue his studies at the College of Philadelphia and at least have the distinction of graduating with the first medical school class there.

Within weeks of Potts's departure, Rush found himself in the middle of another intercontinental family drama. Since the death of Reverend Finley, the College of New Jersey in Princeton had been struggling to replace him as president—and to create some stability in its leadership. Even for a time when so much disease went unchecked, the college had had miserable luck with presidential health. Finley had been its fourth leader in just nine years to die prematurely. The trustees had selected as their next president the Rev. John Witherspoon, a Scottish Presbyterian minister in his early forties. Witherspoon had built a reputation as an enthralling sermonizer and thinker at his congregation in Paisley, five miles outside Glasgow.

But Witherspoon was reluctant to accept the job and bring his family to America. So the trustees asked New Jersey lawyer Richard Stockton, who was in England doing business with Franklin and others, to travel to Scotland and have a talk with Witherspoon. On his way to Paisley in late February 1767, Stockton stopped in Edinburgh to visit with Rush, whom he remembered affectionately from his time in Princeton.

In Paisley, Stockton found Reverend Witherspoon both intrigued by the prospect of the Princeton job and resolute in his opinion that he could never accept it. His wife, Elizabeth, would not consider such a move and refused to even speak to Stockton about it. Her reasons became the subject of much armchair psychology on both sides of the Atlantic over the next six months, while powerful men pronounced what they would do if their wives were similarly uncooperative. Witherspoon explained that his wife had already reluctantly agreed to move the family once for his career and had no intention of going through that again at the age of forty-four. He also said she had "hydrophobia"—a fear of water, somewhat surprising for a woman who grew up on a small coastal island in the Hebrides.

After Stockton left, the reverend wrote to him that Mrs. Witherspoon "continued under such Distress on the Subject that for some Weeks . . . she was scarcely ever half a day out of bed at a time." Finally he agreed he would not force her to go to America. Nobody mentioned the possibility that she might be suffering from depression, even though she had given birth to ten children and had lost five of them, including three over the previous few years: two at childbirth and another at age seven.

Rev. John Witherspoon (there is no existing image of his wife)

Rush couldn't believe that Witherspoon—whose preaching he considered not only transcendent but technically brilliant, because he never used notes—was leaving his beloved alma mater in the lurch. When the trustees started considering other candidates, Rush began writing to Witherspoon himself. Knowing none of the particulars, he was at first confrontational, suggesting that if the reverend didn't agree to take over the school, it would be "ruined" and "the world will impeach you as the cause of it."

Witherspoon was still fielding a great amount of correspondence on the issue of his wife, much of it harsh. He singled out young Benjamin Rush for writing "with much more humanity & Politeness though with no less strength" than the others. Even as he turned down the college's offer yet again, he invited Rush to visit his family in Paisley after his classes ended for the year, and suggested he would enjoy the opportunity to continue their discussion in person.

After another round of international letters, Witherspoon let Rush know that while he was "filled with the greatest Anxiety," he also had a plan, about which he swore the young doctor to secrecy. If Rush spoke to his wife in person, he believed, his contagious enthusiasm might sway her—even though she was now saying that moving to America "would be as a sentence of death." Witherspoon asked Rush to visit them immediately. He wrote the letter and mailed it on a Friday in mid-August; Rush received it and left Edinburgh on Sunday, arriving in Glasgow on Tuesday.

Over the next several days as a guest in the Witherspoons' home, Rush was somehow able to engage Elizabeth in a conversation she had refused to have with anyone for six anxiety-ridden months. It is not known what they discussed, but Rush had developed a unique ability to draw others out; people found themselves revealing personal things to him, as his wide blue-gray eyes transmitted empathy and understanding.

Elizabeth Witherspoon changed her mind. It was still a few months before the couple left for America. But when they got there in the spring of 1768, Reverend Witherspoon was ecstatic and deeply appreciative of Rush. The reception they received, he wrote to him, "even exceeded Your own hyperbolic promises."

Word spread among the college's powerful alumni in Philadelphia and New Jersey that Rush had persuaded the Witherspoons to come. And as the reverend stabilized the school and became its landmark president (serving for over twenty-five years), important people realized that Benjamin Rush had a mind that was going to matter to America.

4

The mind of Benjamin Rush was still, however, easily distracted, given to moments of sparkling insight but also surprising immaturity. Even after Rush had been away from home for almost two years, he still couldn't get past his feelings for Polly Fisher back home, although he knew they would never marry. When his friend from home Thomas Bradford—the son of *Pennsylvania Journal* publisher William Bradford—wrote to tell him of his own romantic interest in Polly, Rush could have stepped aside graciously. Instead, he sent an unnervingly honest letter to Bradford about how much he still loved Polly, revealing that he was still angry that his mother and sisters hadn't let him marry her.

Does the "blessed creature know what pangs of love she has cost me?" Rush wrote to Bradford, Polly's new fiancée. "How often I have walked up and down my room for whole nights . . . thinking upon nothing but her; and above all, could she see my *heart*, my honest heart . . . she may censure and reproach me forever as the worst of men . . . but I will never cease as long as I live to esteem her the loveliest and best woman in the world." After going on like this for another handwritten page, Rush then said, "Still, let us continue friends through life. . . . I hope to see you together in Philadelphia and to enjoy many happy hours' conversation with you. I fancy should I see your lovely spouse. . . . I should be dumb in her presence—my trembling knees and my faltering tongue would refuse to perform their offices. But these I trust will be cured before I return to America."

Bradford wrote back asking for more assurance that his friend would not be his rival for Polly's affections. Rush was genuinely confused by his reaction, in one of the earliest documented examples of a challenge that would follow the young doctor his entire life: while he was perceptive about the feelings and motivations of others, he was sometimes flabbergasted by how people reacted to him. He didn't seem to know his own strength or the impact of his cyclically unchecked emotions and larger-than-life personality.

Ultimately, another tense international letter exchange put the issue to rest, and Thomas Bradford married Polly later that year.

In the meantime, Rush was falling madly in love with someone else he couldn't marry. In Edinburgh he had become friendly with a young Scottish royal named William Leslie, the second son of the sixth Earl of Leven. And as he spent time with Leslie's family, he became smitten with the younger sister, Lady Jane—who was only fifteen. Rush, then nearly twenty-three, explained to a friend that Lady Jane's age was one at which "the Charms of youth—Beauty—& Virtue appear to [the] greatest Advantage. . . . Beauty alone has Charms & Often Beauty is armed with all the additional strength which Education—Virtue—spotless Innocence & Sweetness of Temper give, then its power becomes irresistible."

Lady Jane had a lyrical singing voice, and she spoke and sang with a slight lisp that Rush found captivating, especially when she crooned "The Birks of Endermay," a Scottish favorite.

They had pet nicknames for each other, "Edwin" and "Angelina," inspired by a romantic ballad, "The Hermit," by Irish poet and playwright Oliver Goldsmith, from his popular 1766 novel *The Vicar of Wakefield*. In the ballad, Angelina, the daughter of a "wealthy Lord," meets a hermit in a dale where she has come to die. She tells him of her beloved Edwin, who was young and poor and had only "Wisdom and worth . . . But these were all to me." When the couple can't be together, Edwin disappears from her life and, she assumes, dies of heartbreak. She has come to do the same. "Forbid it heaven!" the hermit cries out because, of course, he's Edwin. Within three stanzas, they are living happily ever after.

That was never going to happen for Rush and Lady Jane: she could never live in America, nor he in Scotland. But they relished each other's company as he finished medical school, ending with his rather gruesome senior thesis, in which he tested a theory about saliva, digestion, and fermentation by throwing up half a dozen different meals and then analyzing his vomit in great detail, as well as the vomit of a friend he asked to participate as a control for the experiment. (It might be best we don't know how Rush assessed that he had "vomited an acid-tasting liquid" after a dinner of "beef, peas, bread and beer" chased down with tartar emetic.)

And perhaps Lady Jane offered solace when the thesis threatened to undermine his career before it began. It wasn't the paper itself that got him in trouble, oddly enough, but its dedication page.

While doing his experiments and writing his thesis (in English, then translating it into Latin, as required by Edinburgh for graduation), Rush had been in touch with his American mentor Dr. John Morgan, who was settling in as head of his new medical school. To make sure that Rush, after graduation, returned to Philadelphia in triumph and full employment, Morgan was holding open the college's chair in chemistry for him. Morgan was also arranging for Rush to become the youngest member of his new Philadelphia Medical Society, which was about to merge with the American Society Held at Philadelphia for Promoting Useful Knowledge—the second generation of Benjamin Franklin's groundbreaking intellectual salon group, the celebrated "Junto," from which many of his "first in America" ideas had sprung. And Rush was certainly bursting with medical ideas (although, as he noted in a letter to a friend, "the theory of physic is like our dress always changing, and we are always best pleased with that which is fashionable").

Dr. Morgan and Dr. William Shippen, Jr., had never gotten over their argument about whose idea it had been to start the medical school in Philadelphia. Now they were at each other's professional throats—at the college and elsewhere in the medical community—

openly criticizing each other for anything they could think of. Since Rush would need the help of both men if he were to succeed when he returned home, he tried not to offend either one. He even wrote to Morgan asking his permission to mention him in the dedication of the thesis, "to prefix your name to it together with Dr. Franklin's, Dr. Black's, Dr. Shippen and Redman's." He went on to tell Morgan, "you cannot conceive, my dear sir, with what pleasure I look forward into life when I think I shall pass through it hand in hand with you."

When Rush wrote the dedication, he first thanked "that most outstanding person Benjamin Franklin" (whom he still hadn't met, but who was a great person for a young Pennsylvanian expat to thank first). Then he thanked Dr. Black, his Edinburgh chemistry teacher, then Dr. Redman, and then:

THOSE DISTINGUISHED MEN,
WILLIAM SHIPPEN, M.D.
AND
JOHN MORGAN, M.D., F.R.S &C.
EMINENT PROFESSORS
IN THE COLLEGE OF PHILADELPHIA
THE FORMER OF ANATOMY,
THE LATTER OF MEDICINE

Apparently, when Morgan received his copy of the dissertation and saw his name listed below Shippen's, he became incensed. We do not have the angry letter he sent Rush, but we do have the first of Rush's several apology letters, dated July 27, 1768. Rush downplayed the whole situation by not mentioning it until he had discussed other matters, including Morgan's advice about spending some time training in London hospitals before coming back to Philadelphia. Rush then began:

> I am sorry to find I have not followed the order in the names which you hint at, in the dedication of my thesis. . . . I thought it a matter of no consequence. Dr. Shippen was my oldest friend and master, and this was the only reason why I put his name before yours. . . . I hope therefore, my good friend, you will overlook my

> omission in placing your name after Dr. Shippen's. My thesis has been read, and is now I dare say forgot forever. No one will remember six weeks hence whose names were mentioned in my dedication.

It was not clear whether Rush was trying to minimize the damage by being dismissive, or if he truly didn't understand how angry Morgan was. He had a tendency toward self-forgiveness, while often forgetting to ask others to forgive him first. This made it hard to be his enemy, but sometimes even harder to be his friend.

By the time Morgan received this weak apology, Rush had moved on to London, where he boarded in a house in the Haymarket—along with a cousin of his from Philadelphia, Thomas Coombe—and was receiving instruction from the medical luminaries of the British Empire. While Edinburgh had the finest medical school, London was where the finest medicine was practiced. Rush worked at Middlesex Hospital and St. Thomas's Hospital alongside the surgical and anatomical legends Dr. William Hunter and Dr. William Hewson (the latter of whom, while Rush was there, finished his landmark study proving that fish had lymphatic systems). He met and became friendly with Dr. John Pringle, who all but created the field of military medicine and was, as Rush reported, "the favorite physician of the Queen and the royal family." Pringle asked him to join the weekly "medical conversation party" held every Wednesday at his home, and he invited him to dine at other times as well.

Rush also became friendly with Dr. John Fothergill, the Quaker physician who had sent the famous plaster casts to Pennsylvania Hospital—and had tried, unsuccessfully, to keep his former students Shippen and Morgan from competing so brutally against each other.

Rush made connections in the arts in London, beginning with a friendship with the well-known Pennsylvania-born portrait painter Benjamin West, who had moved there in 1763 and had recently been named historical painter to King George III. West introduced Rush to, among others, painter Sir Joshua Reynolds, who was president of the Royal Academy of Arts and, the year he met

Rush, was knighted by King George III. Reynolds, in turn, invited Rush to a dream dinner that included the celebrated man of letters Dr. Samuel Johnson, whose essays on literature Rush had read, and whose prototype dictionary everyone used. Among the other guests was Rush's favorite Irish writer, Oliver Goldsmith, whose novel and play had inspired the nicknames between himself and Lady Jane Leslie and who knew something about medicine from working as a young apothecary.

The dinner was most likely one of the meetings of "The Club"—a literary group founded by Reynolds and Johnson five years before, which met weekly for dinner at the Turk's Head Inn in Soho, always promptly at seven p.m. On this particular evening, according to Rush's account, Dr. Johnson arrived late, and immediately interrupted Reynolds, who was trying to console an author friend who had just received a bad review.

Etching of "The Club," with Johnson second from left; Reynolds across from him, third from left, and Goldsmith all the way on the right

"Don't mind them," Johnson bellowed, as he took a seat next to Rush. Nearly forty years his senior, Johnson was tall like the young doctor but much broader and more physically imposing.

"Where is the advantage," he continued, "of a man having a great deal of money but that the loss of a little will not hurt him? And where is the advantage of a man having a great deal of reputation but that the loss of a little will not hurt him? You can bear it."

Rush was intrigued by the way Johnson took control of the conversation and did intellectual battle with anyone who tried to make him relinquish it. Some of his strongest opinions concerned drunkenness, which Rush quickly surmised were well-informed.

Johnson and Goldsmith went after each other all through dinner—which was entertaining but also a little uncomfortable for Rush, because he was seated between them. When Goldsmith posed a question, Johnson made sure that before answering, he first criticized the question for not being "of the most interesting nature."

At one point, Goldsmith queried Rush about the customs of North American Indians—a subject of great fascination on both sides of the Atlantic. Johnson stopped talking to someone else long enough to hear what Goldsmith was asking Rush, then barged into the conversation. "There is not an Indian in North America," he declared, "who would have asked such a foolish question."

"I am sure," Goldsmith shot back, "there is not a savage in America that would have made so rude a speech to a gentleman."

And on it went.

WHILE RUSH NEVER saw Johnson again, he did dine with Oliver Goldsmith on another occasion. The author not only offered insights into Rush's favorite book of his (explaining that the vicar's wife was based on his own mother) but offered a preview of his political poem-in-progress, *The Deserted Village*.

During his time in London, Rush also became friendly with booksellers Edward and Charles Dilly, and he spent much of his free time at their shop and home at #22 Poultry. Rush described it as "a kind of Coffee house for authors," and it became his model for the kind of casual literary mecca he would seek out his entire life—a place where authors and readers talked dramatically about books, some of which the bachelor Dilly brothers went on to publish to great fanfare. (It was also a place where ex-pat Americans could have their mail delivered and held.) The Dillys would later become Rush's publishers in London, but would be best known for publishing the first three volumes of James Boswell's biography of Samuel Johnson, both of whom were regulars.

At one dinner at the Dillys' home, Rush became friendly with the controversial author Catharine Macaulay, England's first major female historian, whose ambitious eight-volume *History of England* was up to book four and becoming increasingly antimonarchical. She and Rush went on to become lifetime friends and correspondents.

Through the Dillys he also connected with the radical politician John Wilkes, who was in prison at King's Bench, where he had been remanded after being expelled from the House of Commons for his views. Rush visited him in prison, for a dinner party attended by more than a dozen of Wilkes's friends in his two-room cell (which included its own library). Rush was impressed that Wilkes was "an enthusiast for AMERICAN Liberty" and was intrigued by his advice about the need to build a new nation that challenged class distinctions. "If you can but preserve an equality among one another," Wilkes told him, "you will always be free in spite of everything. Titles are the bane of an infant country."

These political ideas percolated through Rush's mind in London, even as he was sightseeing. When he and a Danish physician friend visited the House of Lords, it felt to him like "sacred ground," and he found it hard to "arrange my thoughts into some order, but such a crowd of ideas poured in upon my mind." Then they went to the House of Commons where, inside the wood-paneled legislative chamber, he was overwhelmed by the realization that "this was the place where the infernal scheme for enslaving America was first broached."

He asked a guide to show him to the place where he might find comfort—the "very spot" where William Pitt had risen from his seat and delivered his famous call to repeal the Stamp Tax. Rush sat down in what had been Pitt's chair, imagined himself surrounded by "a crowded House," and then slowly, deliberately rose and began delivering Pitt's speech from memory.

"Americans are the *sons*, not the *bastards* of Englishmen!" he called out to the near-empty room. "I *rejoice* that America has resisted."

He couldn't believe that his own voice was echoing against "the very walls" that had reverberated with Pitt's speech "upon that glorious occasion."

5

While Rush wrote in endless detail about his meetings with extraordinary characters in Britain, he curiously left no record of his first meeting with the man whose kindness and introductions had made so many of those experiences possible: Dr. Benjamin Franklin.

It appears something happened to Rush's journals from his time in London and Paris. The Paris journal was rewritten (the only copy that exists is not in Rush's handwriting), and while Rush later rewrote much of his London journal, he omitted all details of the day he actually met Franklin and nearly anything substantive about their interactions during their five months in London getting to know each other.

All Rush said about meeting Franklin in the writing he left is that "it was my peculiar happiness to be domesticated in his family"—which meant he dined often at Franklin's home, a four-story Georgian house at 36 Craven Street near Trafalgar. He also noted that Franklin "once took me to Court with him and pointed out to me many of the most distinguished public characters of the nation. I never visited him without learning something." And Rush explained that when he was preparing to leave London for Paris, Franklin insisted he accept a line of credit in case he ran out of money. Otherwise, Rush hardly left another word about his nearly half a year observing Franklin in London—even though later in life, when they were both in America, Rush appeared to record almost everything Franklin ever said or did in his presence.

This may have been because Rush initially found himself confronting not just the heroic, mythic Franklin he always heard about as a child, but the actual, three-dimensional Franklin, who, at sixty-two, had some of the same self-control issues with women that young Rush recognized in himself. One difference was that Franklin was long-married to a woman, Deborah Franklin, who lived just down the street from Rush's mother in Philadelphia. Two years earlier, when the young artist Charles Willson Peale first visited Franklin's home in London, unannounced, he apparently discovered the great man upstairs with a woman less than half his age sitting on his lap (a scene he sketched in an undated drawing). That woman has been presumed to be Polly Stevenson, the daughter of Franklin's London landlord.

Benjamin Franklin portrait; sketch of Franklin and friend, by Charles Willson Peale

Rush interacted socially with Franklin and Polly, as we know from a letter Franklin penned. In October 1768, a month after the young doctor's arrival in London, Franklin invited Polly and her mother to a daylong excursion on Saturday the twenty-second, beginning bright and early. "Our Reason for going so early is, that having the Day before us, we may do our Business and dine in time, so as to be back by Day light," Franklin wrote. "There is otherwise Danger of our being benighted, as the Days are now short, and you know I don't love Travelling in the Dark after a Day of Pleasure, thinking it like a bad Epilogue to a good Play." The list of nine people he invited ended with "Dr. Rush, and your affectionate friend B Franklin."

Rush likely discussed what he saw in Franklin's company with his cousin, Thomas Coombe, who ran errands for the great man in London and even boarded with Franklin for part of Rush's time abroad. Coombe was the one who delivered, in February of 1769, the letter of credit Franklin arranged for Rush before he traveled to Paris, in case he ran out of money. On February 13, Franklin had written to his banker about the matter, in which he referred to Rush as "a young Physician from Pensylvania, of excellent Character, and a particular Friend of mine" and arranged for him to borrow up to 200 pounds ($33,000). Rush very much appreciated what he called Franklin's "delicate act of paternal friendship."

Besides the line of credit, Franklin sent Rush to Paris with a new set of introductory letters—presumably more glowing now that they actually knew each other. Rush recounted the impact of one such letter with great drama.

His first contact in Paris was Dr. Jacques Dubourg, a sixty-year-old physician who had recently become a close friend of Franklin, after years of translating his scientific writings into French. (Dubourg dabbled in invention himself and would go on to create the first—and probably the only—parasol equipped with a lightning rod.) The tall, moon-faced doctor brought Rush to be presented at the Paris home of Victor de Riqueti, the Marquis de Mirabeau. (Mirabeau's son Gabriel, three years younger than Rush, would grow up to be one of the great spokesmen of the French Revolution.) Dr. Dubourg was ushered into the marquis's house ahead of young Dr. Rush. They were then escorted into a large room, packed with all manner of "ladies and gentlemen of the first literary characters in Paris."

Dubourg gestured toward Rush and cried out, "Violà! Un ami de Mons. Franklin!"—"Behold, a friend of Mr. Franklin!"

Upon hearing that, the marquis himself came running toward them, took Rush by the hand, and assured him, "C'est assez."

Being a friend of Franklin, "that is enough."

This was Rush's introduction to the Coterie, a distinctly Parisian form of intellectual social gathering that utterly fascinated him because the opinions of men and women were equally valued. "Here Ladies and Gentlemen meet only to talk upon Subjects in Science," he wrote in his journal, and *both sexes* participated in the rousing conversations. "Here they forget their little domestic Cares, & amuse one another with their Remarks, upon the News, Politics, witty sayings, Books & etc of the past day or Week. There is nothing stiff or reserv'd in these Companies. Sometimes they all listen to one person Speaking, at other times they form themselves into little Parties—some of them set, some stand & walk up and down the room without any restraint."

Dubourg may have introduced Rush to his friend Denis Diderot at this party, because soon afterward the philosopher entertained the young doctor in his library. If Rush didn't already feel he had "arrived" in the heart of the European Enlightenment, he must have got a special charge when Diderot asked if he wouldn't mind carrying a letter for him back to England. He needed it be delivered to his friend—and Rush's recent acquaintance—David Hume.

Rush was fascinated by how different the French were from the English—they had fewer gender and class divides and were more in touch with their "savage" side. This was, to Rush, a compliment. He felt that "the highest degrees of civilization border upon the savage life. The individuals of the human race are once men, and twice children, so nations are once civilized and twice savage." He thought the French were particularly aware of this, as were Native Americans, Jewish people, and African Americans.

Being in touch with one's savage side wasn't always pretty. During a visit to Versailles, Rush observed the "brutish" teenage dauphin misbehaving during a big formal meal: "he took a piece of meat from his Mouth, which he had been chewing and after looking at it for some time in the presence of near 100 spectators, threw it under the table."

But Rush associated this trait in the French with an admirable level of gender equality. He did find himself surprised by how much makeup French women used—he had never imagined a woman "painting" her face until it was another face. But otherwise, he appreciated the modern women of France. "Much has been said of the want of Delicacy in the French ladies," Rush wrote in his French journal:

> . . . The freedom of their behavior—their using certain Expressions, in Conversation which are look'd upon as indelicate in other Countries; and above all their admitting Gentlemen to pay them Morning Visits in their Bed Chambers, have all been urg'd as Arguments to support the justness of the Censure. For my part I am far from agreeing in the common Opinion . . . [of] the propriety or impropriety of these things. . . .
>
> There is as much real Virtue among the Ladies of France as among the Women of any other Country in the World. Too much cannot be said of the Accomplishments of their Minds: A well bred Woman here is one of the most entertaining companions in the World. Tis not enough for her to understand the Duties of domestic Life. She extends her Enquirys much further, and never thinks her Education complete till She has acquired some general Knowledge of *Geography, Philosophy* and the *Belles Letters*, etc.

In America and England, Rush had heard "declamation against Women reading and Women learning." But his experiences in France reinforced his conviction that education added "much to the native Charms of a Woman," rendering her "in every Respect a more agreeable companion to a Man of Sense. If a Sympathy of Affection only gives such a degrees of Happiness in the married State, how much greater might it be, were there always a Sympathy of Understanding joind with it?"

After a month in Paris, Rush had spent all his own money and a significant amount of what Franklin had loaned him, so he headed back to England. During his carriage ride from Dover to London, the driver suddenly stopped because he heard a voice screaming in the woods for help. Rush jumped out and found a poor pregnant woman lying on the ground wrapped in an old blanket. Ten minutes later he delivered her son. Afterward she was "speechless," took his hand "and pressed it to her lips in the most affecting manor." He never forgot it, and the baby became the first of many children to be named after Benjamin Rush.

Two months later Rush boarded a ship in London, the *Edward*, bound for Philadelphia. At twenty-three, he had been away from home for nearly three years. While he did not experience as much seasickness on the ocean voyage home, he complained of something more upsetting and perplexing: an "inquietude of both body and mind."

At first, he joked about it in his journal, noting that Dr. Franklin liked to quip that there were "three classes of people who did not care how little they got for their money . . . school boys, sermon hearers and sea passengers." But Rush noticed that his appetite was weak, and food didn't taste the same. His mind was "restless" and "unsettled," and reading was the only thing that really helped. Since he had sent his library home on an earlier boat, he relied on the kindness of strangers for books—including a German dictionary someone had brought, from which Rush taught himself that language during the voyage (making it his fifth, after English, Greek, Latin, and French).

The journey took seven weeks. When Rush landed in New York, he was warmly met at the wharf by an old school friend, but he immediately felt disappointed—the people in New York "had less color" than he remembered. They seemed to walk "less erect," and "move with a less quick step than the citizens of London."

That evening and the next day, he felt "an uncommon depression of spirits."

He had experienced such distress at least once before, when he learned of the death of his older brother, James. But this depression after returning home from London in 1769 was worse. It overcame him so powerfully that, for the first time, he "believed the many accounts which have been published, of melancholy and even suicide following similar emotions of the mind." It was one of his earliest insights into how the brain could be ill; it was also a lonely moment for a young man returning to the new world, fearful of its expectations.

6

Back in Philadelphia, Rush moved into a house around the corner from where he grew up—on Arch Street, between Front and Second, two blocks from the Delaware River. His brother Jacob, who was training to be a lawyer, was living there, as was his younger sister Rebecca, who had been "unfortunate in her marriage" and now kept house for her brothers. Their mother and her new husband lived up the street. It was a time of great uncertainty for the freshly minted physician. He had to set up a practice and find some patients to treat.

He also had to make his formal application for the chemistry professorship at the College of Philadelphia medical school that had been held open for him. But this required an active navigation of egos, as Drs. Morgan and Shippen were still angry at each other, and neither was happy with Rush.

Several months before leaving London to come home, Rush had sent the trustees of the College of Philadelphia an "inaugural address" explaining the importance of chemistry to the teaching of medicine. It was a mission statement for the professorship that Morgan had been holding open for him for three years. In this address, Rush somehow managed—yet again—to list Shippen's name before Morgan's. Morgan, again enraged, wrote Rush an angry letter, and Rush wrote back an even angrier letter in which he claimed the whole matter was "accidental." This probably wasn't true; Rush had privately told his cousin Thomas Coombe that this entire situation had grown out of Morgan's "vanity," and he may very well have been poking his ego on purpose.

Dr. John Fothergill, with whom Rush had just been studying abroad, had an inkling that Rush was still too professionally naïve. He wrote a glowing public recommendation for the young doctor's prospective employers. But he also wrote privately to a well-connected friend in Philadelphia that while Rush had "pursued his studies with so much diligence and success" and earned a "testimonial of his worth from me," he may have received too much too soon and could be "spoiled by too early an introduction to public favores." He thought Rush might benefit from having life be a little harder for him than it had been during medical training. "Not that I want to have difficultys thrown in his way," Fothergill continued, "but let him acquire reputation by his own conduct, rather than the too hasty suffrage of his friends."

Rush never found out about this measured critique, but Dr. John Morgan was tired of being patient. He wrote Rush a twelve-page opus of disappointment. It began fairly reasonably:

> When a misunderstanding once creeps betwixt those who have lived on terms of friendship and professed a regard for each other, it is generally productive of such animosity as persons between whom there has never subsisted any like degree of intimacy, seldom know. To prevent, if possible, the evil consequences which would ensue to both from a breach of good understanding and to prepare the way for an amicable explanation and adjustment of some points, not rightfully understood by one or another of us, so as to maintain an uninterrupted harmony for the future, is the design of this letter.

And then Morgan exploded. "If there were any honesty," he wrote, "in those eulogies you have in all your former letters bestowed upon the friendly offices I have without ceasing done for you ever since I knew you and the very confidence which you acknowledged I gave you, I deserved a more generous and polite treatment at your hands than those attempts of wit and those ebullitions of an angry temper to which you have given vent in your last letter."

Morgan went on for page after page, wondering how he could ever trust Rush again, yet doing everything he could to make Rush understand that he desperately *wanted* to trust him. He also pointed out something that had always bothered him: in his letters from London, Rush had made occasional passing comments about their aging mutual mentor, Dr. Redman, that Morgan thought were unkind and showed a lack of professional gratitude. While praising everything he had learned from his teachers at Edinburgh, Rush had claimed, "I cannot say I ever received a single idea from Dr. Redman" and insisted he owed Redman "no obligations. He never conferred a favor upon me of any kind but such as he was bound to do by the common rules of decency."

Rush may have thought Morgan felt a bond with him, after both had been worked hard by Redman during their apprenticeships. Instead, Morgan saw in these comments how little regard Rush could have for people who had helped him. Perhaps he saw the future of how Rush might treat *him* in old age.

In conclusion, Morgan wrote, "All I need to say further at present is that I shall be glad to have done with all disputes and if possible live in peace with all men. Disputes are ever odious, especially among men of science as they lay themselves open to the censure and abuse of even the lowest set of mankind."

Unfortunately Rush didn't get this missive before he sailed for home. Morgan mailed it four days before Rush boarded his ship, and it didn't catch up to Rush until much later. Presumably, the first time he saw Morgan in Philadelphia, he hadn't yet read it and so didn't realize just how much apologizing, perhaps downright groveling, would be needed to right the situation.

Morgan and Rush did somehow figure out how to move on in their professional and personal relationship. On August 1, 1769, Dr. Benjamin Rush was officially named the first professor of chemistry at the College of Philadelphia—and in the American colonies. He would have some time to prepare his first lectures, because the medical school year began in November.

That very same day Rush saw his first private patient, presumably in a first-floor office on Arch Street. Lydia Hyde, a young woman who owned a tea and dry goods store and was friendly with the Franklins, came in for what appeared to have been the hiccups. Hyde was a member of a growing group of independent young women in Philadelphia with whom he would be increasingly associated. (Unlike the female writers Rush already knew from the city and from Princeton—who were married or would later marry—Lydia Hyde remained single by choice her entire life, focusing her energies on her business and on community activism.)

When he finished seeing her, he filled out the first page of his first medical billing ledger as a physician. He was either so nervous or so excited that he made two mistakes in writing the word "Philadelphia" in large letters with his quill pen. He wrote "Philladelpia"— then scribbled in the missing "h" just above. And then he wrote "Miss Lydia Hyde," her treatment, and the charge, three shillings ($15.70). She became his first regular patient, and other members of her extended family began seeing him as well.

His next patient came as a consultation from a slightly older colleague, Dr. James Bayard, who had apprenticed under one of the top physicians at Pennsylvania Hospital, later served as the hospital's apothecary, and now was in private practice. On August 3, Dr. Bayard had Rush accompany him to discuss with a Mr. Carson the treatment of his son. The consultation must have been satisfactory, because two weeks later, Bayard summoned him again, and this case would change his life.

On August 18, Dr. Rush arrived by carriage at a country manor four miles outside the city, where the master of the house had been chained in a room for three months. Capt. John Macpherson was being held in one of his own cottages, confined to a bed of straw while being treated clandestinely for madness. Rush was there as the newest and youngest medical expert to offer input on one of the most challenging cases colonial Philadelphia had seen.

In late 1768, the Scottish-born Macpherson, a forty-two-year-old merchant sea captain whose right arm had been blown off by a cannonball battle some years earlier, began displaying symptoms that deeply worried his wife, Margaret, and their four children. Macpherson had done very well for himself; he and his family had a place in town but spent much of their time in their country home, Mount Pleasant, a Georgian mansion considered among the most beautiful in the colonies. It sat on the Belmont Cliffs overlooking the river and his 160-acre plantation in what was then a rural area north-west of Philadelphia and is now part of the city's Fairmount Park. (He also owned a second forty-acre plantation on Germantown Road near Rising Sun.)

The crisis began when Macpherson came down with what he believed was "an attack of fever"—a common medical description that could mean many things in a world before diagnostic tests and did not refer only to elevated temperature. When his symptoms did not abate, however, those close to him came to believe he was suffering from a mental disorder and might be dangerous to himself and others. Since Macpherson owned a substantial collection of lethal weapons, his family arranged for them to be removed from the house. They were stored, temporarily, in the home of the captain's best friend, John Dickinson.

Lanky with a long face, arched eyebrows, and a ski-jump nose, Dickinson was among the most powerful lawyers in Philadelphia and a major landowner in Pennsylvania and Delaware. Recently, at the age of thirty-six, he had achieved international renown as a political writer, authoring the series of controversial missives known as the *Letters from a Farmer* (or *Farmer's Letters*). They represented the first in-depth legal challenge to the new taxes on businesses that England was levying in the colonies—and they were meant not to foment revolution but to argue that some of the levies weren't legal. Dickinson did not challenge the power of Parliament to regulate trade, but insisted the colonies had legal sovereignty over their internal affairs, which was violated by taxes that were meant only to siphon revenue from America.

The letters were published in America, in England, and in France, originally attributed to "A Farmer in Pennsylvania"—which Dickinson technically was, since he controlled a lot of rural farmland. He later allowed the letters to be published together, under his name, in a hugely influential pamphlet. While Rush was studying overseas, when people learned he was from Pennsylvania, they often asked what he knew of this Dickinson and his letters. At the time, he knew him mostly by reputation.

Capt. John Macpherson (left) and John Dickinson

Dickinson was close to the Macphersons—the captain's will named him executor of his estate and guardian of his children. He also employed the captain's son, John Jr., or "Jack," who was apprenticing in his office to become a lawyer. Jack Macpherson had played a small role in disseminating the *Farmer's Letters*, making multiple hand copies of them in the Dickinson law office before they were available in print. (This was the kind of scut work Jack and other training lawyers complained about when they got together after work; among his friends in this community of young Philadelphia lawyers was Rush's younger brother Jacob, who had attended the College of New Jersey with Jack.)

In 1769, Macpherson began spending and wagering huge amounts of money, issuing a standing dare to race anyone with his schooner on the Delaware for a bet of 10,000 pounds ($1.8 million). He was scribbling increasingly paranoid and hypergraphic ramblings, many in incoherent verse (for which he suggested tunes by which they could be sung). He picked fights with friends over nothing. Most surprising and embarrassing, he had suddenly decided that Dickinson's *Farmer's Letters*—which he had previously praised—had not all been written by Dickinson. He accused his best friend of plagiarizing parts of his internationally famous pamphlet. He did not reveal who he thought the real author was, perhaps suggesting that he had written some of the letters himself.

That spring Dickinson and Macpherson's family—primarily his wife and eldest son but also his brother-in-law, a physician in New York—began discussing whether the captain's mind was failing, and if so, where and how they might find medical help. They did not wish to put him in Pennsylvania Hospital, though that was what many families would have done. Mentally ill patients were warehoused in its basement, chained in unheated cells and partly visible to the public. While the nation's first hospital was primarily for indigent patients, this was the only place where patients of all classes and races were treated together. Madness respected no societal boundaries; it was an equal opportunity destroyer.

The Macphersons believed that this harsh treatment was the best chance to cure "madness." Dickinson, who was well-connected, likely helped the Macphersons arrange for the captain to be treated in this manner in the privacy of his own home. He was imprisoned in the shepherd's cottage next to the manor house, chained to the ground by his ankle and left to sleep on straw on the floor. His one arm was restrained much of the time in a "mad shirt" (an early version of the straitjacket), and he was fed mostly bread and water. The family was not allowed to see him because, as his son explained in a heartbreaking letter to his father, "our presence is incompatible with your safety; for it is well-known, from experience, that persons in your disorder are most injured by the presence of their nearest friends."

Dickinson also apparently helped arrange for many of the top physicians from Pennsylvania Hospital—including Dr. Thomas Bond, the hospital's co-founder, and his colleague Dr. Thomas Cadwalader—to visit Mount Pleasant to assist with Macpherson's diagnosis and ongoing treatment, such as it was. Utterly in shock, Macpherson claimed there was nothing wrong with him, and this had all been a terrible misunderstanding. He did seem to sometimes acknowledge that something might be troubling his mind. He wrote to his wife and son early in his confinement that "my head may be guilty, but God knows my heart is free," and later said that he understood that "whenever I am afflicted with an inflammatory disorder, I know my ideas are more or less deranged, which is the case with most men." But he also believed his biggest problem was a result of what his caretakers had done to him.

"Declare a dog is mad," he wrote, "[and] he will soon be made so, and afterwards killed for being what barbarity made him." He was being treated against his will, he came to believe, because his brother-in-law wanted his money, and his best friend was trying to steal his wife. Dickinson, he claimed, was "the cause of all my misfortunes." He felt certain that "should my unhappy story, become a precedent in these young countries, it will be in the power of a few artful ingenious men of weight, to ruin and confine for life, any person obnoxious to them."

Macpherson also denied that hiding him and his situation away was for his benefit: "I would rather be in the Hospital," he wrote, "than chained here." But it wasn't just that he was chained; he claimed "they also blew stuff into my eyes through a gun barrel, and frequently declared that unless I confessed that I had been mad, they were very certain I would never obtain my liberty."

Young Dr. Rush joined the all-star team helping to treat John Macpherson in his home. The group now included Drs. Cadwalader and Bayard—whom Macpherson didn't like, referring to them as "Dr. FalseHeart" and "Dr. Softhead" respectively—as well as the eminent Dr. Bond and Rush's former teacher, Dr. William Shippen, Jr.

According to Rush's scant record of the case, he attended a meeting with Macpherson to assess his health, presumably in the shepherd's cottage where he was chained. About a week later, Rush and the other doctors returned, just as Macpherson finished writing an epic poem about his circumstances. The last eight verses, he suggested, "may be sung to the tune" of the familiar English "Ballad of Chevy Chase." (The last verse was "Now my good friends, take my advice; Believe I've been bely'd; Remember when you chain a cat; He'll scratch you while he's ty'd.") Macpherson believed the doctors had returned because of a letter that he claimed a slave had smuggled out to Dr. Shippen. This "ingeneous piece of artifice" had got the attention of Shippen, Rush, and Bond, and "these gentlemen soon discovered the fraud, and being a majority, soon after gave me liberty."

What actually happened is unknown, but ten days later Macpherson was apparently unchained but still locked in the cottage. Three days after that, on August 23, 1769, he was released—and immediately demanded that his wife and son be confined for the same 108 days he had been, as retribution.

Macpherson was moved temporarily into an apartment in town at Front and South streets. He was initially chained there, but after several uneventful days he was told his "only guard" would be his "word of honour." Since all his physicians lived nearby, they likely monitored his progress.

Within a few weeks of Macpherson's release, Rush was playing medical shuttle diplomacy between the captain and his estranged family. Rush made "a visit to his wife in the country"—as he wrote in his billing records—on October 3, charging it to Macpherson's account even though the couple were not speaking. He then saw Macpherson five times in five days, treating him with spirits used primarily for nervous disorders, as well as an emetic to empty his stomach and bowels, an alcoholic elixir to stimulate his heart, and a pill for pain relief.

Not long after these treatments, Macpherson began submitting his writings to the newspapers—along with very private letters that his son and friends had written to him, expressing concern about his illness. This quickly undermined the goal of his family and his physicians to keep his condition and treatment out of the public eye. It also meant that any interaction with him could end up in the newspaper, with only his conspiratorial interpretation.

Rush kept treating his wife, but luckily for his fledgling career, he disappeared from Macpherson's accusatory prose. That spring Macpherson published a 105-page pamphlet, including his own writings and some more personal correspondence from his friends and family. Among those reprinted was a heartbreaking letter

Dickinson had written him at the height of his mania, about the challenge for friends and family forcing a loved one into care. Dickinson declared that he "heartily love[d]" the captain and joined his family in feeling "a great deal of grief . . . that you believe all their attempts to relieve you, are cruelties practiced upon you. . . . Your family is not only to be pitied, but also to be commended for taking the best advice and using the properest means for perfectly restoring you to that remarkable strength of understanding that used to give pleasure to all [in] your acquaintance."

Rush was probably relieved to be mentioned in the pamphlet only as one of the "men of truth, sense and humanity" who helped unchain the captain.

He remained involved in the case only to continue taking care of poor Margaret Macpherson, who never reconciled with the husband whose life she believed she had saved. Margaret saw Rush in the late spring of 1770 and died not long after that at the age of thirty-eight. We have no details of her death, except that in his second published pamphlet of letters about his unjustified imprisonment for false madness, Macpherson said he could not "forgive John Dickinson for murdering a lovely and I think virtuous woman, the partner of my bed and the mother of my children." The captain would live another twenty years, partly in England, but mostly on American waters. His second wife believed he had been falsely accused of insanity, but she had to admit that even his sailors "sometimes referred to him as 'Mad Macpherson.'"

This strange case was the first time Benjamin Rush, as a doctor, was forced to confront the realities of mental health care in the 1700s, and wonder if there wasn't a better way to treat madness than chaining people to the floor until they got better. It was also a lesson in just how challenging these patients and their families could be.

But mostly it was Rush's first experience interacting on a professional and very personal level with several men who would go on to change his life, and the life of America, in ways he could never imagine.

7

While assisting with the Macpherson case had been challenging and exhilarating, it was just one case. Generally, Rush was finding the process of building a practice draining and debilitating, a constant cycle of small successes and bigger setbacks.

In the fall, when classes started at the College of Philadelphia medical school, he was able to make money teaching his chemistry course: people bought tickets for his individual lectures or for the whole series at a price of six pounds ($860). The lectures were meant to appeal to the public as well as to serious young academics: they were advertised as "intelligible to the private gentleman, and inquiring artist, as well as to the student of medicine." To prepare for the lectures, Rush wrote in his notebook phrases he hoped would make the material less technical, noting that one could no more "detach" the "parts" of chemistry than describe "a fine woman's face" through just one of her features. Some attendees were soon inspired to apprentice with him, for which they paid him a fee for his time, as well as for room and board in his home. His known connection with Franklin was helpful, as was his membership in the new American Philosophical Society for Useful Knowledge, where thought leaders met every month to float edgy ideas in science, politics, culture, and the arts.

But having fancy friends did not guarantee a fancy practice.

His professors had told him how important it was to treat the poor and unprotected, for free when necessary, and he was happy to do it. He just hadn't imagined what a large percentage of his patients would be from every wrong side of town. His "shop"—the medical office on the first floor of his house—was "crowded with the poor in the morning and at meal times," and he also made many house calls, reckoning that "nearly every street and alley in the city was visited by me every day." Sometimes house calls were dangerous. "Often have I ascended the upper story of . . . huts by a ladder," he wrote, "and many hundred times have been obliged to rest my weary limbs upon the bedside of the sick (from the want of chairs) where I was sure I risqued not only taking their disease but being infected by vermin."

Not only couldn't these patients afford treatments by such a well-trained physician, but they lacked even the money to pay someone else to administer them, as medicine was increasingly practiced à la carte among the upper classes. So Rush often had to do everything. He "often remained . . . long eno' to administer my prescriptions, particularly bleeding . . . with my own hands."

Rush believed that all young doctors needed three things to succeed: a "great man" who lived in town and actively helped recruit colleagues and friends as new patients; "extensive and powerful family connections"; and "the influence of a religious sect or political party." He considered himself lacking in all these areas but especially in religious affiliations. He had come to believe, while abroad, that "all denominations of Christians" could be viewed with an "equal eye," but once he was back home, he realized that being Presbyterian in Philadelphia had financial and social implications: the city was long controlled by Quakers and members of the Church of England (later called Episcopalians). This made him sensitive both to actual religious prejudice and to the nepotism inherent in religious communities. Prejudice and nepotism weren't the same thing, but he often felt like he was on the wrong side of both. He had colleagues and friends who attended Quaker meetings and the "C of E" services at Christ Church, and when they didn't choose him as their doctor, he wondered if religion (rather than his own youth) played a role.

The main institutions in his life were also divided along religious lines. Franklin had envisioned both the College of Philadelphia and Pennsylvania Hospital to be primarily secular when founded, but the college had trustees who were predominantly Church of England, while the hospital managers were mostly Quaker.

As he tried to build his practice, he became aware that Dr. William Shippen, Jr., was turning against him. Shippen was openly telling his medical students not to buy tickets for Rush's chemistry course and loudly criticized him to colleagues. Since Shippen left almost no writing, it's hard to know today why he did this. He could have been unhappy that Rush sided with Morgan on the college faculty, especially since Morgan regarded Shippen's specialty, surgery, as inferior to what he practiced and taught. Or, perhaps they just didn't get along. Either way, Rush felt Shippen was becoming his "enemy." And as a young doctor building a practice, he couldn't afford to have any well-connected enemies.

Rush wrote to his brother Jacob, who was studying law in England, about the problems he was having with Shippen. Jacob replied that he wasn't surprised, since Shippen, in his view, was "a man of . . . cool malice and treachery." But he warned his brother not to overreact, because nothing good could come of it. Anything Rush said would likely only damage himself—not just financially but personally. Jacob wrote, "Suffer me to put you upon your guard against letting any rash or imprudent expressions escape from you. Honest men are frequently betrayed into this error: Villains seldom or never. I have long thought that Dr. Shippen extremely resembles . . . the Cassius of Philadelphia, [and] from a like envy and hatred of you, [he] has attempted to ruin you in your Bread, and has in some measure succeeded. Is it then too much to assert or is it too uncharitable to suppose, that a man who has injured you in your Bread would also injure you in your life, if he thought he could do it with legal impunity."

Jacob was well aware that his older brother, while brilliant, had emotional blind spots. Benjamin, he knew, had no real idea what men of privilege were capable of doing to keep that privilege.

Rush had only one antidote to Shippen's poison: relentless hard work. He seemed to have indefatigable physical and intellectual stamina, requiring only four or five hours of sleep a day. He trained himself to organize his time wisely and aggressively.

And he did his best to avoid distractions of the heart, since his mother and sisters were still insisting he not marry until he was thirty. He consoled himself that his idol, Dr. William Cullen, hadn't married, or blossomed professionally, until relatively late. Cullen had been a relatively obscure surgeon until his late twenties and never "gave any very promising appearances of genius" until then, which Rush believed "Often happen'd to some of the greatest men in the world." His theory was that when "the Faculties of the Mind ripen before the Organs of the Body are able to bear the Fatigue of hard study or closer thinking, they are soon impaired & destroyed."

When matrimony was "not practicable," Rush once wrote, men should seek "the society of chaste and modest women." But that didn't mean he couldn't flirt. One evening an outspoken twenty-two-year-old Quaker woman, Susanna Hopkins, met Rush at a Presbyterian youth prayer meeting in Cecil County, Maryland, where he had come to visit family on his mother's side.

The prayer meeting was held in the upstairs room of a private home, and Susanna Hopkins found the whole thing fascinating (and later recorded it in her diary). It was racially integrated, which surprised her, and there was much more singing than she was accustomed to. And after the meeting ended around nine p.m., the minister left, and a man entered the room with a violin, "the vibration of which soon set some . . . to dancing." She was truly shocked.

One of the dancers turned out to be Benjamin Rush, whom she described as "a sensible, polite young man, and by no means a novice in conversation." She told him she had never expected to see such dancing after the singing of spiritual songs.

He replied that it was all quite "innocent" and that "he could say his prayers and think as good thoughts when he was dancing as at any other time."

Dancing was "a diversion," she told him, "of small importance to . . . how well we thought or prayed."

He disagreed, invoking Shakespeare: What about "Yorick's French Peasant, whose grace after supper was a dance, by way of returning thanks, with joy and gladness, to the beneficent Creator"?

She said she had always thought plays like *Hamlet* "had more of the air of novelty than truth in them" and were "therefore unsafe to be adopted as precedent for the conduct of others." Before Rush could answer, someone came up and swept her away for a dance.

Soon Susanna was looking for a way to escape the dance floor and reconnect with Rush. She excused herself and sat down next to the large stove that was heating the crowded room of thirty-some people, because she knew it would make her feel faint. When "I became sick, . . . I complained [and] the doctor advised me to try some fresh air." She went outside, but was disappointed that he did not immediately follow.

Instead she found herself trapped in an inane conversation with a group of older people about her dress, which one woman noted was "of very good silk" but of a color "rather grave for a young person." This set off a round robin about "why the Quakers dressed so differently than other people," peppered with quotations of Scripture and broad statements about the state of ladies' fashion. One man opined that "plainness best became handsome women; but in proportion as they were wanting in beauty and good qualities, the trappings of dress became more necessary to set them off. . . . Take a right down ugly woman, who has neither sense nor merit, and dress her . . . rough and plain, and she is just nothing at all."

At this point Rush swooped in to save her, declaring that he "could conceive nothing upon earth more like an angel than a beautiful young Quaker, in whose countenance presided mildness and innocence, in a neat plain dress, especially"—and then he looked at her "earnestly" in the face—"when there are added a few strokes which denote the most refined wit and understanding."

Unsure how to take the compliment, she thought of giving him a "nod of thanks, but an after thought prevented me," and she started babbling instead about angelic forms in the Bible. "I told him that my ideas of angelic forms were different; and if we might compare earthly visible beings with invisible heavenly ones, I thought a real Christian, young or old, whose countenance wore that signature, under the exercise of true devotion came the nearest to my conception of an angel."

Susanna extricated herself from the conversation and went back upstairs, deciding that "we had better part while we were friends." She was pleased when the gathering broke up around two in the morning.

Most of Rush's interactions with women involved less dancing. He had become a regular at the literary "attic evenings" held on Saturdays at the city home of Elizabeth "Betsey" Graeme, now considered by many to have been colonial America's first literary salon. The meetings, held at Carpenters' Mansion at 615 Chestnut, had actually been started by her mother, but after her death Betsey took them over, expanded them, and attracted a younger generation of women—along with their male friends who appreciated this unique, fully coed salon. (While wives were invited to some events of the American Philosophical Society, it was an entirely male-run enterprise.)

Elizabeth "Betsey" Graeme

Betsey Graeme had been writing since she was young. She was a close childhood friend of poet and writer Annis Boudinot Stockton, whom Rush knew from Princeton, and the two women had always shared their work and literary passions. "How often when I am reading Mr. Pope's Letters," Annis wrote to Betsey, "do I envy that day the knot of friends that seem'd to have but one heart by which they were united and their greatest pleasure was giving each other pleasure." The original "knot of friends" had included John Morgan (before he became a doctor), Francis Hopkinson (before he became a lawyer, signed the Declaration of Independence representing New Jersey, and designed the original American flag), and Francis's sister Mary, a childhood friend of Betsey's who married John Morgan.

Benjamin Franklin's son William had also been in the group. Betsey Graeme had been engaged to him in the late 1750s and early 1760s, before he went abroad and then returned from England married to someone else. This hurt Betsey deeply but also led her to double down on her life as a writer—becoming, in the estimation of one biographer, "the most learned woman in America." In her pain, she first translated the entire multivolume French epic *The Adventures of Telemachus: The Son of Ulysses* by François Fénelon into English as a diversion. Then her parents encouraged her to travel in Europe, even though her father, a physician, knew her mother was likely terminally ill. Rush had known Betsey's mother as a patient of Dr. Redman and understood that she thought it would be too much for her daughter to watch her die.

Betsey traveled all over Europe and became friendly with a number of literary luminaries—including *Tristram Shandy* author Laurence Sterne, whom she met at the horse races at York. (Seated near her, he noticed she had bet on the smallest horse in the race; when he asked her why, she told him the "race was not always to the swift, nor the battle to the strong," and he was immediately intrigued.) She returned to Philadelphia after her mother died in 1765, then lived with her father not only in their city house but also in their elaborate country home, Graeme Park, twenty miles from town (where the salon also sometimes met).

It is not entirely clear how and when Betsey Graeme and Dr. Rush first became friendly, since she was almost ten years his senior, but they certainly knew a lot of people in common. When Rush joined Graeme's salon, upon his return to Philadelphia, she became one of his closest friends for life. Rush was fascinated by her mind and dazzled by her performances at the salon. She would sometimes read from an epic travelogue of her journeys abroad, a book Rush claimed that her "modesty alone" prevented her from publishing, as even in these circles it was common for women's writing to remain unpublished, available to be experienced only through live readings and private sharing.

But it was more than her writing that appealed to Rush. "The genius of Miss Graeme evolved the heat and light that animated" these events, he wrote. "She instructed by the stores of knowledge contained in the historians, philosophers, and poets of ancient and modern nations, which she called forth at her pleasure. . . . She charmed by a profusion of original ideas, collected by her vivid and widely expanded imagination, and combined with exquisite taste and judgment into an endless variety of elegant and delightful forms.

"Upon these occasions her body seemed to vanish, and she appeared to be all mind."

8

While Rush enjoyed the continental flair of Betsey Graeme's literary salon, he was also coming to appreciate the increasingly homegrown business of American words. To make it as a physician, a businessman, or a public thinker, he decided he had no choice: he must pamphlet or perish.

Both medical and political writing could appear in general newspapers, which were not yet published daily. Essays read by members at American Philosophical Society meetings were also often published there. But a more entrepreneurial and democratic option was to publish a "pamphlet," a booklet of twenty to forty pages that could crystallize an idea large or small—and turn a nice profit if it became popular. While pamphlets had existed for some time, the success of John Dickinson's *Farmer's Letters* had dramatically raised the form's profile and possibilities. Between the publication of Dickinson's individual letters in newspapers and then the pamphlet compilation, they were considered the most widely read writing in the history of the colonies, possibly reaching, according to one estimate, nearly half of America's literate citizens. (Roughly 200,000 people, 10 percent of the total population, were believed to be able to read.)

In the early 1770s, Rush published his first pamphlet. He had written two playful pieces for the local *Pennsylvania Gazette*—the first on drinking and gout, the second on "intemperance in eating." They were presented as "sermons" allegedly discovered in a bundle of writings by a clergyman deceased for "a few years." Rush wrote the pieces posing as another cleric who had found the sermons and recently delivered them at his own church.

When the two pieces proved popular in Philadelphia, he wrote a third "sermon" about exercise, and then gathered them together in a forty-four-page pamphlet. This time he abandoned the whole dead priest story, admitting that the "sermons" had never actually been preached but instead had been written by a physician, still anonymous, for "no other purpose than to excite the attention of the Public to subjects highly interesting to every body." Published in Philadelphia under the title *Sermons to Gentlemen Upon Temperance and Exercise*, the text may very well qualify as the first American self-help book. It was published soon afterward in England, with a

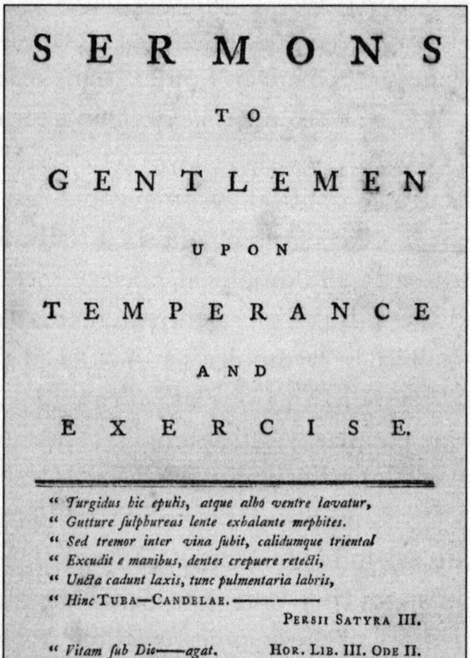

SERMONS

TO

GENTLEMEN

UPON

TEMPERANCE

AND

EXERCISE.

"*Turgidus hic epulis, atque albo ventre lavatur,*
"*Gutture ſulphureas lente exhalante mephites.*
"*Sed tremor inter vina ſubit, calidumque triental*
"*Excudit e manibus, dentes crepuere retecti,*
"*Uncta cadunt laxis, tunc pulmentaria labris,*
"*Hinc* TUBA—CANDELAE.——

PERSII SATYRA III.

"*Vitam ſub Dio——agat.* HOR. LIB. III. ODE II.

PHILADELPHIA:

PRINTED BY JOHN DUNLAP, IN MARKET-STREET.

M. DCC. LXXII.

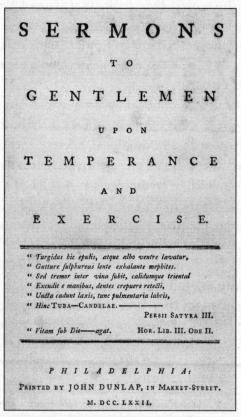

Rush's first pamphlet, Sermons to Gentlemen Upon Temperance and Exercise title that sounded even more like Rush was aggressively trolling for better-paying patients: *Sermons to the Rich and Studious, on Temperance and Exercise.*

The word *temperance* meant something different to Rush in the 1700s than it would a century later. He was concerned about the consumption of wine and hard liquor among young people—unless they were ill and it was being used as medicine. But in adults, consuming wine, even three or four glasses at a sitting, could contribute to good health:

> WINE is principally useful to old people, or such as are in the decline of life. It is hard to fix the limits between the beginning of old age, and the close of manhood. At a medium, the body begins to decline at the age of forty-five or fifty in this climate. Then the hot fit of the fever of life begins to abate, and from the many disappointments in love—friendship—ambition or trade, which most of men meet with by the time they arrive at this age, they generally feel a heavy heart. The decay of the vital heat—the slowness of the pulse—the diminution of the strength, all show that the vigour of the system is declining. Here wine prolongs the strength and powers of nature. It is the grave of past misfortunes—In a word, it is another name for philosophy.
>
> Remember, my aged hearers, if you would expect to enjoy a long reprieve from the infirmities of age, you must begin to use wine moderately, and increase the quantity of it as you descend into the valley of life.

On the subject of food, twenty-six-year-old Rush put himself forward as an early proponent of balancing vegetables and meats. He believed Americans didn't eat enough vegetables and, in his own diet, had already eliminated almost all meat. And he took *very* seriously the issue of *when* people should eat their main meal of the day:

> At present noon is looked upon as the most proper for this purpose. Hence we generally find dinner the principal meal through this country. I am aware of the difficulty of opposing popular prejudices,

> and that it is often much better to swim with the multitude down the stream than to stem it alone. I am aware too of the fate of reformers in religion, politics, and science. Many have lost their characters, their livings, and even their lives, by advancing things contrary to the established opinions of the world. But . . . I will not conceal my sentiments, nor resist what I look upon and feel to be the sacred power of truth.

The main meal should be in the evening, he concluded, so the body could do the work of digestion at rest. "Every full meal," he wrote, "is a stimulous to the whole system, and brings on a temporary fever, which shows itself in that chilliness and quickness of pulse, which are so remarkable after eating." To exercise after that meal would "divide and weaken the powers of nature" in a process that "requires the combined action of them all."

In his sermon on exercise, Rush explained that there were two types of workouts, active and passive. Walking, dancing, fencing, swimming, skating, jumping, tennis, lawn bowling, and quoits (a game played with a round version of a horseshoe) were, in his view, fine active exercises. He also had high hopes for golf, which had not yet become as popular in America as it was in Scotland but could, if played once or twice a week, make a man "live ten years the longer." Horseback riding he considered somewhere between active and passive; sailing and riding in a carriage were both passive.

Talking, however, was in his opinion an active exercise—at least the way he did it, with great vigour, promoting "circulation of the blood thro' the lungs" and strengthening "important organs." So were reading aloud, singing, and laughing. In fact laughing might be the most important active exercise—but only when "the mind co-operates with it." (Polite, fake laughter would not be medicinal.)

The only exercise he was dead set against was running. While walking "invigorates and strengthens the system," he explained, "RUNNING is too violent to be used often, or continued for any length of time. The running footmen in all countries are short-lived—Few of them escape consumptions before they arrive at their thirty-fifth year. . . . I would recommend it to be used as seldom as possible."

While all three "sermons" had a light touch, Rush offered one serious and provocative political statement. On page twenty-eight, in what started as doctorly language seeking to guilt patients into taking better care of themselves, Rush suddenly proclaimed that the reason people of means needed to exercise was that they were employing slaves to do their physical labor for them.

The American, he said, has

> deserted his fields—and his flocks—and sought for some more speedy methods of acquiring fortune—independence—and a superiority over his fellow-creatures. These have been obtained by commerce—war—rapine—and lastly, to the reproach of the American colonies, and of humanity, be it spoken, by the perpetration of a crime, compared with which, every other breach of the laws of nature or nations, deserves the name of holiness, I mean, by SLAVERY. But in exchange for these, he hath given up that greatest of all blessings, HEALTH.

He suggested the wealthy could enjoy health and long life only if they did "of choice" that which "the laboring part of mankind" had to "do of necessity." So all this exercise he was otherwise writing about so blithely was more correctly viewed as "a kind of voluntary labour."

There was nothing Benjamin Rush loved more than offering an inconvenient truth, without warning, in the middle of a conversation. And then he went back to discussing the best time of day for exercise.

THE PAMPHLET WAS a modest success, so Rush soon began work on his next one, usually writing at his desk on the second floor of his house late at night after his brother and sister, and all his patients, were asleep. This time, surprisingly, he made no attempt to hide his politics or to protect his fledgling medical practice from them.

Rush had become friendly with Anthony Benezet, a French-born Quaker in his early fifties who was well-known as an educator and loudly controversial as an abolitionist. Benezet had been calling for an end to slavery in the colonies for some time and had recently founded one of the first schools specifically for free black children. Since Benezet was on the board of managers of Pennsylvania Hospital, he may have met Rush there, or he may have noticed the small but passionate outburst buried in Rush's otherwise lightweight wellness text and thought to approach him about expanding it. As someone committed to abolition for decades, he kept an eye open for any new voice that could assist the cause. The idea of a young physician using the language of science and medicine to justify abolishing slavery might have struck him as something new.

Benezet had recently been lobbying for passage of a law that would tax the importation of new slaves so heavily that it would all but prohibit the practice. He offered Rush information and encouraged him to write something that might help the bill through. Rush wrote a new pamphlet called *Address to the Inhabitants of the British Colonies upon Slavekeeping*. It was received as one of the most blistering rhetorical attacks on slavery ever seen in the colonies.

Publishing such an address in Philadelphia, where one quarter of all the households had slaves, was bold. Some of these slave owners were consequential people in Rush's life, including Benjamin Franklin, John Dickinson (who had eleven, making him the city's second-largest slave owner), and Drs. Thomas Bond and Thomas Cadwalader.

Rush began the pamphlet by declaring that the "intellects of the Negroes" and their "capacities for virtue and happiness . . . their ingenuity, humanity and strong attachment to their parents, relations, friends and country show us that they are equal to the Europeans," including those descended from European immigrants. Slavery, he continued, is "so foreign to the human mind, that the moral faculties, as well as those of understanding are debased, and rendered torpid by it . . . [so any] Vices which are charged upon the Negroes in the southern colonies . . . such as Idleness, Treachery, Theft and the like, are the genuine offspring of slavery, and serve as an argument to prove they were not intended, by Providence, for it."

He directly challenged the notion that "their black color . . . either subjects them to, or qualifies them for slavery . . . when we exclude variety of color from our ideas of Beauty, they may be said to possess every thing necessary to constitute it in common with the white people."

The essay demanded an end to the importation of new slaves. Rush wasn't sure if freeing older and more infirm slaves was actually going to help them or would be for "the good of society." But he was certain that "young Negroes" should be "educated in the principles of virtue and religion—let them be taught to read and write—and afterwards instructed in some business, whereby they may be able to maintain themselves. Let laws be made to limit the time of their servitude, and to entitle them to all the privileges of free-born British subjects."

Rush's arguments weren't all new, but he wrote them forcefully and humanely and brought them together in concise, compelling form. His name wasn't on the pamphlet—he identified himself simply as "a Pennsylvanian"—but his writing was clearly informed by scientific training and a deep understanding of Judeo-Christian history and philosophy. All twelve hundred copies that were printed quickly sold out. Excerpts appeared in newspapers in Pennsylvania and Connecticut.

While no direct responses were published in the newspapers, a competing pamphlet appeared almost immediately under the title *Slavery Not Forbidden by Scripture.* The author identified himself only as a plantation owner in the West Indies. He challenged Rush on various moral and legal fronts but waited until page twenty-one to get to his most fundamental point:

> It is impossible to determine, with accuracy, whether their intellects or ours are superior, as individuals, no doubt, [they have not had] the same opportunities of improving as we have: However, on the whole it seems probable, that they are a much inferior race of men to the whites, in every respect. . . . Slavery, like all other human institutions, may be attended with its particular abuses, but that is not sufficient totally to condemn it, and to reckon every one unworthy the society of men who owns a negro.

Rush immediately wrote a response, *A Vindication*, which he appended to his original pamphlet and republished, still as the pseudonymous "Pennsylvanian." It was an immediate publishing success. Rush's abolitionist friend Anthony Benezet bought the first five hundred copies of the reprint himself.

Word circulated privately that Rush had written these pamphlets, in part because he mailed some copies out with cover letters admitting his authorship. He became something of a celebrity in the abolitionist world and something of a pariah in the doctoring world. For nearly a year, as he continued to mention his identity as the pamphlet's author in private letters that he suspected wouldn't remain entirely private, his practice drew significantly fewer patients: from an average of eighty a month, business dropped by half or more.

Eventually, as he did more writing under his own name—and public lecturing at the Philosophical Society—on medical issues, his business bounced back. But he was left with the feeling that the experience "injured me in another way, by giving rise to an opinion that I had meddled with a controversy that was foreign to my business. I now found that a physician's studies and duties were to be limited by the public, and that he was destined to walk in a path as contracted as the most humble and dependent mechanic."

Rush continued to take notes and save string on ideas concerning slavery. It would be years before he wrote about it again, because, like many Americans, he was getting caught up in the arguments surrounding England's taxation and control over the colonies. But his thoughts would help fuel new directions for the abolitionist movement, as well as his own ideas about human behavior. In these early writings he can be seen trying to work out how being enslaved affects a human being psychologically; his later conclusions would become an underpinning of his theories of the mind and its vulnerabilities.

"Human nature," he wrote in *A Vindication*, "is the same in all ages and countries, and all the differences we perceive in its characters in respect to virtue and vice, knowledge and ignorance, may be accounted for from climate, country, degrees of civilization, forms of government, or accidental causes."

In a correspondence with the British abolitionist Granville Sharp after publication, he took this idea of innate equality a step further, tying it to the concept of a universal "moral faculty."

Rush told Sharp he had "collected a number of facts to show that the *moral faculty* is as essential a power or property of the soul as memory or imagination—That it is equally innate—equally capable of cultivation and equally liable to injuries from causes of a *physical* nature. It is sometimes suspended like memory in sleep, and in certain diseases, and it sometimes outlives the destruction of every other faculty of the mind."

Rush advanced this theory in an attempt to describe the physical and psychological impact of slavery to Sharp. But he also generalized further: if trauma or disease could change or cloud people's thinking, and influence their actions, then the challenges of madness and vice might be better addressed by treating physical illness instead of trying to influence their moral state through religion.

"If the moral faculty can be injured by physical causes, may it not be improved by the same means?" he asked:

> The memory and judgement are strengthened by exercise, and temperance and the imagination is enlivened by a fulness of the blood vessels of the head,—in like manner may not a regimen, or a medicine be discovered which shall improve, or alter the diseased state of the moral faculty? . . . An erring judgement (as in maniacal and delirious patients) has been cured by bleeding—and blistering.

Rush wasn't certain exactly what treatments would be used to prevent the moral faculty from being influenced by physical causes. He just knew these behaviors—addictions, madness—would come to be seen as medical problems.

"Perhaps hereafter," he wrote, "it may be as much the business of a physician as it is now of a divine to reclaim mankind from vice."

9

Rush's medical practice grew, along with the size of his classes and the number of medical apprentices paying for the privilege of working with him. Many of the apprentices bunked at his new home on Front Street just above Walnut, where the front entrance opened onto a crowded cobblestone street and the back windows looked out on the busy port of Philadelphia and the Delaware River.

Rush delivered more papers at the Philosophical Society and wrote signed articles for the newspaper on subjects that he suspected might attract attention and business. He wrote a short paper exploring the "ill effects of drinking cold water," as he had become fixated on the impact of cold, especially cold air, and the cause of colds. Franklin shared his interest, and in the summer of 1773, they corresponded about a theory that came from Franklin's friend in England, Dr. Joseph Priestley, who was researching all kinds of air (on his way to isolating oxygen a year later). At the moment, Priestley was exploring "fixed air," what we now know as carbon dioxide, which, because it was expelled from the lungs, was thought to carry and hold many nasty things. When Rush queried him on the challenges of this fixed air contamination, Franklin speculated that "people often catch Cold from one another when shut up together in small close Rooms, Coaches, &c. and when sitting near and conversing so as to breathe in each others Transpiration [and] . . . the frowzy corrupt Air from animal Substances," rather than from cold and damp. Rush decided to pursue his cold water theory for the moment.

He also published letters in the papers on the treatment of "spasmodic asthma" in children and of gout in adults, and on the usefulness of wort, the sugary liquid created during the mashing process in beer and whiskey making, in treating ulcers. And he went to great lengths to describe the challenge of getting a little girl to throw up all the seeds she had swallowed from a narcotic plant, the thorn-apple, in her family's garden.

These public case reports were useful for drawing attention to his practice, but they weren't what Rush really wanted to write about. Like many in Philadelphia, he was becoming obsessed with colonial politics, as America's relationship with England grew more frictional by the day. For political reasons, Rush even went so far as giving up one of his favorite drinks:

Tea.

In May 1773, in an attempt to bail out the British East India Company, Parliament passed the Tea Act, which gave the tea exporter a near-monopoly on selling to America. The act was wildly unpopular in the colonies, and anger rose in September when reports circulated that the first huge shipment of tea under the new law was headed for America—where ships would land in Philadelphia, Boston, and New York.

In early October, Rush wrote his first essay about colonial tax issues, "On Patriotism." It appeared on the front page of the weekly *Pennsylvania Packet*, under the pseudonym "Hamden." He began by declaring that "patriotism is as much a virtue as justice, and is as necessary for the support of societies as natural affection is for the support of families." Even "the holy men of old," Rush wrote, ". . . were endowed with a public spirit." He proposed to rescue "patriotism from obloquy" with a critique of "the machinations of the enemies of our country to enslave us by means of the East-India Company."

Rush claimed that if the ships heading to the colonies full of taxed tea were allowed to land and unload, "then farewell American Liberty! We are undone forever. All the images we can borrow from everything terrible in nature are too faint to describe the horror of our situation." In a rousing finish, he cried out, "Let us with ONE heart and hand oppose the landing . . . the baneful chests contain in them a slow poison in a political as well as a physical sense. They contain something worse than death—the seeds of SLAVERY. . . . Think of your ancestors and of your posterity."

Only days after the essay was published, Rush was invited to a secret meeting at the home of old Capt. William Bradford, the successful publisher and printer of the *Pennsylvania Journal* and several magazines and books. Rush had grown up with Bradford's son Thomas (who had married Rush's old girlfriend Polly Fisher), but he knew the captain primarily through his proprietorship of the legendary London Coffee House, which the young doctor often frequented. The "coffee house," on the southwest corner of Front and Market, was much more than that. Politicians and merchants used it to transact all types of business, often in their own private booths. Just outside the London Coffee House was the new location of the stand used for the inspection and auctioning of slaves, including new slaves just off the boats from the nearby harbor, and those being offered for sale to new masters. The establishment was the locus of a lot of animated revolutionary and counterrevolutionary conversations.

Bradford, a fiercely patriotic veteran of the French and Indian War, believed that Philadelphians needed to stop this British tea

William Bradford, printer and owner of the London Coffee House at the corner of Front and Market.

from being delivered to the port. One day he got into a discussion about it with Thomas Mifflin, a friend and contemporary of Rush's who, as a young member of the Pennsylvania Assembly, doubted that the citizens of Philadelphia could be convinced to actively resist the tea deliveries.

Thomas Mifflin and his wife

As the economic capital of the colonies, Philadelphia had the most to lose financially from protest. Among its population were two major groups who would resist even a hint of armed revolt. Tories, or loyalists, believed completely in British rule, usually belonged to the Church of England, and felt that if some of the onerous new taxes were changed or repealed, everything would be fine. And many Quakers, who were pacifists, simply did not believe in violence and war for religious reasons. Political liberals in England, and later colonists who supported revolution, were called Whigs.

As the two men stood talking in Bradford's doorway, Bradford boasted to Mifflin, "Leave that business to me. I will collect a few active Spirits at my house tomorrow evening. . . . Be one of them, and we will soon set the city in motion." Among the half dozen "active spirits" was Rush, whose essay suggested he could prove useful in creating a proclamation the city could support. At the London Coffee House on October 14, Rush, Mifflin, and others drafted eight resounding resolutions to present to the public. Rush's hand was clear in their language, which declared that "a virtuous and steady opposition to this ministerial plan of governing America, is absolutely necessary to preserve even the shadow of liberty." The plan to bring East India taxed tea to the colonies was "a violent Attack upon the Liberties of America." It was "the Duty of every American to oppose this." And "whoever shall directly or indirectly . . . aid or abet in unloading, receiving, or vending the Tea . . . is an Enemy to his Country."

After the coffee house summit, the group arranged for a meeting of merchants and leaders at the State House. On Saturday afternoon, October 16, a large crowd gathered there while Rush and his colleagues were inside listening to their resolutions being discussed, then ratified. They took the document outside and read it to the cheering, jeering throng.

Rush had never seen anything like it in his life. He would later describe the day to John Adams as "the first throe of that Convulsion which delivered Great Britain of the United States. . . . The flame kindled on that day soon extended to Boston & gradually spread throughout the whole Continent."

It was in Massachusetts that the words of Rush and his colleagues had the most impact. Several weeks after the Philadelphia meeting, a similar one took place in Boston at Faneuil Hall, with John Hancock as moderator. After much debate, the Bostonians decided they were so in accord with their peers in Philadelphia that they didn't need to write their own proclamation. Instead, they resolved that "the Sense of this Town cannot be better expressed . . . than in the Words of certain Judicious Resolves lately entered into by our worthy Brethren the Citizens of *Philadelphia*." They accepted the proclamation about stopping East India tea shipments as their own.

Many were surprised that the fieriest rhetoric wasn't coming from Boston. Though Philadelphia was the largest and most powerful city in the colonies, and New York the fastest-growing, Boston was the oldest and was seen as the most radical. Importer Henry Drinker, whose firm James & Drinker was supposed to sell some of the East India tea in Philadelphia—until it became politically incorrect to even consider it—wrote to a friend in New York, "Philadelphia leads the way. . . . Boston but feebly follows our Heroes . . . William Bradford & others, who are stiled [styled] the Sons of Liberty." He was referring to the nickname coined in Boston in 1765, during the fight against the Stamp Act, for what was then a very loose underground of disparate revolutionary thinkers, who knew each other primarily through shared rhetoric in anonymously published writings.

Several weeks later, when the tea-laden boats from England arrived in Boston before the other major ports, the words of Rush

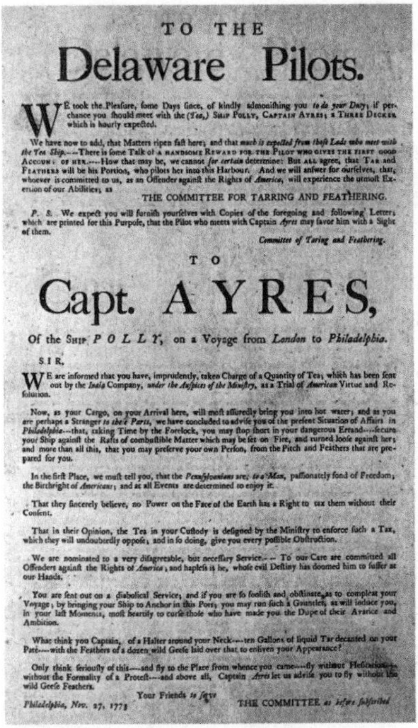
TO THE

Delaware Pilots.

WE took the Pleaſure, ſome Days ſince, of kindly admoniſhing you *to do your Duty*; if perchance you ſhould meet with the *(Tea,)* SHIP POLLY, CAPTAIN AYRES; a THREE DECKER which is hourly expected.

We have now to add, that Matters ripen faſt here; and that *much is expected from thoſe Lads who meet with the Tea Ship.*---There is ſome Talk of A HANDSOME REWARD FOR THE PILOT WHO GIVES THE FIRST GOOD ACCOUNT OF HER.----How that may be, we cannot *for certain* determine: But ALL agree, that TAR and FEATHERS will be his Portion, who pilots her into this Harbour. And we will anſwer for ourſelves, that, whoever is committed to us, as an Offender againſt the Rights of *America*, will experience the utmoſt Exertion of our Abilities; as

THE COMMITTEE FOR TARRING AND FEATHERING.

P. S. We expect you will furniſh yourſelves with Copies of the foregoing and following Letters; which are printed for this Purpoſe, that the Pilot who meets with Captain *Ayres* may favor him with a Sight of them.

Committee of Taring and Feathering.

T O

Capt. A Y R E S,

Of the SHIP *P O L L Y*, on a Voyage from *London* to *Philadelphia*.

SIR,

WE are informed that you have, imprudently, taken Charge of a Quantity of Tea; which has been ſent out by the *India* Company, *under the Auſpices of the Miniſtry*, as a Trial of *American* Virtue and Reſolution.

Now, as your Cargo, on your Arrival here, will moſt aſſuredly bring you into hot water; and as you are perhaps a Stranger *to theſe Parts*, we have concluded to adviſe you of the preſent Situation of Affairs in *Philadelphia*---that, taking Time by the Forelock, you may ſtop ſhort in your dangerous Errand----ſecure your Ship againſt the Rafts of combuſtible Matter which may be ſet on Fire, and turned looſe againſt her; and more than all this, that you may preſerve your own Perſon, from the Pitch and Feathers that are prepared for you.

In the firſt Place, we muſt tell you, that the *Pennſylvanians* are, *to a Man*, paſſionately fond of Freedom; the Birthright of *Americans*; and at all Events are determined to enjoy it.

That they ſincerely believe, no Power on the Face of the Earth has a Right to tax them without their Conſent.

That in their Opinion, the Tea in your Cuſtody is deſigned by the Miniſtry to enforce ſuch a Tax, which they will undoubtedly oppoſe; and in ſo doing, give you every poſſible Obſtruction.

We are nominated to a very diſagreeable, but neceſſary Service.---To our Care are committed all Offenders againſt the Rights of *America*; and hapleſs is he, whoſe evil Deſtiny has doomed him to ſuffer at our Hands.

You are ſent out on a diabolical Service; and if you are ſo fooliſh and obſtinate, as to compleat your Voyage; by bringing your Ship to Anchor in this Port; you may run ſuch a Gauntlet, as will induce you, in your laſt Moments, moſt heartily to curſe thoſe who have made you the Dupe of their Avarice and Ambition.

What think you Captain, of a Halter around your Neck----ten Gallons of liquid Tar decanted on your Pate----with the Feathers of a dozen wild Geeſe laid over that to enliven your Appearance?

Only think ſeriouſly of this----and fly to the Place from whence you came----fly without Heſitation----without the Formality of a Proteſt----and above all, Captain *Ayres* let us adviſe you to fly without the wild Geeſe Feathers.

Your Friends *to ſerve*

Philadelphia, Nov. 27, 1773 THE COMMITTEE *as before ſubſcribed*

The poster of the "Committee of Tarring and Feathering"

and Mifflin helped inspire Samuel Adams and others to carry out the patriotic vandalism that came to be known as the Boston Tea Party. On December 16, 1773, several dozen colonists, some disguised as Native Americans, boarded the three ships in Boston Harbor filled with tea—the *Dartmouth*, the *Eleanor*, and the *Beaver*—and threw their cargo, over three hundred chests of East India tea, into the water. It became the first signature act of the revolt and made the Sons of Liberty, whose identities were still secret, into rising revolutionary heroes.

A week later the tea ship bound for Philadelphia, the *Polly*, was seen in the distance approaching from the south, having navigated Delaware Bay and heading up the Delaware River. A secret group calling itself the Committee on Tarring and Feathering had been issuing broadsides to seamen to be on the lookout for the unadorned black ship, piloted by a "short fat Fellow," Captain Ayres. He was well enough known on this trade route that they had already "calculated to a Gill and a Feather" how much tar would be needed before "we shall heave him Keel out."

Captain Ayres wisely stopped his ship far south of the city, near Chester, where he was met by members of the "committee" and brought by a small pilot boat to meet with angry city officials. After nearly two days in town, including a raucous meeting at the State House on Monday morning, December 27, he agreed to go back to his ship and sail home with his cargo. This deprived Philadelphia's Sons of Liberty, as some now called them, of their own place in Tea Party history, but it energized Benjamin Rush to find his place in the increasingly roiling arguments over colonial rule.

WHILE PRIVATELY BECOMING more politicized, Rush wanted to keep his career as a physician and scientist on track. In 1774, he helped found the Society for Inoculating the Poor, along with several other physicians, to help stop the spread of smallpox—which had killed more than three hundred of the city's 1,334 dead the previous year. Rush had learned the newest way of doing these inoculations, the Suttonian Method, while he was studying in London; it employed a smaller cut and less infected material than the inoculations Cotton Mather had introduced to the colonies in the 1720s, which infected a higher percentage of patients.

Drs. Rush, Bond, Shippen Jr., and others agreed to give free inoculations each Tuesday morning from ten to noon at the State House. It was an act of charity for the physicians, and Rush was in good company. But he was probably the only one of the volunteers who needed the work to bolster his practice, which still included many patients who could just barely pay. He still wasn't yet where he had hoped to be in his career: he was the only professor at the medical school who wasn't on the staff at Pennsylvania Hospital. While the main reason might have been that he was younger than the others, he sometimes felt he was deliberately being held back.

Rush also stayed active as an officer in the Philosophical Society. In February he was invited to give his first annual oration, the main intellectual event in the society's year. He was asked at the last minute, when a colleague fell ill, and chose a subject he had researched very little himself: the "Natural History of Medicine Among the Indians of North America." It is unclear just how many Indians Rush had ever met and spoken to in his twenty-eight years of city-centric life; many of his observations came from secondary sources. But the topic did allow him to offer "a comparative view of their Diseases and Remedies, with those of civilized Nations," which turned out to be a good excuse to explore some of his broader churning ideas about medicine.

At one point during the talk—given to a large crowd of society members and the public—he said that to clarify a point about Indian medicine, he would need to digress into "a history of the operations of nature in . . . the diseases of civilized nations." There were "cases in which nature is still successful in curing diseases," he explained, versus "cases where the efforts of nature are too feeble to do service" or "cases where the efforts of nature are over proportioned to the strength of the disease," in which he included all kinds of fevers and hemorrhages. He also cited cases where "nature is idle," so treatment would be the only hope, including cancer, epilepsy, mania, venereal disease, gout, and tetanus. And there were cases where nature actually "does mischief," including the way it "drives the melancholy patient to solitude, where, by brooding over the subject of his insanity, he increases his disease."

Generally, Rush wasn't sure it was always such a good idea to rely on the "kindness of nature" to guide the treatment of disease. Even a sign as basic as pain could be misleading—there were situations where nature "refuses to send this harbinger of the evils which threaten her," and cases where pain was either much less or much greater than the danger.

In the printed text of the speech, as in many of Rush's longer pieces of writing, the hastily written diversions and footnotes were fascinating or troubling or sometimes both. He was prescient in one footnote: "The late successful inquiries into the laws of the nervous system, and the theories we have built upon them, will probably appear like the outlines of a picture, compared with that COMPLETE SYSTEM of physic which remains to be unfolded hereafter, when we arrive at a full knowledge of the structure and economy of the brain." In another note he railed about the overuse of strong liquor, a medical opinion few would dispute, but then took a political left turn—calling for the end of "the ravages which TEA is making upon the health and populousness of our country."

Rush cut the line about tea before he sent the piece to Benjamin Franklin in England, in hopes that he would write a preface that would help to get it published there. But in July 1774, Franklin wrote back that he thought an essay on the subject of Indian health could hurt Rush's odds of attaining a career goal he desperately wanted: a place in the Royal Society, England's premier scientific institution. Franklin claimed he was about to nominate Rush for the honor and didn't want to take any chances. He recommended delaying publication and politely refused Rush's request to write a preface.

As was typical of their relationship, Franklin's letter moved directly from career issues to science. He excitedly shared some of the latest fixed air experiments using Priestley's ideas—they were carbonating mineral water.

In a blow to his young career, Rush was not accepted into the Royal Society that year. But by the time he found out, he had turned his attention to more pressing matters.

10

In the late summer of 1774, Philadelphia was stinking hot and buzzing about the approach of delegations from all over the colonies for the first-ever Continental Congress. Many of the more established members of the medical community already knew some of the national players and had even arranged to host them at their homes. George Washington, for example, would be staying at the home of Dr. William Shippen, Jr.'s, father.

Benjamin Rush had no such political connections, except for his quiet association with the Philadelphia Sons of Liberty. When that group arranged to head out to meet the most controversial of the arriving delegations—the men from Massachusetts—to escort them into the city, Rush was invited.

On August 29, he and his friend Tom Mifflin, along with several others, rode by carriage out to Frankford, a farm town north of the city. The Philadelphians were probably most interested in meeting Samuel Adams, the fifty-one-year-old former publisher and brewer who was publicly associated with the Boston Tea Party and had more recently organized a boycott of British goods. The primary Massachusetts force behind the Continental Congress and his delegation's elder statesman, Sam Adams was one of the nation's most open proponents of revolution.

But Rush found himself more intrigued by Adams's younger

second cousin, John, a pugnacious attorney. He was, like Rush, brilliant, opinionated, emotional, and occasionally overwhelming, even to himself. But John Adams had the benefit of age—he was ten years Rush's senior—and, at home, the emotional and intellectual anchor of a strong-willed, loving wife, Abigail, and four children. Though he lacked Rush's height and elegance, John Adams was, in almost any group, the most "sensible and forcible speaker."

John Adams

As the two groups sat drinking in a private room in Frankford, the Philadelphians launched into their advice: no matter how much the Bostonians might favor independence, they must never say so in Philadelphia. To the British loyalists and the pacifist Quakers, as well as to representatives arriving from the other middle colonies (New York, New Jersey, Delaware) and the southern colonies, "the idea of Independence is as unpopular . . . as the Stamp Act itself. No man dares to speak of it."

The Philadelphians also told the visiting delegation they shouldn't try to lead the congress. Adams recalled them insisting:

> You are the Representatives of the suffering State. . . . Boston and Massachusetts are under a rod of Iron. British fleets and Armies are tyranizing over you; you yourselves are personally obnoxious to them and all the friends of government. You have been long persecuted by them all:—Your feelings have been hurt; your passions excited; you are thought to be too warm, too zealous, too sanguine, you must be therefore very cautious. You must not come forward with any bold measures; you must not pretend to take the lead. You know Virginia is the most populous State in the Union. They are very proud of their antient [ancient] Dominion, as they call it; they think they have a right to take the lead,

and the Southern States and middle States too, are too much disposed to yield it to them.

By the time everyone finished their drinks, Rush had decided that John was the Adams he needed to get to know better. He let his friends ride into town with Sam Adams and talked his way into the carriage carrying John. They were joined by the most obstinately moderate member of the Massachusetts delegation, Robert Treat Paine, a clergyman turned attorney who admitted to Rush during the ride into town that "his constituents considered him as one of their 'cool devils.'" If John Adams was the designated accelerator of the delegation, Paine planned to be the brake. (Rush wasn't surprised when Paine went on to earn the nickname "The Objection Maker" in Congress, since he "seldom proposed anything" yet "opposed nearly every measure that was proposed.")

During the carriage ride, Rush tried to explain to Adams the kind of people he would meet in Philadelphia: they would express anger at King George and British rule, but they really wanted a return to the pre–Stamp Tax status quo, not a revolution. He specifically warned him about the influential Rev. Dr. William Smith, the Church of England clergyman who was provost of the College of Philadelphia, where Rush taught. Rush said he would find Smith "soft, polite, insinuating, adulating, sensible, learned, industrious, indefatigable"—and a man who would never admit to Adams's face that he was against him, even when he was.

The hero of Pennsylvanians was still John Dickinson, whom Adams looked forward to meeting. As a lawyer, he was interested in Dickinson's *Farmer's Letters*, even if they didn't support revolution.

Rush had Adams's undivided attention, until their carriage pulled into the neighborhood close to Carpenters' Hall—where the convention would be meeting. Even though Adams was, by his own description, "dirty, dusty and fatigued," he could not resist an invitation to go to the new and popular City Tavern, which he had heard was "the most genteel one in America," on Second Street between Walnut and Chestnut. There Rush had to relinquish him to a larger group that included not only Dr. Shippen, Jr., but the very same Provost Smith whom he had just warned Adams about. Along with other members of the South Carolina and Pennsylvania delegations, they all retired to a private room and were served, according to Adams, "a Supper . . . as elegant as ever was laid upon a Table." He was there talking, eating, and drinking until eleven p.m., after which he and Robert Paine retired to the boardinghouse just across Second Street, run by Mrs. Yards, a patient of Rush.

In the coming month, Adams would dine with Drs. Rush, Shippen, and Morgan—all maintaining an uneasy but established truce—together or separately on ten different occasions. Besides currying friendship, all three doctors sought the delegates' medical business; Rush gave Patrick Henry, among others, a smallpox inoculation and eventually "waited upon nearly all the members of this first Congress." Since very few of them show up in his billing logs, he must have been offering a lot of free Founding Father medical advice.

On September 14, Rush held a banquet at his home, which Adams attended along with John Morgan. Rush's sister Rebecca, who did all the cooking and housekeeping, set out what Adams described as "A mighty Feast . . . nothing less than the very best of Claret, Madeira, and Burgundy. Melons, fine beyond description, and Pears and Peaches as excellent." Adams was also impressed by the expansive view of the Delaware River and New Jersey available through the back windows of Rush's home. He wrote in his diary that he had appreciated the banter on the "Absurdities in the Laws of Pensylvania, New Jersey and Maryland," which he found to be "a genteel Topic of Conversation" in the city.

As the Continental Congress headed into its second month, Adams's landlord, Mrs. Yard, became increasingly ill. Rush made house calls nearly every day, in part so he could spend more time with Adams and keep up on the gossip from the congressional meetings.

In his diaries and his letters to his wife, Adams described Drs. Morgan and Shippen, both closer to his own age than Rush, in glowing terms: Morgan was "an ingeneous Physician and an honest Patriot," while Shippen and his father were "sensible, and deep thinkers." But Rush would have been disappointed to learn that

Adams did not describe him—except for his food and the view from his house—in any detail even once during his seven-week stay for the First Continental Congress.

On October 14, the congress adopted the "Declaration of Colonial Rights," resolving that certain acts of the British government were "infringements and violations of the rights of the colonists" and demanding their repeal. They then began debating the creation of a formal "Continental Association," a new quasi-government, the first act of which would be to boycott British imports until all "intolerable acts" were repealed.

During the debate over this first round of congressional decisions, Rush was invited for dinner at the home of Tom Mifflin, who had become an influential delegate for Pennsylvania. Among Mifflin's other guests were John and Samuel Adams—who by then had proven themselves important leaders in Congress—and two rising military men from Virginia. One was Charles Lee, a former British soldier of fortune who now supported independence.

The other was George Washington, a decorated military leader because of his service in the French and Indian War. Washington was then forty-two, as tall as Rush but more broad-shouldered and quietly powerful.

George Washington and a servant

After dinner, John Adams admitted that he assumed Great Britain would ignore the demands to which the Continental Congress had just agreed. During the formal toasting, Adams raised his glass and declared, "Cash and Gunpowder to the Yankies!" Soon, he believed, the colonies would have to pool their money to fund fighting in New England, where he expected the war to first break out. And next to funds, they would need nothing so much as gunpowder.

Rush had been exploring the very political science of gunpowder production for some time, in his role as a chemistry professor. He felt the colonies should take local manufacturing more seriously, in order to become more economically self-sufficient (the very beginning of "Made in America"). But clearly the first item England would stop exporting to America in the event of war was anything that could be used to kill its soldiers. Rush had been experimenting with a method of creating gunpowder from a very plentiful American crop, tobacco. He was writing a paper describing a method to create saltpeter—potassium nitrate, one of the essential components of gunpowder—out of dried tobacco stalks.

It is not known whether Rush brought up this work at Mifflin's table, but his contributions must have made an impression, because George Washington came to Rush's home for dinner the very next day. After Rush's sister cooked for them, they walked over to City Tavern to continue their conversation. Some years later, Washington and Rush would look back on that twenty-four-hour period in late October 1774 and wonder how they could have been both so right and so wrong about each other.

11

During the last week of the First Continental Congress, the members finalized the creation of a formal "association" of colonies and set a December deadline for a boycott of all British imports if the so-called "intolerable acts" were not repealed. They also agreed to meet again for a second congress. After the first congress adjourned on Wednesday, October 26, those delegates who had not already left held a banquet at the City Tavern and invited the local gentlemen who had taken such good care of them, among them Dr. Benjamin Rush.

The conversation that evening, according to Rush, was "animated by the most fervid patriotism." He was especially moved by the toast from the Governor of Rhode Island: "May the fire which has been recently kindled upon the altar of liberty in America, enlighten all nations of the world into a knowledge of their rights."

It was, however, unclear what the congress had actually accomplished. As he was leaving town Friday in the pouring rain, John Adams felt sad to be departing "the happy, the peacefull, the elegant, the hospitable, and polite City of Phyladelphia." Writing in his diary that evening in Bristol, he did not sound optimistic. "It is not likely," he predicted, that "I shall ever see this Part of the World again. but I shall ever retain a most greatefull, pleasing Sense, of the many Civilities I have received, in it."

As the excitement of the congress came to an end, Benjamin Rush was feeling lonely; he would soon turn twenty-nine, and he yearned for love and marriage. Life expectancy in the colonies was under forty years, and in acceding to his mother's wishes and waiting so long to settle down, he was taking an enormous calculated risk. Some close to him had been worried for a while. His cousin Thomas Coombe had pleaded to him, "is there no Maid in the polished City of Philadelphia, whom you covet to call your own? Surely your optics are clouded—your Brain vessels twisted by Study—& your fine Nerves become callous! Spiritus Chemiae, what has thou done! converted the feeling Heart of a Man of Genius into a marble Monument of Stoicism!"

One of his closest single friends, Betsey Graeme, had married for the first time at the age of thirty-five (to a loyalist Scotsman whom Rush had brought to the salon to meet her). Lady Jane Leslie in Scotland was, at twenty-one, still single, which simply served to torture him. Among his correspondence from the fall of 1774 are several torn pages of a letter to her; while it is unclear if they are copies of a letter sent, or evidence that he changed his mind, the sentiment in them is pained.

He feared that someone else "now possesses her heart" and perhaps "the day is fixed for the Consummation." He said he would try to "continue to conceal & attempt to subdue my Passion." But then he changed his mind: "Subdue my Passion, did I say? No, I will not attempt it. When beauty, softness, sweetness of temper, a benevolent heart, an excellent understanding, amiable manners . . . [and] all female excellencies are united together there is both a pleasure and praise in loving."

Among the young women Rush knew in Philadelphia was a plucky, irreverent twenty-four-year-old redhead named Sarah Eve. She was closer to his cousins in town than to his side of the family, and there is some mystery surrounding her relationship with Dr. Rush.

The entire Eve family were patients in his practice, and Sarah took ill during the Continental Congress. For weeks, Rush made almost daily house calls on her, but he was not able to save her;

she died on December 4, 1774. We have no contemporary proof that their relationship was anything more than friendly and professional, and Rush charged Sarah's father fully for her care.

But when part of her diary was published years later, the relative who had inherited it claimed that, according to family lore, there was something more between Sarah Eve and Dr. Rush. A week after her death an unsigned eulogy entitled "A Female Character" appeared in the *Pennsylvania Packet*, richly describing a twenty-four-year-old woman who "belonged to the first order of beings"—a phrase sometimes used by Rush—and who "possessed the most exquisite and delicate sensibility of soul." It described a patient ready to die but magnanimously staying alive because her parents wanted more time with her. "She dreaded the attacks of her pain . . . only because they sometimes extorted groans from her which disturbed her parents. She was reconciled to living, only because her life had become necessary to their happiness."

Rush could have written it. But the Eve family lore that he and Sarah were engaged and would have married on Christmas Eve had she lived seems a little more apocryphal.

WHILE LOVE WAS still elusive, Rush always had the refuge of reading. Given his appetite for volumes on medicine, philosophy, literature, politics, and religion—and his growing side business as an author—he always sought to befriend those who could keep him in books. Bookstores also sold tickets to his lectures.

One bookshop he liked was run by a Scottish immigrant in his late thirties, Robert Aitken. It was on Market Street, just west of the London Coffee House.

Aitken had technically been Rush's first publisher. When he started teaching chemistry at the college, he had needed copies of the forty-eight-page class syllabus (mostly copied from the one Dr. Black had used at Edinburgh). Aitken had printed it. When Rush wrote his controversial pamphlet on slavery, he worked with a better-established publisher, John Dunlap, who also published the *Pennsylvania Packet*. But the Aitken bookshop was just paces from Rush's house and office, and he often stopped there between patients to nibble at new publications and talk about books with fellow customers.

In February 1775, he met "a certain Thomas Paine" there, a thirty-seven-year-old writer who had arrived from England the year before. Paine was down on his luck and hoping to make a fresh start in the colonies as a teacher, either working at a school or offering private lessons in geography to young men and even young women. Rakishly engaging with a mane of thick, dark hair, a larger-than-life nose, and the leathery skin of a journeyman, Paine presented what Rush referred to as "a short letter of introduction from Dr. Franklin," whom he had met in London. (By this point, Rush realized that a *lot* of people had such letters, some more notable than others.)

While awaiting a teaching job, Paine was doing some freelance writing and editing. Aitken was starting his first periodical, which he hoped would become the premier magazine-style publication in America, bringing together stories from the different colonies. Aitken had been trying to sell advance subscriptions for months, taking out ads in newspapers in Philadelphia, Boston, and New York. He proposed so many different names for the publication to see what stuck, that when the first issue finally came out in late February, it had two titles: *The Pennsylvania Magazine: or, American Monthly Museum.*

Aitken hired Paine to help fill the first few issues, finding stories to run and writing about whatever he could think of—under a variety of pseudonyms, so the magazine would appear to have a lot of contributors. Rush's first meeting with Paine was unmemorable, but not long after, Paine wrote an anonymous broadside against slavery that Rush very much admired. Not only did he agree with its sentiment, but he enjoyed the conversation he had with Paine about it in the bookshop.

By this time, the politics in the colonies had experienced a major shift. In the late afternoon of April 24, Philadelphians received the shocking news of the Battles of Lexington and Concord, which had taken place five days earlier. Nearly a thousand British soldiers had marched on two Massachusetts militia outposts and, report-

Thomas Paine

edly without provocation, opened fire. The night before, Paul Revere and several other riders had warned the outposts that the troops were approaching, but they were still stunned by the British actions. One initial report was that six men were dead and at least four injured in Lexington, many more in Concord.

For Rush and so many other colonists, this was the turning point. "The first gun that was fired at an American," Rush wrote, "cut the cord that had tied the two countries together."

That night bells rang all over the city to spread the news of the tragedy, and the next day eight thousand people gathered in front of the State House building and pledged to defend the colonies. Some colonies had already been beefing up their provincial militias, while others debated how to fund a large increase in soldier pay and munitions. Patrick Henry's recent "Liberty or Death" speech at the Virginia Convention meeting at St. John's Church in Richmond was part of that effort. Now even loyalist Quaker Pennsylvania was arming itself.

The timing couldn't have been more perfect to ignite a revolution, because the Second Continental Congress was scheduled to meet in Philadelphia the first week of May. Most of the original delegates were returning—Rush was looking forward to reconnecting with John and Samuel Adams and George Washington—and several important newcomers were joining the process. John Hancock was now a member of the Massachusetts delegation, and for the first time in a decade, Benjamin Franklin was coming home to attend as a representative of Pennsylvania.

When the delegates got to town, Philadelphia felt and even sounded different to them. As a gesture of mourning for the soldiers lost in Lexington and Concord, every bell in the city had been muted.

Yet political conversations were growing louder and more passionate, and Rush found himself in an increasing number of them. While maintaining his medical practice, he made time to "mix freely with" his comrades serving in the Continental Congress and their colleagues. Some friends, like the Adamses, mostly liked talking about the political side of things; others, like Tom Mifflin, Charles Lee, and George Washington, were more likely to talk about military issues. And writer friends such as Tom Paine talked about how best to communicate revolutionary ideas and when it might be safe to do so.

Rush enjoyed moving back and forth between these camps and talking the talk with each of them, cross-pollinating ideas. And he had a rare knack for getting people to speak to him, whether it was at the London Coffee House, at Aitken's Bookshop, at his own supper table, or at Mrs. Yards's rooming house, where he would go after work to gossip with John Adams and others staying there. Some felt Rush could be too exuberant about the ideas they shared with him, and wondered if he was an entirely safe confidant. But he seemed to know *everybody* and almost everything. And there was no question of his commitment to Pennsylvania and the colonies, to freedom, to his religion, and to his loved ones.

He never suggested to his friends in Congress that he would rather have their job than his own. And being in the Continental Congress was a job, one that the colonies paid for but that a person could take only if someone else were able to oversee his farm or plantation or law practice. A sole practitioner physician and college professor probably couldn't do that job without quitting everything.

There were also indications Rush wouldn't necessarily excel at full-time politics. He was too impatient and too certain he was right. Several months earlier he had been given his first political position: he had been elected president of the new United Company for Promoting American Manufactures, which hoped to encourage the manufacture of woolens, cotton, and linens in the colonies, both to create independence from England and perhaps to jump-start a "laudable spirit of industry among the poor."

His first major speech for them turned out to be his last. This may have been because, as he admitted, he only had a "small share of knowledge" about manufacturing. More likely it was that after delivering a fairly straightforward talk about the advantages of more industry in the colonies—one that almost any businessman, loyalist or not, could appreciate—he began a challenging riff about relations with England. "America is now the only asylum for liberty in the whole world," he declared. "The present contest with Great Britain was perhaps intended by the Supreme Being, among other wise and benevolent purposes, to show the world this asylum, which, from its remote and unconnected situation with the rest of the globe, might have remained a secret for ages."

A failure to create new manufacturing, he went on, would be tantamount to a form of slavery. And

> by becoming slaves, we shall lose every principle of virtue. We shall transfer unlimited obedience from our Maker to a corrupted majority in the British House of Commons . . . [and] shall cease to look with horror upon the prostitution of our wives and daughters to those civil and military harpies, who now hover-around the liberties of our country. . . . We shall hug our chains. We shall cease to be men. We shall be *slaves.*

While he then doubled back on more conventional issues of manufacturing, his rousing, somewhat incoherent conclusion focused much more on international politics than on linens.

> I am not one of those vindictive patriots who exult in the prospect of the decay of the manufacturies of Britain. I can forgive her late attempts to enslave us, in the memory of our once *mutual* freedom and happiness. And should her liberty . . . her fleets and her armies and her empire ever be interred in Britain, I hope they will all rise in British garments *only* in America.

The speech was delivered at Carpenters' Hall, and then published in the paper in two parts. But Rush was never again mentioned as a leader or supporter of the organization. If this upset or embarrassed him, he left no writing that suggested so. But it may have informed what he decided to do with his feelings about liberty over the next several months.

The Second Continental Congress spent its first few weeks preparing to raise a colonial militia while moderates, led by John Dickinson, tried to hammer out one last act of conciliation with England. Rush met with George Washington at the London Coffee House, where they discussed the possible creation of a new Continental Army. Rush let him know that if the congress actually went through with it, he and most of his fellow Pennsylvanians would wholeheartedly support Washington as commander in chief.

Washington was given the job on June 15, by an act of Congress, and several days later Rush was invited to a dinner celebrating the general's elevation—and wishing him good luck as he departed to defend Boston from British forces. The dinner was held across town at a restaurant overlooking the city's smaller and less pronounceable river, the Schuylkill. Benjamin Franklin, who at sixty-nine didn't go out much anymore—some rolled their eyes when he appeared to be asleep during congressional sessions—attended the dinner, as did members of several other delegations.

The evening's most memorable guest may have been a new delegate who had just arrived to represent Virginia: Thomas Jefferson, a strong-jawed, charismatic attorney and provincial legislator. Rush and others knew of Jefferson from his pamphlet *A Summary View of the Rights of British America*, which had come out during the First Congress and was debated there, even though Jefferson had not come to Philadelphia to defend it. His pamphlet's argument, that Parliament no longer had a legal right to rule the colonies, had seemed too radical for the initial congress, but now it seemed more in step with the times.

Rush had never met Jefferson before, but they had a great deal in common. Jefferson was nearly three years older than Rush, but they were both appreciably younger than most of the others, and they shared interests not only in politics and law but in science, agriculture, and religion. Jefferson was what Rush might have hoped to be if he had become a lawyer rather than a doctor, and if he had been born into a more prominent family.

Thomas Jefferson (left) and Patrick Henry

After the dinner plates were cleared, the first toast was "to the Commander in chief of the American Armies"—the very concept of which was still so stunning that many in the room, including Washington, didn't seem to know how to react. Washington mumbled a confused thank you, after which everyone "instantly rose, and drank the toast standing. This scene, so unexpected, was a solemn one. A silence followed it, as if every heart was penetrated with the awful, but great events which were to follow the use of the sword of liberty which had just been put into General Washington's hands."

Washington left town the next day to head for New England, accompanied by his new military brain trust: Charles Lee, a general, and Thomas Mifflin, Washington's aide-de-camp who would soon be a general. Thousands gathered to watch them leave, and Rush watched as his friend Tom held the commander in chief's stirrup while he mounted his horse.

When they reached New York, Washington received news of the bloody Battle of Bunker Hill, which had actually begun the day before the celebratory dinner. The British had technically won the battle, which took place in Boston's Charlestown section. But when the colonial troops finally retreated over Bunker Hill and into Cambridge, after running out of ammunition, they knew they had done a remarkable job against the much better armed and trained British forces. The British suffered 226 battlefield deaths with 828 more wounded; only 115 colonial soldiers died, while another 305 were injured, most during the retreat.

It was, to Washington, a hopeful defeat. But he was still far from certain he had the ability to lead the colonies to victory. Not long after the general left Philadelphia, Rush had visited his Virginia friend and colleague Patrick Henry at his rooming house. There Henry described to him a sobering recent scene: Washington, teary-eyed and insecure, admitting he did not feel up to the task of leading.

According to Rush's recollection, Washington had said to his friend, "Remember Mr. Henry, what I now tell you: From the day I enter upon the command of the American armies, I date my fall, and the ruin of my reputation."

12

While the colonies prepared to defend themselves militarily, the Continental Congress also considered John Dickinson's last-ditch attempt at a loyalist solution to the conflict, the so-called Olive Branch Petition. Written in the form of a letter to King George, it laid out Dickinson's belief that the colonies didn't really want independence, just the chance to negotiate fair tax and trade policies with Great Britain. It passed on July 5, 1775, largely because John Adams and some of the other more radical delegates—who were still very much in the minority—decided to simply wait Dickinson out, assuming he and his supporters would eventually accept the inevitable.

The letter was mailed to the king on July 8, and Congress anxiously awaited a reply.

Just over two weeks later, John Adams talked to a young friend from Boston who was heading home and encouraged Adams to send some letters with him. Since Adams hadn't had a moment to write in weeks, he dashed off two short dispatches, one to his wife, Abigail, and the other to his friend James Warren, one of the original Sons of Liberty. In the letter to Warren, Adams described just how exasperated he was with John Dickinson—whom he called a "piddling Genius whose Fame has been trumpeted so loudly . . . [and] has given a silly Cast to our whole Doings." Adams also made it abundantly clear just how useless he believed these attempts at conciliation to be.

In the letter to Abigail, he described the "difficulty and intricacy" of the rebellious work on which the congress needed to focus more wholly: "When 50 or 60 Men have a Constitution to form for a great Empire, at the same Time that they have a Country of fifteen hundred Miles extent to fortify, Millions to arm and train, a Naval Power to begin, an extensive Commerce to regulate, numerous Tribes of Indians to negotiate with, a standing Army of Twenty seven Thousand Men to raise, pay, victual and officer, I really shall pity those 50 or 60 Men." The battle for liberty had so many fronts.

Nobody reading these letters could doubt that Adams believed independence to be the only possible solution to the current conflict. And within a few weeks people on both sides of the Atlantic did read them, because they never made it home. Intercepted in transit, they were sent to Britain as proof of colonial treason, and versions of them ran in newspapers in London and Boston. Rush would later romanticize their publication as the moment when the "independence of the United States was first brought before the public mind." But at the time he had a hard time getting the image out of his head of his friend Adams, walking embarrassed through the crowded streets of Philadelphia, so utterly "alone . . . an object of nearly universal detestation."

Or as Adams himself described it, "the Quakers & Proprietary Gentlemen, took the alarm; represented me as the worst of men, the true-blue Sons of Liberty pitied me; all put me under a kind of Coventry. I was avoided like a man infected with the Leprosy."

The scandal made Rush worry what would happen to his life in Philadelphia—to his practice, to his reputation—if his own feelings about independence became more generally known. And he had plenty of reason to worry, given how bad he was at keeping his political feelings to himself, in conversation, in lectures, after church.

At the same time, Rush had started writing a treatise that he felt was long overdue. He described it as "an address to the inhabitants of the colonies," that would help them "remove" what he believed was "an immense mass of prejudice and error relative to . . . American independence." He wanted to correct "errors" of thinking, which was how Rush viewed long-held, factually challenged opinions. And he knew it would take more than the "ordinary short and cold addresses of newspaper publications" to accomplish that.

This was especially true in Philadelphia, where there were still many Tories and loyalists, as well as Quakers who simply opposed violence. The loyalists needed to understand that a war for independence was not only inevitable but had already started; the pacifists needed to understand the importance of the war being "speedy and successful."

After Continental Congress meetings ended for the day, Rush would listen to John and Samuel Adams rail privately about why the people didn't understand independence. But the doctor felt he knew the answer: nobody had yet directly addressed the "public mind," explaining these issues like a great teacher, rather than prosecuting them like a winning lawyer.

How far Rush got in writing his own declaration of independence is unknown. No manuscript of it has ever been found. But not long after starting to "put some thoughts upon paper upon this subject," he decided, for perhaps the first time in his life, to be intellectually self-protective. He decided to turn the project over to someone who had far less to lose by writing these ideas down and publishing them.

Tom Paine had, by this point, done a creditable job editing and writing for Robert Aitken's monthly *Pennsylvania Magazine*, which was growing in popularity. He had even co-written a piece with Dr. Rush, published under a pseudonym as the featured story in the June issue—a revised and expanded three-page version of his instructions on how to make saltpeter for gunpowder (a subject that interested an increasing number of Americans). Some readers might have guessed Rush was the coauthor because the piece mentioned a dialogue with Dr. Franklin, who "assured me that the manufactury of the salt from the above materials was so simple, that it was carried out entirely by an illiterate old man and his wife." But hardly anyone knew Tom Paine, who wrote almost exclusively under pseudonyms. All the ads for the magazine featured the publisher's name, not the writer's.

One day Rush visited the Aitken shop and got into yet another political discussion with Paine. Before dashing out to see his next patient, he invited the writer to come by his house—there was something he wanted to discuss in private.

Several days later they met at Rush's home on Front Street. The doctor again brought up the subject of independence, and this time asked Paine "what he thought of writing a pamphlet on it."

In one of history's great backhanded compliments, Rush told Paine he was perfect for the assignment because "he had nothing to fear from the popular odium to which such a publication might expose him, for he could live anywhere, but that my profession and connections, which tied me to Philadelphia, where a great majority of our citizens and some of my friends were hostile to a separation of our country from Great Britain, forbad me to come forward as a pioneer of that important controversy."

And so Paine began the process of drafting a pamphlet to explain and sell independence. When he had finished pages that he wanted to run by Rush, he brought the handwritten sheets over to the doctor's home. Rush had to squeeze these sessions into his schedule, between the doctoring, teaching, and studying he crammed into almost every waking hour. Though he slept very little, meetings with his friends in Congress had been taking up all his extra time. He was mostly available later in the evenings, which corresponded to when Paine—who slept as late as possible each morning, and knocked off from work as early as possible each evening—was more likely to be found in a tavern drinking and playing checkers.

In Rush's second-floor study, Paine would read the pages aloud to him. Since they were both tall men prone to making dramatic points with their long arms and hands—and rooms in Philadelphia city homes were generally pretty cramped—they were probably in each other's faces quite a bit. According to Rush's recollections (Paine left no writing about this process), the doctor offered suggestions and feedback but did not rewrite any portions.

As they began, Rush told Paine, just as he had told Adams, that there were two words "he should avoid by every means as necessary to his own safety and that of the public—*Independence* and *Republicanism*." Clearly Paine disagreed; it wasn't possible to sell independence to the layman without actually using the word. Somehow the two managed to move past that issue, because they continued working together.

Other aspects of the draft pamphlet may have made Rush cringe. Paine didn't want to just convince people that America should be independent. He insisted on attempting to undermine the entire history of the British monarchy and the Church of England, in fact the very history of monarchy going back to the Bible. That would not have been quite the brisk polemic on colonial independence that Rush had envisioned. The doctor also disagreed with the sections in which Paine asserted that the new democratic governments, in Pennsylvania and, eventually, the whole nation, should have only one legislative body, not two, and that they should be controlled by "the people": the equivalent of a House of Representatives with no Senate. Rush found this spectacularly wrong-headed and would forever regret how many Pennsylvanians Paine influenced on this subject.

There was one line Paine wrote, and then cut, that Rush missed so much he committed it to memory: "Nothing can be conceived of more absurd than three millions of people flocking to the American shore every time a vessel arrives from England to know what portion of liberty they shall enjoy."

As they edited, Rush continued to share with Paine the ideas bursting from his ongoing dialogues with members of the Continental Congress, particularly Adams. What was said in the congress was supposed to be a secret—members had approved a resolution promising that back in May—but a lot of congressmen weren't really keeping much to themselves, even after they were all required to sign an official Agreement of Secrecy.

When Adams read what Paine had written, his first reaction was "Dr. Rush put him upon Writing on the Subject" and had simply "furnished [Paine] with the Arguments which had been urged in Congress a hundred times."

Paine and Rush likely worked together all through the fall of 1775. Paine was known as a laboriously slow writer; if Rush had been writing the pamphlet, it might have been finished in a week or two.

But the doctor was more focused on another writing project, one that was far more personal. It was a sort of declaration of *dependence*—because he had finally found the young woman he wanted to marry.

13

During the summer of 1775, Betsey Graeme (now officially Mrs. Elizabeth Graeme Fergusson) showed Rush a letter from a young woman she considered almost a daughter—the firstborn of her best friend Annis Boudinot Stockton, in Princeton. She seemed, from the letter, to be very mature for her age, which was sixteen.

Rush was amazed that the voice on the page belonged to little Julia Stockton, whom he remembered from infancy. When Julia was four, she had fallen asleep during the 1763 Princeton commencement, for which Rush had returned to Nassau Hall; at the Stocktons' request, he had carried her back to their house in his arms. Now she was a young woman.

Not long after reading the letter, Rush visited Princeton to get away from Philadelphia's late summer heat. Annis and her husband, Richard Stockton, now a provincial supreme court justice, had invited him to stay at Morven, their mansion near the university. Rush hadn't seen the Stocktons much in the seven years since he and Richard had traveled across Scotland to convince the Rev. John Witherspoon to become president of Princeton. The Stocktons now had six children: Julia; twin daughters, two years younger, Sukey and Polly; eleven-year-old and ten-year-old sons, Dicky and Horace; and a three-year-old daughter, Abigail. They also had a large staff of servants and slaves—including one, Marcus

Marsh, who Annis said she had raised "almost as my own son." His mother, who had been their slave, died not long after Marcus was born in 1765, and the unconventional Annis, who was nursing at the time, decided it would be okay if the "poor fellow . . . nursed at my breast," which he did "numberless times."

From the moment Rush saw sixteen-year-old Julia Stockton, she "attracted and fixed my heart." She had brown hair, dark eyes, "a complexion composed of white and red, a countenance at the same time soft and animated, a voice mild and musical, and a pronunciation accompanied with a little lisp." She was well pedigreed: the educated daughter of a gifted, free-spirited woman and a brilliant, wealthy man. She was also a talented musician, with a lauded singing voice; the first evening of his visit, after dinner, she sang for him. He was stunned when she chose to begin with "The Birks of Endermay," the very song that his Scottish love, Lady Jane Leslie, had sung for him at the same age, in a voice that seemed to have "the same air and lisp" as hers. Rush took this as a sign of divine providence; it apparently didn't occur to him that his friend Betsey had heard the whole story of his crush on Lady Jane many times and may well have suggested the song.

Either way, by the end of the first verse, Julia Stockton had "opened an avenue to my heart." The next day he accompanied the family to church, where Reverend Witherspoon was preaching. Afterward Julia declared that Witherspoon was "the best preacher she had ever heard," with an insight and firmness Rush felt was beyond her years. It was at that moment that he decided they must marry.

As soon as he was home in Philadelphia, he wrote to Annis Stockton to request permission from her and her husband to return and visit Julia, so he might commence a formal courtship. While such a union would bring him "a pretty little fortune" in dowry, he was also smitten.

Courting Julia would be politically challenging for Rush. While he had known her father—his proposed father-in-law—more than half of his life, they held opposing views on independence. Besides his provincial supreme court decisions, Richard Stockton was known for his 1774 treatise "An Expedient for the Settlement of the American Disputes," in which he proposed that the colonies could possibly become independent of parliamentary control while retaining allegiance to the king. But Rush would hardly be the first member of the family who disagreed with him. Annis's brother Elias Boudinot—who had been Richard Stockton's legal apprentice and married Stockton's younger sister Hannah—was now a prominent New Jersey lawyer himself and had been openly pro-independence since 1773. Elias had defended a group of men accused by the East India Tea Company of destroying tea in New Jersey. So the big family dinners at Morven were already politically fraught.

Since Julia had grown up accustomed to great wealth, Rush took another job while courting her. Besides his practice, his teaching, and the paying apprentices he had working for him, he accepted a military appointment as physician and surgeon to the Pennsylvania Armed Boats. This meant that when the colony's small navy was in port in Philadelphia, he would treat any sailors requiring medical attention. He also did rounds at the naval hospital on Province Island, a small island below the city, just where the Schuylkill River flows into the Delaware, which was also where the city ran a quarantine facility for new immigrants.

But mostly what Rush did to win Julia was to write—charmingly, creatively, emphatically, and overwhelmingly. His love letters were so intimate and over the top that Julia hid them from everyone for the rest of her life.

In the earliest letter to Julia that she hid, he wrote:

> I should [be] wanting in gratitude if I neglected to inform you that I daily experience the good effects of my attachment to you upon my temper & conduct in business. I am induced to attend to the rich with new pleasure as my dear Julia will share with me in the reward of my services to them; and I feel more pleasure then ever in attending the poor, since I am persuaded in my care of them that I am drawing down blessings which will descend upon my dear Julia, & her family after I am dead. I love my students better than ever, as I am sure my Julia will esteem me only in proportion as she finds me wise and good. I learn from these things to admire the wisdom & goodness of the supreme being in the institution of matrimony, for I now see that when it is entered into with proper

motives, it not only promotes our happiness in this world but prepares us for the next by the cultivation of those dispositions in our minds which cultivate the happiness of heaven . . .

My dear girl, you have taught me more than I have learned from the pulpit. . . . You have explained an hundred texts of scripture, and have unraveled many mysterious providences for me. Sweet presages these, how much you will teach me hereafter by your precepts and example! You shall check the remaining impetuosity of youth—regulate the ambition of manhood, and guard me against the avarice of age—you shall point out to me the duty & happiness of a life of piety & usefulness. In a word you shall be the little apostle of my heart & family.

A few days later he wrote to apologize that he had told Betsey Graeme Fergusson about his deep love for her—but assuring her that otherwise he had been discreet. "I know eno' of the world to be convinced that mankind in general have as little sympathy with us in our pleasures as they have in our pains, and therefore I have spoken of you upon all occasions with a reserve & moderation that did violence to the feelings of my heart." He went on breathlessly, "You see my dearest girl I write to you, and address you upon all occasions as if we had been old, and intimate friends. As great genius we are told often supplies the want of experience in the military art, so extreme affection supplies the want of a long acquaintance. I lean my *whole heart* upon you—and O! how soft a pillow is the bosom of a female friend!"

In another letter, he chided her for not writing back fast enough, then explained, "I am almost afraid to tell you *how much* pleasure your letter afforded me, least you should reproach yourself for the *pain* you gave me by delaying so long." He went on to compliment her: "you write an excellent letter. You have a most happy way of comprizing a great many ideas in a small compass. Your stile is an exact copy of Dr. [Jonathan] Swift's."

In this same letter he explained he planned to give her an engagement ring that had been a gift of "my noble friend Lord Balgonie, the eldest son of the Earl of Leven." The ring had the Lord's Prayer etched on the outside, and on the inside the date when Rush had left his friend's company in Scotland. He did not mention the true significance of the ring—that it had been given to him by the brother of Lady Jane.

While Rush awaited Julia's letters, his brain would bubble and often erupt. On one occasion, he became so agitated and manic over not hearing from her that he sat down and devised his own new "system" of understanding, not unlike those he studied in medicine. He believed this system allowed him to evaluate and measure perhaps the most ineffable phenomenon: "conjugal happiness."

In a very scientific love letter to Julia, he proposed "a matrimonial thermometer":

> The 1st or lowest degree of conjugal happiness consists in a sympathy in *animal love*. . . . It is but a small degree above the happiness of brutes.—
>
> The 2nd degree of conjugal happiness consists in a sympathy of *manners*. I mean no more than mutual politeness between married people. Although it confers no real happiness, yet it is the best vehicle for it. If it does not prevent disputes, it tends much to soften them, and thus leaves the door to reconcilliation always open.
>
> The 3rd degree consists in a sympathy of *opinions*. The more married people think alike upon all subjects the less danger there is of their disputing. This is of great consequence when the parties are not happy in their dispositions.—
>
> The 4th degree consists in a sympathy of *tastes*. By taste you know is meant a perception of what is proper—beautiful—& sublime in nature or art. When we consider how many objects of taste in building—furniture—gardening—& books of entertainment engage the minds of married people, it will appear to be of great importance that there be a strict uniformity in them.—
>
> The 5th degree consists in a sympathy of *sentiments*. By sentiment you know is meant a perception of what is just, or unjust, right or wrong in actions. It is a moral principle, & therefore requires the most perfect union between married people, especially if they have children. A diversity of opinions in matters which relate to morals will always be supposed by a sense of duty, and therefore will be maintained with more obstinancy than disputes about other

subjects. How many married people have been made unhappy by thinking differently upon the lawfulness, or unlawfulness of teaching children to dance!

The 6th degree consists in a sympathy of *understandings*. This includes an equality of capacity to perceive & relish truth in morals—politicks—philosophy—& religion, and forms an exalted source of happiness in matrimony.

The 7th degree consists in a sympathy of *tempers*. This degree excludes anger—resentment—& pevishness in every shape. It supposes the most perfect uniformity in the *wills* of married people, leading them to just, benevolent—& charitable actions. This is so sweet a source of happiness in matrimony that it only can be exceeded by

The 8th & highest degree of conjugal happiness which consists in a sympathy in *religion*. This includes a sameness of ideas of the attributes & perfections of god with wills—affections, & actions mutually tending toward the honor of the deity, & the advancement of the soul in a resemblance to him.—The happiness of this degree is heightened by a sameness in the mode of worship.

Rush speculated on the various ways one might move either up or down the scale. "I have known married people happy for a few months, or years 'till some new situation or connection in life produced a want of sympathy in some of the degrees of conjugal happiness. I have likewise known people who have been unhappy for a few years after marriage 'till force, or a conviction of superiority in temper—taste—or understanding has produced the necessary sympathies between them."

The goal, for a couple, was what he called "a sympathy of tempers." And he assured Julia that "it shall be the study of my life to cultivate . . . a conformity to you."

As Rush was writing down his novel system for evaluating "conjugal happiness," and Thomas Paine was working on new pages for his pamphlet on independence, John Adams was nearby, being nudged into some resonant writing of his own.

Just across the street from Rush's house, Adams and Virginia delegate Richard Henry Lee, who always wore a black glove on his left hand because he had lost several fingers in a rifle accident, met for drinks after a Congressional session, and ended up discussing just what kind of government the nation should have after it became free. Lee was so impressed with Adams's vision that he urged him to write his ideas down immediately so they could be circulated. While written in the form of a letter to Lee, Adams's document turned out to be, in essence, a first draft of the U.S. Constitution.

"Taking Nature and Experience for my Guide," he wrote, "I have made the following Sketch, which may be varied in any one particular an infinite Number of Ways, So as to accommodate it to the different Genius, Temper, Principles and even Prejudices of different People.

"A Legislative, an Executive and a judicial Power, comprehend the whole of what is meant and understood by Government. It is by ballancing each of these Powers against the other two, that the Effort in humane Nature towards Tyranny, can alone be checked and restrained and any degree of Freedom preserved in the Constitution."

Adams went on to detail his ideas for the three branches of government. He finished by explaining to Lee, "In adopting a Plan, in some Respects similar to this human Nature would appear in its proper Glory asserting its own real Dignity, pulling down Tyrannies, at a single Exertion and erecting such new Fabricks, as it thinks best calculated to promote its Happiness.

"As you was the last Evening polite enough to ask me for this Model, if such a Trifle will be of any service to you, or any gratification of Curiosity, here you have it."

Four days later, Rush was inspired to write Julia a revolutionary love letter. "Many of our future joys, and sorrows will flow I dare say from the good & evil which befall our country," he wrote. "My bosom exults with a new pleasure when I reflect that at a time when all the powers of Europe were united in extirpating liberty from the face of the earth, the congress of America extended all its blessings to an hundred thousand souls. I am more delighted with the sound of liberty than ever since I have enlarged the scale of my existence by a connection with you."

14

Something had changed in Rush's relationship with Adams. In the aftermath of the scandal concerning his intercepted letters about liberty, Adams had a better idea about who his real friends were in Philadelphia. He and Rush had known each other for well over a year and spoke often, but not until after Adams's public embarrassment did he write anything of real substance about the doctor (except for how good the food was at his place). Now suddenly Rush, his opinions, and his foibles seemed to matter more.

"Dr. Rush came in," Adams wrote in the fall of 1775. "He is an elegant, ingenious Body. Sprightly, pretty fellow. He is a republican. He has been much in London." He cited a few of Rush's high-profile correspondents and went on to explain that Rush joined him in complaining about John Dickinson, the main obstacle to Pennsylvania supporting liberty. "He mentions many Particular Instances, in which Dickenson has blundered. He thinks him warped by the Quaker Interest and the Church interest too. Thinks his Reputation [is] past the Meridian, and that Avarice is growing upon him." Rush had also told him that Patrick Henry and Col. Thomas Mifflin, both close to Washington, had been complaining about Dickinson as well.

Yet, while Adams was becoming friendlier with Rush, and appreciated his insider insights, he still wasn't entirely sure about him.

His assessment: "Rush I think, is too much of a talker to be a deep thinker. Elegant not great."

Adams wasn't the only one who wondered if the doctor still saw conversation and debate as too much of a game, and enjoyed the political gossip a little too much as gossip. Rush was such a rapid-fire communicator—who could dash off writing the way he sometimes seemed to talk before thinking—that nobody knew for sure, perhaps including himself, whether he had real vision.

When it came to independence, in any case, the time for talk was ending. Revolution was no longer just an idea to cleverly defend at the London Coffee House or Aitken's bookshop—Americans were now dying over this idea. The pamphlet Rush had been helping Tom Paine to prepare was almost finished, and he would soon have to find someone brave enough to actually print it.

In the meantime, Rush had a wedding and a marriage to plan. He had hoped to be married by Christmas Eve 1775, his thirtieth birthday, but the ceremony was scheduled for the week after New Year's, 1776, at Morven. Meanwhile Rush, his wife-to-be, and her family were busy negotiating how their new life in Philadelphia would work.

Rush had hoped to keep his sister, Rebecca, working in his household, to which the Stocktons agreed. But he needed more help. So he hired a servant named Cyrus, who would attend to the family but mostly oversee the new stable for the horses and carriage that Julia would bring with her.

He also hired a personal maid for the new lady of the house: a thirteen-year-old girl whose mother was one of Rush's financially struggling patients. Mother and daughter had arrived at his office for an appointment, and once the door was closed, the mother quickly admitted she had come "not for physic" but to plead for his favor. Her husband had just returned from prison, and she couldn't support her children. When she heard Rush would be marrying, she hoped he would agree to "bind this little girl to you as a waiting maid for your wife." Then she burst into tears, but Rush was mostly moved by the "innocence & sweetness of the child's countenance."

He wanted to hire her on the spot, but first asked his sister Rebecca, who agreed to the idea. Besides being able to help Julia dress and accompany her on excursions, Rebecca judged the girl to be an "excellent seamstress." Rush was proud of himself for hiring her.

He also undertook a Pygmalion-esque project to create a new library for Julia, brimming with more than one hundred books he thought she should want to read—instead of "all such books as are commonly read by your sex." He had new shelves built in the closet of what would become her room, and before listing her new books, he explained why this was all so important. "If the business of a married woman's life consisted simply in receiving & paying visits—in providing food for a family—or in bringing a number of children into the world, I should pity you in entering so early into matrimony. But I know you have higher objects principally in view. You long to share with me in the pleasure and honor of communicating health & happiness to individuals & the public. You are anxious to cultivate your mind, & to rise above that drudgery to which our sex have consigned yours, and those follies to which too many of your sex have consigned themselves."

Preachiness aside, he seemed eager to propagate the intellectual parity he had so admired in his time in France, and that characterized his friendships with, among others, Julia's own mother. "I know you aim at nothing but to be placed in a situation in which you will soonest arrive at the perfection of your nature in everything."

By this time, the main text of Tom Paine's pamphlet was finished. Rush had better connections, so he arranged to have the prepublication text shared with a short list of revolutionaries, including Ben Franklin and Samuel Adams. Their reactions remain unrecorded—in fact, nobody but Rush ever publicly admitted to reading it, or even knowing about it, before publication.

And with his more extensive history of publication, Rush was able to find Paine a fearless printer. But rather than use one of the better-known publishers he had worked with often, he helped broker a deal with the small shop of Robert Bell, a forty-three-year-old Scottish immigrant. Bell and Paine made arrangements to publish one thousand copies of the pamphlet, which had grown to forty-six pages. It would take almost all the paper Bell kept in his warehouse.

All during the writing, Paine had been calling his work *Plain Truth*, echoing the title of a Franklin pamphlet from decades earlier. But before the manuscript went to the printer, Rush convinced Paine that *Common Sense*—a phrase with a long intellectual and political history going back to Aristotle—would be a much better title. Paine agreed, and on Tuesday, January 9, 1776, the pamphlet was published. It had no byline; the introduction was signed simply "The Author." The first thousand copies sold briskly in Philadelphia, and speculation began immediately over who had written it, perhaps one of the Adamses or Ben Franklin himself.

RUSH MAY NOT have been paying much attention to the publication. The day the pamphlet came out, he traveled to Princeton, after seeing patients, to prepare for his wedding. He and Julia were married on Thursday, January 11, at Morven. The bride was given away by her father, Richard Stockton; the Rev. John Witherspoon, president of Princeton, officiated. Rush, Stockton, and Witherspoon had come a long way since meeting in western Scotland nine years earlier, to try to convince the reverend's wife to sail to America.

The doctor and his bride returned home the next day, and according to his records he (or his apprentices) saw patients that Friday. Julia began the process of putting her new household in order. Her new sister-in-law, Rebecca—who went by her married name, Mrs. Stamper—was still running the place, but there were many more servants, some hired temporarily, others "indentured," meaning they agreed to work for a certain number of months or years at a set price.

Some historians have suggested Rush had a slave at this time, raising the question of whether his 1773 abolitionist broadside was hypocritical. But we have no evidence that he owned slaves before the war. His staff in the 1770s was comprised of servants and overworked apprentices. In his last letter to Julia before the wedding, he detailed his negotiation with one of the new servants, who agreed to the wage of 20 pounds ($3,090), along with room and board, for three years' service. A servant he originally wanted "was seduced from me by the offer of better wages than he demanded of me."

As the Rushes settled in, sales of *Common Sense* took off. Rush must have been astonished and at least a little proud of his part in the publishing phenomenon. He surely knew that the reaction to *Common Sense* was only partially about the writing. The timing had been perfect. Congress was back in session, so many interested in independence were in town and able to send copies home. Also, the local newspapers had just published King George's three-month-old speech calling the rebels "an unhappy and deluded multitude" and promising to send more troops to oppose them.

The pamphlet's success was also a by-product of the emerging competitiveness of the colonial printing industry. When the sales of *Common Sense* took off, Paine thought that as the writer, he could just walk into the publisher and demand all his profits right away. Even when he explained that he wanted to donate his royalties to clothe Washington's troops—who were very cold fighting in February—printer Robert Bell didn't immediately pay out what the author felt he deserved. So Paine decided he would take *Common Sense* elsewhere. He created a second edition by adding more than a dozen new pages and brought it to Rush's friends the Bradfords, likely making a deal over drinks at their coffee house.

To meet the increasing demand, the Bradfords hired two additional printing shops, so they could create six thousand copies very quickly, and start distributing them all over the colonies. But Robert Bell claimed he had the right to publish as many copies as he could sell and printed another thousand right away himself. Between them, the two publishers did more promotion for *Common Sense* than anyone would have otherwise, which drove the patriotic word-of-mouth about how "controversial" the pamphlet was. The rival publishers helped drive its sales into the tens of thousands, and then over one hundred thousand within the first three months. Total sales (after much copying and bootlegging in America and England) were estimated at some half a million.

While the pamphlet was compelling and well articulated, it became popular without the kinds of often-quoted sentences usually associated with such success. Rush believed the pamphlet garnered all the attention simply because it allowed people to finally say the word *independence* out loud, discuss it, and write about it. He would later claim to have had a hand in all the publicity: "the controversy about independence was carried into the newspapers," he wrote, "in which I bore a busy part." Whether the pamphlet actually swayed many Americans toward the cause or just became a totem, objective correlative, and rallying point for those who already believed will never be known. But it became famous in a way possible only in a large, diverse country that was on the cusp of a new form of democracy.

In early 1776, the Rush family started getting more involved in the business of independence. In January, Jacob Rush, back from his legal training in England, took a job as private secretary to John Hancock, president of the Continental Congress.

Then Dr. Rush himself assumed his second political position: he was elected to Philadelphia's Committee of Inspection and Observation. The Continental Congress had called for the creation of these "committees of inspection" all over the colonies, to make sure the decisions of the Congress's "Association"—starting with the boycott of British goods—were carried out locally. The committees grew in power as the decisions the colonies made together increased in number and scale; Philadelphia's committee expanded from forty-three members to a hundred as it regulated prices, reprimanded judges, inspected ships for contraband, closed stores that sold boycotted goods, imprisoned traitors, and even helped raise militias.

The committees quickly became shadow governments, especially in the colonies that were still lukewarm on independence, such as Pennsylvania, as their provincial assemblies couldn't yet be counted on to follow the Continental Congress's agenda. (This was the very beginning of America's federal/state turf wars.) The committees were made up of people outside the mainstream of politics—merchants, teachers, doctors, and now, Benjamin Rush.

Philadelphia's Committee of Inspection had a unique gravity, because Pennsylvania was starting to look like the biggest impediment to declaring independence. All the middle colonies—New York, New Jersey, and Delaware—had a higher percentage of loyalists than New England and the South; in many cases, their delegates to the Continental Congress had not yet been authorized by their elected provincial assemblies to support independence if a vote came. And Pennsylvania in general—Philadelphia specifically—still needed the most convincing. Its committee was therefore sometimes at odds with Pennsylvania's elected provincial assembly. As a way of addressing this, the Philadelphia committee was working to get the counties outside Philadelphia more involved in provincial politics: it was believed that there was more support for independence in the countryside than in town.

Rush found work on the committee frustrating. When the group tried to enact price controls to fight skyrocketing costs for provisions and imported goods, he explained why such market manipulation wouldn't work. He was flabbergasted that they wouldn't listen to him. He tried reading aloud to them from the acclaimed history of England by his acquaintance David Hume, which explained how price controls there had failed and made the economy worse. But "the precedents of Mr. Hume had no effect" on his legislative colleagues. He was almost unanimously outvoted.

This episode made him realize that "men do not become wise by the experience of other people." He was starting to think that "even our own experience does not always produce wise conduct, though the lessons for that purpose are sometimes repeated two or three times."

At the same time he was elected to the committee, Rush was named to the board of physicians charged with selecting surgeons to care for Pennsylvania's battalions. The other board members were men he had been working with almost since the day he returned from medical school, Drs. Bond and Cadwalader from Pennsylvania Hospital, and Drs. Shippen and Kuhn from the medical school.

Dr. Morgan had already left town for a more impressive military appointment: he was named director general of all continental hospitals and chief physician for the Continental Army.

For the most part, Rush experienced the early stages of the war of independence through reading and hearing from friends in the

Boston area about the violence. In Philadelphia, discussions of revolution were still largely theoretical; nobody there felt physically threatened. That was why so many people could still be unsure about their politics on the issue. While history might portray colonists as either strongly for or against the revolution and freedom, at this point many Philadelphians were just against change.

On Monday, May 6, 1776, Philadelphians heard the sounds of war for the first time. Two British warships, the *Liverpool* and the *Roebuck*, normally patrolled far to the south of the city, in Delaware Bay, the entrance to the sea route to the city. But now they suddenly headed up the Delaware River, apparently looking for trouble. The *Roebuck* had forty-four cannons at the ready, the *Liverpool* twenty-eight, and as they slowly approached Wilmington, alarm guns were fired in Philadelphia for the first time, warning people that an attack could be coming soon.

Since nobody was sure how imminent the risk was, life went nervously on for the rest of the day. John Adams used the air of fear to propose, yet again, that those colonies whose delegates had been sent with instructions not to vote for independence should "repeal or suspend them." The motion failed, but Adams kept thinking of other procedural schemes that might encourage, or trick, the reluctant colonies to join the groundswell. The next day the two British vessels reached the mouth of the Christiana River, and orders were given for colonial gunships to defend. And by Wednesday afternoon, Philadelphians could clearly hear cannon fire in the distance as the ships engaged.

The firing went on for nearly four hours, and while one American sailor died during the barrage, neither side's vessels were badly damaged. When the ships retired from fighting with the ebb tide, the *Roebuck* ran aground and was surrounded. But the colonial forces were reluctant to attempt to board the boat without disabling it first, and they had already shot every cannonball they had. So they waited for more ammunition to be delivered.

Unfortunately, when the tide rose that night, the enemy boat was freed and began drifting upriver toward Philadelphia. Colonial forces could not attack because they still didn't have a single cannonball. A small amount of gunpowder was delivered by boat, enough to fire eight cannonballs—whenever they arrived. Later Thursday morning, more gunpowder and forty-five cannonballs arrived, and suddenly the battle was back on.

By this point the ferocious action was close enough to the Wilmington area that people came running to the river's edge to watch. According to one newspaper report, "the novelty of the fight, the gallant behaviour of the officers and sailors, and the important consequences of the contest, afforded a most interesting spectacle to many thousand spectators who stood on the shores." The battle was still close enough to Philadelphia that city residents could hear the firing and see smoke rising. When the colonists ran out of cannonballs again, the sailors desperately began cutting up their blankets, jackets, and stockings, as well as some of the boat's cables and the harder oakum ropes in their netting—anything that could be packed into a cannon to fire at them. By sunset even these makeshift "wads" were gone.

In the meantime, the three colonial sailors wounded in the exchange were taken to the navy hospital, to be treated by Rush and his staff. Rush had seen wounds of war in the past, but only in men hurt in far-away or long-ago fighting. This was the first time he had ever treated patients freshly injured in combat while the fighting was still going on near enough to see, to hear, even to smell and taste the sulfurous smoke in the air from the cannon shots that had maimed them.

The Delaware River fleet was restocked the next day, and the battle continued until the British ships finally turned back. The story of the battle, however, would take on a life of its own, especially after a local publisher released a book about the clash almost overnight: two shillings sixpence ($26.30) for the black and white version, three shillings ninepence ($39.40) for the "elegantly colored" edition. And in Philadelphia, the fight for independence was no longer a subject for agree-to-disagree discussions: it was the Revolutionary War.

15

So far, marriage had not been exactly what Julia Stockton Rush might have reasonably expected. Her new home in Philadelphia was in the middle of an exciting, sometimes overwhelming urban world, so unlike the wide-open space of bucolic Princeton. It was the dead of winter when she moved in, and she had no idea how much wood to put on the fire in a city home. Rush teased her that he couldn't believe how quickly she went through a cord of wood—but then, she had always lived in a mansion with extensive grounds where trees were plentiful, along with staff to fell and chop them. She was also adjusting to smaller quarters; their house had a kitchen, a dining room, a parlor, and master bedroom that still looked as if it had been decorated by an unmarried man: hanging on the wall was the sword that had belonged to Rush's great-grandfather when he fought in Cromwell's army.

As a gesture of his love and newfound wealth (and perhaps to distract her), Rush hired Charles Willson Peale, an artist who had just arrived in town from Maryland and started advertising his services, to paint Julia's portrait.

She posed with one of the many instruments she could play—a handsome, dark wood cittern—next to a table of books, one open and recently put down, as if she could not decide which way to enrich herself first. Her dark hair was pulled up high with a blue

Julia Stockton Rush

ribbon, she wore a blue silk dress, and between her broad, dark eyes and full brows, her porcelain skin, and a knowing half-smile, she looked more mature than seventeen, the birthday she celebrated two months after the wedding.

She and her new husband did not have the kind of time together they would have liked. Rush was seeing patients for office visits and house calls and was involved in more political meetings and heated private conversations than ever. In the spring, there was river combat just a few miles from her new home, and the newspapers were reporting that the British were sending forty-five thousand Hessian troops to America to quell the percolating revolution. It was becoming too dangerous for her to remain in Philadelphia. Rush asked her to rejoin her family and siblings at Morven, far from the threat of war.

Julia left Philadelphia in May, and only then did Rush realize just how accustomed he had become to living with her. They wrote love letters again. "I did not know . . . how much you were a part of myself," he admitted, "and I feel some abatement of my affection for my country when I reflect that even she has deprived me of an hour of my dear Julia's company."

He visited her in Princeton when he could, but with so much family around, the newlyweds felt like they could never be alone together. "I anticipate with you," Rush wrote in late May 1776, "the pleasure we shall enjoy when we have no third person to break in upon our sweet house of social and conjugal happiness. I have a thousand things to say to you. I think, write, talk, work, love—all, all—only for you."

WITH THE LOCAL fear factor still high, John Adams moved again to bring the Pennsylvania delegation into the revolutionary fold. He proposed to the Continental Congress a new resolution mandating that any colony without a government "sufficient to the exigencies of their affairs" should create one immediately. This was vague enough that even John Dickinson and the other anti-independence Pennsylvanians voted for it, since they believed it referred to other, lesser colonies. But in the preamble to the resolution, Adams hid a political time bomb to be used against Dickinson and the other Pennsylvania holdouts at the right time. It was a tricky sentence concerning oaths to the crown, part of a strategy he had been thinking about for a year of "Anxiety, labour, study, Argument and Obloquy."

His preamble declared it was "absolutely irreconcilable to reason . . . for these people of the colonies now to take the oaths . . . necessary for the support of any government under the crown . . . every kind of authority under the said crown should be totally suppressed." When the preamble came up for a vote, it passed 6-4, with Pennsylvania and Maryland abstaining and Georgia absent. Either the Pennsylvania delegates didn't notice or they thought it wouldn't matter that their constitution still called for oaths to the crown and the king's authority, technically putting the commonwealth government at risk, in light of the "exigencies" of its "affairs."

By this point, each colony had an enormous number of moving political parts, multiple centers of authority. Each had an elected provincial assembly as well as local committees of inspection. These governmental bodies shared some members but not all. At the same time, the Second Continental Congress was increasingly acting as a national government—even though the British, in many ways, still maintained overall control. To further confuse matters, some colonies were already drafting their own new constitutions for when independence was declared.

Attorney John Dickinson, for example, was a delegate to the Continental Congress, a member of the provincial assembly, and with Rush, a member of the Philadelphia committee of inspection. Dickinson had come to believe that independence was inevitable, but he also felt that if it came too soon—and he was sure this was too soon—it would fail. He was simultaneously attempting to persuade the loyalist and Quaker-run provincial assembly to be more open-minded, and the forces of independence to move more cautiously. The interplay of those who opposed independence, those who embraced it, and those just trying to delay change amounted to a three-dimensional chess game being played in statehouses and in private gatherings across the colonies.

Rush was becoming an increasingly important player. "God knows I seek his honor and the best interests of my fellow creatures supremely in all I am doing for my country," he wrote to Julia. "General Mifflin and all the delegates from the independent colonies rely chiefly on me"—then he crossed out *me* and replaced it with the name of a colonel from Delaware—"and a few more of us for the salvation of this province. It would be treason in any one of us to desert the cause at the present juncture."

The committee decided, at Rush's urging, to hold a Monday morning rally at the State House—where both the Continental Congress and the Pennsylvania Assembly were meeting, on different floors—to call for independence, using Adams's resolution. By ten a.m. on May 20, some five thousand people were standing in a downpour in the walled yard behind the building. John Adams, who had never seen such a mass meeting in Philadelphia, listened from a first-floor window as his controversial resolution was read "in a loud Stentorian voice that might be heard a quarter of a mile," as he recounted in his diary. The reader got through only the first few words before "the multitude . . . tho so wett," burst out in "three Cheers. Hatts flying as usual."

After reading Adams's resolution, the moderator presented to the assembled throng several new resolutions prepared by Rush and the committee. The most important declared the current government of Pennsylvania to be no way "competent to the exigencies of our affairs." When the sopping crowd unanimously affirmed this resolution, Adams's gambit had succeeded. A call was immediately made to demolish Pennsylvania's current government, renovate, and build another one.

But the Pennsylvania Assembly would not go quietly. The next day it asked for a clarification of the Adams resolution and tried a procedural runaround, proposing that if it agreed to sever from royal authority, it could still remain in charge. This led to a series of private meetings between Rush, John and Samuel Adams, and several others to plan a strategy. They wrote a new document to present to the Continental Congress—which they referred to as a "Memorial," since it memorialized a proposal—that they hoped would further undermine the authority of the state assembly.

Similar events were happening in other colonies: shadow government committees, favoring independence, tried to muscle out the existing governments one county at a time. To people like Rush, this was patriotism. To a great many others, including people Rush had known his entire life and some of his patients, it was treason.

As the politics grew more intense in late May and June, Rush struggled to maintain a balance with his medical work—seeing a few patients first thing in the morning before all the meetings and the constant drafting of statements and pronouncements. Independence, it turned out, required a lot of paperwork.

On Friday, May 24, George Washington came by Rush's house for lunch. The general was in town to speak to Congress about his next military campaign, and how he planned to handle those forty-five thousand new Hessian troops. Rush and Washington "dined *most luxuriously* upon cold ham and salad." Several hours later a Virginia delegate came by for tea, and together they railed against Maryland withdrawing its delegation because it wasn't ready for independence. The delegate proclaimed he would "hate hereafter to breathe the contaminated air of that province" when returning to Virginia.

The next day, as Rush was tending to a patient near Frankford who had summoned him at six in the morning, the "Memorial" was released to Congress as an attempt to finally overturn the power and authority of the Pennsylvania Assembly. It didn't work. Moderates in the Assembly had been circulating a petition all over the province and had amassed some six thousand signatures; they were able to hold the line.

After more fevered meetings and meals and coffees in the neighborhood of the State House, Richard Henry Lee rose in the Continental Congress on Friday, June 7, and read from what would come to be called the "Lee Resolution." He declared, on behalf of his

Virginia delegation, that the "United Colonies" were now "free and independent" and should begin writing a "plan for confederation" and thinking about forming alliances with foreign governments.

Congress reacted to this stunning pronouncement by tabling discussion of it for three weeks because some delegations did not have approval from their colonies to vote. In his notes on the proceedings, Jefferson observed that "the people of the middle colonies . . . were not yet ripe for bidding adieu to British connection . . . [but] they were fast ripening." In the meantime, Congress created a committee to draft a formal declaration of independence, so the colonies would have an actual document to debate, vote on, and possibly approve.

John Adams, Thomas Jefferson, Benjamin Franklin, and delegates from New York and Connecticut were selected to write the declaration. Jefferson took the place of Richard Lee in representing Virginia; some felt it was because he was a much better writer, others that he was better-liked (in part because he had been much quieter in sessions). Franklin was too ill to attend the initial brainstorming meeting, as an attack of gout kept him away for much of May. After the four other men met, Jefferson told Adams that he should take the minutes from this session, and from other meetings that might be useful, back to his room at Mrs. Yards's to write the first draft himself.

"I will not," Adams told him.

"You should do it," Jefferson shot back.

"I will not. . . ."

"Why?"

"Reasons enough," Adams said.

"What can be your reasons?"

"Reason first, you are a Virginian, and a Virginian ought to appear at the head of this business. Reason second, I am obnoxious, suspected, and unpopular," a point Adams didn't recall anyone challenging. "You are very much otherwise. Reason third, you can write ten times better than I can."

"Well," said Jefferson, "if you are decided, I will do as well as I can."

AND SO JEFFERSON gathered up the notes, carried them back to his quarters, and began. He was renting a two-room apartment a few blocks west of where his colleagues were staying—at the southwestern corner of Seventh and Market, on the second floor of the home of bricklayer Jacob Graf, Jr. He slept in one room and wrote in the other, on a slanted wooden box on his desk.

Although Jefferson left no record of his process over the next two weeks, the writing of the declaration has been imagined dramatically over the centuries as a secular version of Moses's trip to the top of Mount Sinai to receive and etch into stone the Ten Commandments. In fact, Jefferson was on deadline not only for a declaration of independence for the colonies but for his edits on the new constitution for Virginia, among other documents he had agreed to help write for the Continental Congress.

And Jefferson was hardly the only person in America—or even in the neighborhood—writing a declaration of independence at that moment. There were quite a few, because each colony needed one as well. His home province of Virginia, for example, had already finished its Declaration of Rights, which began with the assertion that "all men are by nature equally free and independent, and have certain inherent rights, of which, when they enter into a state of society, they cannot, by any compact, deprive or divest their posterity; namely, the enjoyment of life and liberty, with the means of acquiring and possessing property, and pursuing and obtaining happiness and safety." So Jefferson had inherited a substantial palette of phrases to work with.

Rush was waiting to see what Jefferson would come up with, because the doctor had his own declaration to write, for Pennsylvania. The Philadelphia committee of inspection had chosen him, Franklin, and several other delegates to the commonwealth-wide conference to draft a new constitution that would include an open declaration of support for independence.

The Pennsylvania constitutional conference, held in Carpenters' Hall, was Rush's first look at what self-government might be like, what "the people" would do if they were in charge. While the delegates agreed on the need for independence, they agreed on little else; Rush was amazed at just how many things like-minded people could argue about. He was especially upset by the battle over oaths, and to whom Pennsylvanians would or wouldn't have to swear them.

First, the members of the conference wanted anyone voting on the new constitution to take an oath that supported government "on the authority of the people only." No more oaths to the king of England—Rush was fine with that.

But then the conference proposed that anyone who wanted to be a candidate for the Pennsylvanian constitutional convention would have to swear a religious oath—a Christian oath. This would mean that nobody could help write a new constitution guaranteeing liberty, justice, equality, and religious freedom unless they swore: "I profess faith in God the Father and in Jesus Christ his eternal Son, the true God, and in the Holy Spirit, one God blessed evermore; and do acknowledge the Holy Scriptures of the Old and New Testament to be given by divine inspiration."

While Rush wasn't the only attendee who found the proposal offensive, he was, according to meeting minutes, its "chief and zealous opposer." Just because the words of the oath corresponded to his own religious beliefs didn't mean they had any place in a secular document guaranteeing freedom of religion. Rush rose from his seat in Carpenters' Hall on June 21st and argued that there were many men in Pennsylvania who were moral and righteous and even religious, but would still find that oath unconscionable. His friends and patients were among the many who would object.

Rush had been thinking about the role religion would play in the new American democracy. He believed in the Bible as a tool for teaching morality, but he was knowledgeable about other belief systems as well and respected them. He had studied the Old Testament, the "Hebrew Bible," and counted Jews among his friends and patients. He had long lived among Quakers, who didn't believe in taking any religious oaths. He greatly respected many physicians and scientists, starting with William Cullen in Scotland and Benjamin Franklin, who were skeptical about organized religion. Some few publicly identified as Deist, a religious philosophy that acknowledged a God as creator, and perhaps as a force of nature, but that rejected the existence of miracles and other overt divine interventions.

But whether they were Deist or atheist, it didn't matter. Rush didn't believe in religious prejudice: it wasn't Christian. "There are many good men who do not believe in the divinity of the Son of God," he told the conference. "I am not one of that class. But no man whose morals are good should be exempted because he will not take that declaration."

It was one of the first, if not *the* first, public statements in the American debate on separation of church and state. Interestingly, we only know of Rush's pronouncement because it was captured by a fellow conference member, Christopher Marshall, who utterly disagreed with him. Rush had known Marshall, a former Quaker, for years—he was a local druggist and chemist. Marshall felt "blamed . . . buffeted and extremely maltreated by sundry of my friends, as I thought, and who, I believed were really religious persons and loved our Lord Jesus Christ, but now declare that no such Belief or Confession is necessary, in forming the new government."

Ultimately Rush lost the debate over religious oaths in the state constitution, as well as several other arguments. Politically, he was in an odd position: when it came to national or "continental" politics, he was considered a radical because, unlike many Pennsylvania loyalists, he favored independence. But in provincial or "colonial" politics, like this conference of all the committees of inspection in Pennsylvania, he was more of a moderate.

The provincial conference moved on to the one subject almost all of them agreed on: declaring independence. The motion was approved—which had no bearing on the elected state assembly but was an official vote of confidence from the committees. After the vote on Sunday, June 23, Rush was told that he should write Pennsylvania's declaration of independence as quickly as possible. He would have the assistance of seasoned attorney James Smith, another member of the conference.

By this time, the first draft of Jefferson's declaration was circulating among a very small group. Jefferson had sent it to the recuperating Franklin, and it is reasonable to assume that Adams had seen it by now and had possibly shared it with his exuberant physician friend.

Sunday evening, June 23, 1776, Rush went home, sat down at the table in his parlor, and stayed up much of the night writing his own impassioned version. Whenever he felt "languid or sleepy," he briefly stepped out on his balcony overlooking the river for fresh air. He delivered the declaration the next morning:

> WHEREAS, George the third, king of Great Britain, &c., in violation of the principles of the British constitution; and of the laws of justice and humanity, hath by an accumulation of oppressions unparalleled in history, excluded the inhabitants of this *with the other American colonies from his protection*;
>
> And whereas, He hath paid no regard to any of our numerous and dutiful *petitions* for a redress of our complicated grievances, but hath lately purchased foreign troops to assist in enslaving us, and hath excited the savages of the country to carry on a war against us, as also the negroes to embrue their hands in the blood of their masters, in a manner unpracticed by civilized nations, and hath lately insulted our calamities, by declaring that he will show us no mercy until he has reduced us:
>
> And whereas, the obligations of allegiance (being reciprocal between a King and his subjects) are now dissolved on the side of the colonists, by the despotism of the said king, insomuch, that it now appears loyalty to him is treason against the good people of this country:
>
> AND WHEREAS, Not only the Parliament, but, there is reason to believe; too many of the people of Great Britain, have concurred in the aforesaid arbitrary and unjust proceedings against us:
>
> AND WHEREAS the public virtue of this colony (so essential to its liberty and happiness) must be endangered by future political union with or dependence upon a crown and nation so lost to justice, patriotism, and Magnanimity.
>
> We the *deputies* of the people of Pennsylvania, assembled in *full provincial conference*, for forming a plan for executing the resolve of congress of the 15th of May last, for suppressing all authority in this province derived from the crown of Great Britain, and for estab-

> lishing a government upon the authority of the people only, now in this public manner in behalf of ourselves, and with the approbation, consent, and authority of our constituents, unanimously declare our willingness to concur in a vote of the congress, declaring the united colonies free and independent states:
>
> *Provided*, The forming of the government, and the regulation of the internal police of this colony be always reserved to the people of the said colony; and we do further call upon the nations of Europe; and appeal to great arbiter and governor of the empires of the world, to witness for us, that this declaration did not originate in ambition or in an impatience of lawful authority; but that we were driven to it in obedience to the first principles of nature, by the oppressions and cruelties of the aforesaid king and parliament of Great Britain, as the only possible measure that was left us to preserve and establish our liberties and to transmit them inviolate to posterity.

Once Rush's declaration was approved, the provincial conference moved on to hiring 4,500 new soldiers for the state militia, to join the 1,500 already under command. Every colony needed to fortify its own military, as well as support the growing Continental Army. The British fleet was rapidly approaching the Atlantic Coast.

Five days later, on Friday, June 28, 1776, an edited version of Jefferson's Declaration of Independence was shared with the Continental Congress. Adams, Franklin, and the others on the committee had already offered their editing suggestions. Where Jefferson had originally described truths that were "sacred & undeniable," they were now "self-evident." Where Jefferson had written that all men were "created equal & independent . . . [and] from that equal creation they derive rights inherent & inalienable among which are the preservation of life, & liberty, & the pursuit of happiness," the prose had been smoothed and tightened. Now it read: "that all men are created equal; that they are endowed by their creator with inherent & inalienable rights, that among these are life, liberty, and the pursuit of happiness." It was almost finished.

John Dickinson and others still wanted to offer critiques, notably that such a declaration was still premature and too dangerous. Dickinson continued to hover between camps, still declaring that independence should wait but remaining involved, with Samuel Adams and others, on the committee to prepare articles of confederation for the colonies, and with John Adams and Ben Franklin, on the committee to plan to make treaties with foreign governments.

The next day, however, the issue of independence became almost moot.

On Saturday morning, Washington's officers stationed in Manhattan and on Long Island saw signals that forty-five ships from the British fleet were approaching Sandy Hook. And intelligence from Halifax, Nova Scotia—where the fleet had put into port before sailing to attack America—suggested that another seventy-five ships were on their way, not only with more firepower than the fledgling continental navy but carrying tens of thousands of troops that would head directly to New York and then New Jersey.

There was no more time for negotiating with the king. There was only time for winning gloriously or losing horribly.

16

It was hot and rainy on July 1, 1776, as the Continental Congress held its most important debate ever: Should it ratify the Declaration of Independence and formally separate the colonies from Great Britain? As the draft of the declaration "lay on table" in the front of the room, the delegates took their last, best shots, speaking with passion that would either create a nation or put off the decision again. John Adams and John Dickinson, the best trial lawyers in Boston and Philadelphia respectively, dominated the debate, locked in a rhetorical death match not over *whether* the nation should be independent but *when*. Adams had been ready for a year. Dickinson was still acting like a lawyer trying to protect his clients—in this case, the colonies—from themselves.

Dickinson, at forty-three, was only three years older than Adams, but as he rose to give his final appeal to a jury he had once thought of as his peers, he appeared so thin and pale that he looked much older. It was hard to believe that what had begun for him with the *Farmer's Letters* nine years ago was going to end like this. "The Consequences involvd in the Motion now lying before You are of such Magnitude," Dickinson began, "that I tremble under the oppressive Honor of sharing in its Determination. I Feel myself unequal to the burthen [burden] assigned Me. I believe—I had almost said, I rejoice—that the Time is approaching, when I shall be relieved from its Weight. . . .

"My Conduct, this Day, I expect will give the finishing Blow to my once too great and . . . now too diminish'd Popularity. It will be my Lott to know, that I had rather vote away the Enjoyment of that dazzling display, that pleasing Possession, than the Blood and Happiness of my Countrymen—too fortunate, amidst their Calamities, if I prove a truth known in heaven—that I had rather they should hate Me, than that I should hurt them."

He spoke for some time about the reasons to delay. The colonies should first finish the articles of confederation he was drafting for Congress, because the minute they declared independence, all those boats and troops waiting at New York were going to attack. Then he delivered his rousing, scripted finish: "When our Enemies are Pressing Us so vigorously, When We are in so wretched a State of Preparation, when the Sentiments & Designs of our expected Friends are so unknown to us, I am alarm'd at this Declaration being so vehemently presented." He hoped he would not one day be reading "the Doomsday Book of America . . . I should be glad to know whether in 20 or 30 Years this Commonwealth of Colonies may not be thought too unwieldy. . . . I have a strong Impression on my mind that this will take Place."

Dickinson dropped into his chair, spent, and like so many in the hot room, sopping. According to Adams's recollection, nobody said a word in response. Finally, "after waiting some time, in hopes that someone less obnoxious than myself" would say something, Adams "determined to speak."

He gave the same talk he had given so many times before, made the same points he had been making for a year, the ones Thomas Paine had invoked, the ones that filled so many pages in colonial newspapers and declarations, not because they were so original but because they were, to him, common sense.

As Adams was finishing, there was a knock on the chamber door. Three new delegates from New Jersey, weary and wet from riding hard through the mud from Princeton, were admitted and seated.

One was Rush's father-in-law, Richard Stockton, who had only just recently decided to support independence. He was joined by

Rev. John Witherspoon and attorney Francis Hopkinson. Several days before, they had been quietly voted into office to replace the last New Jersey delegates who had been holding out. They had ridden hard to get here in time for their first vote.

As they settled in, Richard Stockton asked what he had missed from his first day in Congress. When told, he asked Adams and Dickinson to repeat their points, so he and the reverend might know them. "All was silence," Adams recalled. "No one would speak: all eyes were turned upon me. Mr. Edward Rutledge [from South Carolina] came to me and said, laughing, 'Nobody will speak but you, upon this subject. You have all the Topicks so ready, that you must satisfy the Gentlemen from New Jersey.' I answered him, laughing, that it had so much the Air of exhibiting like an Actor or Gladiator for the entertainment of the audience, that I was ashamed to repeat what I had said twenty times before, and I thought nothing new could be advanced by me. The New Jersey gentlemen, however, still insist[ed] on hearing at least a Recapitulation of the Arguments."

So Adams quickly summed up his and Dickinson's points—basically, he debated himself—until "the Jersey gentlemen said they were fully satisfied and ready for the Question."

It was simple and profound: Yea or nay on the Declaration of Independence?

The roll was called, and Benjamin Franklin announced that the Pennsylvania delegates had not approved the declaration—the vote was four to three against. Dickinson and the one other possible swing vote, financier Robert Morris, were standing their ground. So the matter was put off until the next day.

The next morning's session of the Second Congress began with the reading of "sundry letters," including one from General Washington and another from the paymaster general with the weekly accounts. Then it was time for the main event. The resolution was read to the chamber: "*Resolved*, that these United Colonies are, and, of right, ought to be, Free and Independent States; that they are absolved from all allegiances to the British Crown, and that all political connexion between them, and the state of Great Britain, is, and ought to be, totally dissolved."

This time Pennsylvania's vote had changed: three to two in favor. John Dickinson and Robert Morris had abstained.

Dickinson did not come to the chamber the day of the final vote. He soon left Philadelphia and, wishing to serve, joined the Delaware militia. From his battalion's posting in Elizabethtown, New Jersey, he drafted a letter in which he expressed extreme disappointment in the way his Pennsylvania colleagues had treated him. Rush, whom he had considered a good friend, and one other had "totally estranged themselves from Me, and . . . did not act kindly with respect to my Reputation." He was especially upset because, regardless of their differences of opinion on the timing of independence, Dickinson felt he had always "entertained as sincere and unsuspicious a Friendship for them as they could wish to lodge in any Bosom . . . [and] on every occasion I religiously performed a friend's Duty in vindicating their Characters from every Reflection that came to my Hearing." He was particularly angry at Rush, and told the unknown recipient of the letter that he was free to tell the doctor that.

The five-year personal relationship between Dickinson and Rush, going back to when the doctor had helped treat Dickinson's manic friend, Captain Macpherson, was now ruptured. But there was a more practical matter at hand. Dickinson's resignation had left the Pennsylvania delegation to the Continental Congress shorthanded, just as the Declaration of Independence was being finalized.

The document went through a few more last-minute tweaks, before it was approved on July 4 and read aloud in public for the first time, to a throng in front of the State House on July 8. Then several hundred copies of it were printed up and distributed. But it had yet to be signed: many members of Congress were away, and Pennsylvania still had a delegate to replace.

Almost two weeks later, a new name showed up in the minutes of the Continental Congress, representing Pennsylvania. There had been no official vote yet in the colony to replace John Dickinson, but someone—possibly Benjamin Franklin—decided to bring in his replacement a few days early.

It was Dr. Benjamin Rush.

Three days later, on Saturday, July 20, he was formally voted into the Continental Congress. At the age of thirty, he was the fourth youngest delegate and the only one whose father-in-law was also a delegate.

The evening of his election, Rush ran into John Adams on the street near a popular meeting place for congressional members, the Indian Queen Tavern. They walked a bit, and Rush began telling his friend how much he admired one of his fellow congressmen, who he believed to be honest and virtuous. Adams stopped short and turned to him. "*That* is saying a great deal of a public character," he exclaimed. "For political integrity is the rarest virtue in the whole world." They continued the conversation back in Adams's room at Mrs. Yards's, where Adams gave Rush a bit of a lecture on how *public* and *private* integrity did not always go together. He mentioned a man in Boston who in his private life was "strictly just" but in his public dealings was completely unprincipled.

While Adams was as jaundiced as ever about politics, he was developing a greater appreciation for his idealistic doctor friend. That evening after Rush left, he wrote home to Abigail about him with none of his previous reservations.

The letter began, appropriately, with Adams suggesting his wife get a smallpox inoculation—doctor's orders. Then as if he had never written to Abigail about Rush before, he wrote, "I don't know how I can better entertain you, than by giving you some Idea of the Character of this Dr. Rush.—He is a Native of this Place, a Gentleman of an ingenious Turn of Mind, and of elegant Accomplishments. . . . This Gentleman is said to be a staunch American, I suppose, truly."

He also wrote to his physician friend at home, Dr. Cotton Tufts, about Rush, whom he referred to as "an eminent Phisician of this City, and a worthy Friend of mine, who with a Politeness and Benevolence, becoming his Character . . . practices with great Success. Several of our Members, have been under his Hands and come out, almost without an Alteration of Countenance."

Several nights later Rush wrote to his friend Maj. Gen. Charles Lee, who was stationed in South Carolina defending

Charleston from sea attack, to tell him he had joined Congress. "I find," Rush admitted, "there is a great deal of difference between sporting a sentiment in a letter or over a glass of wine upon politics, and discharging properly the duty of a senator. I feel myself unequal to every part of my new situation except where plain integrity is required."

He also wrote to Julia, still in Princeton. He was glad his election gave her "so much pleasure." He was still getting adjusted to the audience: "Dr. Franklin alone is enough to confound with his presence a thousand such men as myself. I hope however in a little time to experience the same freedom and confidence in speaking that I observe in other members."

Rush was eager for Julia to return home. He knew her mother wouldn't likely encourage her to return—even before there were safety issues in Philadelphia, Annis had already been pressing her to spend at least one week a month back in Princeton. But, said Rush, "Mama must part with you. . . . I cannot support the burden of public and private business which now lays on my shoulders without you."

The doctor just didn't feel confident managing so much help around the house. "William," one of their house staff, "fell asleep as usual this evening. Betsey walked out, and I was obliged to wait near an hour before I could go out to visit a patient—and at last got one of the neighbors to watch the door." Rush was also taking on new apprentices, renting living space in the home of a Jewish family in the alley behind his own house with some of the hundred guineas ($15,300) the students paid him for their education and upkeep. He figured that between these payments and his new wages in the Congress of 20 shillings ($146) a day, he and Julia might be able "to realize our money in a house or a plantation."

He was rather astonished by his good fortune in the midst of revolution. "Heaven requires only the heart," he wrote. "I was willing to be poor, that my country might be free. The latter I hope will be granted, and contrary even to my wishes I find I am growing rich."

At the same time, Rush was about to take a great risk: he was going to put his name to the Declaration, which had been ratified but never actually signed. On Friday, August 2, most of the Continental Congress members arrived at the Assembly Room in the State House to take their lives into their own hands and pens, to put their names to what was probably the most treasonous document in the history of the British Empire. Only they would ever know what Rush described as "the solicitude and labors and fears and sorrows and sleepless nights of the men who projected, proposed, defended and Subscribed the declaration of independence."

Declaration of Independence *by John Trumbull; inset, Rush is in the middle of the front row, to the left of Elbridge Gerry (hand on chin)*

As he waited his turn, Rush found himself caught up in "the pensive and awful silence which pervaded the house" as they "were called up, one after another, to the table of the President of Congress," John Hancock, to sign what they believed to be "our own death warrants."

There was one moment of gallows humor. Col. Benjamin Harrison, a heavyset fifty-year-old plantation owner and ship builder representing Virginia, was chatting with Elbridge Gerry from Massachusetts, a slender, thirty-two-year-old merchant (whose name and local politics later inspired the term *gerrymandering*).

"I shall have a great advantage over you, Mr. Gerry, when we are all hung for what we are now doing," Harrison chuckled. "From the size and weight of my body I shall die in a few minutes, but from the lightness of your body you will dance in the air an hour or two before you are dead." There were grins all around, before the room again turned solemn.

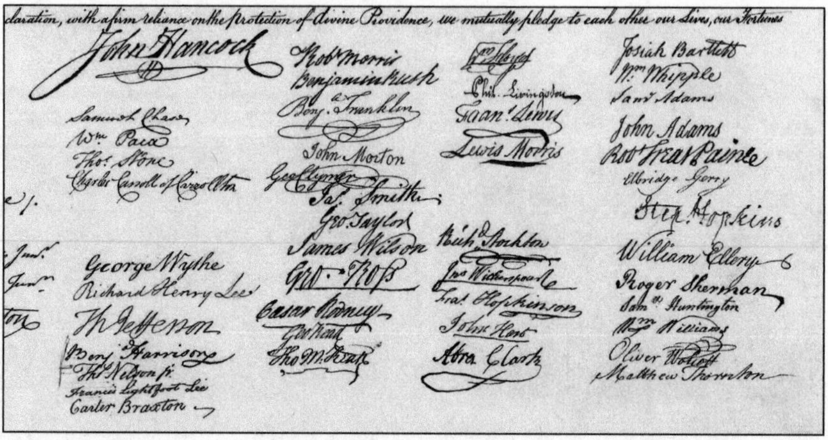

The signatures: Rush signed to the right and just below John Hancock; Benjamin Franklin signed after Rush

17

As Dr. Rush settled into Congress, he realized he liked the intellectual stimulation and the camaraderie more than the politics. He was "surprised to observe how little of the spirit of [the Declaration] . . . actuated many of the members."

It was his habit to speak only from prose written on the right-hand pages of his commonplace books, so he could keep notes on the left-hand pages. During sessions he was often seen scribbling down observations and even the occasional doodle.

Rush's doodling

His first major speech concerned whether a small group of congressional leaders should be allowed to travel to New York to meet with Lord William Howe, the king's commander in chief for North American forces. Howe had just handed Washington's troops their first devastating defeat on Long Island, which Rush described in a long letter to his old friend in France, Dr. Jacques Dubourg (who had first introduced him, as a young medical trainee, to Parisian society).

"Our troops behaved like veterans," he wrote. Three thousand American troops had faced ten thousand British and Hessian troops for six hours; the Americans ceded the day after about a thousand men were killed and taken prisoner, having killed or wounded five hundred British. "One brigade sustained three heavy fires in an open field without moving. When the word of command to 'fire' was given, the enemy gave way, and a total rout was expected, but alas, their numbers supplied their want of order, and our men were surrounded and cut to pieces or taken." Soon after the battle, Britain took possession of Long Island, and Washington's troops were preparing to fall back.

Before forcing his way into Manhattan, Howe paused in his position on Staten Island and sent a message to Congress that he wanted a meeting. The invitation was delivered by a high-profile American prisoner of war: Gen. John Sullivan, whom Howe's troops had captured after overwhelming him on Long Island. Sullivan was released and sent to Philadelphia.

Some congressmen wanted to see if there was one more chance for a negotiated peace before England released the hordes of troops and fleets of vessels they had at the ready. They listened to Sullivan's message from the enemy. As he spoke, Adams turned to Rush, who was next to him, and whispered, "I wish the first ball that had been fired" that day "had gone through [Sullivan's] head."

When he rose to speak against the proposal, Adams referred to Sullivan as nothing more than "a decoy duck." Reverend Witherspoon and several others also spoke against the proposal, and then Rush got up.

"Our country is far from being in a condition to make it necessary for us to humble ourselves at the feet of Great Britain," he said. "We have lost a battle . . . but the city and State of New York are still in possession of their independence. But suppose the State had been conquered, suppose half the States in the union had been conquered—nay, suppose *all the states in the union except one* have been conquered, still let not that one renounce her independence.

"But I will go further: should this solitary state, the last repository of our freedom, be invaded, let her not survive her precious birthright, but in yielding to superior force, let her last breath be spent in uttering the word *Independence*."

His speech sounded patriotic but was also oddly defeatist—the way a nonmilitary orator might talk about war, perhaps more worried about the nobility of the sentiment than about the objective of victory.

After Rush spoke, three southern representatives spoke in favor of taking the meeting with Howe. One targeted Rush directly in his rousing conclusion: "I would much rather live with *dependance*," he bellowed, "than die with *independance* on my lips!"

The measure passed. John Adams, Benjamin Franklin, and Edward Rutledge—the South Carolina representative who, at twenty-six, was the youngest member of Congress—were ordered to go meet Howe. Adams was incensed. That night, when Rush spoke to him at the doorway of Mrs. Yard's, Adams railed, "It would seem as if mankind were made of *slaves*, and the sooner they fulfill their destiny the better!" But he went.

THE MEETING WAS a disaster—although an elaborate and mannered disaster, as Adams recounted to Congress upon their return. It lasted for three hours. Forty-seven-year-old Howe, in his red silk army officer uniform, met their boat with decorum and then walked his guests "between lines of guards of grenadiers, looking fierce as ten Furies, and making all the grimaces, and gestures, and motions of their muskets, with bayonets fixed, which, I suppose, military etiquette requires," Adams recalled. They were taken to a filthy waterfront house that soldiers had commandeered, in which Howe had prepared one "large handsome room, by spreading a carpet of moss and green sprigs, from bushes and shrubs in the neighborhood, till he had made it not only wholesome, but romantically elegant; and he entertained us with good claret, good bread, cold ham, tongues, and mutton."

Lord Howe had been the subject of furor all over the colonies since leading the British troops in the 1775 Battle of Bunker Hill, after which he was elevated to commanding all British forces

William Howe

in America. But while colonists often cursed his name, few had ever seen him. Franklin had met him in London during friendlier times, but for Adams and Rutledge, it must have been surreal to share a meal with the man behind England's assault on their countrymen.

After all the bowing and eating and posturing, the men finally began to talk, and it became clear that Howe had no authority to do anything but listen politely to their grievances. Unless, of course, they agreed to tear up that Declaration of Independence and reestablish their allegiance. Until then, Lord Howe admitted, he wasn't sure in what capacity he was receiving them.

"In any capacity your Lordship pleases except in that of *British subjects*," Adams said.

Lord Howe claimed that "nothing would mortify me more than to witness the fall of America." If that happened, he said, he would "weep for her as a brother."

To which Franklin responded, "I hope your Lordship will be saved that mortification. America is able to take care of herself."

The three rebels returned to their ship, then to Philadelphia. Lord Howe had his troops prepare to attack, full force.

To Rush this was bad news, but the fighting was still far away. The letter he sent Julia recounting Adams's story of meeting Lord Howe also included more mundane matters of work and household challenges. A family had sent for him to visit "four miles in the country," and since Julia had taken their carriage, along with their best horses and driver, with her to Princeton, he had to borrow the carriage of a fellow congressman. He needed a haircut, and with all the staff gone, the maid needed to find him a barber. And his apprentices were failing at their office duties: they were "as irregular in their attendance upon the shop as ever." When he was an apprentice to Dr. Redman, he never would have acted so irresponsibly.

Soon, however, the war became more palpable to him as a physician. In late September, he was appointed to the Medical Committee of the Congress, which put him in an odd position. He would have to oversee the budgets and decisions of doctors he knew well, starting with Dr. John Morgan, who had been director general for all the medical care of Washington's army for the past year, and Dr. William Shippen, Jr., who was trying to depose Morgan.

Morgan, now in his early forties, had military experience, having served as a surgeon in the British Army during the Seven Years' War. As long as the fighting was primarily in New England, he had been successful enough in securing treatment for the sick and wounded, although the hospitals were already experiencing overcrowding, lack of funding, and disorganization, which would continue throughout the war. Morgan and his staff had done their best with the constant challenges of rampant infections for which there were no cures, and the still-primitive tools of field surgery.

Once the fighting moved south to New York and involved more soldiers over wider areas, the hospitals were unable to keep up with injuries, infections, and amputations. The top doctors blamed each other and inevitably Morgan. And the complex structure of the military meant there were many paths to undermining his authority. After all, these doctors had been hired by Congress, not by Morgan—just as the Continental Army was led by Washington, but the generals were appointed by Congress. Besides Washington's troops, there were many state militias that were organized and paid locally and could complain to their local delegates. All this made Morgan's job even more impossible.

Morgan first clashed with Dr. Samuel Stringer, the medical director Congress had hired for the northern army. Stringer was his subordinate but aspired to end-run him.

And then after Morgan had been on the job seven months, Congress decided to hire Shippen as director of the hospitals in what was called the "flying camp": ten thousand troops from middle state militias that could be moved to any trouble spot below New York. Shippen was well connected in Congress—his brother-in-law was Virginia representative Richard Henry Lee, and his family was personally friendly with Washington. So it was easy enough for him to circulate his opinion that Morgan was doing a bad job and he could do better.

It had been more than a decade since the battle over credit for America's first medical school had ruptured the friendship between Morgan and Shippen; the two men, considered the leading medical educators in the colonies, had coexisted for so long that it was easy to forget the sheer depth of their contempt for each other. Washington may have known about the feud, but he had attended enough dinners where the two had been civil to assume they could rise above their differences for the cause of freedom and democracy.

But Shippen knew something Morgan didn't: when the battles in New England began, Washington had dangled the highest medical appointment first in front of him. Shippen had turned it down because of all the travel required. Even after Morgan took the job and slaved away in New England, where his wife Mary moved to be with him, Washington confided in Shippen's brother-in-law, a congressman, that he still wished Shippen had accepted it.

Clearly, Washington was angry about his medical corps. In a September 25, 1776, update to Congress, he decried the "constant bickering" among the surgeons and their superiors, "which tends greatly to the Injury of the Sick." He called them "a disgrace to the profession, the army, and to society."

So as the war intensified and its stakes heightened, as the limitations of the medical service became more obvious, and as the fighting moved closer to where Shippen lived, he began his machinations against Morgan.

Before Rush was even put on the medical committee, Shippen wrote Congress a boastful letter from his post running the flying camp hospital, then in Perth Amboy, New Jersey. "All the wounded from Long Island were now recovered," he reported—as if he had been treating them, which he hadn't—and he claimed an astonishingly low death rate among his patients, which wasn't accurate. Rush, new to Congress and to the committee, and not having seen any of the military medical care firsthand, made no apparent objection when Congress decided to alter the chain of command.

Morgan was effectively demoted to the same level as Shippen, and they were each given half of the battle area in which to handle all medical care. Shippen was given the area below the Hudson River, where the war was moving.

NOW THAT HE was in a position of congressional influence, Rush made it his work to study the medical corps on a structural level. But he was also fascinated by individual case reports. One day in the early fall, he met a colonial soldier who had been returned from capture by Howe's army in New York, and was "much pleased with the fashion of his hair," which had been "cut short all around by General Howe's orders."

Rush recalled that Maurice de Saxe, a famed leader in the German and French army, had written in his 1757 military memoir, "I would have a soldier wear his hair short." He had then gone on to propose something far less practical: after the haircut, each soldier would be "furnished with a small wig, either grey or black, made of Spanish lamb-skin, which he should put on in bad weather." Rush wasn't so interested in field wigs. He was intrigued, however, by the idea that everyone in the colonial military could sport a buzz cut. He wrote to a friend, Col. Anthony Wayne of the Fourth Pennsylvania Battalion, to suggest he start this trend in his own regiment.

"If you begin with yourself," Rush noted, "every private as well as officer must follow your example." Doing this would not only save "time and trouble" but would prevent lice and prevent "a soldier from suffering from the rain, which often keeps the hair wet for hours afterwards." This was the beginning of the standard American GI haircut.

18

In late November 1776, the Revolutionary War became personal for Rush. The Continental Army had retreated from New York, then from north and central New Jersey, and was now trying to hold the line from the Pennsylvania side of the Delaware River. Washington had seen an estimated 969 of his men die, with another 1,781 injured or diseased and 4,624 captured. The British had lost more men—just over a thousand dead, with two thousand wounded and 1,649 captured—but they had won almost every battle. During the most recent fighting in New Jersey, the British forces, and their hired Hessian troops, had ransacked and occupied hundreds of buildings.

Among them were two structures cherished by Benjamin and Julia Rush: her family's home, Morven, and Nassau Hall at the College of New Jersey. Julia's family had evacuated just in time. Before leaving, they buried their silver and other valuables in three boxes on the property. They had no time to hide Richard's papers, but Annis was able to stash away some of her poetry. Richard had left his twelve-year-old son there, along with one of their slaves, to guard the house in case it was spared; when the troops approached, the pair had been able to flee to freedom.

Richard, however, was not so fortunate. He had unwisely chosen to hide, with Annis and Julia's sisters, in a nearby New Jersey town instead of crossing into safer Pennsylvania. The town, Federal Hall, had its share of British sympathizers—one of whom couldn't resist turning in a signer of the Declaration of Independence.

On November 30, 1776, Richard Stockton became the first signer to be captured by the British. The moon-faced forty-six-year-old judge was dragged from his bed at night, tortured, and transported in leg irons to Perth Amboy, then to Howe's headquarters in New York. There he was left to rot, in a cold common jail—surprising, for a noncombatant of his political and social class.

When Rush heard what had happened, he was beyond incensed. "Every particle of my blood is electrified with revenge," he wrote to a friend, "and if justice cannot be done to him any other way, I declare I will, in defiance of the authority of the Congress and the power of the army, drive the first rascally tory I meet with a hundred miles, barefooted, through the first deep snow that falls in our country."

Rush's other close friend in Princeton, Rev. John Witherspoon, had successfully fled with his wife into Pennsylvania. They were safe, but their beloved college was under siege. The British took over Nassau Hall, using the first floor and prayer hall as a barracks and hospital, and the basement as a stable.

Congress adjourned early, on Thursday, December 12, 1776, because British troops were getting too close to Philadelphia.

Rush quickly moved to get seventeen-year-old Julia to safety—especially important because they had just realized, amid the nightmare of her father being taken prisoner, that she was two months pregnant. He arranged for her to stay with the family of a cousin of his mother, Col. Elihu Hall.

The Halls lived on a large plantation called Mount Welcome, comprising some four hundred acres along the Susquehanna River in northeastern Maryland, where the broad river meets Octoraro Creek, not far from where Rush had gone to boarding school. Mount Welcome had a large brick main house overlooking the river, as well as an octagonal bath house and a mill. The plantation had a large staff attending to the family and the farm and was known as a popular place for local gatherings.

The master of Mount Welcome, Colonel Hall, was away with the Maryland militia; Julia stayed with his wife, Catherine, and their many children, the oldest of whom, four boys, were around Julia's age.

Rush arranged for his sisters and his mother to relocate closer to Philadelphia—to Rush Hill, the tiny country home Mrs. Rush had bought eleven miles outside town. His brother Jacob would follow Congress, where he still worked as a private secretary for John Hancock, to Baltimore, where it planned to reconvene in two weeks. Rush had all his books—along with a few prized pieces of furniture, including his mahogany tea tables—moved to the home of a patient who had a farm southwest of the city in Darby, where he thought his possessions would be safe from British invaders.

Rush accompanied Julia, the household staff, and their horses to Maryland. It was a long, cold fifty-mile trip in their carriage, and Julia had just reached the point in her pregnancy when she was likely experiencing morning sickness. Once they were settled into their new surroundings, Rush kissed Julia goodbye, not knowing if they would see each other again.

Rush's servant and groomsman, Cyrus, prepared the horses, and the two of them rode off into uncertainty.

While he was expected to join Congress in Baltimore, Rush had decided to serve in a less political and more practical way. Washington's colonial troops had dug in on the Pennsylvania side of the Delaware River, at the places considered most vulnerable to the enemy—mostly ferry crossings. Washington himself was north of Trenton, near McConkey's Ferry. The Philadelphia militia would cover strategic points south of Trenton, near the Bristol crossing.

Rush learned all this when he got back to Philadelphia, which had largely been abandoned except for those still loyal to the Crown (who expected to soon welcome British troops). The city's economy was devastated, and many buildings were barricaded to prevent looting. Only a few businesses remained open.

While the newspapers had stopped publishing, Thomas Paine found a printer for his latest revolutionary rail, *The American Crisis*, his first new pamphlet since *Common Sense.* He had been scribbling notes on it for weeks while embedded with Washington's retreating troops in New Jersey and then finished it while walking thirty-five miles to secure his dwelling in Philadelphia. It began with what was arguably Paine's most memorable sentence: "These are the times that try men's souls."

Paine went on to describe the situation, which Rush was about to encounter. Washington's Continental Army troops were freezing and dispirited in the brutal winter weather, and many were enlisted only through the end of the year. If they did not agree to reenlist soon, the Revolutionary War would most likely be over, because Washington's army would cease to exist.

Paine addressed this problem directly in his second line: "The summer soldier and the sunshine patriot will, in this crisis, shrink from the service of their country; but he that stands by it now, deserves the love and thanks of man and woman." From there he used every verbal trick and bit of patriotic guilt he could think of to persuade America's ragtag troops to reenlist. The pamphlet was distributed nearly free to the soldiers, and Washington ordered it read aloud. It is unclear exactly how copies made it to Washington's camps so quickly, but it may not be a coincidence that Rush and his servant left Philadelphia the day after eighteen thousand copies were printed.

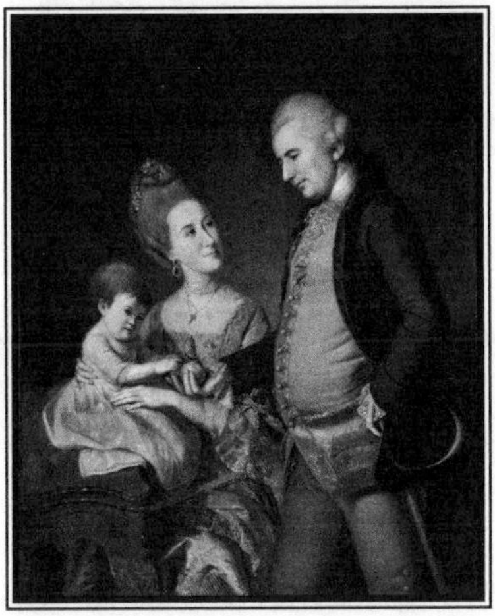

Gen. John Cadwalader and family

Rush and Cyrus traveled, on horseback, about twenty miles, along with the twelve-hundred-man Philadelphia Associators; it was the oldest volunteer militia in the state, first proposed by Franklin in the late 1740s. The Associators were now under the leadership of a gentleman Rush knew from Philadelphia, John Cadwalader—

the son of Dr. Thomas Cadwalader, the Pennsylvania Hospital physician with whom Rush had written the tea tax resolution that helped fuel the Boston Tea Party. General Cadwalader, three years older than Rush, had married well enough that he could leave his dry goods business and focus on a life in the military. He was tall with a friendly face and had inherited the family gut.

Many others Rush and Cadwalader knew had joined the ranks of the militia. Among them was Charles Willson Peale, the exuberant young painter who had recently done Julia's portrait. Before enlisting, Peale had been painting other people in town—including Cadwalader and his brother Lambert, with matching protruding stomachs—and he had already painted two portraits of George Washington, before and after he was made general. While Peale was learning to fight, he also took copious notes and drew sketches.

Charles Willson Peale, self-portrait in uniform, and one of his field drawings from 1776

The Associators set up camp near Bristol, along with another Philadelphia militia, awaiting Washington's orders. Rush spent a few days there "superintending their health, and encouraging them to firmness and perseverances in defense of our liberties and independence," as the main hospital for these troops was over forty miles away, in Bethlehem. In his free time, he was still involved with political matters. From the camp, he wrote to Richard Henry Lee about his concern over the economy of Philadelphia, where the remaining merchants were "refusing Continental money" for fear that when General Howe arrived, it would be worthless.

He also worried about the state of the colonial forces, their size, and the quality of their training and leadership. "Many of the Continental troops now in our service pant for the extirpation of their enlistments . . . [but] the continent cannot spare them," he wrote. We "have a right at this juncture to their services and to their blood. . . . [But] a distrust has crept in among the troops of the abilities of some of our . . . heaven-taught and book-taught generals. . . . We must have an army; the fate of America must be decided by an army."

After several days with the Philadelphia militias, Rush left on the afternoon of December 24, his thirty-first birthday, to visit General Washington's camp fifteen miles away. He and his servant were accompanied by Col. Joseph Reed, a College of New Jersey graduate who had studied there with Richard Stockton, so both of them had much to be upset about as they traveled. Fearful for his father-in-law's life and concerned with the way the war was going, Rush was nonetheless a complete Washington believer. He told people the general "must be invested with dictatorial power . . . or we are undone."

Colonel Reed was not so sure. He admitted to Rush that he had moments of doubt and pain about Washington's leadership. He had, just days before, written the general a letter begging him to do something, anything, "to revive our expiring Credit, give our Cause some Degree of reputation. . . . Our Affairs are hasting fast to Ruin if we do not retrieve them by some happy Event." While a victory would be ideal, in Reed's eyes, "even a Failure cannot be more fatal than to remain in our present Situation."

Rush and Reed stopped for the evening at a farmhouse near where the colonial troops were encamped. The next morning he was ushered into the general's tent for a private meeting.

He had never seen Washington like this before: "He appeared much depressed, and lamented the ragged and dissolving state of his army in affecting terms." Besides offering him support as a friend, Rush was also now, technically, one of the general's superiors. He delivered the "assurance . . . of Congress to support him, under his present difficulties and distresses."

They spent most of an hour together, just the two of them.

While they spoke Washington fidgeted with his quill pen and ink, occasionally scribbling on small shards of paper; Rush wondered what he was writing. Finally, one of the pieces of paper slipped from Washington's hand and fell to the ground, near Rush's feet. He looked down and "was struck with the inscription upon it."

It read "Victory or Death."

What Rush didn't know was that "Victory or Death" was the watchword Washington had chosen to ensure security for the military operation that evening. It would be his last-ditch effort to end this bleak military year with new hope that there would be a United States of America in 1777.

Rush returned to Cadwalader's camp. Late that afternoon, as the sun sank on the horizon, Cadwalader's troops began moving out in tight formations, marching toward the river at Bristol. The other Philadelphia militia split off and headed slightly south to Dunk's Ferry. Washington ordered that they march in "profound silence" and threatened that "no man" could "quit his Ranks on pain of Death."

The same procession was taking place from Colonel Ewing's camp just across the river from Trenton, and from Washington's camp farther north. The plan was to cross the Delaware just after sundown, stealthily set up on the other side before the full moon rose, lie low, then unleash a sneak attack the daybreak after Christmas—a holiday the Hessian troops were known to celebrate excessively.

When Rush left with Cadwalader's troops, he may have known that the operation was already running several hours late: they were supposed to be at the river already. He didn't know, however, that just before leaving with his troops, Washington had received an unsettling letter from one of his highest-ranking generals, Horatio Gates.

General Horatio Gates

Washington had been growing concerned that Gates might have designs on his command. Several days before, he had asked Gates to lead the troops across the Delaware to Trenton. The general had claimed he didn't feel well enough for the task. Washington had thought it odd. Now Gates had sent him a letter postmarked not from his military location but from Philadelphia. And the courier delivering it said Gates wasn't sick at all—in fact, he was on his way to Baltimore to meet with Congress.

Victory or death, indeed.

19

When the continental troops and militias reached their positions on the eastern shoreline, it was already dark, and the moon wasn't yet high enough to illuminate the Delaware. It was bitter cold, but clear enough, and the river looked icy but passable in places.

Then the nor'easter came: first the rain, then the wind, and then the rain froze into hard, stinging pellets. The river tide rose dramatically, and the ice flowed fast, slamming into the rocks and shores. By nine p.m., they had all hoped to be safely on the other side and preparing for sunrise attacks on the Hessians in the villages lining the river, followed by a march toward Trenton for a surprise attack there. But so far not one boat or soldier or cannon or horse had crossed the river, now a frosty operational nightmare.

Rush was with the Associators' militia along the river's edge, shivering and waiting for a break in the weather. Finally Cadwalader gave up on this entry point and had his troops march another six miles to the south, to see if their fellow Philadelphians were having any better luck. There they were able to get a couple of boats into the water.

Around eleven p.m., several of the boats, including one carrying Charles Willson Peale, had dodged the treacherous ice floes and made it most of the way across the Delaware. But as they approached the eastern shore, huge, jagged ice blockades prevented them from making landfall. Some six hundred men reached the other side by crawling across the ice, but when it proved impossible for their artillery or horses to follow, they were forced to crawl back to those boats that hadn't been smashed by the ice or the current and row back to the Pennsylvania side. They all headed back to camp in the dark—which took so long that when another storm hit at daybreak, they were still marching. Finally they arrived and awaited new orders.

The troops trying to cross to Trenton fared the same, as did two of the three forces farther north under Washington. But at the northernmost entry point, McConkey's Ferry, the general caught a break. His troops arrived before the river turned impassable and found Jersey militiamen waiting for them with a variety of vessels—everything from the local ferry to smaller, nimbler boats. Since much of the ice had been forced downriver, where their fellow soldiers were battling it, they stood a better chance of getting across. Many of the boats did not have seats, so the soldiers had to maintain their balance standing while making the eight-hundred-foot crossing. More than a few of them had to be fished out of the Delaware. When Washington reached the other side, he sat down on a wooden box that had once contained a beehive, watched the rest of his troops cross, and contemplated whether to keep moving forward. He decided he had no choice.

Washington Crossing the Delaware *by Emanuel Leutze*

The troops were able to start marching toward Trenton at around four a.m. They scored a decisive victory there, creating some of the first really good news for Washington's forces in quite some time.

Later in the morning, word reached Cadwalader's camp that Washington's troops had, from what Rush was told, "surprised and taken 1000 Hessians." The Philadelphia Associators were so pumped up with patriotic determination that they insisted on trying the river again. This time some eighteen hundred men—including Rush—were able to cross over into New Jersey, then headed north to Burlington, where they spent the night. The next day, late in the afternoon, they marched farther north: the ground was still so icy that Peale slipped and fell hard enough to break the stock of his rifle.

They kept on to Crosswicks, southeast of Trenton. Cadwalader urged Washington to bring his troops back to Trenton from the north, so the Americans could inflict more damage and push the whole British line back. Cadwalader's troops would attack and divert from the other direction. His advice to his commander in chief: "keep up the panic."

Rush left Crosswicks ahead of Cadwalader's troops and proceeded to Trenton by himself, to visit with Washington's troops and see if he could help medically. He found the officers working out of a house at East Front Street and South Montgomery. There he met up with Philadelphian Col. Clement Biddle and an officer he had never met but greatly admired: Gen. Hugh Mercer. Trained as a surgeon in his native Scotland, Mercer, now fifty-six but with the boyish, cheeky face of a grown cherub, had served in the French and Indian War and then practiced medicine in Fredericksburg, Virginia.

Rush "dined and spent the afternoon" with Mercer and Biddle, not realizing it would be "a day which I have ever since remembered." He was moved when Mercer declared, "I will not be conquered. I would rather cross the mountains and live among the Indians rather than submit to the power of Great Britain."

That evening spies brought word that the British army at Princeton was about to attack both Washington and Cadwalader's outposts. Washington called a "council of war" at his quarters, summoning his top leaders, including Mercer, to discuss next steps. Like everyone else, Rush waited to hear what they decided.

Suddenly he was told he was needed at the council of war. When he arrived, Washington explained their dilemma: they couldn't decide whether to call Cadwalader's troops up from Crosswicks to join their fighting force and try and retake Princeton, or leave the Philadelphia Associators where they were, as a possible diversion.

Rush, uncharacteristically humble, said, "I am not a judge of what is proper in the business before this council. But I know one thing well: the Philadelphia militia would be very happy to be under your command, and would instantly obey a summons to join the troops in Trenton." He was thanked for his insight and excused. But just a few minutes later he was called back and asked if he could leave immediately to deliver a letter to Cadwalader. He "readily consented" and by ten p.m. was heading south on a dark road.

Rush was on horseback, accompanied by Philadelphia printer William Hall, a member of the City Light Horse Troops, a small group of affluent volunteers who paid all their own expenses. (William's father, David Hall, had been Benjamin Franklin's partner.) The weather was extremely damp and cold, and the roads were treacherously muddy. The trip took almost three hours, and when they finally got to within a mile of the camp, an armed patrol approached until they were right in each other's faces.

Rush felt a cocked pistol at his chest. "Who are you?" the soldier demanded. Rush recognized him as Sharp Delany, a Philadelphia druggist he had known since he was a medical student, who was now active in local politics.

"An old friend," Rush replied.

"I don't know you Sir," he replied, digging the pistol deeper into Rush's breast. "Tell me your name!" Finally he realized it was Rush, and let him through to see the general.

It was one a.m., and Cadwalader was in bed when Rush was led in to hand him the letter from General Washington. He read it by candlelight and then sprang into action, calling the brigade to prepare to move out.

Rush rode back with them, and by the time they reached Trenton at seven a.m., he was so exhausted, he asked General St. Clair if he could sleep in his quarters for a few hours. Just after he fell asleep, he heard gunfire outside of the general's door. When he opened it, St. Clair appeared, completely composed. He explained that the gun was a signal that the enemy was advancing toward them.

"What do you intend to do?" Rush asked.

"Why, fight them!" he beamed, as he took his sword down from the wall and calmly girded it to his thigh. Rush was surprised by his composure, considering he was headed into battle. Later, when Rush was riding alongside the Philadelphia militia on their way to Trenton to confront the British, he asked a soldier how he felt to be marching into the breach.

"As if I were going to sit down to a good breakfast," the fellow replied.

THE SECOND BATTLE of Trenton was on, and Rush was having his first experience with "the terrible aspect of war . . . all was now hurry, confusion and noise." He watched as a man he had known much of his life, Thomas Mifflin, rode by him now as a wartime general in the heat of battle, in his shiny blue uniform with gold piping and epaulets, his three-cornered hat and his sword dangling at his side. "He appeared to be all soul," Rush thought, as Mifflin galloped ahead to lead the Pennsylvania militia, the soldiers picking up their pace in turn. Another general rode past Rush, calling out thanks for helping at the war council.

The battle began and went on for several hours before the wounded started being brought to Rush for triage. The first soldier he had to treat was from New England. A cannonball had hit him directly in the forearm, and "his right hand hung a little above his wrist by nothing but a piece of skin." Rush asked Peale to help, but the artist-turned-soldier said he was too drunk. He had managed to bring a quarter cask of rum with him, and when the fighting ended for the day, he offered drinks to his compatriots. He was happy to be too inebriated "to assist in cutting off the limbs and dressing the wounds of those unfortunate men."

After Rush and the other doctors treated another twenty patients, there was a temporary break in the triage, during which they tried to get a little sleep on some straw in the same room with their patients, many of whom were groaning in pain from amputations. The sick-burned smell of their cauterized wounds still hung in the air. Rush reflected on what he had just experienced: "for the first time war appeared to me in its awful plentitude of horrors." He wished he could find "words to describe the anguish of my soul, excited by cries and groans and convulsions of the men who lay by my side."

After a couple of hours' sleep, one of his fellow doctors decided to ride to the front lines to see how things were going with the army. Unfortunately, he couldn't find the army. He dashed back, panicked, and he and Rush quickly had their patients loaded onto wagons and taken away, in case the enemy was nearby.

They heard gunfire in the distance as they moved the wounded. Not until the next morning did they find out that Washington and Cadwalader's troops had attacked the British and the Hessians at Princeton—and triumphed.

As Rush and the other doctors approached Princeton, the first thing they saw was "the field of battle still red in many places with human blood," starkly visible on the ice and snow. Washington's troops had already left, on their way north to Morristown. And the British forces were gone as well, having retreated northeast to Brunswick, more than thirty miles back toward New York.

The war, which Lord Howe and his field marshal, General Cornwallis, had thought to be almost over, had only just begun. Howe was stunned, admitting, "I do not now see a prospect for terminating the war but by a general action, and I am aware of the difficulties in our way to obtain it."

For the moment, however, there were many wounded to treat and dead to bury. Rush was first brought in to treat the officer he had befriended just days earlier, Gen. Hugh Mercer. The baby-faced general had led his Virginia militia bravely and gallantly, only to be felled during a crucial battle in the orchard of William Clarke's farm, about a mile and a half from Nassau Hall.

Mercer's troops had been faring well with horses, artillery, and muskets, but they did not have bayonets—so when the British charged them with blades drawn, they were vulnerable. As Mercer's horse was stabbed, he called out a retreat; his troops escaped, but he did not. He was taken prisoner and tortured on the spot, because the British suspected he might be George Washington—he was wearing a blue and gold general's uniform, and they had no idea what Washington looked like. One soldier smashed the side of Mercer's face in with a musket butt, while others stabbed him in the chest and belly with their bayonets. Bleeding and freezing, he was left for dead.

Mercer was dragged to the nearby farmhouse of William Clarke's brother Thomas, where he was attended to by a British surgeon in one of the spare bedrooms. The medical staffs of the warring nations were not considered combatants; in general, they cooperated as best they could. However, since Mercer was under British care, he was technically a prisoner. When Rush got there the next day, Mercer had to be paroled as a prisoner so he could be handed off and cared for by the colonial army.

Rush was cautiously optimistic about Mercer's chances, although the general, himself a physician, wasn't so sure. Rush tended to his seven bayonet wounds, but there was nothing he could do about the blow to the head except give Mercer opium for the ringing pain. When the general was conscious, he discussed which of his wounds was most dangerous. He told Rush he was most worried about his head, and he told another doctor that the stab wound under his right arm "is the fellow that will soon do my business."

There were many other patients at the field hospital on the Clarke farm. Rush treated an American sergeant who had been so charged with adrenaline during the battle that he hadn't realized until it was over that the end of one of his fingers had been shot off. Rush oversaw amputations done on four British soldiers who had been left behind by their retreating forces. The amputations were done by saw, with nothing but rum and opium for anesthesia, and vinegar to sterilize the wounds. Yet all four survived.

Rush insisted on documenting the case of another critical pa-

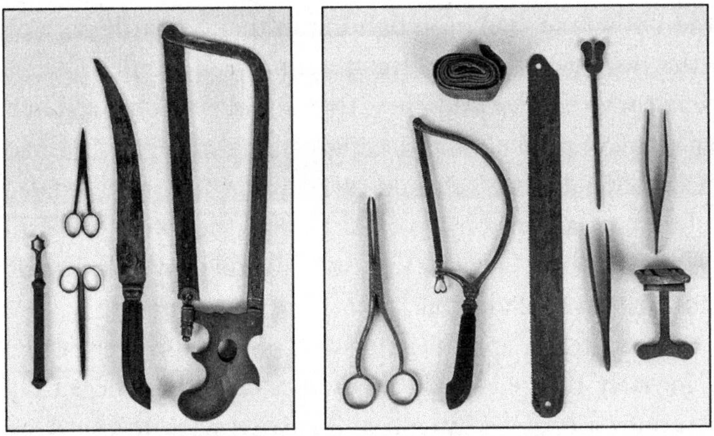

Revolutionary War amputation kits including various bone saws

tient, as proof that the British and Hessians were refusing to follow what everyone understood to be the rules of warfare. Lt. Bartholomew Yates, from one of the Virginia regiments, had suffered an injury during the Battle of Princeton that immediately brought him to the ground. When he saw the enemy advancing on him, he begged "for quarters," meaning he asked to be taken into custody. But instead, as Rush learned:

> A British soldier stopped, and after deliberately loading his musket at his side, shot [Yates] through the breast. Finding that he was still alive, he stabbed him in thirteen places with his bayonet, the poor youth all the while crying for mercy. Upon the enemy being forced to retreat, either the same or another soldier, finding that he was not dead, struck him with the club of a musket on the side of the head.

When Rush reached Yates a day after the battle, he was "in the greatest anguish." From examining him and speaking to others, he had no doubt that his wounds had been inflicted after he surrendered. Several days before, he learned, "the savages murdered a clergyman, a chaplain to a battalion of militia, in cool blood at Trenton after he had surrendered and begged for mercy."

While tending to other patients, Rush was devastated to hear that his Scottish friend William Leslie, the older brother of his beloved Lady Jane, had been fighting in that orchard—as a captain with the Seventeenth Foot. Rush hadn't seen Leslie in years, but they had corresponded and knew they could possibly meet in battle. Using his new privileges as a congressional delegate, he had sent Leslie an official letter he could carry in his uniform. It stated that if Leslie were captured by colonial troops, they were to alert General Washington or General Lee, who would provide him safe passage to Rush in Philadelphia.

Unfortunately, Captain Leslie was killed in the Battle of Princeton. Not only that, his body was temporarily lost, because it was thrown onto a baggage wagon and carried back to the American camp. But one of the first British officers Rush was asked to treat was a captain who had been very friendly with Leslie. When introduced, the captain, who had been wounded in his lungs, gasped, "Are you Dr. Rush? Captain Leslie's friend?"

Rush nodded.

"Oh, sir, he loved you like a brother."

When Rush finally stabilized the most serious patients from the Battle of Princeton at the farmhouse, he got on his horse and rode through what was left of his college town, his wife's hometown. Since Princeton had been evacuated before the British arrived, most of the damage to the college actually had been inflicted by Washington's troops taking it back. Nassau Hall, where the British had set up their headquarters and hospital, was in ruins; not only were many windows blown out, but cannonballs had left large indentations in the stone walls.

In a nice bit of cinematic irony, an American cannonball went through a window and destroyed a portrait of King George. (Peale was later hired to create a *Battle of Princeton* painting to replace it. He painted General Washington with Princeton under siege behind him to his right and, to his left, three stacked, intertwined figures: first a generic American soldier, then an unusually emotional Rush, who is holding General Mercer in his arms.)

Rush was shocked by the devastation of Princeton. "You would think it had been desolated with the plague and an earthquake as well as with the calamities of war," he told one friend. "The College and church are heaps of ruin. All the inhabitants have been plundered."

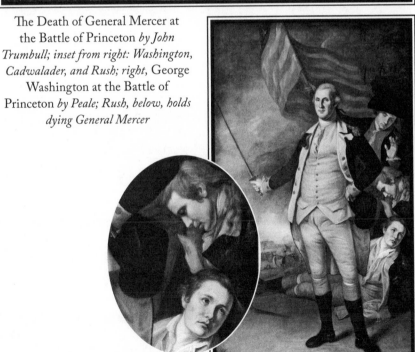

The Death of General Mercer at the Battle of Princeton *by John Trumbull; inset from right: Washington, Cadwalader, and Rush; right,* George Washington at the Battle of Princeton *by Peale; Rush, below, holds dying General Mercer*

He rode on to Morven, which had not been in the battle at all. British and Hessian troops had senselessly trashed, looted, and torched it anyway: "The whole of Mr. Stockton's furniture, apparel, and even valuable writings have been burnt. All his cattle, horses, and hogs, sheep, grain, and forage have been carried away." Two of the three buried boxes of silver and other valuables had been discovered and emptied. Rush believed his in-laws' losses would amount to at least five thousand pounds ($538,000).

He didn't know how he would tell Julia about her pillaged home. But at the moment, the loss of possessions and money seemed relatively insignificant. Julia's father, the master of Morven, was still a prisoner of the British. Nobody knew if he was dead or alive. A friend of Rush's in Congress said they had heard only that Stockton "suffers many indignities and hardships from the enemy, from which not only his rank, but his being a man, ought to exempt him."

20

Over the next few days, as Rush treated patients, he got a chance to see up close how the British Empire handled military medicine. He was impressed that even as the British generals retreated, they left a surgeon and five assistants behind to tend to their wounded—and to their fallen enemies as well.

Rush spent a good bit of time talking to the surgeon, who explained that every captain in the British Army was "obliged to visit the sick of his company at least once a day to see that they want for nothing." Washington's young army did not have any such procedures in place; its patients wanted for almost everything. Rush knew this situation had to change.

"The medical department must undergo a revolution," he wrote to a fellow congressman. He was still thinking about what that overhaul might look like when he got word that his new insights would come too late to save Dr. Morgan: Congress had relieved him of his position. Rush begged his colleagues to suspend filling Morgan's job until he could report on what he had learned in the field.

Just as Rush was ready to leave Princeton, he received the startling news that his father-in-law was back. There had been no ceremony, no prisoner exchange; he just arrived in Princeton after five weeks, looking as if he had aged twenty years and might not live much longer.

The details of his capture, imprisonment, and release were a mystery. Since General Howe recently had proposed a new loyalty oath for those wishing to undeclare their independence, when Stockton reappeared, free, some in Congress assumed he had sworn allegiance to the Crown. Others weren't sure, and when Rush recounted the events in his autobiography years later, all he wrote was that Stockton "was permitted to return to his family upon parole." But in a recently discovered fragment of a letter from Rush to Julia at the time, it was clear the doctor believed his father-in-law had sworn some kind of "oath & obligation . . . to General Howe" and depending on its "nature" he would either "be obliged to take part with General Washington in driving the enemy out of New Jersey or submit to be treated as an enemy of his country."

Stockton, however, was too ill to do much of anything, and immediately resigned his seat in Congress. Later that year, he signed the new "Oaths & Abjurations of Allegiance" the state required of those "employed in the Distribution of Justice," which allowed him to overcome some but not all suspicions of what he had done to gain his freedom.

Rush apparently left Princeton satisfied that his father-in-law was safe and would quickly be reunited with Annis and their children. As he was leaving, he also said goodbye to Hugh Mercer, who was still hanging on. The doctor judged the general "exceedingly weak from the loss of blood" and still in a lot of pain but, he hoped, basically *"out of danger."* So he was profoundly saddened to learn that Mercer died the very next day, groaning in pain, his bedsheets so soaked with blood that the floor in the farmhouse bedroom where he had been treated was permanently stained.

Rush and his servant, Cyrus, rode to Philadelphia briefly, then on to Mount Welcome to see Julia. He was happy to be able to tell her that her father was alive but crushed to describe Richard Stockton's ill health, as well as the condition of her family home. His own health wasn't perfect: his chronic cough was back after so much time exposed to cold winter weather.

The visit was life-affirming to Rush, and the couple were able to belatedly celebrate their first wedding anniversary. Julia planned to accompany her husband to Baltimore for the Congress—with the winter coming full force in New Jersey and Pennsylvania, the troops weren't going anywhere for a few months—but she ultimately decided not to join him. Rush had proceeded only a few miles toward Baltimore when he realized she had made the right decision. The roads were a mess, there were problems with the ferry across the Susquehanna, and the entire fifty-some-mile journey was an icy challenge. When he got to Baltimore, he had trouble finding a place to stay, so he had to crash in a room being rented by one of the New Jersey delegates, Jonathan Sergeant. He understood why one of his fellow congressmen called Baltimore "the Damdest Hole in the World."

The new congressional meeting hall in Baltimore consisted of "a long chamber, with two fire places, two large closets, and two doors . . . a Quaker . . . built it for a tavern" as Adams described it. But Rush hadn't spent much time there before he heard that Pennsylvanians were unceremoniously voting him out of the Continental Congress. His six-month term ran out in February, and he was not going to be reappointed, probably because of his outspoken opinions in the debate over the new Pennsylvania state constitution.

The more "radical" wing of the Pennsylvania government took its inspiration from, among others, Thomas Paine, who had gone from attacking British rule to attacking any kind of meritocracy. The radicals were trying to create a maximally "democratic" constitution, for a state that could be run by "the people" and only by the people. Professional politicians, lawyers, merchants—basically anyone who had experience running a government or a business—were to be distrusted.

Rush openly despised the draft they had prepared, and if that undermined his nascent political career, he didn't seem to care. He felt only "shame and indignation" that his fellow Pennsylvanians were being "called upon to 'reject men of learning' in choosing a body of legislators." He also felt the proposed constitution was built on a rather shaky system of checks and balances; many public servants could be voted out at the public's whim. The legislature would have only one house (as Paine had suggested in *Common Sense*); the executive would consist of a weak council and an elected president, and the judiciary would be appointed by the legislature, not by the executive; judges would serve only seven years and could be replaced by the legislature whenever it chose.

Rush shared the draft constitution with John Adams, who declared, outraged, "The people of your state will sooner or later fall upon their knees to the King of Great Britain to take them again under his protection, in order to deliver them from the tyranny of their own government!" Rush was so desperate to make sure the constitution didn't pass that he reached out to John Dickinson, trying to make amends and encouraging him to use his connections state-wide to save Philadelphia from the will of the radicals. "The eyes of the whole city," he told Dickinson, "are fixed upon you." But Rush put too much stock in the influence of the traditional Dickinson.

He also didn't have Benjamin Franklin to support him. Congress had sent Franklin to France, to try to convince the French to renounce their impartiality and, in the spirit of centuries of Franco-British enmity, help the rebels thwart King George. Franklin was the right man for that job, but his departure from Pennsylvania meant local politics lost its most resonant voice of moderation.

Rush was unable to stop the new constitution. His disappointment was palpable, but it was less clear how upset he was about leaving Congress. Many assumed he was humiliated by being voted out of office after six months, but he said his strongest reaction was relief. He claimed to be "not offended or mortified" by the decision, "for I wished to hold a station for which I was better qualified . . . [and] more useful to my country." In a letter to Julia, he claimed to be ecstatic:

> I have been told since my arrival here [in Baltimore] that our Assembly intend to leave me out of the next appointment of delegates as a punishment for opposing their new government.
>
> Welcome this storm of popular rage! I shall kiss the rod that smites. I never was so weary of public life and never languished more for the sweets of domestic life than since I last parted from you. . . . to exchange a *whole* house for a *single* room—to *request*

> instead of *commanding* when the most trifling favor is wanted—and above all to give up a most affectionate wife for the society of strangers—to lay aside freedom, ease and unbounded confidence in conversation for constant restraint and formality, are circumstances that illy agree with a man of my age and disposition.

The finish of Rush's congressional term in no way ended his insider status, just his responsibility to spend long days in sessions, opining and voting. He also felt freed and inspired to begin a new writing project: a sort of tell-all diary of the American Revolution.

Rush had started taking notes for his book during a controversy that unfolded while he was with Washington's troops. At a meeting in Providence on Christmas Day, four New England states had agreed to impose local price controls. But the Continental Congress wasn't sure that individual states, or groups of states, should be able to manipulate their own prices. Some delegates opposed price controls altogether.

The issue was discussed in Congress during Rush's last days there. Rush's notes captured the ensuing debate in meticulous detail. During his own remarks, he offered a flurry of metaphors on economic issues until one stuck.

"The price of goods may be compared to a number of light substances in a bas[i]n of water," he started. "The hand may keep them down for a while, but nothing can detain them on the bottom of the bas[i]n but an abstraction of the water." Then he switched to medical references. "The continent labours under a universal malady. From the crown of her head to the Soal of her feet she is full of disorders. She requires the most powerful tonic medicines. The resolution before you [approving local price controls] is nothing but an *opiate*. It may compose the continent for a night, but she will soon awaken again to a fresh sense of her pain & misery."

Richard Henry Lee, who favored price controls, countered. "The learned Doctor has mistook the disorder of the continent. He labours under a spasm and Spasms he knows require *palliative* medicines."

When Rush got another chance to speak, after John Witherspoon, John Adams, and several others, he found his way back to Lee's diagnosis. "The gentleman from Virginia has miscalled the malady of the continent. It is not a spasm, but a dropsy. I beg leave to prescribe two remedies for it. 1., Raising the interest of the money we borrow to 6 percent; this like a cold bath will give an immediate *spring* to our affairs, & 2., taxation; This like *tapping* [bloodletting], will diminish the quantity of our money, and give a proper value to what remains."

Besides the speeches, Rush captured more intimate drama. "I sat next to Jno. Adams in Congress," one of his earliest notes read, "and upon my whispering to him and asking him if he thought we should succeed in our struggle with G. Britain, he answered me, 'Yes—if we fear God and repent of our sins.'"

In his last days as a congressman, Rush offered opinions on, among other subjects, General Howe's most recent proposal for a one-sided peace conference with the British, and the question of whether Washington and his generals, appointed by Congress, should be able to choose their officers. Rush was against both. He was concerned about the military becoming too independent and powerful and not working for Congress. "If this motion is passed," he declared, "I shall move immediately afterwards that all the civil power of the continent may be transferred from our hands, into the hands of the army, & that they may be proclaimed the highest power of the people."

John Adams spoke soon afterward, sharing an idea publicly that many in Congress had only whispered about privately: the fear that overblown patriotism was turning the commander in chief into some kind of superhero—or worse, a newfangled democratic king. "I have been distressed," Adams said, "to see some members of this house disposed to idolize an image which their own hands have molten. I speak here of the superstitious veneration sometimes paid to Gen'l Washington. Altho' I honour him for his good qualities . . . in this house I feel myself his superior. In private life I shall always acknowledge that he is mine."

Rush wanted to accomplish just one more thing before leaving Congress. For some time, he had been lobbying General Washington on the need to inoculate American soldiers against smallpox.

On February 13, 1777, in a formal letter to the general on behalf of the medical committee, he requested that Washington order all his troops to be inoculated. He suggested that until this was done, the southern troops that were heading up from Virginia to join him in New Jersey and Pennsylvania should not travel through Philadelphia "where the infection now prevails." Washington agreed.

By making sure the troops were inoculated, this three-paragraph letter may well have saved more lives than anything else done by Rush or any other physician involved with the Revolutionary War.

Two days after he sent the letter, Rush went out for a last big dinner with his congressional colleagues. He was joined by John and Samuel Adams, Reverend Witherspoon, Richard Henry Lee, and several others. While the food was unremarkable, they all took notice of the decor. Before the struggle for independence, a portrait of King George III had commonly hung in public places. But once the war began, many places had taken them down. In Baltimore, however, it was popular to leave the portraits hanging upside down as what John Adams referred to as "Topsy Turvy Kings." In this establishment, beneath the inverted monarch were written these lines:

Behold the Man who had it in his Power
To make a Kingdom tremble and adore
Intoxicate with Folly, See his Head
Plac'd where the meanest of his Subjects tread
Like Lucifer the giddy Tyrant fell
He lifts his Heel to Heaven but points his Head to Hell.

On Rush's last day, his final duty as a congressman was to present the new plan for Continental Army hospitals. The plan was based on the British model, with one chief executive physician, more organization, and better pay for doctors. Rush had been advocating such changes for some time—as had Dr. Morgan, for even longer, before his ouster. He believed that if properly overseen and funded, the British model could transform military medicine.

But Dr. William Shippen, Jr., had also written a plan for military hospitals. Just after it became clear Rush wouldn't be reelected, Shippen arranged for his plan to be submitted to Congress, accompanied by two letters of recommendation from General Washington himself.

Shippen's plan deviated from the British model in the area of procurement, or the purchase and distribution of supplies. The king's army had a specialized director of procurement, which allowed the director-general to focus on treatment; in Shippen's plan, the director-general was in charge of everything. Rush argued hard against this in committee and to Washington himself. He believed that the purveying of materials had to be separated from medical oversight. "In vain did I plead publickly and privately for adoption of this system," Rush said. "Such was the temper of Congress at that time that its British origin helped to produce its rejection."

Equally important as its structure, the new system needed someone more qualified than Shippen to be the new, all-powerful director-general of Continental Army hospitals. The service needed its own Washington, its own Adams or Jefferson, someone who had shown himself to be both a leader and a revolutionary genius, someone worth following while the new nation was making up the rules as it went along. But Shippen had had a grand total of six months' experience in the military—the past six months. And unlike John Morgan, he had never been in charge of anything in his life. Still practicing medicine with his more formidable father, he was a bright and eloquent teacher but also a preternaturally privileged socialite and a not terribly hard-working doctor. As director-general, he was the obvious choice only to the nonphysicians he had charmed.

There wasn't much Rush could do, however. His days in Congress were over. He had no choice but to help Shippen's proposal work its way through committee and get to the floor of Congress. Once the new plan was approved, Rush would be seeking an appointment to serve in the new system.

21

As soon as Congress adjourned, Rush and his servant jumped on their horses and headed back to Mount Welcome to join Julia, who was now nearly five months pregnant. They accompanied her and her staff back to Philadelphia—which was considered safe enough, for the time being, that Congress could reconvene there. Unfortunately, the Rushes had already packed up their house and moved everything of value to safety, so they couldn't go home. The entourage headed instead for Rush Hill, his mother's property well outside the city, to be reunited with her and Rush's sister.

Rush Hill was much less elaborate than Mount Welcome, but it was just as beautiful and welcoming. When John Adams visited in the summer, he wrote to Abigail that "it is the most airy, and at the same Time the most rural Place in Pensilvania. The good Lady has about sixty Acres of Land, two fine orchards, an excellent Garden, a charming Brook, beautifull Meadows and Clover in Abundance." Rush Hill was a place of "perfect Peace," which was exactly what Benjamin and Julia Rush needed.

They spent a few weeks there, catching up on all the astonishing things Rush had experienced and planning their next steps. Rush expected to soon be offered a major role in the new military hospital system, and Julia was going to have a baby in a few months.

Then Rush returned to Philadelphia alone. The city was quite a bit more active than it had been when he left in December—Congress was meeting, and some of the newspapers were being published again, although from remote locations. But everyone knew it was only a matter of time before the British made a military move, whether by land or by sea or both, on Philadelphia, the capital of the revolution. Rush had to rent a room, since his house was boarded up. He reconnected with friends from Congress and did a bit of local political writing. But mostly he waited to see what job he would be offered in the new military medical system.

On April 7, 1777, Congress voted to reorganize the military hospitals into four geographical "departments": the Middle Department, from the Hudson River to the Potomac; the Eastern Department, east of the Hudson River; the Northern Department, which extended up to Lake Champlain; and a Southern Department, to be created if the war extended below the Potomac. Four days later, Congress announced the new leadership. Shippen, as expected, was appointed director-general, at the generous salary of six dollars ($143) a day and nine rations, or nine times the amount of food and supplies a regular soldier received every day.*

Dr. Benjamin Rush was appointed surgeon-general of the Middle Department, where the most troops were stationed and the most combat was currently taking place. He would be paid five dollars ($119) a day and six rations. (By comparison, a bricklayer or carpenter in Pennsylvania at that time might earn a dollar [$23.80] or less a day.) It was technically the third-ranking job in the department, but the two positions above were unfilled, so he was for all practical purposes the physician-general. His old friend from medical school, Dr. Jonathan Potts, filled the same position in the Northern Department.

Upon accepting the appointment, Rush closed out his private

---

* One "ration" consisted of "1 pound of beef, or 1/2 pound of pork or 1 pound of salt fish, per day; 1 pound of bread or flour, per day; 3 pints of peas or beans per week, or vegetables equivalent . . . ; 1 pint of milk, per man per day; 1 half pint of rice, or one pint of Indian meal, per man per week; 1 quart of spruce beer or cider per man per day, or nine gallons of molasses, per company of 100 men per week; 3 pounds of candles to 100 men per week, for guards; 24 pounds of [soft] soap, or 8 pounds of hard soap, for 100 men per week."

medical practice. On the last page of his ledger he wrote: "Here ends the chapter."

Before he started his new job in the hospitals, however, there was something he needed to say about preserving the health of soldiers, and prevent them from requiring his care. He sat down to compose a manifesto, and its first sentence would reverberate not only through the rest of the Revolutionary War but through every American war to come.

"Fatal experience has taught the people of America the truth . . . that a greater proportion of men perish with sickness in all armies than fall by the sword."

Rush indicted Washington and the "officers of the army" for not paying enough attention to soldier wellness. He then laid out a plan that, rather than focusing on the practice of medicine by physicians, addressed what soldiers could do themselves, or what their officers could do for them, to improve their health.

Much of his advice might seem obvious today. But in 1777 it was startling news to American soldiers that they should wear their hair short; change their clothes more often, especially their socks; eat more vegetables; drink less alcohol; wash their hands and faces every day and their whole bodies several times a week; change the hay they slept on; and dry their blankets in the sun. Along with these dictums, Rush insisted that soldiers keep the area around their tents "perfectly clean of the offals of animals and of filth of all kind," and that they avoid "unnecessary fatigue" by performing all "daily exercises . . . maneuvers . . . [and] also all marches . . . in the cool of the morning or evening in the summer."

Rush recommended helping sentries stay awake at their posts by ensuring that they were properly fed, garbed, and rested, and that they were relieved often (especially "in very hot, cold, or rainy weather"). Based on current theory that the smoke from burning wood, gunpowder, and even sulfur had "a singular efficacy in preserving and restoring the purity of the air," and thereby prevented the spread of fevers, he recommended soldiers often be near prescriptive fires.

While most of the manifesto was advice for the soldiers themselves, at the end he returned to his call to leaders. "The principle study of an officer, in the time of war, should be to save the blood of his men," he wrote. ". . . If it be criminal in an officer to sacrifice the lives of thousands by his temerity in a battle, why should it be thought less so to sacrifice twice their number in a hospital, by his negligence?"

It was an unprecedented piece of public health writing—a *Common Sense* for preventive medicine. And Rush published it as boldly as he had written it. He might have submitted it to the commander in chief or to his new superior, Dr. Shippen, so it could be quietly digested by congressional committees and incorporated into the army's orders. Instead, before he actually started work as surgeon-general of the Middle Department, he gave the text to his printer friend John Dunlap, who had been publishing his *Pennsylvania Packet* from a press in Lancaster.

Dunlap turned the front page of the April 22, 1777, issue over to the unsigned declaration that everyone knew had been written by Dr. Benjamin Rush: "Directions for preserving the HEALTH of SOLDIERS; recommended to the confederation of OFFICERS in the ARMY of the UNITED AMERICAN STATES."

Several generals told Rush his manifesto should be published as a pamphlet that could be circulated throughout the army, and plans began to make that happen. But in the meantime, in his new job, Rush found himself fighting for the rights and health of the injured and sick soldiers. One of the military hospitals now under his supervision was in Philadelphia, at the House of Employment building at Eleventh and Spruce. Rush began supervising and treating patients there in late April, and in early May a terrible epidemic broke out among the patients and staff—which he described as "a fatal hospital fever." (Also called "jail fever," it was most likely a form of typhus.)

Symptoms of "jail fever" began, according to one of Rush's fellow doctors who contracted it, with a "listlessness of the whole body, and a peculiar sensation of the head, as if it were tightened or compressed by a hook." The "febrile attack" ran "very high in the beginning, so as to warrant bloodletting," but after several days "the pulse begins to sink, a dry tongue, delirium and the whole train of nervous and putrid symptoms intervene. . . . Besides an obstinate delirium, I had a crust on my tongue as thick as the blade of a knife, and black as soot." The skin on his back and hips became so delicate and bedsore that it "wore off," and it was "necessary to patch those parts with common plaster." He was treated with mercury, Peruvian bark, wine, "volatile salts," and blistering. "At the acme of my disorder," the doctor recalled, "eleven surgeons and mates all gave me over, and only disputed how many hours I should live. Providence ordered otherwise [and] my friend, Dr. Rush, paid kind attention to me."

Eventually he improved enough that he could start drinking, and "my tongue soon after began to moisten on the edges; and in the course of some days the whole crust fell off and left it so raw and irritable that I was obliged to hold skinned almonds in my mouth to abate the irritation." All the hair fell off his head and skin, and when it started growing back, "instead of my former straight hair I had an entire new suit, that curled beautifully."

Not all of Rush's fellow doctors were as fortunate. "Several of the attending surgeons and mates died of it," Rush recalled. Their burials were especially hard.

Desperate to keep his patients and colleagues alive, Rush reached out to Shippen and made what he believed was a perfectly reasonable request: more rooms, to isolate contagious patients from each other. "This was denied," Rush reported, in what he described as "the beginnings of sufferings and mortality in the American army which . . . nearly destroyed it." He was astonished that a fellow doctor, especially one with a new, broadly expanded budget, would ignore his medical advice and put soldiers at risk.

"A physician who practices in a hospital or elsewhere should have no check upon his prescriptions," Rush declared (in what would become one of his most often-quoted lines). "Air, water, fire, and everything necessary to the relief or cure of the sick should be made to obey him." Trying to be a good soldier and not to make waves, Rush didn't complain right away to Washington about Shippen's inaction.

When he did reach out to his commander in chief, it was with strategic advice. On May 13, 1777, he wrote to Washington because he heard that the American troops would soon be on the move, after a very quiet winter and early spring. He suggested the general wait a bit longer, on the theory (promoted by one of his favorite British authorities, Dr. John Pringle) that the "variable weather of the spring" engendered more illness than the "uniform heats of summer or colds of winter":

> I hope your Excellency will excuse the liberty I am about to take in Suggesting that your troops will probably suffer from being so early exposed. . . . the difference in the proportion of sick in an Army in the latter end of April, and the middle of may is as 1 to 32 in the former and 1 to 36 in the latter case. . . . If your Excellency can possibly delay encamping your men a few weeks longer I am sure you will save the lives of many hundreds by it, besides retaining as many more in your Service who might Otherwise be rendered unfit for duty. . . . With sincere wishes that you may begin and close the campaign with much honor to yourself, and lasting Advantages to our country, I have the honor to be with great regard your Excellency's most Obedt Hble Servant

Washington got right back to Rush: "[I] am much obliged to you, for communicating your judicious observations on the inconveniences of an early incampment," he wrote. "They are perfectly correspondent with my own ideas, but how far they can be allowed to operate must depend upon many other considerations and circumstances. . . . I shall however endeavour to defer incamping 'till the weather becomes a little more settled and temperate."

The general put off the encampment order for another week and also ordered a new troop health assessment, comparing the number of soldiers in hospitals with those listed "*Sick absent* . . . [because] I very much suspect, that a great deal of pay is drawn for sick Absent who do not exist."

During this time, Rush did some political writing opposing the new Pennsylvania constitution, but most of his efforts stayed focused on the military hospitals. In the first months after his appointment, much of the fighting moved outside his coverage area, so he spent his time overseeing the hospitals in Philadelphia and Bethlehem, as well as in Morristown, New Jersey, where Washington had his headquarters.

At noon on a day in early July, dozens of armed ships and galleys lined up in the Delaware River, cannons and guns aimed directly at the city of Philadelphia. At one p.m., the order was given to fire. Each ship fired thirteen cannons, and while the noise was deafening, echoing through the cobblestone streets, they caused no damage—because there were no cannonballs. They were American ships, there to help celebrate the nation's first-ever Independence Day. The thirteen cannons symbolized the thirteen states. Each one was fired three times, greeted in town, according to newspaper reports, by "loud huzzas that resounded . . . through the city."

At three p.m., a large and elegant dinner was held at the City Tavern for Congress and their many guests, including military and state officials and what the newspapers called "strangers of eminence." (Adams mentioned being there in a letter to his daughter; Rush was likely there, too.) After the meal and the toasts—each one, according to the newspaper, "followed by a discharge of artillery and small arms" by troops lining Second Street, "and a suitable piece of music by the Hessian band"—there was a procession of several horse troops and artillery corps. When darkness fell on the first day of celebration of American independence, every bell in the city was sounded, and a grand exhibition of fireworks began and ended with the firing of thirteen rockets.

After the festivities, Philadelphians who supported liberty displayed lit candles in all their windows. John Adams was utterly delighted. "I think it was the most splendid illumination I ever saw," he wrote. To be sure, "a few surly houses were dark," he admitted. But that was a patriotic exaggeration—in truth, a lot of the windows were dark. Loyalist and pacifist Philadelphians remained unhappy about the war and refused to light candles even though rebel revelers threw rocks through many unilluminated windows. But considering how hastily this whole celebration was put together, Adams was "amazed at the universal joy and alacrity that was discovered, and at the brilliancy and splendour of every part."

The next day the *Pennsylvania Evening Post* concurred. "Everything was conducted with the greatest order and decorum, and the face of joy and gladness were universal. Thus may the fourth of July, that glorious and ever memorable day, be celebrated throughout America, by the sons of freedom, from age to age till time shall be no more. Amen, and amen."

22

Days after the festivities, over eighteen thousand British and Hessian troops boarded ships from various points between Sandy Hook, New Jersey, Staten Island, and lower New York. As General Howe contemplated his next move, the troops sat in those boats, in the searing summer heat, for more than two weeks. Everyone knew Howe's goal was Philadelphia, but there were several ways to approach the city by water, each requiring a substantial amount of marching and sailing time. While the general cogitated, his troops roasted.

Since Washington's troops—and people in Philadelphia—knew well that Howe's boats were still sitting in the harbor, Rush decided it would be safe for him to sneak away for a few days to be with Julia for the birth of their first child. He left Philadelphia for Mount Welcome on July 14, according to notes he scribbled on the flyleaf of the second notebook of his revolutionary tell-all. He arrived in time to welcome his son into the world, at just before one a.m. on Thursday, July 17.

They decided to name him John, after Rush's father and grandfather. (During his early childhood, they would call him "Jack" or "Jacky," but the nickname wouldn't stick.) Three days after the birth, Benjamin and Julia Rush attended John's christening at the First Presbyterian Church.

For a couple who had been apart almost as much as they were together during their year and a half of marriage, these shared experiences were particularly powerful. Rush reveled in the peculiar happiness of fatherhood at the age of thirty-two. These were among the best days of his life, and he savored them for as long as he could—which turned out to be about a week.

He left on July 24, when word arrived that General Howe's troops had departed Raritan Bay: 266 ships of various sizes carried all those British and Hessian soldiers, their horses, and provisions for the next three months, as well as three hundred rounds of ammunition for each cannon. They appeared to be heading south, but nobody knew for sure where Howe planned for them to disembark. (He himself was on land strategizing and scouting possible locations.) Washington's troops had been inching northward, in case Howe decided to go up the Hudson River and attack there first, but as soon as they confirmed the boats were headed in the other direction, they reversed course.

Suddenly everyone was heading toward Delaware, because that was the logical place from which Philadelphia could be reached and defended. Rush returned briefly to Philadelphia and then joined Washington and his troops in Morristown, New Jersey. According to reports from Rush's department, about 26 percent of Washington's soldiers, most of whom hadn't seen action in months, were already ill, many of them with dysentery and intractable "putrid" diarrhea. "Multitudes melted away, as it were, of this miserable complaint, and died," one of Rush's physicians would recall. There were shortages of almost everything.

Much of the advice Rush had offered for the health of soldiers was still being discussed in Congress. No one questioned his ideas, but they were not easy to implement or pay for in an army that still didn't have enough uniforms, shoes, or proper weapons.

Rush remained patient that these were problems without easy answers, the shared challenges of a young nation and the imperfections of modern medicine. He was doing his best to contain his frustration without griping and pointing fingers—and also trying hard to get along with Dr. Shippen. Since General Washington and his former colleagues in Congress seemed genuinely concerned about the problems faced by the medical department, he focused on simply doing his job. His reports were accurate yet mild and encouraging. His passions were focused primarily on patient care. He kept his growing fears largely to himself, sharing them only with his wife and John Adams, both of whom he could count on for discretion.

In early August, Washington traveled to Philadelphia ahead of his troops so he could meet with Congress. He was also there to connect with an important visitor from France, the nation the rebels were hoping would support their cause. The visitor—sort of a military tourist—was the nineteen-year-old Marquis de Lafayette, whom Congress had agreed to appoint as volunteer general so he could absorb the passion of the conflict and maybe do a little fighting. Not only wouldn't he be paid, but he agreed to pay the military the tens of thousands of dollars required to take care of himself and his staff. The marquis had been two years old when the British killed his father at the Battle of Minden in 1759, and he had spent his youth pledging to take revenge. He hoped fighting with the Americans would fulfill that pledge, and upon meeting in Philadelphia on August 5, he and Washington took an instant liking to each other. The marquis was looking for a new father figure, and Washington took the precocious Frenchman under his wing.

The young Marquis de Lafayette and one of his servants

At the time, Washington and his generals were mostly trying to figure out where the hundreds of British ships that had departed the New York area were going to land, and how General Howe's troops would commence their attack. Parts of the armada were sometimes visible from land—and both spies and common citizens would send intel to Washington's headquarters. But often the only evidence of their progress was what they threw overboard, which later washed ashore.

Sometimes this included their dead horses. As the ocean voyage continued in the grueling August heat, the British had to sometimes decide whether to give fresh water to their troops or to their horses. Dozens of carcasses were discovered, first on the shores of southern New Jersey, including Cape May—which was at the height of its season as the area's first major seaside resort.

The ships initially turned west below Cape May, threatening to come into the Delaware Bay and then head up the Delaware River, the most direct route to Philadelphia. But then General Howe changed his mind and sent them farther south, to take the longer and more challenging approach up the Chesapeake. Soon John Adams was writing to Abigail about "many dead Horses . . . thrown overboard from the Fleet, no doubt," along the eastern shore of Maryland. Slowly, the British were coming.

At three a.m. on August 24, 1777, Washington's troops, most of whom had relocated just outside Philadelphia in the Germantown area, broke camp and set up in a marching formation over ten miles long. Some eleven thousand soldiers divided into brigades—each with its own field musicians, fifes and drums, and its own artillery, wagons, and horses—and began in columns of twelve down the York Road, still damp from a night rain. Setting a steady pace, they moved toward the center of town. Hours later the troops began entering the city along Front Street.

Washington was at the lead, on his horse; Benjamin Rush, his servant, and his staff, also on horseback, followed later in the procession. (Washington's orders specifically stated that only male military personnel could march, and not the women "belonging to the army," which included laundresses, soldier's wives, and others who took care of "a multitude of feminine tasks, good and bad, to ease the lives of the soldiers.") The parade moved down Front, past the house where Rush had grown up, the London Coffee House, and the Aitken Bookshop, where the revolution had been debated and published into being. Just before passing Rush's current home—which was just ahead of them on the left, boarded up—it turned right at Chestnut Street, so Washington and his troops could be reviewed by the Congress, waiting at the State House five blocks away. They were finally going to see the fighting force they had been supporting financially for several years—in all its glory but also its shortcomings.

Lafayette had got a preview of this display some weeks earlier, when Washington ordered his troops to pass for the review of the Frenchman and his entourage. He described them as "eleven thousand men, poorly armed and even more poorly clothed" who "offered a singular spectacle." Their uniforms were far from uniform. While the British and Hessians all wore proper "red coat" outfits, rebel soldiers did their best to wear something blue or brown or, if they were riflemen, green. "In this motley . . . state, the best garments were *hunting shirts*," Lafayette reported incredulously. Still, he believed they were (or were slowly becoming) "fine soldiers, led by zealous officers."

Philadelphians lined the parade path, some to encourage the soldiers, others to say goodbye. Both the townspeople and the congressmen had terribly mixed feelings. John Adams hoped this parade and the subsequent offensive might "make an entire and final Seperation of the Wheat from the Chaff, the Ore from the Dross, the Whiggs from the Tories." If the British failed to take Philadelphia, it would "give Lustre to our Arms and Disgrace to theirs." But if they succeeded, Adams wasn't sure that would be all bad. The Declaration of Independence hadn't settled the long-running friction between New England and the Middle States, between Protestant Boston and Quaker Philadelphia, over which was the true heart and soul of America and its revolution. While Rush and Franklin love-hated their city like so many of its most devoted citizens, Adams mostly hated it. If the British took Philadelphia, he thought, "it will cutt off this corrupted city, from the Body of the Country." He also knew that once the British controlled the city, "it will take all their Force to maintain it."

Like most others who saw the parade, Adams was both hopeful and worried. "Our soldiers have not yet, quite the air of soldiers," he said. "They dont hold up their Heads, quite erect, nor turn out their Toes, so exactly as they ought. They dont all of them cock their Hats—and such as do, don't all wear them the same way." (In order to bring some measure of uniformity to the "bare feet, and rags, every man wore a green sprig in his hat," according to one account.) But he had to admit he liked the spectacle. He thought it made "a good Impression upon the Minds of the timourous Whiggs for their Confirmation, upon the cunning Quakers for their Restraint and upon the rascally Tories for their Confusion."

Washington acknowledged Congress as he passed the State House, then continued his march another twenty-five blocks to the bank of the Schuylkill River, where a temporary floating bridge had been erected, allowing the troops to cross and then head south along the river to Chester and points south. By now it was clear that Howe's ships were in Chesapeake Bay, which extended like long, gnarled fingers deep into Virginia and Maryland. At the top of the middle finger, the one closest to Philadelphia, was the area called Head of Elk, the source of the Elk River. This was the most logical spot for Howe's forces to end their torturous five-week journey and finally put their feet on land again.

The marching orders of Washington's troops were to protect the sixty-some miles between there and Philadelphia. For the first time in the war, the full force of both sides would meet face to face. The unknowns would be strategy, firepower, and grit.

British troops set up along the west bank of the Elk River in Maryland. Meanwhile the colonial troops gathered near Wilmington, Delaware, then moved southwest closer to the Delaware-Pennsylvania border, to set up their forward operations near the crossings, or "fords," over the Brandywine Creek. They took over the old Birmingham Friends Meeting House, which was expected to be a good mile or more northwest of the action. A large stone building with a tall A-frame roof, this was where Rush would work; it was set up as a hospital but also a headquarters for directing whatever care was possible in the field (besides dragging wounded soldiers away, as was done over the ground, on one's shoulders, or in an open cart to the hospital). A log building next to it was used as a school, and a large stone wall around the property protected them both and the Quaker cemetery.

Birmingham Meeting House

Washington, Lafayette, and a few others rode ahead to scout the situation. Lafayette later reported being stunned at how close Washington was willing to come to Howe's forces. "General Washington imprudently exposed himself to danger," Lafayette wrote in his journal, "After a long reconnaissance, he was overtaken by a storm, on a very dark night. He took shelter in a farmhouse, very close to the enemy. . . .

"Because of his unwillingness to change his mind"—clearly Washington and his French protégé had argued about it—"he remained there with General Green[e] and M. de Lafayette." Lafayette referred to himself in the third person in his writing. "But when they departed at dawn, [Washington] admitted that a single traitor could have betrayed him." In fact, the owner of that house did turn out to be a loyalist. If not for his desire to sleep in on a rainy day, he could easily have exposed Washington's whereabouts.

The steady rain, it turned out, also interfered with Howe's plans to start advancing with his troops at three a.m. Since the British later commandeered this farmhouse as a headquarters, Washington and Lafayette might easily have been captured.

As many days passed and the ammunition dried—heavy rain was a huge setback, especially for American troops who didn't always have proper protection for their gunpowder—there were a handful of small incursions, military foreplay, in preparation for the main battle to halt the enemy's progression. The location was shaping up to be the area around the Brandywine Creek crossing known as Chadds Ford.

Washington had, by this time, fortified the twelve thousand troops he had paraded through Philadelphia with three thousand more men, including local militias' marksmen and artillery gunners stripped from every outpost north along the Delaware above Philadelphia. He was sure he had enough manpower and firepower to turn back Howe and his travel-weary troops, though he knew the British had more better-trained men, as well as superior small arms.

Many of Washington's soldiers had brought their own long flintlock hunting rifles, which were more accurate but could not accommodate bayonets and were slower to load than British muskets, which shot slightly larger metal balls. For longer-distance damage, both sides had cannons, mortars, and howitzers, which shot cannonballs, shells, and small exploding bombs. But as the enemy drew close, cannonballs could be replaced with "grapeshot"—iron or lead balls wrapped in a small canvas bag, then mounted on a wooden base with a dowel in the middle for easier loading. The grapeshot blew apart right out of the cannon and had a wide kill range.

There were a lot of different ways to send a soldier to his death—or to the field hospital. At the Birmingham Meeting House, Dr. Rush already had his hands full with soldiers sick from heat exhaustion and dysentery. On the morning of September 11, 1777, empty wagons were already set up behind each battalion to carry injured soldiers immediately off the battlefield and into the care of Dr. Rush and his staff. He was ready for the first wave of wounded from the most important battle, so far, in the war for independence.

23

When the first shots were fired in the Battle of Brandywine, at about six a.m. on September 11, 1777, George Washington was certain he knew how it would go. The British, under the leadership of General Howe and Lord Cornwallis, were going to charge the rebels directly at Chadds Ford and dare them to not be overwhelmed. Washington packed all eight of his divisions along two miles of the eastern shore of the Brandywine, above and below Chadds Ford, and waited for the fifes and drums and the explosion of redcoats by the thousands.

For the first few hours, Washington's men held their own. The general could be seen riding or walking back and forth along the front lines, cheering on his men, who returned the favor by shouting to and even applauding him. The Marquis de Lafayette "was received with acclimations that should have promised victory." During a lull in the fighting in the late morning, both sides regrouped and reloaded, but the rebels felt optimistic about their chances.

Just before noon Washington was handed a note from Lt. Col. James Ross, whom he didn't know well but who possessed an impressive patriotic lineage: his father, Philadelphia lawyer George Ross, had signed the Declaration of Independence, and his cousin by marriage, Betsy Ross, had just months before sewn what some would later claim was the first American flag, which they were carrying into battle.

Ross had written his note nearly an hour earlier, at eleven a.m. He claimed to have spied "a large body of the enemy" marching several miles due north, rather than directly into the maw of Washington's fortifications. Some five thousand redcoats with artillery were heading to a point along the creek where they could cross unnoticed—which Washington knew would give them access to his largely unprotected northern flank.

Ross guessed that General Howe was with this group, and not with the soldiers Washington had been fighting all morning. He had heard it from some locals, who had heard it from an unlikely source: Joseph Galloway, a mousy-looking Philadelphia lawyer in his late forties who had been the longtime speaker of the Pennsylvania Assembly, a close friend of Franklin's, and even a member of the First Continental Congress before turning deeply loyalist. He was now a member of General Howe's entourage, compiling and interpreting British intelligence reports about his own country—about as clear a traitor to the revolution as there was. Yet he apparently couldn't help leaking Howe's secret plan of attack.

Washington sent out notes to see if anyone could confirm this sighting, then walked with a couple of his attendants into a field above the house where he was stationed to get a better look. Unfortunately, by doing so, he gave enemy sharpshooters on the other side of the creek a good look at him. Soon British cannonballs were pounding the field, and Washington was fortunate to dodge back inside before being hit.

While Washington was changing his strategy, General Howe, Lord Cornwallis, and their troops crossed the Brandywine several miles to the north of him at Jefferis Ford, heading toward Washington's unprotected flank. In their clean red uniforms, carrying their glistening weapons, they marched down the main road to the drumbeats in perfect formation.

This was Birmingham Road, which ran directly over Birmingham Hill and past the Birmingham Meeting House—where Dr. Rush was treating patients, far—he thought—from imminent danger. But as he heard fifes in the distance, he began to realize that the war, like the recent bad weather, had suddenly changed direction. He was drenched in blood from surgeries and amputations, his wide blue-gray eyes red and tired from the endless hours. The meetinghouse had made an excellent hospital, with so many wooden benches for soldiers to lie on or, with an unhinged door laid across, for use as makeshift surgical tables. In the cemetery outside, they had already dug a pit for the bodies of those who didn't survive, and for the severed limbs of those still hanging on.

Rush's staff included Dr. Lewis Howell of New Jersey—whose twin brother, Maj. Richard Howell, was several miles away fighting against the British with General Maxwell's division. They had just been ordered to cross Brandywine Creek at Chadds Ferry, three hundred yards downstream of the ford, where the water was only waist deep, to try to push the enemy back. In the meantime, Washington ordered another division to start moving north toward Birmingham Hill.

Instead of being safely behind the lines, the Birmingham Meeting House was now almost exactly in the middle of the battlefield.

About 8,000 British and Hessian troops with artillery and full regalia were approaching from the north. About 4,000 American soldiers were approaching from the south, including two divisions of 1,500 that Washington had just diverted in their direction. All the defenseless medical team could do was keep working on their patients. Finally, according to a letter Dr. Howell sent to his father, the surgeons were startled by the sounds of three guns in the distance. Every man stayed at his post and kept working, and for the next half hour there was no more firing. Then they heard bursts of small arms that turned out to be Howell's brother's division fighting downriver. When General Stirling's division arrived to defend Birmingham Hill, he set off what Dr. Howell called "the heaviest firing I ever heard . . . continuing a long time, every inch of ground being disputed."

Only the white hospital flags spared them from the onslaught as the American divisions held the line. While the troops dug in to hold the position, a group of Virginia sharpshooters positioned themselves just behind the cemetery wall that ran next to the meetinghouse, so they could shoot, duck, and reload. This went on for some time until, as Dr. Howell described, "our people at last gave way . . . [and] fought them retreating in good order." Rush and the other doctors ran out to gather the nearby wounded and drag them to safety. In doing so, they saw another problem: the British and Hessians were marching directly toward the meetinghouse from the other direction.

Rush and Howell realized they were in grave danger of being captured. Rush knew what could happen if he were taken prisoner and his captors realized he was a signer of the Declaration of Independence. He was still haunted by the way his father-in-law had looked after his release from captivity. Only weeks before, Rush had watched his first child being born. He was too young to be rendered more dead than alive by imprisonment and torture.

Rush and Howell were later both cryptic in describing what happened next. Rush wrote that he "nearly" fell "in the hands of the enemy in my delay in helping off the wounded." Howell described "my escape from the enemy after having been among them." The British stole Howell's horse, saddle, and bridle, even his coat and hat. But they let him live. "Dear Father," Dr. Howell wrote home afterward, "I am happy in being able to inform you that I still exist."

Clearly both men had the scare of their lives and narrowly avoided capture. Then, just as quickly as the British and Hessian soldiers swarmed around the meetinghouse, they moved on. They had Washington's troops on the run; their goal was to follow and mow down everything in their path.

Unfortunately, this left Rush and Howell behind enemy lines. It wasn't safe. Their horses had been taken. They did their best to stabilize their remaining patients, then prepared to leave, taking with them anyone who could walk. They moved as quickly as they could, searching for Washington's retreating troops. They walked along battlefields strewn with revolutionary soldiers and their enemies—dead, dying, bleeding out everywhere—as well as metal spheres of various sizes, from musket balls to grapeshot to cannonballs. The smell of smoke and gunpowder was inescapable. It pained them to leave so many men behind, but they had no choice.

Rush made it back to safety, but many Americans did not. Washington lost almost 10 percent of his entire army that day—over 300 killed, 600 wounded, and 400 captured. One of the wounded was the Marquis de Lafayette, who had taken a musket ball to the leg but insisted on continuing to fight and later riding off without medical care. Only days later did he allow a doctor to look at his wound.

Washington and Lafayette at the Battle of Brandywine
(with Rush kneeling to treat Lafayette's leg wound) by J. B. Stearns

Reports of British losses varied wildly but were higher. Of the original force that had attacked Washington head-on in the morning, over 900 were killed, wounded, or captured, and the flanking column that attacked later and won the day lost more than a thousand.

The Americans were saved from worse losses only by darkness. As Washington rode away toward Chester, he turned to his aide Timothy Pickering on the next horse and said somberly, "Why 'tis a perfect rout." After they got settled in Chester, Washington wrote to John Hancock and Congress just before midnight: "I am sorry to inform you, that in this day's engagement, we have been obliged to leave the enemy masters of the field."

THE NEXT DAY Washington received a note from General Howe. "The Number of wounded Officers and Men of your Army in this Neighborhood, to whom every possible Attention has been paid, will nevertheless require your immediate Care, as I shall not be so situated as to give them the necessary Relief. Any surgeons you may chuse to send to their Assistance upon Application to me, in consequence of your Orders, shall be permitted to attend them."

Washington wrote back that he would be sending Dr. Rush, along with two of his other staff physicians, two volunteer doctors, and a "Mate in the Hospital" to help them. After what Rush had just been through, it must have been surreal and traumatizing to ride behind enemy lines under safe passage from General Howe, on a fresh horse, to care for barely alive soldiers—some in custody, some dying on the battlefield exactly where they had fallen.

The British who oversaw this humanitarian visit were intrigued and a little baffled by how talkative and level-headed Rush was, as he worked on the wounded soldiers. They were especially surprised at how vocal he was about the rebel cause while behind enemy lines. "Their principal surgeon [was] a very clever fellow . . . who came in with a flag of truce to visit the wounded prisoners," wrote one British captain, Robert FitzPatrick. He marveled that though Rush "acknowledged the defeat to have been complete," he still "spoke with the greatest confidence" of a colonial victory, vowing that "all possibility of accommodation [with the king] . . . was as remote the day after the battle as it ever had been since the declaration of independence."

It was daring for Rush to even mention the declaration, given what he knew from General Mercer's death and his father-in-law's capture about how the king's men sometimes treated the enemy. Yet Rush, surrounded by armed enemy soldiers, went right on talking, as if it was his first chance to explain to the British how they had turned something fixable into a revolution. Rush said that all Americans, Whigs and Tories alike, agreed that "a few concessions" by the king and Parliament "would have put an end to the whole business." But once the declaration was signed, there was no turning back.

Rush, of course, also talked about medicine with the British. "I was much struck," he would recall, "in observing the difference between the discipline and order of the British and the Americans." He was touched when British officers thanked him for the care he had given to some of their colleagues similarly stranded after the Battle of Princeton.

Rush traveled back to Washington's headquarters and then went on to his Middle Department hospitals, where, in Bethlehem, his patients included the Marquis de Lafayette. Rush didn't speak much about his boasts to the British about the eventual victory of the American Revolution. But he did talk a lot, better informed than ever, about how far the American medical corps had to go before it could compete with the machine-like systems of the British. His intention was not to disparage the revolution or its medicine but rather to describe a goal to which they must aspire. After yet another military setback, there should have been general agreement on the American side that everyone needed to do *much* better.

Yet Rush was surprised to discover that his hard-won insights about British discipline—medical and otherwise—sounded to many like unconstructive criticism. When he "lamented" the differences between the rebels and British, "it gave offense and was ascribed to fear and to lack of attachment to the cause of my country." Yet he couldn't stop himself from continually noting how much better Washington's forces would have to be if they were going to win.

Over the next few days, Washington backtracked his troops from Chester, always making sure they were in position to stop a straight-on assault on Philadelphia. Howe craftily countered him, in a chess match through southeastern Pennsylvania farm country. One day the troops lined up on opposite sides of the Great Valley near Goshen and began a battle that was rained out by a nor'easter—which may have saved Washington's troops a defeat, but also compromised more than four hundred thousand musket cartridges. Several days later one of Washington's generals, Anthony Wayne, got wind of a possible enemy action from a couple of townspeople in Paoli, where his brigade had made camp. He wasn't sure what to make of the information, from a "Mr. Bartholamew" who "visited us" in the evening and "insinuated that our situation was a little Dangerous." But later, after midnight on September 21, he realized he should have listened.

The British made a brutal attack in the dark, after the Americans had gone to sleep. The troops had been ordered not to load their muskets—in case one went off by mistake and warned the Americans—so they relied on their bayonets and swords instead. It became an especially bloody, horrific assault with hand-to-hand fighting that, according to many reports, violated all norms of combat. General Wayne's soldiers were slashed to death, many of them after they tried to surrender.

One American officer, who was briefly captured but managed to escape with his life, said he saw the British "cut & hack some of our Poor men to pieces after they had fallen into their hands and scarcely shew the least mercy to any." Nearly two hundred men were killed, wounded, or captured in a few hours, in what would be called the Paoli Massacre.

It was now only a matter of time before the British marched into Philadelphia, however much more resistance they might encounter en route. Before heading there, though, Howe wanted to damage the Continental Army's winter stockpiles. One was in Valley Forge, along the Schuylkill River. The other was farther west, bigger and safer, in Reading. Washington had to decide which to protect more aggressively; he chose Reading, so the British looted Valley Forge before heading toward the city.

The Continental Congress voted to adjourn and relocate to Lancaster. One of its last orders before leaving the State House was that all the bells in the city—including the two in the clock tower above them—be taken down and hidden, since the most precious commodity in the city was metal that could be melted down into balls for muskets or cannons. The bells were loaded onto wagons and carried to Allentown, where they were hidden in various church basements.

While the Rushes had never moved back into the city after leaving in 1776, many others had—and now they needed to flee. Charles Willson Peale took leave from the Pennsylvania Militia to resettle his family. He arranged for lodging near Reading, and then, finding that his family had already left the city, returned to town and packed. "As the Wagons were waiting," Peale wrote, "I hurried what things I could hastily pick up & shoved them off." The family sped out of town behind galloping horses, narrowly missing the approaching British soldiers.

Some older Philadelphians didn't make it. Legendary botanist John Bartram, who had been named "His Majesty's Botanist" by George III during friendlier times, and whose "Bartram's Garden" along the river was considered the greatest horticultural achievement in North America, became increasingly agitated as the British approached. At seventy-eight, he was not in excellent health, but it was still a shock when he dropped dead not long after finding out the British were just twenty miles away.

Early in the morning on September 26, 1777, General Howe led his forces along almost the same path Washington and his troops had traveled less than three months earlier. In lockstep formation, wearing perfect uniforms and marching to painstakingly precise fife and drums, the king's men marched into Philadelphia. Those who were upset kept it to themselves, but many were astonished that Washington had given Howe the city without a fight. Thomas Paine, who remained in the city, was among the most furious, writing to Franklin in France of his incredulity that Washington had let the British walk into Philadelphia without a shot being fired.

Washington's assistant Timothy Pickering, by contrast, expressed what many non-Pennsylvanians were thinking: "I feel in some way reconciled to Howe's entering Pennsylvania and Philadelphia," he wrote, "that the unworthy inhabitants (of which 'tis apparent a majority of the state is composed) may experience the calamities of war, which nothing but their own supineness and unfriendliness to the American cause would have brought on them. Perhaps Heaven permits it in vengeance for their defection, that their country should be the seat of war."

After several days of dashing between military hospitals to treat the seven hundred newly wounded soldiers from Brandywine and Paoli, Rush scribbled a note to Adams and did not mince words. "My dear friend," he wrote, "we are on the brink of ruin."

He went on to rail about the images he couldn't get out of his head from his hours behind enemy lines. He mentioned how kind some of the British doctors had been to wounded enemy prisoners. But he strongly cautioned Adams, "You must not attribute this to their humanity. They hate us in every Shape we appear to them. Their care of our wounded was entirely the effect of the perfection of their medical establishment, which mechanically forced happiness and satisfaction upon our countrymen perhaps without a single wish in the Officers of the hospital to make their Situation comfortable."

On his way to Trenton, Rush had visited Washington's army, where he was outraged that not one sentry had asked who he was as he walked into camp and up to a general's tent. While visiting, he heard endless stories of what was going wrong—including over a hundred soldiers who had drunk themselves into a stupor the night before.

He ended his letter to Adams—in which he sounded deeply agitated, his mind flurrying with what he was certain were solutions to all these problems—by sending love to his friends and colleagues in Lancaster, and writing, perhaps to himself: "Adieu, my dear friend. May you never Sleep sound 'till you project and execute Something to extricate and save your country."

Washington had decided to make a Hail Mary attempt to retake the nation's capital. He planned a sneak attack on Germantown, just north of the city, hoping a victory there might allow his troops to continue down and retake Philadelphia. Because of where Howe had deployed his men, the rebels actually had a numerical advantage. And the Philadelphians among Washington's men had a special knowledge of the area around their own city. Gen. John Cadwalader was one of several locals who dressed as redcoats to sneak into the area.

Unfortunately, local loyalists were snooping for the British. One of them was Rush's provost from the College of Philadelphia, Dr. William Smith—the very gentleman he had warned Adams about the day they had met three years earlier. Smith betrayed Washington in a way that even the appreciative enemy found puzzling. He rode up to a British captain at his post on Ridge Road, between the city and Germantown, and asked if he could take a walk with the officer, a man he had never met before. Smith then told him, "My friend, I confess to you that I am a friend of the States and no friend of the English government, but you have rendered me a friendly turn. You have shown me that humanity which every soldier should not lose sight of. You have protected my property. I will show you I am grateful."

Smith, deeply conflicted about the war, had apparently decided to thank a random British officer for sparing his home by warning him he was in danger. "The enemy approaches, friend, God bless your person!" Smith babbled. "The success of your arms I cannot wish.—Friend! General Washington has marched up to Norriton today!—Adieu! Adieu!"

He rode away, and the captain stood in disbelief for a moment. Then he ran to let his superiors know. When General Howe was told, he made clear that this was the first he had heard of such an attack; now he would be ready and waiting. Sure enough, the Battle of Germantown on October 4, 1777, was another American disaster. That night in four hours of close fighting, Washington lost more men to death, injury, and capture than he had in an entire day at Brandywine.

More than 150 soldiers were killed at Germantown, among them twenty-six-year-old Maj. James Witherspoon, whom Rush knew well, since he was the eldest child of the Rev. John Witherspoon. James Witherspoon's death was particularly horrible: a six-pound iron cannonball hit a signpost on a road where he was riding, ricocheted through the neck of a brigadier general's horse, passed through the general's own thigh, and then smashed full on into Major Witherspoon's head.

Several days after the defeat, Rush found himself dining with Washington and his generals at a temporary camp. He did his best to make pleasant conversation but privately he took note of every detail about the meal that unnerved him, which he later scribbled in his diary.

"Dined with the commander-in-chief of American army," he wrote, taking care not to use Washington's name. He respected the general greatly as a man, and genuinely liked him. But he sympathized with the growing number of congressional and military leaders who were disappointed with Washington's recent leadership, and he worried that he was being "out-generaled," as Adams had grumbled to his wife. Both Adams and Rush were also increasingly nervous about Washington's growing star power in a country that knew it didn't want a king but wasn't sure how it would be governed without one.

Rush noted there was "no wine—only grog" at the meal, and that there were "knives & forks eno' for only half the company," so the others had to wait until they were finished eating. Inspecting everything and everyone for clues to the recent string of harsh defeats, Rush was even annoyed that Washington had given "the head of his table to one of his aids-de-camp," as he wrote in disbelief, "and sat 2d or 3rd from him on his left side."

He then made a list of the "State and Disorders in the American army." He began, "the commander-in-chief at this time [is] the *idol of America*," then went on to claim that Washington was overly influenced by his top generals and even by one of his aides, "a young man of 21 years of age," Col. Alexander Hamilton.

Rush offered this assessment of Washington's four major generals, Greene, Sullivan, Stirling, and Stevens: "the 1st a sycophant to the general, timid, speculative, without enterprise; the 2nd, weak, vain, without dignity, fond of scribling, in the field a madman. The 3rd, a proud, vain, lazy, ignorant, drunkard. The 4th, a sordid, boasting cowardly sot."

As for the troops, they appeared "dirty, undisciplined, & ragged." In the last line of Rush's diary entry, he offered a restaurant review of Washington's table: "bad bread; no order; universal disgust."

Rush was demoralized. "We lost a city—a Victory—a campaign by that want of discipline and system which pervades every part of the army . . . ," he wrote to Adams. "Be not deceived, my dear friend. Our army is no better than it was two years ago."

In his heart, Rush still believed in Washington almost as much as he believed in the revolution itself. But *something* had to change; someone had to answer for the failures. Perhaps changes among the major generals could be the answer. "The Spirit of our men is good. Our Officers are equal nay superior to Howe's. A few able major generals," he wrote, "would make them a terror to the whole power of Britain."

Four days after Rush sent that letter, there was finally good military news—from the northern army. The Battles of Saratoga, along the border between Canada and New York on the Mohawk and Upper Hudson Rivers, had ended with the first decisive American victory. The British general, John Burgoyne, had surrendered to the American forces in Saratoga, which were overseen by Horatio Gates and a younger general with whom he endlessly argued, Benedict Arnold. (Arnold was injured in the leg before the final battle.) The victory at Saratoga offered some hope to an otherwise dejected Continental Army. News of the victory also made its way to the King of France, who for the first time considered that it might be wise to cultivate a relationship with the American revolutionaries, with whom he shared an enemy.

24

Rush was fraying at the edges. He hadn't slept in his own home in nearly a year. He hadn't seen his wife or his closest revolutionary ally, John Adams—his personal and political reality-checkers—for months. He was overseeing the care of more patients than he had treated during his entire career, and they were dying faster than he could keep up, in some cases from diseases acquired in his hospitals. Regardless of the recent victory at Saratoga, the revolution on which he had bet his life and his country seemed in danger of failing.

His brain was racing; he was certain he knew how to fix everything but felt he had the power to fix nothing. Shippen ignored his requests and proposals. And while Rush had the ear of many in Congress and the army, they never seemed to do what he suggested.

He was now thirty-two, but felt so much older—weary from work and travel, struggling with his recurring cough, and extremely worried about the war. He wasn't alone in feeling discouraged. It had been nearly a year and a half since the Declaration of Independence was signed, and revolutionary fatigue had set in. Some days fewer than half of the Continental Congress showed up, and many members were considering whether to run for reelection.

John Adams, for one, had quietly decided it was time for him to move back home, practice law again, and tend to his wife, family, and farm. He was instead told in November that Congress was going to ask him to join Benjamin Franklin in Paris, so he headed home to Quincy to prepare for that move.

Rush found himself increasingly isolated as the pressures on him mounted. Besides overseeing the Middle Department hospitals, he occasionally saw combat. In mid-November, he spent one of the longest days of his life taking care of the wounded on site during the end of the battle for Fort Mifflin. The fort, situated on Mud Island in the Delaware River south of Philadelphia, was one of the last holdouts against British domination of all routes to the city. The British had thought they could take the fort in a few days, but it held up under bombardment for an astonishing month and a half—a feat that may have saved the revolution from being quashed by the end of 1777.

At Fort Mifflin, Rush was an eyewitness to the fortitude of American soldiers "under the most complicated dangers and sufferings . . . showers of balls, bombs, and carcasses were the smallest part of them." The temporary fortifications were demolished, and all but one cannon had been silenced. "Their barracks and blockhouses were burnt and shattered to pieces, so that the whole garrison (500 in number) were reduced to the necessity of lying under the cover of a stone wall . . . on the wet ground without fire or any other covering than a blanket. Yet under these circumstances did these brave fellows appear cheerful and declare to the last that they would never yield the island."

Fort Mifflin finally did fall, several days after Rush left. Afterward he declared, "Britain in the height of her glory . . . never saw her sons perform more gallant exploits than the ragged sons of liberty performed who fell in defense of that island."

Rush was next sent to Princeton, to oversee the New Jersey hospitals. Regardless of the friction between them, Dr. Shippen may have realized that Rush needed some time with his family and the opportunity to work from a familiar place. Julia had just arrived from Maryland with their son John. They were going to stay with her parents at Morven, which they were rebuilding.

Rush gushed about the reunion in a letter to Betsey Graeme Fergusson. "My dear Julia . . . I have not a wish that is not gratified in her," he wrote, and John, "dear boy . . . He is so good-tempered that he seldom or never cries. He spends his whole time in sleeping, eating, and pulling his mama's caps and handkerchiefs to pieces."

Despite his cheerful words, all was not well with Rush. His emotions were labile and contagious. Julia didn't know her husband all that well yet; he kept to himself much of the strain of his work and wartime experiences. Under different circumstances, his father-in-law might have been able to help him cope with his anxieties and rein in his manic energy. But Richard Stockton was still a living ghost and could barely help himself.

There was a growing desperation in the letters Rush wrote from Princeton. He accused Shippen of dramatically mismanaging budgets for the military hospitals and supplies, while personally living high on the hog. He even relayed a rumor that Shippen was reselling the medicinal wine meant for treating patients. On the military front, Rush believed that Washington should elevate the generals who had been successful in the northern battles in Canada, New England, and New York, and demote those who had lost so many battles in the Middle States. Rush particularly favored Horatio Gates, whom he had got to know fairly well, and Brig. Gen. Thomas Conway, whom he knew by reputation.

Conway was Irish born and trained in the French military before coming to America. After the Battle of Brandywine, he had composed a controversial letter to Gates that listed thirteen reasons for the loss—one of which was an overt criticism of Washington as a "weak general." Word of the letter, and of this key phrase about Washington, spread through the military and congressional gossip chain for weeks.

Rush mentioned the existence of the phrase in a letter to Adams as early as October 21. The way he heard it, Conway had written: "A great and good God . . . has decreed that America shall be free, or ________ and weak counsellors would have ruined her long ago." Rush was careful to leave a blank so as not to repeat the words "weak general."

On November 5, someone passed a version of Conway's comment to Washington himself. Washington dashed off a note to Conway, seeking an explanation:

> Sir,
>
> a Letter which I receivd last Night, containd the following, paragraph.
>
> In a Letter from Genl Conway to Genl Gates he says—"Heaven has been determind to save your Country; or a weak General and bad Councellors would have ruind it."
>
> I am Sir Yr Hble Servt.

Conway wrote back immediately, only half-denying authorship. "I Believe i can attest that the expression *Weak General* has not slipped from my penn," he told Washington, but "if it has," he wanted to make his feelings about his commander in chief clear. "You are a Brave man, an honest Man, a patriot, and a Man of great sense," he began, but "although your advice in council is commonly sound and proper, you have often been influenc'd by men who Were not equal to you in point of experience, Knowledge or judgment." The letter in question had been written to his colleague General Gates, he explained, with whom he spoke "my mind freely" about "several Measures pursued in this army" with which "I found fault"—suggesting that surely no one would be surprised after so many defeats that top generals would be discussing what had gone wrong. He offered to have Gates show Washington the original letter. (Gates later confirmed to Washington that Conway had never written "weak general"—but he had conveniently lost the letter.)

Brig. Gen. Thomas Conway

Conway offered to resign and return to France, where there had been talk of a war with Britain. Instead Congress gave him a new job as inspector general. But Washington clearly felt injured by the episode. In the meantime, the debate over whether Conway had written these two words took on a life of its own. Anyone who criticized Washington openly raised suspicion that they were part of a mutinous "Conway Cabal."

Rush's preoccupation with military discipline continued, primarily over how it affected life in his overcrowded hospitals. Amid disheartening defeats and colder temperatures, drinking problems were on the rise among both active soldiers and convalescents. The drinking and rowdiness contributed to the increase in hospital fevers and other infections and led to rising casualties. Rush begged one of Washington's generals, Nathanael Greene, to send some officers to the hospitals to keep the soldiers in line. "Physicians and surgeons," Rush explained, "possess no power" to discipline or punish members of the military. And besides, "a soldier should never be suffered to exist a single hour without a sense of his having a master being impressed upon his mind."

Rush later wrote of this time, "Many hundred . . . were buried every week in different villages in Pennsylvania and New Jersey. The scene was shocking to humanity and alarming to the friends of the Revolution. . . . I should at this time have retired from the public service, to avoid sharing in the guilt I witnessed. . . . But I loved my country and the brave men who had offered their lives for its defense too well to shrink from what I conceived to be my duty."

On December 2, Rush wrote directly to Dr. Shippen requesting an officer be dispatched to the hospital in Princeton to maintain order among the patients. It was a pretty friendly letter, the last one that would ever pass between them.

A week later Rush wrote a long letter to a New York delegate to Congress, William Duer, explaining his belief that the Continental Army should adopt the system used by all European armies, splitting Dr. Shippen's job into two: a chief physician and inspector general, and then a purveyor general. He claimed he wasn't making this proposal "to hint anything to the prejudice of the present director general." Rather, he felt Congress had given Shippen a position no single man could do properly.

But he also took shots at his boss, claiming that when he told Shippen about the dangerous overcrowding in the hospitals, his response was "I am the *only* judge of that, and your *only* business is to take care of all I send there." And he told Congressman Duer that "Dr. Shippen has taken pains to represent my complaints of the sufferings of the sick as intended to displace him." Shippen, Rush had heard, was saying the only reason anyone was criticizing him was that they wanted his job. In fact, the military physicians who agreed with Rush—and there were many—just wanted Shippen to *do his job.*

To prove that he was interested only in "the happiness of my distressed countrymen and the honor of my country," Rush boldly offered to quit "as soon as the campaign is closed . . . [and] seal my disapprobation . . . with my resignation."

THE NEXT WEEK Washington's troops, beaten physically and mentally, trudged to Valley Forge—many of them barefoot—to set up camp for the winter. But not enough food, cold weather clothing, or medical supplies had been stored for them there. The site offered little shelter: they had to build their own log huts. It was as if they were in a prison camp of their country's own making.

Rush did not visit Valley Forge initially because it didn't have its own medical facility: the sick were to be sent to one of the hospitals he was overseeing from Princeton. He remained in the warmth of Morven through the last weeks of 1777, able to celebrate both his thirty-second birthday and Christmas with family there. He relished his time with Julia and baby John, and had a chance to talk with Annis about the sad state of affairs of their mutual friend Betsey Graeme Fergusson, whose loyalist husband had abandoned her to support England. Rush kept writing letters to those in power, despite not receiving timely and proper answers.

The day after Christmas, he wrote a long letter to Washington offering a deeper explanation of his concerns about the state of the army hospitals, and noting that the situation was about to get worse along with the weather. "There cannot be a greater calamity for a sick man than to come into our hospital at *this season* of the year.

Old disorders are prolonged and new ones contracted among us. This last is so much the case that I am safe when I assert that a great majority of those who die in our hands perish with fevers caught in our hospitals."

He laid out a plan to address overcrowding, including providing more initial care for sick soldiers in the camps, where the "air and diet" were probably healthier than in the hospitals. He described the shortages of supplies, medicine, food, blankets, and hospital gowns; the lack of security and officer supervision of hospitalized soldiers; and the structural challenge that too many nonmedical responsibilities were under the director-general's control.

When he didn't hear back from Washington in a week, he took it upon himself to leave his posting in Princeton and travel to York, Pennsylvania—where Congress was now meeting—to plead his case with whoever would listen. He felt he needed to do this before resigning his post in the military hospitals.

On the way, he spent a night at Rush Hill visiting with his mother and sister, then went to Valley Forge to inspect conditions there. He couldn't believe what he saw. The encampment was "dirty & stinking," and the men were "dirty & ragged" as well as hungry. There was no forage for the horses, and many had died.

Washington and his generals were all living in nicer houses outside camp. Rush spent the night at the home of General Sullivan, who reportedly told him, "Sir, this is not an army—it is a mob."

From there, Rush went to Lancaster, where he spent several days among friends from Philadelphia who had temporarily relocated there, then continued on to York, where Congress was meeting.

He arrived there on January 8, 1778, and quickly contacted several friends on the medical committee. They assured him that his letters had been seen, his concerns were understood, and Congress had already been urged to act on some of his requests. They were also scheduling a session later in the month to allow both Rush and Shippen to testify, in hopes that the two of them could put their differences to rest. He was urged to put aside any thoughts of resigning his post.

A number of members of Congress, Rush discovered, were

ready to voice concerns about Washington's leadership. He told Julia in a letter, "Nothing is talked of here but a reformation of every department in the army." People spoke openly about the "rupture between General Gates and General W——g——n" (for some reason, Rush declined to write Washington's name in this sentence but not elsewhere) as well as Conway's self-banishment for "speaking disrespectfully of the Commander in Chief." Rush's perception was that Congress was acting "a prudent part" by consulting Washington "in everything" while remaining "determined to support the authority and influence of Gates and Conway."

It was one thing to write a candid letter to his wife. But while he was in York, away from family, close friends, and anyone else who might talk him out of it, Rush sat down in his rooming house on January 12 and wrote an odd, dangerously irreverent letter to Patrick Henry, who was now the governor of Virginia. Years before in Philadelphia, Henry had told him of Washington's fear that he might fail as commander in chief. More recently, Rush had heard from General Gates that Henry had shared concerns about Washington's leadership at the beginning of the war.

Rush didn't know Henry well. He had served as his physician at times and considered him a collegial peer, but they hardly corresponded regularly. And Rush knew that, as a Virginian, Henry likely remained loyal to Washington, warts and all. Yet he decided to air his grievances to him anyway.

He may have written to Henry exactly because he was close to Washington, out of frustration that he hadn't heard from the general in the nearly two weeks since sending his day-after-Christmas letter. The painful irony was that Washington, on the very same day Rush was writing to Henry, was finally replying to the doctor from Valley Forge. But Rush had no way of knowing this, and his patience was at an end. The letter he wrote Henry included nothing terribly new, but it was, like many things Rush wrote, more dramatic and intimate than most missives on the subject, which made it all the more spectacularly wrongheaded.

"The common danger of our country first brought you and me together," Rush began:

> I recollect with pleasure the influence of your conversation and eloquence upon the opinions of this country in the beginning of the present controversy. You first taught us to shake off all our idolatrous attachment to royalty, and to oppose its encroachment upon our liberties with our very lives. By these means you saved us from ruin. . . . But, sir, we have only passed the Red Sea. A dreary wilderness is still before us, and unless a Moses or a Joshua are raised up in our behalf, we must perish before we reach the promised land.

He went on to describe some of the new nation's problems:

> Her representation in Congress [has] dwindled to only twenty-one members. Her Adams [and] . . . her Henry, are no more among them. [As for] her army—what is it? . . . Discipline unknown or *wholly* neglected. The quartermaster's and commissaries' departments filled with idleness and ignorance and peculation. Our hospitals crowded with 6000 sick but half provided with necessaries or accomodations, and more dying in them in one month than perished in the field during the whole of the last campaign. The money depreciating without any effectual measures being taken to raise it.

On it went. And then Rush asked, "But is our case desperate? By no means. We have wisdom, virtue and strength *enough* to save us if they could be called into action. The northern army has shown us [with the recent victory at Saratoga] what Americans are capable of with a GENERAL at their head." He suggested that one of the northern army generals, perhaps Gates or Conway, "would in a few weeks render" the rest of the army "an irresistible body of men." He even quoted the radioactive line from Conway's letter, about the "_______ and weak counsellors" almost ruining America.

He finished by cheekily explaining that his letter, while unsigned, was from "one of your Philadelphia friends" whose identity Henry absolutely had to keep secret: "A hint of his name, if found out by the handwriting, must not be mentioned to your most intimate friend. Even the letter *must* be thrown in the fire. But some of its contents ought to be made public in order to awaken, enlighten and alarm our country."

Rush never heard back. He had no way of knowing what Henry thought about the letter, or if he had burned it as requested. It is entirely possible that after writing it, Rush forgot about it. He was capable of writing passionately with dispassion.

SEVERAL DAYS LATER, Rush received the reply from Washington that he had been waiting for. It was entirely cordial, acknowledging Rush's concerns and suggesting that some could be promptly addressed while others, which grew out of the "peculiarity of our circumstances," might take more time. He told Rush he had dispatched a field officer to the hospitals to investigate: "Among the many necessary reforms in the military line. . . . I shall always be ready to contribute all in my power, towards rendering the situation, of those unhappy people who are under the necessity of becoming the inhabitants of [hospitals], as comfortable as possible."

Washington's general orders for January show he sent an investigator with orders to look into every in-hospital issue that Rush had raised. He would soon order many of the changes Rush had requested, immediately adding more guards for the hospitals, better triage for sick soldiers before they were sent to the hospital, new procedures for keeping track of patient admission and discharge back to camp, and clothing needed during care.

This could have been the end of Rush's risky round of letters challenging his superiors in the name of his sick patients. But then Shippen went on the counterattack. Instead of appreciating the improvements Rush had instigated, he took it all personally. He sent Congress a letter flatly denying any wrongdoing. He also questioned whether Rush's trip to York to lobby Congress represented a "long absence from his duty without leave at this important period," raising the possibility of a formal complaint.

Shippen's most outrageous claim, however, concerned the status of the military medical service: "I flatter myself . . . that our sick are not crowded in any hospital . . . that very few die—that no fatal disease prevails, and that the hospitals are in very good order. . . . Some amendments to our system may be made, but Doctor Rush, from his ignorance of the state of our Hospitals and not knowing his duty, has not hit upon any of them."

Rush's reaction was to demand that their upcoming private audience with Congress instead be made a public hearing. Congress denied the request, ruling that he and Shippen would testify in a closed session.

Rush's closest friend in Congress, whom he needed more than ever, was not available to help him. Adams was back in Massachusetts at his farm, preparing to leave for Paris. On January 22, Rush let him know he intended "to lay down my commission." He seemed reconciled to it, almost relieved. He predicted the meeting in Congress would end with Shippen "acquitted honorably and my complaints dismissed as groundless, malicious, etc. But times must alter, or this is a ruined country. Nothing but integrity in private and justice in public bodies can preserve a republic. If calamities are necessary to teach us wisdom and virtue, I wish God would rain down shows of them upon us." He joked about Adams's upcoming sojourn: "While you are *gazed* at for your American-manufactured principles . . . I shall be secluded from the noise and corruption of the times and spending my time in the innocent employments of husbandry on a farm in Jersey with an amiable wife and rosy boy."

But by the time his hearing began, five days after that letter was sent, Rush had changed his mind: he wanted to keep his commission after all. He also wanted to beat Shippen.

He began well enough in front of the congressional committee, where at three p.m. he read a long letter critical of the hospital system. But his presentation then veered into a more direct attack on Shippen. He wasn't spending enough time visiting hospitals and seeking to understand their problems. Also, while some of the hospitals were short of medicinal wine, he had personally bought some of the military's stock and resold it for more than three times what he paid—along with other misappropriation of provisions. There was ample evidence for these claims, but the more Rush talked, the more it sounded to the congressmen as if his issues with Shippen were more personal than medical. And given the current dismal state of the war effort—and the fact that Congress had already fired one Philadelphia doctor from this position because he didn't work well with others—they were not likely to make another such change.

Rush vowed that he wasn't after Shippen's job, but most assumed that was exactly what he wanted. He claimed that the problem was not "want of harmony" between them, but that he had "lived so long in harmony with him" that to do so any longer "would have been high treason against my country." Rush didn't see this as an ultimatum, because he believed the facts were on his side. He was also certain that his critiques of the military hospitals were indisputably correct, and anyone fighting them was just trying to score political points and would eventually have to relent.

There is some question as to how clearly Rush was thinking at this point. The evening after he testified, he wrote a long letter to Julia, recounting a conversation he had in York with General Gates, who by then was doing everything he could to make the Conway controversy go away. Rush wrote that he had told Gates flat out, "if I thought that he alone could save America, I would vote for his being" elevated to Washington's job.

Gates had certainly schemed for such a result, but he was horrified by the doctor's naïveté about the danger of such talk during a war. He turned to Rush and declared, "You would do better to vote to have my throat cut."

After saying that, Gates likely would have been even more shocked to learn that Rush was writing this all down in a letter, which could be intercepted and lead to grave consequences for both of them. Upon receiving it, Julia, seeing that it risked his reputation, hid it permanently with her most personal documents.

THE NEXT DAY in Congress, William Shippen, Jr., responded to Rush's testimony. According to Rush's recounting (there is no official record of their testimony), Shippen told Congress about the situation and criticized Rush, his thirty-two-year-old former protégé. At the end of his testimony, Dr. Shippen announced that he could no longer work with Dr. Rush. Congress would need to decide between them.

A five-man committee was appointed to address the situation; its chairman was Rev. Dr. John Witherspoon. He may have been chosen because he was so close to Rush and his wife's family, but things were no longer the same between the Rushes, the Witherspoons, and the Stocktons. Witherspoon, who had lost his eldest child at the Battle of Brandywine, had soured on the Stocktons because he believed Richard had signed an oath to the British. The British had commandeered his university, and now the American army hospital system had taken it over, with Rush overseeing it.

When they met privately, Witherspoon asked Rush if he planned to follow through with his earlier threats to resign. Rush said no. Several congressmen, as well as Washington himself, had told him that many of his suggestions for the medical department were being implemented, and if that were true, he was ready to keep serving.

Witherspoon, however, told him it would be best if he resigned. When Rush kept asking why, he finally admitted that the doctor had made too many enemies in the department to continue. Rush said he didn't care how many friends he had—"do not think," he declared, "to terrify me into a resignation by the fear of being dismissed by the Congress. You have suffered enough in the opinion of the public by dismissing Dr. Morgan without a trial. I dare you to dismiss me in the same manner."

Witherspoon told Rush he "had been deceived," that Shippen's responsibilities were never going to be significantly altered. Only "very trifling" changes would be made in the medical department.

Rush sat for "about an hour" to ponder the situation, then began to compose his resignation. He wrote for a long time, filling up page after page, some two dozen in all. Then he wrote a second version, which consisted of one sentence. This he submitted to Witherspoon.

"Finding it impossible," he said, "to do my duty any longer in the department you have assigned me in your hospitals in the manner I would wish, I beg the favor of you to accept of the resignation of my commission." At the afternoon session on January 30, 1778, Congress accepted his resignation.

25

Rush was devastated, feeling betrayed by people he thought were his friends and brothers in arms—especially Witherspoon—and equally betrayed by his own judgment. Desperate for another way to serve the revolution, on his way out of town, Rush wrote to Witherspoon that he was thinking of joining a proposed expedition to invade Canada, under the leadership of Conway and the Marquis de Lafayette. Witherspoon responded quickly that the members of Congress he discussed this with were "at a loss what Station or Character you could sustain" in that effort.

Rush and his servant rode to Lancaster, where he immediately threw himself into an ironically timed assignment. Just as the medical committee was forcing him out of the hospital system, the Board of War wanted to publish his essay on the health of soldiers as a pamphlet and give one to every Continental serviceman. Rush used the opportunity to expand on a few points, insert observations he'd made during his experiences in combat, and tweak some of the language. Mostly he wanted to add advice for the bitterly cold winter of 1778. He was especially concerned that when it was cold, soldiers were less likely to relieve themselves far enough away from where they slept and ate, so camps needed to be moved more frequently.

Rush noted that soldiers needed to exercise more when they weren't in battle, especially in the winter: "Idleness is the bane of a soldier," he wrote. "It exposes him to temptations not only to every kind of military vice, but to every species of military disorder."

Mostly Rush wanted to speak directly to the soldiers, now that he had been tricked out of his position officially overseeing their health—physical and mental—which was, ultimately, all he had ever cared about:

> Consider that your country and posterity look up to you for the preservation of the only means of establishing the liberties of America. The wisdom and eloquence of writers and orators have long since yielded to the more powerful oratory of our sword. All our hopes, therefore, are in our Army. But if any thing can be added to these motives, consider further, that there is scarcely a soldier under your command who has not a mother, a wife, a sister, or a child. These helpless members of society made great sacrifices to their country when they urged the beloved objects of their affection to follow the recruiting drum to the camp. Whenever, therefore, your duty requires that you should attend to the health of your men, imagine you see one or perhaps *all* of their female and helpless connexions standing at the door of your tents or quarters, and beseeching you . . . to attend to every thing which reason and conscience tell you are necessary for the preservation of their health and lives.

Several days after finishing his edits on the *Health of Soldiers* pamphlet, Rush received a letter from Adams, who apparently wasn't yet aware of his resignation.

"I have received so many of your Letters," Adams wrote, ". . . containing such important Matter, in So masterly a style, that I am ashamed to confess I have answered but one of them, and that only with a few Lines. I beg you would not impute this omission to Inattention, Negligence, or Want of Regard, but to its true Cause a Confusion of Business. I beg Leave to assure you that I hold your Correspondence, inestimable, and will do every Thing in my Power to cultivate it."

But his advice was far too late. "I am very glad you have not laid down your Commission and I conjure you, by all the Tyes of Friendship to your Country, not to do it. Men who are sensible of the Evils in the hospital Department are the most likely to point them out to others, and to suggest Remedies—Patience! Patience! Patience. The first the last and the middle Virtue of a Politician."

It must have devastated Rush to read these words, because he had already realized his resignation had been a huge mistake. He felt that even more strongly when Congress released the orders for restructuring the medical department: most of the changes Rush had argued for, had put his career and reputation and life on the line for, had been approved. Congress even noted on the record that the changes were being made in response to "letters from Dr. Shippen, Dr. Rush, and others."

Procurement for the Middle Department, specifically, was taken away from Shippen, who would be "excused from the duty of providing supplies"; that duty would be put in the hands of an independent deputy. The physicians running each regional department would be given more control over care in their own areas. Shippen himself was directly ordered to "frequently visit the hospitals in each district" to make sure that "the regulations are carried into effect."

When he read these orders, despite the good news, Rush understood that Witherspoon had completely deceived him. He wrote to a friend on the medical committee, "Had I expected such a change would have been made in the system, I should not have resigned my commission. And I beg it as a favor that you inform the members of the committee as well as our friends in York town, that I was induced to take that step by . . . Dr. [Witherspoon]." He asked his friend to pass on his thanks to the committee for addressing his complaints and concerns—which, for his patients, was ultimately what mattered.

While in Lancaster, Rush also heard from Dr. Shippen. The letter has been lost, but Rush's response suggests that Shippen tried to threaten him with a court-martial. Rush informed Shippen, "I have no revenge in me," but his actions belied this. He checked in at the military hospital in Lancaster, looking for evidence of Shippen's crimes of mismanagement. He then went to Allentown and Bethlehem, where he asked doctors at each hospital to write letters and swear affidavits.

Word spread that Rush wouldn't back down about Shippen and also that he was spouting off about Gates; the talk reached Williamsburg, Virginia, where Patrick Henry hadn't burned Rush's incendiary letter and didn't know quite what to do with it. Rumors about the "Conway Cabal" had continued, with some whispering that Washington was facing a coup attempt at any moment. Henry decided he had better share Rush's month-old letter with Washington and sent it to him at Valley Forge, including a disclaimer that he did not recognize the author's handwriting or identity. Henry sent Washington the letter on February 20; when he didn't hear back from him after a week, he wrote again.

By this time, Washington had also received a letter from the Marquis de Lafayette, who reported that "john adams Spoke very disrespectfully of your excellency in boston. . . . Give me leave to say my opinion, my dear general; those ennemy's of yours are So low So far under your feet, that it is not of your dignity to take much notice of 'em."

Washington also received a long letter from Rush himself, who announced he would "think myself inexcusable" if he resigned his commission "without informing your Excellency" why. He then launched into a detailed critique of Shippen, including a letter from four other military physicians accusing Shippen of stealing wine and food meant for patients, lying to Congress about the number of men who died in their care, and almost never showing up at the hospital.

After several pages trashing Shippen, Rush congratulated Washington on the changes being made in the military system, which were already, in Rush's estimation, producing "the most salutary effects." He also enclosed a copy of his new pamphlet on the health of soldiers, closing his letter with "the warmest Sentiments of regard, and Attachment" as "your Excellency's most Affectionate humble servant."

This profession of warmth, attachment, affection and humility only made it worse when, later in March, Washington caught up to Henry's first note and the "anonymous" letter, written in the exact same hand as the one he had just read from Rush. Until then, Washington had always considered the doctor a friend.

"That I may have erred in using all the means in my power for accomplishing the objects of the arduous exalted station with which I am honored, I cannot doubt," Washington wrote back to Henry:

> Nor do I wish my conduct to be exempted from reprehension farther than it may deserve. Error is the portion of humanity, and to censure it, whether committed by this or that public character, is the prerogative of freemen.
>
> However, being intimately acquainted with the . . . Author of the Letter . . . and having always received from him the strongest professions of attachment and regard, I am constrained to consider him, as not possessing . . . a great degree of candor and honest sincerity . . . [even if] his views in addressing you, should have been the result of conviction and founded in motives of public good. This is not the only secret, insidious attempt, that has been made to wound my reputation. There have been others equally base, cruel and ungenerous.

Just as Washington was finishing this letter—in which he chose not to reveal Rush's identity—the second one from Henry arrived.

To this he replied with the backstory of a situation he had tried hard to keep secret:

> The Anonymous Letter, with which you were pleased to favor me, was written by Doctor Rush, so far as I can judge from a similitude of hands. This Man has been elaborate & studied in his professions of regard for me; and long since the Letter to you.
>
> My caution to avoid anything that could injure the service, prevented me from communicating, but to very few of my friends, the intrigues of a faction, which I know was formed against me, since it might serve to publish our internal dissentions; but their own restless zeal to advance their views, has too clearly betrayed them, and made concealment on my part fruitless. I cannot precisely mark the extent of their views, but it appeared in general, that General Gates

> was to be exalted, on the ruin of my reputation and influence. This I am authorised to say from undeniable facts, in my own possession, from publications, the evident scope of which, could not be mistaken, and from private detractions industriously circulated. . . . But I have good reasons to believe that their machinations have recoiled most sensibly upon themselves.

He named Conway "a very active, and malignant partizan" in the scheming and also suspected Thomas Mifflin's involvement. What they had done, Washington could almost understand. It was wrong, but this was what ambitious military people sometimes did when war wasn't going well. And while the word "cabal" was tossed around, it is unlikely Washington ever believed there would be a true attempt at a coup.

But what Rush had done was something different. It was personal. He had hurt the general deeply.

RUSH RETURNED TO Princeton just as every soldier in the army was receiving his pamphlet. He was, simultaneously, the most publicly famous and well-regarded he had ever been, and the most privately destroyed. He had no idea what to do next, except to care for his wife and his son.

He was only thirty-two. Maybe it wasn't too late to become a lawyer.

He discussed the possibility with his father-in-law. And in the weeks that followed, he certainly started acting like a lawyer, traveling all over Pennsylvania, New Jersey, and Maryland, meeting with friends but also collecting stories from doctors and hospital staff members—anything that would support his contention that Shippen was not only a mismanager but a scoundrel and that the only way to deal with him now was with a court-martial.

Luckily, it was the quietest time the nation had seen since the war began. Washington's troops remained in Valley Forge from December 1777 through the late spring of 1778. Despite a few minor battles, his generals spent most of this time drilling them, really for the first time, with the help of the Marquis de Lafayette and several other imported battle experts. This basic retraining would allow Washington's army to engage at a higher level from this point on in the war.

America was also able to negotiate a treaty with France during this period. In February, the king recognized the United States as a sovereign nation, in a deal negotiated by Benjamin Franklin. In the late winter, he was joined by John Adams, who brought along his ten-year-old son John Quincy when Abigail decided not to come. Franklin and Adams were in Paris together when the mutual defense deal that the two nations had signed went into effect. Britain declared war on France, and France became America's first international ally.

In the meantime, the British occupation of Philadelphia became more and more challenging, without providing great strategic advantage. In April, Gen. William Howe was relieved of his duties as commander in chief of the British forces in America. He had, technically, submitted a letter of resignation in the fall, claiming he was not receiving adequate support. But now it was clear that for two years in a row, he had failed to subdue the ragtag rebel army that the British vastly outnumbered in manpower and firepower. He was replaced by one of his generals, Henry Clinton, as both sides made their plans for war season.

As Rush was preparing to begin the study of law in earnest, the British announced they would be evacuating Philadelphia. Suddenly he could go home and be a doctor again. Since the British retreat was likely to come back through Princeton, Rush left town on May 27, 1778, with Julia and John and their servants. He took them back to Mount Welcome in Maryland, which he assumed would be safer—especially since Julia was now two months pregnant with their second child. He left the family there, and then he and Cyrus rode back to Philadelphia to open up the house.

When they reached the farmhouse in Darby where Rush had hidden his library and his favorite furniture, he made a startling discovery: at some point during the occupation, General Howe had lived in that house. Moreover he had left Rush a bizarre souvenir: Howe had used the doctor's prized mahogany tea tables to write his dispatches home to England. Rush knew because he could read some of the writing in the ink that stained the tabletops. He and Cyrus loaded these possessions into a wagon.

General Clinton had ordered the British forces to return to New York, and as Rush restored the Front Street house, the retreat was under way. Clinton had chosen not to use ships, not even to move baggage and supplies, but instead to journey over land. The British were therefore marching with all their stuff in a dead-summer heat that reached one hundred degrees. Washington thought that made them vulnerable, especially to his newly trained forces, and decided to attack them at Monmouth, New Jersey. Some of his generals weren't entirely supportive of the plan, but Washington was motivated.

On June 28, 1778, the two sides fought valiantly on several fronts, all day, to a near-draw. Each side lost just over a hundred men to death, half of whom died of heat stroke, not wounds, with several hundred wounded or missing. Among the American wounded was artilleryman William Hays, whose thirty-three-year-old wife, Mary, had been living with the army since Valley Forge. During the battle, she and other women brought buckets and pitchers of water from a nearby spring to cool down the soldiers and swab the cannons. When her husband fell, Mary reportedly stepped in for him, swabbing the cannons with water the others brought. That day she earned the nickname "Molly Pitcher."

After the Battle of Monmouth, the British continued on their way to New York. The Americans finished retaking New Jersey, and the war headed into its second phase. This time the United States had France as its ally, which would make all the difference.

Rush returned to Maryland to fetch his family, and on July 21, 1778, they walked back into their Philadelphia home and commenced the updated version of their previous life, with a one-year-old son and another baby on the way. Philadelphia was festering with the stink of summer and occupation—which did have one unfortunate upside. "The filth left by the British Army in the streets," Rush noted, "created a good deal of sickness." He "quickly recovered" his business "with a large accession of new patients" and was able to attract a new crew of apprentices.

In August, an epidemic began of what Rush called "a bilious fever" and was most likely typhus. Unfortunately, Rush got sick. Within a few days, he was too ill for his assistants to care for him—and Julia, pregnant, had to stay away from him. His most trusted fellow physicians were called in to treat him: Dr. John Morgan, with whom he had reconnected while waging war against Shippen; Dr. John Redman, to whom both Morgan and Rush had apprenticed; and Dr. Adam Kuhn, Rush's colleague at the medical school before it had closed down for the war.

During the worst of his illness, in mid-September, Rush was deliriously ill for eleven straight days. Rumors circulated in town that he was dead.

"I was . . . ," he later recalled, on "the brink of the grave. My physicians . . . shook their heads as they went out of my room. My friends could do little more than weep at my bedside. I made my will and took leave of life. But in the extremity of my danger it pleased God . . . to break the violence of my disease."

While the fever broke on September 24, he was still incapacitated for another five or six weeks: "My recovery was slow, and the loss sustained by my long confinement was considerable." It seems likely that some form of secondary depression prolonged his convalescence, which kept him from getting out of bed for weeks at a time. Rush detailed his long illness, and his treatment for it, in a commonplace book about his "physical history."

He returned to practice near year's end and started selling tickets for new lectures in chemistry, which he hadn't given in some time. He was also called to help a family member who was sicker than he was: his father-in-law, who came to Philadelphia to show him a growth on his upper lip that he had been keeping secret from his wife.

Rush diagnosed Richard Stockton with cancer and arranged for him to be operated on—all without telling Julia or her mother, at Stockton's request. (Stockton's cover story, which was true, was that he was in town helping Betsey Graeme Fergusson with the legal nightmare of wresting her family estate back from her estranged loyalist husband.) Stockton's family found out only after the surgery: during his convalescence in Philadelphia, they moved in with the Rushes. One benefit was that Annis Stockton could help out during the last weeks of Julia's pregnancy.

It was a challenging way to end perhaps the most challenging year of Rush's life. But at least everyone was together during the holidays. They remained together until New Year's Day 1779, when Julia gave birth to their daughter Anne Emily.

And Benjamin Rush began a new year able to feel hopeful again.

part two

AMERICAN HIPPOCRATES

26

For the next five years, Benjamin Rush struggled to recenter himself, to keep a distance from politics and live "a most unrepublican life, wholly devoted to my family and my patients." This was not easy. Much was in flux in Philadelphia, as in Boston and New York: every place the war passed through would spend years settling into a new normal. It was like the aftermath of a once-in-a-century flood—the water had receded, but the ground beneath them, once fully submerged, was still mushy and would take awhile longer to become solid again.

When Rush later looked back on this challenging period, he tried to assess the impact on the human body of the events of the American Revolution. "The minds of the citizens of the United States were wholly unprepared for their new situation," he wrote. "The excess of the passion for liberty, inflamed by the successful issue of the war, produced, in many people, opinions and conduct which could not be removed by reason, nor restrained by government. For a while, they threatened to render abortive the goodness of heaven to the United States, in delivering them from the evils of slavery and war. The extensive influence which these opinions had upon the understandings, passions, and morals of many of the citizens of the United States, constituted a species of insanity."

While he meant this to describe the citizenry, it was also a fairly honest diagnosis of himself.

Rush returned to teaching, but in 1779 the commonwealth dismissed the trustees of the College of Philadelphia—they were mostly loyalists in the Church of England. The school was replaced by the University of the State of Pennsylvania, which was supposed to be more secular, but its provost, Rev. John Ewing, and its trustees were largely Presbyterians. In theory, that was better for Rush, but the Presbyterians had their own divisions. Reverend Ewing was the more old-school leader of the First Presbyterian Church of Philadelphia and tied to the politically radical Pennsylvanians; the Rush family worshipped at the Second Presbyterian Church, which was considered part of the more modern, spiritual, "New Light" Presbyterian movement, and the doctor was a republican. Rush initially refused to teach at the new school. He eventually conceded, but friction with Ewing was inevitable.

The new university went through growing pains, as Rush and John Morgan tried to settle in at the reconstituted medical school. Both were initially distracted by their insatiable desire for vengeance against William Shippen. Morgan spent several years pushing for the director-general to be court-martialed, and Rush allowed himself to be sucked back into the fray. In early 1780, as Washington's troops wintered in Morristown, New Jersey, Shippen was arrested and charged there. His court-martial began in March, and Rush came up from Philadelphia to testify.

On March 20, he gave testimony for just an hour before proceedings ended for the day—after which he was invited to share a meal with George Washington. It was the first time they had spoken in the two years since Rush had privately criticized the commander in chief's strength as a leader and publicly resigned his commission.

If Washington had any agenda beyond a casual meal—for example, to tacitly remind Rush they were in the middle of war and nothing good would come of trashing Shippen in a military court, since Americans were supposed to be fighting *the British*, not each other—it was lost on the doctor. In his brief notes about the day, Rush wrote only, "Dined with Gen'l Washington. The General uncommonly cheerful—talked chiefly of the affairs of Ireland." He later wrote that Washington "treated me with a degree of attention which led me to believe he had magnanimously forgotten my letter to Governor Henry." It was probably wishful thinking on Rush's part that all had been forgiven, but Washington seemed to be acknowledging that he and the doctor were still bonded as fellow members of a select fraternity and needed to move on.

Rush testified for five hours the next day, and another five and a half the day after that, holding nothing back. The legal proceedings continued, on and off, for several months, making Morgan and Shippen, and to a slightly lesser degree Rush, look petty and vindictive—especially when the war resumed in North and South Carolina as the weather warmed, and they were still offering testimony about possibly pilfered wine from three years earlier. Washington just wanted the medical infighting to end.

Shippen was acquitted of all charges but only by a single vote, so Washington threw the final decision on him to Congress, because "the Medical Department is in such disorder already." Some congressmen made it clear that they believed Shippen was "reprehensible" and had been involved in "speculation in some articles," but ultimately they upheld his acquittal and reappointed him for another year.

Morgan and Shippen continued dueling, in letters published in the *Pennsylvania Packet*. Rush couldn't resist writing to Shippen, rubbing open every old wound and ending with "your reappointment . . . after the crimes you have committed, is a new phenomenon in the history of mankind. It will serve like a high-water mark to show posterity the degrees of corruption that marked the present stage of the American Revolution."

The university announced it would offer Shippen his old teaching position back when he retired from the military. Morgan and Rush both said they would quit, but Provost Ewing ignored them. (Later Shippen did join the faculty.)

The affair changed Morgan, who was never really the same. Still a talented doctor, and important in the Philadelphia medical community, he nonetheless seemed broken inside.

Rush wanted to avoid that fate, hoping to chalk the whole experience up to his own "indiscreet zeal for justice and humanity." He would not "repent" his actions, nor would he forget what had been "so injurious and distressing to me." Rather, he would focus on what he had achieved: "the alteration I effected in the hospital arrangements was the means of saving many lives. It saved likewise . . . several millions of dollars annually to the United States."

While this was going on, Julia Rush, pregnant with her third child, took the high road—and became more involved in the war effort than her husband. She joined a national group of prominent wives—including Martha Washington and the spouses of several governors—to raise money for America's troops.

"The women of America have at last become principals in the glorious American Controversy," Rush wrote Adams. ". . . My dear wife who You know in the beginning of the war had all the timidity of her Sex as to the issue of the war . . . was One of the ladies employed to sollicit benefactions for the Army. She distinguished herself by her Zeal and Address in this business." In fact, Julia was "so thouroughly enlisted in the cause of her country" that she reproached him for being less involved.

During her fundraising in the summer of 1780, Julia gave birth to another son. They named him Richard, after her father—in the hope of bringing him some small measure of happiness, since his cancer had returned and was spreading quickly. Julia's mother, Annis, described his last months as particularly torturous. She found herself "totaly Confin'd to the chamber of a dear and dying husband, whose nerves have become so Iritable as to not be able, to bear the Scraping of a pen, on paper in his room, or Even the folding up of a letter, which deprives me of one of the greatest releifs I could have."

Richard Stockton's death in early 1781 deeply affected Julia and her family; her twenty-year-old single sister Sukey came to

Philadelphia and moved in with the Rushes. The doctor suddenly had a more prominent role in the family, and Julia had many more responsibilities—although with those came a substantial inheritance, which they needed because the economy in Philadelphia was weak, and many men were still at war. Julia quickly got pregnant again, with a daughter named for Rush's mother, Susanna, who died after just four months. She then became pregnant with another daughter—named Elizabeth, for Betsey Graeme Fergusson—who also died after four months. So much loss in such a short time was devastating.

THERE WAS GOOD news, finally, from the war, as Washington's troops did better and were augmented by a dramatic influx of troops from France, fighting on multiple fronts. Battles in the North and the West were stalemated, but the summer of 1781 saw the combined American and French forces finally make a breakthrough in the South. Since the dark winter of 1778, Rush had gradually grown more optimistic, and during these last battles, a new phrase sneaked into his correspondence: "all will be well."

When the British were defeated in October 1781 at Yorktown, Virginia, and Cornwallis surrendered, the war was effectively over. Peace talks began in Paris, with Franklin and Adams playing major roles. They sought to negotiate not only British acknowledgment of the United States and an American amnesty for its loyalists, but a dramatic expansion of territory, extending the nation west to the Mississippi River and north well into Canada. They negotiated under the authority of the Articles of Confederation, a provisional constitution that had enabled congressional decision making since 1777, although it had never been formally ratified. That finally happened in 1781, and America became a free confederation of states.

Rush was ecstatic over the victory, but he also viewed the end of the fighting as the true start of the American experiment. The new nation would be free to create the republican government it had fought for—and equally free to mess it up.

The next steps would involve new federal and state constitutions, and the basic structures of this new democracy would be the subjects of broad, passionate debate. But Rush was just as concerned with how Americans would rise to their new personal responsibilities as public citizens—how they could best become what he called "republican machines."

He was particularly fascinated—and worried—about the challenge of teaching responsibility and morality and the place of faith in a nation that, until very recently, had religious freedom but also had a state church and a monarch with divine rights. Rush believed the most important force in turning Americans into secular "republican machines"—with an appreciation for both faith and freedom of religion—would be education, both the existing private institutions and all the new public schools that would need to be created. He saw public education as the major missing cornerstone of the new nation—and that meant public education for everyone, regardless of class, gender, ethnicity, or race.

Rush was especially concerned with how education in the new America would expand beyond the crowded eastern port cities—and he was not happy with the politics at the University of the State of Pennsylvania.

So in 1782, he began his first postwar effort to be a more "republican machine" himself: he set out to raise the money and the political will to create the nation's first "back-country" college. The nation's westernmost educational institution would be located in the far off Scotch-Irish village of Carlisle, Pennsylvania—which he had not yet visited—on the site of a struggling grammar school. He wanted to name the school for John Dickinson, with whom he was once again aligned in Pennsylvania politics (against Tom Paine and the radicals), along with his wife Mary. Rush's original name for the school was John and Mary's College, which Dickinson himself rejected because it sounded too much like the College of William and Mary in Virginia. He later settled on Dickinson College instead.

Mostly, however, Rush focused on his family and medical obligations: his private patients, his lectures on chemistry, and volunteer care at the Philadelphia Alms House, a Quaker institution that offered a free clinic as well as food and housing for the poor.

But one position in the city's medical establishment eluded him: he was still the only professor at the medical school who had not been invited to join the prestigious, all-volunteer medical staff of Pennsylvania Hospital. He had guest lectured there and filled in during rounds, but no permanent place seemed forthcoming. In the late summer of 1783, a spot opened on the staff because John Morgan, still losing interest in his work, quit over a dispute with the hospital's board of managers regarding a decision to offer free treatment for venereal disease, which he claimed would contribute "rather to the growth than the diminution of immorality."

The first days of September 1783 were momentous for Dr. Rush. On Wednesday, September 3, he officially joined the staff at Pennsylvania Hospital. That day he discharged six patients, admitted three, declared one dead (a French seaman named Jean), and looked in on the other forty-five. Twenty-seven of them had an L next to their names in hospital managers' records, which meant they were "lunatics."

That same Wednesday, the Treaty of Paris was signed in France, officially ending the Revolutionary War. In the final negotiation, Adams and Franklin had not been able to annex Canada as they had hoped. But they did double the size of America, extending the western borders of New York, Pennsylvania, Virginia, North and South Carolina, and Georgia to the borders they maintain today, and adding territory all the way to the Mississippi River that would become Ohio, Michigan, Kentucky, Indiana, Tennessee, Illinois, Wisconsin, and parts of Alabama, Mississippi, and Louisiana.

The peace also eased communications between the countries, so Rush could more reliably receive letters from his friends and mentors in England, Scotland, and France. One of the first was from Dr. William Cullen at the University of Edinburgh. Rush wrote back gleefully: "the events of the late war have not lessened my attachment to my venerable master. The members of the republic of science all belong to the same family. What has physic to do with taxation or independence?"

Rush also heard from John Adams, whose traveling secretary carried the letter to America along with his main task—bringing the actual Treaty of Paris to Congress. "I hope the States are Settling fast into order, and that all will go well," Adams wrote. "This Treaty . . . was all We could obtain . . . but I assure you We were very glad to get the Hand put to this. I was in hopes to have Soon Seen you in Philadelphia, but Congress have had the Goodness to resolve upon a Commission . . . which will detain me, I know not how long." It would be nearly five more years.

On Tuesday, September 9, the final charter for Dickinson College was approved, and Rush began work in earnest to develop a curriculum that would create Americans who deserved and understood the responsibilities of their new liberty.

Not long after that, Julia realized she was pregnant again. It was quite a couple weeks.

The Rushes were now living in a large rented property at the corner of Second Street and Lodge Alley, which ran between Second and Third just south of Chestnut, not far from their previous home. (In fact, in Rush's entire life, he never lived more than six or seven blocks from where he grew up.) The three-story main house had a one-story building attached as a kitchen; a second three-story building had its own kitchen for boarders and staff; another smaller one-story building would be used for Rush's medical office; there was a garden and greenhouse and a stable large enough for six horses and two carriages. According to Rush's taxes that year, they were keeping only two horses of their own and one cow, as well as a carriage in which two or three could sit, and his single-seat "chair" for house calls. (He may have rented the other stable space.)

They were renting, in part, because Rush was buying property in the country to create his own "Cottage Farm" retreat, in a different spot than his mother's Rush Hill. As far back as his love letters courting Julia, he had dreamed of "our little cottage," in which they would "pass a rainy day, or a winter's evening in reading alternately to each other select passages from the most useful, or entertaining books." He bought over a hundred acres northeast of the city, in what was then Oxford Township, and started building his summer dream house there.

Rush increasingly spent his time and energy at Pennsylvania Hospital. Now thirty-eight, six years older than the hospital itself, he would become indispensable to its recovery after the war. As the wunderkind of the first generation taught by the landmark hospital's physicians, he now represented the proud medical heritage of a new nation and aspired to the mantles of both of its founders: not only Dr. Thomas Bond but Benjamin Franklin.

He was still a tall, striking figure and spellbinding talker, but time, war, illness, and fatherhood had changed his countenance. His face was fuller, his hair had turned prematurely gray from illness, and his hairline was receding, further exposing his big head. At the end of 1783, he sat for a portrait by Charles Willson Peale, who had moved his family back into the city and was developing a gallery at his house down the street. He had originally commissioned the portrait back in 1776, when Peale painted Julia, but waited until now to have it done (in part, perhaps, because he could better afford to pay for it).

Rush decided to use the portrait to recast himself as a man of letters, science, and philosophy. He was portrayed sitting in his study at a small wooden table, looking up with a half-smile as if just interrupted from writing a sentence—which reads, "We come

Rush portrait by Charles Willson Peale

now gentlemen to investigate the cause of earthquakes." His graying hair is tied tightly back, and he wears a comfortable salmon-colored dressing gown sometimes called a banyan, which was used in portraiture to show the subject's body being at ease, allowing his mind more freedom.

Behind him is a bookshelf draped in emerald fabric; the titles, chosen to be clearly visible, include the works of his medical hero Thomas Sydenham; a French-language version of the Bible; two books by Benjamin Franklin (*Experiments and Observations*, his writing on electricity, and *Philosophical Works*); the British political essays of Sir William Temple and Sidney Algernon; works of seventeenth-century French theologian Blaise Pascal, English philosopher and Deism critic Joseph Butler, philosophers James Beattie and Thomas Reid, and several others. The titles were a declaration not only of his extensive library but his diverse intellectual and scientific influences.

As for Rush's face, it wasn't the most engaging rendering ever done of him, nor was it as typically animated as Peale's other work. But the painting made Rush appear exactly as he wanted to see himself: as a man of science, philosophy, and literature, surrounded by ideas.

27

Rush's rounds at Pennsylvania Hospital became a new cornerstone of his life. They were done at least twice a week—staff physicians did not see patients every day—and Rush quickly became known for starting his rounds at eleven a.m. with obsessive punctuality.

A guest invited to observe Rush giving rounds during his early years on staff was struck by both the size and grandeur of the hospital and the sheer drama of watching him work and teach. There were still very few hospitals of any kind in America, and since they were largely for indigent patients, they almost never featured such splendid architecture. "Such is the elegance of these buildings, the care and attention to the sick, the spacious and clean apartments, and the perfect order in every thing," the visitor wrote, "that it seemed more like a palace than a hospital and one would almost be tempted to be sick if they could be so well provided for."

Rounds began on the second floor ward—a broad room with high ceilings and large windows—where female patients were treated. There were two rows of beds, with chairs and small tables between them. When Rush entered the ward, there was "the most profound silence and order," even though he was being trailed by more than twenty people, including several physicians "and all the young students in Physic in the City."

Pennsylvania Hospital when Rush joined the staff in 1783: painting (left) of original building viewed from undeveloped south of town; front view of 8th Street entrance

The process was quite formal. Every patient was in a bed or a chair, their dressings "all ready to be taken off and exposed to view the instant the Doctor came to them." When Rush approached a patient, he was quickly brought up to date on everything that had happened before and after hospitalization; then the apothecary described all the medicines that had been employed. Rush offered his observations "in every case worthy of notice," pointing out "its nature, the probable tendency, and the reason for the mode of treatment." Everyone then followed him down the staircase to the first floor, the all-male ward, where the process was repeated. He explained that a number of the cases were chronic patients, many with "swellings and ulcerations," which he said were the result of "their drinking spirituous liquors," as he never failed to remind them that "the greater proportion of his patients in the city . . . originated from the same cause."

The rounds finished in the lower, partially underground story, where Rush and his students "took a view of the Maniacs" in their locked ward, which had individual locked cells, "about ten feet square, made as strong as a prison." Each cell door had "a hole, large enough to give them food . . . which is closed with a little door secured with strong bolts." Each cell had a window high up on the wall, with a large iron grate inside to prevent the patient from reaching and breaking the glass. The ward was filled to its capacity of about thirty patients, men and women.

"Some of them were extremely fierce and raving, nearly or quite naked; some singing and dancing; some in despair," the visitor noted. "Some were dumb and would not open their mouths; others incessantly talking." He found it "curious indeed to see in what different strains their distraction raged . . . [a] distressing view of what human nature is liable to."

As for his private practice, Rush had been treating patients in his office and at their homes for more than a decade, and he had recently taken on a partner—his young cousin James Hall—to handle the more routine work. But the experience of interacting regularly with the city's most serious cases moved and upset him. The endless assault of illness deepened ideas he had developed while treating the wounds of war. Even during peacetime, hospital medicine was a battlefield.

The single most devastating illness, Rush quickly figured out, also appeared to be the most preventable. In 1784, after less than a year on the hospital staff, he published a ten-page pamphlet called *An Enquiry into the Effects of Spirituous Liquors upon the Human Body, and Their Influence upon the Happiness of Society*, which offered one of the first modern descriptions of the effects of chronic alcohol use. Spirituous liquors, originally used primarily as medicine, now created a *need* for medicine. They could produce "a sickness at the stomach, and vomiting in the morning," he said, along with a tremor in the hands, such that "persons who labour under it are hardly able to lift a teacup to their heads," edema, and "obstruction of the liver."

Overuse of spirits, he said, could also instigate "madness . . . with all its terrors and consequences." Rush was certain that:

> Spirituous liquors destroy more lives than the sword. War has its intervals of destruction—but spirits operate at all times and seasons upon human life. . . . [They] fill our church yards with premature graves . . . fill the Sheriff's docket with executions . . . [and] crowd our jails. . . . [They] produce debts—disgrace and bankruptcy. Among farmers they produce idleness with its usual

> consequences, such as houses without windows—barns without roofs [and] . . . half clad dirty children without principles, morals or manners. . . . A people corrupted by strong drink cannot long be a *free* people.

Rush was not against all alcoholic beverages, and his pamphlet reflected the realities of 1784. Low-alcohol wines were the aspirin of the day, so discouraging their use would not only be impractical but might be seen as tantamount to malpractice. Nor was drinking wine, beer, or cider considered problematic, especially since city water wasn't always so healthful. "Few men ever become *habitual* drunkards upon wine," Rush said. Its effects "upon the *temper* are likewise in most cases directly opposite to those . . . of spirituous liquors. It must be a bad heart indeed that is not rendered more chearful and more generous by a few glasses of wine." Rush himself drank wine with supper almost every day.

The drink Rush most recommended was "vinegar and water sweetened with sugar or molasses," not only for warm-weather refreshment but also to help combat addiction to distilled spirits. Otherwise, abstinence was the key. "No man was ever *gradually* reformed from drinking spirits," he said. It was important to "leave them off *suddenly and entirely* . . . avoid tasting [or] . . . even smelling them until long habits of abstinence have subdued [one's] affection for them." To prevent "any inconveniences from the sudden loss of their stimulus upon his stomach"—liquor was viewed primarily as a stimulant—Rush recommended drinking "plentifully of camomile or of any other bitter tea, or a few glasses of sound old wine every day."

He was optimistic that abstinence—or the current medical version of abstinence, which included wine and weak beers—could cure addiction: "I have great pleasure in adding, that I have seen a number of people who have been *effectually* restored to health—to character—and to usefulness to their families and to society by following this advice."

While the pamphlet was meant for the general public, Rush hoped his colleagues would read it as well. Since the war ended, the entire hospital seemed to be developing a drinking problem;

the board of managers was amazed to see their bills for wine and rum skyrocketing. Some of this represented proper medication, but Rush had no doubt that some of it represented a dramatic overmedication of the patients and self-medication of the staff.

Next to alcoholism, what intrigued and horrified Rush most in his rounds were the patients locked in the basement cells. He felt immediately that the circumstances these patients lived under were absolutely unacceptable. But the "lunatics," who most people still viewed as damned rather than diseased, presented a unique and troubling situation. They weren't truly in the hospital to be treated, because nobody knew for sure what their treatment should be. They were in the basement primarily to keep them safe from society, and society safe from them. The first step in improving their situation would simply involve warehousing them more benevolently. But even that proposition was challenging; nobody seemed to have the slightest idea how to proceed.

Rush had first encountered this problem in the mid-1760s, when he visited the hospital as an apprentice to Dr. Redman. In 1765 Thomas Perrine, a mentally ill sailor, had escaped from his basement cell, run through the hospital to the top floor—a decorative cupola overlooking Eighth Street—and simply refused to come down. The hospital brought him bedding and began to feed him up there—which they did for the next nine years. According to hospital records, he never left the cupola for any reason, not even to warm himself near a fire during the coldest winters. He was also "noted for his long nails, matted beard and hair."

Twenty years later most psychiatric patients were still locked in the basement. There they spent most of their days overseen by the "cell keeper," a nonmedical staffer paid about three pounds ($306) a month—the same as the hospital's gardener—to keep order and keep the patients safe, sometimes with the help of a nurse. It was the hospital's most thankless work; cell keepers were often drunk on the job and frequently had to be replaced. The hospital had only fifteen basement cells—each of which could accommodate two patients sleeping on straw on the floor—so some mental health patients had to be cared for in the regular wards, which only added to the challenge.

One of the hospital's more appalling practices had been to allow members of the general public to pay four pence ($1.70) to come in and gape at the lunatics. The managers considered the fee a step in the right direction: before it was instituted, a great "Throng of People . . . led by Curiousity" could descend on the basement to bait the patients for free. But in August 1784, one of Rush's former students, Dr. John Foulke—now a member of the junior staff—campaigned to change the rules. Soon only two people could visit the basement at a time, and under no circumstances were they allowed to talk to the patients. But their visits were still overseen only by the cell keeper, who often bent the rules. And management oversight of "lunatics" was as lax as ever; their treatment had been supervised by aging founder Thomas Bond, who died in 1784 at the age of seventy but wasn't replaced for several years.

In the meantime, Rush and other younger doctors tried to figure out how to improve living conditions in the cells. Given space constraints and challenged finances after the war, no change would come easily. But Rush had something more ambitious in mind than just making these patients more comfortable. He sought a more radical kind of progress: to actually better understand what was wrong with those locked in the basement and even one day know how to treat them as patients, not as prisoners.

Rush discussed some of these broader ideas about patient care with the doctors and trainees at Pennsylvania Hospital. According to notes from some of his private lectures to the staff, as early as 1783 he began describing madness in new ways. Instead of viewing aberrant, antisocial, or self-destructive behaviors as the result of immorality or lack of self-control, he talked about them in the language of medicine. He told the medical staff and students that melancholia, or depression, was "a disease of the body as well as the mind," and that mania was a "disease of the brain." Both illnesses had "various causes," including "hereditary disposition." At a time when most viewed lunacy as demonic possession or lack of will or character, these were surprising ideas.

Rush and his colleagues were also coming to appreciate the importance of talking, and listening, to the occupants of the cells. One of the first psychiatric patients he encountered was a woman in her late sixties named Hannah Garrett Lewis, who was admitted around the same time Rush joined the hospital staff. He may have recognized her, because she was well known on the streets of Philadelphia for her incessant public preaching, which she had done for decades, since the death of her husband in the 1740s.

Her illness was first noticed by her fellow Quakers at the Philadelphia Meeting House, who characterized her as "under Great Indisposition of Mind." She had powerful delusions, believing herself to be the eldest daughter of George II and the rightful heir to his throne, with her tiny one-windowed home her "castle." Her many erratic behaviors included eating broiled mice and cats, catching mosquitoes and flies, tearing off their heads or wings and keeping them in a jar "for the presumption of daring to bite the King's daughter."

Hannah was poor but not destitute: she had inherited some money from her father, which she spent down until she had to survive on 15 pounds ($1,500) a year. And that was enough to allow her to come to Pennsylvania Hospital as a paying patient (which most of those being treated for mental illness were not). A fellow Quaker had brought her there and paid her "security"—patients weren't admitted unless someone agreed to pay their burial expenses if they died there. But since her community was no longer able to take care of her, she could spend the rest of her life there.

Rush diagnosed Hannah Lewis with a "mania" in her charts, which he also described in a case report as "grief induced madness . . . in middle life" triggered by "the loss of her husband." She was one of the first patients whom Rush and others on the staff really tried to talk to, to better understand her thought processes and what Rush viewed as "errors of thinking."

Hannah Lewis's case presented physicians with a unique opportunity to try to treat the most publicly mad woman from the streets of Philadelphia as an actual patient with a psychiatric illness, taking her delusions and thought disorders seriously as symptoms and studying them in the hope of healing her.

IN THE AFTERMATH of the war, a great deal of healing was still needed all around. In the spring of 1784, Rush received a letter from Lady Jane Leslie, who was now a wife and mother. She yearned to understand more about her brother David's demise at the Battle of Princeton seven years earlier. She knew very little about his last days or his death or even what had happened to his body.

David had always carried a picture in his breast pocket, and Lady Jane wondered if Rush knew anything about it—perhaps someone had given it to him. She still hoped there might be a chance to get it back.

Rush didn't know what had become of David's personal effects—he assumed they had all been stolen. But he did know exactly where his body was, because he had personally taken care of his burial. In fact, her letter reminded him that he had held off on erecting a tombstone because of "the insecure state of graveyards during the war." Now, seven years later, he could finally take care of it.

Rush then offered Lady Jane a surprisingly intimate view of his own life, providing us with a rare real-time snapshot of him in his late thirties. He told her about his very happy marriage, and their children, including the two that were "no more" and another that was on the way. He described how well he was doing financially, admitting that "I got a pretty little fortune with Mrs. Rush and have added to it from the income of my business so as to produce an estate which, if thrown in to cash, would yield about three hundred pounds [$30,100] a year sterling."

Rush then shared something surprising: Julia was "no stranger" to their teenage romance in Scotland and had "more than once" wept over (he used the word "bedewed") their old love letters. But she had ultimately come to believe that Rush's heart was "more valuable to her" because it had been "so long and so faithfully preserved" by Lady Jane: "she knows that she owes her conquest in part to [you]."

It was a strange thing to admit but typical of Rush's extreme candor about relationships and his fascination with the mechanics of human emotion.

28

On September 14, 1785, Benjamin Franklin returned to Philadelphia for the first time in nine years. When his ship, the *London Packet*, arrived in the port, his son sent a small boat out to fetch him, and he was greeted at the Market Street wharf by "a crowd of people with huzzas" who then followed him "with acclamations quite to my door." Franklin was seventy-nine and not in great health—one reason why, during his time in Paris, he contributed a last major invention: bifocal glasses. But his presence immediately energized Rush and many others.

His return came at just the right time, because the original alliance of the states was beginning to fray due to monetary and land disputes not clearly addressed in the Articles of Confederation. Philadelphia's intellectual and political elite felt unmoored, as the city was no longer the meeting place of Congress, now called the Confederation Congress; it had moved to New York.

The American Philosophical Society, for which Franklin had been serving as president in absentia, seized on the impact of his return to signal that intellectual life in the new, free United States had officially begun—and to renew its own ambition to be the nation's premier forum for "useful knowledge." The society also hoped to finish fund-raising for a new freestanding headquarters next to the State House, so it revived its annual oration, which had been given only twice since the beginning of the war.

At its December 2, 1785, meeting, the society invited Benjamin Rush to deliver the oration, "as early in the year as may be convenient for him." He readily agreed, both to honor Franklin and "to atone for my long absence from the temple of science."

Rush dove into a more active role in the group, to help fill out its scientific offerings. At the December 16, 1785, meeting, he delivered a paper on a recent bilious fever outbreak just after another member read a paper from Berlin comparing "the Vegetation of different plants." In early January, Rush was elected an officer of the society for the first time since before the war, as was scientist David Rittenhouse (best known for his expertise in astronomy) and his fellow physician Adam Kuhn.

Then at the February 3 meeting, Rush presented a quickly written paper on "Doctor Martin's Cancer Powder," which some considered a "quack medicine" since its label claimed it could cure *all* cancers. Rush and his young partner, Dr. Hall, tested the powder and determined it to be largely arsenic—considered a legitimate treatment for cancerous sores but ineffective for more life-threatening tumors. Rather than dismissing the product's overreaching claims as quackery, Rush felt there was a lesson to be learned from it. Physicians and patients, he thought, had to understand the difference between skin cancers (which could be treated topically), cancers of internal organs (for which "the knife should always be preferred"), and cancers "that taint the fluids, or infect the whole lymphatic system" (which were still largely incurable). Too many people, he worried, considered cancer untreatable, but pronouncing "a disease incurable, is often to render it so." Others too often "neglected" tumors and sores from "an apprehension that they are incurable," or out of misguided advice "to let them alone." There were many kinds of quackery.

Two weeks later the Philosophical Society met to discuss the relaunch of the annual oration. Rush had told them he was ready, after weeks in which "every leisure moment from the duties of my profession [was] taken up in preparing it." The society agreed to print up one thousand tickets and put ads in the newspapers. The subject of the lecture was not announced; Dr. Rush himself was the draw.

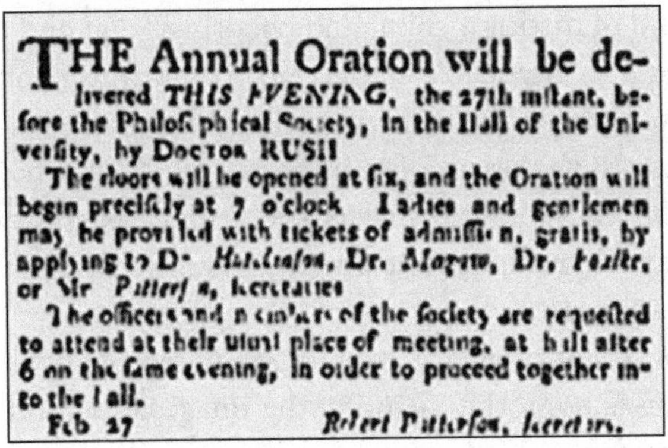

THE Annual Oration will be delivered THIS EVENING, the 27th inſtant, before the Philoſophical Society, in the Hall of the Univerſity, by DOCTOR RUSH

The doors will be opened at ſix, and the Oration will begin preciſely at 7 o'clock Ladies and gentlemen may be provided with tickets of admiſſion, gratis, by applying to Dr *Hutchinſon*, Dr. *Magaw*, Dr. *Foulke*, or Mr *Patterſon*, Secretaries

The officers and members of the ſociety are requeſted to attend at their uſual place of meeting, at half after 6 on the ſame evening, in order to proceed together into the Hall.

Feb 27 *Robert Patterſon, Secretary.*

Ad in The Pennsylvania Packet *the day Rush gave his oration at the American Philosophical Society*

AT AROUND FIVE p.m. on Monday, February 27, 1786, Rush arrived at Franklin's house on Market to meet with his fellow society officers. For the formal procession, the fifteen of them walked together two blocks in the late afternoon chill to the Hall of the University, at the corner of Fourth and Mulberry (now Arch). As they entered the hall, a crowd of Philadelphia's brightest and socially finest greeted them—what the society's minutes described as "a very respectable assembly of gentlemen & ladies."

Julia Rush was likely not among them, since she was about to give birth to their seventh child at any moment.

After paying a glowing tribute to Franklin, Rush announced that he was taking as his subject "An enquiry into the influence of physical causes on the moral faculty." It was a subject he had been thinking about for more than a decade—since casually suggesting to a fellow abolitionist that it might explain some of the physical and psychological effects of slavery—and he had drafted an essay over seven years before. But he had waited and cogitated, because these were not ideas to voice lightly, even as they were evolving. Rush was fairly certain his talk was going to upset people. "I foresee, that men who have been educated in the mechanical habits of adopting popular or established opinions will revolt at the doctrine I am about to deliver," he said, though he hoped that "men of sense and genius will hear my propositions with candour."

Rush began by defining the "moral faculty" as the "power in the human mind of distinguishing and choosing good and evil . . . virtue or vice." He then laid out the crux of his argument: that there were "physical causes" for many actions that had previously been viewed through the prism of morality and will. Much of what was labeled immorality could, in fact, be a manifestation of physical illness—requiring medical treatment, and prayers that the medical treatment worked.

"Our books of medicine contain many records of the effects of physical causes upon the memory, the imagination and then judgment," he said:

> Their derangement has received different names, according to the number or nature of the faculties that are affected. The loss of memory has been called "amnesia;" false judgments upon one subject has been called "melancholia;" false judgment upon all subjects has been called "mania;" . . . Persons who labour under the derangement, or want, of these powers of the mind, are considered, very properly, as subjects of medicine; and there are many cases upon record that prove that their diseases have yielded to the healing art.

These conclusions were rooted in his observations at the Pennsylvania Hospital, where he had grown only more convinced that the "lunatics" and "madmen" were misunderstood and unfairly excluded from the possibility of treatment. If these cases were medical in nature, he understood, they could no longer be viewed exclusively through the prisms of morality and faith.

Personally, Rush had long been both fascinated and awed by the seemingly arbitrary dividing lines between science and religion. At the same time, he remained a man of deep personal faith, wrestling with the clash of religious and secular forces in many arenas. He and his wife were raising young children and thinking about how they should be brought up as citizens in a new republic, while organized religions were adjusting to the new realities and liberties of American life. He supported using the Bible to teach moral behavior, but he also believed in secular education. He was, in essence, trying to work out for himself the basic battle between religious belief and religious freedom—while addressing some of the world's leaders in worshiping at the altar of science. Almost everything he had to say in this lecture, he knew, would be blasphemous to someone he respected. Yet he forged ahead:

> If physical causes influence morals . . . may they not also influence religious principles and opinions?—I answer in the affirmative, and I have authority, from the records of physic, as well as from my own observations, to declare, that religious melancholy and madness, in all their variety of species, yield with more facility to medicine, than simply to polemical discourses or causistical advice.

Rush roundly dismissed prescribing prayers or scolding to address "fevers and madness," "hysteria and hypochondriasis," and any conditions inducing "preternatural irritability—sensibility—torpor—stupor—or mobility of the nervous system." It was "vain to attack these vices with lectures upon morality. They are only to be cured by medicine. . . . [and] laws for the suppression of vice and immorality will be as ineffectual as the increase and enlargement of jails."

Rush even talked about the rise of "humane societies," which attempted to rescue and revive people who were drowning, including many who attempted suicide. He found self-harm—those "crimes . . . most disgraceful to human nature"—to be horrifying. But he was intrigued by theories on how to combat self-destructive behavior, especially among adolescents. Suicidal thinking might be contagious, he suggested, "often propagated by means of newspapers," which he wasn't sure should cover self-harm or "the proceedings of our courts . . . when they expose, or punish, monstrous vices."

But since restraining the press was unlikely, he was deeply committed to preventing and, when possible, reversing suicidal acts: medicine "has penetrated the deep and gloomy abyss of death, and acquired fresh honors in his cold embraces."

Then, as he began winding down his address after twenty-five pages, he said:

> I am not so sanguine as to suppose that it is possible for man to acquire so much perfection from science, religion, liberty and good government as to cease to be mortal; but I am fully persuaded that from the combined actions of causes, which operate at once upon the reason, the moral faculty, the passions, the senses, the brain, the nerves, the blood and the heart, it is possible to produce such a change in the moral character of man, as shall raise him to a resemblance of angels—nay more, to the likeness of God himself.

That paragraph neatly summed up what Rush was coming to recognize as the challenge of his life, as well as the life of his new country. The next step in the ongoing American Revolution was to figure out how to balance, as best as possible, "science, religion, liberty and good government."

As Rush predicted, his oration received a powerfully mixed reaction. During the speech, there was a crowd control issue in the hall—the society's notes refer to the need "to prosecute such of those concerned" with what it described as a "roit [sic]" (which meant the writer either misspelled *riot* or misused the word *roit*, meaning to walk around idly).

Perhaps more surprising, something about the speech really bothered Benjamin Franklin. Just days after Rush delivered it, a cryptic note arrived at his home:

> My dear Friend,
>
> During our long acquaintance you have shown many instances of your regard for me, yet I must now desire you to add one more to the number, which is, that if you publish your ingenious discourse on the moral senses, you will totally omit and suppress that most extravagant encomium on your friend Franklin, which hurt me exceedingly in the unexpected hearing, and will mortify me beyond conception, if it should appear from the press.

Confiding in your compliance with this earnest request, I am ever my dear friend, yours most affectionately,

B. Franklin.

Rush quickly wrote back to Franklin, apologizing for whatever he had done to offend. He explained that he had shown the talk beforehand to their mutual friend and society officer David Rittenhouse, who told him he shouldn't "Alter one word of it."

Still, Rush was willing to make any changes Franklin wanted. "All your requests," he said, "have with me, the force of commands." He was anxious for the society to follow through on its plan to publish the lecture as a pamphlet, which wasn't going to happen if Franklin was displeased.

Over the next week, Rush became suddenly and deathly ill. He described his condition to various friends as "an attack of a fever," or "a severe attack of pleurisy" but did not elaborate. What is certain is that he feared he was about to die at the age of forty—which would make the publication of his "moral faculty" lecture the very last of his life. He hoped Franklin would agree to let him "send my last, as I did my first publication into the world, under the patronage of your name."

With Rush's life hanging in the balance, Julia gave birth to their seventh child—a boy they named James—on March 15. In the meantime, Franklin either softened or approved changes in the essay, because on April 12, the pamphlet was published. Its title page and all the newspaper ads included a quote attributed to John Locke, paraphrased from his *Second Treatise on Government*:

> Human Knowledge, under the present circumstances of our beings and constitutions, may be carried much further than it has hitherto been, if men would employ all their industry, and labor of thought, in improving the means of discovering truth. Morality is the science, and business of Mankind.

And the dedication page read:

TO
HIS EXCELLENCY
BENJAMIN FRANKLIN, ESQ.
PRESIDENT
OF THE
SUPREME EXECUTIVE COUNCIL
OF
PENNSYLVANIA,
THE FRIEND AND BENEFACTOR
OF
MANKIND,
THE FOLLOWING ORATION IS RESPECTFULLY INSCRIBED,
BY HIS GRATEFUL FRIEND,
AND HUMBLE SERVANT,
THE AUTHOR

Rush wrote a preface admitting that he was floating a radical argument, one that he was still coming to grips with himself. But the mission and the desire of the Philosophical Society, he said, was to encourage "useful ideas"—to boldly go where no thinkers had gone before. But given his already rocky reception, he also sought to temper his claims a bit. He was "so far from proving physical influence as a substitute for religious, moral, or rational instruction" that he offered the idea "only as a reinforcement to the obligations of reason and religion." And he was "sensible that in this new, and difficult inquiry," he had "only performed the drudgery of a pioneer; those who come after [me] upon this subject, will find a way opened, for extensive and important observations, and will probably enjoy with more certainty, than the author, the fruits of their labors."

Nevertheless, he made a prediction: if these new ideas had "the same operation upon the mind of the reader, that they had upon the mind of the author, they will at first be doubted—afterwards believed, and finally they will be propagated."

29

Rush's "moral faculty" pamphlet sold out its initial printing, and a second edition was quickly ordered, along with a printing in England. As he wrote to a friend from his sickbed, "It has had a quick sale and extensive circulation in this country. As it contains some new opinions in religion and morals, as well as in physic, it will stand in need of the protection of my friends in London to preserve it from the rage of criticism. If political prejudice blends itself with literature, I shall find no mercy from British reviewers."

Rush recuperated throughout the spring, and as soon as he was feeling up to it, he began writing again, this time with new urgency. He seemed to appreciate how little time he might have left to help deliver on the promises of the Revolution, and how much there was to get done. Discussions were heating up about new constitutions, the basic structures of government, and the political relationships between the states and the nascent federal political establishment. But he found himself equally if not more interested in the issues that, constitutions notwithstanding, communities and individuals would need to address through volunteerism, social action, philanthropy, and public pressure.

Education, *public* education, was the key. It was through an enlightened educational system that citizens could ask the big questions of democracy, learn the responsibilities of being republican machines, and meet the challenges of moral education in a secular democracy—or at least intelligently discuss them.

Rush's first foray into education, the founding of Dickinson College, had been successful: the school was up and running. (His travels to far-off Carlisle yielded a secondary, personal benefit: he had done some investing in the vast and inexpensive real estate of central Pennsylvania.) But he had been forced to pull back from Dickinson due to political and religious infighting, some of which pitted him against his provost at the University of the State of Pennsylvania, Rev. John Ewing.

Now Rush didn't want simply to start another school: he was thinking bigger. He wanted to create a public school system in Pennsylvania, which would be the nation's first. To jump-start this process, he published a new pamphlet, *A Plan for the Establishment of Public Schools and the Diffusion of Knowledge in Pennsylvania; To Which Are Added Thoughts Upon the Mode of Education Proper in a Republic.*

There were already a handful of public schools around the nation. (The Boston Latin School, the first, had been in existence for over 150 years.) But Rush was calling for something much more ambitious: a complete public school system for all children and teens in Pennsylvania. His plan called for the creation of a university system linking the University of the State of Pennsylvania and Dickinson College with an as-yet-to-be-established college in Pittsburgh, as well as the nation's first college for non-English-speaking immigrants, with all teaching in German. (This last, which Rush was already trying to help create in Lancaster, would be called Franklin College, later Franklin & Marshall.)

Rush proposed creating free primary and secondary schools in every township and an academy in each county to prepare students to enter college. The colleges and schools would have public libraries, and this diffusion of knowledge would be expected to create more local newspapers.

These schools were to teach not only young men but young women as well. "Women . . . must concur in all our plans of education . . . or no laws will ever render them effectual," he declared.

Women were to be taught not only "the usual branches of female education" but also "the principles of liberty and government; and the obligations of patriotism." Rush had always personally favored women's education, but this was the first time he honed statements about it for a policy-making audience:

> The opinions and conduct of men are often regulated by the women in the most arduous enterprizes of life, and their approbation is frequently the principal reward of the hero's dangers, and the patriot's toils. Besides, the First impressions upon the minds of children are generally derived from the women. Of how much consequence, therefore, is it in a republic, that they should think justly upon the great subjects of liberty and government!

As for the curriculum in these schools, Latin and Greek, the "learned or dead languages" of traditional education, would still be taught, but the main focus would be proficiency in the language of America, English, for reading, writing, and public speaking. English was the language that would most help the next generations succeed, whether they farmed or went on to the study of "law, physic, or divinity."

Crucially, the schools had to figure out a way to teach religion, because without it "there can be no virtue, and without virtue there can be no liberty, and liberty is the object and life of all republican governments." Certain "paradoxical opinions" of "modern times" held that it was "improper to fill the minds of youth with religious prejudices of any kind" because they should be allowed "to choose their own principles" once arriving "at an age in which they are capable of judging for themselves." While he personally preferred the teaching of his own religion, Christianity, he made it clear that "the history of the creation of man, and of the relation of our species to each other by birth," as "recorded in the Old Testament," the Hebrew Bible, "is the best refutation that can be given to the divine right of kings, and the strongest argument that can be used in favour of the original and natural equality of all mankind." Ultimately he would rather have "the opinions of Confucius or

Mahomed inculcated upon our youth, than see them grow up wholly devoid of a system of religious principles."

During the hottest part of the summer, Julia took the younger children to Morven, where her mother could dote on all of them. The older boys—John, nine, and Richard, six—remained in town with their father and a skeleton staff at the house. The boys liked riding with Rush on the small horse-drawn carriage he used to make house calls. And John especially was fascinated by Pennsylvania Hospital, where he followed his father through the upstairs wards and the surgical area. Rush was a little surprised when John "stood by me and saw a painful and bloody operation performed a few days ago without an emotion." At his age, Rush couldn't stand the sight of blood.

On Tuesday, August 23, Rush allowed John to accompany him to the basement to visit the mentally ill patients. All fifteen cells were occupied, two apiece. There were seven nonpaying patients, three of whom had been there twenty years or longer, and more than twenty paying patients, almost all of whom had come since the war ended. The windows at ground level allowed little ventilation from the hot summer air when the doctor and his precocious son, trailed by all of Rush's apprentices, descended past John Tire, the cell keeper.

"This morning," Rush wrote to Julia, John "went with me into the cell of a young woman once handsome and of a respectable family. She was chained to the floor. Upon seeing a potato in John's hand which the steward of the hospital had given him, she asked him for it and accompanied her request with tears. John advanced at once and gave it to her. She instantly filled her mouth with the whole of it, and for half a minute it seemed as if it would have choked her. John viewed her as if he had been petrified."

The nine-year-old remained silent until they left the hospital and were sitting comfortably in Rush's "chair"—the carriage—heading home. Then he erupted with questions for his father: "What is the cause of madness?" he asked, "And what caused the madness of the poor woman we just saw? Can you cure madness? How long does it last? Do people die from it?"

Intrigued by his son's passion and compassion, Rush offered what answers he could, then noted that the young man "seemed devoted to physic."

"Yes," John replied, "I will be nothing but a doctor."

Rush marveled that a boy his age could understand so much. "I have great pleasure in his conversation upon many subjects," he told Julia. "With a vivacity bordering upon folly, he seems to possess a solid and correct judgement. His memory is almost without [limit.]" John reminded him a lot of himself.

BY THE END of 1786, Rush was writing like there was no tomorrow—which perhaps he felt was the case, following his recent brush with mortality. He had developed new powers of concentration, working not just after everyone was asleep but also amid the daily hustle and bustle of his household, where five children under the age of ten were underfoot.

His output during this time was breathtaking, in volume and depth. And it came at an opportune moment in American publishing. After the reinvigoration of the Philosophical Society, one of Franklin's young protégés, a twenty-six-year-old Irish immigrant named Mathew Carey, took it upon himself to create, in Philadelphia, some of the first publications recognizable as magazines rather than newspapers or journals or almanacs.

Carey had published controversial political writing in his native Ireland as early as his midteens, making the British government unhappy by criticizing Parliament. At twenty-one he moved to Paris, where he worked in Franklin's printing office for a year before returning home, and at twenty-four, he smuggled himself onto a ship to America by dressing as a woman. In Philadelphia, he slowly began a publishing enterprise, funded in part by $400 ($9,890) the Marquis de Lafayette had given him to start his business. He opened a bookstore, started a newspaper, and then decided the new nation needed a national magazine, so he started *The Columbian Magazine (or Monthly Miscellany containing a view of History, Manners, Literature and Characters of the Year).*

Mathew Carey

For a prolific, ambitious writer like Rush, there was nothing quite like a new editor with pages to fill. One of his first pieces for *Columbian Magazine*—which he may have written for Carey but, just as likely, had written in a commonplace book to amuse himself and then offered to the voracious young editor—may have been a bit of self-diagnosis. "On the Different Species of Manias" was an inventive satire in the style of one of his literary heroes, Jonathan Swift, for which he retrofitted as social commentary diagnostic ideas that he was trying to introduce into the hospital. It listed twenty-six ways America had gone mad.

Dr. William Cullen, he explained, had divided madness into two forms: "mania," or "universal madness," and then "melancholia," a "partial madness" further divided into subcategories. Rush said this was "certainly too limited" for all the "partial insanity" he saw in the world. He wanted to provide a list of these near-madnesses "in the language of our country, because I wish to be understood by men of all classes, and by both sexes." He proposed a new definition of mania as a "want of perception, or an undue perception of truth, duty or interest," and went on to describe twenty-six different varieties.

First was "The Negro Mania," which though it had "formerly prevailed in the eastern and middle, is now confined chiefly to the southern states," where inhabitants:

> mistake their interest and happiness in supposing that their lands can be cultivated only by Negro slaves. . . . There is no reason why rice and indigo may not be cultivated by white men, as well as wheat and indian corn. It is true, if the owners of the soil in the Carolinas and Georgia, cultivated their lands with their own hands, they

> would not be able to roll in coaches, or to squander thousands of pounds yearly in visiting all the cities of Europe, but they would enjoy more health and happiness in a competency acquired without violating the laws of nature and religion.

Another kind of mania was the obsession with owning land and horses ("often an object of greater attachment with persons who are afflicted with this disorder, than a wife or a mistress"). Still another was "Liberty Mania," with which he might have been diagnosed himself: it "occupies the time and talents so constantly, as to lead men to neglect their families for the sake of taking care of the state. Such men expect liberty without law, government without power, sovereignty without a head, and wars without expense." Its corollary was "Monarchical Mania," found among "people who believe that 'a king can do no wrong.'" And of course republicans (like himself) were likely to contract "Republican Mania," because "every man, who attempts to introduce a republican form of government, where the people are not prepared for it by virtue and knowledge, is as much a madman as St. Anthony was, when he preached the Gospel to fishes."

"Donation Mania" afflicted those who "impoverish their families, by extravagant contributions to public undertakings, or who neglect their relations at their death, by bequeathing their estates to hospitals, colleges, and churches." Three different manias involved firearms: "Military Mania" (whose sufferers "remember nothing in history but the details of sieges and battles, and . . . consider men as made to carry muskets"), "Duelling Mania" ("men whose ideas of honor amount to madness"), and "Hunting Mania." "Gaming Mania" plagued those who needed to bet on everything, and "Virtuoso Mania" tormented those with "an extravagant fondness for the monstrous and rare productions of nature and art." "Rambling Mania" beset people "who are perpetually changing their country houses or occupations, and who are always praising the absent, and abusing the present good things of life."

Rush diagnosed "Love Mania" in "all marriages, without a visible or probable means of subsistence," because they are all "founded in madness." "Pride Mania" affected "every man who values himself upon his birth titles, or wealth, more than upon merit." He was especially amused by the "Dress Mania," for which one needn't go to "the cells of a hospital to see madmen or mad-women" because "every place of public resort nay, every street in our city is filled with them." A man "demands a court of enquiry to prove the insanity of his sister, in order to sequester her estate. 'What has she done?' says the court. 'Why look at her hat, her craw and her bishop! Do they not proclaim her madness?'"

Near the end of this prepsychiatric romp, Rush identified "Humane Mania." How "strange," he noted:

> that an excess of humanity should often produce those irregularities in behaviour and conduct, which constitute madness! . . . Persons afflicted with this madness, feel for every species of distress, and seem to pour forth tears upon some occasions, from every pore of their bodies. Their souls vibrate in unison with every touch of misery, that affects any member of the great family of mankind.
>
> Gracious heaven! if ever I should be visited with this species of madness, however much it may expose me to ridicule or resentment, my constant prayer to the divine fountain of justice and pity shall be, that I may never be cured of it.

Writing and publishing this bitingly whimsical list, and another for Carey's magazine on phobias, must have put the Rush household in the mood for numbered badinage. Among Rush's papers from the time are husband-and-wife lists of each other's most salient (or irritating) attributes as spouses.

Julia wrote hers first, titling her four-page work "A List of my husband's Dr. Rush's faults kept by me Julia Rush—wife of the above named Dr. Rush." Among them:

1. He is too passionate
2. He is too impatient in health and too peevish in sickness
3. He suffers his servants to do as they please
4. He gives too little attention to his children
5. He spends most of his evenings from home in political club

6. He suffers every body to cheat him that he deals with
7. He neglects to collect his debts, except when pressed by necessity, or the want of market money
8. He is too preoccupied with Dickinson College

In response, Rush filled seven notebook pages with "A List of Mrs. Rush's excellent Qualities taken down by her husband Dr. Benjn. Rush." These included:

1. She is a most affectionate, dutiful, obsequious wife to her husband when in health and a most faithful nurse to him in sickness
2. She has very agreeable and correct manners—having never been known to say or do an improper thing.
3. She excels in all kind of domestic knowledge and accomplishments. She sews well—makes all her children's clothes, understands perfectly the composition of all the different kinds of pudding, can preserve meat by smoke or salt, and makes excellent pickles.
4. If perhaps she has any fault at all it is her tendency to put too much wood on the fire. We burn as much as a cord and a half more wood in a season than any of our neighbors. But this is because of her farm-breeding at Princeton where firewood was to be had for nothing but the cost of cutting and hawling [hauling]

One of the most unusual pieces Rush wrote for *Columbian Magazine* during this firestorm of creativity was "The Paradise of Negro-slaves—A Dream." His life, he claimed, had been changed by a powerful dream about slavery, which he decided to publish after reading a new British essay on abolition. He had actually dreamed it several years earlier, right after the death in 1784 of Anthony Benezet, his friend and mentor in abolition work. Benezet had yet to be replaced on the front lines of racial politics. Rush himself had not written much about slavery in some time.

Dr. Rush rarely put much stock in dreams. In his moral faculty oration, he had dismissed them as "nothing but incoherent ideas, occasioned by partial or imperfect sleep" But this one he had recorded for posterity. In it, he was transported to a country of extraordinary "cultivation and scenery" that was "inhabited only by negroes . . . [who] appeared cheerful and happy." As he approached "a beautiful grove where a number of them were assembled for religious purposes, I perceived at once a pause in their exercises and an appearance of general perturbation." They "fixed their eyes" on Rush, and then "a venerable-looking man" stepped forward and addressed him.

"Excuse the panic which you have spread through this peaceful and happy company," he said. "We perceive that you are a *white man*. That colour, which is the emblem of innocence in every other creature of God, is to us a sign of guilt in man."

But after realizing just which white man Rush was, the elder "ran up and embraced me in his arms" and introduced him to a variety of former slaves. They were, in paradise, making sense of and peace with their lifetime of enslavement and torture. And they had messages they wanted Rush to take back to their cruel masters: it was not too late to repent.

One slave, Scipio, asked Rush to tell his master that "his sin is not too great to be forgiven. Tell him his once miserable slave Scipio is not angry at him, he longs to bear his prayers to the offended majesty of heaven, and when he dies, Scipio will apply to be one of the convoy that shall conduct his spirit to the regions of bliss appointed for those who repent of their iniquities." Other slaves offered memories of terrible mistreatment, each one ending with the looming possibility of redemption.

Perhaps the most heartbreaking story he heard was from a woman who "was called upon to suckle my Master's eldest son." To make sure this happened most "effectually, my own child was taken from my breast and soon afterwards died."

She explained that her "infant master" thrived under her care and grew up a handsome young man. But when his father died, "I became his property. Soon after this event, he lost 100 at cards. To raise this money, I was sold to a planter in a neighbouring state."

The woman said she would never forget "the anguish with which my aged father and mother followed me to the end of the lane when I left my master's house, and hung upon me when they bid me farewell." Her new master put her to work in the field; not long after, she caught a fever and died.

"Say, my friend," she asked Rush, "is my first young master still alive? If he is, go to him and tell him his unkind behaviour to me is upon record against him. The gentle spirits in heaven whose happiness consists in expressions of gratitude and love will have no fellowship with him. His soul must be melted with pity or he can never escape the punishment which awaits the hard-hearted equally with the impenitent in the regions of misery."

Near the end of his dream, Rush and the slaves in paradise saw "a little white man" coming toward them from the opposite side of the grove. "His face was grave, placid and full of benignity. In one hand he carried a subscription paper and a petition, in the other he carried a small pamphlet on the unlawfulness of the African slave trade." While he was trying to deduce who "this venerable figure" could be, everyone began "running to meet him, the air resounded with the clapping of hands." And suddenly Rush awoke from his dream with a name on his lips: "Anthony Benezet."

There the article ended, with an exhortation to honor and further Benezet's work. But privately, the dream had a different resonance for Rush. It was as if his late abolition hero had come back from the grave to haunt him, not only for putting on hold his efforts against slavery, but for doing something even worse.

Rush now owned a slave.

AMONG THE LARGE staff attending to Benjamin and Julia Rush and their children was an African-born cook named William Grubber. Rush had purchased him from a Scotch-Irish sea captain, David McCullough, whom he may have known from his work as a navy physician. There is no record of when Rush purchased William, or "Billy," as he often called him, and no ready explanation for why he did so, since he was openly hostile to slavery his entire adult life. Grubber was most likely purchased in 1779 or early 1780—just as Pennsylvania was passing the Act for the Gradual Abolition of Slavery, which stopped the sale of new slaves in Pennsylvania. It had no immediate impact on slaves like Grubber, who had previous owners, because it didn't mandate freeing slaves for another twenty-eight years. It was nonetheless a landmark: the first act to abolish slavery ever passed by a democracy.

Buying a slave at this time was a strange thing for Rush to do in every sense, since he already had paid servants and apprentices helping run his household—and much to lose if his purchase became publicly known. Yet even after the publication of his dream of the "Paradise of Negro-slaves," no one seems to have publicly seized on the odd hypocrisy of the situation.

Some historians have confused William Grubber with other members of Rush's household staff named William or Billy—of which there were several—and claim he owned a slave in the 1770s, when Benezet had him write his first abolitionist pamphlet. But a 1775 city document (a "constable return") shows that he did not. Grubber does not appear in the doctor's own account books until December 10, 1780, when Rush noted that "Black Bill" had left to start working aboard the ship of a "Capt. Angus" for a monthly rate of seven dollars ($129) a month—the first month of which appears to have already been paid to Rush.

It is possible this was all part of a plan for Grubber to buy his freedom; it was not uncommon for abolitionists to buy slaves in order to free them, legally, and have them work off the debt over time. But there was a longer history of slaves who were rented out for income—to farms by rural owners, to ships by city dwellers who lived near ports. Rush left no detailed record of his purchase, just several entries over the years marking when Grubber went to work at sea with various captains, in between periods when he worked as a cook in the Rush home. The city's annual tax records, which counted both slaves and indentured servants, do not list Rush as having a slave—although records for some tax years are missing. Regardless, the details of his "ownership" of Grubber remain a bit of a mystery.

Rush's feelings about him, however, are somewhat better docu-

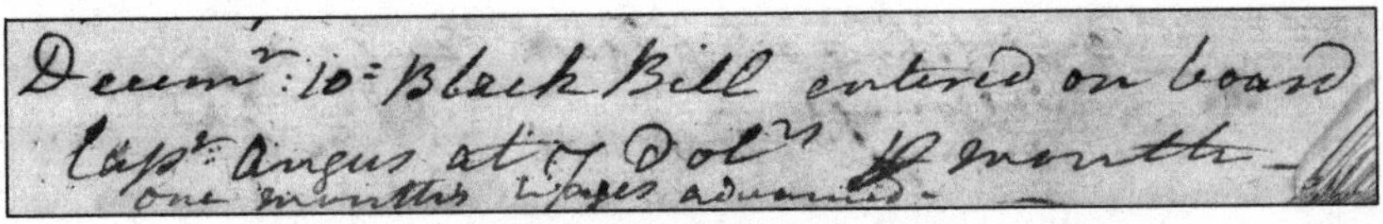
Decemr: 10 = Black Bill entered on board Capt. Angus at 7 Dolrs ℔ month —
one months wages advanced —

First mention of William Grubber, "Black Bill," in Rush's December 1780 financial log

mented. According to one of his commonplace books, "when I first bought his time," Grubber was "a Drunkard and swore frequently. In a year or two he was reformed from both of these vices, and became afterwards a sober, moral man and faithful and affectionate servant. His integrity extended to trifles, and was of the most delicate nature."

Grubber appears to have spent more time working at sea than in the Rush home. But there was no way around the truth of an arrangement that most likely awakened Rush with a start on more than one occasion, wondering what Anthony Benezet might think of him: he was an abolitionist with a slave.

But now that the battle lines were being drawn for replacing the Articles of Confederation, Rush had to rejoin the battles he had put aside to focus on family and medicine. The Constitutional Convention was coming to town, and once again, the whole world would be watching Philadelphia.

30

To raise the curtain on the year of the Constitutional Convention, Mathew Carey started another magazine, this one centered on politics. Titled *The American Museum*, it debuted with a new essay by Benjamin Franklin, another by John Dickinson (writing, once again, as "A Farmer"), a reprint of Thomas Paine's *Common Sense*, and a particularly bold essay by Dr. Benjamin Rush. Simply titled "Address to the People of the United States," it signaled Rush's return to active public life on national issues after years on the periphery.

"There is nothing more common," he began, "than to confound the terms of *the American revolution* with those of *the late American war.* The American war is over: but this is far from being the case with the American revolution. On the contrary, nothing but the first act of the great drama is closed. It remains yet to establish and perfect our new forms of government; and to prepare the principles, morals, and manners of our citizens, for these forms of government."

He then proceeded to walk readers through many issues the convention needed to address if the states truly wished to be united. The states had to give up the right to print their own money. The federal legislature should have two houses, one with only one delegate per state, the other based on population. Elections should be annual, and the two houses were to elect the president annually. But politicians should be able to serve multiple terms, as "the custom of turning men out of power or office, as soon as they are qualified for it, has been found to be . . . absurd." He called for an expanded post office system and proposed that newspapers always be mailed postage-free: "They are not only the vehicles of knowledge and intelligence, but the sentinels of the liberties of our country."

One of Rush's biggest fears for the young nation was that the men who had founded it were losing their energy and stamina to continue with the process of creating a more and more perfect union. He wanted to make sure that Washington, Adams, and other founders who were well into their fifties would accept the first elected positions in the new democracy.

> I am extremely sorry to find a passion for retirement so universal among the patriots and heroes of the war. They resemble skillful mariners, who, after exerting themselves to preserve a ship from sinking in a storm, in the middle of the ocean, drop asleep as soon as the waves subside, and leave the care of their lives and property, during the remainder of the voyage, to sailors, without knowledge or experience. Every man in a republic is public property. His time and talents—his youth—his manhood—his old age—nay more, life, all, belong to his country.
>
> PATRIOTS of 1774, 1775, 1778—HEROES of 1778, 1779, 1780! come forward! your country demands your services! . . . Lovers of peace and order, who declined taking part in the late war, come forward! your country forgives your timidity, and demands your influence and advice! . . . Hear her proclaiming, in sighs and groans, in her governments, in her finances, in her trade, in her manufactures, in her morals, and in her manners, "THE REVOLUTION IS NOT OVER!"

After Rush threw down this gauntlet, some might have expected him to get back into politics, but he didn't seem to want that anymore. Perhaps he felt elected office didn't suit his temperament and conflicted with his obligations, or perhaps he had other ideas about how he could make a difference.

Rush had been spending a good bit of time with the aged, ailing parent of liberty, Benjamin Franklin, since his homecoming. While they had known each other for nearly twenty years, they now for the first time lived in the same town, as adults and as peers. As a physician, Rush had a more sympathetic perspective on Franklin's infirmities than some others, and he wanted to learn what he could from him before he was gone. So he had dinner with him as often as possible and always jotted down notes afterward.

One night Franklin told Rush he had known ten years before the Declaration of Independence that "Britain would drive the colonies to independence" because, during a visit to England in 1756, he was told by prominent jurist Charles Pratt that it would happen. At another meal, Franklin told Rush he was certain that "tobacco would, in a few years, go out of use," and swore that in his eighty-one years he "had never snuffed, chewed, or smoked." A discussion of foreign credit rates produced the Franklin maxims that "credit produces idleness and vice" and "all debts should [be] like debts of honor . . . irrecoverable by law." He talked to Rush about his hearing problems, and how he had experimented with different ways of holding his hand to his ear to see which helped the most.

Their time together coincided with the reinvigoration of the city's intellectual life, but also with Rush's apparent decision that the best way for him to be a good citizen, a good man, a republican machine, was to emulate Franklin's early civic life, when he had periodically started voluntary associations to address problems government couldn't or wouldn't handle. He had helped create the Library Company, the Pennsylvania Hospital, and the Philosophical Society. Someone needed to do that again, on a larger scale, at a faster pace, with the good of a new country, not just a city, in mind—and to do it as a man of faith as well as a scientist. So on top of his family and his career and his writing, Rush was going to catalyze efforts to provoke thought, enable change, and heal in ways an individual doctor could not.

One night in February during a dinner at the City Tavern, Franklin, Rush, Thomas Paine, David Rittenhouse, Francis Hopkinson, and several others decided to start a new organization: the Society for Promoting Political Inquiries. It would be a nonpartisan group to study and discuss new theories of government and new challenges of governing—a sort of Philosophical Society for politics. They wrote up bylaws, Paine drafted a "preamble," and Rush was designated to deliver the society's first paper at its inaugural meeting, which would take place at Franklin's home a few weeks later.

At the meeting, on March 9, Franklin invited his guests into his library, which they were curious about because he had, after all, created the country's first lending library. One member was intrigued that while his collection was extensive, in English and French, the books themselves "were not, in general, expensively bound. The outside of a book was evidently not regarded by him."

Rush then presented his paper, on one of his new and controversial interests: the "Effects of Public Punishments Upon Criminals, and Upon Society." He detailed his reasons for opposing the death penalty. But the centerpiece of his argument concerned the impact of all public punishments, not just execution, on the minds of prisoners. A new state regulation, the Wheelbarrow Law, allowed courts to sentence criminals to public work gangs instead of to prison. Convicts in work gangs wore special uniforms to mark them as criminals. Rush felt this form of punishment subjected them to psychological damage that would likely increase recidivism.

"Far from preventing crimes by the terror they excite in the minds of spectators," he wrote, such public punishments "are directly calculated to produce them." He was against mandatory sentencing for a similar psychological reason: criminals would be more likely to commit crimes if they knew exactly what punishments they could expect. He thought incarceration and even forced labor should be more solitary, to encourage reflection. But he doubted much would change in the overcrowded penal system anytime soon. "The human mind," he wrote, "seldom arrives at truth upon any subject, till it has first reached the extremity of error."

Until change came, Rush decided to do what he could personally to lessen the shame of prisoners. He started politely engaging the "wheelbarrow men" whenever he could.

One day a group of these prisoners were cleaning the street in front of Rush's house, and one man asked him for a penny. "I told him I had none," he later wrote Julia, "but asked him if a draught of molasses beer would not be more acceptable to him. He answered in the affirmative. I called Billy [presumably William Grubber], who cheerfully (honest soul!) ran to the cellar and brought up one of his black *gugs* (as he calls them) full of beer, and poured him a quart mug full."

Rush offered the beer to the dozen or so prisoners in the group. While they were drinking, one man "took a large dog in his arms and played with him in the most affectionate manner." It gave Rush hope that he could be reformed and did not deserve such cruel punishment: "A heart is not wholly corrupted and offers at least one string by which it might be led back to virtue that is capable of so much steady affection even for a dog. The conduct of the dog excited my admiration and conveyed a faint idea by his fidelity of that infinite love which follows the human species, however much reduced by distress, debased by crimes, or degraded by the punishments of a prison, of ignominy, or of pain."

Rush emerged as the dominant voice of the Society for the Promotion of Political Enquiries, as Franklin grew quieter. Some members appreciated this: "Dr. Rush, who had great powers of conversation, commonly took the lead," recalled one member, while "Dr. Franklin, though very attentive, said but little after the subject was broached."

Other members wished Rush would shut up more often. "His writings and incessant talking," noted one, "disturbed us very much."

As Rush gained even more public visibility then he had had in Congress, this love/hate reception of his promiscuous talking, writing, and thinking also grew. His opinions—political, religious, social, and scientific—had a great many detractors, and some ill will accrued to him from enemies of his friends and associates. He was, for some, an acquired taste.

None of this stopped him from forging ahead in civic life. In early 1787, he helped found the first American medical society, the

College of Physicians. There had been previous state medical organizations but never a national body; he and the other organizers modeled it on the British Royal College of Physicians. The group involved most of the physicians who had just finished creating the Philadelphia Dispensary for the Medical Relief of the Poor—the nation's first such dispensary. Rush was one of the largest donors to help buy the land for the dispensary, and he also volunteered there. The College of Physicians honored John Redman with its first presidency; Rush and his now rather professionally punch-drunk mentors Morgan and Shippen were among the senior fellows.

Rush also joined Franklin in re-energizing the nation's first major abolition group, the Pennsylvania Society for Promoting the Abolition of Slavery and for the Relief of Free Negroes Unlawfully Held in Bondage, or, as it was better known, the Pennsylvania Abolition Society. While the doctor had joined the organization several years earlier, he didn't become an active member until 1787, when he was made an officer. Much of the society's work involved paying for lawyers to help African Americans buy their freedom or prove that they had already purchased it. They also advocated for black equality and an end to racial prejudice. Rush and Franklin (along with John Dickinson) made plans to lobby the Constitutional Convention to include language abolishing slavery and offering full voting citizenship to free blacks.

As the Abolition Society prepared for the convention, two former slaves from Delaware, Absalom Jones and Richard Allen, created their own political group, the Free African Society of Philadelphia. Jones, who was Rush's age, had been born enslaved to a plantation owner who later moved with him to Philadelphia; Allen, in his late twenties, had been born a slave on the Delaware plantation of a prominent Philadelphia lawyer and judge. Both had taught themselves how to read and write and had bought their freedom in Philadelphia in the early 1780s.

Jones and Allen were interested in religion as a path to inclusion and education and were testing the limits of racial equality as the only black preachers at the nation's oldest Methodist church, St. George's United Methodist Church, at Fourth and New streets.

They preached only early in the morning and had been ordered to run services in a sedate, moderate style—nothing too fiery or ecstatic. Once they started to attract more parishioners of color, the church instituted segregated seating, directing black worshippers to sit only along the walls.

The Free African Society was founded not so much to address these inequities but as a more secular community action group to support black families. But its efforts soon led to more direct advocacy. Neither Rush nor Allen and Jones left any written record of having met each other as early as 1787, but Philadelphia's small group of white abolitionists and free activist blacks—who all lived a few blocks from one another—were all set to contest the limits of religious freedom and liberty.

Absalom Jones (left) and Richard Allen

As the convention approached, Rush was shocked to discover that the Pennsylvania Assembly was not even considering Franklin for its list of delegates. He informed several committee members, especially his friend Thomas Fitzsimmons, that he thought their conduct both "ungrateful and impolitic." Fitzsimmons said that several of Franklin's friends had claimed his health precluded him from serving, and they didn't want to embarrass him with public exposure; Rush insisted they invite him anyway, not only out of respect but because Pennsylvania would be a key state in ratifying the Constitution—just as it had been during the vote on independence—and Franklin was still the state's unquestioned international star.

Rush then went to see Franklin privately, to make sure he would accept the better-late-than-never invitation if it were extended. Franklin must have assented, because in late March a surreal scene unfolded on the floor of the Pennsylvania Assembly, as several prominent Philadelphians who had worked with Franklin for years, like financier George Morris, tried to offer plausible explanations for why they had left the great man off the ballot. His fragile health was brought up, but Morris claimed the "stronger" reason was that at the time of selection he had been "apprehensive" that there would even be a constitutional convention, and "therefore it was not so material who was appointed." Now that the event was set (and right down the street from Franklin's house), Morris assumed everyone would be "desirous of having his excellency added."

Soon afterward Franklin was among those selected to represent the state in the writing of the Constitution. Without actually serving at the Convention, Rush was still helping shape its process—and repaying his debts.

THE CONVENTION BEGAN on May 25, after representatives straggled into Philadelphia over many days. George Washington was unanimously elected president of the proceedings, which most believed would end with him becoming the nation's first chief executive, either by election or appointment, depending on how the Constitution read. Franklin was the ranking Founding Father and elder statesman; the fact that he had to be carried to the sessions on a sedan chair lifted by four strong convicts from the nearby prison added to the drama.

Neither John Adams nor Thomas Jefferson attended—both were still in Europe, representing the new nation diplomatically. But their feelings were well known, especially those of Adams. He had put together, from letters and essays written in his various diplomatic posts, a book, *Defense of the Constitutions of Government of the United States of America*, which explored in nearly four hundred pages (just the first volume) the constitutions of nations current, past, and ancient and compared their philosophical systems. One of his strongest desires was for a bicameral (two-house) legislature, which for him was the cornerstone of checks and balances. Since Rush agreed wholeheartedly, he helped get the book reprinted in Philadelphia, with plenty of copies available at local bookstores, so Adams could harangue delegates in absentia.

Over the next two months, the Convention wrestled with the basic premises of a federal government, working largely from ideas that had bubbled up during state constitutional processes. While its delegates agreed on three branches of government—executive, legislative, and judicial—they had to make choices on the number of executives (one president or a committee); the number of legislative bodies and their division of responsibilities; the workings of a "supreme court" and a federal court system; which officers would be elected versus appointed and by whom; how long terms would last; and how easily officials could be removed. As for the chief executive, should he be appointed by the legislature, elected by popular vote, or by an "electoral college" representing the voters of each state?

Rush socialized with visiting representatives, and proved a popular host. Whether he was the ultimate insider—having served with many of these men in Congress, in combat, or as a physician—or the ultimate busybody (or both), he was an excellent source of information. But these proceedings were tightly closed, so he received less gossip from inside the State House than he was accustomed to. His closest friends on the inside, Franklin and Dickinson (now representing Delaware), appear to have used his predictably loose lips in a different way than Adams had once done. Adams had needed him to help foment outrage and sell revolution in the nation's largest city and most powerful state. Now Franklin and Dickinson needed him to spread the word that everything was going pretty well—even when it wasn't.

Rush turned out to be capable of a little more cautious optimism than he had had as a younger man. A new phrase had infiltrated his lexicon: "all will be well." He was now a father of five, and Julia was pregnant again. Every time he and Julia lost a child, or he became deathly ill and survived, they had grown more reliant on belief and prayer and hope. So his friends found him more open to trusting their process, to saying, in many different ways, "all will be well"—sometimes in the hope that saying so would make it so.

Among the delegates who sought Rush out was George Washington, who came by the house for tea; after a pleasant conversation, he left with a handful of the doctor's recent pamphlets. Rush also got to know some of the convention's rising younger players. James Madison, the protégé of Jefferson, arrived with a constitutional plan that expanded on Virginia's and became the template for much of the U.S. Constitution. Alexander Hamilton, the protégé of Washington, had strong ideas about the new nation's fiscal woes.

As the weeks went by, Rush followed the discussion of slavery with interest but soon tempered his expectations of progress. The Pennsylvania Abolition Society and its supporters failed to gain any traction since nearly half of the Convention delegates were slave owners. The compromise reached was that the southern states agreed that the regulation of slavery could be a federal issue—as long as the government promised not to use that regulatory power to outlaw the Atlantic slave trade for at least twenty years. They also agreed to allow a slave to be considered three-fifths of a person when counting heads for legislative and Electoral College representation; if slaves had counted only as property, southern states would have had fewer votes.

Rush did not rail publicly against this unequivocally disappointing outcome, knowing that slavery was a subject that would be revisited again and again. Instead, he focused on the fact that the emerging structure of government, especially the bicameral legislature, seemed to be conforming to what he supported.

He hoped that all would be well with the Constitution. Because even as he followed the trials of its birth, he was trying to build America in other ways and questioning some of his own founding principles.

31

Among the causes Rush championed during the Convention year was education, which was a state and local issue. He boldly proposed that Philadelphia start its own system of free public schools, funded by a tax on "all estates in the city"—a plan more immediately feasible than the similar one he had proposed earlier for the whole state. He also spoke out strongly for women's education, as the recently opened Young Ladies Academy of Philadelphia drew students from all thirteen states and aimed to be the first national school to take the education of women as seriously as that of men. Rush helped raise money and attention for the school by giving a public lecture, "Thoughts on Female Education," to visitors to the academy on the occasion of its first quarterly exams.

"The elevation of the female mind, by means of moral, physical and religious truth, is considered by some men as unfriendly to the domestic character of a woman," he explained. "But this is the prejudice of little minds, and springs from the same spirit which opposes the general diffusion of knowledge among the citizens of our republics." He cited frivolous and expensive fashions as evidence of male efforts to "divert the ladies from improving their minds," and he charged his audience to rebel: "It will be in your power, LADIES, to correct the mistakes and practice of our sex upon these subjects, by demonstrating, that the female temper can only be governed by reason, and that the cultivation of reason in women, is alike friendly to the order of nature, and to private as well as public happiness."

Young women, he said, needed to learn "the English language," both in speaking and writing, legibly and grammatically; "figures and bookkeeping," geography, vocal music, and dancing; and "the reading of . . . history, biography and travels . . . poetry—and moral essays."

And this led him to the subject that was increasingly on his mind: the role religion might play in education and science. He was still trying to balance the separation of church and state, in which he believed as firmly as ever, with his fear that in a more secular republic the teachings of the Bible could become lost. His vision for public schooling fell squarely between the two poles. "It will be necessary," he said of the Ladies Academy curriculum, "to connect all these branches of education with regular instruction in the christian religion." He believed "our pupils should early be furnished with some of the most simple arguments in favour of the truth of christianity. A portion of the bible (of late improperly banished from our school) should be read by them every day, and such questions should be asked, after reading it, as are calculated to imprint upon their minds the interesting stories contained in it."

He also declared his belief that "Christianity exerts the most friendly influence upon science, as well as upon the morals and manners of mankind." This may have represented more of what he prayed for than what he believed as a scientist, but he was trying to thread an important and challenging needle. "Whether this be occasioned by the unity of truth, and the mutual assistance which truths upon different subjects afford each other, or whether the faculties of the mind be sharpened and corrected by embracing the truths of revelation, and thereby prepared to investigate and perceive truths upon other subjects, I will not determine, but it is certain that the greatest discoveries in science have been made by christian philosophers, and that there is the most knowledge in those countries where there is the most christianity."

Ultimately, Rush ventured, "those philosophers who reject christianity, and those christians, whether parents or schoolmasters, who neglect the religious instruction of their children and pupils, reject and neglect the most effectual means of promoting knowledge in our country."

Rush wrote and spoke about these concepts as if he had reached hard and fast conclusions. But he was often just thinking out loud—sometimes very loud—and offering early drafts of his ongoing thought process. His discussion at the Young Ladies Academy of the role of religion in secular education came during a particularly rough period in his own religious life. His spiritual integrity was coming under attack from Dr. John Ewing, the prominent minister of the First Presbyterian Church and his provost at the medical school.

Rush and Ewing had known each other for years, and while there had always been friction between them, they had generally navigated it. Many of their disagreements came from the "New Order" schism between Ewing's First Presbyterian Church and the Second Presbyterian Church culture in which Rush grew up. But now that Rush was becoming more of a public voice in some religious debates, Ewing was becoming his fierce and nasty critic.

Whenever Rush talked about religion in public education, he always acknowledged the various Christian "sects," as he called them. He was watching them adjust to independence, especially Church of England congregations trying to shift into what would become known as American "Protestant Episcopal." Rush was a fan of all religious oratory and was known to visit various services—including those of the Universalist Rev. Elhanan Winchester, who preached on Sundays at a hall at the university—just to expose himself to differing perspectives. He liked to chat with clergy after services about their sermons, since they shared techniques and tricks with his medical lectures. He would joke with preachers about what he called the "clergyman's setting-pole," which was the use of the phrase "I say" and then a long pause—during which they were presumably trying to figure out what to say next.

Ewing decided that Rush's religious tolerance and his familiarity with other clergy was a kind of betrayal. He accused Rush of putting the interests of Quakers and Episcopalians above his own faith's, and he even advised Presbyterians to stop using him as a doctor. In response, Rush offered to present evidence to the Presbyterian synod of Ewing's "lying, drunkenness, and unchristian language," and it devolved from there.

Their public frictions escalated, as Ewing published attacks on Rush under an alias in the newspaper, and Rush responded at length. They argued partly about religion, partly about politics, partly about money, and partly about power. Their war of words became so public that when Judge Francis Hopkinson lampooned it in a satirical one-act play about a certain "doctor of divinity and doctor of physick" in the *Pennsylvania Packet*, everyone knew who he was describing.

In May 1787, Rush's Presbyterian church ordained a new junior minister, Ashbel Green, an engaging twenty-five-year-old graduate of the College of New Jersey. Rush liked him, but when Green invited Reverend Ewing to help conduct his ordination, Rush very noticeably refused to attend the event or the dinner afterward. So he didn't hear for some time—it was a very busy summer—that the diners had discussed how the First and Second Presbyterian churches might develop more "friendly intercourse," maybe even sometimes swapping Sunday pulpits. Which could mean that Ewing would preach during the Rush family's Sunday worship.

When it came to national religious politics, Rush was spending more time that summer talking with Philadelphia's most prominent Jewish lay leader, Jonas Phillips, a well-known merchant and president of the city's first synagogue, Mikveh Israel. Rush had been treating Phillips's family for years, and they had recently invited him to their daughter's wedding. It was the first time he had seen a Jewish marriage ceremony, and afterward he sent Julia a long letter, describing its rites like a fascinated anthropologist. He marveled at the Hebrew prayers, the hats, the "freedom with which some" congregants "conversed with each other" during the entire service, the parchment wedding contract, the "beautiful canopy composed of red and white silk," the breaking of the wineglass and the "general shout of joy," even the way "Mrs. Phillips put a large piece of cake into my pocket" when he was leaving, so Julia could eat some.

(This letter, and another he wrote after attending the circumcision ceremony of Phillips's first grandson, represent some of the earliest American cross-cultural writing on Jewish practice.)

Jonas Phillips had previously been involved with Rush in protesting the religious oath in Pennsylvania's constitution. After his daughter's wedding, Phillips had time to play a far larger role in the Constitutional Convention: he filed a formal petition that the new federal constitution avoid all religious oaths or tests in any aspect of the nation's new laws. His activism would be credited for helping the passage of Article VI of the Constitution, which included the phrase "no religious test shall ever be required as a qualification to any office or public trust of the United States."

In the midst of the convention, Rush's medical partner, James Hall, suddenly quit, leaving for a marriage (which Rush predicted would be unhappy) and to begin his own practice in another city. With him would go some of the freedom Rush had enjoyed to pursue writing and voluntary work. The day he left, Hall took Rush's hand "but was unable to bid me farewell. His eyes filled with tears, and he attempted in vain to give utterance to his affection and grief." Rush had said goodbye to a great many apprentices and students, but Hall's departure was surprisingly painful—especially since Julia and the children were away at Princeton for the summer.

"He has left a blank in every part of the house," he wrote to Julia. "I feel without him as if I had lost my right arm." He was bursting with insights—just down the street they were writing the Constitution—but he had nobody to share them with. "To a mind like mine, which so soon (perhaps from its slender size) becomes plethoric with ideas and which delights so much in communicating them, it is a new and peculiar hardship."

Hall's departure may have been one reason Rush decided to buy a new house for the family—and a new building for his office—on the east side of Third Street, just south of Walnut. It was a handsomer property, the two-story main house replete with trappings of taste—molding and wainscoting, pediments and cornices, an open newel staircase with a twist bannister. The property also included an older, two-story building with a step-down basement, which would be used for Rush's medical office, as well as a kitchen and sleeping chambers.

He bought the new house without Julia seeing it first, then made an even bigger decision while she was still away: he quit the family church. He finally heard that Reverend Ewing was going to be more active from the pulpit of Second Presbyterian, so he decided he and his family could no longer worship there. He quit the church in a letter, because "when a man of 40 years of age changes his place and mode of worship, he ought to be able to give good reason for it."

The Rushes joined St. Peter's Episcopal Church, which was associated with Christ Church down the street, the parish Rush had attended as a child. Both churches were overseen by Bishop William White, who was a couple years younger than Rush, had been a longtime junior clergy member in Philadelphia and chaplain for the Continental Congress, and then in the 1780s emerged as the leading local voice for the transition from state church to "Protestant Episcopal." He had recently been ordained as the first Episcopal bishop of Pennsylvania. While not known as a dramatic sermonizer, he was a religious, social, and political powerhouse; he had been a driving force in the creation of the Philadelphia Dispensary where Rush did volunteer care. The doctor found Bishop White's church, for the time being, much more to his liking.

Bishop William White

IN THE FALL of 1787, amid all this change came a major shift in Rush's life at Pennsylvania Hospital: he was officially put in charge of all patients with mental illness, inheriting the province of the hospital's late founder, Dr. Thomas Bond.

"I have lately obtained the exclusive care of the maniacal

patients in our hospital," he wrote to a physician friend in London, Dr. John Lettsom. While he always had been fascinated by the patients in the basement cells, now he could focus more intensely on how best to care for them and how to conceptualize what they were suffering—both in terms of physiology and of what we would today call psychology. To Lettsom, he referred to the position as "this desperate undertaking."

Rush first used his new clout to improve conditions in the cells. There was a long-standing belief that lunatics didn't feel hot or cold and so didn't need heat; he convinced the hospital board that this was demonstrably wrong. In the winter of 1787–88, stoves were purchased and installed to warm the basement, one in between every two cells.

Rush had studied the history of theories of madness: How Hippocrates and the ancients had believed it "derived from a morbid state of the liver." How it was later viewed as "a disease in the spleen," and for many years in England and New England, those affected were "said to be spleeny." How a French theory blamed "the effect of a disease of the intestines, and particularly of their perotineal coat."

In Edinburgh Dr. Cullen had taught Rush the predominant theory there, that madness was "the effect of a disease in the nerves." Rush had also become interested in the theories of Dr. David Hartley, the late English physician, philosopher, and very-Christian scientist. Hartley had ideas about the physiology of the brain, especially the vibration of nerves, which caused associations that were the mechanics of psychology, and irregularities (or imperfections) of which explained madness.

None of these theories suggested useful treatments—and none successfully combated the conventional wisdom that located madness on the moral rather than the medical spectrum. They just suggested where the possession manifested in the body.

Picking up where his "moral faculty" lecture left off, Rush could now explore the possibility that the cause of and the solution to his patients' ills were essentially physical. In some more recent thinking, he noted, "madness has been placed exclusively in the mind," which suggested it was neither moral nor material but psychological in nature. He split the difference, hypothesizing that in his patients it involved both "the nerves" and "that part of the brain which is the seat of the mind."

In his search for the physical roots of madness, Rush developed an idea that it was "seated primarily in the blood vessels of the brain." Blood flow, he was coming to believe, was the key to understanding all disease, and pulse the key to understanding blood. (Not for many decades would germ theory be developed, or any other concept of how infections move through the body *in* the blood.) Pulse was one of the few things inside the body that physicians could easily measure from the outside—and do something to change. Assessing the strength of the pulse, Rush had been taught, was the key to diagnosis, and modifying the pulse by medicine or by reducing blood volume through bleeding was the cornerstone of practical treatment.

Dr. Bond himself had told a story of performing bloodletting on one of the hospital's lunatics, although it sounded more like an experiment in psychology than a medical treatment. A preacher in a "state of madness," claiming to be "possessed of devil" who he could feel in his body "constantly in aches and pains," had once called upon Bond. The doctor found his pulse to be "full and tense," and he told the preacher to "sit down in his parlour [and] let him open a vein in his arm." As soon as the blood began flowing, the preacher cried out, "I am relieved, I felt the devil fly out of the orifice in my vein as soon as it was opened." According to Bond, "from this time he recovered rapidly from his derangement."

Rush had no illusions of a panacea, but he started treating mental illness with the era's standard medical practices, including bloodletting, purging, wine, bark, and mercury, along with some of the preventive medicine he espoused—eating less meat and more vegetables, exercising, and not drinking spirituous liquor. An early favorite treatment was one he understood to be employed by Native Americans. "The remedies on which I place my chief dependence are the warm and cold baths," he wrote to Dr. Lettsom. "In some cases I have used them after the Indian method—that is, I direct the cold to succeed the use of the warm bath while the patient is in the lowest state of debility and the highest state of irritability from the action of the warm water."

He wanted to see if any of these measures could help break cycles of mania and depression, anxiety, agitation, and psychosis. "I shall carefully record the effects of these and other remedies upon my patients," he promised Lettsom, "and if any new facts should occur I shall not fail of communicating them to you."

Among the hospital managers who most supported his efforts was Samuel Coates, a successful Quaker merchant in his mid-thirties who volunteered at the hospital out of a sense of community, as he had several years before at the Library Company of Philadelphia. Coates was brought in to help the hospital reform its finances, but he had a personal fascination with patients of mental illness. At the age of six weeks, one of his parents' maids, who had shown some signs of instability, had kidnapped and run away with him; when the maid was found, she had to be prevented from throwing baby Samuel out a second-story window. He had been thinking about what he called "derangement" ever since.

Samuel Coates

Rush and Coates were a good team. Coates was not afraid of the mentally ill patients; he was interested in speaking to them, even when it was difficult, and he carried around a notebook to write down what they told him and told each other. Coates had no medical training; he kept these notes out of a genuine curiosity and later would use them to write some of the first mental health case histories. Rush would be forever grateful for his observations. But mostly Rush was pleased to have a powerful friend on the board of managers who agreed with him about the importance of making medical progress on diseases of the brain and mind, and bringing these patients out of the basement and into the light.

32

The first draft of the constitution was almost finished. Much of it had been written by a newcomer Pennsylvania delegate, whom Rush didn't know well. Gouverneur Morris had represented New York in the Continental Congress and, after being voted out of office there, relocated his law business to Philadelphia. On September 8, he and the other members of the Committee of Style and Arrangement, which included Alexander Hamilton and James Madison, were given the rough first draft to polish. Over the following days Morris wrote and attached what became known as the Preamble:

> We the People of the United States, in Order to form a more perfect Union, establish Justice, insure domestic Tranquility, provide for the common defense, promote the general Welfare, and secure the Blessings of Liberty to ourselves and our Posterity, do ordain and establish this Constitution for the United States of America.

On September 17, 1787, the proposed Constitution was signed by all but four of the remaining delegates: three out of protest, and John Dickinson because he was sick and couldn't attend the signing. (A fellow delegate forged his signature for him.) It was published in the *Pennsylvania Packet* the next day and sent to Congress to be transmitted to the states for ratification, which would take several months.

During that time, the debate over "Federalism"—advocacy of a strong central government that would take some powers from the states—began getting louder, and the first anti-Federalist letters were anonymously published. Alexander Hamilton, James Madison, and John Jay countered with *The Federalist*, an ongoing series of essays from the pseudonymous "Publius" that would eventually total eighty-five, written and published during the ten-month process of ratification and later collected as *The Federalist Papers*.

Rush was seen as a Federalist—his "Address to the People of the United States" had a Federalist slant—and in Pennsylvania the anti-Federalists were the same "radicals" he had been opposing for years: they were still calling for less government control in general, unicameral legislatures, easily replaced executives and judges, and a general lack of meritocracy.

While Rush had been somewhat distant to the writing of the Constitution, he was pleased to find himself nominated as a delegate to the state convention to ratify it—especially since, once again, Pennsylvania's approval was considered crucial but uncertain. The anti-Federalists who had created the state constitution that Rush so hated (including Thomas Paine) were now in the minority, but they still had a loud divisive voice. Nineteen of them held up a vote even to discuss the procedure for choosing a delegation for a state convention to approve: one day two of them had to be physically dragged into the State House.

On October 10, Rush spoke to promote his candidacy as a delegate pledged to support the Constitution and the ratification process. He spoke in a style that the next day's newspaper called "elegant and pathetic" (meant as a compliment, in the sense of evoking pathos) about all the "advantages which would flow from the adoption of the new system, of federal government." He highlighted the "advancement of commerce, agriculture, manufactures, arts and sciences, the encouragement of emigration, the abolition of paper money, the annihilation of party, and the prevention of war" having been "ingeniously considered" in the document, and argued that ratification was crucial.

Rush ended his remarks with a dramatic flourish. "Were this

the last moment of my existence," he proclaimed, "my dying request and injunction to my fellow citizens would be to accept and support the offered Constitution."

Several weeks later the city would vote for him to represent it at the state ratifying convention. Two days after that vote, Julia gave birth to a son. They named him William. He appeared to be in good health.

When the state convention began two weeks later, Rush stopped the proceedings to "request the attendance of some minister of the gospel . . . to open the business of the convention with a prayer." The "sect or persuasion" of the clergyman didn't matter to him—he just "hoped there was liberality sufficient in the meeting to unite in prayers for the blessing of Heaven." He did not feel this violated his strong position separating church and state; having a clergy member offer a convocation was not the same as asking legislators to swear an oath to Jesus and the Bible.

His request for an opening prayer was denied as "absurd superstition." But he went on to have another immediate impact: he was named the first delegate to the committee to formulate the rules for the convention. So he would have a hand in everything.

He made his first remarks during a discussion of whether the Convention had the right to revise this new Constitution before voting on it. His fellow Philadelphia delegate, James Wilson, said no: "Shall we . . . contemplate a great and magnificent edifice, condescend like a fly, with a microscopic eye, to scrutinize the imperfections of a single brick?" Another delegate said yes, they should "examine and compare the materials . . . rejecting everything that is useless and rotten."

Then Rush stood up to make their mission clear. "We are not, at this time, called upon to raise the structure," he said. "The house is already built for us, and we are only asked whether we choose to occupy it? If we find its apartments commodious, and, upon the whole, that it is well calculated to shelter us from the inclemencies of the storm that threatens, we shall act prudently in entering it; . . . otherwise, all that is required of us is to return the key."

But the Convention refused to stop debating whether revising the Constitution was an option, so Rush stood again and was adamant. The arguments and counterarguments had all been heard before, and the "expense and procrastination" of going through it all again "would be intolerable. We can have no view either to a revision or a repeal, and therefore protests can only serve to distract and perplex the state." He offered a metaphysical appeal that struck some as imaginative and others as hyperreligious, saying he saw "the hand of God" in the creation of the United States and its Constitution, just as "God had divided the Red Sea to give a passage to the children of Israel, or had fulminated the Ten Commandments from Mount Sinai!"

For the nation to truly be a republic, he reminded the delegates, some state sovereignty would have to be sacrificed. There was considerable discussion about why the Constitution did not contain a Bill of Rights, to lay out which rights were guaranteed by the federal government, and which were left to the states; the authors had decided to table this until after the structure of the government was approved.

But Rush wasn't convinced such a bill could really ensure rights. "All Bills of Rights have been broken," he claimed. "There is no security for Liberty but in *two* things: *Representation* and Checks."

Just before the final vote, he told the convention that ratification by a majority wasn't enough: "Nothing short of an unanimous vote can indeed complete my satisfaction. And, permit me to add, were that event to take place, I could not preserve the strict bounds of decorum, but . . . [would fly] to the other side of this room, cordially embrace every member, who has hitherto been in opposition, as a brother and a patriot. Let us then, Sir, this night bury the hatchet, and smoke the calumet of peace!"

Like many Rush speeches, it raised as many concerns as it quieted. Several more hours of debate ensued until, finally, a vote was taken. Pennsylvania, arguably the powerful state in the union, ratified the Constitution, 46 votes for, 23 against. Delaware had, technically, ratified five days earlier, unanimously, but it was the smallest state in the union. Pennsylvania's ratification led the nation.

In the coming weeks, as other states considered the Constitution, Rush and fellow Philadelphia delegate Wilson stumped for it. The anti-Federalists took to attacking them in print. One anonymous writer called Rush "Doctor Puff, the paragraphist," and accused him of "the fabrication of extracts of letters, paragraphs, correspondents, etc., etc. . . . [He] has scarcely slept since his appointment, having received orders to work double tides; beneath his creative pen thousands of correspondents rise into view, who all harmonize in their sentiments and information about the new constitution."

Rush worked tirelessly for the Constitution until early January, when he and Julia became distraught as their infant son's winter cold developed into a pleurisy. His breathing became increasingly labored, and on January 15, baby William Rush died at the age of two months. Julia was "much afflicted from the loss of our youngest boy," he wrote to a friend, and the couple sought comfort, as they had before, in prayer.

They decided to make a religious statement: they were re-baptized together in the Episcopal church by Bishop White. "[I] submitted to confirmation with my dear wife in the month of February 1788," Rush recalled, "and a few days afterwards received the blessed signs of the death of Jesus Christ in St Peter's Church. I was deeply impressed with this solemnity."

Unfortunately, just after receiving the sacrament, Rush became ill himself. "In consequence of rising a night or two before [the ceremony] and going out too thinly clothed, I was attacked upon my return from church by a severe pleurisy. . . . [It] nearly put an end to my life. I realized death." He took to his bed for nine days and was certain he wouldn't leave it alive: "I not only settled all my worldly affairs but gave the most minute directions with respect to everything that related to my funeral."

He was surrounded by his family during waking hours. William Grubber, who was back from sea, stayed up with him through the nights. When the infection finally broke, Rush was quick to credit God even over his medical treatment. "It pleased God to enable me to do this with an uncommon degree of composure, for the promises of the Gospel bore up my soul above the fear of death and the horrors of the grave. O! my friend, the religion of Jesus Christ is indeed a reality. It is comfortable in life, but in a near view of the last enemy its value cannot be measured or estimated by the pen or tongue of a mortal."

But he soon felt some of his religious fervor dissipating. "It pleased God to restore me," he later wrote, "and for some time afterwards to continue upon my mind a considerable sense of divine things." The next year, however, brought revisions to the Episcopal liturgy—a revised prayer book that altered "the forms of baptism, and the communion service, the former admitting infant regeneration [the belief that dying babies are reborn before they die] and transubstantiation [the belief that the wine and wafer actually, physically, become the blood and body of Christ]." Rush wasn't sure he believed in all that.

He stopped attending the Episcopal church as fervently and had the children rebaptized—this time by Presbyterian ministers. "I still attended public worship in the Episcopal church and occasionally in Presbyterian churches," he said, "but alas! with coldness and formality. I was under the influence of an unholy temper, and often wounded the peace of my mind by yielding to it."

Not long after his recovery, Rush took a long-overdue step: he filled out the "manumission" papers required to free William Grubber from slavery:

> I, Benjamin Rush of the city of Philadelphia, Doctor of physic, having purchased a negro slave named *William* of Capt. David McCullough, and being fully satisfied that it is contrary to reason, & religion to detain the said slave in bondage beyond such a time as will be a just compensation for my having paid for him the full price of a slave for life, I do hereby declare that the said *William* shall be free from me, & from all persons claiming under me, on the twenty-fifth day of February in the year of our Lord One thousand seven hundred & ninety four.

In witness thereof, I have here unto set my hand & seal, on this twenty fourth day of May, 1788.

Benjamin Rush

The manumission was witnessed by Dr. Samuel Powel Griffitts, who had been Rush's student (and would later be active in the Abolition Society), and Dr. Benjamin F. Young, who had been his apprentice. There is no record of a reaction to Rush's filing these papers. In fact, there is no record that anyone but these two young doctors and Julia ever knew William Grubber was a slave rather than just another servant in the Rush household.

It is also unknown why Rush chose not to free Grubber right away. His stated belief that slavery was "contrary to reason & religion" is hard to square with manumission papers setting the date for Grubber's freedom more than five years in the future.

Several weeks after Rush filed the manumission, Grubber left again to work at sea. "Billy my black boy went with Capt. Angus to granada at 5 dollars [$142] a month," Rush wrote in his ledger.

In June 1788, the ratification of the Constitution was nearly complete. It had hit a roadblock in Massachusetts and several other states concerned with making sure powers not delegated to the federal government would be kept by the states, and with making absolutely sure that the human and civil rights—speech, religion, press—would be included in a Bill of Rights. They agreed to ratify only with assurances that amendments to the Constitution would be proposed following the first election, as soon as the government was functioning. In late June, the ninth state, New Hampshire, ratified, which allowed the new government to begin planning for that election.

Independence Day 1788 was the first celebration of the nation united under its new Constitution. The "Federal Procession" in Philadelphia began on South Street at Third and wended a nearly three-mile course to Union Green (on a country estate then called Bush Hill, now around Seventeenth and Spring Garden). The parade was so long and involved that it took Francis Hopkinson three full newspaper pages to describe the eighty-eight different regiments, trade groups, floats, and other walking, riding, and rolling spectacles. The highlight was an actual thirty-three-foot long, twenty-gun warship, renamed for the event as the *Federal Union*, which had been mounted on a long carriage pulled by ten horses. On board were its twenty-five crewmen, commanded by Capt. John Green, along with four hired boys dressed up as midshipmen.

One of the four boys was Rush's oldest son John, just two weeks away from his eleventh birthday, who waved to the crowds for hours. Rush's brother Jacob, now a state judge, was also in the parade—waving in his robes from a twenty-foot float honoring the Constitution, featuring a thirteen-foot-high bald eagle, its "breast emblazoned with thirteen silver stars . . . and underneath thirteen stripes" and in its talons, an olive branch and thirteen arrows.

The *Federal Union* ended up being moored in the middle of Union Green, where hundreds of tables had been set up for anyone who wanted to be part of a Fourth of July picnic. Some seventeen thousand people ate there; James Wilson offered a spirited oration, after which there were lively toasts, each "announced by the trumpets and answered by a discharge of artillary." Rush was very pleased that all these toasts were made without what Rush referred to as "Antifederal" spirituous liquors. Only "American Porter, beer and cyder" were allowed.

After the long patriotic day, Rush described the event to Elias Boudinot, his mother-in-law's brother and a lawyer in Elizabeth, New Jersey, in a lengthy letter that was quickly published in the *American Museum*. The letter became known for one exquisitely quotable sentence, but the whole captured the weight of the occasion. Rush said the procession began in "solemn silence," and stirred in him "a greater number . . . or combination of passions" than had ever before "seized" at his "soul." And he was sure the event provided all kinds of catharsis for others: "the patriot enjoyed a complete triumph," and:

> The benevolent man saw a precedent established for forming free governments in every part of the world. The man of humanity contemplated the end of the distresses of his fellow citizens in

> the revival of commerce and agriculture. Even the selfish passions were not idle. The ambitious man beheld with pleasure the honors that were to be disposed of by the new government, and the man of wealth realized once more the safety of his bonds and rents against the inroads of paper money and tender laws.

Rush was particularly touched when seventeen leading members of the city's clergy marched by:

> arm in arm . . . to exemplify the Union. Pains were taken to connect ministers of the most dissimilar religious principles together, thereby to show the influence of a free government in promoting Christian charity. The Rabbi of the Jews locked in the arms of two ministers of the gospel was a most delightful sight. There could not have been a more happy emblem contrived of that section of the new Constitution which opens all its power and offices alike not only to . . . Christians but to worthy men of *every* religion.

Watching the marching multitudes made Rush think again about the role of powers larger than man in the creation of the nation. Many remarked, he said, that "Heaven was on the federal side of the questions." And the ratification of the Constitution was doubtless "a solitary event in the history of mankind." The "Union of the States [was] . . . as much the work of a Divine Providence as any of the miracles recorded in the Old and New Testament."

And then in a sigh of patriotic relief, he wrote: "'Tis done! We have become a nation."

That line captured the moment in history so well that it took on a life of its own. It was initially quoted by people who saw it in *American Museum*, but others would later suggest that Rush had said it at the signing of the Constitution, even though he wasn't there.

It was, like many of Rush's best lines, just one he dashed off to someone he hoped would share his enthusiasm.

Inspired by the city's liquor-free mass picnic, Rush decided to publish a new version of his pamphlet *An Enquiry into the Effects of Spirituous Liquors on the Human Body, and their Influences upon the Happiness of Society.* He had learned from writing for Mathew Carey's magazines that readers seemed to respond to lists and charts, sometimes even more than to prose. So to help market the new pamphlet, he combined his ideas about temperance with the idea he came up with when courting Julia—systematizing a concept through a "thermometer."

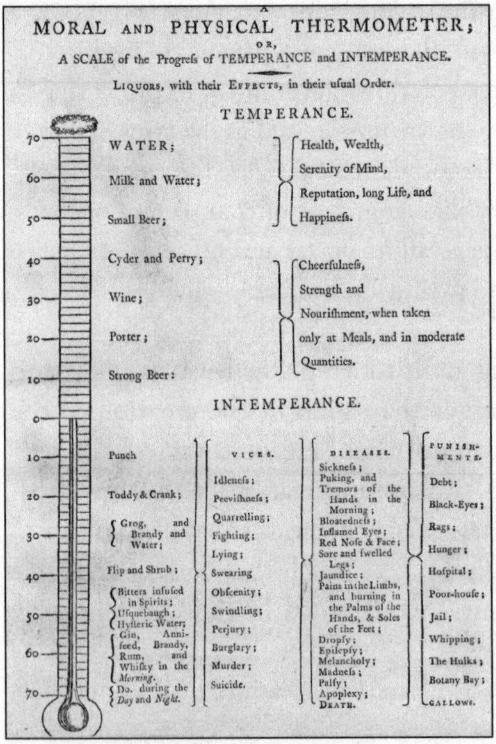

Rush's "Moral and Physical Thermometer"

This time, instead of measuring marital love, he fashioned an ingenious full-page chart he called "A Moral and Physical Thermometer," which showed the slippery slope of alcoholic beverages. At the top were water, vinegar and water, and small beer—associated with health, wealth, serenity of mind, reputation, long life, and happiness. Following these were cider, wine, porter, and strong beer—associated with cheerfulness, strength, and nourishment, when taken with meals in moderate quantities. Then things turned dark. Strong punches, toddies, grogs, slings, bitters infused with spirits, and other spirituous liquors (including "pepper in rum") led to the vices of fraud, anarchy, hatred of just government, murder, and suicide; the diseases of madness, palsy, and epilepsy; death; and the punishments of jail, the whipping post, and the gallows.

33

Just before Independence Day, John Adams returned to America for the first time in nearly a decade, after representing the nation in France, Britain, and Holland. He went directly to his farm in Braintree, Massachusetts, where Rush wrote to welcome him home. They had exchanged mostly short letters over the years Adams had been away, and Rush was anxious to rekindle their intimacy—so the letter covered everything from international, national, and state politics to personal matters delivered in the emotional shorthand of old friends: "My dear Mrs. Rush joins me in most respectful Compliments and congratulations to Mrs. Adams. We count five living out of eight children." The letter finished, "with every possible mark of respect and esteem, I am, dear sir, your Affectionate Old Friend and humble servant."

Rush didn't hear back for more than five months, until in early December a letter arrived, full of apologies. "A multiplicity of avocations have prevented me, from answering your friendly letter of the 2d. of July," Adams wrote, "till I am almost ashamed to answer it, at all."

And with that, the friendship between the two men was not only rekindled but deepened—because they had so much to catch up on, and because so much was happening in their new country.

With the Constitution ratified, the nation's first presidential election was set to begin on December 15, 1788, with the popular vote for electors in each state, after which the Electoral College would make the decision in early January. Whoever got the most electoral votes would be president, and whoever came in second would be vice president (and, according to the Constitution, president of the Senate). There was no question of George Washington winning the presidency. But it wasn't clear who, among Adams, John Hancock, John Jay, and several others, would come in second. Only ten states had electors, since two hadn't yet ratified the Constitution, and one (New York) had failed to appoint its electors quickly enough.

The seat of the government was now in New York, where the Congress had been since 1785, but the competition was on for the location of the new permanent capital. Philadelphia was, of course, lobbying heavily for the government to return to the site of its founding. In the meantime, Congress and the president would work out of a grand building in lower Manhattan: Federal Hall at Wall Street and Nassau. The two houses of Congress convened there first on March 4 but adjourned for lack of a quorum. They reconvened in early April, elected leaders, and began their work as the electoral votes were officially counted.

Washington won in a landslide. John Adams came in second, with more votes than the five other candidates combined, and was made vice president. He was sworn in to office on April 20, 1789, and Washington was formally inaugurated on April 30.

Adams lived and worked in the nearby Richmond Hill mansion, at Varick and Charlton Streets, and from there carried on a steady correspondence with Rush. They shared intellectual and political insights as well as well-informed gossip and innuendo. They complained about everything and everyone who disappointed or annoyed them.

Their correspondence became especially passionate in 1789, when the first book about the nation's founding was published: *History of the American Revolution*, by a former student of Rush's,

Dr. David Ramsay. Rush had helped Ramsay, a physician in South Carolina, with the two-volume book, yet was scarcely mentioned in its seven hundred pages. Ramsay included Rush in his list of the "most distinguished writers in favour of the rights of America," along with Adams, Jefferson, Franklin, Dickinson, and Paine, and he did credit Rush—not Shippen—for the changes in the military medical department. But that was all.

Adams was covered more extensively, but hardly to his liking. "The History of our revolution will be one continued Lye [lie] from one End to the other," he railed:

> The Essence of the whole will be that Dr Franklin's electrical Rod, Smote the Earth and out Spring General Washington. That Franklin electrified him with his Rod—and thence forward these two conducted all the Policy Negotiations, Legislation and War. These underscored Lines contain the whole Fable Plot and Catastrophy. If this Letter should be preserved, and read an hundred Years hence, the Reader will say "the Envy of this J.A. could not bear to think of the Truth!" He ventured to Scribble to Rush, as envious as himself, Blasphemy that he dared not speak, when he lived.

Venting aside, what distinguished Rush's and Adams's correspondence was how attentive they were to their friendship and to the importance of their dialogue. One day Rush received a letter in which Adams disagreed with him on who should be chief justice of the Supreme Court. Adams favored New Yorker John Jay, while Rush favored his Philadelphia ally James Wilson. Rush began his reply, "I find you & I must agree, not to disagree, or we must cease to discuss political questions."

Adams wrote back immediately, "No! You and I will not cease to discuss political questions: but We will agree to disagree, whenever We please, or rather whenever either of Us thinks he has reason for it."

Adams and Rush wrote often about the role of the democratically elected president, the only position in the new government they felt was truly without historical precedent. Their discussion, initially, was over what the chief executive should be called. When

Adams suggested that language such as "His majesty, the President" could be appropriate, Rush replied that he abhorred "all Titles."

They exchanged several follow-up letters, but the issue apparently stuck in Adams's craw because he brought it up again a month later. "I will take a little more notice of a Sentiment in one your letters," he wrote:

> You say you "abhor all Titles." I will take the familiar freedom of Friendship to say I don't believe you.—Let me explain my self.—I doubt not your veracity, but I believe you deceive yourself, and have not yet examined your own heart, and recollected the feelings of every day and hour.—What would you say or think or feel, if your own Children, instead of calling you, Sir, or Father, or Papa, should accost you with the title of "Ben"? Your Servant comes in, and instead of saying my "Master! my hat is much worn, would you please to give me a new one;" cries "Ben! my old hat is all in rags, and makes you the laughing stock of the Town! give me a new one."—What think you of this simple manly republican Style?

The issue of how the first elected leader of their new nation would differ from a monarch, once in office, had fascinated and vexed Adams since the earliest days of the revolution. And by even bringing up the subject, he was criticized by some as appearing to support a form of American monarchy. Rush noted in his next letter that he had been discussing this very subject with their mutual friend Thomas Jefferson during his recent visit to Philadelphia. "In my notebook," Rush said, "I have recorded a conversation that passed between Mr Jefferson & myself . . . of which *you* were the principal subject. We both deplored your Attachment to monarchy, and both agreed that you had changed your principles since the year 1776."

In fact, that wasn't exactly what Jefferson had said to him. In the notebook entry concerning the visit, Rush wrote that Jefferson "still professed himself attached to republican forms of government, and deplored the change of opinion on this subject in John Adams, of whom he spoke with respect and affection as a great and upright man." For the first years they knew each other, Adams, Jefferson, and Rush had fought on the same side, holding the same basic opinions on liberty and unity and republicanism. Now the nation's goals were more fragmented, and words like *republican* and *federalist* were becoming labels for a different spectrum of views—or sometimes just ways of disagreeing.

On a more personal level, this meant that Rush was starting to find himself in between the exuberant Adams, a northerner whom he loved intellectually and emotionally but didn't always agree with, and the more reserved Jefferson, a southerner with whom Rush, in theory, had more in common politically and shared a fascination with science. (Their correspondence and conversations often started with national affairs and segued into questions such as whether Europe or America had more species of deer.)

Perhaps sensing an unresolved issue, Adams, in his next letter, refused to let the monarchy discussion go. He felt Rush didn't fully appreciate his position—and he wanted to be very clear with his friend, who he assumed might be called upon again to explain precisely what the vice president thought (for example, to Jefferson):

> My Friend Dr. Rush will excuse me if I caution him. . . . I am a mortal and irreconcileable Enemy to Monarchy. I am no Friend to hereditary limited Monarchy in America . . . Don't therefore my Friend misunderstand me and misrepresent me to Posterity.—I am for a Ballance between the Legislative and Executive Powers and I am for enabling the Executive to be at all times capable of maintaining the Ballance between the Senate and House, or in other Words between the Aristocratical and Democratical Interests—Yet I am for having all three Branches elected at Stated Periods, and these Elections I hope will continue.

Adams did worry, however, that one day in the future elections might be corrupted, even fixed, and the nation could be forced to consider its electoral alternatives. "If the time should come when Corruption shall be added to Intrigue and Maneouvre in Elections and produce civil War," he told Rush, "then in my opinion Chance will be better than Choice for all but the House of Representatives."

Rush was feeling his own sense of political cynicism. Adams

had asked him if he was interested in a position in the government when it moved to Philadelphia. The doctor said absolutely not, that he was doing his best to ignore public affairs—especially the still-contentious fight over the new Pennsylvania constitution—to focus on medicine and his family. However honest that was, Rush was candid about why politics wasn't for him:

> Sir, I learned . . . from you, to despise public opinion. . . . So much did I imbibe of this Spirit from you, that during the whole of my political life, I was always disposed to suspect my integrity, if from any Accident I became popular with our Citizens for a few weeks or days. . . . The experience I have had in public pursuits, has led me to make many discoveries in the human heart that are not very favourable to it . . . "a politician can never suffer from his *enemies.*"—The folly—the envy—and the ingratitude of his friends are the principal sources of his sufferings.

The slings and arrows of Rush's brief brushes with elected or appointed positions had taken their toll on him. Home was where his heart was, and he was trying to keep it there. "Heaven has been profuse in its gifts of family blessings to me," he explained. "My dear Mrs Rush is every thing to me that a friend—a companion & a wife should be to any man. Our children are affectionate—& dutiful—& promising as to their capacities for acquiring knowledge.—Nineteen out of twenty of my evenings are spent in their Society."

Rush knew he had been among the rising stars of his generation; "I see many men high in power or affluent in office, Who in the year 1776 considered me as one of the firebrands of independence," he wrote. But he felt ready to let go "the midnight Studies which I devoted for 16 years to my Country," for steadier pursuits. "I see nothing before me during the remainder of my life, but labor and Self denial in my profession—and yet I am happy. I envy no man—and blame no man."

In response, Adams spoke foremost to Rush's touching portrait of family, with a candid admission of his own. "The charming Picture you give me of your Domestic Felicity," he wrote, "delights my inmost soul: but revives in me a lively regret for the ten years of my life that I lost—when I left my Children to grow up without a Father." That said, Adams still hoped Rush would one day return to politics.

Rush responded:

> I thank you for your polite wishes to see me restored to public life. There was a time when I would have accepted of an Appointment Abroad. . . . I have meditated with great pleasure upon the pains I should have taken in such a situation to employ my leisure hours in collecting discoveries in Agriculture—manufactures—and in all the useful arts and sciences, and in transmitting them to my American fellow Citizens. But the time is past—for my accepting of that or of any other appointment in the Government of the United States.—I already see a System of influence bordering upon corruption established in our Country, which seems to proclaim to innocence & patriotism to keep their distance.

To reiterate that his family was a worthy refuge, he painted a picture for Adams of what was going on around him as he was writing:

> At the same table where I now sit, I have had the pleasure of seeing my dear Mrs. Rush deeply engaged in reading [Xavier] Millot's Account of the manners—& laws of the Ancient Egyptians—my Eldest son—plodding over [Charles] Rollin's history of Cyrus—and my second boy just beginning [Oliver] Goldsmith's history of England. In the course of the evening, frequent applications were made to me to explain hard words by my boys. One of them who has just finished Ovid at School, asked me—"if there was such a river as the Nile, or such a Country as Egypt." My Answer to this question led me to express my hearty disapprobation of that mode of education which makes the first knowledge of boys to consist in fables, and thereby leads them to reject truth.
>
> I must not forget to mention that my eldest daughter (between 11 and 12 years of age) composed a part of this family picture. She was employed in sewing, but partook in all the conversation of the evening. . . . A compassionate heart is the principal feature in her

> Character. Her little allowance of spending money is chiefly given away to the poor. To both her parents she is dutiful and affectionate in the highest degree. In the Absence of her Mama, she makes tea for me, and sooths me with a hundred little Anecdotes picked up in her schools or in company.

Rush's seventy-five-year-old mother was also among his household. "She is often indisposed in body," he admitted, "but all the powers of her mind are in their full Vigor."

"I have," he concluded, "erected & decorate my little bower. Its shade is already refreshing, and its odors truly delightful."

At some point during one of their many discussions of how the Revolution would be remembered, Rush revealed to Adams that he had been keeping notes for a history book he might someday write. He had already written character sketches of all his fellow members of the Continental Congress, he said, and the generals with whom he had interacted, and he offered to let Adams read some of them.

Adams asked for his own sketch, of course, at which Rush turned cagey; he shared the first few lines, then pulled back, admitting that he:

> intended to have conclude[d] this letter by transcribing your character from my notebook—but upon reading it over, I find so many things said in favor of your principles & conduct in the years 1775 & 1776, that I should be suspected of flattery should I send you a copy of it. I shall give you a specimen of the manner in which I have observed in drawing characters by sending you that of your colleague Robt; Treat Paine's—whose name follows yours in the notebook.

Adams approved of what Rush wrote about his fellow Massachusetts delegate Paine. He also elaborated on a couple of points concerning the few lines about himself that Rush had shared but apparently left it at that. Rush wrote back, "In consequence of the

Contents of your last letter, I shall make no material alterations in your political Character." From then on, however, Adams knew—and he may have been the only one who knew—that Benjamin Rush would one day write a definitive book on the Revolution. At the very least, he was gathering material to establish himself as a sort of Boswell for some of the Founding Fathers.

During this fertile period, Rush and Adams both had deeply affecting dreams about their own places in public life (which they chose not to share with each other until years later). In Rush's dream:

> I imagined I was going up Second Street, in our city, and was much st[r]uck by observing a great number of people assembled near Christ Church, gazing at a man who was seated on the ball just below the vane of the Steeple of the Church.
>
> I asked what was the matter;—One of my fellow citizens came up to me, and said, the man whom you see yonder, has discovered a method of regulating the weather, & that he could produce rain, & sun shine, & cause the wind to blow from any quarter he pleased. I now joined the crowd in gazing at him. He had a trident in his hand which he waved in the air, and called at the same time to the wind which then blew from the north east, to blow from the north West.
>
> I observed the Vane of the Steeple while he was speaking, but perceived no motion in it. He then called for rain, but the Clouds passed over the city without dropping a particle of water. He now became agitated & dejected, and complained of the refractory elements in the most affecting terms. Struck with the issue of his conduct—I said to my friend who stood near to me, "The man is certainly mad."
>
> Instantly a figure dressed like a flying Mercury descended rapidly from him, with a Streamer in his hand, and holding it before my eyes bid me read the inscription on it. It was "De te fabula narratur." ["This story is about you" from Horace.]
>
> The impression of these words was so forcible upon my mind, that I instantly awoke, and from that time I determined never again to attempt to influence the opinions & passions of my fellow Citizens upon political Subjects.

The man who believed he could change the weather was, in fact, just a weather vane.

Adams had a much different kind of dream. It began with him mounting "a lofty scaffold" at Versailles, about to address a huge audience of some "five and twenty millions at least"—not of people but throngs of wild animals, livestock, birds, and fish of all species, the entire Royal Menagerie. His goal was to convince them to live together in peace, under the principles of "Liberty, Equality and Fraternity, among all living Creatures." He had been laboring over the speech for some time, and before beginning, he threw "my eyes round" to connect with his audience and bowed. He started speaking: "My beloved Brothers! We are all Children of the Same Father, who feeds and cloaths us all," he began. "Why Should We not respect each others rights and live in peace and mutual Love!" But he had barely gotten these words out before:

> the Elephant pouted his Probosis at me in contempt, the Lion roared, the Wolf howled the Cats and Dogs were by the Ears, the Eagles flew upon the Turkies, the Hawks and Owls upon the Chickens and Pidgeons. The Whale rolled to swallow twenty at a mouthful and the Shark turned on his Side to Snap the first he could reach with his adamantine Teeth. In a Word Such a Scene of Carnage ensued as no Eye had ever Seen, and no Pen or Pencil ever described. Frightened out of my Witts, I leaped from the Stage and made my Escape; not however without having all my Cloaths Torn from my back and my Skin lacerated from head to foot. The terror and the Scratches awakened me and convinced me forever, what a Fool, I had been.

The dream was no doubt inspired by the French Revolution (which had been rising steadily since the Bastille was stormed in July 1789). But for Adams, it also seemed to have more personal implications. Rush claimed his dream was part of what convinced him to stay away from politics, but Adams's was more a commentary on the public life he was unable to leave, though it often left him feeling as though torn to pieces by wild animals. The latter turned out to be more predictive. He didn't date the dream exactly, but it could have been from around the time early in his presidency when Washington became ill, and Adams was considering that he might have to assume the job.

LATELY RUSH WAS feeling like his life was being spun around by the winds of fate, as several of his guiding lights died, in quick succession. On a Thursday afternoon in the autumn of 1789, he was called to the home of Dr. John Morgan, who though only in his mid-fifties was in deteriorating health. Rush had still seen him around the medical school but had grown distant from the doctor who, twenty years before, had single-handedly delivered to him his first major credential, his professorship in chemistry. He was pained and saddened to find Morgan "dead in a small hovel, surrounded by books and papers, and on a light dirty bed. He was attended only by his washerwoman, one of his tenants. His niece . . . came in time enough to see him draw his last breath."

The image of Morgan dying this way devastated Rush. "What a change from his former rank and prospects in Life!" he wrote. "The man who once filled half the world with his name, had now scarcely friends enough left to bury him."

He was selected to eulogize Morgan for the medical school. Not long afterward he was given Morgan's professorship. While the other professors covered specific subjects such as anatomy, chemistry, and *materia medica*, Morgan's position had always been much broader: his lectures encompassed the experience of becoming a physician. Obtaining his professorship was a huge step in Rush's professional career: from this position, in the intellectual center of the United States, he would essentially oversee the medical education of the first generation of American physicians. Here he could become a Cullen for America.

Unfortunately, he would not have Cullen to guide him. Less than five months after Morgan's funeral, Rush's medical idol died in Scotland at the age of seventy-nine.

Dr. Cullen's death was marked worldwide, and Rush wrote an

elogium for Philadelphia. He reconsidered Cullen's contribution to the history of medicine: his system was the one every physician knew, even if they chose to deviate from it.

Several months before the deaths of Morgan and Cullen, Rush had published his first full-length book, a collection of his most popular essays titled *Medical Inquiries and Observations*. It became the first American medical book known widely across the country, as well as in Europe. Physicians and patients in other cities began contacting him, asking for diagnoses by mail, just as acolytes always had with Cullen. Some solicited free advice; more included cash or coins with their letters, which he always donated. It was clear from the book that Rush did not yet have a complete "system" of his own, even though he was thinking more and more about the primacy of pulse and blood. If anything, the book put the medical world on notice that he was a growing force to contend with, and perhaps someday a Morgan or even a Cullen.

Then on a Sunday in mid-April 1790, Benjamin Franklin died at eighty-four, in the most expected yet most resonant loss for Philadelphia. Rush had not been his physician but was in contact with his caregivers and knew he had suffered with a "stone in his bladder" and "a pleurisy which terminated in the abscess in his lungs," diagnosed from what he painfully coughed up in the days before his death. As the last word on their long debate about dangerous air, Rush noted that Franklin's "pleurisy was caught by lying with his windows open." Rush was pleased to learn that Franklin "possessed his reason to the last day of his life" but disappointed that he "spoke nothing of his future existence or expectation beyond the grave." He had held out a slim hope that Franklin would call to Jesus with his last breaths, or invoke an afterlife, but he was a scientist and a Deist to the end—and to Rush, forever a member of "the first class of beings."

The next day Rush went to Franklin's house to see the corpse before burial. His fifty-two-year-old son-in-law, Richard Bache, escorted him to where the body was laid out. "It was much reduced," he noted, "but not changed. Had his beard been shaved after his death, he would have looked like himself, but this was forbidden by Mr. Bache."

Rush asked for a lock of Franklin's hair, a common keepsake, and Bache assented. So Rush cut some for himself and enough to mail to two of Franklin's closest friends abroad, Richard Price in England and the Marquis de Lafayette in France.

Two days later Rush marched in the funeral procession, with the assembled members of the many societies in which he and Franklin were officers or active. (Many would need to scramble to elect new presidents to replace Franklin.) Some twenty thousand lined the streets to watch the march, which ended at the Christ Church cemetery at Fifth and Arch streets, where Franklin was buried in the most visible location on the burial ground's northwest corner.

Rush's family plot was on the other side of the cemetery, against the eastern wall. There was some comfort in knowing that someday, he and the great man would be together again. But it was the end of an era—several eras, actually—for his city.

Only weeks after Franklin's funeral, however, Philadelphia was reborn, for at least the next ten years. In a stunning piece of political compromise, New Yorker Alexander Hamilton—the thirty-five-year-old secretary of the treasury and an increasingly aggressive political animal—brokered a deal with Jefferson, then secretary of state, and his fellow Virginian, Congressman James Madison. The new federal government would assume the debt of the Revolutionary War—a key to the federal banking system Hamilton imagined—while the country's permanent capital would be located in the South (or far enough south that slavery was still allowed).

A site along the Potomac River was selected for the federal district, with land donated from Virginia and Maryland, to become the capital starting in 1800. Rush immediately lobbied Adams to rethink the long-range plan. He was certain the nation's elected leaders would regret being "dragged in a few years to the banks of the Potowmac where negro slaves will be your servants by day—

mosquitoes your centinals by night, and bilious fevers your companions every summer and fall—and pleurasies, every spring."

But Rush was thrilled about the deal Hamilton had made for the ten years until the permanent seat of government could be designed and built. The capital was moving from New York to Philadelphia, the country's birthplace. The city hadn't hosted the government since the summer of 1783, when Congress moved after an embarrassing protest by soldiers over back wages. Even though it was starting to be edged out by New York as the most populous city in America, Philadelphia was still very much the nation's intellectual and financial powerhouse. And for the next ten years, it would be the undisputed center of the rapidly expanding American universe.

34

Abigail Adams had never met this Benjamin Rush with whom her husband so boisterously corresponded. When she moved to Philadelphia in the fall of 1790, now the wife of the vice president, she had been concerned that people would be solicitous of her because of her husband's position. But she and John and Benjamin and Julia became fast friends.

Abigail must have written to her sister, Mary Cranch, about how well they got along, because Mary expressed her pleasure that the Adamses had found in the Rushes "friends where you can visit free from the shackels of so much ceremony as your station subjects you to." Rush became their family doctor but also, perhaps more usefully, their first source for Philadelphia lore, logistics, and gossip. Abigail described him to her sister as "my intelligenser, dr. Rush, who knows everybody and their connections."

In the spring Abigail decided six months in Philadelphia was enough and moved back to Massachusetts to take care of the farm. But her relationship with the Rushes was set, and she was pleased her husband had such a family in Philadelphia he could count on.

In general, Rush stayed away from the pomp and circumstance of the government, which was largely centered around Congress

Hall—a newly expanded courthouse building at Sixth and Chestnut, where the House of Representatives and the Senate met—and the President's House (and office), just over a block away on Market near Sixth. He met Adams sometimes for meals and saw Jefferson at Philosophical Society meetings, but mostly he stayed busy teaching, taking care of his private patients, and working at the hospital.

He was now teaching at the new University of Pennsylvania, which had been created when the old College of Philadelphia (which closed after the war and briefly reopened in the late 1780s) merged with the newer University of the State of Pennsylvania, where Rush had been working more recently. The unified University of Pennsylvania was a more powerful institution, where his local, national, and international profile could broaden further. He was appointed to be both professor of the institutes of medicine and of clinical medicine (applied physiology as well as clinical practice), and was joined on the new faculty by his longtime colleagues Dr. Adam Kuhn (theory and practice of medicine) and Dr. William Shippen, Jr. (anatomy, surgery, and midwifery), along with several of their brightest former students, Caspar Wistar, Samuel Griffitts, and Benjamin Barton.

Classes for the new medical school were held at Surgeons Hall at Fifth and Walnut streets, and Rush found himself engrossed—and sometimes overwhelmed—by the pressure of lecturing on broader and more challenging subjects, after years of boilerplate teaching of chemistry. Rush was also expected each fall to write and deliver the "Introductory Lecture to courses of Lectures upon the Institutes and Practise of Medicine"—an original talk on an important and medically inspirational topic. It took a lot of writing, practicing, and memorization to appear effortless in front of his students; he had to turn down invitations because of the work.

Rush was especially unhappy, one Wednesday evening, to turn down, because of a teaching conflict, an invitation to dine with Jefferson. They were supposed to continue their exciting conversation about sugar maple trees, which they wanted to start planting as a way of expanding American agriculture while simultaneously de-incentivizing the slave trade from the West Indies. (The plan was eventually presented to the Philosophical Society but never took root.)

At Pennsylvania Hospital, Rush's work in the basement was starting to attract notice. His friend Thomas Mifflin, the newly elected governor of Pennsylvania (the first-ever governor under the new state constitution), came for a visit and recognized Hannah Lewis from her years on the street—and thought she might remember him. They got into a feisty conversation. He introduced himself as governor, and she introduced herself as "King George the second's daughter. And do you say you are the governor? . . . Who signed your commission? I never did."

When he explained "the people" had elected him, she said, "I wonder what they could see in your face to make you a governor for let me tell you that you are a very ill looking fellow." He gave her a pair of spectacles he had brought her, which she suggested he might have stolen but was happy to have back. "I may never get anything else," she said, "so I may as well keep them." Her thinking was still disordered, but she was much better than when she had been trying to live on her own.

The first international public notice of Rush's work with mental illness appeared in a book by the French writer Jacques-Pierre Brissot, who had visited America and among his *New Travels in the United States of America* had spent some time with "the enlightened and humane Dr. Rush."

He was impressed by what the doctor and his staff had been able to accomplish in the challenging below-ground space. Each patient, he noted, "had his cell, with a bed, a table, and a convenient window with grates. Stoves are fixed in the walls, to warm the cell in winter. . . . These unhappy persons are treated with the greatest tenderness; they are allowed to walk in the court; are constantly visited by two physicians. . . . None of these fools were naked, or indecent. . . . These people preserve, even in their folly, their primitive characteristic of decency.

"What a difference," he declared, "between this treatment and the atrocious regulations to which we condemn such wretches in France! where they are rigorously confined, and their disorders scarcely ever fail to increase upon them."

Brissot noted that Rush was experimenting with "a kind of swing chair for their exercise." Most likely the chair spun the patient back and forth, in an attempt to better regulate blood flow in the body and brain. Rush must have heard about it when its inventor, young British physician Joseph Mason Cox, was studying at Edinburgh, and had one made in Philadelphia to try out.

Rush had told Brissot that he sought to move the patients into new, less prison-like quarters at ground level. He had been talking to the hospital administration about it for some time, privately begging them for a more humane building and gardens. A year after Brissot's visit, but before his book was published, Rush went public with his complaints, in a bold letter to the board of managers, which also ran in the newspaper. He wrote that "patients afflicted by Madness, should be the first objects of the care of a physician. . . . I have attempted to relieve them, but . . . my attempts . . . which at first promised some Improvement were soon afterwards rendered Abortive by the Cells of the hospital." The cells were too damp in the winter and too warm in the summer, and since they got almost no ventilation, the "smell of them is both offensive and unwholesome." Most patients contracted a cold within weeks, and "several have died of Consumption in consequence."

Using the cells "any longer for the reception of mad people," he declared to the board, "will be dishonourable both to the Science and Humanity of the city of Philadelphia." He urged them to raise money immediately for new facilities, which represented the best hope that "many of them might be Relieved by the use of remedies which have lately been discovered to be effectual in their disorder."

Rush's oldest child, John, was still planning on becoming a doctor, and in the spring of 1792, he was accepted to study at the College of New Jersey, where, at fourteen, he would begin as a sophomore.

While Rush was excited for him, he was also nervous. As a first-time father who hadn't had one of his own growing up, he realized he was learning on the job; two years earlier, when John was twelve, Rush had written to a clergyman about his childrearing ideas, which he suspected were unique. "I have discovered that all corporal Corrections for children above three or four years old are highly improper," he wrote. He had come to the determination "that *solitude* is the most effective punishment," not least because John had "more than once begged me to flog him in preference to confining him." He had once confined John and his brother Richard "in separate rooms for two days. The impression which this punishment has left upon them I believe will never wear away, nor do I think it will ever require to be repeated."

Rush thought John, at the college, shouldn't live with other students and so arranged for him to board with the Princeton family of Dr. Walter Minto, the chair of mathematics and natural philosophy. In a letter both pedantic and anxious, Rush asked Minto—who was also to be John's professor—to be "taking charge of him and superintending his morals as well as his studies. I shall expect that he will *study* constantly in your house and never enter the College except when he goes to say his lessons or perform some academic exercise. On no other condition can I consent to sending him to Princeton." For boys John's age, he considered "*college life* and *college society*" to be "fatal" to their morals and manners.

Rush also felt compelled to describe John's personality in more detail. "He is a lad of promising talents and has of late become more inquisitive and studious than formerly," he wrote. "His temper, though a little quick, is not violent, and soon gives way to a firm spirit of government in his superiors. As yet his morals are pure." He added, oddly: "He has a taste for music. I have indulged him with a flute, but under two conditions—that he give up his gun, and that he never touch his flute except in the evening." He told Dr. Minto that he and Julia were deeply grateful for his help because John, their firstborn, was, in the words of Virgil, "spes gregis"—the hope of the flock.

John Rush turned fifteen that summer, and he lasted at Princeton a total of four months. On Monday, September 10, the faculty met to discuss the shocking news that four students had been found "playing cards on Sunday evening," the Sabbath. Their punishment was to "read a confession before the whole college assembled at evening prayers," which the four of them did the next day. They promised to "restore all the goods & money . . . we have won from each other & never to indulge ourselves in the like practice while subject to the discipline of the college."

The three other offenders returned to their classes, properly chastened. John Rush was withdrawn from Princeton by his parents. Rush told Minto that because of John's:

> public disgrace. . . . he can never recover his character so as to appear to advantage either with his masters or among his fellow students, [so] I have concluded to take him home. I . . . shall always ascribe it not less to the depravity of his mind than to the temptations and opportunities of vice which are inseparably connected with a number of boys herding together under one roof without the restraints which arise from female and family society.

Rush closed the letter, "We shall always retain a grateful sense of your kindness to our poor deluded boy." It is unclear whether withdrawing John was an overreaction to the reported gambling or there was more to the story than made it into the official report. But Rush had already expressed concern about John's nature, and the incident seemed to confirm his worries. John returned to Philadelphia to study at the University of Pennsylvania, under his parents' watchful eyes.

Rush also took steps to restrain John from other risky or un-Christian activities, which included not only card playing and drinking of alcohol but attending or participating in live theater, which troubled some clergy. Not long after returning home, Rush had John sign a document, which his mother and aunt witnessed, in which he agreed to "renounce all claim or demand whatsoever to the Theatre & I do further promise that I will not go to the said, or any other whatever" for a period of the next "four years three months and twelve days"—until he was twenty-one. If he broke the promise, he would be "forfeiting a valuable gold watch."

By this point, the Rushes had a new son and tempted fate by naming him Benjamin Jr., as they had their last son, who had died in infancy less than two years before. There were now six children in the house under fifteen, four boys and two girls—and Julia was pregnant again.

They had also moved again, just across the street, to the northwestern corner of Third and Walnut. It was a fine, large house, an easy walk to the hospital and the medical school. The only problem was the neighbors. The Alexander Hamiltons were renting their old house across the street. (In the 1790 census Rush's name can be seen crossed out and Hamilton's written in.)

Rush and Hamilton disagreed, vehemently, on nearly everything. Rush loudly opposed many of the decisions Hamilton had made as secretary of the treasury; he had always feared aggressive government fiscal actions, going back to debates on state price controls. More important, Rush had started out as a federalist with a small "f," when that meant supporting a union with a strong central government over the demands of radical states' rights partisans. But Hamilton increasingly claimed his own form of bigger government as Federalism with a capital "F," drawing battle lines among those who had fought together for independence.

Hamilton seemed, to Rush, to want an adversarial two-party system, positioning himself as the driving force of the winning side through his cabinet position and access to President Washington. He and the newspapers that supported him were coming to see Federalism as the adversary, even as the enemy of Republicanism, the more populist view of government of which Jefferson was becoming the standard-bearer. Rush sided with Jefferson (and James Madison) in disagreeing not only with many of Hamilton's strategies but also with his brand of political infighting in Washington's cabinet. He conceded that Hamilton was a "visionary" in some of his "principles and projects" and was

Alexander Hamilton

almost frighteningly capable of getting things done. But he also thought he was a manipulative back-stabber and bomb-thrower who all but "looked forward to a civil war."

Adding to the friction was that not long after they became neighbors, the nation experienced its first financial disaster, the Panic of 1792—which Rush blamed entirely on Hamilton. As part of his plan to consolidate the war debt and stabilize the federal government, Hamilton had convinced Washington to let him start the Bank of the United States (later known as the First National Bank). This involved the selling of "scrip," or stock, each share of which cost $25 ($661) initially with three later payments. But widespread speculation developed, leading to what Rush described in 1791 as "the bursting of the bubble."

Rush, like many, had invested in scrip. In a commonplace book, he mentioned selling two shares for $450 ($11,900) at eight a.m. on an August morning—and then watching the value of his other shares fall to $320 ($8,460) by evening. Eventually, he lost enough that he had to quietly sacrifice the family's Cottage Farm in Oxford County.

The Hamilton and Rush families, meanwhile, didn't care about the political squabbles of their fathers. The secretary's wife and children got along well with the doctor's wife and children. Hamilton was twelve years younger but had married much younger, so they had several children the same age. His oldest son, Philip, was friends with Rush's second son, Richard.

Far from these domestic affairs, the French Revolution intensified, putting at risk the relationship with the French that had allowed the American Revolution to succeed. It was the first true international issue to confront the United States. Jefferson and Rush were torn: they had friends in the French aristocracy, but they also believed in democratic revolution. When King Louis XVI was beheaded on January 21, 1793, the whole world worried—especially as France declared war on England (and the Dutch Republic), making America's two largest trading partners arch adversaries once again. Hamilton feared anarchy or a possible second revolution in

America; he also wanted to maintain international neutrality. So Hamilton pushed for Federalist political and financial actions to keep America out of the conflict, and for a military buildup. Jefferson and Rush feared and attacked these actions, as "Democratic-Republicans," so called after the party Jefferson and Madison had recently founded, marking the beginning of America's two-party system.

The capital was politicized as never before. Several newspapers developed for each partisan camp, as Philadelphia publishers realized they could sell copies by fanning the flames of controversy. Those willing and able to use the papers to their advantage gained extra power but paid for that influence by being more aggressively targeted themselves. Benjamin Rush had a high-profile national voice but did not also hold a high office or own a newspaper, so he was especially vulnerable. His powerful friendships notwithstanding, attacking him was less risky.

Still, Rush dealt with his fear of a foreign war fearlessly. He wrote a satirical piece entitled "Plan of a Peace-Office for the United States" in which he argued that since the government had a standing Department of War, it should also have a countervailing Department of Peace, with its own cabinet secretary.

Among the secretary of peace's first actions, including the spread of more peaceful and Christian thought, Rush proposed general demilitarization and even gun control (echoing, by coincidence or not, his concern with his son John's fascination with firearms).

"To subdue that passion for war" he wrote, ". . . a familiarity with the instruments of death, as well as all military shows, should be carefully avoided." He proposed that local militia laws be repealed and military reviews halted; he thought uniforms and titles from the Revolutionary War should be discouraged from being used. After all, military reviews "tend to lessen the horrors of a battle by connecting them with the charms of order; militia laws generate idleness and vice, and thereby produce the wars they are said to prevent; military dresses fascinate the minds of young men, and lead them from serious and useful professions . . . military titles feed vanity, and keep up ideas in the mind which lessen a sense of the folly and miseries of war."

To once and for all "affect the minds of the citizens of the United States with the blessings of peace," he suggested that a few inscriptions be painted over the door of the office of the U.S. Department of War:

> 1. An office for butchering the human species.
> 2. A Widow and Orphan making office.
> 3. A broken bone making office.
> 4. A Wooden leg making office.
> 5. An office for the creating of public and private vices.
> 6. An office for creating a public debt.
> 7. An office for creating speculators, stock jobbers, and bankrupts.
> 8. An office for creating famine.
> 9. An office for creating pestilential diseases.
> 10. An office for creating poverty, and the destruction of liberty, and national happiness.
>
> In the lobby of this office let there be painted representations of all the common military instruments of death, also human skulls, broken bones, unburied and putrefying dead bodies, hospitals crowded with sick and wounded soldiers, villages on fire, mothers in besieged towns eating the flesh of their children, ships sinking in the ocean, rivers dyed with blood, and extensive plains without a tree or fence, or any object, but the ruins of deserted farm houses.
>
> Above this group of woeful figures,—let the following words be inserted, in red characters to represent human blood,
>
> "NATIONAL GLORY."

As if the article weren't controversial enough, it was published in *Banneker's Almanac*, a new publication edited by a free black writer, Benjamin Banneker.

Among the political tensions, racial strains were worsening in Philadelphia, especially in houses of worship that Rush attended. The reception of black parishioners, some of them his own friends and patients, was increasingly uneasy, he noted. This friction had been coming for some time.

Two years earlier, Rush had quietly met with a dozen free black men who wanted to start their own congregation. At their request, he wrote out a basic "plan for church government" for them, but they weren't quite ready to move forward. However, Episcopal leader Bishop White must have heard about the draft plan, because a week later he confronted Rush on the street and "expressed his disapprobation to the proposed African church." White said the proposal "originated in pride," and that if they went through with it, he would no longer officiate at black funerals.

Over a year after their first meeting with Rush, several African American religious leaders published a small notice in a local paper, the *Gazette of the United States*, announcing a fund-raising effort for the nation's first black church. It was addressed "to the Friends of Liberty and Religion in the city of Philadelphia" from "the Representatives of the African Church in said city"—and was widely assumed to have been the "plan" drafted by the doctor.

One of these leaders was Absalom Jones, who, with his fellow former slave Richard Allen, had created the Free African Society in 1787 and had been preaching at St. George's local Methodist church for years. Soon after the Free African Society purchased two lots on Fifth Street south of Walnut, they were inspired to make a bold move.

One Sunday, the black congregants at St. George's were informed that from then on, they would be allowed to sit only in new balconies that the church had just put in. Confused, the worshippers went to the seats they normally used, along the walls on the main floor. Richard Allen knelt down and began his prayers when he was disturbed by "considerable scuffling and low talking." He looked up to see Absalom Jones being lifted bodily out of the pew by white church trustees, saying "you must get up—you must not kneel here."

Jones pleaded that the trustees "wait until prayer is over," but they refused. So, as soon as the prayer was over, Allen recalled, the black congregants "all went out of the church in a body."

The date of the "Saint George's walkout" has never been firmly established, but it is known to have happened around February 12, 1793. This was the day the U.S. Congress, driven by southern states, passed the Fugitive Slave Act, which made it easier for slave owners to reenslave blacks who had fled—and also led to some demonstrably free blacks being kidnapped back into service.

The Fugitive Slave Act was likely the reason Rush, in May 1793, wrote a signed letter of emancipation and recommendation for William Grubber:

> I do hereby certify that the bearer, William Grubber, formerly my servant, has been duly emancipated according to law in Pennsylvania. Whilst he lived with me he was sober, honest, and faithful. He leaves me with the affections, and best wishes of every member of my family; and I do hereby recommend him to the protection, and friendship of all persons who love integrity, and goodness of heart in their humble, as well as in their more distinguished forms.
>
> Benjamin Rush MD
>
> Professor of Medicine in the University of Pennsylvania

The tone of the document suggests that Grubber had already been legally free for some time. While Rush's 1788 manumission of Grubber set 1794 as his date of liberation, this document shows he was freed at least a year earlier. How much earlier is unknown, because no official document exists, and Rush most likely gave this letter to Grubber so nobody could take him under the Fugitive Slave Act.

Meanwhile Rush continued to be active in the Abolition Society and in fund-raising for the African Episcopal Church of St. Thomas, the city's first black church and the nation's first black Episcopal church. (During this time, Richard Allen asked the Abolition Society to help him start a new business: a nail company. They gave him a fifty-pound [$7,460] loan, payable in eighteen months.)

Toward the end of August 1793, Rush was invited to celebrate the raising of the roof for the new church—at a remarkable dinner. It was held a mile from town, down Second Street, under the shade of large trees.

The dinner began with a hundred white people involved with the church project—primarily carpenters but also some donors—sitting down at a long table, where they were served dinner by free black congregants. Rush was asked to sit at the head of the table. After a plentiful dinner finished off with very good melons, Rush offered two rousing toasts, to cheers: "Peace on earth, good will to men," and then, "may African churches everywhere soon succeed African bondage."

After the toasts, the white attendees rose, and a hundred black men and women took their seats. Then the white guests served *them* dinner. Rush would have been among the servers, but the church elders insisted he sit back down with them. "Never did I witness such a scene of . . . virtuous and philanthropic joy," he wrote. "Billy Grey [church leader William Grey] in attempting to express his feelings was checked by a flood of tears." He described one of the elders' toasts: "'May you live long, and when you die, may you not die eternally.'"

Rush felt strongly that free blacks in prison should be able to share in the triumph of the new church, too. So he had arranged, earlier in the day, to have "a large wheelbarrow full of melons" sent to the prison, with a note explaining they were for "persons who are suffering in the jail for their offenses against society." He hoped that while they were "partaking of this agreeable fruit they will remember that BEING who created it still cares for them, and that by this and other acts of kindness conveyed to them by his creatures, he means to lead them to repentance and happiness."

All in all, he said, it was "a day to be remembered with pleasure as long as I live."

Unfortunately, it was the last pleasurable day he would have for a while.

35

The night before the Free African Society dinner, Rush had been sitting in his parlor, bone-tired, writing a letter to Julia with troubling news.

Near the end of almost every summer in Philadelphia, people suddenly began worrying about illness, wondering what a cough or an ache might mean. But this August something more fearsome seemed to be happening.

"A malignant fever has broken out in Water Street," Rush wrote. The illness had "already carried off twelve persons" on one block—one of whom died only twelve hours after the first symptom appeared. Rush had treated eleven patients so far; three had already died, while the others were barely holding on.

He prayed the fever wouldn't spread "beyond the reach of the putrid exhalation which first produced it." All the deaths were concentrated in one small area close to the river, north of Market Street, and doctors as well as port officials initially believed that the disease was caused by a toxic air "produced by some damaged coffee which had putrefied on one of the wharves." At the moment, nobody was sick except those who lived within a summer breeze of the contaminated coffee. So Rush hadn't panicked. Two of his sons, eleven-year-old Richard and two-year-old Ben, were still there at the house with him, and John was on his way home from vacation;

he had no worries for them. (The rest of the children, including their new seventh child, a daughter named Julia, were with their mother visiting their uncle Richard's house in Trenton.) Rush's sister, Rebecca, and his mother were still with him in Philadelphia. Their twenty-eight-year-old servant Marcus Marsh—who had been born at Morven as a slave, grew up with Julia, and was freed after Richard Stockton's death but had kept working for the family, now in the Rush house—stayed, even though he was just getting over an influenza. Dr. Rush was reasonably certain that all would be well.

But then the illness spread, block by block, toward his house. "The fever," Rush wrote, "has assumed a most alarming appearance. It not only mocks in most instances the power of medicine, but it has spread through several parts of the city remote from the spot where it originated." He remembered the 1762 yellow fever epidemic from his apprenticeship and had seen a few lesser outbreaks since. He knew the symptoms to watch for in patients, and the sad inevitability that when their eyes turned yellow and their vomit black, there was no hope. Just that morning Rush witnessed a scene that reminded him of histories he had read of the black plague: a young merchant and his only child died almost simultaneously, the wife frantic and inconsolable with grief. And he had lost nine other patients in different parts of the city.

In going over his clinical notes, Rush realized he had been seeing early cases of yellow fever for weeks. As early as August 5 a fellow physician, Dr. Hodge, had asked him to attend to his sick child, who died of the fever two days later. Not long afterward he treated his old girlfriend Polly, who had been married for over twenty-five years to his friend Tom Bradford, for what he now suspected could have been the same illness. She, luckily, survived.

On August 19, after several more of the early patients died, Rush consulted on the case of a prominent society woman with a junior colleague, Dr. Foulke, and the same Dr. Hodge whose son they had just lost. The patient died the next evening, and as the doctors were leaving her room, Rush turned to Foulke and Hodge and said, "I suspect all is not right in our city."

On August 25, he met with his fellow doctors at the College of Physicians to discuss the growing epidemic. Many of them didn't show up, because, as Rush noted, they were already "flying from the city." But those who attended all pored over their medical books, trying to come up with answers and figure out a course of action. While these doctors all had histories of personal clashes with one another, they generally agreed about what should be done to prevent and treat the illness. Rush was selected to write up the college's prescriptions, the first of which was "to put a stop to the tolling of the bells" for funerals—since so many people were dying.

They also recommended that people avoid "unnecessary intercourse" with people who were infected, and that a mark (a small red flag) be placed on the front door or window of any house with an infected person inside. Infected people were to be placed in the center of large and airy rooms, in beds without curtains, their linens frequently changed and washed and "all offensive matters" removed from near them. For the poor, it was suggested the city create a new "large and airy hospital."

They recommended the dead be buried as privately as possible, and the streets and wharves of the city be kept "as clean as possible" to prevent "contagion." Preventive measures included avoiding "all fatigue of body and mind," as well as "*standing* or *sitting* in the sun" in a "current of air, or in the evening air." Dressing too warmly was recommended; intemperance was not.

It was also the opinion of the college that building fires would be ineffectual, but burning gunpowder could potentially impede the fever. While vinegar and camphor were useful disinfectants, using them "too frequently upon handkerchiefs, or in smelling bottles," could be dangerous. (In the aromatherapy department, citizens were soon eating or rubbing themselves with garlic, smoking constantly or chewing tobacco, and even dipping pieces of rope into tar to wear around their necks.)

While Rush wrote up the college's recommendations, they were not published under his name. They were signed by the college's vice president, Dr. Shippen. But since Shippen had fled the city for his own safety almost immediately after the meeting, Rush became the leading spokesman for the directive.

He wrote to Julia that he hoped the recommendations would "do good, but I fear no efforts will totally subdue the fever before the heavy rains or frosts of October." Until then, he asked her to pray for him. "I hope I shall do well," he said. "I do not neglect to use every precaution. . . . I even strive to subdue my sympathy for my patients; otherwise I should sink under the accumulated loads of misery I am obliged to contemplate. You can recollect how much the loss of a single patient once a month used to affect me. Judge then how I must feel in hearing every morning of the death of three or four!"

John and Richard were still at home, but when he returned from making house calls, they wouldn't come near him, afraid of being infected by his clothes. He realized the boys had to leave. He sent the older two to Julia at Trenton, and one of the servants, Becky, took two-year-old Ben to William Bradford's farm outside the city. Rush's sister and mother insisted on staying to help. His apprentices were doing their best to put on brave faces.

Rush was now working ridiculous hours and making little progress—patients continued to die. He asked Julia to tell the children he loved them. "For some days past," he admitted, "my mind has been so occupied with the immense objects now before me that I had almost forgotten them."

On August 29, only a week after he had been celebrating the church roof-raising, Rush came to a dreadful realization: the fever was everywhere in the city. The stories that circulated were more and more shocking; publisher Mathew Carey reported that "a man and his wife, once in affluent circumstances, were found lying dead in bed, and between them was their child, a little infant, who was sucking its mother's breasts. How long they had lain thus, was uncertain." Rush was having the hardest time watching young people, the age of his own children, die. He was spooked by the image of "a solitary corpse" lying across the seat of a horse-drawn carriage, with nobody attending its progress down the street.

He himself was dashing all over town to make house calls, often just to confirm a death. Sometimes people would stop his chair in the street and beg him to come to their houses. With many doctors gone from town, he consolidated a small team he could count on.

Thirty-one-year-old Caspar Wistar, who had been a student of his and Shippen's and now taught at the medical school, was particularly helpful, and one of Rush's apprentices, Johnny Stall, slept and ate with him, relieving him when needed.

But none of the common remedies for such fevers—bark, wine, blistering, cool baths—were working at all. On September 3, he tried a more aggressive treatment, purges, using salts and crème of tartar. But they were "ineffectual to open the bowels." So he turned to small amounts of calomel, mercury chloride, and jalap, the Mexican tuber, downed with some "chicken water or water gruel." This "mercurial antidote" seemed promising, and he recommended it to others—including fellow physicians who were ill, among them Caspar Wistar.

Each day Rush was astonished to be still alive. Morning prayers had never seemed so moving and resonant, as he did them on his way to absurdly early house calls. While waiting for Rebecca to give him a quick breakfast before leaving, he jotted a few lines down to Julia—but there was a knock on the door. "Adieu," he scribbled. "The delay of a minute seems a year to a patient after a physician is sent for."

For the next few days, Rush was convinced that his "mercurial antidote" could be the cure for everyone. But other physicians were skeptical—some, to his frustration, would even "rail" against his "new remedy." Dr. Hutchinson, the doctor in charge of the docks and naval vessels, argued publicly with Rush on a few issues concerning the fever, and then, when he got sick himself, refused to try Rush's treatment.

Hutchinson was the first prominent physician to die of yellow fever. Since he practiced at the docks, he had probably been infected early on. But Rush assumed he had died because he had been too arrogant to listen to him. He was coming to believe that anyone who wouldn't try his methods was doing so for political or personal reasons. There was some truth to this, because almost everything the doctors said and thought, and everything their critics in office and even their patients said, was finding its way, often in sensational form, into the newspapers.

Still, some physicians disagreed with Rush on medical grounds, feeling that his treatments were too aggressive and risky. They grew only more convinced when, once he realized purges alone weren't stopping the disease, Rush added light bloodletting. And then when that didn't work, he purged and bled more aggressively than ever before. To him, it was still standard practice for a physician with a failing treatment to explore whether a higher dose might work, especially in a dire situation. And this situation was beyond dire—it was turning into the worst epidemic in history.

Rush came across an old bound manuscript Franklin had given him, in which the Virginia doctor John Mitchell chronicled yellow fever epidemics in 1737 and 1741. Mitchell claimed that in certain yellow fever cases, he tried bleeding and purging even when the patient already had a somewhat faint pulse—regardless of the fact that bleeding was generally thought of as a way to reduce a pulse that was too strong. Instead of making these weakened yellow fever patients worse, however, the bleeding seemed to make them better. This convinced Rush that such measures were worth trying, however counterintuitive they were. (And while he didn't say so, the fact that the manuscript was from Franklin's library probably felt like divine intervention.)

So when weaker treatments failed, Rush tried these more aggressive purges and took more blood. Patients were now panicking at the first sign of anything they thought might be yellow fever, so even before they developed yellow skin and black vomit, he used light purges and bloodletting as preventive measures (paired with careful attention to the patient's nourishment and cleanliness).

Physicians who disagreed with him used different courses of treatment; most tried purges, fewer of them bloodletting. Two who doubted Rush, Dr. George Stevens and Dr. William Currie, published a pamphlet recommending nothing more than fresh air, mild purgatives, and laudanum or ammonia to encourage perspiration. Whenever Rush heard about patients who had died after relying on the milder treatments in this pamphlet, he became angry that they hadn't listened to him and at least tried bloodletting. And whenever any of Stevens's and Currie's patients recuperated, they immediately questioned why anyone would try Rush's harsher methods.

Of course, none of these physicians really knew how to prevent or treat yellow fever. (Even today, no treatment reliably targets the yellow fever virus. Some recover on their own while being kept hydrated and comfortable, and the rest die.) They also didn't know the true source of the disease—it was carried by infected mosquitoes. Intense debate broke out over whether it was contagious, passed from patient to patient by contact or through the air. They also debated where it had originated: Had it been brought to Philadelphia on a ship from another city or country, in contaminated coffee or in passengers? Or was its origin in Philadelphia itself? In the absence of actual information, partisan rancor filled the void, turning the debates into a nasty zero-sum game.

When Alexander Hamilton and his wife, Elizabeth, both became ill, they chose to be treated by Dr. Stevens.

Jefferson assumed Hamilton's illness had been caused by sheer fear. If Hamilton was in danger at all, he wrote to Madison, "he puts himself so by his excessive alarm. He had been miserable several days before from a firm persuasion he should catch it. A man as timid as he is on the water, as timid on horseback, as timid in sickness, would be a phænomenon if his courage, of which he has the reputation in military occasions, were genuine. His friends, who have not seen him, suspect it is only an autumnal fever he has."

Whether the Hamiltons actually had yellow fever cannot be proven, but on September 11, after they felt better, they touted Dr. Stevens's milder course of treatment. Hamilton wrote a public letter saying Stevens's "mode of treating the disorder varies essentially from that which has been generally practiced—And I am persuaded, where pursued, reduces it to one of little more than ordinary hazard." The Federalist press praised Stevens and called his treatment the "Federalist cure."

Rush was incensed, both medically and politically. "I think it probable," he wrote to Julia, "that if the new remedies had been introduced by any other person than a decided Democrat and a friend of Madison and Jefferson, they would have met with less opposition from Colonel Hamilton." (Washington and Adams avoided the yellow fever crisis: Adams was in Philadelphia only when Congress was in session, and Washington fled town with his family on September 10 but was kept apprised by cabinet members.) On the same day Hamilton wrote about Dr. Stevens, the *Federal Gazette* published a long letter from Rush's friend and colleague Adam Kuhn, which also endorsed common treatments Rush had moved on from; he felt beset from all sides.

On the very day Hamilton and Kuhn's letters came to light, September 11, an announcement appeared on the front page of several local papers from black leaders Absalom Jones and Richard Allen. Since many of the city's white physicians, nurses, and others involved in health (and death) had fled, they wanted people to know the black community stood ready to help: "As it is a time of great distress in this city, many people of the Black colour, under a greatful remembrance of the favour received from the white inhabitants, have agreed to assist them as far as in their power for the nursing of the sick and burial of the dead." The ad listed the home address for both Jones and Allen.

Rush had encouraged Allen and Jones to offer their services, in a letter dated "September 1793":

> My dear friends,
>
> It has pleased God to visit the city with a malignant & contagious fever, which infects white people of all ranks, but passes by persons of your color. I have therefore taken the liberty of suggesting to you whether this important exemption which God has granted to you from a dangerous & fatal disorder does not lay you under an obligation to offer your services to attend the sick who are afflicted with this malady. Such an act in your society will [crossed out: render you acceptable to] be very grateful to the citizens, and I hope pleasing in the light of that God who will see every act of kindness done to his creatures whom he calls his brethren, as if done to himself
>
> From your sincere friend
> B Rush

At the time, Rush believed it to be a medical fact that black people were immune to yellow fever. He was likely the author of a short item in the *Daily Advertiser*, signed "Benezet," which quoted his medical source—a "late Doctor Lining" from South Carolina—confirming that "black people . . . in not one instance have been infected."

The day after Jones and Allen's advertisement, Rush dashed off a letter to the College of Physicians to justify his methods. ("I have bled twice in many, and in one acute case four times, with the happiest effects.") Then, impetuously, he wrote to the *Federal Gazette*, offering detailed medical advice to the entire city. He shared his controversial "antidote," which was still only days old and had been tested on a few dozen patients. He suggested that if patients were unable to be seen by the city's few remaining physicians, they could arrange for the purges and bloodletting themselves.

For some reason, he offered this advice while referring to himself in the third person: "Dr. Rush . . . hopes this information will be attended to, as many of the sick suffer greatly from the want of the assistance of bleeders and of the attendance of nurses and friends."

To avoid stoking panic, Rush assured readers that "the risk from visiting and attending the sick, in common cases, at present is not greater than from walking the streets." Leaving the city was no longer necessary, he said, "because the disease is now under the power of medicine." But he did suggest that those who had fled should not return until after the first frost.

His writings had an immediate impact. As George Washington's personal secretary, Henry Knox, informed the president several days later, "Doctor Rush's success . . . is great indeed. I understand that he has given his medicine to upwards of 500 patients. He does not pretend to say they have all had the yellow fever but many undoubtedly had, and he lost only one since he adopted his new mode. He has acquired great honor in visiting every body to the utmost of his power. but his applications have been so general that it was utterly impossible to attend to all of them. But he directs the medicine and the apothecaries [prepare] it."

In another dispatch, Knox was more succinct: "Everybody whose head aches takes Rush."

ON SEPTEMBER 12, Rush was up at six a.m. scribbling a note to Julia; it was probably the only time during the day when his house of sick apprentices, sick family members (his sister worse than his mother), sick nurses, and sick patients, sprawled over every available bed and chair, were relatively quiet.

"After a restless night," he wrote, "I am still alive and preparing for the awful duties of the day. Yesterday exceed any of the days I have seen for distress and death in our city. . . . I send you these few lines only to let you know that I am still wonderfully supported in mind and body, but that I stand in greater need than ever of the prayers of all good people." Just a day or two later, people would start saying Dr. Rush looked a little yellow himself.

"My eyes are tinged of a yellow color," he admitted the next day. "This is not peculiar to myself. It is universal in the city. Even the Negroes who do not take the disease"—which, as late as September 13, he still believed because he hadn't yet seen a black patient with it—"discover that mark of infection in their eyes. . . . Yet under all these circumstances, and upon a diet consisting wholly of milk and vegetables, I enjoy, as to my feelings and activity, a perfect state of the health."

And the next day he had his first attack of the fever.

His own treatment was administered to him at once. He was given purgatives and then bled and proceeded to convince himself he was cured. He had been living on two hours of sleep a night. He was physically wasted and cycling from buzzy excitement to depression as his beloved city experienced a disaster to match any biblical plague.

Pennsylvania Hospital and the Almshouse decided it was too dangerous to treat yellow fever patients, so a separate facility was set up at Bush Hill, the mansion on the grounds where the picnic had been held after the Constitution was approved. After a few weeks of dysfunction at Bush Hill, Stephen Girard, a French-born banker and philanthropist, stepped up to help fund and run the facility. Among the doctors working there were Currie and Stevens, but the Bush Hill hospital employed all the standard treatments of the day—including, at lower "doses," bleeding and purges. On its staff were several of Rush's trainees who needed paid work. (At this point, Rush was largely working for free.)

Bush Hill became seen by some as an alternative to Rush, even though it was a hospital for the poor, and Rush was mostly treating private patients in their homes or his home. In political circles Bush Hill became Federalist; since Girard was French and his best-known doctor, Stevens, was from St. Croix in the French Caribbean, Rush described their approach as "the French remedies" to make them sound vaguely un-American. (Rush and Girard also had history, although it's unclear how it affected the situation. Rush had been treating Girard's wife, Mary, in the basement cells of Pennsylvania Hospital, for several years.)

In the meantime, black aid workers were now roving the death-strewn streets of Philadelphia, asking how they could help. They carried bodies to the graveyard—the old plague phrase "bring out your dead" was most likely heard from workers helping Jones and Allen—and Rush taught some of them basic nursing (and lancing) procedures.

They witnessed heartbreak every day. Once Allen was called to a woman's house to get her body for burial. "On our going into the house, and taking the coffin in, a dear little innocent accosted us with—'mamma is asleep—don't wake her!' But when she saw us put her into the coffin, the distress of the child was so great, that it almost overcame us. When she demanded why we put her mamma in the box, we did not know how to answer her, but committed her to the care of a neighbour, and left her with heavy hearts."

Allen would also never forget the racial aggression toward the black aid workers. "A white man threatened to shoot us, if we passed by his house with a corpse. We buried him three days after."

Rush's letters to Julia in late September were a jumble of reports on his own health and death tolls: "among the late dead are our neighbor Thos. Anthony, Mr. Walker, Mr. Ketland's friend, all Ross the blacksmith's family, Cornl. Barnes, Henry Pratt's wife, Mrs. Wigton, and Emily Bullock. Near twenty persons have died in Pear Street alone." He admonished her to make sure the children, so long displaced from home, were keeping up with their reading.

On September 23, at about twelve-thirty p.m., Rush lost his first staff member: "my dear and amiable pupil Johnny Stall breathed his last." He himself was growing weaker and weaker. "You cannot conceive with what difficulty I climb a pair of stairs," he told Julia. "I carry a vial of Lisbon wine with me in my pocket, and when I am faint wash my mouth with a spoonful of it. It acts as powerfully on my whole system in that way as a pint of wine in my stomach would have at any other time."

Several days later he admitted to Julia that he now realized he had been tragically incorrect about black immunity to the fever. "The Negros are everywhere submitting to the disorder," he said. "Rich. Allen . . . is very ill. If the disorder should continue to spread among them, then will the measure of our sufferings be full. . . . O! that God would rend the heavens and come down! and save our guilty city from utter desolation!"

Within twenty-four hours, Rush learned that his last standing apprentice—Dr. John Redman Coxe—had been sent home with the fever, joining his grandfather, Rush's mentor John Redman, who also had it. Far worse was Rush's dread for his sister, Rebecca, who, "overcome with fatigue and anxiety, retreated to her bed, where she is very ill." She refused to take his, or anyone's, treatments and continued refusing for the next three days. "This infatuation with respect to the existence or danger of the disorder," he told Julia, "seems to be one of its most characteristic symptoms."

36

On the last day of September 1793—the worst month of Dr. Rush's life—he received a letter from a terrified Julia, for which she apologized because she was "so much agitated that I can scarcely write intelligibly":

> My dear Dr. Rush,
>
> I have endeavored to keep up my spirits thru the whole of this great calamity with which we are visited. and my friends all say I have done it wonderfully—but your two last letters have been almost too much for me. . . . I think in your weak state to be exposed to so much contagion from within and without, will be too much for you.
>
> You had an attack it is true—but it was so mild as not to risk communicating the disease. I fear your mother and sister have gotten it by nursing those that have been so much worse—divine power I know can preserve you, notwithstanding these circumstances are so much against you. . . . Think how I must feel. I have not slept above three hours for two nights past.

Julia feared that Rush was living in a house teeming with contagion, with every sick apprentice or patient increasing the danger to him. She also was concerned about all the different people—and the types of people—overrunning her house. If an apprentice was sleeping:

> in the tea room I must request that you will get your mother or sister to give a little heed to my clothes. I need my chest of drawers to be lock'd in that room, as all my drawers are unlocked. If that room is an hospital and black nurses about the house, I shall have a poor account of them I fear.
>
> I hope you will not take any more into the house. If you get sick again yourself, which I very much fear, what shall I do when I come to you, with the house full of sick men. I should feel no fear in coming to you, but the idea of so many sick and dying in the house create a perfect horror in my mind.

Mostly, however, she and the children were panicked that Rush would die, and that any letter she sent him could be the last. The letter finished:

> Adieu my dearest friend. I tell your children if we were all as worthy of the divine favor as you are I should not have a fear for you—for if the worst should happen our loss would be your . . . gain. But if you are called from us, it will be for the punishment of our sins. . . . [I pray that] god in his infinite mercy to avert so great a calamity and permit us to meet again under more favorable circumstances
>
> I am in all situations,
> Yours sincerely,
> Julia Rush

When he got this letter, Rush found a semiquiet place in the house to respond:

> My dear Julia,
>
> You write like a spectator only of the distresses of our city. What is a little furniture, a few clothes, a whole city, or even the globe

> itself compared with one human life. Had I believed that certain death would have been the consequence to myself and the whole family of taking [apprentices] Johnny Stall and Ed Fisher into the house, it would have been my duty to have done it. Neither of them had another home . . . and had I shut my doors upon them, they must have perished in the streets. Remember, my dear creature, the difference between the law and the gospel. The former only commands us "to love our neighbors as ourselves," but the latter bids us love them *better* than ourselves.

He did not go so far as to challenge her mentioning "black nurses about the house."

By the time Julia got this response, she had received another letter from her husband with the horrible news: Rush's sister, Rebecca Stamper, had died. Julia had grown close to Rebecca over the years, loving her as a maternal figure and at the same time pitying her for having been so unlucky in life and marriage that her lot was to care for brothers (and later her mother).

After telling Rush how sorry she was for the loss and how happy she was that he still lived ("I am denied the melancholy pleasure of sharing your sorrow—but if your life is spared all other affections are light in my estimation"), she did want to let her husband know she was rather offended by what he had written to her:

> Your letter . . . does me injustice. I do not feel like [a] spectator on your calamites however I may write, but if you will look again on the letter, you will find, I do not put clothes in competition with human life. I only lamented the necessity you were driven to, of introducing so much contagion in to your own house. . . . And it was on the account of your aged mother and your weakly sister's exposed situation and from the fear of your relapse that I was induced to mention the subject. . . . In the conclusion, and not as if I valued them more than a human life, I beg'd a little attention might be paid to my clothes, which were all exposed. . . . I well know that their being secured would not risk a life . . . but to have you suppose for a moment that I want feeling for the distresses of the whole city would hurt me much [more] than the loss of all my clothes & furniture.

During the first week of October, as hundreds continued dying each day, doctors kept debating whose "antidote" worked best. As he drove his chair up Arch Street, "I cast a look at the grave of my dear, dear sister. If I survive the present calamite [calamity] I will adorn it with healing plants and water them with my tears."

As Rush's letters reached a plateau of repetitious sadness, Julia felt a little more comfortable talking about the children. Neither she nor her husband had seen their two-and-a-half-year-old son, Ben Jr., for some time, since he had been taken out of town. (One day Rush got a letter from someone who had seen Ben, which reported that the boy complained, "I have no Papa.") A few of the children were with Julia's uncle in Trenton, while the older boys had moved with her to Morven. She was especially concerned about John, now sixteen, raising issues about his behavior in a way that sounded like she and Rush had discussed them before:

> Our son John you know wants a little opus from you now and then—he does not read as much as I could wish—tho he makes fair promises—a letter to him or a postscript to one of mine from you would not be amiss.
>
> I have no material cause of complaint against him, but you know how he teases me at times about cloaths and that it is best for him to be reminded that he is not out of the reach of your authority. Some hints as to his general treatments of servants will come in well—not as if a complaint had been made, but as if these things had occurred at some wise moment. . . . His transgressions in these ways have not amounted to much but I would wish them avoided entirely, and a letter from you at this time, I know, would have more effect than common.

Unfortunately, Julia's presumption that her husband was ready to think about disciplining his boys was premature. His fever returned at one a.m. on October 10, when he was:

> attacked in a most violent manner with all the symptoms. . . . Seldom have I endured more pain. My mind sympathized with my body. . . . At 2 o'clock I called up Marcus and Mr. Fisher, who

> slept in the adjoining room. Mr. Fisher bled me, which instantly removed my pains, and then gave me a dose and a half of the mercurial medicine. It puked me several times during the night and brought off a good deal of the bile from my stomach.

Rush spent the next day at home, and when his pain returned, he asked to be bled again. The next night he grew still sicker and had what he called a "fainty fit" that reminded him of the night he almost died in 1788. After surviving the fit, he dreamed about Julia and family.

"I dreamed that I saw you at a distance at a window in a house . . . with a countenance healthy and pleasant, without the least tincture of that sallow gloom which pervades the face of every Philadelphian," he explained in a letter the next day. "I made signs to you that I would first go home and prescribe for my patients, and that I would come up to you in the evening. But ah!—I awoke soon afterwards, and that evening did not come."

While lying in what might be his deathbed, Rush gave orders to his apprentices and his mother, wrote sparingly, and repeatedly sent Marcus to the post office, hoping for a letter from Julia.

"The disease continues to rage, with I fear unabating mortality," he wrote, before falling asleep after two paragraphs. Marcus slept in his room with him, just as William Grubber—who was now away at sea—had done during his previous illnesses. Marcus was there "to hand me a little bit of food in the middle of the night, for I have become so much a child, or an old man, in constitution that I am obliged to eat often or I become weak and fainty," he continued in the letter the next day:

> My patients know this so well now that many of them hand me a glass of milk and a crust of bread as soon as I enter their houses, just as they hand other people a glass of wine. I cannot tell you how much we all owe to Marcus. His integrity, industry and fidelity deserve great praise. . . . It has been a great alleviation of our distress that he has remained with us. Half the servants in the city have deserted their masters.

Rush was in bed for another day or two before he started regaining his strength and seeing patients. On the morning of October 21 he arose thrilled at how nippy the weather was. Perhaps the only thing he and his fellow physicians agreed on was that fall weather would quash the epidemic—although all were wrong about why, based on their respective incorrect theories on how the disease was spread. (In fact, mosquitoes stop breeding in the cold.)

Two days later, however, it was warm and muggy again, which:

> revived the disease [so] that the mortality is nearly as great as before the late rain and cold weather. 700 have died since the 11th of October, 3,400 have died since the first of August. . . . I feel the distresses of my fellow citizen[s] the more of my being unable to assist them, and from my hearing constantly of some of them being murdered by large and ill-timed doses of bark and wine.

Knowing that Rush was running short of cash—he hadn't been charging patients during the entire epidemic—his friend from the hospital board and the basement cells, Samuel Coates, came by the house and offered to lend him 50 pounds ($7,460). "I shall probably require it," he told Julia, "for I have only a few dollars in the house, and this is not a time to ask for money from my patients. I have expended since the commencement of this disorder nearly 200 pound [$29,800] in cash and have contracted some debts. In what manner a part of it has been spent, I shall not mention. I regret only that it was not 2000 pounds [$298,000]."

People all over the country had read about Rush's bravery and commitment. Julia wrote "there is great sympathy in New York in your sufferings," and a friend of hers there had told her "you are all but prayed for by *name* in most of the churches." But in Philadelphia he felt like a pariah, which pained him:

> I am supposed to have created a great many friends and a large fund of gratitude among my fellow citizens. This is far from being true. The relations and patients of the physicians whose practice I opposed have taken part with them in their resentments, and I am

> now publicly accused at every corner of having murdered the greatest part of the citizens who have died of the present disorder.

He was thinking about leaving Philadelphia, to try teaching and practicing in New York, at Columbia College (later Columbia University). If offered a chair, he said, "I should prefer ending my days there (if I survive the present calamity) to continuing in Philadelphia, where I see nothing before me but strife and misery." Rush was depressed, but that didn't mean there wasn't some truth to his claim. He even seemed ready to cut ties to the fraternal organization he had helped start, the College of Physicians.

Julia chose to ignore his negativity and focus on the future, now that there might be one: "When you have done the utmost to committing to the sick, something is due to your own family, whom you have not seen for these months and when the disease is going on there will be an interval in which you can be spared, and must come to us. Oh, with what joy will you be received by me, from whose thoughts you have never been for five minutes separated."

Rush was looking ahead in at least one way; he had decided to move his family out of the house where so many had died, to one around the corner. If all went well, Julia would never have to see what her house had turned into during the epidemic. Later that evening, Sam Coates came by and said, for the first time he could remember, no graves had been dug at the Friends' burying ground all day, and there had been no admissions or deaths at Bush Hill. Maybe it was almost over.

In the meantime, Rush was praying more and rereading the Old Testament psalms. One night he was reading the 102nd Psalm, "a prayer of the lowly man when he is faint and pours forth his plea before for Lord," and found himself weeping. Another day he pored over the 37th Psalm, "Do not be vexed by evil men, do not be incensed by wrongdoers," and felt "rebuked, humbled and comforted" by it. "I find I am a perfect Jew in unbelief," he said.

Two days later Richard Allen and Absalom Jones came to the house to visit. After most of the white doctors had stopped being able to treat patients, they had taken it upon themselves to procure "the printed directions for curing the fever," and then had gone "among the poor who were sick, gave them the mercurial purges, bled them freely." They had, in their own estimation—and Rush agreed, as he wrote Julia—"by those means save[d] the lives of between two and three hundred persons."

In the same letter, Rush told Julia he was thinking of writing a book, in which he would elaborate on things that had happened during the worst of his illness that he hadn't shared with her: "The history of the circumstances under which life was preserved in me will form an interesting memoir in the account of the disease which I expect to publish as soon as I have strength and time enough for that purpose."

Rush probably didn't realize that his editor and friend, Mathew Carey, had been saving string for a book about the yellow fever epidemic and was already having it printed. The day before it was published, Julia came from Princeton to the northern suburbs of Philadelphia to pick up their son Ben.

She had hoped Rush would meet her there, but he was called away to see a patient and sent his apprentice, Fisher, with a note giving her the choice of coming back to town—where Rush promised to sleep in a different room, unsure it was yet safe to touch her—or waiting until he could come out to see her. It is unknown what happened, because this note ended the longest and most revealing correspondence of their lives. The last line of Julia's last yellow fever letter involved a medical issue that would otherwise have deeply frightened her, but in comparison to what they had just lived through, seemed mild: baby Julia seemed to be coming down with the whooping cough.

THE NEXT DAY Mathew Carey published *A Short Account of the Malignant Fever Lately Prevalent in Philadelphia.* It came out just as Governor Mifflin announced that the epidemic was officially over. The book sold out almost immediately, in part because its appendix included one of the first comprehensive listings of the "most noted inhabitants" of Philadelphia who had died. (There was much speculation about the total number of yellow fever deaths; the best estimate remains just over five thousand, or about 10 percent of the population of Greater Philadelphia. Almost all the deaths were among the white population; Philadelphia was approximately 6 percent black at the time, and the estimates of black yellow fever deaths were in the same range.)

Carey's book refueled every fight that had just died down in the medical and political communities and instigated a new one between the races: he reported that the black men and women who had been so heroic had also overcharged many people and plundered some of their houses.

So everyone was back to business as usual in the nation's capital, in the new world of the American media.

Over the next weeks, Rush set out to rebuild his eroded life and business. Julia and the children were no doubt greatly relieved that he moved them to a new, larger three-story mansion at 98 South Fourth Street. Known as the longtime home of Judge Edward Shippen IV, the spacious, airy home had five rooms on the third floor, four on the second, and a large parlor room in the rear of the first floor, with a hearth. The front of the mansion was forty-two feet wide, and it sat on a lot 275 feet deep, which also had a large second building for the kitchen and Rush's office, and a garden where, unlike his previous home, nobody had ever emptied bowls after bloodletting. (The mansion was haunted in its own way, however; Judge Shippen's daughter Peggy had been married there to Gen. Benedict Arnold in 1779, the year before his treasonous defection to the British.)

The Judge Shippen Mansion

Rush did not respond publicly to Carey's book, which was revised several times after each printing sold out in a week or two. But he no doubt encouraged the book-length response to it written by Absalom Jones and Richard Allen. Their book, *A Narrative of the Proceedings of the Black People, During the Late Awful Calamity in Philadelphia, in the year 1793: and a Refutation of Some Censures, Thrown upon Them in Some Late Publications*, was published on January 24, 1794, and became a landmark in many ways. It was the first copyrighted book ever written by African Americans, and it was also the first time black authors challenged a prominent white journalist—and some of Philadelphia's more racist (yet unnamed) citizens—in print.

The book showed exactly what Jones and Allen and other black Philadelphians had done during the yellow fever epidemic in great detail. The two of them had handled a great many of the city's burials, and they knew the location and cost of every coffin. After Rush got sick, they had handled much of the bleeding and purging around the city and had coordinated nursing efforts.

"We feel a great satisfaction in believing, that we have been useful to the sick," they wrote, "and thus publicly thank Doctor Rush, for enabling us to be so. We have bled upwards of eight hundred people, and do declare, we have not received to the value of a dollar and a half, therefor: we were willing to imitate the Doctor's benevolence, who sick or well, kept his house open day and night, to give what assistance he could in this time of trouble."

They admitted that, among all races, some people had overpaid for services out of desperation, and even that some dead people's homes had probably been looted. But they expressed outrage that anyone would suggest that *mostly* black people had done any of this—because they hadn't.

After this staunch defense, they included a bolder postscript: "An Address to Those who Keep Slaves, and Approve the Practice." It began:

> THE judicious part of mankind will think it unreasonable, that a superior good conduct is looked for, from our race, by those who stigmatize us as men, whose baseness is incurable, and may therefore be held in a state of servitude, that a merciful man would not doom a beast to; yet you try what you can to prevent our rising

> from the state of barbarism, you represent us to be in, but we can tell you, from a degree of experience, that a black man, although reduced to the most abject state human nature is capable of, short of real madness, can think, reflect, and feel injuries, although it may not be with the same degree of keen resentment and revenge, that you who have been and are our great oppressors, would manifest if reduced to the pitiable condition of a slave. We believe if you would try the experiment of taking a few black children, and cultivate their minds with the same care, and let them have the same prospect in view, as to living in the world, as you would wish for your own children, you would find upon the trial, they were not inferior in mental endowments.
>
> We do not wish to make you angry, but excite your attention to consider, how hateful slavery is in the sight of that God, who hath destroyed kings and princes, for their oppression of the poor slaves; Pharaoh and his princes with the posterity of king Saul, were destroyed by the protector and avenger of slaves. . . . When you are pleaded with, do not you reply as Pharaoh did, "Wherefore do ye Moses and Aaron, let the people from their work, behold the people of the land, now are many, and you make them rest from their burdens." We wish you to consider, that God himself was the first pleader of the cause of slaves.

Within six months of the book's publication, Jones and Allen had opened not only the first black church in the nation's capital but the first *two.* The African Episcopal Church of St. Thomas opened on July 17 under Jones's supervision. (Rush presumably was there—according to church records, he paid to reserve his own pew, and the visiting white Episcopal pastor, Samuel Magaw, thanked the doctor for helping him with his sermon.) But by then, Richard Allen had decided he wanted to have his own congregation with a different denomination. After further fund-raising, he bought a building at the corner of Sixth and Lombard streets and turned it into the Mother Bethel African Methodist Episcopal Church (AME), which opened on July 29.

The African Episcopal Church of St. Thomas (left) and the Mother Bethel AME Church

THAT SUMMER RUSH published his own 363-page opus on the epidemic: *An Account of the Bilious Remitting Yellow Fever, as It Appeared in the City of Philadelphia in the Year 1793.* He explained in the preface that it had been delayed "by the want of health" and that he had gone ahead and published it "under the great disadvantages, of having been hastily copied from my notes, amid frequent professional interruptions," only because the end of summer was fast approaching, and if the yellow fever returned, he wanted the nation's capital, and all American port cities, to have his account as a resource.

Rush's book took on all the debates he had waged with other physicians—although he claimed he was only doing it "to prevent the revival of certain opinions and modes of practice by bringing them forward under the patronage of respectable names," and he insisted he was "more minute with my own mistakes, than those of other Physicians." He also said he didn't use the names of any other physicians or patients until they "were given to the public by their authors, during the prevalence of the fever." He reprinted in the book all the major letters written by his colleagues, as well as those written *about* them by high-profile patients—anything in the press he felt had influenced public opinion.

This allowed him, he felt, to point out any number of medical mistakes and injustices attributable to others. But he seemed equally interested in clearing the air about the treatment of one high-profile patient: Hamilton. The treatment protocol used by his doctor, Stevens, would not cure yellow fever, in Rush's opinion: the treasury secretary's case "was either very light, or Mr. Hamilton owes more to the strength of his constitution, and the goodness of heaven, than most of the people who recovered from the disorder." He also critiqued finer points in his colleague Dr. Kuhn's published letter.

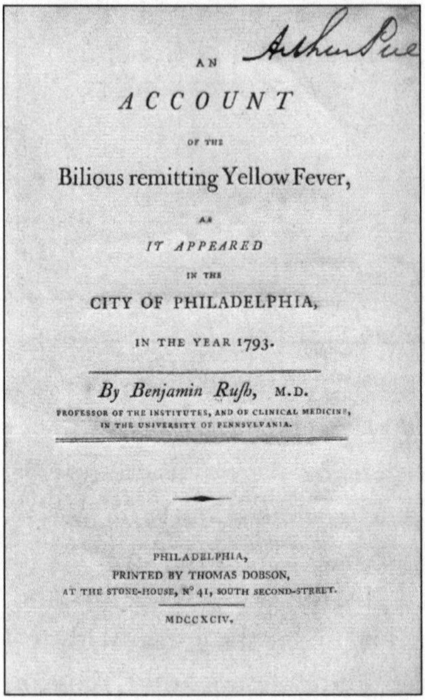
AN
ACCOUNT
OF THE
Bilious remitting Yellow Fever,
AS
IT APPEARED
IN THE
CITY OF PHILADELPHIA,
IN THE YEAR 1793.
By Benjamin Rush, M.D.
PROFESSOR OF THE INSTITUTES, AND OF CLINICAL MEDICINE, IN THE UNIVERSITY OF PENNSYLVANIA.
PHILADELPHIA,
PRINTED BY THOMAS DOBSON,
AT THE STONE-HOUSE, N° 41, SOUTH SECOND-STREET.
MDCCXCIV.

First edition of Rush's book on the yellow fever epidemic

He was arguing that medical knowledge should not be spread, half-baked, through the lay media. But he spared himself criticism for doing the same thing—and doing it again, now, in a book for the public. His excuse was that other physicians had prescribed in the press first, to which he had responded with more correct information. He also simply believed he was right.

After 337 pages of sober analysis, Rush shared his own journey through the fever—which he thought was a ripping good tale:

> Narratives of escapes from great dangers of shipwreck, war, captivity, and famine, have always formed an interesting part of the history of the body, and mind of man. But there are deliverances from equal dangers, which have hitherto passed unnoticed; I mean, from pestilential fevers. I shall briefly describe the state of my body and mind, during my intercourse with the sick in our late epidemic. The account will throw additional light upon the disorder, and probably illustrate some of the laws of the animal economy. It will moreover serve to furnish a lesson to all who may be placed in similar circumstances, to commit their lives without fear, to the

> protection of that BEING who is able to save to the uttermost, not only from future, but from present evil.

This version was darker than the one he told Julia in his letters; he hadn't wanted her to know just how bad things were. The afternoon his sister, Rebecca, died, he explained, he had had to leave the house an hour later, get into his carriage, and spend the rest of the day visiting patients. Ever since, he had been haunted by whether his "sense of duty, or . . . grief" should dominate his memory of this: "I have approved, and disapproved of this act, ever since." Rebecca had been a rock for him for decades; she had taken care of him ever since he began practicing, twenty-four years before. "My whole heart reposed itself in her friendship," he wrote.

After her death:

> I declined in health and strength. All motion became painful to me. My appetite began to fail. My night sweats continued. My short and imperfect sleep, was disturbed by distressing, or frightful dreams. The scenes of them were derived altogether from sick rooms, and grave yards. I concealed my sorrows as much as possible from my patients, but when alone, the retrospect of what was past, and the prospect of what was before me, the termination of which was invisible, often filled my soul with the most poignant anguish. I wept frequently when retired from the public eye.

Twenty-four brutally honest pages later, Rush brought the reader up to date on his health. "My convalescence was extremely slow," he wrote, but the "early warmth of the spring, removed those complaints, and I now enjoy, through divine goodness, my usual state of health."

He made a theatrical finish. "But wherewith shall I come before the great FATHER and REDEEMER of men," he asked, "and what shall I render unto him for the issue of my life, from the grave?"

He paused. Then: "Here all language fails."

And finally a quote from the Scottish poet James Thomson: "Come then, expressive silence, muse his praise."

37

When Rush returned to his teaching and his work in the hospital in 1794, he received some good news: Pennsylvania Hospital finally began construction on a new West Wing for patients with mental illness, the building he had been asking for since he took over their care in 1787. His patients would live in heated, well-lit rooms—still locked, when necessary, but also in view of gardens. Once the structure was finished, Rush felt he would have a better idea of how well his treatment innovations actually worked.

The timing was ripe, as care for madness was being discussed more seriously at a handful of facilities around the world. It is unclear how much the field's major innovators knew of each other's work in real time, but as they began publishing more actively in the early 1800s, a movement emerged. Rush hadn't published much on the subject yet, besides his 1786 oration on the "influence of physical causes upon the moral faculty" and his November 1789 letter to the managers of Pennsylvania Hospital demanding better care facilities. But he had been privately sharing insights with physicians in England and Scotland who knew of his work.

On December 11, 1794, the French physician Philippe Pinel read his paper "Memoir on Madness" to the Society for Natural History in Paris. Pinel, like Rush, was almost fifty; he had trained first in religion and eventually switched to medicine. He had made a patchwork living in Paris teaching mathematics, translating one of Cullen's books into French, and editing a French medical publication, *Gazette de Santé* (Journal of Health), where he wrote primarily on hygiene but a few pieces on mental disorders, a subject that had interested him since the illness of a close friend in the early 1780s. After the journal closed, he had done some consulting at a nursing home for patients with mental illness, where the owner was not interested in his ideas about improving care.

In late 1793 Pinel was hired to take over an all-male hospital in Paris, Hospice de Bicêtre, where some two hundred mentally ill men were warehoused in one of the wards. He tried to improve conditions and after a year published on his efforts to "restore alienated reasoning" with what he called *traitement moral*, meaning "psychologic" but also more "ethical" treatment. He believed such patients could one day be treated almost entirely with psychological interventions rather than the "rough treatment" associated with "the old regime," which ran the hospital as "no more than a place of sequestration and imprisonment for a class of dangerous men who needed to be segregated from Society." Mental illness was often curable, he argued, suggesting that physicians should carefully observe patients and speak to them before creating a diagnosis and prognosis.

Philippe Pinel

Pinel did not, in this first talk, discuss the notion of "unchaining" patients, for which he and his associate Jean-Baptiste Pussin would become known in the early 1800s. In fact, in this initial work, Pinel accepted that some patients had to be restrained, for their own safety and the safety of those who treated them. The challenge, as he put it, was to "dominate agitated madmen while respecting human rights."

Pinel used baths, purgatives, and bloodletting as treatments, but he preferred, whenever possible, to use purely psychological interventions. He felt that bloodletting, especially, was overused and later wrote a dramatic condemnation often taken out of context: "the blood of maniacs is sometimes so lavishly spilled, and with so little discernment, as to render it doubtful whether the patient or his physician has the best claim to the appellation of madman." Yet in the rarely quoted sentences following that one, he conceded that "it is a well-established fact that paroxysms of madness . . . are in many instances prevented by a copious bleeding . . . and the experience of hospitals authorizes the free use of the lancet."

It is unclear when Pinel and Rush came to know about each other's work and interests—neither acknowledged the other until the early 1800s, after Pinel published his first book in 1801. In the 1780s, it would have been more likely that Pinel had heard of Rush, through editing his French medical journal. Rush may have heard about Pinel's 1794 paper through his contacts in Paris, although it was not widely circulated at the time. But they would have completely agreed with each other on the need for more benevolent care for madness. Pinel was most interested in treating the mind, while Rush believed both the brain and the mind had equal importance, but they were slowly rowing in the same direction against the same strong currents.

They were soon to be joined in England by a Quaker tea merchant named William Tuke, who in 1791 was outraged by the death of a woman with mental illness in an asylum in his hometown of York, and began advocating for the local Quaker meeting to create a better facility for its own members. Several years later he founded and funded the York Retreat, based entirely on psychological treatment.

Tuke would likely have heard about what was happening at Pennsylvania Hospital, with its strong Quaker roots, while researching his own facility. And by 1794, Rush's books were known in England and Germany. A new edition of *Medical Inquiries and Observations*, opening with his "moral faculty" lecture, had been published in London, and his yellow fever book became well-known (and aggressively reviewed).

As for Rush and his staff in the cells, they were just happy their patients would soon have a new home, with a view of the gardens.

In the summer of 1794, the renowned British scientist Joseph Priestley and his family moved to America. Rush had corresponded with him for years and was excited about the idea that Priestley would move to Philadelphia, get involved with the Philosophical Society, and be available for fascinating conversations about science and religion. With Rush's pull at the University of Pennsylvania medical school, he was able to arrange an offer for Priestley to become a professor of chemistry.

On July 3, 1794, Priestley came to the Rushes' home for dinner. They exchanged stories about their old friend Franklin and talked a lot about religion. Rush enjoyed discussing what people believed, even if it made almost no theological sense to him. He and Priestley talked about Deists, who had confused Rush ever since he realized his hero William Cullen probably was one. Deists did not believe in the more supernatural aspects of religion and in the Bible as divine revelation—but Rush, after surviving yellow fever, was going through one of his stronger periods of believing. Rush had parted ways with Thomas Paine over his Deist and frankly antireligious writings, including *The Age of Reason*, the first part of which had recently been published. But Rush also had to admit that some of his best friends were Deists. (In the 1770s, Priestley had done some aggressively Deist editing of one of Rush's favorite writers, David Hartley—filleting *Observations of Man,* the philosophical physician's 1,066-page opus from 1749, by deleting much of his most religious writing and retaining his "theory of the human mind." Hartley's entire book had recently been reissued; Rush had heavily marked-up copies of both in his library.)

Priestley said Franklin used to joke that he had "made many Deists." The chemist "acknowledged a belief only in the Being of a God and a particular providence." Did he, Rush asked, believe in the doctrine of final restitution or just annihilation when life ended? Priestley said he believed in annihilation of the wicked but offered a scientific perspective, using "the analogy of some plants and animals which have perished for ever on our globe."

After the dinner, Rush was even more excited that Priestley would come and join the faculty at the university. So he was crushed when the famous scientist wrote a few days later to tell him he preferred a quieter life in the country and was buying land in rural Northumberland County, near what is today Sunbury, Pennsylvania. Rush never really understood his reasons, but one could have been a desire to stay away from the city's newspapers, since he had a history of drawing angry attention with his ideas.

Not long after Priestley set foot on American soil, a pamphlet was published attacking him. It was so cruel and controversial that the printer refused to put his own name on it, let alone an author's name. But it got some attention and sold on both sides of the Atlantic, so a pseudonym was attached to later editions: "Peter Porcupine." Nobody knew who this Porcupine was, but his pamphlet had surely helped dash Rush's hopes of spending more quality time with the renowned Dr. Priestley. They would have to continue their conversation by post.

In the late summer of 1794, the usual seasonal rise in illness triggered fear of another yellow fever epidemic—which, fortunately, did not materialize. This did not stop doctors from arguing again about its treatment and contagion. Mathew Carey published an updated edition of his yellow fever book, and in response, Rush did likewise. He used the opportunity to lengthen his yellow fever book, and his publisher also reissued a longer version of his essay collection. These were published as volumes I and II of *Medical Inquiries and Observations*, a title Rush had developed as a way of branding his medical writing.

This was all part of his effort to build his own system of physic, for which his yellow fever experience had inspired fresh insights. There were, he felt, too many different diagnoses and treatments. And he was starting to think that the reason for this was the belief, possibly mistaken, that there were many kinds of fevers. Maybe, he proposed, there was only *one fever* with a range of symptoms. (*Fever* in Rush's time referred not only to an elevation in temperature but also to a general inflammation.)

Rush was also more convinced than ever of the centrality of blood and pulse in medicine, believing that the bloodletting he and others had done during the epidemic was the reason many more didn't die. Such theories were still works in progress, but as he approached age fifty, he wanted to wrestle more with bigger ideas.

JULIA, AT THIRTY-FOUR, was pregnant for the twelfth time. Her mother was still holding on to Morven—which had become a sort of country literary retreat for Princeton, where the Washingtons and others stayed when they were in town—and was proud of the way her eldest child balanced motherhood and literary interests. Annis wrote to her of Mary Wollstonecraft's book *A Vindication of the Rights of Woman*, which Julia had read, that perhaps its message was timelier in Europe; as a wealthy widow, it seemed American "women have their equal right of everything."

Annis was also watching over her grandson Richard, who, in the Rush family tradition, had matriculated to the College of New Jersey at age fourteen. Richard was a more level-headed young man than his older brother, John, and living with Annis—who had taken care of him on and off over the years—seemed effective in keeping him from the temptations of college. Having just watched what Philadelphia's physicians went through, it was no surprise that he was thinking about law as a career, though he also wanted to write. His grandmother Annis—the widow, sister, and mother of so many lawyers—encouraged both.

On April 9, 1795, Rush's old Philadelphia friend Tench Coxe called at his office with an offer. Rush had known Coxe since they were boys; he had been a groomsman at Ben and Julia's wedding, and he had done well in the Washington administration, serving first as Hamilton's assistant secretary of the treasury and then as federal revenue commissioner. Coxe came to talk about David Rittenhouse, who was in ill health and was planning to resign from the job Washington had given him in 1792, as founding director of the U.S. Mint in Philadelphia, overseeing the coining of currency. The position paid 750 pounds ($116,000) a year for far less than full-time work. The administration wanted Rush to take it.

While Rush had never sought an appointment from the federal government, he had always wondered why he hadn't had any offers. Now his suspicions were confirmed: the offer had come not long after Alexander Hamilton left the administration to return to New York to practice law (and figure out his next political play). Adams had advocated on Rush's behalf, knowing his friend's finances were still challenged since the epidemic. And if Washington had allowed the offer to be made, perhaps this meant the commander in chief had finally forgiven Rush. (If so, it was most likely the result of lobbying by Rush's mother-in-law, who not only hosted the First Family at Morven, but had been corresponding with Washington for years, sometimes sharing patriotic poems she had written.)

"I declined the offer on the steps of my door without deliberating a moment upon it," Rush wrote in his commonplace book. He told Coxe it would "expose me to the calumnies of my brethren, who would say it interfered with my business . . . [which] was more profitable to me than three times the value of the office." The position would also hamper his ability to train John in physic, endangering his dream that his oldest would one day join him in his practice. And it could hurt his chances of finishing his "new system."

In addition, Rush wrote, there were "secret objections . . . I did not mention." He may have feared being in public office again after nearly twenty years, especially now that the print media had become so voracious in its appetite for controversy.

Three months later, on July 2, 1795, Rush's mother, Susanna, died. She was seventy-eight, and had been living with him and Julia for some time. As Rush relayed in a letter to Betsey Graeme Fergusson, she had "retained the vigor of her faculties to the last day of her life." A few hours before her death, she asked for Rush, who was out working; he made it home just in time to say goodbye. "I saw her draw her last breath . . . her last words were 'Sweet Jesus!' . . . and oh! my dear madam, never did my heart swell with so many and such various emotions."

A month later, on August 1, Ben and Julia Rush welcomed another child, whom they named Samuel. They enjoyed the newborn for a week or two before yellow fever season—or fear of yellow fever season—set in.

THE SEASON'S FIRST victim was the U.S. attorney general, forty-year-old William Bradford, Jr., whom Rush had known for most of his life. He was the brother of publisher Tom Bradford, and he was married to Julia's cousin, the daughter of Annis's brother Elias Boudinot. William Bradford died of a "malignant fever" on August 23, 1795, while Rush was caring for him. Rush witnessed his last words; he had, in his career, heard many last words, but these would prove the most controversial.

Bradford was quite wealthy and had rewritten his will several times over the years—the most recent revision, from 1793, had been signed but not witnessed. When it was brought to him on his deathbed to finalize, he tore it up in a fit of delirium. Later in the day, when he appeared to be sane—according to Rush—he declared his desire to die without a will, which would leave his money split by his wife and his brother. He also signed three promissory notes: one to his sisters, one to a woman nobody knew, and a third giving $1,000 ($20,100) to Rush, to use for charitable purposes.

When the will was probated, the question of its validity came down to Rush's testimony as to whether Bradford was sane when he made those last bequests. Rush believed so, but he also stood to benefit financially by claiming that. Tom Bradford was satisfied with his testimony, because it allowed him to share in his brother's large estate. Julia's uncle, Elias, however, was livid that Rush's testimony forced his daughter, Bradford's widow, to split more of his estate.

This situation created Pennsylvania case law on the question of legal and medical definitions of sanity. The court accepted Rush's testimony and upheld a physician's right to give it. It also contributed to Rush's fascination with the intersection of medicine and law. But the case over Bradford's last words would remain in litigation for the next sixteen years. And the emotional wound it caused in Julia's family would never heal.

OTHERWISE, YELLOW FEVER season passed relatively smoothly in Philadelphia in 1795; the more significant outbreaks were in New

York and Norfolk. Rush instead focused more on the treatment of madness. "I have lately discharged six and cured eight patients of mania in our hospital," he wrote to his former apprentice, John Redman Coxe, in January 1796. ". . . They were all recent cases. When the new building is completed, I shall undertake the cases of chronic madness with which you know the Hospital abounds. My remedies for the recent cases were bleeding . . . strong purges, low diet, kind treatment and the cold bath." He was pleased to report that "my late success in the treatment of mania has brought me an increase of patients in that disorder."

Rush had received a letter from Dr. Francis Willis, the British caregiver who treated George III during his first attack of mania in 1788. Physicians would later debate the cause of the king's attack (some would speculate porphyria), but at the time Willis was more interested in discussing theories of treating madness with Rush.

Willis, now in his seventies, had distinguished himself by running a popular rural sanitarium for wealthy patients near Bourne, Lincolnshire, where much of the treatment involved fresh air and light farmwork. But he was also known to be able to control patients with an aggressive, almost bullying style of psychological intervention. He did often use purgatives, blistering, baths, and other medical techniques of the day—but they were, in his eyes, just ways to prepare his patients for the real treatment, his intense psychological therapy. That was where he disagreed with Rush, who saw the medical and psychological interventions both as treatment. It was the beginning of a debate in mental health care that would never end.

John Rush had finished college and then apprenticed under the careful supervision of his father. Now nineteen, John was sent on a sea voyage for his health—as a surgeon on a British indiaman (a type of trade ship) bound for Calcutta.

Rush thought his son's journey possibly "premature" but "necessary for him." He and Julia wrote out several pages of "directions and advice" that they arranged for his captain to deliver to him after a week at sea. It was the counsel of a father who had forgotten what it was like to be young, and a mother who had never really had the chance to be. On morals: "Read in your Bible frequently. . . . Avoid swearing and even an irreverent use of your Creator's name. *Flee* youthful lusts." On health and diet: "*Never* taste distilled spirits of any kind, and drink fermented liquors very sparingly." In summation:

> Be sober and vigilant. Remember at all times that while you are seeing the world, the world will see you. . . . Whenever you are tempted to do an improper thing, fancy that you see your mother and father kneeling before you and imploring you with tears in their eyes to refrain from yielding to the temptation, and assuring you at the same time that your yielding to it will be the means of hurrying them to a premature grave.

Then they both signed it.

With John gone, Rush focused on some of his problem protégés. Most challenging among them was Charles Caldwell, his former apprentice who was now trying to finish his degree at the University of Pennsylvania medical school. Caldwell had done everything he could to court favoritism from Rush, even writing about the doctor's lectures fawningly in the newspaper. But Rush ended up favoring other students, whereupon Caldwell developed a sort of academic fatal attraction for him. He claimed that Rush had stolen an idea from him—the notion that cold water from rain could effectively treat certain fevers—and used it in a lecture. Caldwell proceeded to write his thesis on the subject, so he could accuse Rush of plagiarizing from him. Rush held up Caldwell's degree, because he wasn't sure his student had a firm grip on reality. Their interaction became Penn medical school legend.

According to Caldwell, at one point Rush, "almost hysterical with rage," said to him, "Sir, do you know either who I am or who you are yourself when you presume thus arrogantly to address me?"

To which Caldwell said he replied, "Know you sir? O! no; that is impossible. But as respects myself, I was, this morning, Charles Caldwell; but indignant, as I now am, at your injustice, call me, if you please, Julius Caeser, or one of his descendants!"

While they later made some peace, Rush would always see Caldwell as a reminder of how emotionally fraught a teacher-student relationship could become. He had been mentored by doctors who couldn't control their emotions. He didn't want to become one of them.

In June 1796, Rush got news that his longtime scientific colleague David Rittenhouse had died. Rittenhouse was one of his last links to the scientific legacy of Franklin and the original "useful knowledge" movement—which, as president of the blooming Philosophical Society, he had been able to keep alive admirably. The society selected Rush to write and deliver the official elogium to Rittenhouse, whom he viewed as a "a man of immense genius . . . modest, amiable, just, a friend of liberty, a true republican." Honored to be chosen, he was scheduled to deliver it at a meeting late in the year.

Meanwhile the presidential election of 1796 approached, the first in which voters would choose between multiple candidates and two political parties, the Federalists and the Democratic-Republicans. Rush felt optimistic about how it would go. "All is calm at present in our country," he wrote to a friend in London. "Mr. Adams and Mr. Jefferson are talked of as successors to General Washington at the approaching election. The former it is said will be the successful candidate." Adams was running as a Federalist, Jefferson as a Democratic-Republican. Hamilton supported the third candidate, Charles Pinkney from South Carolina, as a spoiler for vice president—in hopes of keeping Jefferson from getting the job and as a possible stepping-stone to the presidency.

Rush was torn. His republican politics were increasingly with Jefferson, but he was much closer personally to Adams, who had the support of the Federalist Party—but was more unpredictable than the New York establishment preferred. Some were still accusing Adams of believing in some form of American monarchy—mostly to criticize him for being unsure about the will of the people, but also not trusting the Federalist elites to run the country.

Rush was mostly happy that his two Founding Father friends

would likely both live in Philadelphia for the next four years, and that Adams's wife, Abigail, could return as first lady. He was trying not to obsess over the details; he admitted to a friend in London that he hadn't even voted during the "general suffrage for electors." In the general election, Adams won. Jefferson, coming in second, would be vice president if he accepted the place before the March inauguration.

A week before Christmas 1796, the Philosophical Society met to honor David Rittenhouse at the First Presbyterian Church. The gathering had an even more special meaning: George Washington attended, in one of his last public appearances in Philadelphia as president.

Rush began by lamenting the "mournful occasion. Death has made an inroad upon our Society. Our illustrious and beloved President, is no more." Rush portrayed Rittenhouse as he knew him, as the ultimate republican scientist who especially loved the stars and would long be remembered for the observatory in the city that bore his name.

He spoke for thirty-five pages about Rittenhouse's life, family, and accomplishments, and republican spirit. Then he veered into some of his favorite—and to a Federalist crowd, confrontational—republican rhetoric. "The obligations of patriotism are as universal and binding, as those of justice and benevolence," he said, "and the virtuous propensities of the human heart are as much resisted by every individual who neglects the business of his country. . . . Man was made for a republic, and a republic was made for man, other wise Divine Power and goodness have been wasted." Rush made no apology for holding and sharing such sentiments, claiming that had he "said less" about Rittenhouse's politics, "thousands of my fellow-citizens would have accused me, of an act of treachery to his memory. May the time never come in which the praises of our republican government shall not be acceptable to the ears of an American audience!"

While the speech was a little Jeffersonian, the bipartisan audience received it well, and the Philosophical Society made plans to publish it as a pamphlet.

A week after the speech, and two days after Rush's fifty-sixth birthday, Pennsylvania Hospital unveiled its new West Wing, which was devoted entirely to the treatment of mental illness. Rush's patients were moved from their dank cells into airy rooms. The bottom-floor windows appeared to be partly below ground from the street, but actually a broad dug-out walkway around the building gave the windows full light and ventilation.

It had been seven years since Rush first called for such a modern facility, but it was finally here.

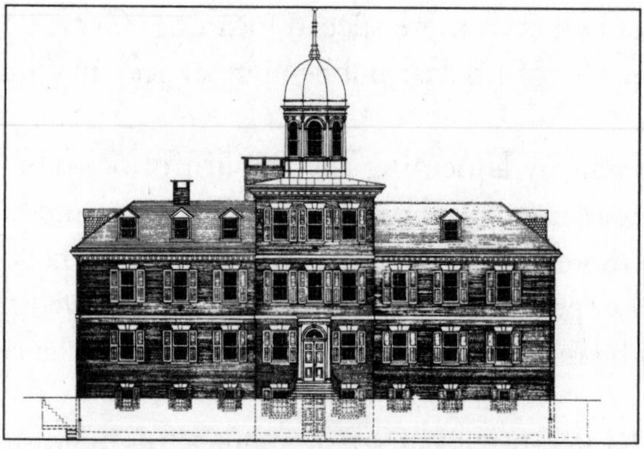

The new Pennsylvania Hospital West Wing

Rush spent New Year's Eve 1797 with John Adams. As Adams described the evening to Abigail, "Dr. Rush's Tongue ran for an hour. So many Compliments, so many old Anecdotes." Rush assured him that his election "had given vast Satisfaction in this City and State. Even those who had voted for another had a great Affection for me."

Rush told Adams he had been shown a letter from Jefferson to Madison, in which Jefferson discussed being "told there was a Possibility of a Tye between Mr Adams and himself." If that happened, Jefferson asked Madison to "use all your influence to procure for me the Second Place, for Mr Adams's Services have been longer, more constant, and more important than mine." According to Adams, Rush then "ran on with his Compliments to me and Sarcasms upon" Washington, saying the country would "rise in the Estimation of the World and of all Europe, from the 4th. day of March next." That was the day Washington's term ended, and Adams would be inaugurated.

"It hurt me to hear this," he admitted to Abigail, but Rush's "old Griefs and Prejudices Still hang about him. He got disaffected to Washington during the War."

Rush told Adams that when it came to his election for president, he had "been neutral." He had made it a rule that whenever Adams or Jefferson was "traduced" in his presence, he had "vindicated" them both. Rush said he hoped Adams and Jefferson would "go on affectionately together and all would be well."

NOT LONG AFTER New Year's, a copy of Rush's newly published memorial to David Rittenhouse fell into the hands of the writer known as Peter Porcupine, who had announced himself by attacking Joseph Priestley but now was coming after other public figures with full force.

"Porcupine" was a pudgy, furry-headed English fellow named William Cobbett, who paid his rent by teaching school in Wilmington, Delaware, but dreamed of being a muckraking essayist who would one day turn America on its head and make it want to go back to Mother England, as he believed it should. When he got going in print, Cobbett could be brilliantly funny and mean. On this day, he turned his review of the Philosophical Society's pamphlet into a yellow and feverish slam on Rittenhouse, Rush, and everything he despised about America.

William Cobbett, aka "Peter Porcupine"

"The remorseless Dr. Rush shall bleed me till I am as white as this paper before I'll allow that [Rittenhouse was] . . . doing good to mankind," he spewed. He called Rush's speech "a dry uninteresting narrative . . . so glaring a departure from the truth that it will attract but little more respect for his memory than the hogwash toasts of the factious Society of which he was president."

Rush and his fellow society members largely ignored the screed, and for the next few months, Peter Porcupine ignored Rush while tearing into others. From writing individual pamphlets, in March 1797, he moved on to producing his own daily newspaper, *Porcupine's Gazette*, which combined a modicum of actual reporting with brutal, and sometimes hilarious, antiestablishment essays and riffs. A running gag included fake letters from invented characters skewering real people, which readers may or may not have understood were satire. But they liked what they were reading in *Porcupine's Gazette*, and it became popular. It focused its attacks mostly on Jefferson and Adams—and America in general, which Cobbett had not forgiven for declaring independence. But he was capable of attacking almost anyone in authority, for having too much power or making too much money.

People liked Peter Porcupine; even Abigail Adams found some of his writing amusing, regardless of how her husband was targeted. Rush, too, may have chuckled at it—at first. He wouldn't have agreed with the political slant, but he paid attention to loud new voices.

By the summer of 1797, Rush was feeling some confidence that the worst of his challenges might be behind him. John had returned from his navy posting in India and was now working as one of his apprentices. Richard was just turning seventeen and about to become the first of his children to graduate from Princeton, the youngest in his class. (His debate subject during commencement exercises: "Is it probable, from the present state of society, that modern eloquence will rival the ancient?") Richard was planning to apprentice in the office of a prominent Philadelphia lawyer. The rest of the family was well.

Rush delivered a paper at the Philosophical Society that he suspected might be controversial, so he discussed it beforehand with

Jefferson. The paper, a version of which he had presented years earlier at the Abolition Society, theorized on why black people had dark skin; he told Jefferson that he hoped his theory would encourage whites to treat African Americans "with humanity, and justice." Black skin was not a racial difference at all, he hypothesized, but perhaps was left over from earlier generations inflicted with a disease that darkened the skin. The only disease he could think of that did that was leprosy.

If dark skin was a form of leprosy, or the inherited remnant of it, then "all the claims of superiority of the whites over the blacks, on account of their color, are founded alike in ignorance and inhumanity." Disease wasn't anyone's fault, and "instead of inviting us to tyrannize over them, it should entitle them to a double portion of our humanity, for disease all over the world has always been the signal for immediate and universal compassion."

Being Rush, he continued conjecturing. What if the disease accounted for the different ways black people looked? "The big lip and flat nose . . . the wooly heads" could all be "symptoms of the leprosy." He wondered aloud if interracial marriage was a good idea, since it could "tend to infect posterity with any portion of their disorder."

One Rush historian has generously suggested the lecture was the most egregious example of Rush's propensity for being "as Dr. Johnson said of Pope as a metaphysician, 'in haste to teach what he had not learned.'" One could also argue that he was pursuing the mandate of the Philosophical Society, and Franklin's Junto before it, to seek "useful knowledge" by throwing ideas against the wall to see what stuck. Either way, it stands as perhaps the most spectacularly wrong-headed address of Rush's career, as both a doctor and an abolitionist.

Rush was probably fortunate the lecture was delivered at a summer meeting of the society, which were not as well attended. He may also have been saved by a medical emergency: just days after the talk, the first cases of another yellow fever epidemic were reported in Philadelphia.

38

One of the first painful deaths in the 1797 outbreak was Rush's friend Dr. Nicholas Way, a physician in Wilmington whom he had known since they were boys and who was later among his early medical students.

On August 27, Way "was seized after a ride from the country in the evening air with a chilly fit and fever." The next day Rush was called to see him and advised "the usual depleting remedies," bleeding and purgatives. But Way was reluctant, feeling his fever was just a "common remittent" and not yellow fever. The next time Rush visited, he brought a colleague, in the hope the two of them could persuade Way to take all the treatments prescribed. He agreed only to six small bleedings over two days, much less than the doctor ordered.

"Our combined exertions to overcome his prejudices against our remedies was ineffectual," he wrote. On the sixth day of Way's illness, Rush "saw the sweat of death upon his forehead, and felt his cold arm without a pulse." He died a few hours later.

Way was well known in Philadelphia—besides his large private practice, he was the treasurer at the U.S. Mint—and his death reignited all the debates from 1793 about the best way of treating the fever, in particular the critiques of bloodletting and purging. This time around, as the attacks against Rush mounted, he proved more vulnerable.

Since the opening of the hospital's new wing, Rush had become better known for treating mental illness—which made him a target for stigmatizing comments about clinicians who treat "madmen" being mad themselves. "Rush behaves like a Man escaped from Bedlam," wrote a merchant in a mid-August letter to Timothy Pickering, who was just about to start as John Adams's secretary of state:

> He has told two Gentlemen of my acquaintance within two days past to *fly*, for Contagion was every where and that respiration could not be performed without the utmost hazard.
>
> One of the persons laughed at him, the other whose nerves were not so strong was very much affected. If I should hear such language from him I shall advise him to have his head shaved and take his seat in the Hospital. . . . I am not disposed to be severe upon him, but such speeches coming from *him* will do our City more injury than . . . good.

Julia's uncle, Elias Boudinot, put aside his anger over the William Bradford, Jr., will litigation to express concern (also to Pickering) that Rush's "mind is greatly clouded by the present appearance of the disorder. He seems determined if he should live thro' this Visitation of the City, to retire from the City." One way to keep Rush in Philadelphia, and make sure he could support his family if he really was ill, would be to give him the easy job at the mint left open by Dr. Way's death. It was a less taxing job than the one Rush had turned down several years earlier, but now Boudinot felt certain the doctor had no choice but to "gladly accept the Office of the Treasurer of the Mint."

Whether Boudinot came up with the idea of Rush filling the job—for which Adams, working from his home in Quincy, began receiving dozens of applications the moment Way died—or was asked to do so by Rush, Julia, or Annis (or all three) is unknown. But clearly many around Rush were concerned for his physical and mental well-being and hoped the president would look favorably on the idea.

Adams was disposed toward giving Rush the job, but first he

asked Oliver Wolcott, Jr., his treasury secretary, what he thought. Wolcott wrote back that based on his public service, "celebrity of character," and a "disposition [that was] naturally benevolent," Rush was "certainly superiour to any of the Candidates who have been named."

This was helpful, but Adams appeared to have already made up his mind. His friendship with Rush transcended politics, and he didn't hesitate to throw the doctor a financial life preserver. He instructed Wolcott to select Rush "on Account of ancient Merits and present Abilities. Of his Integrity and Independence, I have a good opinion." And he reassured Pickering on September 18 that he had "known, esteemed and loved" Rush for over twenty years. But it was another two months before the commission was officially announced, during which time Rush seemed more and more uneasy and had trouble attending to his business. He was also becoming obsessed with what was being written about him in the newspapers.

It made his blood boil. A longtime Federalist editor, John Fenno, was losing circulation to *Porcupine's Gazette*, and so to out-Cobbett Cobbett, he went after Rush and what he called his "lunatic system of medicine," announcing that bloodletting had been inspired by the guillotines of the French Revolution.

Cobbett, delighted to be able to one-up a journalistic competitor, responded with a fake letter to his own paper, allegedly from "A Tavern Keeper" whose sales were suffering from the epidemic, and was looking into bloodletting and purging as a better business. The next day he ran a short piece called "Medical Puffing," which began with a vaguely Swiftian couplet that Rush might have enjoyed if it hadn't been targeted at him: "The times are ominous indeed, When quack to quack cries, *purge* and *bleed*."

It went on:

> Those who are in the habit of looking over the gazettes, which come in from the different parts of the country, must have observed, and with no small degree of indignation, the arts that our remorseless *Bleeder* is making use of to puff off his preposterous practice. He has, unfortunately, his partisans in almost every quarter of the country. To them he writes letters, and in return gets letters from them:

> he extols their practice, and they extol his; and there is scarcely a page of any newspaper that I see, which has the good fortune to escape the poison of their prescriptions.—Blood, blood! Still they cry, More blood!—In every sentence they menace our poor veins. Their language is as frightful to the ears of the alarmed multitude, as is the raven's croak to those of the sickly flock.

Several days later Cobbett published another letter from his imaginary bartender, this one telling of a customer who had recently bought Rush's book on yellow fever and was persuaded to change careers to bloodletting. The customer pointed out that it was harder to make a living peddling "villainous liquors" than the "quiet business. . . . of the lancet, because you know . . . *dead men never tell tales*."

The imaginary bartender replied that he was hiring "a few nurses," a reference to the black men and women who were again helping Philadelphia's physicians. "They will never desert their patients, as I have engaged to supply them with excellent gin and have also promised them the pillage of such of my patients who be determined to die."

Cobbett began to call Rush "Doctor Sangrado," a reference to an evil quack physician who bled patients dry in a popular French novel of the early 1700s. While the name "Sangrado" was Spanish, this was another way of attacking Rush's Jeffersonian and therefore "French" leanings.

Many wrote to the papers in defense of Rush. One letter proclaimed, "Those feeble attacks which have been made on our *American Hippocrates*, can have but little effect in blotting or injuring his fame." After all, words in a daily newspaper were "short-lived, ephemeral . . . limited to the existence of a single day." The writer compared "the torrents of abuse," the "desire of wounding his feelings as an individual [and] . . . his reputation as a physician" to attacks on George Washington: "the tongue of malice will as ineffectually shed its venom as it did at the time when our late illustrious president retired from the chair of government."

As the yellow fever death toll rose, so did tensions. On October 2, 1797, out of desperation to curb the media attention, Rush began legal proceedings against William Cobbett and *Porcupine's Gazette* (as well as John Fenno and his *Gazette of the United States*, a case he later dropped). His friends strongly cautioned him against this, but he believed, in these earliest days of American media law, that the suit, for slander, would prevent the periodicals from covering him until the case was adjudicated. He was sadly mistaken.

JOHN RUSH COULDN'T take it anymore; the medical practice he was training to take over was being pilloried. When an article attacking his father appeared on October 6, John sent an angry note to Dr. Andrew Ross, a longtime enemy of Rush's, who he believed was the source. Then John saw Dr. Ross on the street, and they got into an argument: after Ross called him "an impudent puppy," John punched him, setting off a street brawl which ended with Ross challenging Benjamin Rush to a duel—because he was sure the father had put his son up to it.

Rush declined the challenge, but a few days later he began exploring an exit plan from Philadelphia. His friend and former student Dr. John Rodgers was now a prominent member of the medical school faculty at Columbia in New York; Rush asked if there might be a position for him there. "If you think there is any chance of the above proposition succeeding, you are at liberty to commend it in confidence to some of the regents of the University. If not, you will please to burn this letter."

Four days later the faculty at Columbia voted unanimously to appoint Rush as their new chair of medicine. But the board of trustees had to approve the appointment, and unfortunately for Rush, Alexander Hamilton was a prominent board member. Just before Rush's appointment was to be voted on, Hamilton insisted the matter be postponed. There is no known documentation, from Hamilton or Rush, that explains what happened. Hamilton may not have wanted the controversies surrounding Rush to be brought to his city and his college, and he was probably aware that many people who liked and respected Rush were worried about his state of mind.

Or perhaps Hamilton did it just to spite Rush, something he was not above.

Either way, Dr. Rush didn't wait to find out—although his friend on the Columbia faculty, Rodgers, implored him to. He said they stood ready to take Hamilton on, and see "whether the old leaven of Bigotry & political resentment shall triumph or not." Rush thanked him for his support but explained he could not accept the appointment "after the obstacles that have been thrown in the way of it by Mr. Hamilton." In fact, Rush said, "it is peculiarly gratifying to me to learn that the opposition to my appointment has come from that gentleman."

Rush took the treasurer's job at the U.S. Mint, just a few blocks from his home. All the work there was done by hand, or by horses turning the mill in the basement where the gold and silver were stored. Rush oversaw the costs of designing, printing, and coining money; he had an office on the second floor, below the laboratory where materials were tested, and he had to be there for only "a few minutes . . . three or four times a week." It was a good, easy job, and after he got it, he went to see John Adams—who he sometimes had to remind himself was president—to thank him.

Adams lived in the same President's House that Washington had—a huge, three-and-a-half-story brick mansion on Market Street near Sixth. It was handsome and imposing on the outside, but when Adams moved in, he was amazed at the "deplorable condition" of the furnishings. "There is not a chair to sit in," he wrote Abigail. "The beds and bedding are in a woeful pickle." Even after some refurbishment at government expense, he and Abigail hated the pomp and circumstance of state events held there.

Rush sat with Adams and said he had been thinking about their new working relationship. He must "act towards him," he had decided, as sixteenth-century French surgeon Dr. Ambroise Paré did when King Henry of France asked him to be his family physician. Dr. Paré said he would do it as long as he never had to "see a battle" or "change his religion." Rush begged Adams "in like manner to be forever excused from taking a part in any political controversy." Adams just smiled.

With the extra money coming in, Rush and Julia bought a new country home for summers and, one day, for retirement. The cottage stood two and a half miles north of town, at the corner of Timber and Slumb lanes (now Fifteenth Street and Cecil B. Moore Avenue, near Temple University). It was beautiful countryside with a stream nearby. The small, sturdy brick dwelling had one big common room downstairs and one large sleeping room upstairs, as well as a big, dry cellar. The frame building nearby included a kitchen and a well. Rush named the property Sydenham in honor of his first medical hero, the seventeenth-century British physician Thomas Sydenham—whose devotion to extreme "heroic medicine" he had come to appreciate only more as his career progressed. (People sometimes referred to Rush as "the American Sydenham," which in some medical circles was less than complimentary.) Rush referred to the property as his "Sydenham Hut," but it wasn't going to stay a hut for long; he had plans to build out and improve almost every inch of it and to have Julia design gardens around it, as her mother once had at Morven.

In the spring of 1798, twenty-one-year-old John Rush was made a navy surgeon, just in time for the Quasi-War with France, an undeclared war with occasional sea skirmishes that began after the United States stopped repaying its old war debt. In case the Quasi-War turned into a real war, Adams brought both Hamilton and Washington out of retirement and gave them top jobs in the military.

John did not yet have a medical degree, but his years of study with his father led to him being hired as a full surgeon, rather than the position he might have deserved and have been better prepared for, a surgeon's mate.

In the late summer, when yellow fever season began for 1798, John was stationed in Marcus Hook, south of Philadelphia on the Delaware, where the navy was isolating some sixty sailors who caught the fever onboard the *USS Ganges* and the *USS Retaliation*. One patient was a nineteen-year-old seaman named James Clark, who was given the standard treatment—a light bleeding, followed by a purge, and the next day a smaller purge and a rubdown with mercury—but did not survive and was declared dead. Later in the day, John Rush walked by Clark's open coffin and noticed that the "lifeless" corpse seemed to be regaining some of its coloring. He checked the pulse—nothing. He put a small mirror under the nose—nothing again. But he thought he detected some warmth in the torso, so he ordered the body to be warmed up the fastest way he could think of—covering it with warm ashes from the kitchen fires. And he told his surgeon's mate to pour some warm brandy down the dead man's throat every half hour. Then he went to attend to his other patients.

The next day John checked on his "dead" patient and found him sitting up, sipping soup. The "brandy treatment" became young Dr. Rush's first published paper.

Rush may have heard this story from John himself, since Marcus Hook wasn't far from town. Dr. Rush was in and out of Philadelphia that summer from Sydenham. In August, when the fever spread—at a rate almost as deadly as 1793—Rush stayed at the cottage directing construction and repairs. He occasionally visited patients, but mostly he received news from the front lines as doctors he had trained fought the good fight. Julia was in Princeton with most of the children; Richard, working in a law office, helped his father on the side with preparing medicines.

"Even the retirement and silence of our little hut," he wrote Julia, did not prevent his "poor heart" from aching over the news of deaths of people they knew, including one of his newest apprentices. Nearly 3,500 Philadelphians lost their lives to yellow fever that year, only 1,500 fewer than in 1793. But Rush's life during this outbreak was much different. He and Richard would take a carriage into town about nine in the morning and were always back at "our hut" before sunset.

As for John, the temper that had always worried Rush and Julia soon began undermining his naval career. That fall he got into an argument with another officer, Lt. Archibald McElroy, and ended up challenging him to a duel. McElroy refused, but he did reach out to his father, who reached out to Dr. Rush. John wrote his father a long and defensive letter about the incident.

It wasn't his last. By the spring, either by his own choice or the navy's, John Rush stopped being a surgeon—"quitted physic," as his father described it. He became a regular navy line officer and remained at sea. "Our Eldest Son has received his Leiutenant's Commission in the Navy with great gratitude," Rush explained to Abigail Adams, "and I hope he will not dishonor it."

Not long afterward the Rushes' freed slave William Grubber returned from sea: he still lived with them when he wasn't sailing. Grubber was very ill, and when Rush could no longer care for him at home, he arranged a bed for him at Pennsylvania Hospital. He was signed in as poor, his illness listed as "venereal disease." Rush agreed to pay for his clothes there and for the cost of his burial if he died ($3 [$61] for a coffin).

Grubber was in the hospital for a week, and on June 17, 1799, he died. After the burial, Rush wrote in his commonplace book:

> This day died and was buried in the city burying ground Wm. Grubber, a native African whom I bought, and liberated after he had served me 10 years. He lived with me occasionally afterwards, and after returning from sea always made my house his home. . . .
>
> In a fit of sickness which I had in 1787 it was expected I should die. William refused to go to bed on the night in which he expected that event would take place, and added, "If massaw [master] die, put me in de grave with him. He be de only friend I got in dis world." He obtained some of my hair secretly, and had it put into a ring in London, which . . . he gave to one of the maids to keep for him, with an injunction "not to tell me of it."

Whatever his former slave's reality of the situation had been, Rush had made his peace with his version of it.

During the last two years Philadelphia was the U.S. capital, Rush really appreciated having Adams and Jefferson in town.

He especially enjoyed talking to Jefferson about religion, because unlike his thoroughly Deist scientific friends, with no hope of considering the idea of divine intervention, Jefferson had what Rush appreciated as a more nuanced view. They had several provocative dialogues at Jefferson's residence, about the relationship of republicanism to faith in the young nation.

"I have a view of the subject," Jefferson told Rush, "which ought to displease neither the rational Christian or Deist; & would reconcile many to a character they have too hastily rejected." Presumably he was referring to Jesus, whose original teachings he seemed to feel had been lost in later writings requiring belief in supernatural events. Jefferson was also concerned that the clause in the Constitution that "secured the freedom of the press [and] covered also the freedom of religion, had given to the clergy a very favorite hope of obtaining an establishment of a particular form of Christianity thro' the US."

The problem, as Jefferson saw it, was that "every sect believes its own form the true one . . . but especially the Episcopalians & Congregationalists." Yet the "returning good sense of our country threatens abortion to their hopes," because ". . . I have sworn upon the altar of god eternal hostility against every form of tyranny over the mind of man."

While Rush wasn't sure about separating the biblical Jesus from his miracles, both men clearly agreed how important it was to, in Rush's words, "keep religion and government independant of each other. Were it possible for St. Paul to rise from his grave at the present juncture, he would say to the clergy who are now so active in settling the political Affairs of the world: 'Cease from your political labors—your kingdom is not of this world. . . . Christianity disdains to receive support from human Governments.'" Rush pressed Jefferson to publish on his religious ideas, his "creed"; the vice president promised to write something when he had time.

Rush also enjoyed talking to Jefferson about science, agriculture, and history—all very intellectual, not so emotional. Their scientific chats could range from Jefferson's idea that perhaps the recurrent yellow fever epidemics meant that men weren't supposed to live in cities as big as the ones in America, to Rush's obsession with "muskmelon seeds," which he wanted to share with Jefferson, because he thought they were "of a quality as much Above the common melons of our Country as a pine Apple is superior to a potatoe."

With Adams, Rush tried to stay away from politics—not easy because they had spent so many years talking about it—and focused on more personal matters. Both of them had sons who had once shown promise but were now descending into darkness. Adams's son Charles was in worse shape than John Rush. Now in his late twenties, Charles had struggled for years with alcoholism and the consequences of his drunken excesses, and neither John nor Abigail (who had lost a brother to the disease) knew what to do—nor, after Charles married, did his wife. Adams described Charles as a young man "cutt off in the flower of his days, amidst very flattering Prospects by causes which have been the greatest Grief of my heart and the deepest affliction of my Life."

Rush, at the time, was the nation's expert on alcoholism and its treatments and was trying to figure out where drunkenness "short of insanity" fit into the care he was giving at Pennsylvania Hospital. But Charles refused treatment or abstinence. Adams was angry at the behavior of his son, yet he also blamed himself for the many years he lived apart from him. He was so frustrated that he cut off communications with Charles, although Abigail continued to speak to him. Their dysfunctional family dynamic may have been part of Rush's inspiration, several years later, to propose a separate "asylum for drunkards to be called Sober House," where "persons addicted to the excessive use of . . . liquors, in which they might be reformed or accommodated where they could no longer injure themselves or others."

Rush did his best to be supportive of Adams. When current politics—national and family—were too oppressive, he shifted the conversation to the "old days" of the Revolution.

And Rush had developed a deeper friendship with Abigail Adams, always referring to John Adams, in their correspondence, as "our friend" or "your best friend," as if they were conspiring behind-the-scenes on his emotional behalf. He would send her advice on health matters and, sometimes, would talk about political challenges, reaching out to her when the president was too busy. They also talked about family—the Rush children and the Adams children knew each other well, and although Charles Adams had left Philadelphia for New York, their younger son Thomas was still in town and would visit him and Julia. Rush also offered medical advice, promising Abigail that if the yellow fever looked like it was coming back, he would "*whisper* in your son's ear the necessity of flight."

IT'S UNLIKELY THAT either Jefferson or Adams wanted to talk about Rush's upcoming court case against William Cobbett. Everyone he knew felt it was a mistake to take the issue to trial, especially as he was trying to step away from the controversies of public life.

But Rush felt at least one reason for optimism: the Alien and Sedition Acts, which Adams had signed into law. The Alien Act allowed for the imprisonment or deportation of hostile foreigners, which Rush could use against Cobbett since the angry Brit was not a U.S. citizen. And the Sedition Act's proposed limitations on the press—it banned the printing of false statements critical of the American government—helped create an environment that could favor Rush in the case. The acts had also created a possible conflict with the ten-year-old and largely untested First Amendment; Rush was a strong supporter of a free press, but he did not think what Cobbett wrote and invented was protected. The Rush-Cobbett trial would be one of the first high-profile slander trials under the Constitution.

The trial itself, in December 1799, wasn't nearly as dramatic as what had led up to it. Rush chose not to testify, while Cobbett didn't even attend; he disappeared from town, hiding out in New York. He didn't want to provide good stories for his competitors, he said. But the tide had clearly turned on him. A popular cartoon showed him as a monstrous, scribbling porcupine, with the following verse:

> See Porcupine, in Colours just Portray'd
> Urg'd by old Nick, to drive his dirty trade,
> Veil'd in darkness, acts the assassins part,
> And triumphs much to stab you to the heart.

The far greater drama of the moment—about which no one in the courtroom knew—was that by the second day of the trial, George Washington was seriously ill at Mount Vernon. He had contracted an infection after working on his farm in the rain. It began as a sore throat and steadily worsened, making breathing difficult. Even as a parade of doctors testified on behalf of Rush, sharing dramatic stories of being cured themselves by his methods, Washington was being treated with a strong course of fluids, an enema, four rounds of bloodletting, a potion of vinegar and sage tea, blistering, and an emetic to produce vomiting.

One of Washington's three doctors, Elisha Dick, had been a student of Rush's and, according to some reports, had objected to one of the bleedings. He also supported another doctor's suggestion that Washington have a tracheotomy, because he believed there was a blockage in his airway. Whoever was right, it was too late to save the first president. He died on December 14, 1799, at the age of sixty-seven, though his death was kept quiet for several days.

The day Washington died, Rush's trial went to the jury. It deliberated for two hours and returned with a verdict against Cobbett. Rush was awarded $5,000 ($103,000) in damages, and since Cobbett had disappeared, the property he left in the house he had rented in Philadelphia was seized.

Dr. Rush seemed to have received some justice. Perhaps he could enjoy some peace—it would be a good way to end a challenging period in his and his family's life, a hopeful way to welcome the new century.

Late in the day on December 18, word spread from Alexandria that Washington had died. The news arrived so late in Philadelphia that only one paper could jam in a quick notice, on page three. The next day it was in every newspaper, and the nation began making plans to mourn its first hero.

There was debate on how to mark the occasion—how did a new democratic nation bury its first elected president? President Adams proclaimed a period of mourning, and military officers were to wear a black crepe band on their left arms for five months. Congress continued meeting, but members wore black, and the chambers were shrouded. Mrs. Adams announced that women should wear "white, trimmed with black ribbon, black gloves and fans as a token of respect," but wives of government officials should wear all black. The mayor of Philadelphia called for all bells in the nation's capital to be muffled for three days. Business meetings were put off, and theater productions were closed down for a week.

The day after Christmas was the first official memorial to the president. Gen. Richard Henry Lee delivered the funeral elogium—which became famous for his description of Washington as "first in war, first in peace, first in the hearts of his countrymen." Rush thought Lee's speech was "sensible and moderate, but . . . deficient in elocution and pathos."

Washington's death could have put an end to the twenty-plus years of insider controversy concerning his relationship with Rush and the letter he had written during the war. But just before he died, Washington had made sure his feelings about the doctor would live on for posterity.

After Patrick Henry's death, which came just six months before the president's, a mutual friend of theirs in Virginia wrote to Washington seeking information about Henry's reputation and his contribution to the Revolution. Washington responded that the most "unequivocal proof" of Henry's honor and loyalty was when he had warned him about Rush's letter, which he called "an attempt which was made by a Party in Congress, to supplant me in that command."

Washington said that if the friend was unable to find Rush's letter among Henry's papers, "I will furnish you a copy." So the letter would live on.

39

William Cobbett tried to get a new trial in Pennsylvania and failed. From New York, he published a farewell issue of *Porcupine's Gazette*—his first public writing in over two months. He went over the trial, reprinting everything Rush had sued him over in minute detail. And then, on page ten, he made an accusation that was astonishing even for him: he said Benjamin Rush was responsible for killing George Washington.

Deep in a riff about "*Rush's practice* (that sublime practice, that infallible art, for ridiculing which I am to pay 5,000 dollars)," he wrote that "THE DEATH OF GENERAL WASHINGTON" was caused by treatment "in precise conformity to *the practice of Rush*."

Based on an article in one of the New York papers describing Washington's treatment and death, he continued:

> Thus, on the fatal 14th of December, on the same day, in the same evening, nay, in the very same hour, that a Philadelphian court & jury were laying on me a ruinous fine for having reprobated the practice of Rush, GENERAL WASHINGTON *was expiring while under the operation of that very practice*. On that day the victory of RUSH and of DEATH was complete; but their triumph was but of short duration, for while I have continued on my course unchecked by the judgments, the seizures, the attachments of Rush. . . . Gen-

eral Washington has, I hope, broken the chains of the grim tyrant, Death, and soared into the realms of immortal glory.

Two months later Cobbett published a pamphlet in New York under the title "The Rush-Light" that brought together all his old and new writing against Rush. The day the pamphlet came out in Philadelphia, John Rush just happened to have arrived home, on leave from the navy. He was still in his uniform when he started reading it, along with nineteen-year-old Richard, who had recently finished his legal apprenticeship and passed the bar.

When John discovered there was a chapter about him—in which Cobbett fancifully retold John's street brawl defending his father's honor, the victim this time proclaiming "I affirm this John Rush to be an impertinent puppy, a waylaying coward, a liar, and a rascal"—he dashed to catch the next stage to New York before anyone could stop him.

Drawing of John Rush in uniform, artist unknown

Cobbett also claimed that back in 1793, a certain physician had refused to be bled, at which point Dr. Rush had become hysterical. Richard Rush stormed out of the house and tracked the physician down. When he found him, he screamed at him and may have hit him. (In Rush's letter recalling this event, he wrote the word "assaulted" and then crossed it out and wrote "insulted.") Richard was taken into custody, and Rush was beside himself.

"This I fear," he wrote, "is the beginning of my family troubles from the feelings of my sons."

Dr. Rush dispatched a note to a college friend of his in New York, lawyer Brock Livingston, begging him to intercept John before he did anything rash. "His spirit is uncommonly firm and determined, and his resentments are keen upon the present occasion. I tremble therefore for the consequences of a meeting between them. The design of this letter is to call upon you as a *friend* to find him out and by persuasion or the force of law to arrest him in his present undertaking. He will probably be met with in a sailor's *undress* near Cobbett's door."

Rush also told Livingston he had been advised to file suit against Cobbett in New York, and he asked if Livingston thought that was a good idea. "You are a father," he wrote. "*Feel* and *act* as you would wish me to do for your children in a similar situation." In case Livingston decided to move quickly with a writ, Rush included $10 ($206) for expenses and begged him not to tell John that his father had written to him.

After receiving the letter, Livingston discovered John at a theater where he expected to confront Cobbett. He was able to calm him down; John asked a friend from the army, Capt. John Stille, to go talk to Cobbett in his place. What happened in their confrontation is a matter of dispute. Cobbett wrote an angry public letter to the secretary of war, James McHenry, to report that Stille had threatened him with "a bludgeon cane" before he had scared him off with "an iron poker."

Stille responded with his own published account, that Cobbett had appeared to him "armed with a large iron rod," and told him that he assumed John Rush had sent him seeking a "compromise" or "accommodation." Stille described their conversation, but as far as his choice of weapons, he reported that what he had drawn from his pocket was a copy of Cobbett's pamphlet, from which he read a few lines aloud. "Some few words ensued, the particulars of which are not material. I then left him."

Cobbett later claimed in a letter that he had gone for legal advice to Alexander Hamilton, who told him he had nothing to fear, legally, in New York. He said Hamilton "refused any fee, and . . . told me, that he should think himself honoured in defending me." Nothing more came of this affair, and Cobbett returned to England later that year, where he started another newspaper.

John Rush, temporarily saved from himself, returned to his

navy duties. His father and mother hoped that all would return to calm. They likely took it as a sign when, only months after William Cobbett fled the country, Julia became pregnant again. It would be her thirteenth pregnancy to come to term. She was forty-one years old and already a grandmother: their oldest daughter Emily and her husband, lawyer Ross Cuthbert, had recently welcomed a child.

The Rushes' baby turned out to be a healthy boy. Perhaps surprisingly, they gave him Cobbett's first name, William.

By then, Philadelphia was winding down as the capital of the United States. The new White House—still under construction—became the stage for the last acts of the hugely contentious presidential election of 1800, which pitted Adams against Jefferson. The popular election was brutal not only because of what was at stake, and because of Adams's and Jefferson's long friendship, but also because it lasted so long: each state chose its own date for the general election, so voting went on from the spring into the fall.

At the peak of the popular election, Rush inadvertently ran afoul of Adams. A former mutual friend of theirs, Tench Coxe, who President Adams had relieved of his federal position and was now publicly supporting Jefferson, brought up in a newspaper article the old charges that Adams favored monarchy over democracy. He claimed Rush had told him Adams still felt that way.

Rush immediately and emphatically denied it, while Coxe shot back that he was only denying it because Adams had given him a job at the Mint.

The episode did not affect the popular vote, which Adams lost handily. But the allegation certainly made Adams angry—so angry that Rush felt the need to reach out to both the president and his wife. His letter to Abigail showed the depth of his consternation: "I cannot express to you the distress which I continue to suffer from this cruel Act of Mr Coxe," he wrote. "I am consoled . . . not only by a Consciousness of my integrity towards Mr Adams, but by the universal indignation and horror which Mr Coxe's friends as well as enemies express." He swore that everything he had ever said about her husband was "calculated to beget esteem and respect . . . there is no One circumstance in my political life, that I review with half the pleasure that I do the uninterupted friendship with which he has honoured me for six & twenty years."

Abigail, from Massachusetts, tried to calm Rush's fears:

> I am sorry that you should have felt yourself so wounded tho to be assailed in the house of our Friends is a calamity of the bitterest kind. . . . I pray you my dear Sir do not give yourself any further uneasiness upon the Subject of your Letters, which I shall forward to the President, more as proofs of your attachment, than with an intention of removeing any unfavourable impression which the report of Mr Cox could excite.

A week later Rush met John Adams in person and tried to make amends. Afterward he wrote again to Abigail, saying her letter had brought his "distressed family great Consolation," which was "much encreased by the friendly manner in which my dear and venerable friend Mr Adams received me last evening. . . . My dear Mrs: Rush joins in the most affectionate regard and gratitude with my D[ea]r madam. Your Sincere friend, Benjn: Rush."

Four days later lame duck President John Adams moved into the White House in what was being called "Washington-City." Only weeks after arriving there, he received the news he had been dreading for years. His son, Charles, had been found dead in New York, at thirty. Charles was buried in New York with full military honors. A one-sentence obituary was published, mentioning no age, cause of death, or surviving wife and children, just that he was the second son of the president. If Adams ever corresponded with Rush about his death, the letters have been lost.

JEFFERSON, FOR HIS part, took his leave of Rush and Philadelphia in a long letter that acknowledged that they would probably never again speak face to face. "It would be a great treat to recieve you here," he wrote on his way to the new capital, "but nothing but sickness could affect that: so I do not wish it. For I wish you health & happiness, and think of you with affection. Adieu."

Rush wrote a long, philosophically sighing response. Jefferson had voiced his worry that the country and government they had built were under siege; Rush agreed. "Representative & elective Government appears to be a discovery of modern times," he said. "It has met with the fate of many Other discoveries which have had for their Objects the melioration of the Condition of man. It has been opposed, traduced, and nearly scou[r]ed from the face of the earth."

He shared with Jefferson that his ancestor John Rush had fought in Cromwell's army, and the family still had his sword. "To the sight of his Sword, I owe much of the Spirit which animated me in 1774, and to the respect & admiration which I was early taught to cherish for his Virtues, and exploits, I owe a large portion of my republican temper and principles." Democracy was, at least, an idea and an inheritance worth fighting for. He pointed out that the "science of medicine abounds with instances of new truths being treated in the same manner."

He ended abruptly. "Excuse the length of this letter," he wrote. "My pen has run away with me.—Pray throw it in the fire as soon as you have read it. Not a line of it must be communicated to a human Creature with my name."

And with that he said goodbye, except to note that he would, in the new year, get Jefferson those muskmelon seeds.

JEFFERSON, HAVING WON the popular vote along with his vice presidential candidate, New York senator Aaron Burr, now faced a more contentious Electoral College vote. Federalists who had supported Adams in an "anyone but Jefferson" effort decided to give their votes to Burr instead. Even with Hamilton in the surreal position of begging Federalist electors to choose Jefferson (because he despised Burr), the vote ended up tied, forcing the House to make the decision.

On Wednesday, February 11, as the rest of Washington was snowed in, House members arrived to choose the new president.

The first vote brought Jefferson one vote short of a victory, so the vote was taken again, with the same result. Then another with the same result. By three a.m. they had taken nineteen votes, all with the same result. So they started again the next day.

During this standoff, the Rushes were more focused on personal matters: over the course of just seventeen days in February 1801, they had to absorb the deaths of both Julia's mother, Annis Stockton Boudinot, and their close friend Elizabeth Graeme Fergusson. Rush eulogized Betsey Fergusson, whose last decades had been harsh (and who would have to wait more than a century before scholars rediscovered her writing and salons). Many eulogized Annis, who had a rich literary life after losing her husband.

In Washington, the House continued with more ballots on Thursday and on Friday—still deadlocked. By Saturday, they had voted thirty-three times. Finally, on Saturday evening, a Federalist from Delaware, James Bayard, offered to abstain to end the deadlock. But he would do it only if Jefferson, who hadn't been heard from, would agree not to purge Federalists from the government. It took two more days to verify the deal, and on the seventh day of voting, on the thirty-sixth ballot, Bayard abstained and Jefferson became president.

Abigail Adams packed her things. On her way home from Washington for the last time, she stopped in Philadelphia and had dinner with the Rushes. Her husband was not with her; he was staying in Washington until the last moment of his presidency, filling jobs and making judicial appointments. (His eleventh-hour appointment of Federalist John Marshall to the Supreme Court, who would become the longest-serving chief justice in history, was arguably the most influential decision of his presidency.) There is no record of what Abigail Adams talked about with Rush and Julia.

Adams left Washington on the morning of Jefferson's inauguration; he couldn't stay and watch and pretend. Unlike Abigail, he did not make time to stop in Philadelphia.

In fact, he would never see Benjamin Rush again.

Rush didn't hear from the Adamses for several months, although he sometimes bumped into their son Thomas in town. In one encounter, he gave Thomas a new piece he had written to send to his parents; when he didn't hear back from them, he decided to break the silence and write. Perhaps still nervous about addressing John directly, he wrote to Abigail. He included the article, about the life and recent death of a war compatriot whom Adams had known—a patriotic piece about the old days.

Rush told Abigail that Julia was taking care of their new baby "at our little farm." Lieutenant John had "returned from Sea after escaping death from a battle (in a British vessel in which he was a passenger) and from a yellow fever." John was about to leave the navy and proposed to go to sea as a master of a merchant ship.

He also told Abigail that he had been collecting "some of the most remarkable Opinions, and speeches of our friend in the years 1774, 1775, 1776 and 1777 upon public questions. In more impartial times, they shall be committed to the press. At present, they would only provoke hostility and Abuse."

Abigail wrote back a few weeks later, apologizing that she hadn't been feeling well. In the undated letter (likely late in August 1801), she thanked Rush for the soldier profile, which, she said, "will be read with pleasure by all Lovers of virtue, honor and patriotism." She went on:

> but my dear Sir these days of prosperity, Luxury and dissipation are not those in which such characters flourish. We have an intire new Theory in Religion, Morals & politicks, corresponding with our State of Society. They will have their preponderance until [heaven] in wrath punishes us for talents misemployd. blessing and benefits intirely thrown away, and this fair land, once the abode of freedom, becomes the prey of some bold Tyrant all the Social feelings which bind man to man & humanize Society, are wearing away; and bitter party Spirit of Calumny and falshood are linked together to lay prostrate all those kind affections without which Life is a curse instead of a blessing do not most of the evils described grow out of our Government, and shall we not ever long be convinced that the

passions of men are not held and restrainded by silken cords, by the still small voice of reason that Liberty which is unrestrained is a plethora in the political constitution.

Then Abigail made it clear that she didn't want Rush sharing any "annecdotes which relate to our Friend." She was emphatic about it:

> Truths are not always to be spoken. At the present period they would be scoffd at; persecution has followd that Spirit of independance which would not be domineered over by any party, but which undeviatingly pursued that System which has produced the unexampled prosperity of the country. let others act with the Same candour and firmness.

With that, Benjamin Rush, and John and Abigail Adams, quietly stopped communicating altogether.

Rush remained in regular contact with Jefferson, corresponding on science, religion, politics, and more often than not, the president's gastrointestinal issues. They spent a lot of time discussing Jefferson's diarrhea, both his symptoms and myriad ways they might be addressed.

He corresponded with medical colleagues around the world, and with his hundreds of former students, who now made up a large percentage of America's physicians—and for whom he was the American Cullen, the American Sydenham. And he was in contact with hundreds of perfect strangers, who wrote to the famous Dr. Rush seeking medical advice. When he decided his finances no longer allowed him to respond to these letters for free, he wrote explaining this to prospective postal patients, hoping they might stop writing. Instead, word spread that the letters seeking advice should come with cash in them. He ended up donating the money anyway.

Rush stayed in touch with James Madison, especially after he was made Jefferson's secretary of state, in part because his son Richard thought there might be a position for him as a secretary to a foreign minister. While Richard was in private practice in the early 1800s and did some legal work, he spent most of his time at home, devoted to the study of literature, history, government, and law, and developing his skills at writing and public speaking. He was hoping for an opportunity for foreign travel, but the family couldn't afford it.

Rush pleaded his son's case to Madison, who promised to put the matter in front of Jefferson, but that was the last they heard of it. Disappointed, Richard doubled down on his studies for the next five years, later boasting that "I read the whole of Johnson's writing from the beginning to end, *twice.*" (He decided that Johnson's "was not the style for a man of affairs.")

In the fall of 1801, Rush wrote to Alexander Hamilton and his wife after their son Philip was killed in a duel—he had been defending his father's honor against a local detractor. While Hamilton and Rush did not speak, their sons Philip and Richard had maintained a long friendship, sharing, among other things, the experience of living up to the dreams of demanding fathers who happened to have founded a nation. Philip had been to the Rushes' home not long before his death; he and Richard were both writing for a new Philadelphia-based magazine, *Port Folio.*

"You do not weep alone," Rush wrote to the Hamiltons. "Many, many tears have been Shed in our city on your account." (Over four months later, Hamilton did respond: "I felt all the weight of the obligation which I owed to you and to your amiable family, for the tender concern they manifested in an event, beyond comparison, the most afflicting of my life. But I was obliged to wait for a moment of greater calm, to express my sense of the kindness.")

But among all these correspondents, for the next four and a half years, Rush heard not one word from John Adams.

Rush continued to write essays and case reports, and his older pieces were republished in the United States, England, and Europe—along with his *Medical Inquiries and Observations.* But much of his creativity and energy went into his lectures. He still delivered them from large portfolios on which every left page was blank, so that he could take notes on what occurred to him and what students asked. He lectured sitting down on a stage, but his performances were considered dramatic and intense because of the way he used his hands and his voice. One former student, during a professional visit to Philadelphia, slipped in to see his old professor in action:

> His hair, braided, and secured behind with a black ribbon, was now silver white and the invidious artist, Time, had been silently busy on his temples [but] . . . his penetrating grey eye continued to emit the living lustre . . . of genius. . . . He was chain bound in the spell of enthusiasm—Transfixed—agitated—absorbed—lost in the variety, and overwhelmed by the intensity of his emotions, the Hippocrates of America stood before me, his lofty and upraised brow was deeply impressed with the seal and signet royal of *unbought* nobility. . . . It filled me with tumultuary and superstitious emotion. I was on enchanted ground and my friend was the grand Magician who animated and governed and directed the sorcery of the scene. Such was Rush.

While much of his curriculum was the same every year—training physicians from scratch being a noble and repetitious practice—Rush looked forward each fall to writing and delivering a new "Introductory Lecture to courses of Lectures upon the Institutes and Practice of Medicine" to start the school year. He had been writing them since 1791, the debut of the University of Pennsylvania medical school.

He had begun that first lecture, "On the Necessary Connexion Between Observation, and Reasoning in Medicine," by claiming that medical education in America was now preferable to that of Europe, then held forth as the title promised: "Physicans have been divided into empirics and dogmatists. . . . The former pretend to be guided by experience, and the latter by reasoning alone in their prescriptions." But the only way to avoid error was to combine the two. Moreover if a teaching of his was proven wrong, "I shall publicly retract it. I am aware how much I shall suffer by this want of stability in error, but I have learned from one of my masters [Rev. Samuel Finley] to 'esteem truth the only knowledge, and that labouring to defend an error, is only striving to be more ignorant.'"

In the years to come he gave a lecture on Hippocrates; another "On the duty and advantages of studying the diseases of domestic animals, and the remedies proper to remove them"—which would be considered the beginning of veterinary medicine; another on "the vices and virtues" of being a physician, "the pains and pleasures of a medical life," and the "means of acquiring business and . . . causes which . . . occasion the loss of it." One year he even took on "the duties of patients to their physicians," which, among his advice on specific ways to follow doctors' orders, also explained the right way to fire your physician.

In 1802, Samuel Coates asked him to lecture on "the construction and management of hospitals." Among the innovations Rush called for were "a room formed in the manner of an amphitheatre for surgical operations," which led, two years later, to the building of a circular surgical amphitheater in Pennsylvania Hospital, the first in America.

He also said it was time to build a separate, humane hospital facility in Philadelphia for "persons affected by madness." This call would help instigate the creation in 1813 of the landmark private Quaker Friends Hospital and then, in 1841, to the Institute of Pennsylvania Hospital, the nation's first asylum and the birthplace of what became the American Psychiatric Association. But when Rush wrote this in 1802, he was likely responding to the recent publication in France of Philippe Pinel's *A Treatise on Insanity*, which detailed his work in Paris and his expanding views of *traitement moral.* William Tuke's York Retreat was also becoming more successful. These initiatives weren't well known to the public, but the physicians working with madness and its care were starting to recognize one another.

Not long after his 1802 lecture, one of his students, William Darlington—whose notes from hospital rounds with Rush are the only ones known to have survived—described following Rush and his retinue as they visited the psychiatric patients in the new building. "Dr. Rush remarked," he noted, "that he has always considered it a sign of returning Reason, when a maniac becomes desirous to see, or hear from his family, or friends—or discovered any solicitude on hearing their names mentioned. One of these we saw was almost overcome when his wife was introduced to him." Darlington was also interested in the detailed psychological profile Rush offered his students of a patient named Thomas Willis, a carpenter "admitted for derangement, occasioned by poverty and other distress." He explained that "Dr. R. observed that we should talk a great deal with deranged patients; and we should always in the early & violent stages of mania, seem to agree with their notions. We should admit their *premises*, but draw a *different inference*; which may generally be done. To oppose them at first would be like opposing a northeast storm."

Rush told the students, as they walked through the hospital, a tougher-love story about "a maniacal patient," he had once had, who "wished to kill himself in his own house with a pistol or knife." Rush had assured the patient that it was "perfectly right to kill himself, but that he had better go to some private place to do it." The man agreed and accompanied the doctor to the hospital, where, as soon as he was in a cell, he "demanded a pistol." Rush then told him he supported his desire to die, "and even urged the propriety of his being killed, but told him it would be wrong for him to commit *suicide*; and that he had better let another person dispatch him."

Better, Rush said, that he "be *bled to death* as it was a very easy mode of dying."

"Done, Doctor!" said the patient, who held out his arm. A large quantity of blood was taken, which knocked him out, and "a *mad shirt* was put on him to prevent his loosing the bandage." The next day the patient was suddenly "very much afraid of dying—and requested protection against some persons he thought intended to kill him!!!!" Rush explained to his students, "We should never attempt to ridicule the ideas of maniacs, except in the last stage of convalescence."

Rush had also developed new ideas for long-term care. During rounds, Darlington recounted, he had explained a novel proposal that he was trying to get the hospital to adopt, for when patients improved and were ready to be released. In order to ease their transition back to their lives, Rush proposed that the hospital should hire "a person whose business shall be to lead Maniacal convalescents home. . . . It is as much a remedy as the hot or cold bath . . . [and] will increase the cure. Novelty after confinement produces too much action—patients after going home apparently cured, have committed murder—The keeper should accompany them."

As the nation's expert on madness, Rush was concerned about a public scourge he considered to be a bizarre form of suicide: dueling. In early 1803, he called a local alderman, Robert Wharton, to help thwart the plans of two of his students. As they were going to duel the next morning, the alderman came at eleven p.m. and arrested them both. He "bound them over" until they agreed not to go through with it.

Rush's younger brother, Jacob, now president judge of the Third Circuit Court in Reading, had just written a blistering jury charge that made a comprehensive legal argument against dueling, which he lamented "has become a fashionable vice in our country" and is "illegal . . . immoral . . . irrational . . . [and] impious." When someone is killed in a duel:

> it is generally speaking, the most aggravated species of murder; because it is accompanied with every circumstance of cool preparation, that a spirit of revenge can dictate. In such extreme abhorrence does our law justly hold this offence, that not only the principal, that is, he who *actually* kills the other, is guilty of murder, but his *second* also; because he takes part with him, and by his *presence* becomes a principal in the first degree.

There was no difference, Judge Rush railed, "between the bloodthirsty highwayman, who murders for the sake of gold, and the duellist, who murders for the sake of revenge." Unfortunately, the dueling mania didn't seem to be going away.

In February 1803, Thomas Jefferson, while negotiating the Louisiana Purchase, wrote to Rush with an unusual request. Would the doctor be willing to offer some medical and cultural mentorship to "about 10 chosen woodsmen" who would "undertake the long desired object of exploring the Missouri & whatever river, heading with that, leads into the Western ocean"?

The expedition was to be led by Capt. Meriwether Lewis, Jefferson's secretary, who was "brave, prudent, habituated to the woods, & familiar with Indian manners & character. He is not regularly educated, but he possesses a great mass of accurate observation on all the Subjects of nature which present themselves." Jefferson wanted Rush to (as Franklin had always admonished) "be very useful" and "state for him [Lewis] those objects on which it is most desireable he should bring us information." He asked Rush "to prepare some notes of such particulars as may occur in his journey & which you think should draw his attention & enquiry. He will be in Philadelphia about 2. or 3 weeks hence & will wait on you."

(The remainder of the letter, which made Rush the de facto medical director for the Lewis and Clark expedition, concerned more details about Jefferson's diarrhea—which the president had recently deduced was most predictably triggered by eating certain seafood: "while fish & sturgeon affect me powerfully, neither oysters nor crabs do." Jefferson had also come to believe that being on a horse was a remedy, and "daily rides of an hour or two keep me free from inconvenience from the visceral weakness.")

Rush wrote back, "I shall expect to see Mr Lewis in Philadelphia, and shall not fail of furnishing him with a number of questions, calculated to encrease our knowledge of subjects connected with medicine." He also pointed out to the president that "you were in the practice formerly of washing your feet every morning in cold water in cold weather. It is possible that practice so salutary in early and middle life, may not accord with your present age. The bowels sympathize with the feet above any other external part of the body, and suffer in a peculiar manner from the effects of cold upon them."

Three months later, twenty-nine-year-old Meriwether Lewis arrived in Philadelphia and called on Rush. They discussed not only the medical challenges of a long expedition with no doctor in the group but also what Rush knew, and wanted to know, about Native American culture and medicine.

Rush especially wanted Lewis to find out about the mental health of the people he encountered while heading west. He asked Lewis to inquire of each tribe what they knew about madness and suicide; he especially wanted to know if suicide was common, and if it was "ever from love."

While Rush had written and lectured on this subject in the past, he may have been more comfortable discussing it with Lewis because, by all accounts, the young man was known to have strong and sometimes unstable moods. Jefferson knew Lewis had been "subject to hypocondriac affection" since "early life" and while working with him in Washington he saw that he was prone to "sensible depressions of the mind." He may have recognized in Rush someone who understood such problems and sympathized with them.

After meeting with Rush, Lewis met with colleagues in the Philosophical Society, including physician Caspar Wistar (who was more of an expert on surgery and anatomy than Rush), botanist Benjamin Smith Barton, and geographer Robert Patterson. And then merchant Israel Whelan took him to twenty-seven different shops, where they purchased everything the expedition might need, until he filled his Conestoga wagon with 3,500 pounds of essentials.

Among them were lots and lots of what Lewis called "Rushes Pills"—which the explorer would later say he "found . . . sovereign" in treating his constipation and other stomach ailments. Rush didn't sell the pills, nor did he benefit financially from them; since the 1793 yellow fever epidemic, all Philadelphia apothecaries carried purging pills made to Rush's specifications. The pills were famous (and infamous) for exploding all blockages.

After Lewis headed back to Washington, Rush sent him a detailed list, which he copied from his commonplace book, called "Questions to Merryweather Lewis before he went up the Missouri." These were primarily about "physical history and medicine," the "morals" and "religion" of the Indians (and any "affinity between their religious ceremonies and those of the Jews," since some, although not Rush, believed Native Americans descended from the lost tribes of Israel). Three weeks later Rush wrote out a second list, "Directions for Mr. Lewis for the Preservation of the Health of those who were to accompany him." It included the advice that "when you feel the least indisposition," he should fast, rest, drink fluids, and sweat and, if that didn't work, "take a purge of two pills every four hours until they operate freely."

Rush mailed the second list directly to the president, to pass on to Lewis. "His mission is truly interesting," he wrote to Jefferson. "I shall wait with great solicitude for its issue. Mr: Lewis appears admirably qualified for it. May its Advantages prove no less honourable to your Administration, than to the interests of Science!"

John Rush may have helped his father make these lists, because at the age of twenty-six, he had quit the navy and come home to pursue a medical degree. "So anxious was he to return to my house and business," Rush wrote in his commonplace book, "that he said 'he would supply the place of one of my men servants, and even clean my stable rather than continue to follow a sea life.'"

John may have been suddenly inspired to seriously pursue a career path leading to a partnership in his father's practice. But he also knew that his teenage brother, James, now at the College of New Jersey, was interested in physic; so John could have been thinking about fortifying his birthright to the family business. Either way, he worked hard at the University of Pennsylvania medical school, graduating in 1804, with a thesis on "The Causes of Sudden Death and the Means of Preventing It." He dedicated it to his father.

Among the causes of sudden death, John included several involving mental health. One was "Sudden and violent emotions of the mind," such as "the return of a long-absent and favourite son from his travels, [which] once produced death in a father." He made a second category for "Derangement producing suicide" and noted he had "ascribed this cause of sudden death to a disease, for such is its contrariety to the natural principles of action in man, that I believe it rarely takes place in the perfect exercise of his reason." As far as prevention went:

> where there is reason to apprehend a sudden death from suicide, persons suspected of it, should be narrowly watched, and all the means of death should be removed out of their sight, or they should be removed from them. Solitude should be prevented, and cheerful society, or a cheerful glass, should be advised. The excitement of a strong emotion of terror and pity has prevented it in two instances, when the patients were just about throwing themselves into a river.

John went on to write a second paper, called "Elements of Life, or the Laws of Vital Matter," which began as a talk at the Medical Society of Philadelphia and then was published as a pamphlet. John strongly praised his father's work in mental health (in language that suggests he had heard his father privately assess his own impact): "Madness, a disease of the mind, was perhaps never understood, and seldom cured," John wrote, "until a professor, distinguished alike for talents and piety, announced, that the cause of it was a morbid and irregular action of the blood vessels, which excited correspondent actions in the nerves. His numerous cures of it demonstrate, at least, that it proceeds from a physical cause."

Young Dr. John Rush was then offered a staff position at Pennsylvania Hospital. But, much to everyone's surprise, he turned it down. And soon afterward he left Philadelphia with a friend of his father, Maj. Pierce Butler, to relocate to Charleston, South Carolina, where Rush's former student Dr. David Ramsay lived and could keep an eye on him.

As always, John Rush's parents hoped that all would be well.

THE ELECTION OF 1804 was full of jolting surprises—none of which had to do with whether Jefferson would be reelected, because he was clearly going to win by a landslide. In July, the nation's dueling craze reached its zenith when Jefferson's vice president

Aaron Burr—who was running for governor of New York—met Alexander Hamilton, his longtime political and personal enemy, at the dueling grounds on the west bank of the Hudson River, in Weehawken, New Jersey. Before going to the duel, Hamilton wrote a statement in which he disparaged dueling—which had already taken his son—and explained it was his intention to "*reserve* and *throw away* my first fire" and perhaps even his second, "thus giving a double opportunity to Col Burr to pause and to reflect."

Hamilton shot and missed; Burr aimed for Hamilton and shot him in the stomach. Hamilton—who was considered a likely presidential candidate to replace Jefferson after his second term—died the next day. Rush wrote about the tragedy in his commonplace book with surprising evenhandedness, describing Hamilton as:

> learned, ingenious, and eloquent, and the object of universal admiration and attachment of one party, and of hatred of the other party which then constituted the American people. He was greatly and universally lamented . . . on his deathbed he condemned this duelling in strong terms. . . . Col. Burr visited Philadelphia the week afterwards, went into company, and walked the streets with apparent unconcern.

Several weeks after the Burr-Hamilton duel, Rush found himself in the very odd position of begging the chief justice of the Supreme Court to cut some lines out of a book he was writing. It was the upcoming third volume of Marshall's epic biography *The Life of George Washington*. The first two volumes had come out earlier that year, not long after the Marshall Court established the concept of "judicial review" of constitutionality in the landmark case *Marbury v. Madison*.

Rush had heard that the next volume was going to include, in an appendix on the Conway affair, the letter he had written to Patrick Henry about Washington in 1778, along with Henry and Washington's responses to it. The copy Washington had given Patrick Henry's friend had made its way to Marshall.

The book was being widely read—in fact, Rush's own family

had been devouring the first two volumes. And Rush was apoplectic that everyone he knew would read the letters and think he had been unsupportive of Washington during the darkest days of the Revolutionary War. He urged the chief justice in the strongest possible terms not to reprint the letters and offered a long explanation of what had really happened.

But the third volume was already at the printer—too late for Marshall to respond to Rush's pleading. Still, the chief justice had already deleted a handful of references, including Washington's revelation that Rush was the author.

Nobody who had ever heard about the letter—and by this time many had—was fooled by Marshall's clumsy deletions. But at least all those experiencing the hagiographic retelling of the Washington story for the first time wouldn't know the commander in chief believed Rush had tried to undermine him just before the turning point in the war.

40

The letter was completely unexpected. It arrived in mid-February 1805, with a playful postmark from Massachusetts: "Mount Wollaston—Alias Quincy."

"Dear Sir," it began. "It seemeth unto me that you and I ought not to die without saying good-bye or bidding each other Adieu."

It was, at last, John Adams. "Pray how do you do? How does that excellent Lady Mrs: Rush; How are the young ladies? Where is my Surgeon & Lieut? How fares the lawyer?" As if no time had passed, he picked up their conversation where it had left off nearly five years earlier.

Adams mentioned Rush's controversial idea that, in an epidemic, all other diseases are subsumed by, and turn into, one plague. "I cannot help thinking," he went on, "that Democracy is a distemper of this kind, and when it is once set in motion and obtains a majority it converts every thing, good bad and indifferent into the dominant Epidemic." Then he put a few questions to Rush's conscience:

> Is the present State of the Nation Republican enough? Is virtue the principle of our Government? Is honor? Or is ambition and avarice adulation, baseness, covetousness, the thirst of riches, indifference concerning the means of rising and enriching, the contempt

> of principle, the Spirit of party and of faction, the motive and the principle that governs? These are Serious and dangerous questions; but serious men ought not to flinch from dangerous questions.

He signed off saying "my family unite with me in presenting respects and assurance of old regard to you and yours."

Rush professed surprise, but he probably had suspicions as to why Adams had written. His son John Quincy had visited Philadelphia during another fall of raging fevers and reported to his father that he had "pass'd a couple of hours" with Rush, "whose accounts were truly melancholy." While John Quincy noted that it had been "a Season uncommonly sickly," he may also have been suggesting Rush himself was melancholy.

John Quincy's father had been achingly depressed, unable to get much done, and anxious about his life and legacy. His wife and children had encouraged him to write a book—a memoir, a history of the revolution—but he had claimed to his son Thomas that he had little to say "worth reading." He recalled that Rush had kept "an elaborate Collection of Biographical Memoirs of those Men," but "to me, the Undertaking would be too painful. I cannot bear to reflect upon the Scenes I have beheld. The Sincere have been allways tortured by the Sinister: and Sometimes even by the Sincere. Such is the Lot of humanity."

Adams replied to John Quincy about the rampant illness, which he saw as both medical and metaphorical. "There are Some deleterious Effluvia in the American Atmosphere . . . which engender political Delirium, and Spread Contagion endemically or epidemically, from one Man and one State to another," he wrote. "The vile Corruption has Seized and mortified Massachusetts at last." By this he meant not so much fever as the enemies of Federalism.

"If I had been with you," he told John Quincy, "and heard the Jeremiades of Dr Rush, I would have congratulated him or rather complimented him upon the universal diffusion of his adored Republicanism. I presume his Soul is entranced with Raptures." Presumably missing his friend's jeremiads and raptures, a few weeks later Adams broke their silence.

Rush wrote back at once:

My much respected & dear friend

Your letter of the 6th: instant revived a great many pleasant ideas in my mind. I have not forgotten—I cannot forget you. You and your excellent Mrs Adams often compose a subject of conversation by my fire side. We now and then meet with a traveler who has been at Quincy, from whom we hear with great pleasure, not only that you enjoy good health, but that you retain your usual good spirits, and that upon some Subjects, you are still facetious.

He brought Adams up to date with his family. His oldest daughter, Emily, was married and lived in Montreal. His second daughter, Mary, had, against his and Julia's initial wishes, married a captain in the British Army and would soon be living abroad. John had "lost his health" after graduating from medical school and was now in South Carolina, where he hoped for better prospects for his life and career. Richard was still at home, studying and dabbling in law.

As for himself, "I live like a Stranger in my native state," he said. "My patients are my only acquaintances,—my books my only companions, and the members of my family, nearly my only friends." He felt outcast, he confided, due to his belief that the seasonal fevers were not brought in on boats from other countries but were rather of "domestic origin" and should be addressed by public health measures including better sanitation. The letter finished with "cordial and affectionate regards."

Adams quickly wrote back, asking which British captain Rush's daughter had married. (It was Thomas Manners.) He assured Rush that he would see his married daughter, that John would "do well," and that he needed to be patient with Richard, because it sometimes took the legally inclined a while to find themselves. Besides, "No civilized Society can do without Lawyers."

WITH THAT BEGAN a dialogue about America's past and future that would influence the history of the country—even as it remained, at its core, an intimate record of friendship between two men. The correspondence began privately, but after a few months, both acknowledged that the letters were developing a small audience.

At the end of the sixth letter, Rush left as a P.S.: "I hardly need to suggest that certain parts of this letter must not be read out of your own family." Adams wrote back, "I cheerfully agree to confine your Letter to my family upon condition that you confine mine to yours." In his next letter, Rush assured Adams, "None of your letters are read out of my family." And he explained, "You see I think aloud in my letters to you, as I did in those written to you near 30 years ago, and as I have often done in your company. I beg again they may be read only in your own family. I live in an enemy's Country."

Some of what they were writing, both knew, could prove scandalous in the hands of political enemies—or, worse, historians who would decide their posthumous fate. Rush noted the letters "deeply interest my Son Richard," who still harbored political ambitions. As the letters continued, Adams and Rush both referred to their respective family audiences as "the fireside," as that was where the missives were usually read aloud. These chosen few got to watch two cranky, opinionated old Founding Fathers replay their revolution.

In one of his earliest letters, Rush recounted his 1790 dream, in which he found himself to be a weathervane atop of Christ Church, and which he had taken to mean that he should leave public office. Interestingly, Adams wrote back saying, "I admire the Brilliancy of your Invention, when asleep. I know not whether [A]Esop or Phaedrus . . . have given us a more ingenious fable than yours. . . . The Structure and application of the Fiction are very clever."

As the correspondence deepened in 1805, Rush brought up his longtime plan for a book entitled "Memories of the American Revolution," for which he had collected notes since the event. "But perceiving how widely I should differ from the historians of that event," he admitted, "and how much I should offend by telling the truth, I threw my Documents into the fire, and gave my pamphlets to my son Richard."

Rush (first three portraits) and Adams (bottom right) as rendered by various artists around the time they reconnected

He claimed that all he had preserved were his character sketches of the signers of the Declaration, "part of which," he reminded Adams, "I once read to you while you were President of the United States. From the immense difference between what I saw, and heard of men and things during our Revolution, and the histories that have been given of them, I am disposed to believe with Sir R. Walpole that all history (that which is contained in the bible excepted) is a romance, and romance the only true history."

Adams was shocked and disappointed at this news:

I am extreamly Sorry you relinquished your design of Writing Memoirs of the American Revolution. The burning of your Documents was, let me tell you, a very rash Action, and by no means justifiable upon good Principles. Truth, Justice and Humanity are of eternal Obligation and We ought to preserve the Evidence, which can alone Support them—I do not intend to let every Lye impose upon Posterity.

He challenged Rush on one point—his inclusion of Hamilton in a list of Founding Fathers:

You rank Colonel Hamilton among the Revolutionary Characters. But why? The Revolution had its beginning its middle and its End before he had any thing to do in public affairs. . . . You Say that Washington and Hamilton are idolized by the Tories.—Hamilton is: Washington is not. To Speak the truth, they puffed Washington like an air Balloon to raise Hamilton into the Air. Their preachers, their orators, their Pamphlets and Newspapers have Spoken out and avowed publicly Since Hamiltons death, what I very well knew to be in their hearts for many Years before . . . that Hamilton was every thing and Washington but a Name.

From this point on, each of Rush and Adams's letters included, often in impassioned detail, memories for the books that neither of them would ever write. After almost a year of renewed correspondence, Rush noted as much:

I am pleased in reflecting that I destroyed all the documents and Anecdotes I had collected for private memoirs of the American Revolution. I discover from your letters that I have seen nothing but the "Scenery of the business," and know but little more than what servants who wait upon table know of the secrets of their masters families, of the springs of the events of the war, and of the administration of the general Government since the year 1791.

While he was probably underplaying what he knew, he understood that this was a way to keep Adams talking.

More than dredging up the past, Rush mused on what he had learned from it:

> There is Quackery in every thing as well as in medicine, and it is because Politicians neglect to form principles from facts, that so many mistakes are committed in calculations upon the issue of commotions in human Affairs. Louis the 14th: lamented that we were only fit to live in the world, when we were called to leave it. I feel the truth of this remark daily in myself as well as see it in others. *Learned* men, I now find know what *was*—*weak* men know what *is*, but men made *wise* by reflection, only know *what is to come.*

THINGS DID NOT go as planned for young Dr. John Rush in South Carolina. He was unable to develop a practice as hoped and felt injured by an engagement that fizzled. He decided to return to the military and asked his father to recommend him to the secretary of the navy. Rush did so reluctantly: his letter mentioned two glowing recommendations John previously received at sea, yet admitted "both these certificates are mislaid [presumably by John] . . . but I do hereby vouch for the correctness of them as above stated." Within two weeks John was named a sailing master and put in command of Gunboat #18 sailing out of Boston.

"Very contrary to my wishes & advice," Rush wrote to Adams, John has "returned to the navy."

On Gunboat #18, John Rush earned the respect of his fellow officers as a skilled seaman. But they recognized in him a deep and profound melancholy—which he led them to believe had been caused by "an estrangement from his father." He described himself to navy colleagues as "the degenerate son of an eminent and respectful father, as a failure to the fair reputation of his brothers and in short . . . as a blackguard."

During the next two years, John went on to command several other gunboats and was promoted. In the meantime, his former role as the heir apparent to his father's practice was taken over by his third brother, James, who was studying medicine at the University of Pennsylvania before going to Edinburgh. Richard, for his part, became known as a lawyer and a writer. Still living at home, he remained in touch with John Quincy Adams, who he hoped might one day help him get a federal appointment—though his father was dead set against it.

Rush's children had often heard him rail against politics: "I entreat [my sons] to take no public or active part in the disputes of their country beyond a vote at an election. If no scruples of conscience forbid them to bear arms, I would recommend to them rather to be soldiers than politicians. . . . In battle men kill, without hating each other; in political contests men hate without killing, but in that hatred they commit murder every hour of their lives."

Richard Rush

Rush also didn't want his ambitious, talented second son to be thinking about leaving home. Now that his oldest daughter, Emily, was married, and Julia was becoming more involved as a grandmother to Emily's son and daughter (regularly visiting Canada to spoil them), Richard had become his closest everyday confidant.

In October 1807, the Rush family received shocking news from the navy: John had been in a duel, and there had been a fatality.

The duel took place in the late afternoon of October 1, aboard Gunboat #18, in port at New Orleans. John Rush's opponent was a fellow officer and close friend, Lt. Benjamin Turner. A third-generation navy man from Massachusetts, Turner was twenty-seven, three years younger than John, and had distinguished himself in battle on the *USS Constitution* during the Second Attack on Tripoli, Libya, in 1804. According to multiple navy sources (and what John told his father), Turner had refused to accept a recent duel challenge and became upset over being labeled a coward for it.

John Rush had been helping him work through his feelings

about that situation, as had other officers who thought he made the right decision. So it seemed incomprehensible when Lieutenant Turner then challenged Rush to a duel.

John had no plan to shoot his friend; he assumed that when the moment arrived, neither would aim at the other. But just before the event, he was told that Turner had claimed he would "kill or be killed" and felt he had no choice but to aim true. Turner died at the scene, and soon afterward both families discovered what the two friends had been fighting about. According to a letter sent by one of the sailors onboard at the time, "the quarrel was some trifling argument about Shakespeare plays."

Several days later another detailed letter from an eyewitness ran in major city newspapers from Boston to New Orleans: "This morning at 10 o'clock, I shook Lt. Turner by the hand, and this evening at eight I held in my hand a ball that had passed through his heart." The eyewitness explained how this "dreadful affair" had unfolded: "A number of officers were amusing themselves in their quarters last evening playing cards when Lieut. Rush came in and was asked to play, he declined, with a quotation from Shakespeare. Some criticism was made on it by Turner, and an argument of some warmth took place—disagreeable reflections were made, bad language ensued, and this morning Turner sent Rush a challenge."

They met early that evening, and on the word *fire*, "Turner's pistol flamed and Rush's snapped. . . . They both fired almost at the same instant, and Rush's ball passed quite through Turner's body and lodged in the left sleeve of his shirt."

Turner staggered, cried out, "I am a dead man," and fell into John Rush's arms.

He died almost immediately, and John, frantic but still holding him, wailed, "My dear friend! Why would you force me to do this? Let me declare in your dying ear . . . that I did not wish to meet you, and . . . shall mourn your death as that of a brother!"

John was briefly incarcerated by the navy, but soon after an investigation cleared him of wrongdoing, he was given another command. Benjamin Rush shared the story and his feelings about the situation with several friends—interestingly, when he told Adams, he referred to Turner as "the infatuated young man." But he was entirely supportive that John had had been in the right.

For a few months, it seemed as if John had survived this traumatic incident relatively unscathed. But by the end of the year, he was corresponding with his mother and Richard about new struggles. John framed them as financial disagreements with his father, but as always seemed to be the case, there was also something more.

"Let me my dear son again entreat you, not to cherish chagrin or irritation against your best friends, or the world," Julia wrote him just before Christmas 1807. "Rouse you like a strong minded man, and resolve that you will be independently limitting your expenses to your income, let that be what it may, and here let us drop this subject."

WHILE INCREASINGLY CONCERNED about John, Rush knew things could be worse. His longtime friend Col. Timothy Pickering had a son about the same age, William, whom Rush had been treating for "derangement" at Pennsylvania Hospital for months.

Pickering had lived in Pennsylvania for many years but now represented Massachusetts in the U.S. Senate. His son William was twenty-two, and both he and his parents remembered noticing changes in his mind during his late teens—what one Pickering family member would describe as "occasional slight melancholy hallucinations." William also grew despondent and anxious over what he described as "an offense toward his parents"—but they could not guess what the offense had been.

Over the next years, his symptoms became so regular that his periods of wellness seemed intermittent. He was admitted to Pennsylvania Hospital on September 27, 1807, as an unpaid "poor" patient, but Rush agreed to pay his security.

William was one of many patients Rush had known personally before finding them in his care. The wife of philanthropist Stephen Girard, Mary, was still his patient. Since 1800, he had been treating writer and artist Richard Nisbett, the same Nisbett who had written an audacious challenge to Rush's first published antislavery piece in the early 1770s. He had treated painter Charles Willson Peale's son Rembrandt. And now he was trying to cure William Pickering, who had spent much of his childhood living near the Rushes while his father served as postmaster general, then secretary of war, and then secretary of state under Washington and Adams.

In March 1808, Rush wrote to Pickering with an update. So far nothing had helped his son, but they were trying a new exercise treatment called a "gyrater"—a board on which a patient lay down, then was spun on a pivot, with the goal of circulating more blood to the brain. William "submits to it patiently and pleasantly," Rush wrote. "In his stage of derangement it will be well if he discovers signs of amendment after using it six months." He assured Pickering that William was "treated with kindness by all the officers of the Hospital. His name is a protection to him."

Not long afterward Rush was asked to treat a far more unlikely patient: Dr. William Shippen, Jr., who summoned him to his deathbed. His former mentor and adversary no longer held power over him. At seventy-one, Shippen had been ill for some time: first vertigo kept him from the social engagements he so enjoyed, and then he developed an infection diagnosed as "an anthrax." By the time he sent for Rush, a soreness in his esophagus made swallowing nearly impossible, and he hadn't spoken in some time.

"He retained his reason, but not his speech, to the last hour of his life," Rush wrote in his commonplace book. "He was my enemy from the time of my settlement in Philadelphia in 1769 to the last year of his life. He sent for me to attend him notwithstanding . . . which I did with a sincere desire to prolong his life." While Shippen was mute, Rush spent some of his last hours on earth prompting him to acknowledge repentance and forgiveness, a silent confession. Shippen, Rush claimed, "gave signs to certain questions that were proposed to him, that he died a believer in the Gospel, and that in all his hopes of happiness were founded on the merits of Jesus Christ. Over his faults, etc, let charity cast a veil."

Dr. Shippen died at six p.m. on July 11, 1808, at his home in Germantown. Afterward Rush wrote, "Peace and joy to his soul for ever and ever."

Several months later, when Rush drafted his annual introductory lecture, he felt compelled to append a small soliloquy:

> An event has occurred since we last met in this room, which it would be improper to pass over in silence. The most ancient, and most prominent pillar of our medical school, is fallen; and the founder of anatomical instruction in the United States is no more. Hung be his theatre in black! and let his numerous pupils in every part of our country, to whom he first disclosed with peculiar elegance and perspicuity, the curious structure of the human body, unite with us in dropping the tribute of a grateful tear to his memory!
>
> To all the members of his profession his death should teach a solemn and useful lesson, by reminding them that the knowledge, by which they benefit others, will sooner or later be useless to themselves.
>
> To me, whom age has placed nearest to him upon the list of professors, his death is a warning voice. The next summons from the grave will most probably be mine. Yes, gentlemen, these aids of declining vision [pointing to the reading glasses propped on his forehead] and these gray hairs remind me, that I must soon follow my colleague and your preceptor to the mansions of the dead. When that time shall come, I shall relinquish many attractions to life, and, among them, a pleasure which to me has no equal in human pursuits: I mean that which I derive from studying, teaching, and practising, medicine.

It soon became clear that John was struggling again, this time with troubles from which his father could not bail him out. Richard ran interference for him with the family—he was becoming a good lawyer for all kinds of tricky situations—but could not heal the wound between his father and his older brother.

"Beg my father not to assume my debts," John wrote to Richard. ". . . I would rather answer for them in jail." He resented that his parents were forcing him to live on his navy salary, while he heard they were helping his younger brother Ben start out in business, giving him what John believed was "forty times the draw I wanted." He was under the impression that one of his married sisters had asked their father to change his will to benefit her "and strike me out." He had consulted with an estate attorney in Boston, William Minot, about his rights; Minot, in turn, reached out privately to Richard, concerned about John's demeanor, dysfunction, and obsession with his father.

John was acting out not only in the family but in his navy post as well. First he committed relatively minor infractions: he was cited for "gunplay," after two local planters reported that "two muskets were fired from Gun Vessel #20 on their negroes who were harmlessly going to the market." Later he failed to report a fight between two of his men. By the fall of 1808, the navy was worried that he might take his own life. In October, he was hospitalized for mania and self-destructive behavior in New Orleans. He suffered a brief "attack of insanity" and did make at least one suicide attempt.

There is no evidence in Rush's writing, even to Adams, that the doctor knew anything had worsened with John. Most likely the navy chose to keep its concerns about him from his father, hoping he was suffering only temporarily. John's siblings may have kept the information from their parents as well. In late September, his younger sister Julia wrote John that she was pleased to hear about his "re-established" health. But John's siblings didn't seem to understand the severity of the situation; as late as December 1808, Richard was writing to John as if the main issue were his obsessive concern about his father's money and how much he could borrow or inherit.

But finally Richard decided the situation was beyond his abilities and understanding as a sibling. "I will not pursue any further the subject of our late letters," Richard wrote to John in early December. "I put the one last received from you into the hands of my Mother and Father, and it must be for them to decide upon it. Upon this, or any other subject, I hope never to have a dispute with a brother." He did, however, encourage John to hold on to his commission and try to weather his personal storm, noting the real possibility of a coming naval war. He begged his brother to be "patient and resolute," and to remain focused on career goals that were still, even with his setbacks, attainable. Richard said he believed "the day will come when I shall pay my respects to you on your arrival on the Delaware as . . . admiral of your fleet."

On December 15, 1808, John received orders to "settle your accounts with the Purser on this station and repair to the city of Washington, where you will report yourself to the Honorable Secretary of the Navy." Instead, John began cutting shallow gashes into his skin and refused to stop. He was taken back to the hospital in New Orleans, but the staff there were almost too afraid of him to treat him. The navy apparently still did not alert the Rushes, though John was on full lockdown and suicide watch for over two months, during which he occasionally escaped, found something sharp, and cut himself again.

Finally, on February 20, 1809, a new physician at the hospital, Samuel Heap—who had been a classmate of John at the University of Pennsylvania—felt compelled to write to Dr. John Syng Dorsey, who had been ahead of them in medical school and was now assistant professor of surgery. "Our fellow student John Rush has since the 15th of December been insane, [and] has made several attempts to destroy himself," he said. This was "the third time I have had him under my care since my arrival at this place. . . . The great uncertainty of his recovery from the present attack induces me to wish he might be sent to Philadelphia in order that he might derive the advantages of his father's attention. Our hospital is by no means calculated for persons in Mr. Rush's situation."

While it is unclear if Dorsey contacted Rush, John's supervising officer did so several weeks later, on March 7, 1809. Just that morning, John had cut his throat, with a razor he had been hiding:

> The situation of your son is at present the most deplorable. He is now and has been for some time past in a state of insanity; and in consequence of his having made several attempts on the life of

the surgeon, and others in the hospital, it was found necessary to confine him. . . . It is quite uncertain whether he will survive the injury he has done himself.

John did survive: in fact, in a second letter to Dorsey, Dr. Heap speculated that as a doctor, John probably knew where to cut his neck so it would bleed heavily but not kill him: "He made an incision on the left side of his trachea with a razor, about four inches in length but superficial, fortunately no artery was [damaged], the hemorrhage notwithstanding was very profuse." John subsequently improved enough under Dr. Heap's care that the navy (and likely his father) let him remain there until he was well enough to transport.

By June 1809, it was decided he could travel, and his doctors were optimistic that his health could still be restored if he returned home to family and friends. They were also certain that treatment by the famous Dr. Benjamin Rush was John's best hope. "Your acquaintance with the 'anatomy of the human mind,'" one navy physician wrote Rush, "will enable you to do more for him than any other man on earth could."

But when John was finally brought to the harbor to leave, he discovered his boat was delayed. By the time it was ready, he had grown so anxious that the captain was no longer willing to have him as a passenger. John was returned to the hospital and stayed there until the navy, and the Rush family, could figure out the best place for him. He pleaded not to go back to Philadelphia, where he knew he would face the indignity of becoming his father's patient.

Two months later Benjamin Rush admitted to John Adams what had been going on: "My Eldest son John, since his unfortunate duel, has lost his health, and with it . . . I feel this affliction in the most sensible manner." John would be coming home after all.

"John's Misfortune I deplore," Adams responded. "I Sympathize with you, and with the keener sensibility as I have experienced the Feelings and Reflections of a Father in Circumstances perhaps Still more desperate, calamitous, and afflicting." Adams was referring to his son Charles's death from alcoholism. "Parents must have their Tryals. I am now experiencing Another."

John Quincy had just set sail for St. Petersburg with his family, after being named U.S. minister to Russia. The separation, Adams said, was "tearing me to Pieces. A more dutiful and affectionate Son there cannot be. His Society was always a cordial and a Consolation under all Circumstances. I maintain my Serenity however. I can only pray for his Safety and Success."

Rush had some idea what he was talking about: Richard was getting married, to Catherine Murray, the daughter of a prominent physician in Annapolis. While they wouldn't be living far away—they planned to live in the house next door to Rush's—it would still end nearly a decade of Rush having to himself the attention of his smart, engaging, protective second son.

Soon Rush wrote back to Adams with good news: "I have great pleasure in informing you that my son John has recovered from his late attack of insanity, and is now doing duty in the navy," though "a gloom still, I have heard, hangs upon his spirits."

He mentioned that the biographer of the late Thomas Paine had contacted him. Rush had been out of touch with Paine during his last years, but was willing to share his version of the writing of *Common Sense*, which was not well known. He trusted that the writer would "do Paine justice," he told Adams, covering "his errors and crimes as well as extol his talents and Services to our Country." He then encouraged Adams, again, to consider writing a memoir: "The young people of our Country born since the year 1774 & who compose a majority of our citizens would receive every thing that came from your pen upon the Subject of American Independance with great Avidity."

Adams was pleased to hear about John: "I hope his gloom will wear off." He was less pleased about the biography, which he felt was "of uncertain utility. The sooner Paine is forgotten perhaps the better."

Rush was editing two massive books that he wanted to be published before the 1809 school year began, ostensibly so his three hundred or more students could purchase them. One was a new edition of *The Works of Thomas Sydenham*, and the other a dramatically expanded third edition of his *Medical Inquiries and Observations*. The latter had now grown to four separate volumes and required the efforts of eight different Philadelphia publishing houses to print. He was buried in so many proof sheets that he joked he was turning into a proof sheet.

When he finally sent the books off to the printer, he sat down to write Adams about something he had been pondering for a long time. They had already exchanged nearly a hundred letters in the four years since reestablishing their friendship. But this one, Rush believed, could save the legacy of the Revolution.

41

Rush's October 17, 1809, letter to Adams started slowly. He offered a new insight into their ongoing discussion of whether the sons of great men can themselves become great—as they parsed a quote about renowned thinkers having "neither ancestors nor posterity." He promised a copy of his new book.

Then, in the third paragraph, he began narrating a vivid dream:

> What book is that in your hands said I to my son Richard a few nights ago in a DREAM?
>
> "It is the history of the United States sir said he. Shall I read a page of it to you?"
>
> "no no said I—I believe in the truth of no history but in that which is contained in the old & new testaments."
>
> "But Sir—said my Son, this page relates to your friend Mr Adams."
>
> "Let me see it then said I." I read it with great pleasure, and herewith send you a copy of it.

The page Richard wanted to read to Rush, in this dream, was the year in review for the current year, 1809. According to Rush's dream, it read:

Among the most extraordinary events of this year was the renewal of the friendship & intercourse between Mr John Adams and Mr Jefferson, the two expresidents of the United States. . . . A difference of opinion upon the Objects and issue of the French Revolution seperated them during the years in which that great event interested and divided the American people. The predominance of the party which favoured the french cause, threw Mr Adams out of the Chair of the United states in the year 1800, and placed Mr Jefferson there in his Stead. The former retired with resignation and dignity to his Seat at Quincy where he spent the evening of his life in literary and philosophical pursuits surrounded by an amiable family and a few Old and Affectionate friends. The latter resigned the Chair of the United States in the year 1808 sick of the cares and disgusted with the intrigues of public life, and retired to his Seat at Monticello in Virginia where he spent the remainder of his days in the cultivation of a large farm agreeably to the new System of husbandry.

In the month of November 1809 Mr: Adams addressed a short letter to his Old friend Mr: Jefferson in which he congratulated him upon his escape to the shades of retirement and domestic happiness, and concluded it with assurances of his regard and good wishes for his Welfare. This letter did great honor to Mr Adams. It discovered a magninimity known only to great minds. Mr Jefferson replied to this letter, and reciprocated expressions of regard and esteem. These letters were followed by a correspondence of several years, in which they mutually reviewed the scenes of business in which they had been engaged, and candidly acknowledged to each other all the errors of Opinion & conduct into which they had fallen during the time they filled the same stations in the Service of their country. Many precious aphorisms, the result of Observation, experience, & profound reflection it is said are contained in these letters. It is to be hoped, the World will be favoured with a sight of them, when they can neither injure nor displease any persons or families whose ancestor's follies or crimes were mentioned in them.

These gentlemen sunk into the grave nearly at the same time, full of years, and rich in the gratitude and praises of their coun-

> try (for they outlived the heterogeneous parties that were opposed to them) and to their numerous merits and honors posterity has added, that they were Rival friends.

Rush then simply ended the letter, "With affectionate regard to your fire side in which all my family join I am Dr: Sir your / sincere Old friend." He waited to see what Adams would say.

The Adams family loved a good Benjamin Rush dream letter—there had been quite a few of them in the past years. "A Dream again!" Adams wrote back. "I wish you would dream all day and all Night, for one of your Dreams puts me in spirits for a Month. I have no other objection to your Dream, but that it is not History. It may be Prophecy."

Adams claimed there had "never been the smallest Interruption of the Personal Friendship between me and Mr. Jefferson that I know of." This assertion was questionable, since the former presidents hadn't spoken or communicated in nine years.

"You should remember that Jefferson was but a Boy to me," he wrote. "I was at least ten years older than him in age and more than twenty years older than him in Politicks. I am bold to say I was his Preceptor in Politicks and taught him every Thing that has been good and solid in his whole Political Conduct. I served with him on many Committees in Congress in which we established some of the most important Regulations." They had also lived together in France for two years in the mid-1780s, along with Franklin, and had remained close for a long time.

"If I were disposed to be captious," Adams said, "I might complain of his open Patronage of . . . my most abandoned & unprincipled enemies; But I have seen Ambition and Party in so many Men of the best Character of all Parties that I must renounce almost all Mankind if I renounce any for such Causes. Fare them all well. Heaven is their Judge and mine."

Having planted the seed, Rush watched to see if it would grow. When Adams didn't write to Jefferson immediately—disproving the history book in the dream, which stated they would reconnect a month after Rush's letter—he chose, uncharacteristically, to be patient through another season.

Fall was the busiest time for the Rush family in any case. Lectures began again, and Rush's books came out. The family gathered for Christmas and Dr. Rush's fifty-fourth birthday. Rush wrote his son James—now studying at Edinburgh—a long holiday letter. But before he could send it, Julia commandeered some of the remaining space on the last page for her own message, which included regards from his other siblings, his new sister-in-law, and even some of the servants. Only one Rush family member went unmentioned: his brother John. But then, nobody had heard much from or about him in a while.

In late January of 1810, the navy reached out to Dr. Rush, letting him know that somebody would need to come fetch John. He had been discharged from the military and was being shipped from New Orleans to Washington, where he would need help getting home. A captain who knew John suggested to Rush that he send Richard, who would have "sufficient authority to prevent any excesses; for I am informed that at times, if John chance to get a little liquor, he wants more, and it always makes him worse."

This was the first time, at least in an official letter, that anyone discussed John having a problem with alcohol—although Rush may not have been surprised. One of John's outstanding bills for a month's lodging in New Orleans listed charges for many bottles of porter and brandy, as well as six separate purchases of gin by the half pint.

Instead of Richard, Rush sent his younger son Ben, as well as a servant, to pick up John. When he arrived home, the family was stunned by how he had changed from the clean-cut navy man they remembered. As Rush recounted to Adams:

> He arrived in Philada in a state of deep melancholy & considerable derangement. His Appearance When he entered his father's house was that of the King of Babylon described in the Old

> testament. His long, and uncombed hair, & his long Nails and beard rendered him an object of horror to his afflicted parents & family.
>
> No entreaties could induce him to utter a word to any of us. After three days Spent in unsuccessful Attempts to Alter his Appearance, we sent him to the Pennsylva. hospital, Where he has been ever since.

After being admitted, John seemed to Rush "much improved not only in his appearance, but in the health of his mind. Though still gloomy, he submits to be shaved, & dressed, and walks out daily in the garden of the hospital. At times he converses in the most lucid & agreeable manner." While Rush thought there was a chance his son could recover, he was honest with Adams: John would probably "end his days in his present situation."

Notably, for a physician who had spent many years thinking about the biological and hereditary underpinnings of madness and alcoholism—and wrestling with his son's unstable temper and moods—he seemed to put all the blame for John's condition on the duel that had taken his friend's life. "Could the advocates for duelling, and the idolaters of the late general Hamilton press into the Cell of my poor boy," he declared, "they would blush for their folly & madness in defending a practice and palliating a crime which has rendered a promising young man wretched for life—and involved in his misery, a whole family that loved him."

Rush had always taken his patients' cases to heart, but seeing John in his hospital pushed him to a new level of empathy—and ambition. He had been making progress in the treatment of mental illness with the support of Samuel Coates and the managers, as well as his brightest and most compassionate former students. But now he redoubled his efforts to find new therapies, new cures.

Rush was keenly aware that he might not live much longer. His health had never been fully robust; he had spent many of his days around the sickest people in the nation, and his lifelong cough still periodically brought up blood. Just recently, he had quietly asked the aptly named surgeon Dr. Philip Syng Physick—a former student and now a medical school colleague—to remove a tumor from his neck.

The "low diet" that had kept him fit as a younger man now made him appear almost skeletal, and he had lost much of his long gray hair.

One consequence of Rush's notoriety was that institutions, admirers, and former students commissioned portraits of him, and then variations on those portraits. Each new version, created in oil, watercolor, or etching, portrayed him a bit older. His most famous later portrait was created by Philadelphia artist Thomas Sully, who started with a bust image that a former medical student commissioned in 1809. Then another former student ordered a copy of the same Rush head in a painting with Pennsylvania Hospital in the background. Eventually Rush sat for Sully as he painted a dramatically lit watercolor, full body, of him sitting in his study. Later, when Adams saw one of the many etchings made of this Sully portrait, he was shocked at how much his friend had aged.

"The last time I Saw him in March 1801," he wrote, he was "as upright as a Reed and his Countenance no less animated than Intelligent. But his Portrait now exhibits . . . the decrepitude of Old age worn out by long labours in the cause of humanity."

Watercolor study for Rush's last portrait by Thomas Sully

Rush was prepared for posterity. His recent publications had put his literary estate in order—and ensured that his legacy would not fast recede, as those of Morgan and Shippen already had. And while he had destroyed much of his writing about the Revolution, what he hadn't mentioned to Adams was that before burning all those pages, he had copied many of them into a private autobiography, to be read by his children after he was gone. He had compiled this book back in 1800, after the Cobbett trial, at one of the lowest ebbs of his life. It might have read differently had he written it later, after a couple of years of exchanging letters with John Adams: there they recounted even the darker periods in their ongoing dual autobiography with fresh energy and humor, read in fireside installments by their rapt families.

But as much as Rush played the elder sage, he had one thing left to do. He wanted to accomplish something powerful and lasting to improve the lot of those suffering from "diseases of the mind." For years, he thought he had accomplished enough in this area. But watching his son in the hospital, shuffling seemingly soulless back and forth along the same exact floorboards every day, made him keenly aware of how much was left undone.

For the first few months of John's hospitalization, Rush hoped that the treatments he had already devised, which had been successful for many patients, would work for his son: warm and cold baths, wine, gentle purges, bloodletting, "low diet," exercise, perhaps some time on the old swing chair machine (although that device had fallen into disfavor because patients sometimes hurt themselves on it) or the more recent gyrator. There was also, he thought, some value in talking with medical staff and with manager Samuel Coates, who still visited psychiatric patients.

While John was getting his hair cut one day, Coates listened in and jotted in his notebook:

> The barber on combing John's hair, pleasantly remarked to him, that it was becoming quite grey "but never mind" added he. "Grey hairs are honorable you know."
>
> "Yes," replied John Rush emphatically, "and sometimes, honor makes grey hairs." It is probable that Rush alluded to the duel in which he killed his intimate friend, the sole cause of his lunacy.

The hospital staff apparently embraced the notion that John's duel was the "sole cause" of his condition. They ignored, to the public at least, all his years of unusual behavior: a duel leading to insanity was the best way to get empathy. But privately, Benjamin and Julia acknowledged that they had been struggling with John's emotional volatility for a long time. And occasionally Rush would describe symptoms and delusions unrelated to the duel: for example, John's insistence that he owned or was inheriting a large estate in New Orleans.

After four months in the hospital, John generally seemed improved; his ongoing delusion about his Louisiana mansion led Rush to begin describing him as "deranged at present upon but one subject only." So the family made hopeful plans to bring him home, thinking that if he could function away from the hospital, he might convalesce somewhere in the country. When he finally came home in September 1810, he was quiet and withdrawn but also capable of engaging in conversation that interested him. But that didn't last. After only a few days, he voluntarily returned to the hospital.

During this time, inspired by his son, Dr. Rush devised his most famous—and in some corners infamous—treatment device, the Tranquilizer. He invented it because he felt he could no longer watch the most turbulent patients bound, writhing in straitjackets. "In this state they often lie whole days and nights, and sometimes in a situation which delicacy forbids me to mention," he wrote to a colleague.

"To obviate these evils and at the same time to retain all the benefits of coercion," Rush had a cabinetmaker fashion an armchair that let a patient to be restrained while sitting up straight, which allowed access to the body for treatments—it was difficult to bleed or take the pulse of someone in a "mad shirt." It could be outfitted with a hole in the seat for waste, especially important when a patient was taking purgatives. The Tranquilizer could also be used with a wooden box around the head to block visual stimulation.

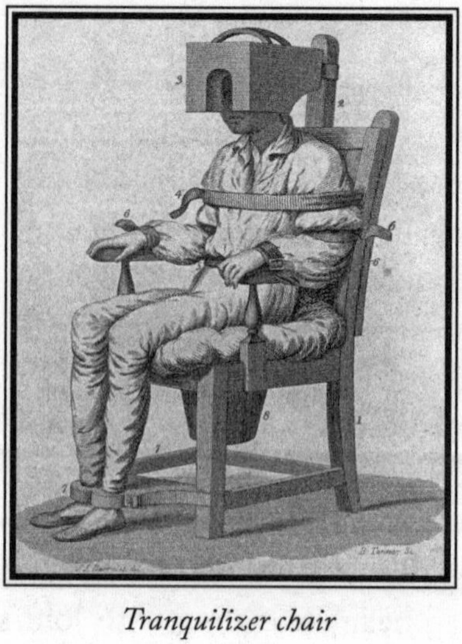

Tranquilizer chair

The patient's position was "less irritating to his temper, and much less offensive to the feelings of his friends, than in a straight waistcoat," Rush claimed, and "the body of the patient in this chair, though in a state of coercion, is so perfectly free from pressure that he sometimes falls asleep in it." He had, so far, tried it only on the most "violent state of madness" but he had no doubt it would be helpful with other diseases, such as "epilepsy, headache, vertigo wakefulness and sleepiness."

Many who treated severely mentally ill patients considered the chair a breakthrough, but those who believed no patients should be restrained—as much a social criticism as a medical outlook—regarded it as a symbol of cruelty in care. By this point, Philippe Pinel's book had been translated into English. Pinel's *traitement moral* involved unchaining patients at his Paris asylum—specifically those who had never needed restraint in the first place and suffered from other kinds of cruel and dehumanizing conditions: some were mentally ill, some were intellectually disabled from birth, others suffered from head injuries and other factors. Rush and the physicians at Pennsylvania Hospital had made many of the same improvements years earlier, as had others at more modern facilities in Europe. (And Pinel still had to physically restrain some patients when they were floridly ill.)

But even if critics of the Tranquilizer doubted it embodied *traitement moral*, Rush was on a path similar to Pinel's: to make the public more aware of mental illness, to better describe its possible causes and treatment, and to impress upon their nations the importance of funding care in humane conditions.

To that end, on September 24, 1810, Rush published a bold letter to the managers of Pennsylvania Hospital demanding more support for treating diseases of the brain. "There is a great pleasure in combatting with success a violent bodily disease," he wrote, "but what is this pleasure compared with that of restoring a fellow creature from the anguish and folly of madness and of reviving in him the knowledge of himself, his family, his friends and his God! But where this cannot be done, how delightful the consideration of suspending by our humanity their mental and bodily misery!"

Rush listed his demands, knowing they would not be fulfilled immediately. He asked for several small, solitary new buildings for those in the highest state of madness, so they could heal separately from other patients. He asked that psychiatric patients be separated by sex on different floors. He asked for "certain kinds of labor, exercize and amusements . . . which shall act at the same time upon their bodies and minds," or what later became known as "occupational therapy." He asked that "an intelligent man and women be employed . . . to direct and share in their amusements and to divert their minds by conversation, reading, and obliging them to read and write upon subjects suggested from time to time by the attending physicians," formalizing Samuel Coates's rudimentary "talk therapy."

No visitors, he insisted, should be allowed in to see or talk to "the mad people" without an order from their physicians. "Many evils arise from an indiscriminate intercourse of mad people with visitors. . . . They often complain to them [about the hospital] . . . and at times in so rational a manner as to induce a belief that their tales of injustice and oppression are true." It was also an invasion of privacy: illness that "might have been concealed in individuals and in families is thereby made public," and those who were becoming ill might feel discouraged from seeking care. A young gentleman Rush knew, who "felt the premonitory signs" of mental disease, insisted he "would rather die" than "be gazed at and pitied in the cell of a hospital." Rush was haunted that "to prevent this poignant evil," the young man had "discharged a musket ball through his head."

Rush recommended new feather beds and mattresses and armchairs for the cells, and that each cell should have its own toilet apparatus, a "close-stool with a pan half filled with water" to absorb smells.

He concluded his appeal in the most personal way possible. He reminded the board that he had been asking for many of these things for years, "long before it pleased God to interest me in their adoption by rendering one of my family an object of them."

SEVERAL WEEKS LATER, when classes began at the medical school, Rush delivered his introductory lecture for the year, "The Study of Medical Jurisprudence," in which he explored the illnesses that could incapacitate one from exercising civil rights, as well as the responsibilities of physicians and families. The lecture focused primarily on "those states of the mind which should incapacitate a man to dispose of his property, to bear witness in a court of justice, and exempt him from punishment for the commission of what are called crimes by the laws of our country." Although he described these situations in technical terms, anybody who knew Rush understood that many of the challenges he raised were inspired and informed by his career of treating "intellectual derangement," from his first case as a young doctor, Capt. John Macpherson, to his last and most heartbreaking patient, Lt. John Rush.

After inventing the Tranquilizer, writing his open letter to the managers, and delivering this talk on medical jurisprudence, Rush realized that his recent version of *Medical Inquiries and Observations* was not going to be his final book after all. He dove back into the literature, into his own lectures and case files, to create something unique: the first American book specifically on mental illness and addiction.

He wanted to write it not only for physicians and asylum keepers, as Pinel had done so successfully in France, but for the general public as well, in language that would allow patients and their families, doctors, clergy, and politicians to discuss the new medical and psychological ways of understanding madness. He wanted it to help people begin to comprehend how these illnesses felt—by invoking everything from the medical literature to, if necessary, Shakespeare's *King Lear.*

Just after New Year's 1811, after waiting more than a year for John Adams to reach out to Thomas Jefferson, Rush took the next step himself: he wrote to Jefferson at Monticello. It was a lengthy letter, long overdue—it had been over a year since Jefferson had written him—and began with sharing news of work as well as his family's recent challenges (which he knew Jefferson would appreciate because "you are a father").

Then Rush brought up Adams. "Your and my Old friend Mr. Adams now & then drops me a line from his Seat at Quincy," he wrote, in a touching understatement. "His letters glow with the just Opinions he held in the patriotic years 1774, 1775 & 1776." He quoted a paragraph from a letter Adams had just sent him, bemoaning the banking system: "A bank that issues paper at interest, is a pick pocket, or a robber."

Finally, Rush made his entreaty:

> When I consider your early Attachment to Mr Adams, and his to you; when I consider how much the liberties & Independance of the United States owe to the Concert of your principles and labors, and when I reflect upon the sameness of your Opinions at present, upon most of the Subjects of Government, and all the Subjects of legislation, I have ardently wished a friendly and epistolary intercourse might be revived between you before you take a final leave of the Common Object of your Affections.
>
> Such an intercourse will be honourable to talents, and patriotism, and highly useful to the cause of republicanism not only in the United states but all over the world. Posterity will revere the friendship of two Ex presidents that were once opposed to each Other. Human nature will be a gainer by it. I am sure an Advance on your Side will be a Cordial to the heart of Mr. Adams. Tottering over the grave, he now leans wholly upon the Shoulders of his old revolutionary friends The patriots generated by the funding System, etc, are all his enemies.

Rush's desire to reunite Adams and Jefferson was much bigger than a mere hope of reconnecting old friends. He considered these two "the North and South poles of the American Revolution." While many had written and spoken and fought for independence, Rush believed it was Adams and Jefferson who had "*thought* for us all." Their speeches, their opinions, and even their private conversations represented to Rush "the great political, moral and intellectual Atchievements of the Congresses of those memorable years." Their divisions beginning in the 1790s accelerated his fears that partisanship was shaking the still-hardening foundations of American democracy. If America's first truly elected presidents—Washington having been more elevated than voted for—could not put the nation they had created above politics, what hope did America have?

After reading Rush's letter, Jefferson was moved to look over the history of his relationship with the Adamses, including his last correspondence with Abigail, seven years earlier, when she had attempted to mend the friendship. He went so far as to include this correspondence when he wrote back to Rush, to let him know he took seriously his efforts at Founding Father family therapy, and to prove that he had not been the impediment to reconciliation. His response, over two thousand words long, teemed with memories of both his happiest and his most challenging days with Adams, and how they had all once been members of President Washington's government, until circumstances (and Hamilton) turned them against each other.

Jefferson recalled a crystallizing dinner with Adams and Hamilton in the early 1790s, during which the two of them argued loudly about constitutional politics. Around the room "portraits of remarkable men" hung on the walls, among them "Bacon, Newton & Locke. Hamilton asked me who they were. I told him they were my trinity of the three greatest men the world had ever produced. . . . He paused for some time: 'the greatest man, said he, that ever lived was Julius Caesar.'"

Jefferson declared to Rush, "Mr. Adams was honest as a politician as well as a man; Hamilton honest as a man, but, as a politician, [he believed] . . . in the necessity of either force or corruption to govern men."

Now Rush knew that Jefferson was open to "reviving a farewell intercourse with Mr Adams"—as long as Adams made the first move. While he was deeply concerned that his two friends reconnect "before you meet in another world," as he wrote to Jefferson, he knew healing took time.

Rush was feeling hopeful because his family finally had some good news. His son Richard and his wife Catherine just had a baby boy, whom they named Benjamin. And several days later, Richard was named attorney general of Pennsylvania, which would keep him and his family in Philadelphia for the foreseeable future. Rush and Julia would, for the first time, be able to watch one of their five grandchildren grow up close to home.

During the first months of babysitting a third-generation Benjamin Rush, the doctor prepared a new book: a collection of his introductory lectures going back to the early 1790s. They were his least-known talks, as each had been delivered only once, to the incoming medical school class, yet he knew they were among his most accessible and—he hoped—timeless writings, imparting the lived wisdom of medicine, science, and human nature. The lectures were less about Rush's system than about being a doctor and being a patient.

At the end of the manuscript, he threw in two more unpublished talks, one on "the pleasures of the senses" and the other exploring "the pleasures of the mind," after which he paused to philosophize.

"Is it possible," he asked, "that such an immense and ingenious contrivance, for the enjoyment of corporeal and mental pleasure"—namely the body, the brain, and the mind—"should have been given to us, to last no longer than the ordinary term of human existence in this world?" Wasn't there an "exact correspondence" between "all our capacities" and "the ineffable pleasures of a future world"? And if so, was it "probable that a wise and good Being, whose means and ends are so exactly suited to each other . . . will finally waste or throw away the costly and beautiful apparatus he has given us for the enjoyment of corporeal and mental pleasures?"

He stopped for a moment, mentally gathering his pages. "But I am wandering from the subject of our lectures," he said. "Let us be good here; and we shall be wise hereafter."

Not long after the book came out, Rush's plan for a peaceful anecdotage was rocked. At two p.m. on March 11, 1811, a friend ran into Rush's office and breathlessly announced that one of his sons was about to fight a duel.

It wasn't John—he hadn't escaped; it was Richard.

When Richard was elevated to attorney general, the governor had passed over the longtime assistant in the office, lawyer Peter Browne, who thereafter argued often with his new boss. Finally Browne challenged Richard to a duel—and he accepted, without saying a word to his father. When Dr. Rush did hear about it, he was told only that Richard had crossed the Delaware River, so he didn't know where to go to try to stop him.

He went out looking for his son; "the anguish of my Soul" during the next hours "of suspense was undescribable." Julia was beside herself, as were the two of their teenage children at home, Julia and Benjamin. After more than an hour of futile searching, Rush came home and awaited news.

At about four p.m., Richard walked into the Rushes' house, uninjured and nonplussed. He had "discharged his pistol in the air," he said, and not much else. He never explained why he had put himself in harm's way.

Rush wrote in his commonplace book, "Glory and praise to God, for his deliverance from the consequences of his folly and madness!" But the incident had to make him wonder how well he really knew Richard, whom he relied upon as his chosen son.

Not long afterward Rush was made aware of a catastrophe in the Adams family: John and Abigail's oldest daughter, forty-six-year-old Nabby, had a large lump protruding from her left breast. They hadn't told him about it because she had, at first, kept it a secret, then relied on local physicians, who told her they could treat it with medicine—even as the lump grew so large, she could see it in the mirror. Her husband, Colonel Smith, never an Adams family favorite, had also discouraged more aggressive treatment.

Adams initially led Rush to believe the situation was under control. But soon Abigail and Nabby wrote directly to him for medical advice, and he told them Nabby needed surgery immediately. "Let there be no delay in flying to the knife," he said. "After the experience of more than 50 years in cases similar to hers, I must protest agst [against]: all local applications, and internal medicines for her relief. . . . It shocks me to think of the Consequences of procrastination in her case."

Nabby's husband finally assented, and a local surgeon performed the operation in a second-floor bedroom in the Adams's house, without anesthetic. Nabby was belted into a reclining chair with her left arm raised above her head as her breast was sliced off from the bottom up with a sharp razor. Unfortunately, removing it revealed that the tumor had spread to her lymph nodes, where hard knots of it had to be removed.

Nabby slowly recovered from the operation, then was buoyed by a letter from Rush ten days after the surgery. "All my family rejoice with yours in the happy issue of the operation," he wrote, and now it was time to help excite in Nabby "a belief that her Cure will be radical & durable. I consider her as rescued from a premature grave."

John and Abigail remained nervous about the cancer, but they had reached the age where they were going through so many deaths among their friends and relatives as to "make the Excision of a Ladys Breast appear but a Small Affliction." Adams himself had also been hurt in an accident while "going out in the dark in my Garden to look for the Comet, I Stumbled over a Knot in a Stake and tore my Leg near the Shin in Such a manner that the Surgeon with his Baths Cataplasms, Plaisters and Bandages has been daily hovering about it." He had been stuck with his leg propped up on the sofa all day.

So Adams had plenty of time to write supportive letters when Richard came to Rush with the news he knew would break his father's heart: he and his family were leaving Philadelphia, so he could accept a job President James Madison had arranged for him with the federal government. Richard was being appointed Comptroller of the Department of Treasury. The position meant walking away from an income his father estimated at "nearly 4000 dollars [$77,000]" a year from his state office and private practice, and it meant sacrificing time to write. He also wouldn't even be able to live with his wife and Rush's namesake grandson; his family would live in Annapolis with Catherine's parents while Richard rented a place in Washington. But it would be a stepping stone for his political ambitions.

Rush turned out to be even angrier than Richard predicted.

He all but threatened to disown him. When Adams heard about the appointment, he dashed off a letter that began, "Shall I congratulate or condole with you on the appointment of your Son to be Comptroller of The Treasury?"

"You have touched me in a sore place," Rush soon replied. After explaining why family and friends opposed Richard's decision, he recounted his own dissent:

> I pointed out the vexatious dangers, and poverty of political & Official life, and mentioned the distress & obscurity in which many old patriots and servants of the public were now ending their days in many parts of our Country and that the Acceptance of the Office now offered to him would be an act of Suicide to his family.—Lastly I implored him by my Affection for him, by my Age, by my gray hairs, by the prospect of my Death, which must according to the Course of Nature take place in a few years, and of the importance of his presence and patronage to his mother, & to my young Children when I shall be called from them.—
>
> But Alas!—all these Arguments & importunities were employed to no purpose. There was One insurmountable Objection to them. His Wifes Connections live near Washington, and her Wishes were to be near them.

Rush knew a thing or two about strong women, as he ruefully concluded. "There are two Classes of female tyrants—Termagants, and Syrens. My son's Wife belongs to the latter Class. She is the most facinating woman, and ardently beloved by her husband, & 'Where love enters' you know, 'he will rule alone. And suffer no co-partner in his throne.'"

When it was clear Richard would not change his mind, Rush sat down and rewrote his will. He had already done this once before, because even if John improved, he would never be able to take over his father's business as they had once hoped. Richard had been given "the rank and priviledges of primoginiture." Now he had to change that and designate his third son, James, as his primary heir.

James was a smart, engaging young man of twenty-five who had recently returned from his studies in Edinburgh and would one day become a perfectly good doctor. But he was not a star as Richard was. And Rush had become accustomed to the idea that, after he was gone, the family would be run by a brilliant lawyer, not by a fledgling doctor trying to hold on to a practice not his own. Everything he had spent a lifetime building for his family felt suddenly endangered.

AMID HIS ARGUMENTS with Richard, Rush received a saving grace of a letter postmarked from Virginia. While spending time at Poplar Forest—his retreat from the bustle of business at Monticello—former president Jefferson had been thinking about Rush's last letter, when a friend of his from Washington serendipitously mentioned that he had visited the Adams home in Braintree. The friend recounted that during a long conversation about the old days, Adams had railed against a great many things, including "the unprincipled licenciousness" of the press's coverage of Jefferson.

At that point, the friend reported, Adams said, "I always loved Jefferson, and still love him."

Jefferson told Rush, "This is enough for me. I only needed this knowledge to revive towards him all the affections of the most cordial moments of our lives." He wanted to let Rush know that:

> in your letters to mr. Adams you can perhaps suggest my continued cordiality towards him, & knowing this, should an occasion of writing, first present itself to him, he will perhaps avail himself of it, as I certainly will should it first occur to me. No ground for jealousy now existing, he will certainly give fair play to the natural warmth of his heart. . . .
>
> I have thus, my friend, laid open my heart to you, because you were so kind as to take an interest in healing again revolutionary affections, which have ceased in expression only, but not in their existence. God ever bless you and preserve you in life & health.

With that go-ahead, Rush intensified his shuttle diplomacy. He casually informed Adams that Jefferson—with whom "I exchange letters Once in six, nine or twelve Months"—had written about him. He quoted at length from Jefferson's letter, then pushed Adams harder:

> Permit me Again to suggest to you,—to receive the Olive branch which has thus been offered to you by the hand of a Man who still loves you. . . .
>
> Fellow labourers in creating the great fabric of American Independance, Fellow Sufferers in the Calumnies and falsehoods of party rage!—Fellow heirs Of the gratitude, and Affection of posterity!—and Fellow passengers in a stage that must shortly Convey you both into the presence of a Judge with whom the forgiveness and love of enemies is the condition of Acceptance. . . .
>
> Embrace—embrace each Other!—Bedew your letters of reconcilliation with tears of Affection and joy.—Bury in Silence all the Causes of your seperation. Recollect that explanations may be proper between lovers, but are *never* so between divided friends.
>
> Were I near to you I would put a pen into your hand, and guide it.

The next day Rush wrote to Jefferson, quoting what he had written to Adams. He also told Jefferson about Richard leaving and lamented that the nation seemed headed for its first war (over England's incursions with the Indians in the still-disputed Northwest Territories, a side conflict of the Napoleonic Wars). The world needed as much peace as it could get.

Then Rush wrote to Adams again, but their letters crossed. When Rush received the one Adams had written Christmas Day, he had to be disappointed. "I never was so much at a loss how to answer a Letter, as yours," Adams began. ". . . I perceive plainly enough, Rush, that you have been teazing Jefferson to write to me, as you did me some time ago to write to him. You gravely advise me 'to receive the olive Branch' as if there had been War. But there has never been any hostility to my Part, nor that I know, on his. When there has been no War, there can be no room for Negotiations of Peace."

He then went on for several pages describing all the ways he and Jefferson were still at war. Many were substantial, a few just plain funny:

"Jefferson and Rush were for Liberty and Strait Hair. I thought curled Hair was as Republican as strait." He concluded, "You often put me in Mind that I am soon to die. I know it and Shall not forget it . . . But why do you make so much ado about nothing. Of what Use can it be for Jefferson and me to exchange Letters. I have nothing to Say to him, but to wish him an easy Journey to Heaven when he goes."

Rush wrote back the next day about how hard it was going to be for him without Richard. "Independently of his affection and kindness to me," he said, "his office kept the libellers of my reputation in Awe."

On New Year's Day 1812, Adams finally capitulated. He sat down to write to Jefferson.

He opened the short letter with a joke, noting that since Jefferson was a "friend to American Manufactures," he was sending him "two Pieces of Homespun," which turned out to be a two-volume set of his son John Quincy's lectures. He told Jefferson that "All of my family whom you formerly knew are well." He ended with an olive branch for the new year:

> I wish you sir many happy New Years and that you may enter the next and many Succeeding years with as animating Prospects for the Public as those at present before Us. I am Sir with a long and Sincere Esteem your Friend and Servant
>
> John Adams

ADAMS WAITED FIVE days before posting the letter and neglected to tell Rush what he'd done. When Jefferson wrote back, he began a little stiffly—he assumed Adams really was sending him "homespun" and so went on unnecessarily about American milling. But the rest of the letter was warm.

Jefferson also wrote to Rush the same day: "As it is thro' your kind interposition that two old friends are brought together, you have a right to know how the first approaches are made. I send you therefore a copy of mr Adams's letter to me & of my answer."

It was another two weeks before Adams acknowledged what had happened, but he did so much more dramatically:

> Mr Dreamer!
>
> Your Dream is out, and the Passage you read in the History that Richard was reading is come to pass. . . .
>
> Mr Mediator! You have wrought Wonders! . . . You have brought again Babylon and Carthage long Since annihilated, into Fresh Existence! Like the Pythoness of Endor you have called up Spirits from the vast deep of Obscurity and Oblivion, to a new acquaintance with each other!
>
> Mr Conjuror! In Short the mighty defunct Potentates of Mount Wollaston and Monticello, by your Sorceries and Necromances, are again in Being. Intercource and Commerce have been restored by your Magic, between Neutrals, whose Interests and Reputation has been long Sacrificed by the Systems of Retalliation adopted by two hostile and enraged and infuriated Factions.
>
> Huzza! you will Say, but what does all this Rhapsody mean? Nothing more nor less than that a Correspondence of thirty five or thirty Six years Standing interrupted by various Causes for some time, has been renewed in 1812 and no less than four Letters have already passed between the Parties.

Adams went on to try to help Rush come to grips with his son's departure. He believed that Richard would someday soon be treasury secretary, then perhaps a Supreme Court justice, or vice president, or even president:

> Compose yourself, Rush. Richard will do well. Young Men must judge for themselves in the last resort. The Authority of Parents must not always be absolute. . . . The World was not made for Us Old Men. Young Men have their Views and Feelings and must Judge for themselves: and I believe their decisions are more correct and impartial than ours.

Rush responded, "I rejoice in the correspondence which has taken place between you and your Old friend Mr Jefferson." He complimented Adams's rhetorical flight: "I admire, as do all my family, the Wonderful Vivacity, and imagery of your letters. Some men's minds wear well, but yours dont appear to wear at all."

WEEKS AFTER THE reconnection of friends and legacies, Adams brought up Rush's own legacy—a subject they had, in all these years, never explored in depth. "In my Opinion there is not in Philadelphia a Single Citizen more universally esteemed and beloved by his Fellow Citizens than Dr Benjamin Rush," he began. "There is not a Man in Pensilvania more esteemed by the whole State. I know not a Man in America more esteemed by the Nation. There is not a citizen of this Union, more esteemed throughout the litterary Scientifical and Moral World in Europe Asia and Africa."

All that said, however, there is "not a Tory and Scarcely a Whig in America but Talks about Dr Rush and will tell twenty absurd and ridiculous Stories about him as well as John Adams." For example, he had recently spoken to a gentleman who declared "that General Washington was a Hypocrite!" When Adams asked for proof, the man mentioned, among other things, that Washington had appointed Rush "to lucrative and respectable Office" at the U.S. Mint.

When Adams asked the man why that was hypocritical, he said, "I know that he thought Dr. Rush a Villain," and when pressed, he said he knew of another man, a "most intimate Friend" of the president, who had heard Washington say "that he had been a good deal in the world and Seen many bad Men, but Dr Rush was the most black hearted Scoundrel he had ever known."

Adams told the man that it had been he, as president, who appointed Rush, not Washington, and that he considered Rush "one of the best Men in the World." Which caused the man to retract the detail about the Mint, but not Washington's feeling about Rush.

Adams pointed out to Rush that plenty of others would always be upset with "one of your earliest Offences . . . your opposition to Negro Slavery."

> Your Posterity and mine, I doubt not, my Friend will be teased and vexed with a Million of Such Stories concerning Us When We shall be no more. In the Struggles and Competitions of fifty or Sixty years in times that tryed mens Hearts and Brains and Spinal Marrow it could not be otherwise. The Pelts of Friends no less than the hatred of Ennemies, could not fail to produce a great deal of Such invenomed Froth.

Adams had a simple prescription for his friend: "Let me hear no more of your Jeremiads. Let Us Sing O be joyfull all the rest of our Lives."

Rush could not consider such advice before, finally, saying his piece about Washington. His letter back began, "I did not require the anecdote you have communicated to me in your letter of last month to know that I had incurred the hatred of General Washington. It was violent & descended with him to the grave."

He then replayed almost every interaction he had with Washington—except, in any detail, the circumstances of the letter to Patrick Henry. He did, however, offer an impassioned description of something he had been unable to ever get out of his mind since the war:

> I still see the Sons of our yeomanry brought up in the lap of plenty, and domestic Comforts of all kinds, shivering with Cold upon bare floors without a blanket to cover them, calling for fire,—for water,—for suitable food and for medicines—and calling in vain, I still hear the complaints they utter against their Country,—I hear thier Sighs for thier fathers fire Sides, and for a mother or Sisters Care. Thier dying groans still peirce my ears. I see them expire.

After many pages, he closed with:

> When Calvin heard that Luther had called him "a Child of the devil," he coolly replied, "Luther is a Servant of the most high God." In Answer to the epithet which G: Washington has applied to me ["black-hearted scoundrel"], I will as coolly reply, He was the highly favoured instrument whose patriotism and name

contributed greatly to the establishment of the independence of the United States.

He asked Adams to destroy the letter after he read it and not to share it with his family—because it could get back to his own family, who, he said, "have descended with the multitude down the Stream created by the homage paid to GW: and I have taken no pains to bring them back again. He is welcome to their praises and Admiration. They know only that I am not one of his idolaters, and that I ascribe the Success of our Revolution to a Galaxy." Then he crossed out "a Galaxy" and replaced it with "an illustrious band of Statesmen—philosophers—patriots & heroes."

Not long after this exchange, Rush found himself in a conversation with Julia about his correspondence with Adams. She teased him about how important the letters had become to the men over the years. To her, they seemed less like Founding Fathers trading wisdom than "two young girls" writing "about their sweethearts."

42

After school finished in the spring of 1812, Rush devoted much of his time to his opus on mental health, "the result of the reading, experience and reflections of fifty years upon all the forms of madness, and upon all the Other diseases of the mind."

Rush was moving quickly to install James as the heir to his private practice, his hospital practice, and his teaching. After a long period of silence, he renewed his correspondence with Richard, though their letters were mostly about Richard's job, which his father still felt he could still quit, and his personal life. Richard's wife, Catherine, was pregnant again and having a much rougher time than with her first child; she and baby Benjamin were still living at her parents' home in Annapolis, so he remained alone in Washington, a city he despised as "a meagre village; a place with a few bad houses, extensive swamps, hanging on the skirts of a too thinly peopled, weak and barren country."

But Richard was learning a lot about politics. His office controlled the purse strings for the treasury, and he was figuring out how much a family name and connections, combined with a shrewd legal mind and an ease with writing and public speaking, could lead to success in Washington. In May, as war with England approached, he suggested that President Madison urge Jefferson out of retirement and name him wartime secretary of state—much as

President Adams had named former president Washington senior officer of the U.S. Army during the late 1790s. The smart play reinforced to James Madison—who had known Richard since he was a child—that he might be a surprisingly useful adviser.

So Richard moved up quickly, even in the wake of tragedy: in June, the day after the United States declared war on Britain, his wife delivered a stillborn baby.

Richard became Madison's de facto spokesman on the war, and in late June was told he would deliver the July 4 address to Congress on the situation. Panicked, he wrote to his father for advice and anecdotes, many of which found their way into his speech.

Father and son remained as close as they could be from such a far distance. But there is no indication they ever saw each other again.

As Rush worked on his final book, waves of sentiment overwhelmed him. Several medical emergencies had previously convinced him he was about to die, but he was now experiencing the slow, strong ebb of old age. In June, he wrote a poem for Julia, which he signed "by her husband 36 years after their marriage"—even though their wedding anniversary had been in January, and her fifty-third birthday in March. It was based on one of their favorite poems, "To Mary," by the British poet William Cowper.

When tossed upon the bed of pain
And every healing art was vain,
Whose prayers brought back my life again?
my Julia's.

When shafts of scandal 'round me flew
And ancient friends no longer knew my humble name,
Whose heart was true?
my Julia's.

When falsehood aimed its poison dart
And treachery pierced my bleeding heart,
Whose friendship did a cure impart?
my Julia's.

When hope was weak and faith was dead
And every earthly joy was fled,
Whose hand sustained my drooping head?
my Julia's.

When worn by age and sunk in years,
My shadow at full length appears,
Who shall anticipate my cares?
my Julia.

When life's low wick shall feebly blaze
And weeping children on me gaze,
Who shall assist my prayers and praise?
my Julia.

And when my mortal parts shall lay,
Waiting in hope the final day,
Who shall mourn o'er my sleeping clay?
my Julia.

And when the stream of time shall end,
And the last trump my grave shall rend,
Who shall with me to heaven ascend?
my Julia.

Several weeks later Rush had to visit a patient nine miles out of the city. He brought his youngest child with him, William, who had just turned eleven. The patient lived only a few miles from the family farm where Rush had been born in 1745 and lived until the age of five, so they paid a visit. The front entrance of the house looked different, but the owners kindly said he and his son could look inside—where it felt more familiar, and he took William upstairs to see the room where he had been born. He sat for a while in the common room, thinking of the conversations his ancestors had had there. He looked for a cedar tree that his father had planted near the door. The owner said it had been cut down but had been used to build a piazza in front of the house. Rush walked over to it and hugged one of the pillars. He asked about his father's apple orchard and was directed to "a few larger Struggling apple trees that Still bore fruit, to each of which I felt something like the Affection of a brother."

He then visited the small family graveyard, where his grandfather, the gunsmith, was buried. His name was James Rush; he and Julia had named their son, the physician, after him. Rush stood and looked at the grave for a long time, while his son picked cherries from a tree supposedly planted by Rush's father.

When they got home that evening, Rush gathered the family to tell them of his day. They listened, he later told Adams, "with great pleasure"—especially after William produced a pocketful of cherries and passed out the fruit of the family tree.

IN THE FALL of 1812, Rush published *Medical Inquiries and Observations, upon the Diseases of the Mind.* The title was meant to link the book to his life-long medical text project, but most people referred to it by the shortened name embossed on the spine: *Rush on the Mind.* It was a late-career effort by the most celebrated doctor in America to bring all his credibility as a physician, a scientist, a revolutionary, and a man of faith to the most vexing and painful problem of all: mental illness, and society's failure to understand and care for some of its most marginalized members.

"In entering upon [this] subject," Rush began, ". . . I feel as if I were about to tread upon consecrated ground." He wanted, once and for all, to dispel the view of "madness" as a failure of will or belief or philosophical perspective, and to recast "mental derangement" as a disease of the brain that could—periodically or sometimes permanently—distort or create "errors" of perception of the world. He wrote in a style he felt was "accommodated to the 'Common Science' of Gentlemen of all professions as well as medicine."

The diseases of the mind had "hitherto been enveloped in mystery," he wrote to Adams:

> I have endeavoured to bring them down to the level of all the other diseases of the human body, & to show that the mind and the body

are moved by the same causes & Subject to the same laws. For this Attempt to simplify the 'medicini mentis' I expect no Quarter from my learned brethren. But time I hope will do my Opinions justice. I believe them to be true and calculated to lessen some of the greatest evils of human life.

He reviewed historical theories of madness, from Hippocrates to Cullen, then offered his own (and without naming names, included Pinel and several British physicians for whom "madness has been placed exclusively in the mind"). But instead of spending many pages discussing where mental illness sat in the body, he shared a career's worth of patient anecdotes and insights, exploring all possible "causes" and predisposing events tied to "intellectual derangement," and perhaps most ambitiously, explaining what it was like to experience various mental illnesses.

Among the medical causes, or triggers, were head injury, tumor, water in the brain, epilepsy, palsy, vertigo, headache, gout, dropsy, consumption, pregnancy, malnourishment, and "profuse evacuations." But the single biggest cause of mental illness that he had seen at Pennsylvania Hospital was "excessive use of ardent spirits"—an issue for more than a third of the patients in the mental health ward.

Several cases of madness appeared linked to "inordinate sexual desires and gratifications," especially, onanism—which was "more frequently" problematic "with young men than is commonly supposed by parents and physicians." Some cases of mental illness had been triggered by "certain cutaneous eruptions" and the trauma of becoming "repelled" by one's own skin. He had seen patients become deranged after "intense study, whether of the sciences or the mechanical arts . . . [and] real or imaginary objects of knowledge," like those who sought "the means of discovering perpetual motion, of converting base metals to gold, of prolonging life . . . , of producing perfect order and happiness," or who researched "the meaning of certain prophesies in the Old and New Testaments." He had seen madness brought on by "the frequent and rapid transition of the mind from one subject to another. It is said that booksellers have sometimes become deranged from this cause."

But madness was "excited . . . most frequently by impressions that act primarily upon the heart," which included "joy, terror, love, fear, grief, distress, shame from offended delicacy, defamation, calumny, ridicule, absence from native country, the loss of liberty, property and beauty, gaming, and inordinate love of praise, domestic tyranny, and, lastly, the complete gratification of every wish of the heart." A clergyman in Maryland "became insane in consequence of having permitted some typographical errors to escape in a sermon which he published upon the death of General Washington."

Rush quoted research from Pinel about the reported causes of madness for the 113 patients with mental illness in his Paris hospital. He said Pinel cited thirty-four triggered by "domestic misfortunes," twenty-four by "disappointments in love," thirty by "the distressing events of the French Revolution," and the rest by what Pinel "calls fanaticism." When Rush conducted the same study among fifty patients in his own hospital, he found more balance between cases with "mental" and "corporeal" causes. Of the mental cases, seven were caused by disappointments in love, seven by grief, seven by the loss of property, five by "erroneous opinions in religion," two by jealousy, and one by terror. On the physical side, five were caused by intemperance, three by masturbation, two by pregnancy, two by "repelled eruptions," one by fever, one by "an injury to the head," and one by sun exposure.

Rush had grown interested in the concept of hereditary predisposition to madness—which he especially associated with suicidal behavior. In his latest study of his patients, only five seemed to have hereditary disease. But he had treated families with multiple members affected, including one in which three members came to the hospital for treatment the same day.

A colleague had also written him about twin brothers who had fought together in the Revolutionary War, went on to have successful careers, marriages, and young families in different cities, and then one of them, a member of the general assembly in Vermont, took his own life by cutting his throat "from ear to ear." Two years later, the other brother got up one morning, asked his wife to take a ride with him, went to shave before they left, finished, wiped his razor, and then went to put it away—when his wife heard a strange noise like water on the floor. She found him dying with his throat cut. When this was reported to the rest of the family, it triggered derangement in both their mother and their two sisters.

No possible causal factor was too far-fetched for Rush to study. He had found that a disproportionate number of his patients had dark hair—and he had heard the same thing from other doctors. Fifty-six of his seventy-nine patients had light-colored eyes, even though only six of them had light-colored hair. He studied the age of onset of mental illness—prompted, most likely, by a study Pinel had done of French patients in the 1790s. Rush found that over 86 percent of his patients had become ill between twenty and fifty, more than the 50 percent–plus that Pinel had recorded. During those years, he thought, the blood vessels and nerves were "in a highly exciteable state," and the mind was "more easily acted upon by mental irritants" including "family afflictions . . . [and] disappointments in the pursuit of business, pleasure and ambition." Madness almost never appeared before puberty, he thought.

He also observed that patients with mental illnesses "seldom live to be old." The one exception he could recall was Hannah Lewis, his first psychiatric patient as a staff physician at Pennsylvania Hospital in 1784. She had died in the hospital in 1799 at eighty-seven. Over fifty, Rush believed, people were more protected from the onset of mental illness because their "blood-vessels lose their vibratility from age" so the "causes of madness make but a feeble and transient impression upon their minds." Their bodies "revert to that state which takes place in children," which Rush felt protected them.

Women were "more predisposed to madness than men," Rush explained, because of the impact of "menstruation, pregnancy, and patruition" on their bodies and the impact of "living so much alone in their families" on their minds. He had become aware of this early in his career when the hospital treated a woman "who was deranged only during the time of her menstruation, and who in one of those periods hung herself with the string of her petticoat." He cited statistics from several hospitals and asylums about the proportion of male to female patients, and the possible reasons for this (including whether men or women were more likely to be sent to a hospital in the first place). He speculated that perhaps women were more subject to madness from "natural causes" while men were more likely to be triggered by "artificial" causes, such as "the evils of war, bankruptcy and habits of drinking."

More important than gender, in any case, was marital status: "single persons," he declared, "are more predisposed to madness than married people." He believed this to be true of many diseases and sometimes would recommend that patients, especially single people with chronic illnesses, get married as part of his treatment. "The absence of real and present care" from a mate "gives the mind leisure to look back upon past, and to anticipate future and imaginary evils." Single people were likely more prone to madness because of "the inverted operation of all the affections of the heart upon itself, together with the want of relief in conjugal sympathy from the inevitable distresses and vexations of life, and for which friendship is a cold and feeble substitute."

Moreover "certain states of society . . . opinions, pursuits, amusements and forms of government" could predispose people to derangement. In the United States, "madness has increase[d] since the year 1790," which he blamed on "the number and magnitude" of "objects of ambition and avarice." He singled out "the funding system, and speculations in bank scrip" and noted the alarming suicide rate in New York—which meant, to politically attuned readers, he was partially blaming Alexander Hamilton for its rise.

Rush was careful to specify that derangement was often partial or episodic. He thought it unfortunate that people used the term *hypochondriasis* for "the lowest grade of derangement," which, given its implied accusation of fraud, "is always offensive to patients who are affected with it." Rush used the term for patients who, while seeming to be fine otherwise, had ongoing "errors" of thinking or "erroneous opinions" on certain subjects. Some patients erroneously believed they had physical afflictions, such as consumption, cancer, impotence, venereal disease. He once treated a sea captain who believed "he had a wolf in his liver." Others were convinced that "animals were preying upon different parts of their bodies." He had one patient who believed he had been "transformed into glass," and another who was certain that "by discharging the contents of his bladder he shall drown the world."

To treat these myriad conditions, Rush provided a list of interventions. Some, like bloodletting, were physical, "intended to act directly upon the body," while others were psychological, acting "indirectly upon the body, through the medium of the mind." He held the two categories to be equally important, requiring great balance and the judgment of a worthy doctor.

Rush on the Mind went on for three-hundred-sixty-seven pages, reading like what it was, a first draft thrown together from thirty years of notes. There were repeated ideas and disorganized sections, and Rush apologized for failing to cite all his sources. Yet, on almost every subject, sometimes just in passing, there were flashes of insight on issues that have always vexed people with mental illnesses and addictions, as well as those who care for them.

Studded throughout, too, were tiny, powerful moments from the author's years at Pennsylvania Hospital—such as his description of the day in June 1806, when, during a total eclipse of the sun, he recalled "a sudden and total silence in all the cells of the hospital."

Rush also recounted his vivid journeys into patients' minds:

> The associations of a madman are often discordant, ludicrous or offensive, and his judgment and reason are perverted on all subjects. He sometimes attempts to injure himself or others. Even inanimate objects, such as his clothing, bed, chairs, tables, and the windows, doors and walls of his room, when confined, partake of his rage. All sense of decency and modesty is suspended, hence he besmears his face with his own excretions, and exposes his whole body without a covering. . . . What is called consciousness in his mind is at this time destroyed in his mind. He is ignorant of the place he occupies, and of his rank and condition in society, of the lapse of time, and even of his own personal identity.

It reminded him of a passage in *King Lear*, Act IV: "I am mainly ignorant. What place this is and all the skill I have Remembers not these garments; nor I know not Where I did lodge last night. Do not laugh at me." Rush quoted the play several times. "The reader will excuse my frequent references to the poets for facts to illustrate the history of madness," he explained. "They view the human mind in all its operations, whether natural or morbid, with a microscopic eye; and hence many things arrest their attention, which escape the notice of physicians."

Rush went out on a lot of limbs, hoping to provoke conversation. One can only imagine what his religious mentors would have made of his discussion of visual and auditory hallucinations. After offering physical explanations for why people might "see" and "hear" things that weren't there, he speculated on whether the prophets and apostles in ancient times had actually seen and heard "the supernatural voices and objects" ascribed to them in the Bible, or whether these might have been "produced by a change in the natural actions of the brain." In all cases where "miracles were necessary to establish a divine commission or a new doctrine," he pointed out, they had to have been seen by at least two or three people.

Finally, in the middle of an exegesis on whether those with mental illness should be held personally and criminally responsible for their actions when deranged, Rush just stopped writing.

He picked up his pen just one more time, and scribbled this:

> Here the reader and the author must take leave of each other. Before I retire from his sight, I shall only add, if I have not advanced, agreeably to my wishes, the interest of medicine by this work, I hope my labours in the cause of humanity will not alike be unsuccessful; and that the sufferings of our fellow creatures, from the causes that have been mentioned, may find sympathy in the bosoms, and relief from the kindness, of every person who shall think it worthwhile to read this history of them.
>
> THE END

Not long after *Rush on the Mind* was published, the doctor attended the funeral of a patient on a cold, damp November day. Soon afterward his cough, which Julia described as "constitutional with him on the slightest cold," came back with a vengeance. While it seemed under control during the day, he suffered harsh spells at night and upon rising. He tried to combat them by taking a drink of warm molasses and water, mixed with brandy or lime juice, before bed—sometimes with a few drops of laudanum to help him sleep.

Julia had grown so accustomed to his coughing, especially during the winter months, that she accepted his self-diagnosis that this was just another passing bout. She remained optimistic even after he suddenly stopped drinking his daily "one to two glasses of good Madiera," and then even the "small table beer of which he was fond, and always used at his dinner."

Besides being ill, Rush was upset by the reception to his book.

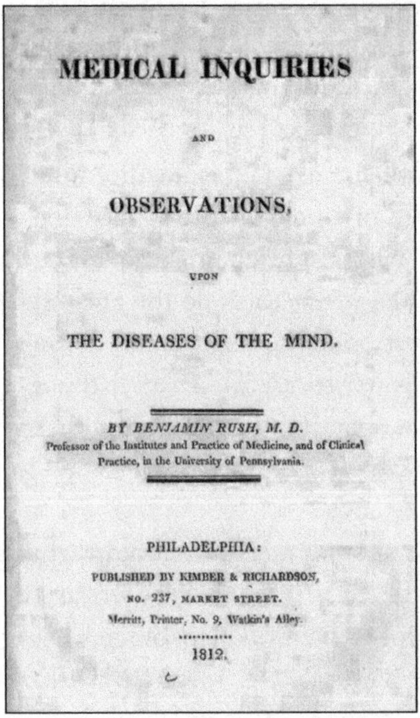
MEDICAL INQUIRIES

AND

OBSERVATIONS,

UPON

THE DISEASES OF THE MIND.

BY BENJAMIN RUSH, M. D.
Professor of the Institutes and Practice of Medicine, and of Clinical Practice, in the University of Pennsylvania.

PHILADELPHIA:
PUBLISHED BY KIMBER & RICHARDSON,
NO. 237, MARKET STREET.
Merritt, Printer, No. 9, Watkin's Alley.

1812.

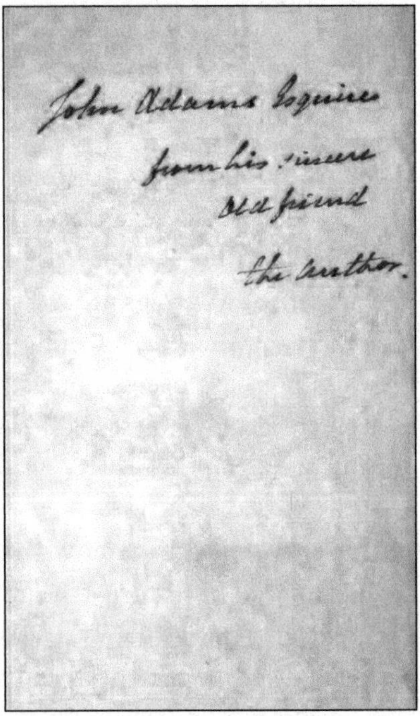

The copy of Medical Inquiries and Observations upon the Diseases of the Mind *that Rush inscribed to Adams, writing: "John Adams Esquire, from his sincere old friend, the author"*

"It has been well-received by many of my fellow Citizens, and particularly by some Gentlemen of the bar," he told Adams, "but not a single physician in our city . . . has taken the least Notice of it." Adams was not surprised. Before he even saw it—Rush's publisher failed to send the former president an advance copy promptly—he predicted that his friend's book would be met with "Reproaches, vilifications and Lies and Slanders . . . You will be accused of Materialism and consequently of Atheism. They are all mad as I am, and we Shall all see ourselves in Some or other of your Theories and then We Shall all call you a Blockhead and Swear that We are as rational Men as ever existed, as an Inhabitant of Bedlam once Swore to me, that he was."

But Adams wanted Rush to know, with all "the Sincerity of my heart," that the controversial subject he had dared to tackle was "one of the most important, interesting and affecting, that human Nature and terrestrial Existence exhibit. And you will merit everlasting Thanks of your Species, for your Attempt to investigate it, whatever your present Success may be."

After reading the book, Adams said it would:

> run mankind still deeper into your Debt. . . . If I could afford the expence, I would advertize a reward of a gold Medal to the Man of Science who should write the best Essay upon the question whether the Writings of Dr Franklin, or Dr Rush do the greatest honour to America, or the greatest good to Mankind. . . . You would not have been so industrious nor so useful, if you had not been persecuted. These Afflictions are but for a moment and they work out greater Glory.

He followed this letter with one about a recent dream, in which he had found himself in the middle of a play, "advertised as the most extraordinary that ever was represented on Any Stage," being performed at an open theater in the "vast plain of Virginia," with all eight million American citizens in attendance. It was a play about America itself, "this overgrown Colt of a Nation . . . [that had] no feeling of its Strength nor any Sense of its Glory." At the height of the dream's action, Adams "obtained a Speaking Trumpet, and made a Motion, which was carried that the Play Should be dismissed," and the country should "resolve itself into a Committee of the whole House on the State of the Nation, Dr Rush in the Chair."

Rush thanked Adams for his support and kind words about the book, noting that his friend had "so far outdreamed me in your last letter, that I shall be afraid hereafter to let my imagination loose in that Mode."

Julia was pushing Rush to retire to Sydenham and let James run the medical practice, but he felt he couldn't afford to quit just yet. Though they were financially secure—largely from Rush's real estate investments, which had allowed them to pay off their large house on Fourth Street, and the smaller one next door they were renting out—they still had three children living at home: young Julia, who was twenty; Samuel, who was seventeen; and William, who was about to turn twelve.

Their second daughter, Mary, who was now twenty-nine and had been married to British Capt. Thomas Manners for nearly a decade, had recently moved back home with her two young children while her husband fought in the War of 1812. "Should her husband fall in battle (which is Alas! not improbable, for he is now at Queenstown or in the neighbourhood of it with his regiment)," Rush told Adams, ". . . his whole family would remain with me for life with but a scanty inheritance from him."

So Rush kept working through the winter, even as his cough got worse. Julia kept telling him that "his labors and his advancing years required more generous living." She noticed that while he still "ate plentifully of buttered toast, and buckwheat cakes," he ate very little meat and drank nothing more than water, tea, or coffee. He claimed that this diet allowed him to continue working after dinner, as he had done since he was thirty, but Julia begged him to eat more because "his dieting plan was more likely to injure him now." She urged him to try the wine, but every time he did, it seemed to make him cough. While he still claimed to have no "apparent disease," he "looked pale and reduced," and she feared the overall "sinking of his system."

Julia also noted that her husband had recently "burned a great many letters."

On March 6, 1813, Dr. Benjamin Rush missed rounds at Pennsylvania Hospital. Over the years, he had opted out of rounds before—he sometimes sent James in his place. But he hadn't missed rounds for the past six months, even as his colleagues noticed he was weakening. So when he missed rounds again on March 10, and then on March 13, 17, 20, and 24, they had reason for concern.

Dr. Rush reappeared for rounds on Saturday, March 27, and saw dozens of patients, including seventy-three suffering from mental disease—nearly half of the entire population of the hospital. While over thirty of them had been admitted during the previous year, he had been treating quite a few for a decade or more, and a handful had been there during his entire thirty years on the Pennsylvania Hospital staff.

Most important to Rush, he saw John for the first time in almost a month. John had been in the hospital's locked mental health wing for over two and a half years. It was beyond even his father's most optimistic hope that he might recover, or respond to the treatments he received when his dark mood worsened or his thoughts grew more disordered than usual.

John spent his days pacing and talking to himself, in a low voice but with expansive, theatrical movements of his hands and arms. He walked back and forth in such a tight, uniform line that he was wearing down several floorboards inside, and doing the same thing on a boardwalk outside where the patients were allowed on pleasant days. The staff referred to these deeply grooved boards as "Rush's Walk" and sometimes showed them to visitors to illustrate the impact of serious mental illness.

That Saturday Rush visited his son, finished up his hospital business for the day, and went home.

Two weeks later, Benjamin Rush wrote his last letter to John Adams—although he didn't realize it because he felt as well as he had over the past few months. Adams, more than a decade his senior and often in challenged health, seemed more at risk. Whenever either of them ended a letter with a cryptic comment about dying soon, it wasn't Rush they were referring to.

Of the 223 letters they had exchanged since reconnecting in 1805—letters their wives loved to watch them retrieve from the post, because they were so excited to open them—this last one wasn't in any way exceptional. Rush acknowledged that he had given publisher Mathew Carey a piece Adams wanted him to consider. Then came some talk about the War of 1812 (now in its second year) and excitement about a naval victory. No longer against the war, Rush now said that "the year 1812 will I hope be immortal in the history of this world for having given the first Check to the overgrown power and tyranny of Britain and France. Russia and the United States may now be hailed as the deliverers of the human race." (Richard's superior had just been sent to Russia as a minister, leaving Rush's thirty-two-year-old son to, as the newspaper put it, "superintend the department.") Rush talked about war loans, and about his son Ben returning home from abroad, and then said, "Adieu."

Before mailing his pages, he added a postscript about two new pieces of writing he had begun. His students had requested them, and he wanted to write them quickly, "Knowing that my time is Short and that the night of imbecillity of mind or death is fast approaching."

FOUR DAYS LATER, on the Wednesday before Easter, Rush returned home from seeing patients at around seven in the evening, ate a quick dinner of buckwheat cakes and coffee, and then repaired to his writing desk, where he was drafting a new book on personal hygiene. Julia wandered in and out of his room, offering tea but mostly just keeping an eye on him, until nine p.m., when she discovered him away from his desk, sitting close to the fire; he said he "feared he was getting a chilly fit." She told him it was time for bed, and while preparing warm water for his feet, she also warmed his heavy coat by the fire and made him more tea. They walked up the stairs together, Julia in the lead holding a candle. She got him into bed, wrapped in his heated coat and blankets, but within twenty minutes he was complaining of chills and fever. Soon after he reported pains in his limbs, and after midnight he said he felt a sharp pain on his right side—and asked Julia to call him a bleeder. She talked him out of it, saying it was too soon and he "was too pale and thin to bleed upon every little fit of pain that occurred." She finally coaxed him to sleep.

Julia felt strange denying a bleeder to the doctor who had advised generations of physicians to let blood early and often. "I do not know why," she later admitted to Abigail Adams, "but I did feel a great reluctance." But the next morning he was clearly worse, so a bleeder was summoned at seven a.m.; he took twelve ounces. Rush said he felt better and began sweating away his fever.

Later that morning Dr. John Syng Dorsey, the twenty-nine-year-old surgeon, stopped by the house to consult James about a medical concern of his own. While he was in the house, Julia asked him to look in on Dr. Rush, who had been his teacher, and see if he agreed with the bleeding. He said it had been the right thing to do but did not recommend doing it again. He diagnosed Rush with typhus and told Julia to prepare some "generous wine whey"—warm milk mixed with wine and water—which seemed to help. But Rush never regained the strength to leave his bed. He disagreed with Dorsey about the typhus diagnosis, guessing rather that the pulmonary tuberculosis he believed had ebbed and flowed in his body for years was finally reaching its acute stage.

Later that evening, he told Julia the pain in his right side had returned. The doctors tried a blister in the area, to no effect. His cough returned, and he took more laudanum to sleep. He slept most of the next day, which was Good Friday, but on Saturday morning he awoke very early in pain and demanded another bleeding. Julia was afraid to let him be bled without a doctor seeing him first, because "if he should sink under bleeding I could never forgive myself."

Dr. Dorsey arrived and was against it but agreed to send for his uncle and Rush's friend, Dr. Philip Syng Physick, for a second opinion. Physick concurred that opening a vein was a mistake—no matter how much Rush asked for it—and instead performed a cupping on the side where Rush's pain was, and took four ounces of

blood from there. Rush said he felt more comfortable but remained weak. Every few hours Julia tried to get him to eat wine whey and drink porter, as the doctors had suggested.

By Sunday morning, Easter, Rush said he was feeling better, and "when the Doctors came," Julia recalled, "they congratulated me on his being in safe way." Before heading to church, "the children came in," and "he kissed the girls and shook hands with his sons, and said he hoped to be down among them in a few days." He told Julia he was happy he "could think again" after days of pain. When afternoon Easter services ended, Bishop William White paid Rush a visit; they spoke for fifteen minutes and the bishop offered a short prayer. When he left the room, he was certain Rush was out of danger, and that he would be seeing him soon. The doctors returned and said they were pleased with his progress.

Rush too believed the worst was over and told Julia he was "thankful to be spared yet a little longer" to his family. But he also said that "if god had done with him here, he was perfectly resigned to his will and ready to go."

At nine p.m., the doctors returned again, and Julia "soon awoke to the horrors." Her husband's pulse had grown faint, and he needed strong stimulants poured down his throat and applied externally. He was given brandy until it made him cough, he was blistered on his body—then rubbed with cloths soaked in turpentine to dry the blisters. Regular blisters were applied to his wrists.

On Monday, Julia felt her husband was "sensible of his immediate danger, but meek, resigned and collected." Rush called in James to tell him where to find the legal papers he would need, explained his responsibilities as new head of the house, and gave him some final career advice. James, now twenty-seven, had shadowed his father for many months and occasionally filled in for him, but it was only just dawning on him that he was about to become "Dr. Rush." His father's last words to him were "Be indulgent to the poor."

A message was sent to Richard in Washington, even though it was unlikely he could make it back in time. Rush said goodbye to his other children, and then Julia came to the bedroom alone. They

had been together for nearly thirty-seven years, since she was sixteen. Now he took her hand, looked at her with his wide, blue-gray eyes, and said, "My excellent wife, I shall leave you, but your son will take care of you as I have charged him to do so."

Then he raised his eyes to heaven, and repeated a phrase from the litany of the Episcopal Church, Matthew 13: "By the Mystery of thy holy incarnation, by the holy nativity and circumcision, by the baptism fasting and temptation, by thine agony and bloody sweat, by thy cross and passion, by thy precious death and burial, by the glorious resurrection and ascension, and by the coming of the holy ghost, blessed Jesus wash me from the defilements of sin and receive me into thy everlasting arms."

A third doctor came to visit, James Mease, another former apprentice. He came primarily to pay his respects but did manage to get his mentor to drink some porter.

Rush lasted for a few more hours "in a tranquil and happy state," either sleeping or silently raising his hands, wiping cold sweat from his face with a handkerchief he would not let go of. Then "at seven minutes after five in the evening," Julia recalled, ". . . without a struggle or a groan he took his flight to an happier region. . . . A more quick, happy death no mortal was ever favored with, perfectly rational to the last moment—he put the seal to the piety and usefulness of his life by his composure and resignation in death."

With that, Julia Rush said goodbye to her one and only love.

"But oh . . . ," she thought, "what an aching heart is left to me."

EPILOGUE

Five days after Rush's death, John Adams stepped out of his home in Quincy to meet the morning post. As Abigail watched from a window, he looked through the mail and, disappointed at seeing nothing from Rush, opened a letter from a medical student acquaintance who was taking classes with Rush in Philadelphia.

The letter, as she described the scene, bore "tydings that rent his heart," and as he read it, John Adams cried out, "O my friend, my friend, my ancient, my constant, my unshaken Friend, My Brother, art thou gone, gone forever? Who can estimate thy worth, who can appreciate thy loss? To thy Country, to thy Family, to thy Friends, to Science, to Literature, to the World at large? To a Character which in every relation of Life shone resplendent?"

By the time Adams found out that Rush had even been ill, his friend had already been buried. The funeral was held on Thursday, April 22, at four p.m., and before it began, there were mourning processions from the Philosophical Society and the Society for the Abolition of Slavery, as well as the Pennsylvania Hospital staff and a group representing the African American churches he had helped found.

"The citizens testified their grief for his loss by the manner they assembled at his funeral," said one newspaper story. "Nothing of the kind has occurred since the death of Franklin, and Washington."

The standing-room-only funeral was held in Christ Church, after which Rush's casket was carried several blocks to the church's burial ground at Fifth and Arch. He was buried next to his father and not far from the grave of Benjamin Franklin.

Richard Rush hurried home from Washington but, sadly, arrived just after his father was buried. "I reached his disconsolate house," Richard wrote a friend, "just as the funeral obsequies were over, and the gates of the tomb shut forever upon me."

A few hours after attending the funeral, Dr. Physick sat solemnly in one of the upstairs rooms of his home. He was contemplating a world without Dr. Rush, and what it would mean to Philadelphia, to medicine, and to his own practice, since the great doctor had opened doors for him since the early 1790s.

It was late, and Physick was lost in his thoughts, when he was suddenly summoned to come downstairs. An "unusually large" man stood in his entrance hallway waiting for him.

He abruptly asked the surgeon: "Do you want Dr. Rush?"

"What do you mean?" Physick asked, recoiling. "Dr. Rush is dead!"

"I will have him at the College for you at nine o'clock tomorrow morning, for twenty dollars [$317]," the burly laborer replied. He assumed Physick would want to use Rush's body for a dissection demonstration, so he was about to head over to Christ Church to dig him up.

Physick, shocked and terrified, told the man he was not interested, and that he should leave Rush's body alone. Years later, when Physick was dying, he made his son promise that his own grave, not far from Rush's in the Christ Church Burial Ground, would be guarded "for a sufficiently long time to insure" that his "remains would be valueless for the purposes of any enterprising resurrectionist."

A DELUGE OF tributes to Rush appeared in newspapers, magazines, and journals across the country. "His death is a public and private calamity," wrote one paper. "In him, Science has lost one of her most distinguished Sons; Philanthropy a brother; the U. States a patriot of the Revolution; the sick the afflicted and the poor, ah! how incalculably great is their loss of this most beloved Physician, who, like the good Samaritan, went about to the last, doing good and administering to the *body* as well as to comfort the *soul*."

The First African Baptist Church declared that "the excellent Dr. Rush, great as a Physician, and zealous as a Christian, was the *coloured man's* friend. Actuated by the purest benevolence and patriotism, often has he destroyed the chain, vindicated the cause and banished the tears of the oppressed. The grateful African will often utter, and teach his children to utter, the name of RUSH."

Jefferson wrote to Adams, "Another of our friends of 76. is gone, my dear Sir, another of the Co-signers of the independance of our country. and a better man, than Rush, could not have left us, more benevolent, more learned, of finer genius, or more honest."

Adams responded, "I lament with you the loss of Rush. I know of no Character living or dead who has done more real good in America." He wrote to other friends about the late doctor. "You know much of Benj. Rush as a Physician and as a Professor," he told Dr. Benjamin Waterhouse, "but it is impossible you Should thoroughly know his Biography as a Statesman. From 17[7]4 to his Death he acted an important Part on the political Theatre. He has Suffered more and gained less in Fame, Fortune and Feelings by the Revolution than almost any other Man."

Adams compared the accomplishments of Rush and Franklin during the Revolution and afterward and elaborated on the subject to Richard:

> Dr Rush was a greater and better Man than Dr Franklin: Yet Rush was always persecuted and Franklin always adored. . . . Why is not Dr Rush placed before Dr Franklin in the Temple of Fame? Because Cunning is a more powerful Divinity, than Simplicity. Rush has done infinitely more good to America than Franklin.

Both have deserved a high Rank among Benefactors to their Country and Mankind; but Rush by far the highest.

City and state medical societies commissioned memorial lectures about Rush, and many held an official period of mourning, during which members wore a black crepe band on one arm—some for thirty days, others for sixty or ninety. The memorial lectures became popular pamphlets and books. Ads appeared in newspa-

Various copies of Rush's last portrait (including, bottom left, one with Pennsylvania Hospital in background) and one of several copies of his bust (by cousin William Rush)

pers for commemorative etchings of Rush, and medical schools and individual admirers ordered oil paintings or watercolors or etchings of Rush portraits. Some paid Thomas Sully or Charles Willson Peale to create new versions of their portraits of him (Sully did one with Pennsylvania Hospital in the background); others had lesser painters or lithographers create facsimiles.

During the last year of his life, Dr. Rush had sat for a terracotta bust of himself, created by his cousin, the sculptor William Rush. He was quickly commissioned to make more of them.

Rush's family and close friends had other priorities. The first was the question of Rush's position as treasurer of the U.S. Mint. As word spread of his death, President Madison received dozens upon dozens of letters, each briefly eulogizing Dr. Rush and then asking after the low-work, high-pay political appointment.

Only a handful of people, including Adams and Physick, wrote to ask that Madison honor Rush's memory by appointing his son James. But Madison had another reason to consider James for the job. If he wanted to keep Richard Rush in Washington, he had to ensure that his acting treasury secretary and increasingly trusted adviser would not be forced to move back to Philadelphia to take care of his family. Eight days after Rush's death, the president named Dr. James Rush treasurer of the U.S. Mint.

Another challenge was what to do with Dr. Rush's many, many letters.

Jefferson quickly reached out to Richard to ask if he could have several of his back. Two were from 1811, in which he discussed reconnecting with Adams with Rush's help. Few people knew just how long and entirely the two ex-presidents had been estranged, and Jefferson wanted to keep it that way, by making sure these letters remained "unseen and unknown." Although he didn't say so specifically, this signaled that he didn't want the family sharing the story of how Rush had brought Adams and him back together—not because he didn't appreciate the "kind intervention," but because, he wrote, "I have too many enemies disposed to make a lacerating use of" the letters narrating the "friendship revived."

The other letter he wanted was from 1803, in which he had described at some length his controversial ideas about Jesus and organized religion. It was an intellectual artifact of the discussion he and Rush began in Philadelphia during his vice presidency (which Jefferson had appreciated as a distraction "to the afflictions of the crisis through which our country was then laboring"). The dialogue had become deeper and more interesting to both of them after Joseph Priestley, not long before his death in 1804, shared an essay he had written comparing Socrates and Jesus, which prompted Jefferson to start sketching out more of his ideas.

Since that time Rush had never stopped pestering Jefferson to finish what he was writing and publish on the subject. He still hadn't, but he didn't want anyone to see this letter until he decided what to do. The family couldn't find the letters, but Richard told him that, according to his mother, the doctor had burned a number of papers in the weeks before his death.

Soon after he heard that his letter to Rush about Jesus was likely destroyed, Jefferson began a correspondence with Adams on some of the same religious ideas. There weren't many people he could trust with his views on Christianity, which revolved around his belief in a human, not a supernatural, Jesus, and a critique of the corruptions of organized religion. It was as if Rush had willed his role in the conversation to Adams.

On August 9, 1813, after the former presidents exchanged several impassioned letters on religion and politics, Adams admitted to Jefferson that part of the reason he was fanning the flames was that "I wish it may Stimulate You, to pursue your own plan which you promised to Dr Rush," to create a piece of writing that would allow a public discussion of these ideas.

Three days later Richard wrote to Jefferson that Julia had discovered a stash of Dr. Rush's most secret correspondence and had found the 1803 letter. He returned it, along with an admonition that "often have I heard my father express a wish, that . . . in addition to all you have already done and written for [the country] . . . , you would yet favor it with something more, some work upon its past history, or peculiar interests, to be made the medium of the further treasures of your knowledge, and the still riper reflections of your wisdom."

From then on, both Adams and Richard encouraged Jefferson to complete the work on Christianity he had "promised" Dr. Rush. Several years later, it was finished, and the resulting book was as audacious as any of them could have wished. Jefferson had sliced up sections of the New Testament, especially the gospels, to remove all the miracles, leaving only the story of Jesus the man. It became known as "The Jefferson Bible," and was the last major work of religious freedom from the Founding Fathers.

Rush would have completely disagreed with its premise, but undoubtedly would have taken "peculiar happiness" in discussing it at great length with the author.

AT THE END of the first paragraph of Rush's autobiography, he had written, "it is my wish that it may not be read out of the circle of my family, and that it may never be published." But that had been in 1800, thirteen years before his death. His family now believed he would have wanted at least parts of his book to be read.

John Adams very much encouraged them. "I rejoice that Dr Rush has left his own Life in writing," he wrote to a Rush family friend, saying he hoped it would be published and "do honour to this youthful and inconsiderate Nation."

Sometime in early 1814, James, who was overseeing the estate for Julia, sent the handwritten manuscript of *Travels Through Life: an Account of the Sundry Incidents & Events in the Life of Benjamin Rush* to Richard in Washington. By this time, Richard had risen in the government: President Madison had offered him his choice of cabinet positions, either treasury secretary or attorney general. He chose attorney general and became, at thirty-three, the youngest-ever cabinet member in American history. (He was a year younger than Hamilton, who was treasury secretary at thirty-four, and three years younger than Robert Kennedy, who became attorney general at thirty-six.) His political ascension surely came to mind as he contemplated which of his father's strong feelings should become a matter of public record.

Richard went through the manuscript twice, marking in pencil the sections he wanted deleted—which included anything critical of the nation's major political players, living or recently deceased. He excised the saga of his father's resentments toward Washington and Shippen and his battles over the military medical service. James had a new, shortened version made based on the edits and sent it back to him; Richard added to the cuts his father's railings against Cobbett and all the physicians who had opposed him during the yellow fever epidemics. At some point after that second redaction, James reconsidered publishing the book at all.

Later that summer, on August 24, 1814, the British attacked the U.S. Capitol and set part of it on fire. Richard escaped on horseback with President Madison and several other cabinet members, who watched from a distance as the White House burned to the ground.

It was another two years before Dr. James Mease, Rush's protégé and the last doctor to treat him, informed Adams that he wanted to publish a book of Rush's letters and hoped he would approve and share some of their correspondence.

Adams, who had encouraged publication of the autobiography, responded frankly, "I know not how you could have conceived a project more victorious or more patriotic." Yet "I shudder at the thought" of those letters being published. He said he would consider sharing them if Mease secured written consent from Julia Rush, "which I know will not be given without the advice of her children."

It is unclear how far Mease or Adams went in seeking the family's permission over the following months. But if Richard ever considered the project, he would likely have vetoed it. His career had taken another sharp upward turn: when James Monroe became president in March 1817, he kept Rush as attorney general and also named him acting secretary of state, until John Quincy Adams could return home from England and take the job permanently. During that time he negotiated the Rush-Bagot Treaty, which ended the combat with Britain on the Great Lakes that was related to the War of 1812.

Later that year Richard succeeded John Quincy as U.S. minister to Great Britain and moved his family to England. The job meant his family would spend eight years away from the United States, which proved to be challenging for them: Catherine gave birth to two daughters who died before the age of four. But he was actively involved in the discussions leading to the Monroe Doctrine, which ended American isolationism and made the United States an official player in halting the spread of European colonialism.

While Richard was away, just after the fifth anniversary of Dr. Rush's death in 1818, Julia decided to have his original love letters to her from their courtship sewn into a small book. In it she wrote, on an open space in one of the letters:

> I have frequently determined to commit these letters to the flames as I know they are fit for scarsely any eyes but those to whom they are addressed, and as yet no others have seen them. But as I have daughters, it may not be unacceptable for them, when both their parents are no more, to learn the principles upon with their attatchtment and friendship was founded, at their father's request I kept mine during his life time, but destroyed them since his death, not thinking them worth preserving. I also destroy'd after his death many I received from him, both before and since my marriage because many things were in them I had not wished to appear—but they all breathed the same strain of affectionate partiality to me, and of benevolence and charity to all around him, and of piety to God. —such a friend and husband, few women have had to loose.

Richard and his family returned to America in 1825, called back by newly elected President John Quincy Adams, who made him his treasury secretary. John Quincy won the hotly contested election against southerner Andrew Jackson, in a decision by the House after an Electoral College deadlock. During that time the Marquis de Lafayette made a year-long visit to America. Now in his late sixties, the French general wanted to revisit the country he had helped to create as a young man. He and his traveling road show toured every state (now up to twenty-four, Missouri being the most recent) and made well-publicized visits to John Adams and Thomas Jefferson. His extended stay in the country, talking about his pride and amazement at what America had accomplished, set off a great wave of Revolutionary nostalgia.

In Philadelphia, his visit triggered a concerted effort to finally stop moping about the city's loss of the capital to Washington and instead start embracing its legacy as America's birthplace. The Pennsylvania State House had been condemned after the state capital moved to Harrisburg; the structure remained standing only because of a newspaper drive in 1816 to stall its demolition. During Lafayette's second visit to the area, during the weeks surrounding July 4, 1825, Philadelphians began referring to the building with pride as Independence Hall.

Among the events Lafayette blessed with his patriotic presence were two dinners to welcome Richard and his family back to America: an intimate affair at Franklin Hall, and two days later a huge banquet in the grand ballroom of the new Washington Hall Hotel, where Richard and his family, Lafayette and his family, Bishop White, and many other foreign and local dignitaries "sat down, about 6 o'clock, to a table groaning, as usual with the weight of the feast, while the glasses sparkled on the board," according to one newspaper report. "The utmost hilarity and decorum prevailed, and the evening was most agreeably spent, while many toasts and sentiments were delivered, enlivened by the music of the Marine Band."

They toasted Washington, they toasted "the ex-presidents," the current president, the governor, and the honoree Richard Rush, who gave a little speech. Then they toasted General Lafayette, who praised the city of Philadelphia, the press, and the memories of William Penn and Benjamin Franklin; the publisher Mathew Carey toasted Lafayette and Washington; and Lafayette jumped back in to toast the kindness of American ministers abroad.

Finally, a Mr. Pelvey rose to offer the toast it seemed time had forgotten. He raised his glass and proclaimed: "To the memory of Benjamin Rush!"

Much to their own astonishment, John Adams and Thomas Jefferson outlived Benjamin Rush by thirteen years, sharing at least another 280 letters after his death, letters that might never have been written without his intervention.

Much to the even greater collective astonishment of the nation, the two former presidents died on the same day, almost exactly as Rush had predicted in his dreamed history book from the future, which read, "These gentlemen sunk into the grave nearly at the same time." He had failed to predict, however, that they would die on the fiftieth anniversary of their singular, world-rocking achievement: the adoption of the Declaration of Independence.

Neither man knew the other was dying on July 4, 1826. At around one p.m., eighty-three-year-old Jefferson died in his bedroom at Monticello, of multiple ailments. Later that afternoon, ninety-year-old John Adams was lying peacefully in his deathbed in Quincy, Massachusetts. He had been quiet for several hours, when he suddenly stirred and spoke his last words to comfort himself and his nation. "Thomas Jefferson," he whispered, "survives."

After a long silence, he began losing his breath, gasping to his granddaughter "Help me, child! Help me!" At 6:20 his weak pulse gave out, and he was gone.

As the nation found out about the double loss, a meeting was called at City Hall in Washington, D.C. President John Quincy Adams could not attend, as he had already left the city to be with his family. So on July 11, Richard Rush stood to speak for the government.

It was the second address Richard had given about Jefferson in a week. Even as he was dying on July 4, Rush had been addressing the House of Representatives on his behalf, requesting funds to address the former president's personal financial challenges. Now he was here to say goodbye to the men he had been hearing about since he was old enough to talk: his father's "North and South poles of the American Revolution."

He began by marveling that Adams and Jefferson had lived to see the fiftieth anniversary of the nation's birth at all. "Who could have supposed? What imagination could have conceived," Rush asked, of both men surrendering "their mortal existence . . . at the very moment when millions of their countrymen were [paying] . . . grateful homage to their shining worth, their Revolutionary glories.

"Nothing like [this] has occurred before, and it will not be matched again. It is impossible!" he declared. ". . . We should pronounce it romantic, did we not believe it providential.

"*Adams & Jefferson!*" he cried out. "*Jefferson & Adams!* . . . The light of the south and the light of the north have gone down, but the glory remains. Co-heirs of eternity, as they were partners in earthly fame—alike illustrious in life, in death they have not been divided. Let not then, their country divide in the testimonials of respect, and honor, and gratitude, due to their memories."

His father would have loved it.

Several weeks later, a handsome young man with thick black hair, a dramatic chin, and a confident air about him was brought into Pennsylvania Hospital by staff physician Samuel Gross, and led to the West Wing. Edwin Forrest had grown up in Philadelphia performing in small local theaters and had recently made his debut in New York playing Othello to some acclaim. To capitalize on that, he took the ultimate Shakespearean risk: to play one of the oldest, most challenging characters in theater, King Lear, at the age of twenty.

To do so, Forrest needed to study madness. He asked Dr. Gross, who he had met in town, if he could get in to observe the most famous person with mental illness in Philadelphia: "a Mr. Rush."

Gross arranged for a visit, and early one afternoon, after the steward let them pass the checkpoint, "in a trice we were at the desired spot." Forrest "stealthily studied" John Rush "through the grating in the heavy iron door" that blocked the corridor from the rest of the hospital. Now in his late forties, having been in the hospital for over fifteen years, John appeared to Forrest and Gross to be "an old man, although he was still erect, with a handsome, open, manly countenance." They watched as he paced back and forth for hours, hands behind his back, muttering under his breath.

The only word they thought they could make out sounded like "Turner," which they were told was the name of the friend John had killed in a duel. It is unclear if they were told the duel was over a passage from Shakespeare.

Forrest was allowed to come back several more times to observe John Rush, until he, in the doctor's words, "came away perfectly convinced of the madness of Lear." But he also left with a much better understanding of human nature, that John Rush and Lear were men with illnesses, not madmen.

Forrest debuted the role on the New York stage on December 27, 1826, just after what would have been Dr. Benjamin Rush's eighty-first birthday. The first performance was an unreviewed benefit, but when the production began its run in Boston, it was an immediate sensation. For an American, a young American, to do a credible version of the most challenging part in British theater was itself a kind of revolution.

The critic from the *Boston Commercial Gazette* declared that Forrest:

> seemed to have read and conned the part for himself; he conceived and sustained it without imitation and with a single reliance on his own resources. The wild paroxysm of grief with which he burst forth in the following speech was admirable: "I have full cause of weeping; but this heart shall break into a thousand flaws, or ere I'll weep: O fool *I shall go mad!*" The frenzied enunciation of that last line has not been surpassed by any representative of Lear. The sublime insanity of the old king was well sustained, and the whole character in fine evinced a chastened temperament and reflection which we confess we were not prepared to see.

Edwin Forrest's rendition of King Lear became the cornerstone of his career as the first internationally renowned actor born in the United States. He became known for a bold, vigorous style of acting that was considered peculiarly American—developed in large part from his study of Benjamin Rush's son.

The doctor would have loved that, too.

AFTERWORD

The Afterlife of Benjamin Rush

After the deaths of Adams and Jefferson in 1826, Rush's most controversial writings remained in the possession of Julia and her children for another thirty years. These included his autobiography; his candid, state-by-state sketches of the "Characters of the Revolutionary Patriots"; and his most personal correspondence with Adams, Jefferson, Washington, and others. It is unclear whether Richard Rush or his mother had the stronger hand in keeping this material from the public, but Richard had the most to lose if his father's posthumous opinions caused controversy.

Julia Rush, late in life portrait

In 1827, John Quincy Adams ran for reelection against Andrew Jackson. When his vice president, John Calhoun of South Carolina, switched parties to run with fellow southerner Jackson, John Quincy selected Richard Rush as his running mate. It was the first time that two northerners ran against two southerners, presaging a divide that would end in civil war. Adams and Rush were soundly defeated.

Richard spent the next decades pursuing diplomatic and legal work on behalf of different American cities, and sometimes for the U.S. government. In 1836, President Jackson sent him to England to retrieve the massive trust of wealthy scientist James Smithson—over $500,000 ($13,600,000) that had been left to create an "establishment for the increase and diffusion of knowledge among men" in America, but had been detained by the British. (Richard sued on behalf of the United States in the British Court of Chancery, won the case, and sailed back with the gold, more than 100,000 sovereigns, which was stored at the U.S. Mint, where his brother James was still treasurer, until it could be used to create the Smithsonian Institute.)

Dr. Benjamin Rush, meanwhile, lived on in the thousands of students who carried on his traditions and in his books, which were standard texts in several fields for decades. One of the greatest ongoing tributes to his memory took place in a city that did not exist when he died: Chicago. Rush Medical College was chartered in 1837, just before the city itself was chartered, and became the dominant medical school in the West through much of the 1800s (after which the "West" became the Midwest). It later combined with the University of Chicago and other Chicago medical institutions, and was also the inspiration for the naming of "Rush Street," which became a busy city thoroughfare.

In 1845, Rush's younger sons Samuel and William again raised the issue of publishing his autobiography; Samuel needed the money. Richard was still against it, and James—who had since married one of the richest women in Philadelphia, and had a social reputation to uphold—apparently sided with him. The family tabled the issue and went no further with it, even after their mother died in 1848, in her late eighties.

Benjamin Rush's bookplate

It was only after Julia's death that Rush's papers were passed on to the next generation. James inherited the bulk of his professional materials; he had already merged his father's library with his own, and he now inherited his medical and business correspondence and ledgers, several commonplace books, and many letters to and from his father.

But many papers had been separated out. Julia had hidden away the letters she considered most private: besides the early love letters, she had their correspondence during the yellow fever epidemic, his 1778 letter to her about the possibility of having Washington replaced, and letters from John before he became ill. The autobiography, the descriptions of the Founders, and his most closely held political and personal correspondence were not in the archive James inherited, either. They were in the possession of one of his brothers.

Richard presumably still had access to all of his father's archives. He had, during his career, produced quite a lot of writing—several books and many pamphlets, the best-known of which was a memoir of his time as American envoy to England. In 1857, at the age of seventy-seven, he decided to publish one more book. He was in a perfect position to bring together everything he knew about his father, and all the materials he had access to, and write the definitive account of Dr. Benjamin Rush and his role in so many American revolutions. The danger of jeopardizing his own political ambitions had passed, and his father's legacy remained self-evidently relevant. While some of Rush's medical ideas were by now outdated, his insights into preventive military medicine were still considered revolutionary, his writing about physician training and diseases of the mind had been more and more widely recognized, his wrestling with the separation of church and state spoke to an ongoing debate, and his ideas about slavery had never been more modern: the nation was about to go to war over them.

Instead, Richard Rush chose as the topic of his last published book the domestic life of George Washington. It was a short volume he had written earlier and put aside, based on letters Richard acquired from the widow of Washington's private secretary and friend, Tobias Lear. Richard published it in 1857 and then, reportedly, burned much of his other writing. If he ever did any major writing about his father, it has never been found (and since Richard and Dr. Rush lived apart for less than two years, there aren't many letters between them). Richard died in 1859, at the age of seventy-nine.

James outlived his elder brother by ten years. James and his wife, Phoebe Ridgway, had no children, so when she died in 1857, he inherited her fortune—and devised a will leaving a million dollars ($29 million) for a grand new building in her name on South Broad Street: the Ridgway Library (now Philadelphia's High School of the Performing Arts). Its primary goal was to house the Library Company of Philadelphia, but James also charged it with caring for those of his father's papers that he controlled, and which he spent the last years of his life painstakingly organizing. The building also housed James's papers (even today the Library Company must keep his sole book, *The Philosophy of the Human Voice*, in print to satisfy his bequest)—and contained the crypt where his wife was buried and where he would join her.

The massive, largely impractical building was finished in 1887, and James's archives were made available there. (The Library Company is now in a smaller building on Locust Street; the crypt came with it and is under the lobby.)

The remaining Rush papers ended up in the hands of Samuel's daughter Julia Williams Rush, who had married into the wealthy and prominent Biddle family. The papers sat, presumably in Julia's home, for decades, although every once in a while someone would note what a shame that was.

During the hundred-year anniversary of the College of Physicians, also in 1887, there was much storytelling about Dr. Rush and the early days. When all the lectures and speeches from the event were published, the commemorative address, by Dr. S. Weir Mitchell, included this footnote:

> Rush left letters, diaries, and also biographic memoirs of his contemporaries without which no man can fitly judge him or them. Friends, relatives, and executors have been chary of pub-

lishing these records. Some of them I have read, and I think it only just to a great man that we should know all that there is of him to know. He was too great, too productive, too various to lose esteem on account of anything he may have said or written of Washington.

Many who attended the anniversary of the College of Physicians were now also members of a younger, more robust group: the thirty-year-old American Medical Association (AMA), which had just recently begun publishing its journal. The AMA decided that among all the statues being erected in Washington to honor American history, there should be one of a physician. They chose Dr. Benjamin Rush, and by the late 1880s a committee had been formed to raise the money for the bronze.

Rush's image was also appropriated by another medical group, which began in Philadelphia in 1844 as the Association of Medical Superintendents of American Institutions for the Insane. It was founded by Rush's mental health heir, Dr. Thomas Kirkbride, at the Institute of Pennsylvania Hospital, the stand-alone facility for diseases of the mind that Rush had called for in the early 1800s. As its fiftieth anniversary approached in the 1890s, it was renamed the American Medico-Psychological Association, and it adopted as its logo a sketch of Rush with thirteen stars over his head. The group later became the American Psychiatric Association.

In the early 1890s, Julia Rush Biddle's husband, Alexander Biddle, ordered transcriptions of two sets of the papers his wife had inherited: a selection of the letters John Adams had written to Rush (without any of his replies) and a selection of the letters Rush had written to his wife during the yellow fever epidemic (without any of her replies). These were privately published in 1892 under the nondescript title *Old Family Letters: Copied from the Originals for Alexander Biddle*. The volume called "Series A" included the Adams letters; series B was "Old Family Letters Relating to the Yellow Fever." Fifty copies were printed of each.

Alexander and Julia Rush Biddle died in the late 1890s, and

their Rush holdings were passed down to their children. In 1905, their forty-two-year-old son Louis had printed, just for family members, Rush's autobiography—the edited-down version Richard had prepared in 1814—along with some extracts from the doctor's commonplace books and a family geneology.

At around the same time, the AMA presented its statue of Dr. Rush, created by sculptor Roland Hinton Perry, to President Theodore Roosevelt. The project had gained the attention of the medical director of the U.S. Navy—where both Benjamin and John Rush had entered military service—so the statue was installed, on a tall pedestal, outside the Navy Bureau of Medicine. (It is now inside a secure State Department complex, less easily seen.)

The statue was a tribute to Rush's legacy, but his image also appeared in a more popular and accessible location: cigar boxes. The Philadelphia-based Sulzberger, Oppenheimer & Co. began manufacturing a new premium cigar called the "Benjamin Rush," with a gilt cartoon of the doctor on the inside of its wooden box.

Rush on the APA logo, and as the face of a brand of cigars

While the Rush books the Biddle family had made were private, a copy or two leaked out to historians over the next decades. This led first to a 1918 philosophy thesis on Rush's contributions to education, and then a 1934 biography, and a long biographical chapter in a history of "doctors on horseback." Each of these raised a theme that would run through writing on Rush: a strong belief that history had misunderstood him; had not taken him seriously enough as a founder, a writer, a teacher, and a revolutionary in politics, medicine, religion, public health, and philosophy.

In the early 1940s, the last of the children of Julia Williams Rush Biddle died, and the estate hired a Manhattan auction house to hold one of the largest sales of Revolutionary and post-Revolutionary "signature" documents ever. There were more than nine hundred lots, sold at three massive auctions during the summer and fall of 1943, involving multiple examples of previously unknown signed letters from every major and minor Founding Father. The sale literally altered the history of American history, not only leading to new writing on Rush but also fueling a revival of interest in John and Abigail Adams and other founders.

Many of the most important items were, luckily, purchased by publicly minded institutions. The autobiography, which went for $7,000 ($99,200), ended up in the hands of the American Philosophical Society. But many other lots were bought by private investors, and some were never seen again—and live on, so far, only in the few lines quoted from them in the auction catalogues, or the handwritten recollections of those paying attention to the sale for historical reasons.

One of those was a thirty-two-year-old Harvard-trained English-literature professor named Lyman H. Butterfield, who was teaching at Franklin & Marshall College in Lancaster, Pennsylvania. An indefatigable researcher, Butterfield had no hobbies and didn't drive a car. His obsession was exploring intellectual and historical connections; his wife, Betty, sometimes worked with him. (They had two young children: their son, Fox, grew up to be a famous *New York Times* correspondent.) Butterfield convinced Franklin & Marshall to acquire, from the person who bought it at the Biddle auction, a previously unknown 1787 letter Rush wrote to his mother-in-law about his visit to Lancaster for the inauguration of the college. Butterfield published the letter and an analysis in 1944, and was soon hired by the Philosophical Society to undertake a survey of the newly fortified Rush papers, to commemorate the two hundredth anniversary of the doctor's birthday in 1945.

Butterfield began publishing the next year: a thirty-five-page survey of the letters, as well as things he found in the collection that delighted him. He regaled friends with Rush's description of his literary dining in London, and then produced a little book not much longer than its title: *Benjamin Rush's Reminiscences of Boswell & Johnson: Originally Published in the Port Folio and from Thence Newly and Faithfully Corrected for the First Time by L.H. Butterfield, Esqr. on the Occasion of a Dinner Given at the Four Oaks Farm for a Company of Ladies & Gentlemen who Assembled on Dr. Johnson's Natal Day to Do Him Honour Sept. 18, 1946, Over Against the Traffick Circle Near Somerville, in New Jersey.*

Butterfield soon moved to Princeton, as an associate editor of the Thomas Jefferson letters, but he also undertook the editing of the first collection of Rush's letters. He had become fascinated and perplexed by why his contributions to medicine, literature, politics, philosophy, religion, and science were not better known, and he churned out papers and talks examining Rush's life over the next years. He also assisted other Rush scholars, including the authors of two books that changed the way Rush was viewed and, for many, brought him into view for the first time.

One was *Bring Out Your Dead* (1949), a lively, popular account of Rush through the prism of the yellow fever epidemic. Written by John Powell, a Philadelphia library director who had previously published a little-known biography of Richard Rush, *Bring Out Your Dead* is one of the landmark books in the genre of narratives built around microreporting on a historic event. It sold briskly and reads like any such modern book, with one exception: Powell declined to include any specific citations, proudly declaring that "all footnotes have been cut out of this book, under the impression that they annoy more readers than they help." He included a list of sources, but without details of how any were used. This is unfortunate because Powell was an opinionated storyteller. He described Rush as "Philadelphia's most amazing citizen . . . the greatest among great teachers . . . a father of modern psychiatry . . . founder of an American tradition . . . [and] to this day the most important single figure in the history of medicine in the new world." He also suggested that Rush acted as he did during the epidemic because "he had no common sense," which sounded more like a line from Cobbett than a historian's synthesis.

Powell might have had a different take on Rush if he had been able to read the book being prepared at the same time as his own: a new, extraordinarily well-annotated version of Rush's autobiography, with the passages Richard had cut out restored, and with all his known commonplace books appended, also annotated. *The Autobiography of Benjamin Rush* came out just months before *Bring Out Your Dead*, edited by a renowned physician and scientist in Baltimore, fifty-nine-year-old Dr. George Washington Corner, who ran the Department of Embryology at the Carnegie Institute and was one of the researchers responsible for the development of the birth control pill. Corner's book provided the first in-depth picture of Rush's life as seen through his own personal writing.

Dr. Corner and Lyman Butterfield shared much information, insight, and Rush-iana during these years; the autobiography project and the letters project fueled each other. Butterfield's two-volume, 1,295-page book *Letters of Benjamin Rush* was published in 1951. It was a landmark in revealing Rush as a writer, doctor, and man. It also established Butterfield as what the *New York Times* would later call a "heroic" scholar, who had helped create "a new standard of historical research that emphasized thoroughness and painstaking annotation of all available material."

Butterfield hoped that after his book was finished, he would be able to produce what he referred to as a "Union Catalogue" of not only all of Rush's writing, but all the letters written to him. Butterfield noted that such catalogs were already being created around Abraham Lincoln, Theodore Roosevelt, and Thomas Jefferson. Washington had been catalogued from the moment he died. He assumed this would be how all history would be done in the future, to "prevent waste and duplication of effort by scholars."

Unfortunately for Rush's legacy, everything Butterfield learned editing the doctor's letters led to the job offer of a lifetime: he was hired as editor in chief of the John Adams letters in 1954, charged with doing for the Adams family what he had trained to do in the Rush archives. His lifetime of work on the Adams letters is one of the biggest reasons why Americans today know so much about John and Abigail Adams. Butterfield was the consultant for *The Adams Chronicles*, the series that PBS created in 1976 for the bicentennial, and when David McCullough published his vastly popular biography of Adams in 2001, Butterfield was the first person he credited.

Corner's *Autobiography* and Butterfield's *Letters* became the standard sources on Rush, but they were locked in their times of publication, 1948 and 1951. When Butterfield predictably acquired more letters by Rush after his book came out, they were not added to the book, but rather published in harder-to-find Pennsylvania history journals. The same was true of letters to and from Rush family members, including the correspondence between John Adams and Richard Rush and between Julia Rush and Abigail Adams.

The only major piece of new broad scholarship was in 1966, a compilation of the letters between Rush and Adams after they reconnected in 1805, titled *The Spur of Fame*. While the editors, John Schutz and Douglass Adair, were more interested in Adams than Rush, the two-hundred-eighty-five-page book was lively, and suggested much more could be learned by putting the annotated letters of the Founding Fathers together, as the dialogues they were. (The "Founders Online" project from the National Archive has, since 2010, allowed researchers to do the same with the work of all the major founders, as it has brought together their papers in digital transcription.)

In the meantime, a book on the Rush-Cobbett battle and trial, *A Verdict for the Doctor*, was published in 1958, and a biography of Rush by a physician in 1966. In 1972, prominent historian David Hawke published an incisive but idiosyncratic Rush biography that chose to stop telling the doctor's story in 1790, when Benjamin Franklin died (after which four more pages cover the last twenty-three years of Rush's life). Two later, smaller books soon followed on Rush's religious and philosophical views.

More significant to Rush's medical legacy was the work, from the 1960s into the 1980s, of Dr. Eric "Ted" Carlson, at Weill Cornell Medical Center in New York. Starting in 1958, Carlson ran what would become the Institute for the History of Psychiatry and its Oskar Diethelm Library. Carlson wrote and cowrote many papers about Rush's life and his medical and mental health ideas, and was the first to wrestle with John Rush's mental health. He also edited two invaluable scholarly books, one bringing Rush's "moral faculty" essay new attention and another publishing for the first time, with full annotation, many of Rush's lectures on the mind.

What Butterfield did for Rush as a Revolutionary historian, and Hawke did for Rush's political half-life, Carlson did for Rush as medical historian. Later in their careers, Butterfield and Carlson each began work on his own Rush passion project. Carlson's book was to be more a medical intellectual history, while Lyman Butterfield dreamed of a new, full biography, which surely would have gone where no Rush book had gone before. Not only was Butterfield the world's expert on Rush, but he had, almost as a hobby, kept his hand in the doctor's world during all his years editing Adams. He still talked about the doctor's underappreciated story and contributions, and he had reams of outlines and exhaustive notes to himself about where the book should go.

NOT LONG AFTER his retirement in 1975, Butterfield realized that the Rush family had been holding out on him. Just after the bicentennial, the doctor's most socially prominent descendant—Julia Rush Biddle Henry, whose skeletal frame and larger-than-life hairdos had attracted fashion photographers for years, including Diane Arbus—suddenly produced from some hiding place in her Chestnut Hill mansion a large collection of letters to and from Dr. Rush and Julia that nobody had known existed. They were donated to the Rosenbach Library in Philadelphia.

These were, clearly, from Julia Rush's most private stash, many from her husband or her mother. Butterfield and his colleague Whitfield Bell, a historian for the American Philosophical Society, arranged for seventeen of them—the courtship letters Julia had stitched together—to be published in 1979 in a small private book called *My Dearest Julia*.

By then, Butterfield was in ill health, and—surprisingly—very little scholarship has been done with these letters since, even after more letters Julia had kept secret turned up several years later in a donation to the Philosophical Society. Among these two donations were the letters Julia wrote back to Rush during the yellow fever epidemic, and the shocking letter Rush wrote to Julia in early 1778 about the possibility of forcing out Washington, which my researchers and I transcribed, we believe, for the first time. But there is much more historical work to be done on this collection, and more Rush-related letters remain in private hands.

Lyman Butterfield died in 1982 at the age of seventy-two. His research was boxed up and donated to the Massachusetts Historical Society, where nobody unsealed his voluminous Rush files for more than thirty years. I had the fascinating honor of being the first to request to see what he gathered and wrote. He hadn't gotten very far in his book, but his notes and outlines proved an invaluable guide to the arc of Rush's life and his connections to Adams and other founders. Butterfield also left notes concerning letters and writings that nobody has seen since he did.

I had a similar experience with the research of Ted Carlson, who died suddenly in 1992—after which his files sat in storage at the Diethelm Library for decades, untouched, I believe, until I asked to see them. Carlson left a mostly complete manuscript of his book using Rush's life and ideas to explore the history of medical philosophy. While intriguing, his work is unfortunately unsourced; he left no notes or citations. The same is true for an orphaned Rush biography by Philadelphia historian Claire Fox—author of the first major bibliography of Rush's writing—who was writing it when she became ill with Alzheimer's. Fox died in 2010 at the age of eighty-six; her research materials were not preserved, and the only manuscript copy of her book, *Lancet and Pen*, is in the College of Physicians library.

Since the loss of Butterfield and Carlson, there haven't been many Rush-obsessed academics. In the late 1980s, historian Michael Meranze edited a new edition of the collection Rush published during his own life, *Essays Literary, Moral and Philosophical*. And in 1993, on the two-hundredth anniversary of the yellow fever epidemic, the College of Physicians held a conference called "'A Melancholy Sense of Devastation': the Public Response to the 1793 Philadelphia Yellow Fever Epidemic," which led to an engaging group of papers representing some of the most modern scientific and medical assessments of Rush's ideas and treatments, and offering researchers and writers a new prism through which to view his life and times.

More recent books include a slim, speculative volume on the dreams of Adams and Rush by a psychoanalyst, two general biographies, and a legal study by Philadelphia-area literature professor Linda Myrsiades dissecting the Rush/Cobbett trial.

With few exceptions, the major works of Rush scholarship are long out of print. Some libraries have them, but mostly you buy old copies on eBay and hope the covers are still attached. The letters Rush wrote to John and Abigail Adams, Jefferson, Franklin, Madison, and Washington are now included in the Founders Online archive with fresh transcriptions. But these represent just some 230 missives among well over a thousand known to exist. And, unlike the founders with major academic papers projects, none of Rush's other autobiographical writing, which connects so many dots between founder stories, is included except as footnote references. So Rush researchers often have to settle for scholarship that hasn't been updated since 1951.

In 2014, Dickinson College held a conference called "The Republics of Benjamin Rush," to mark (a year late) the two-hundredth anniversary of the doctor's death, organized by historians at Dickinson and the McNeil Center for Early American Studies at the University of Pennsylvania. Not only were fifteen original papers written for the conference, but five scholars were invited to respond to them with prepared remarks and discussion. That meant twenty fresh, thoughtful pieces of Rush scholarship introduced over two days, which triggered so many provocative discussions and suggested all kinds of intriguing next steps.

The conference was not recorded, unfortunately, and only six of the papers were later published in a special issue of *Early American Studies*. So you really had to be there. Luckily, I was—the lone non-academic presenter, at the very beginning of my book research. Among the other presenters were editors from the Thomas Jefferson Papers at Princeton and the George Washington Papers at the University of Virginia. As we spoke, it was impossible not to wonder if there would ever be such a project to take the Rush papers as seriously as those of the other founders and their families—creating a digital version of the Rush Union Catalogue that Lyman Butterfield dreamed of. It could make the writings by, to, and from Rush as accessible as they are enduring, challenging, lively, and occasionally infuriating.

At the end of the conference, we all filed out of the main entrance of the Stern Center where, fifty feet ahead, you can't miss the bronze statue of Benjamin Rush. It's an exact copy of the one the American Medical Association commissioned for Teddy Roosevelt, but it's in a much more accessible location, on a low pedestal you can even sit on. Which I did, and the campus photographer took a picture of me there, still wearing my name tag. It reminds me of how electrified I felt after that conference, buzzing with determination to bring Rush's astounding story to the public, and utterly stunned at how much work I had ahead of me.

NOTES

Abbreviations Used

Characters:

BR: Benjamin Rush

JSR: Julia Stockton Rush

JA: John Adams

BF: Benjamin Franklin

TJ: Thomas Jefferson

GW: George Washington

RR: Richard Rush

JD: John Dickinson

AA: Abigail Adams

JQA: John Quincy Adams

Major Sources:

Letters: *Letters of Benjamin Rush*, edited by L. H. Butterfield, American Philosophical Society/Princeton University Press, 1951.

Autobiography: *The Autobiography of Benjamin Rush, His "Travels Through Life" Together with His* Commonplace Book *for 1789–1813*, edited by George W. Corner, American Philosophical Society/Princeton University Press, 1948.

My Dearest Julia: The Love Letters of Dr. Benjamin Rush to Julia Stockton, Rosenbach Foundation/Neal Watson Academic Publications, 1979.

Founders Online: Founders Online, the National Archives' central online database to access papers of Washington, Jefferson, Franklin, Madison, Hamilton, and the extended Adams family—and many with whom they corresponded, https://founders.archives.gov; it is the easiest place to view the most up-to-date transcriptions of letters and diaries—so even though Butterfield is a primary source, the versions of the letters he edited that appear on Founders are more completely cross-referenced than his 1951 edits, and are more accurately transcribed. Founders post many letters as "Early Access," meaning they have been transcribed professionally but not yet annotated or prepared for publication. We have marked these "EA," and since the Founders is often updated, they were rechecked in early 2018.

Butterfield Papers: Lyman H. Butterfield Papers, Massachusetts Historical Society, includes all of Butterfield's working papers for his many Rush-related publications in the 1940s and 1950s (before he became editor in chief of the John Adams Papers), and his previously unknown files for the book he hoped to write on Rush, and the Rush Union Catalog he envisioned so that Rush's papers would get similar attention and scholarship as those of other major Founding Fathers.

Hawke: *Benjamin Rush: Revolutionary Gadfly* by David Freeman Hawke, Bobbs-Merril, 1971; the landmark twentieth-century biography of Rush (which stops in 1790, and was also written before the last major caches of Rush family correspondence—including Rush's love letters to Julia—was discovered beginning in the late 1970s).

Note: Many of Rush's writings were published multiple times, sometimes in multiple versions, and there were changes even between when a piece of writing appeared in a newspaper and was then made into a pamphlet or included in a book. Wherever possible I cite the earliest possible version, and re-create the writing of that edition.

Rush Papers Major Repositories:

APS American Philosophical Society, Philadelphia

LCP Library Company of Philadelphia

HSP Historical Society of Pennsylvania, Philadelphia

RSB Rosenbach Library, Philadelphia

COP College of Physicians, Philadelphia

MHS Massachusetts Historical Society, Boston

Prologue

1 **well-worn carriage**: JA, entry for August 29, 1774, Diary, Founders Online EA.

1 **"sufficient"**: JA to AA, August 28, 1774, ibid.

1 **six shirts**: JA, entry for August 30, ibid.

1 **Frankford**: JA, entry for August 29, 1774, ibid.

2 **"You must not utter"**: JA to Timothy Pickering, August 6, 1822, Founders Online.

2 **one of the only**: Ibid. There are several retellings of this meeting, and in the last one there is mention of another attendee, John Bayard, who was not elected to the First Continental Congress, but was elected to a later Congress.

2 **"activity of intellect"**: Hall, *The Port Folio* 18, p. 311.

3 **"peculiar happiness"**: Rush, *Autobiography*, p. 55. Peculiar happiness was one of Rush's favorite phrases; this is its first appearance in his autobiography, but it is often used in his letters.

4 **"cold and reserved"**: Adams, entry for August 29, 1774, Diary, Founders Online; Rush, *Autobiography*, p. 110.

4 **"fine beyond description"**: Adams, entry for September 14, 1774, Diary, Massachusetts Historical Society.

5 **"Fatal experience"**: *Pennsylvania Packet*, April 22, 1777.

5 **"republican machines"**: This phrase, which Rush began using in the mid-1780s in discussions about the kind of Americans public education should turn people into, first appeared in his 1786 essay "A Plan for the Establishment of Public Schools."

5 **"science, religion, liberty"**: Rush, "Moral Faculty," p. 37.

6 **"We are indeed a"**: BR to JA, June 27, 1812, Founders Online EA.

7 **"He aimed well"**: Rush, *Autobiography*, p. 148.

7 **"I read with delight"**: TJ to BR, April 8, 1813, Founders Online.

8 **"Mr. Washington would never"**: JA to TP, August 6, 1822, ibid EA.

8 **"our armies"**: Ibid.

9 **"American Hippocrates"**: This phrase appears in many of Rush's obituaries, as well as in writings during his life and long after, either to praise Rush or criticize him (the latter compare him to Hippocrates to make fun of his use of bloodletting). A good example of the phrase as praise can be found in Gross, *American Medical Biography*, p. 404.

9 **"bigots in religion"**: TJ to James Mease, August 17, 1816, Founders Online.

10 **"shudder"**: JA to James Mease, August 24, 1816, ibid EA.

10 **"Father of American Surgery"**: Gross, *Eminent American Physicians*, p. 404.

11 **"acceptable men"**: Rush, "Thoughts on Common Sense, April 3, 1791," in Rush, *Essays, Literary Moral & Philosophical*, p. 256.

Chapter 1

15 **"first *unwelcome* noise"**: BR to JA, July 13, 1812, in Rush, *Letters*, p. 1150.

15 **Christmas Eve, 1745**: The date of Rush's birth (and his age at certain milestones) is recorded different ways by different sources, in part because he wasn't always exact in describing his own age, but also because the British Empire adopted the Gregorian Calendar in 1752 and that technically moved it to January 4, 1746 (in what is called "new style"). There is no indication he celebrated his birthday any day but Christmas Eve, and we have attempted to always fact-check his age against the "old style" December 24, 1745, birthday.

15 **"conversations about wolves"**: Ibid., pp. 1150–151.

15 **"pious people"**: Ibid., p. 1151.

16 **"a talent for observation"**: Rush, *Autobiography*, pp. 26–27, 147.

16 **"small but deep creek"**: Hawke, *Rush*, pp. 8–9; BR to JA, July 13, 1812, in Rush, *Letters*, p. 1150.

17 **"Those who knew me"**: Rush, *Autobiography*, p. 36.

17 **property in Philadelphia**: Ibid., p. 27.

17 **decided to leave the farm**: Hawke, *Rush*, p. 8.

17 **Philadelphia had just overtaken**: Friis, "Series of Population Maps," pp. 463–70.

18 **just published a paper**: Isaacson, *Franklin*, pp. 136–39.

18 **number 82 N. Front Street**: Personal correspondence with J. M. Duffin (Senior Archivist, University of Pennsylvania Archives) based on his innovative Mapping West Philadelphia website, www.archives.upenn.edu/WestPhila1777/, as well as city directories and insurance documents; he and the site helped us determine all Rush family addresses.

18 **wide avenue**: Smith, "Philadelphia: The Athens of America," in *Life in Early Philadelphia*, pp. 3–29.

18 **either side**: Roach, "Benjamin Franklin Slept Here," p. 173.

18 **Christ Church**: "History and People," Christ Church Philadelphia, https://www.christchurchphila.org/history/.

18 **Franklin worshipped there**: "Christ Church Seating Plan, 1760,"

Greater Philadelphia Geohistory Network, http://www.philageohistory.org/rdic-images/view-image.cfm/ChristChurch.PewChart1760.Front.

18 **Presbyterian . . . on the farm**: D'Elia, *Rush*, p. 9.

18 **"heard divine worship"**: Rush, *Autobiography*, pp. 162–63.

18 **Pennsylvania State House**: Nash, *The Liberty Bell*, pp. 1–3.

18 **port of Philadelphia**: Childs, "The Port of Philadelphia," in *Philadelphia City Archives Newsletter*, no. 26, October 1975.

19 **the Dock Creek**: Olton, "Philadelphia's First Environmental Crisis," p. 92.

19 **John Rush unexpectedly died**: Rush, *Autobiography*, p. 27.

20 **Father and son were buried**: Author communication with Christ Church Burial Ground coordinator John Hopkins.

20 **"a likely negroe woman"**: *Pennsylvania Gazette*, October 24, 1751.

20 **expanded version**: *Pennsylvania Gazette*, December 31, 1751.

20 **An ad several years later**: *Pennsylvania Gazette*, August 21, 1755.

21 **auction stand**: Author's correspondence, Anna "Coxey" Toogood, historian, Cultural Resources Management, Independence National Historical Park (INHP), 1/8/2018 (the location of the main auction stand at this time is often misidentified in historical books, because it later moved to the better-known London Coffee House at the corner of Front and Market).

21 **"at the Sign of the Blazing Star"**: Rush, *Autobiography*, p. 27n17.

21 **quit Christ Church**: Rush, *Autobiography*, p. 163.

21 **Tennent**: Tennent, *The Danger of an Unconverted Ministry.*

22 **"genius for learning"**: Mason, *Selections of the Late Susanna Mason*, pp. 47–53.

22 **"a young man of promising"**: Rush, *Autobiography*, pp. 27–28.

22 **china shop**: *Pennsylvania Gazette*, August 21, 1755.

22 **"rough, unkind"**: Rush, *Autobiography*, pp. 27, 167. Dates are deduced from Rush's mention of their being married for sixteen years and Morris's death in 1771.

22 **West Nottingham Academy**: Rush, *Autobiography*, pp. 28–29n23.

22 **The school building**: "Then and Now," West Nottingham Academy, https://www.wna.org/page/about/then-and-now.

23 **"a doubt"**: Rush, *Autobiography*, pp. 29–31.

24 **"early part"**: Ibid., p. 164.

24 **"occasioned by bad health"**: Ibid., pp. 32–33.

24 **College of New Jersey**: McLachlan, *Princetonians, 1748–1768*, p. 319.

25 **fifty-eight students**: Ibid., p. xix.

25 **Samuel Davies**: Rush, *Autobiography*, p. 35; "Samuel Davies" and "Jonathan Edwards" in The Presidents of Princeton University, 2013, https://www.Princeton.edu/pub/presidents/.

25 **"It was my happy lot"**: Rush, *Autobiography*, p. 36.

26 **"should be done directly"**: Rush, *Sixteen Introductory Lectures*, p. 355.

26 **Richard Stockton**: Bill, *House Called Morven*, pp. 16, 24.

26 **Stockton likely reached out**: Rush, *Autobiography*, p. 116.

26 **Stockton family**: Bill, *House Called Morven*, p. 9.

27 **"so fruitful and uncommon"**: Annis Boudinot Stockton, "Addressed to Col. Schuyler," *New York Mercury*, January 9, 1758; Stockton, *Only for the Eye of a Friend*, p. 84.

28 **Morven**: Bill, *House Called Morven*, p. 23.

28 **Rush attended the valedictory**: Leitch, *Princeton Companion*, p. 110.

28 **"imbibe and cherish"**: Davies, *Religion and Public Spirit*, p. 7.

28 **"ingenious"**: *Pennsylvania Gazette*, October 9, 1760.

Chapter 2

29 **study the law**: Rush, *Autobiography*, pp. 36–38.

30 **apprenticeship was the only**: Radbill, "Medicine in 1776," pp. 1–8; Blanco, "Diary of Jonathan Potts," pp. 19–21.

30 **do no Damage**: James Franklin: Indenture of Apprenticeship, November 5, 1740, Founders Online.

31 **Popular medicines included**: Hawke, *Rush*, pp. 27–28; Watson, *Annals of Philadelphia*, pp. 370–91.

31 **For bloodletting**: Hawke, *Rush*, pp. 27–28. DePalma, "Bloodletting," p. 136.

32 **Cupping meant attaching**: Hawke, *Rush*, p. 28.

32 **indigent**: Hawke, *Rush*, p. 28; Williams, *America's First Hospital*, pp. 7–15.

33 **the principles of "modern"**: Brodsky, *Rush*, p. 29.

33 **keep the accounting books**: Rush, *Autobiography*, p. 38.

33 **waking hours**: Ibid.

33 **Herman Boerhaave**: Appendix I: "Medical Theories," Rush, *Autobiography*, p. 362.

33 **too "humoral"**: Ibid.

34 **one discovery**: Powers, *Inventing Chemistry*, p. 108.

34 **"because God was their"**: Rush, *Autobiography*, p. 79.

34 **Thomas Sydenham**: Ibid., p. 38; Bleakley, "Force and Presence."

34 **"laudanum"**: Cook, "Sydenham, Thomas," https://doi.org/10.1093/ref:odnb/26864.

34 **A murderous array**: Bleakley, "Force and Presence," pp. 3–4.

34 **professionally criticized**: Rush, *Letters*, p. 700n12.

34 **Rush toiled**: Rush, *Autobiography*, pp. 38–39.

35 **Davies had preached**: Davies, *Sermons on Important Subjects* 2, p. 139.

35 **"When the silver locks"**: BR to Enoch Green, 1761, in Rush, *Letters*, p. 3.

35 **implored Reverend Finley**: Leitch, "Samuel Finley," *A Princeton Companion*, p. 182.

35 **"perfectly cured"**: Rush, *Autobiography*, p. 28.

35 **seeing twenty a day**: BR to JSR, September 1, 1793, in Rush, *Letters*, p. 646. BR quotes a record from his experience as an apprentice.

35 **"seized with a sudden"**: Redman, *An account of the yellow fever*, p. 15.

36 **"heroic medicine"**: Rush, *Autobiography*, p. 695.

36 **role of a physician**: D'Elia, *Philosopher of the American Revolution*, p. 19.

36 **"cases where the efforts"**: Rush, "Natural History of Medicine Among the Indians," *Medical Inquiries*, p. 35.

36 **"malt liquors and wine"**: BR to Vine Utley, June 25, 1812, in Rush, *Letters*, p. 1142.

37 **William Shippen, Jr.**: Corner, *William Shippen, Jr.*, p. 96.

37 **"What a pity"**: Eve and Jones, "Extracts from Journal of Eve," p. 26.

38 **"the most dry"**: Norris, *Early History of Medicine*, p. 38.

39 **coroner's jury had handed over**: Hawke, *Rush*, p. 32.

39 **"Dr. Shippen's anatomical"**: Corner, *William Shippen, Jr.*, p. 100.

39 **he not marry**: BR to Thomas Bradford, April 15, 1768, in Rush, *Letters*, p. 53.

40 **"the favor of God"**: Rush, *Autobiography*, p. 164.

40 **"friend and master"**: BR to John Morgan, July 27, 1768, in Rush, *Letters*, p. 62.

40 **Dr. John Morgan**: Hawke, *Rush*, p. 35.

40 **Rush knew about**: Bell, *Patriot-Improvers*, sketches for "John Morgan," "John Redman," and "William Shippen."

41 **"affable and courteous"**: Morgan, *Journal*, pp. 26–27.

41 **reached out to trustees**: Bell, *Patriot-Improvers*, p. 331.

41 **"low drudgery"**: Bell, *John Morgan: Continental Doctor*, p. 113.

42 **controversial proposal**: Hawke, *Rush*, pp. 36–37.

42 **"who promised to unite"**: "Shippen to the Trustees of the College, Sept. 17, 1765," in Corner, *William Shippen, Jr.* pp. 109–10.

42 **he privately queried**: Louis, "Shippen's Unsuccessful Attempt," pp. 218–20.

42 **his superior**: Corner, *William Shippen, Jr.*, pp. 108–11.

43 **As a keen reader**: Hawke, *Rush*, p. 40.

43 **"the only woman"**: BR to Thomas Bradford, April 15, 1768, in Rush, *Letters*, p. 53; BR to Thomas Bradford, June 3, 1768; ibid., p. 60.

44 **"O *Franklin, Franklin*"**: BR to Ebenezer Hazard, November 8, 1765, in Rush, *Letters*, pp. 18–19; Van Doren, *Franklin*, pp. 320–22, 330.

44 **"anxious impatience"**: BR to Ebenezer Hazard, March 29, 1766; ibid., p. 23.

44 **"Americans are the sons"**: BR to Ebenezer Hazard, October 22, 1768; ibid., p. 68.

45 **"sat up with him"**: Rush, *Autobiography*, p. 33.

45 **"the hand of heaven"**: Ibid., p. 37.

45 **"by the hand"**: BR to Ebenezer Hazard, July 2, 1766, in Rush, *Letters*, p. 24.

45 **"the distressing office"**: Rush, *Autobiography*, pp. 25n and 33.

Chapter 3

46 **At noon**: Rush, *Edinburgh Journal*, LBP, p. 2.

46 **Jonathan Potts**: Blanco, "Diary of Jonathan Potts," p. 124.

46 **"billows swell"**: BR to Thomas Bradford, September 2, 1766, in Rush, *Letters*, p. 26.

47 **"with the greatest compassion"**: Blanco, "Diary of Jonathan Potts," p. 123.

47 **"convusion fitts"**: Rush, *Autobiography*, p. 40.

48 **They arrived in Edinburgh**: Rush, *Edinburgh Journal*, LBP, pp. 2–23.

49 **To earn a degree**: Rieder and Louis-Courvoisier, "Enlightened Physicians," pp. 584–90.

49 **institutes of medicine**: Jackson, *Introductory lecture to the course of the institutes*, pp. 1–8.

49 **Dr. Joseph Black**: Rush, *Autobiography*, p. 42n11.

49 **Morgan had told him**: BR to John Morgan, November 16, 1766, in Rush, *Letters*, pp. 28–31.

49 **"first school of physic"**: Rush, *Edinburgh Journal*, LBP, pp. 54–55.

50 **the very top professor**: Thomson, *Lectures and Writings of William Cullen, M.D.*, 1, pp. 144–61.

50 **different medical systems**: Rush, *Autobiography*, pp. 362–65.

50 **"warmly reproved"**: Rush, *Edinburgh Journal*, LBP, pp. 61–63.

50 **"wanting"**: Ibid., pp. 66–68.

51 **"deep and affecting sense"**: Rush, *Autobiography*, p. 164.

51 **"Letters of recommendation"**: BF to BR and Jonathan Potts, December 20, 1766, Founders Online.

52 **"ingenious moral essays"**: Rush, *Edinburgh Journal*, LBP, p. 23.

52 **"rather ungenteel"**: Ibid.

52 **pining for Polly Fisher**: Rush, *Letters*, p. 55n1.

52 **Gracey Richardson**: Blanco, "Diary of Jonathan Potts," pp. 122, 126.

53 **Richard Stockton**: Butterfield, "Witherspoon," pp. 26–27.

53 **"hydrophobia"**: Richard Stockton to Annis Boudinot Stockton, March 17, 1767, in Butterfield, *Witherspoon*, pp. 32–33.

54 **"continued under such Distress"**: John Witherspoon to Richard/Annis Stockton, April 18, 1767, ibid., p. 39.

54 **preaching he considered**: BR to Jonathan Bayard Smith, April 30, 1767, in Rush, *Letters*, pp. 37–38; Butterfield, *Witherspoon*, p. 42.

54 **"ruined"**: BR to John Witherspoon, April 23, 1767, in Rush, *Letters*, p. 36.

54 **"with much more humanity"**: Witherspoon to BR, April 29, 1767, in Butterfield, "Witherspoon," pp. 41–42.

54 **"filled with the greatest Anxiety"**: Witherspoon to BR, August 4, 1767, ibid., pp. 49–51.

55 **"even exceeded Your"**: Witherspoon to BR, September 8, 1768, ibid., p. 78.

Chapter 4

56 **"blessed creature know"**: BR to Thomas Bradford, April 15, 1768, in Rush, *Letters*, p. 53.

57 **asking for more assurance**: This exchange is inferred from Rush's follow-up letter. Bradford, June 3, 1768; ibid., p. 60.

57 **"the Charms of youth"**: Rush, *Edinburgh Journal*, LBP, pp. 82–92.

57 **lyrical singing voice**: BR to Lady Jane Wishart Belsches, April 21, 1784, in Rush, *Letters*, pp. 328–29.

57 **"The Hermit"**: Goldsmith, *The Hermit*, pp. 14–42.

58 **"vomited an acid-tasting"**: Musto, "Rush's Medical Thesis," pp. 121–38.

58 **mentor Dr. John Morgan**: BR to John Morgan, January 20, 1768, in Rush, *Letters*, p. 49; BR to Morgan, July 27, 1768; ibid., p. 61.

58 **Philadelphia Medical Society**: Bell, "John Morgan," *Patriot-Improvers*, pp. 1–15.

58 **"theory of physic"**: BR to Jonathan Bayard Smith, April 30, 1767, in Rush, *Letters*, p. 41.

58 **Morgan and Dr. William Shippen, Jr.**: Bell, *Patriot-Improvers*, pp. 16–31, 331.

59 **"to prefix your name"**: BR to John Morgan, January 20, 1768, in Rush, *Letters*, p. 50.

59 **THOSE DISTINGUISHED MEN**: Musto, "Rush's Medical Thesis," p. 131.

59 **"I am sorry to find"**: BR to John Morgan July 27, 1768, in Rush, *Letters*, p. 61.

60 **Haymarket**: Hawke, *Rush*, p. 65; Rush, *Autobiography*, pp. 52–54.

60 **landmark study**: Rush, *Autobiography*, pp. 52–53.

60 **"the favorite physician"**: Rush, *Autobiography*, p. 54.

60 **"medical conversation party"**: Ibid., pp. 53–54; BR to John Morgan, October 21, 1768, in Rush, *Letters*, p. 66.

61 **dream dinner**: Rush, *Autobiography*, pp. 58–59.

61 **Dr. Samuel Johnson**: Ibid.; *Reminiscences of Boswell and Johnson*, pp. 5–10.

61 **Oliver Goldsmith**: John Foster, *The Life and Times of Oliver Goldsmith*, 1. pp. 75–76.

61 **"The Club"**: Chancellor, *The XVIIIth Century in London*, p. 127.

61 **"Don't mind them"**: BR to James Abercrombie, April 22, 1793, in Rush, *Letters*, p. 632.

62 **dine with Oliver Goldsmith**: Rush, *Autobiography*, p. 60.

62 **"a kind of Coffee house"**: Ibid., pp. 62–63; Butterfield, "American Interests of the Firm," pp. 284–86, 290.

63 **Catharine Macaulay**: Ibid., p. 287; BR to Catherine Macaulay, January 18, 1769, in Rush, *Letters*, p. 71n1.

63 **John Wilkes**: Rush, *Autobiography*, p. 61.

63 **"an enthusiast for"**: BR to unknown recipient, January 19, 1769, in Rush, *Letters*, p. 72.

63 **"sacred ground"**: BR to Ebenezer Hazard, October 22, 1768, ibid., p. 67.

Chapter 5

64 **Rush's journals**: Rush, *Autobiography*, pp. 58–59n52, 66n78. In Lyman Butterfield's research notes, there is a card that reads "In MS Journal of Trip to France he concludes "My observations upon London etc are the subject of another volume." Butterfield then writes "Where is it?" Good question.

64 **"it was my peculiar"**: Rush, *Autobiography*, p. 55.

64 **a four-story Georgian**: Huntington, "Franklin's Last Home," pp. 49–52.

64 **"once took me to Court"**: Rush, *Autobiography*, p. 55.

64 **a line of credit**: Ibid., p. 66.

65 **self-control issues**: Isaacson, *Franklin*, pp. 119–21.

65 **Charles Willson Peale**: Ibid., pp. 242–43.

66 **"Our reason for going"**: BF to Mary Stevenson, October 20, 1768, Founders Online.

66 **"young Physician"**: BF to Smith, Wright, & Gray, February 13, 1769, Founders Online.

66 **"delicate act"**: Rush, *Autobiography*, p. 74.

67 **introductory letters**: Ibid., p. 67.

67 **Dr. Jacques Dubourg**: Owen, "Jacques Barbeu-Dubourg," pp. 331–33.

67 **"ladies and gentlemen of"**: Rush, *Autobiography*, pp. 67–68.

67 **"Here Ladies and Gentlemen"**: Rush, *Paris Journal*, LBP, p. 17.

67 **Denis Diderot**: Rush, *Autobiography*, p. 69.

67 **"the highest degrees"**: Rush, *Paris Journal*, LBP, pp. 23–25.

68 **"Much has been said"**: Ibid., pp. 9–10.

69 **"speechless"**: Rush, *Autobiography*, pp. 73–76.

69 **"uncommon depression"**: Ibid., p. 78.

Chapter 6

71 **"unfortunate in her marriage"**: Rush, *Autobiography*, p. 78.

71 **"inaugural address"**: James Gibson, *Dr. Bodo Otto and the Medical Background of the American Revolution*, pp. 186–91.

72 **"vanity"**: Thomas Coombe to Benjamin Rush, July 20, 1768, Rush Manuscripts 33, p. 44, LCP.

72 **"pursued his studies"**: Butterfield, "Reputation of Rush," p. 4.

72 **"When a misunderstanding"**: Quotes from this letter are from Gibson's transcription (on which Butterfield relied as well), about which Gibson himself comments that "the grammatical construction of this letter is so involved that it is difficult to understand, and impossible to parse. In order that it might be more easily read, some liberty has been taken with the arrangement . . ." The letter itself is in Rush manuscripts, vol. 25, p. 1.

73 **"I cannot say I ever"**: Flexner, *Doctors on Horseback*, p. 63.

73 **first professor of chemistry**: Hawke, *Rush*, p. 86.

74 **Lydia Hyde**: Rush, Ledger Book, 1769–1883. LCP; Wulf, *Not All Wives*, pp.184–87.

74 **Dr. James Bayard**: Morton and Woodbury, *History of Pennsylvania Hospital*, p. 526.

74 **Capt. John MacPherson**: Merriam, *Macpherson of Philadelphia*, p. 6.

74 **he had suddenly decided**: Ibid., p. 8; John Macpherson to the Public, March 10, 1787, Nead Papers, 1785–1789, LCP.

77 **in its basement**: Williams, *America's First Hospital*, pp. 64–66.

77 **"our presence is incompatible"**: Macpherson, *Macpherson's Letters*, p. 3.

77 **top physicians**: Williams, *America's First Hospital*, pp. 2–5.

78 **"my head may be guilty"**: Macpherson, *Macpherson's Letters*, p. 2.

78 **"Declare a dog is mad"**: Ibid., p. 6.

78 **against his will**: Macpherson to the Public, March 10, 1787, Nead Papers, 1785–1789, LCP.

78 **"the cause of all my"**: Macpherson, *Pennsylvania Sailor's Letters*, p. 5.

78 **"they also blew stuff"**: Macpherson to the Public, March 10, 1787, Nead Papers, 1785–1789, LCP.

78 **"Dr. FalseHeart"**: Macpherson, *Pennsylvania Sailor's Letters*, p. 7.

78 **"may be sung"**: Macpherson, *Macpherson's Letters*, p. 14.

79 **"only guard"**: Ibid., p. 15.

79 **"a visit to his wife"**: Rush Ledger, 1769–1883, HSP.

79 **submitting his writings**: Merriam, *Macpherson of Philadelphia*, p. 11; Macpherson, *Macpherson's Letters*, pp. 1–105; Macpherson, *Pennsylvania Sailor's Letters*, pp.1–64.

80 **"heartily loved"**: Macpherson, *Macpherson's Letters*, p. 11.

Chapter 7

81 **six pounds**: *Pennsylvania Journal*, September 5, 1771.

81 **"detach" the "parts"**: Hawke, *Rush*, p. 87.

81 **Some attendees were soon**: Ibid.

82 **"shop"**: Rush, *Autobiography*, pp. 83–84.

82 **"great man"**: Ibid., pp. 78–79.

83 **Shippen was openly telling**: Hawke, *Rush*, p. 91.

83 **"a man of . . . cool malice"**: Jacob Rush to BR, January 24, 1771, Rush manuscripts, 34, pp. 44–45, LCP.

84 **"gave any very promising"**: Rush, *Autobiography*, p. 323.

84 **"not practicable"**: Rush, *Diseases of the Mind*, p. 349.

84 **"the vibration of which"**: Mason, *Selections from Letters and Manuscripts*, pp. 45–53.

86 **"attic evenings"**: Slotten, "Elizabeth Graeme Ferguson," p. 261n4; Rush, "Life and Character of Mrs. Ferguson," p. 523.

86 **at Carpenters' Mansion**: Lippincott, *Early Philadelphia*, p. 37.

86 **"How often when I am"**: Slotten, "Elizabeth Graeme Ferguson," p. 262.

87 **Franklin's son William**: Ousterhout, *Most Learned Woman*, pp. 63, 71.

87 **"the most learned woman"**: Ibid., pp. 1–27.

87 **she first translated**: Rush, "Life and Character of Mrs. Ferguson," p. 521; Ousterhout, *Most Learned Woman*, p. 25.

87 **Rush had known Betsey's**: Ibid., p. 128.

87 **too much for her daughter**: Rush, "Life and Character of Mrs. Ferguson," pp. 521–22.

87 **"race was not always"**: Ibid., p. 522.

87 **Graeme's salon**: Rush, *Autobiography*, p. 321.

87 **"modesty alone"**: Rush, "Life and Character of Mrs. Ferguson," p. 523.

87 **"The genius of Miss Graeme"**: Ibid.

Chapter 8

89 **most widely read**: Kaestle, "John Dickinson's Farmer's Letters," p. 353.

90 **drinking and gout**: *Pennsylvania Gazette*, December 26, 1771.

90 **"intemperance in eating"**: *Pennsylvania Gazette*, January 9, 1772.

90 **forty-four-page pamphlet**: Rush, "Temperance and Exercise."

91 **"WINE is principally useful"**: Ibid., p. 19.

91 **"At present noon"**: Ibid., pp. 11–12.

92 **"live ten years"**: Ibid., p. 33n1.

92 **"circulation of the blood"**: Ibid., p. 33.

93 **"deserted his fields"**: Ibid., p. 28.

93 **friendly with Anthony Benezet**: Jackson, *Benezet*, pp. 120–26.

94 **a law that would tax**: BR to BF, May 1, 1773, in *Rush Letters*, p.79.

94 **consequential people**: Nash, "Slaves and Slaveowners," p. 250.

94 **"intellects of the Negroes"**: Rush, *Address to the Inhabitants*, p. 1.

95 **concise, compelling**: Hawke, *Rush*, p. 107.

95 **twelve hundred copies**: Rush, *Address to the Inhabitants*, inside cover.

95 **"It is impossible to determine"**: Nisbet and Sparhawk, *Slavery Not Forbidden*, pp. 3, 21.

96 **A Vindication**: Rush, "A Vindication," Address to the Inhabitants, https://quod.lib.umich.edu/e/evans/N10229.0001.001/1:4?rgn=div1;view=fulltext

96 **significantly fewer patients**: Hawke, *Rush*, p. 108.

96 **"injured me in another"**: Rush, *Autobiography*, p. 83.

97 **"moral faculty"**: Woods, "Correspondence of Rush and Sharpe," p. 6.

Chapter 9

98 **apprentices bunked**: Gibson, "Apprenticed Students," *Transactions & Studies of the College of Physicians of Philadelphia*, 14(3): pp. 127–32.

98 **"ill effects of drinking cold"**: *Pennsylvania Journal*, August 9, 1770.

98 **Franklin shared**: BF to BR, July 14, 1773, Founders Online.

98 **"people often catch Cold"**: Ibid.

98 **He also published**: "Spasmodic Asthma," *Pennsylvania Journal*, December 14, 1769; "Gout," *Pennsylvania Gazette*, December 26, 1771; "thorn apple," *Transactions 1*, American Philosophical Society (1771), pp. 318–22.

99 **reports circulated**: *The Massachusetts Gazette*, October 4–11, 1773: Benjamin Labaree, *Catalyst for Revolution: The Boston Tea Party 1773*, p. 11.

99 **"On Patriotism"**: Rush, "On Patriotism," *Rush Letters*, p. 83.

100 **Rush was invited**: BR to JA, August 14, 1809, in *Spur of Fame*, p. 150; date determined because BR mentions meeting Mifflin, also at that meeting, in a letter he wrote October 10, 1773, to William Gordon.

100 **the stand used for**: James Gigontino, "Slavery and the Slave Trade," *The Encyclopedia of Greater Philadelphia*.

101 **Tom Mifflin**: BR to JA, August 14, 1809, Founders Online EA.

101 **"that business"**: There are multiple accounts of this exchange; I am using BR's 1809 account as my primary quote source, but the events are corroborated by Stone (1891) and various articles in the *Pennsylvania Journal*. BR to JA, Aug 14, 1809, in Rush *Letters*, pp. 1013–15; Stone, F. D. (1891, "How the Landing of Tea Was Opposed in Philadelphia by Colonel William Bradford," *The Pennsylvania Magazine of History and Biography* (1877–1906), pp. 15, 385.

101 **October 14th**: Ryerson, *The Radical Committees of Philadelphia*, p. 34.

101 **eight resounding resolutions**: *Pennsylvania Packet*, January 3, 1774.

102 **October 16**: *Pennsylvania Journal*, October 20, 1773.

102 **"the first throe"**: BR to JA, August 14, 1809, *Spur of Fame*, p. 150.

102 **Faneuil Hall**: *Pennsylvania Journal*, November 17, 1773.

102 **"Philadelphia leads"**: Henry Drinker to Pigou & Booth, November 18, 1773, Drinker Family Papers, HSP.

103 **the *Polly***: Stone, "How the Landing of Tea Was Opposed in Philadelphia by Colonel William Bradford," pp. 4, 15.

103 **Committee on Tarring**: "To the Delaware Pilots . . ." *Early American Imprints*, Series I, No. 12943 (1773).

103 **"short fat Fellow"**: King, *Ten Thousand Wonderful Things* p. 38.

103 **two days in town**: *Pennsylvania Journal*, December 29, 1773.

104 **Society for Inoculating the Poor**: *Pennsylvania Journal*, February 2, 1774.

104 **Suttonian Method**: Rush, *Autobiography*, p. 80n.

104 **first annual oration**: Hawke, *Rush*, pp. 112–15; Rush, *Medecine among the Indians*, p. 10.

105 **Franklin wrote back**: BF to BR, July 22, 1774, Founders Online.

106 **not accepted**: Hawke, *Rush*, p. 115.

Chapter 10

107 **Washington, for example**: "September 1774," *The Diaries of George Washington*, Founders Online.

107 **Tom Mifflin**: JA, entry for August 29, 1774, Diary, A, Founders Online.

108 **"forcible speaker"**: Rush, *Autobiography*, p. 140.

108 **"the idea of Independence"**: Adams to Timothy Pickering, August 6, 1822, Founders Online EA.

108 **"You are the representatives"**: Ibid.

109 **carrying John**: Rush, *Autobiography*, p. 144.

109 **"soft, polite, insinuating"**: JA, entry for Monday, August 29, 1774, Diary, Founders Online EA.

109 **"dirty, dusty and fatigued"**: Ibid.

110 **"a Supper . . . as elegant"**: Ibid.

110 **Mrs. Yards**: Hawke, *Rush*, p. 117; JA, Residents of Delegates in Philadelphia, April 1776, Founders Online.

110 **Adams would dine**: JA, entries for August–October 1774, Diary, Founders Online.

110 **"waited upon nearly all"**: Rush, *Autobiography*, p. 110.

110 **"A mighty Feast"**: JA, entry for September 14, 1774, Diary, Founders Online.

110 **Mrs. Yard, became increasingly ill**: Hawke, *Rush*, p. 117.

110 **"an ingeneous Physician"**: JA, entry for October 14, 1774, Diary, ibid.

110 **"sensible, and deep"**: JA, entry for September 3, 1774, Diary, ibid.

111 **"Declaration"**: First Continental Congress' Declaration of Rights and Resolves. In *Civil Rights in America*. American Journey. Woodbridge, CT: Primary Source Media, 1999. *U.S. History In Context*.

111 **Rush was invited**: Rush, *Autobiography*, p. 111.

111 **"Cash and gunpowder"**: Ibid., p. 111.

112 **method of creating gunpowder**: *Pennsylvania Packet*, November 28, 1774.

112 **Washington came to Rush's**: GW, entry for October 1774, Diary, Founders Online.

Chapter 11

113 **During the last week of the First**: Hawke, *Rush*, pp. 118–19.

113 **the local gentlemen**: JA, entry for October 28, 1774, Diary, Founders Online.

113 **"animated by the most"**: Rush, *Autobiography*, p. 112.

113 **"the happy, the peacefull"**: JA entry for October 28, 1774, Diary, Founders Online.

114 **life expectancy**: *A Population History of North America*, p. 159.

114 **"is there no Maid"**: Butterfield, "Love and Valor," p. 5.

114 **Betsey Graeme, had married**: Ousterhout, *Most Learned Woman*, p. 140.

114 **"now possesses her heart"**: BR to Lady Jane Leslie, September 28, 1774, Rush Manuscripts, 39, p. 27.

114 **Sarah took ill**: Eve and Jones, "Extracts from the Journal of Miss Sarah Eve," p. 21.

115 **"A Female Character"**: *Pennsylvania Packet*, December 12, 1774.

115 **engaged and would have**: Eve and Jones, "Extracts from the Journal of Miss Sarah Eve," pp. 19–21.

115 **"Tom Paine"**: Rush, *Autobiography*, p. 113; Rush, *Letters*, p. 1010n4.

116 **"a short letter"**: BR to James Cheetham, July 17, 1809, in Rush, *Letters*, p. 1007.

116 **broadside against slavery**: *Pennsylvania Journal*, March 8, 1775.

116 **Battles of Lexington and Concord**: Hawke, *Rush*, p. 129.

117 **initial report**: "April 24, 1775," *Extracts from the diary of Christopher Marshall*, pp. 18–19.

117 **"The first gun"**: Rush, *Autobiography*, p. 112.

117 **bells rang**: "The Liberty Bell," *Philadelphia: History of Its Growth*, section 4.

118 **a gesture of mourning**: Hawke, *Rush*, p. 130.

118 **"mix freely with"**: Rush, *Autobiography*, p. 112.

119 **"laudable spirit of industry"**: Hawke, *Rush*, p. 128n8.

119 **"America is now"**: *Pennsylvania Evening Post*, April 11 and 13, 1775.

120 **George Washington**: Rush, *Autobiography*, p. 112; BR to JA, February 12, 1812, in Rush, *Letters*, p. 1120.

121 **"to the Commander in chief"**: Rush, *Autobiography*, p. 112.

122 **"Remember Mr. Henry"**: Ibid., p. 113.

Chapter 12

123 **a young friend from Boston**: JA to James Warren, July 24, 1775, Founders Online.

123 **"piddling Genius whose Fame"**: Ibid.

124 **"difficulty and intricacy"**: JA to AA, July 24, 1775, Founders Online.

124 **"independence of the United"**: Rush, *Autobiography*, pp. 142–43.

124 **"the Quakers & Proprietary"**: JA to Timothy Pickering, August 6, 1822, Founders Online EA.

124 **"the inhabitants"**: Rush, *Autobiography*, p. 113.

124 **help them "remove" . . . "an immense"**: BR to James Cheetham, July 17, 1809, in Rush, *Letters*, pp. 1007–10.

125 **"public mind"**: Ibid., p. 1008.

125 **"put some thoughts upon"**: Rush, *Autobiography*, p. 113.

125 **"assured me that"**: *Pennsylvania Magazine*, June 1775, p. 266.

126 **"what he thought of"**: Rush, *Autobiography*, p. 114.

126 **later in the evenings**: Hawke, *Paine*, p. 40.

126 **"he should avoid"**: William Duane to TJ, November 26, 1802, Founders Online.

127 **Other aspects of the draft**: Adam and Charles Francis Adams, *The Works of John Adams* 2, p. 507.

127 **"Nothing can be conceived"**: Rush, *Autobiography*, p. 114.

127 **a resolution promising that**: Agreement of Secrecy, November 9, 1775, Founders Online.

Chapter 13

129 **showed Rush a letter**: Rush, *Autobiography*, p. 116.

129 **six children**: Bill, *House Called Morven*, p. 22.

129 **Marcus Marsh**: Manumission letter from Annis Stockton, March 2, 1798, NARA 870.

130 **"almost as my own"**: Annis Boudinot Stockton to BR, November 3, 1793, Rush manuscripts 36, p. 120, LCP.

130 **"attracted and fixed"**: BR to Lady Jane, April 1, 1784, in Rush, *Letters*, p. 325.

130 **"the same air and lisp"**: Ibid., p. 326.

130 **"the best preacher"**: Rush, *Autobiography*, p. 116.

130 **politically challenging**: *Only for the Eye of a Friend*, pp. 19–20.

131 **physician and surgeon**: Rush, *Letters*, II. Chronology, p. 90.

131 **treat any sailors**: BR to Owen Biddle, [n.d.], Ibid., p. 94; W. Kenneth Patton, *U.S. Naval Hospitals Historical Survey*, pp. 7–9.

131 **"I should be wanting"**: BR to JSR, October 25, 1775, in Rush, *My Dearest Julia*, pp. 3–6.

132 **"know eno'"**: BR, ibid., pp. 7–9.

132 **"I am almost afraid"**: BR to JSR, November 12, 1775; ibid., pp. 12–16.

133 **"matrimonial thermometer"**: BR to JSR, November 15, 1775; ibid., pp. 16–17.

135 **a first draft**: JA to Richard Henry Lee, November 15, 1775, Founders Online.

135 **"Many of our future joys"**: BR to Julia, November 19, 1775, in Rush, *My Dearest Julia*, p. 20.

Chapter 14

136 **"Dr. Rush came in"**: JA, entry for September 24, 1774, Diary, Founders Online

137 **hoped to be married**: Rush, *My Dearest Julia*, pp. xiv–xv.

137 **Cyrus**: BR to JSR, December 28, 1775, ibid., p. 40.

137 **"not for physic"**: Ibid., pp. 39–41.

138 **"If the business"**: BR to JSR, December 29, 1775, in Rush, *My Dearest Julia*, p. 42.

138 **a fearless printer**: Rush, *Autobiography*, p. 114.

138 **one thousand copies**: Liell, *46 Pages*, p. 82.

139 ***Common Sense***: Rush, *Autobiography*, p. 113.

139 **traveled to Princeton**: Rush, *My Dearest Julia*, p. xv.

139 **returned home**: Hawke, *Rush*, p. 141.

139 **"was seduced from me"**: Rush, *My Dearest Julia*, p. 46.

140 **"an unhappy and deluded multitude"**: King George III, *His Majesty's Most Gracious Speech*, Library of Congress, https://loc.gov/item/2005578.

140 **colonial printing industry**: Liell, *46 Pages*, pp. 92–95.

141 **"the controversy about"**: Rush, *Autobiography*, p. 115.

141 **Jacob Rush**: McLachlan, *Princetonians, 1748–1768*, p. 527.

141 **Committee of Inspection and Observation**: Hawke, *Rush*, p. 142.

142 **Dr. Morgan had already**: *Pennsylvania Packet*, January 29, 1776.

142 **"the precedents of"**: Rush, *Autobiography*, pp. 116–17.

143 **the *Liverpool* and the *Roebuck***: Hawke, *Rush*, p. 149.

143 **"repeal or suspend"**: Ibid., p. 150.

143 **Christiana River**: *Pennsylvania Packet*, May 9 and 11, 1776.

143 **nearly four hours**: Ibid., May 20, 1776.

144 **"the novelty of the fight"**: Ibid., May 13, 1776.

144 **residents could hear the firing**: Hawke, *Rush*, p. 150.

Chapter 15

145 **She was also adjusting**: BR to JSR, June 1, 1776, in Rush, *Letters*, p. 102.

145 **Rush hired Charles Willson Peale**: Sellers, *Charles Willson Peale* 1, p. 128.

146 **Hessian troops**: Richard Bache to BF, May 7, 1776, Founders Online.

146 **"I did not know"**: BR to JSR, May 27, 1776, in Rush, *Letters*, p. 96.

146 **"I anticipate with you"**: BR to JSR, May 29, 1776, ibid., p. 99.

147 **a new resolution**: Hawke, *Rush*, pp. 150–52.

147 **"sufficient to the exigencies"**: May 10, 1776, *Journals of the Continental Congress* 4, pp. 341–43.

147 **"Anxiety, labour"**: JA, entry for May 10, Founders Online.

147 **"absolutely irreconcilable"**: May 15, *Journals of the Continental Congress* 4, pp. 357–58.

148 **"God knows I seek"**: BR to Julia, May 29, 1776, in Rush, *Letters*, pp. 99–100.

148 **By ten a.m. on May 20**: Ibid.

148 **"in a loud Stentorian"**: Hawke, *Rush*, p. 153.

148 **"the multitude."**: JA to James Warren, May 20, 1776, Founders Online.

148 **But the Pennsylvania Assembly**: Hawke, *Rush*, pp. 154–55.

149 **"dined *most luxuriously*"**: BR to Julia, May 27, 1776, in Rush, *Letters*, p. 96.

149 **"hate hereafter to breathe"**: Ibid., pp. 96, 98n6.

149 **the "Memorial" was released**: Ibid., pp. 96–97.

149 **Moderates in the Assembly**: Hawke, *Rush*, p. 155.

150 **"the people of the middle"**: Jefferson, "Notes on Congress, June 8, 1776," Founders Online.

150 **initial brainstorming**: Isaacson, *Franklin*, p. 311.

150 **"I will not"**: JA to Timothy Pickering, August 6, 1822, Founders Online (though Adams offers two descriptions of this scene in his writings, I used the later letter to Timothy Pickering to re-create this dialogue).

151 **on deadline**: See discussion of the month of June in *Journals of Continental Congress*, vol. 5.

151 **"all men"**: George Mason, Declaration of Rights, 1776, Personal Papers Collection, Library of Virginia, http://edu.lva.virginia.gov/dbva/items/show/184.

152 **"I profess faith in"**: Hawke, *Rush*, p. 159; *Diary of Christopher Marshall*, pp. 72–73, 79n2.

153 **"There are many good"**: Marshall to JB, June 30, 1776, HSP.

153 **"blamed . . . buffeted"**: "Marshall Remembrances, June 28, 1776," p. 90.

154 **"Whereas, George the third"**: *Proceedings of the Provincial Conference*, PA Archives, pp. 576–77.

155 **"sacred & undeniable"**: *Journals of the Continental Congress* 5, p. 472.

156 **On Saturday morning, Washington's**: McCullough, *1776*, p. 135.

Chapter 16

157 **hot and rainy**: Tom Moore, Weather on July 4, 1776 (The Weather Company, 2017), https://weather.com/holiday/july-fourth/news/weather-holiday-philadelphia-temperature-4th-of-july.

157 **"The Consequences"**: Powell, "Speech of John Dickinson," p. 458.

158 **"after waiting some time"**: Adams, "Monday July 1, 1776," *Diary*, Founders Online.

159 **"All was silence"**: Ibid.

159 **"sundry letters"**: July 2, 1776, *Journals of the Continental Congress* 5, p. 506.

159 **"*Resolved*, that these United"**: Ibid., p. 507.

160 **Dickinson did not come**: Calvert, "Myth-Making," p. 474.

160 **"totally estranged themselves"**: Transcript courtesy of the John Dickinson Writings Project. See also Dickinson to unknown, August 25, 1776, in Calvert, *Complete Writings of Dickinson*, p. 1.

160 **a new name**: July 17, 1776, *Journals of the Continental Congress*, 5, p. 572.

160 **he was formally voted into**: Ibid., p. 596.

161 **"*That* is saying a great deal"**: BR to JA, April 13, 1790, in Rush, *Letters*, p. 547.

161 **"I don't know how"**: JA to AA, July 23, 1776, Founders Online.

161 **"an eminent Phisician"**: JA to Cotton Tufts, July 20, 1776, ibid.

162 **"I find"**: BR to Charles Lee, July 23, 1776, in Rush, *Letters*, p. 103.

162 **"so much pleasure"**: BR to JSR, July 23, 1776, ibid., p. 105.

163 **"the solicitude and labors"**: BR to JA, July 20, 1811, Founders Online EA.

163 **"I shall have a great advantage over you"**: Ibid.

Chapter 17

165 **"surprised to observe"**: Rush, *Autobiography*, p. 119.

166 **"Our troops behaved"**: BR to Barbeu Dubourg, September 16, 1776, in Rush, *Letters*, pp. 110–11.

166 **"I wish the first ball"**: BR to JA, April 13, 1790, ibid.

166 **"a decoy duck"**: Ibid.

166 **"Our country is far"**: Rush, *Autobiography*, p. 120.

167 **"I would much rather"**: Ibid.

167 **"It would seem as if"**: BR to JA, June 29, 1805, Founders Online EA.

167 **"between lines of guards"**: McCullough, *Adams*, p. 156.

167 **"large handsome room"**: Adams, *Works of John Adams*, p. 377.

168 **"In any capacity"**: BR to JSR, September 14, 1776, in Rush, *Letters*, p. 109.

168 **"four miles in the"**: Ibid.

169 **Morgan, now**: Flexner, *Doctors on Horseback*, p. 14; "John Morgan," U.S. Army Medical Department, Office of Medical History, http://history.amedd.army.mil/surgeongenerals/J_Morgan.html.

169 **"flying camp"**: Hawke, *Rush*, p. 170.

170 **he still wished**: GW to Richard Henry Lee, November 8, 1775, Founders Online.

170 **"constant bickering"**: GW to John Hancock, September 25, 1776, ibid.

170 **"All the wounded"**: Duncan, *Medical Men*, p. 140.

171 **"much pleased"**: BR to Anthony Wayne, September 29, 1776, in Rush, *Letters*, p. 117.

171 **"I would have a soldier"**: Maurice de Saxe, *Reveries on the Art of War*, p. 6.

171 **"If you begin"**: BR to Anthony Wayne, September 29, 1776, in Rush, *Letters*, p. 117.

Chapter 18

172 **three boxes**: Ellet, *Women of the American Revolution* 3, p. 16.

173 **"Every particle"**: BR to Richard Henry Lee, December 30, 1776, in Rush, *Letters*, p. 122.

173 **Nassau Hall**: Barber and Howe, *Historical Collections of New Jersey*, pp. 265–67.

173 **Mount Welcome**: Johnson, *History of Cecil County, Maryland*, p. 480.

174 **relocate**: Rush, *Autobiography*, p. 123.

174 **ferry crossings**: Fischer, *Washington's Crossing*, p. 191.

174 **city's economy was devastated**: BR to Richard Henry Lee, December 21, 1776, in Rush, *Letters*, p. 120.

175 **secure his dwelling**: Nelson, *Paine*, p. 107.

175 **"The summer soldier"**: Paine, "The American Crisis," *Pennsylvania Journal*, December 19, 1776.

175 **John Cadwalader**: Charles Willson Peale, *Portrait of John and Elizabeth Lloyd Cadwalader and Their Daughter Anne*, Philadelphia Museum of Art.

176 **"superintending their health"**: Rush, *Autobiography*, p. 124.

176 **main hospital**: Duncan, *Medical Men*, p. 172.

176 **"refusing Continental money"**: BR to Robert Henry Lee, December 21, 1776, in Rush, *Letters*, p. 120.

177 **"Many of the Continental troops"**: Ibid.

177 **"must be invested"**: Ibid.

177 **"to revive our expiring"**: Col. Joseph Reed to GW, December 22, 1776, Founders Online.

177 **"He appeared much depressed"**: Rush, *Autobiography*, p. 124.

178 **"profound silence"**: Fischer, *Washington's Crossing*, p. 208.

Chapter 19

181 **Some six hundred men**: Fischer, *Washington's Crossing*, pp. 208–16.

182 **"surprised and taken"**: Rush, *Autobiography*, p. 125.

182 **Peale slipped and fell**: Sellers, "Charles Willson Peale," p. 277.

182 **"keep up the Panic"**: John Cadwalader to GW, December 27, 1776, Founders Online.

182 **Rush left Crosswicks**: Rush, *Autobiography*, p. 125.

182 **"dined and spent"**: Ibid., p. 126.

182 **"council of war"**: Ibid.

183 **City Light Horse Troops**: Fischer, *Washington's Crossing*, p. 279.

183 **David Hall**: Rush, *Autobiography*, p. 168n21.

183 **Philadelphia druggist**: "Sharp Delany" in Simpson, *The Lives of Eminent Philadelphians, Now Diseased*, p. 308.

183 **"Who are you?"**: Ibid., p. 127.

184 **shiny blue uniform**: seen in John Trumbull, *The Death of General Mercer at the Battle of Princeton* (1791).

184 **"his right hand"**: Rush, *Autobiography*, p. 128.

184 **"to assist in"**: Peale, *Autobiography*, p. 205.

185 **"for the first time"**: Rush, *Autobiography*, p. 128.

185 **"the field of battle**: Ibid., p. 128.

185 **"I do not now see"**: Fischer, *Washington's Crossing*, p. 360.

186 **"is the fellow"**: Woodward, "Dr. Benjamin Rush in Princeton: 1777–8," p. 4.

187 **"for quarters"**: BR to Richard Henry Lee, January 14, 1777, in Rush, *Letters*, p. 127.

188 **"Are you Dr. Rush?"**: Rush, *Autobiography*, p. 129.

188 **"You would think"**: BR to Richard Henry Lee, January 7, 1777, in Rush, *Letters*, p. 127.

190 **"suffers many indignities"**: BR to Richard Henry Lee, December 30, 1776, ibid.

Chapter 20

191 **"obliged to visit the sick"**: BR to Richard Henry Lee, January 14, 1777, in Rush, *Letters*, p. 127.

191 **"The medical department"**: Ibid., p. 129.

192 **"was permitted to return"**: Rush, *Autobiography*, p. 130.

192 **"oath & obligation"**: Greiff and Gunning, *Morven*, p. 34.

192 **"exceedingly weak"**: BR to Richard Henry Lee, January 14, 1777, in Rush, *Letters*, p. 127.

192 **permanently stained**: William Stryker, *The Battles of Trenton and Princeton*, p. 297.

192 **Cyrus**: Rush, like any physician (or congressman), did not often travel alone, but he usually did not acknowledge, in letters or journals, there was a servant or groomsman with him. I was reminded of this early on when I came across a mention of Rush in the Pennsylvania Archives, Sixth Series, which included the "Muster Rolls Relating to the Associators and Militia of the City of Philadelphia," which noted on p. 54 that on July 31, 1777, "Doctor Benj. Rush, left with his negro." So I have, in several places, reminded the reader that unless Rush specifically said he was traveling alone, I assumed he was with his groomsman, Cyrus.

193 **crash in a room**: BR to JSR, January 24, 1777, in Rush, *Letters*, p. 130.

193 **"the Damdest Hole"**: Morris, *The Confidential Correspondence*, p. 12.

193 **"long chamber"**: Adams, diary entry for February 7, 1777, Founders Online.

194 **"The people of your state"**: Rush, *Autobiography*, p. 142.

194 **"The eyes of the whole city"**: BR to JD, December 1, 1776, in Rush, *Letters*, p. 119.

194 **"not offended or mortified"**: Rush, *Autobiography*, p. 131.

196 **"I sat next to Jno. Adams"**: BR to JA, February 24, 1790, in Rush, *Letters*, p. 534.

196 **"If this motion is passed"**: Rush, *Autobiography*, p. 131.

196 **"I have been distressed"**: BR to JA, April 13, 1790, Founders Online.

196 **"where the infection now prevails"**: BR to GW, February 13, 1777, ibid.

197 **"Topsy Turvy Kings"**: JA, entry for February 16, 1777, Diary, ibid.

198 **Shippen's plan**: Duncan, *Medical Men*, pp. 192–93.

198 **"In vain did I plead"**: Rush, *Autobiography*, p. 131.

Chapter 21

199 **"it is the most airy"**: JA to AA, June 2, 1777, Founders Online.

200 **April 7, 1777**: "Reorganization of the Medical Department, 1777," Office of Medical History, pp. 194, 199.

200 **rations**: Bureau of Labor Statistics, *History of Wages*, p. 53.

200 **Potts**: Duncan, *Medical Men*, pp. 199–200.

201 **"Here ends the chapter"**: Rush, entry for April 12, Ledger, Rush Manuscripts 64, LCP.

201 **"Fatal experience"**: *Pennsylvania Packet*, April 22, 1777.

202 **"Directions for preserving"**: Ibid.

202 **"a fatal hospital fever,"**: Rush, *Autobiography*, p. 131.

202 **"jail fever"**: Duncan, *Medical Men*, chap. 1, pp. 14–15.

203 **"This was denied"**: Rush, *Autobiography*, p. 131.

203 **"A physician who practices"**: Ibid.

204 **"I hope your Excellency"**: BR to GW, May 13, 1777, Founders Online.

204 **"am much obliged to you"**: GW to BR, May 16, 1777, ibid.

204 **"*Sick absent*"**: GW, Circular to the Brigade, May 20, 1777, ibid.

205 **"loud huzzas"**: *Pennsylvania Evening Post*, July 5, 1777.

205 **"strangers of eminence"**: JA to Abigail Adams 2nd, July 5, 1777, Founders Online.

205 **"I think it was"**: Ibid.

206 **"Everything was conducted"**: *Pennsylvania Evening Post*, July 5, 1777.

Chapter 22

207 **eighteen thousand**: Townsend, *Brandywine: Eyewitness Accounts*, pp. 3–5.

207 **left Philadelphia**: Hawke, *Rush*, p. 202.

207 **"Jack"**: BR to JSR, November 10, 1777, in Rush, *Letters*, p. 166.

208 **266**: Michael C. Harris, *Brandywine*, p. 67.

208 **returned briefly**: Hawke, *Rush*, p. 202.

208 **26 percent**: Duncan, *Medical Men*, p. 212.

208 **"putrid"**: Ibid., p. 13.

208 **"Multitudes melted away"**: Hawke, *Rush*, p. 205.

209 **Marquis**: "George Washington and the Marquis de Lafayette," Mount Vernon, http://www.mountvernon.org/digital-encyclopedia/article /george-washington-and-the-marquis-de-lafayette/.

210 **"many dead Horses"**: JA to AA, August 29, 1777, Founders Online.

210 **marching formation**: McGuire, *The Philadelphia Campaign* 1, p. 127.

210 **eleven thousand soldiers**: Harris, *Brandywine*, p. 108.

210 **"belonging to the army"**: Ibid., p. 109.

211 **"eleven thousand men, poorly"**: Note in General Orders, August 8, 1777, Founders Online.

211 **blue or brown**: McGuire, *Battle of Paoli*, p. 7.

211 **"make a final and entire"**: JA to AA, August 1, 1777, Founders Online.

211 **"it will cutt off"**: Ibid.

211 **"Our soldiers have not"**: JA to AA, August 24, 1777, ibid.

212 **"bare feet, and rags"**: Fisher, *The Struggle for American Independence* 2, p. 20.

212 **"good Impression"**: JA to AA, August. 23, 1777, ibid.

212 **Birmingham Friends Meeting House**: McGuire, *The Philadelphia Campaign* 1, p. 196.

213 **"General Washington imprudently"**: Harris, pp. 119–20.

Chapter 23

215 **six a.m.**: McGuire, *The Philadelphia Campaign* 1, p. 175.

215 **"was received with acclimations"**: Harris, *Brandywine*, p. 169.

216 **"a large body"**: From Lieut. Col. James Ross to GW, September 11, 1777, Founders Online.

216 **Birmingham Meeting House**: McGuire, *The Philadelphia Campaign* 1, p. 193.

217 **"heaviest firing"**: Agnew, "Sketch of Governor Richard Powell, of New Jersey," pp. 222–24.

218 **"nearly" fell "in the hands"**: Rush, *Autobiography*, p. 132.

218 **"Dear Father"**: Agnew, "Sketch of Governor Richard Powell, of New Jersey," pp. 222–24.

219 **entire army**: Harris, *Brandywine*, p. 368.

219 **900**: Ibid., p. 369.

219 **"Why 'tis a perfect"**: Ibid., p. 365.

219 **"I am sorry to inform"**: GW to the President of Congress, Twelve O'Clock at Night, September 11, 1777, in *The Writings of George Washington*, p. 57.

220 **"The Number of wounded"**: General William Howe to GW, September 12, 1777, Founders Online.

220 **"Mate in the Hospital"**: "GW to General William Howe, September 13, 1777," ibid.

220 **"Their principal surgeon"**: Harris, *Brandywine*, p. 271.

220 **"a few concessions"**: McGuire, *The Philadelphia Campaign* 1, p. 271.

221 **"I was much struck"**: Rush, *Autobiography*, p. 133.

222 **"visited us"**: "Col. Hartley's Testimony," McGuire, *Battle of Paoli*, p. 203.

222 **brutal attack**: McGuire, *The Philadelphia Campaign* 1. p. 309.

222 **"cut & hack"**: Ibid., p. 314.

222 **two hundred**: Ibid., p. 317.

223 **"As the Wagons"**: McGuire, *The Philadelphia Campaign* 2, p. 4.

223 **his incredulity**: Thomas Paine to BF, May 16, 1778, in *Pennsylvania Magazine of History and Biography* 2 (1878), p. 283.

223 **"I feel in some way"**: Pickering, *The Life of Timothy Pickering* 1, p. 165.

224 **"My dear friend"**: BR to JA, October 1, 1777, Founders Online.

225 **"My friend, I confess"**: McGuire, *The Philadelphia Campaign* 2, pp. 56–57; for "William Smith," p. 56; for "James Witherspoon," pp. 84–85.

226 **"Dined with the commander-in-chief"**: Rush, "Historical Notes of 1777," p. 147.

226 **"no wine—only grog"**: Ibid.

227 **"We lost a city"**: BR to JA, October 13, 1777, Founders Online.

227 **"The Spirit of our men"**: Ibid.

Chapter 24

229 **in Paris**: McCullough, *Adams*, pp. 172–74.

229 **Fort Mifflin**: Rolph, "Fort That Saved America."

229 **"under the most complicated"**: BR to James Searle, November 19, 1777, in Rush, *Letters*, p. 166.

229 **"Britain in the height"**: Ibid.

229 **"My dear Julia"**: BR to Betsey Graeme Fergusson, December 24, 1777, in Rush, *Letters*, p. 177.

230 **He accused Shippen**: BR to JA, October 21, 1777, in Rush, *Letters*, p. 159.

230 **"weak general"**: Rush, *Letters*, Appendix I; Butterfield's appendix is the most in-depth description of the Conway affair from Rush's perspective; this letter itself was never found, but first reference to it appears in GW to Brigadier General Thomas Conway, November 5, 1777, Founders Online.

230 **"A great and good"**: BR to JA, October 21, 1777, Founders Online.

231 **"Sir, a Letter"**: GW to Thomas Conway, November 5, 1777, ibid.

231 **"slipped"**: Thomas Conway to GW, November 5, 1777, ibid.

232 **"Physicians and surgeons"**: BR to Nathanael Greene, December 2, 1777, in Rush, *Letters*, p. 168.

232 **"Many hundred"**: Rush, *Autobiography*, pp. 133–34.

232 **requesting an officer**: BR to William Shippen, December 2, 1777, in Rush, *Letters*, p. 169.

232 **"He claimed he"**: BR to William Duer, December 8, 1777, ibid., p. 171.

233 **"I am the *only* judge"**: BR to William Duer, December 13, 1777, ibid., p. 175.

233 **"the happiness of"**: BR to William Duer, December 8, 1777, ibid., p. 171.

233 **to talk with Annis**: BR to Betsey Graeme Fergusson, December 24, 1777, ibid., p. 177.

233 **"There cannot be a greater"**: BR to GW, December 26, 1777, in Rush, *Letters*, p. 180. Rush later recounts the same letter in his autobiography, p. 134, but transcribes it slightly differently.

234 **"dirty and stinking"**: Rush, "Historical Notes of 1777," p. 148.

234 **"Sir, this is not"**: Hawke, *Rush*, p. 213.

235 **"Nothing is talked of"**: BR to JSR, January 15, 1778, in Rush, *Letters*, p. 185.

236 **"The common danger"**: BR to Patrick Henry, January 12, 1778, ibid., p. 182.

237 **"peculiarity of our circumstances"**: GW to BR, January 12, 1778, Founders Online.

237 **he would soon order**: General Orders, January 15, 1778, ibid.

237 **"long absence from"**: William Shippen to Congress, January 8, 1778, in Duncan, *Medical Men*, p. 283.

238 **"to lay down my commission"**: BR to JA, January 22, 1778, in Rush, *Letters*, p. 190.

239 **"want of harmony"**: BR to John Morgan [June, 1779], in Rush, *Letters*, p. 225. The exact date of this letter is unclear.

239 **"if I thought that he alone"**: BR to JSR, January 28, 1778, Rosenbach.

240 **"do not think"**: BR to John Morgan [June, 1779], in Rush, *Letters*, pp. 225–28.

240 **"Finding it impossible"**: BR to Henry Laurens, January 30, 1778, in Rush, *Letters*, p. 198.

Chapter 25

241 **"at a loss what Station"**: John Witherspoon to BR, February 2, 1778, in *Letters of Delegates to Congress* 9, *February 1, 1778–May 31, 1778*, Library of Congress Historical Collections.

241 **his essay on the health**: Rush, *Letters*, p. 146n1.

242 **"I have received so many"**: JA to BR, February 8, 1778, Founders Online.

243 **"letters from Dr. Shippen"**: Entry for February 6, 1778, in Owen, "Legislative and Administrative History," p. 268.

243 **"excused from the duty"**: *Journals of the American Congress* 2, p. 433.

243 **"Had I expected such"**: BR to Daniel Roberdeau, March 9, 1778, in Rush, *Letters*, p. 204.

243 **"no revenge in me"**: BR to William Shippen, February 1, 1778, in Rush, *Letters*, p. 197.

244 **Henry decided**: Patrick Henry to GW, February 20, 1778, Founders Online.

244 **"very disrespectfully"**: Lafayette to GW, February 27, 1778, ibid.

244 **"think myself inexcusable"**: BR to GW, February 25, 1778, Founders Online.

245 **"That I may have erred"**: GW to Patrick Henry, March 27, 1778, ibid.

245 **"The Anonymous Letter"**: GW to Patrick Henry, March 28, 1778, ibid.

246 **Rush returned**: Rush, *Autobiography*, pp. 123–24.

248 **"The filth left"**: Ibid., p. 138.

249 **"bilious fever"**: BR to David Ramsay, November 5, 1778, in Rush, *Letters*, p. 218.

249 **"the brink of"**: BR to David Ramsay, November 5, 1778, in Rush, *Letters*, p. 218.

249 **"My recovery was slow"**: Rush, *Autobiography*, p. 138.

249 **"physical history"**: Rush, *Autobiography*, p. 169. (This notebook, sadly, has been lost.)

249 **Rush diagnosed**: Bill, *A House Called Morven*, pp. 48–50.

Chapter 26

253 **"a most unrepublican"**: BR to JA, October 19, 1779, Founders Online.

253 **"The minds of the citizens"**: Rush, *Medical Inquiries and Observations*, p. 186.

254 **the commonwealth dismissed**: Butterfield, "Rush and John and Mary's College," p. 30.

254 **Second Presbyterian Church**: Henretta, Edwards, and Self, *America*, p. 157.

255 **"Dined with Gen'l"**: Rush, "Notes and Queries," p. 249.

255 **"treated me with a degree"**: BR to John Marshall, September 5, 1804, in Rush, *Letters*, p. 888.

255 **"testified for five hours"**: Hawke, *Rush*, p. 238.

255 **"the Medical Department"**: "To the President of Congress, July 15, 1780," in Washington, *Writings of Washington*, p. 19.

255 **"your reappointment"**: BR to William Shippen, November 18, 1780, in Rush, *Letters*, p. 260.

256 **"indiscreet zeal"**: Rush, *Autobiography*, p. 137.

256 **"The women of America"**: BR to JA, July 13, 1780, Founders Online.

256 **"totally Confin'd"**: Tarkington, "Young Literary Princeton," p. 22.

257 **Rush was ecstatic**: BR to Nathanael Greene, October 30, 1781, ibid., p. 266.

258 **"republican machines"**: Rush, *Plan for Establishment of Schools*, p. 27.

259 **during rounds**: Pennsylvania Hospital Manager's Notes, p. 25.

259 **"rather to the growth"**: Morton and Woodbury, *History of Pennsylvania Hospital*, p. 468.

259 **officially joined the staff**: Pennsylvania Hospital Manager's Notes, p. 33.

259 **"the events of the late war"**: BR to William Cullen, September 16, 1783, in Rush, *Letters*, p. 310.

260 **"I hope the States"**: JA to BR, September 14, 1783, Founders Online.

260 **final charter**: Charter of Dickinson College, September 9, 1783, Dickinson College Archives and Special Collections, http://archives.dickinson.edu/document-descriptions/charter-dickinson-college.

260 **Second Street**: Garvan et al., Mutual Assurance Company, p. 76.

260 **three-story main house**: "To Be Let," *Pennsylvania Packet*, March 16, 1786, p. 3.

260 **Rush's taxes**: "Middle Ward, 1787," Philadelphia Co. Tax.

260 **"our little cottage"**: Author correspondence with researcher Leslie B.

Potter based on her unpublished manuscript, "Benjamin Rush and His Forgotten Country Estate," May 9, 2009, prepared for the DAR.

261 **banyan**: Fortune, "'Studious Men are Always,'" p. 40.

Chapter 27

263 **"Such is the elegance"**: Cutler, *Life, Journals and Correspondence* 1, p. 238.

265 **"a sickness at the stomach"**: Rush, *Enquiry into Effects of Spirituous Liquors*, p. 4.

267 **bills for wine and rum**: Williams, *America's First Hospital*, p. 118.

267 **Thomas Perrine**: Ibid., p. 64; Morton, *History of Pennsylvania Hospital*, p. 134.

267 **"noted for his long"**: Ibid.

267 **"cell keeper"**: Williams, *America's First Hospital*, p. 111.

268 **Dr. John Foulke**: Morton, *History of Pennsylvania Hospital*, p. 131.

268 **"disease of the body"**: Pennsylvania Hospital, Medical Staff Lectures recorded by Reading Beatty 1779–1783.

269 **Hannah Garrett Lewis**: Rolph, "Strange Insanity of Hannah Lewis."

269 **"under Great Indisposition"**: Anishanslin, *Portrait of a Woman*, p. 218.

269 **"for the presumption"**: Samuel Coates's Memorandum Book, p. 3.

269 **"grief induced madness"**: Rush, *Medical Inquiries and Observations, upon Diseases of the Mind*, pp. 40, 58.

Chapter 28

271 **"a crowd of people"**: Hattem, "When Franklin Came Home."

272 **"as early in the year**: *Early Proceedings*, p. 135.

272 **"long absence"**: Rush, *Upon the Moral Faculty*, p.1.

272 **"insecure graveyard"**: BR to Lady Jane Leslie, April 21, 1784, in Rush, *Letters*, p. 325.

272 **"the vegetation"**: *Early Proceedings*, p. 135.

272 **"the knife should"**: Rush, "Late Dr. Hugh Martin's Cancer Powder," in *Transactions* 2, p. 95.

272 **"every leisure moment"**: BR to John Montgomery, December 28, 1785, in Rush, *Letters*, p. 377–78.

273 **"An enquiry into"**: Rush, *Inquiry into the Influence of Physical Causes*, p. 1.

273 **"I foresee, that men"**: Ibid., p. 16.

276 **"During our long acquaintance"**: BF to BR, March, 1786, Franklin Papers.

277 **"alter one word"**: BR to BF, March 3, 1786, ibid.

277 **"an attack of a fever"**: BR to John Dickinson, April 14, 1786, in Rush, *Letters*, p. 384.

277 **"a severe attack of pleurisy"**: Hawke, *Rush*, p. 320.

277 **"send my last"**: BR to BF, March 11, 1786, Franklin Papers.

277 **"Human Knowledge, under"**: *Freeman's Journal*, April 12, 1786, p. 1.

Chapter 29

279 **"It has had a quick sale"**: BR to Richard Price, April 22, 1786, in Rush, *Letters*, p. 385.

279 **republican machines**: Rush, *Plan for Establishment of Schools*, p. 27.

282 **"stood by me"**: BR to JSR, August 23, 1786, in Rush, *Letters*, p. 394.

282 **"This morning"**: Ibid.

282 **"What is the cause"**: Ibid.

283 **Mathew Carey**: Allen, "Mathew Carey."

284 **One of his first pieces**: Rush, "On the Different Species of Manias," *Columbian Magazine*, December 1786.

286 **"A List of my husband's"**: assorted poems, "Rush on Wives," in the Lyman Butterfield Papers at Mass Historical. An example of the riches in the Butterfield Papers, since the historian had access to materials that are now in private hands or lost. These lists are mentioned in the catalog for the third and last part of the 1943 Parke-Bernet auction of the Alexander Biddle Papers (p. 99), but what Butterfield wrote on these cards is more in-depth than the catalog copy. He also recorded who bought them; I tracked down a descendant of the purchaser, but his office was unable to help me see the lists in full. There are many Rush-related items that, at the moment, can only be known through their listings in these catalogs (and Butterfield's notes).

288 **"cultivation and scenery"**: Rush, "Paradise of Negro-Slaves," p. 316.

289 **William Grubber**: Rush, Ledger Book, p. 98.

289 **David McCullough**: Entry for August 11, 1777, "Minutes of the Navy Board," in Linn and Egle, *Pennsylvania Archives*, p. 38.

290 **slaves who were rented out**: Library Company of Philadelphia private seminar with Dr. Richard Newman and Nicholas P. Wood, PhD, to discuss Rush's slave and missing documentation, December 1, 2015.

290 **tax records**: Tax Records, Philadelphia City Archives.

291 **"when I first bought his time"**: Rush, *Autobiography*, p. 246.

Chapter 30

292 **another magazine**: *The American Museum, or Repository of Ancient and Modern Fugitive Pieces* 1, no. 1 (January 1787), https://babel.hathitrust.org/cgi/pt?id=uc1.b5219233;view=1up;seq=7.

292 **"There is nothing more"**: Ibid., pp. 8–11.

294 **"Britain would drive"**: Rush, "Excerpts from Papers of Rush," p. 24.

295 **"were not, in general"**: Wharton, *Memoir of William Rawle*, p. 18.

295 **"Far from preventing"**: Rush, *Enquiry into Effects of Public Punishments*, p. 5. This paper would, years later, cause Rush to be credited (or blamed) for the rise of "solitary confinement" in American prisons, beginning with the landmark Eastern State Penitentiary in Philadelphia, which opened in 1829.

295 **"I told him I had none"**: BR to JSR, August 22, 1787, in Rush, *Letters*, p. 437.

296 **"Dr. Rush, who had"**: Wharton, *Memoir of William Rawle*, p. 25.

296 **"His writings and incessant"**: Vinson, "Society for Political Inquiries," p. 188.

297 **Philadelphia Dispensary**: *Account of the Philadelphia Dispensary*, US National Library of Medicine, http://resource.nlm.nih.gov/2567006R.

297 **Pennsylvania Abolition**: Meeting Notes, August 30, 1784, Pennsylvania Abolition Society Papers, 15, HSP.

297 **Absalom Jones and Richard Allen**: Newman, *Freedom's Prophet*, p. 60.

298 **"ungrateful"**: Hawke, *Rush*, p. 344.

299 **"apprehensive"**: "Proceedings of the General Assembly, March 27, 1787," *Pennsylvania Packet*, April 9, 1787.

301 **nearly half of the Convention**: Mintz, "Constitution and Slavery."

Chapter 31

302 **"The elevation of the female"**: Rush, *Thoughts upon Female Education*, p. 25.

304 **"clergyman's setting-pole"**: Ashbel Green, *The Life*, pp. 192–93.

305 **"lying, drunkenness"**: BR to Ashbel Green, August 11, 1787, in Rush, *Letters*, p. 433.

305 **"doctor of divinity"**: "Scene, Philadelphia," *Pennsylvania Packet*, March 1, 1785.

306 **circumcision ceremony**: BR to JSR, June 27, 1787, ibid., p. 429.

306 **avoid all religious oaths**: "Jonas Phillips to President and Members of the Convention, September 7, 1787," Founders' Constitution at the University of Chicago, http://press-pubs.uchicago.edu/founders/documents/a6_3s11.html.

306 **"but was unable"**: BR to JSR, August 23, 1786, in Rush, *Letters*, p. 395.

307 **"when a man of 40"**: BR to Ashbel Green, August 11, 1787, ibid., p. 433.

308 **"I have lately obtained"**: BR to John Coakley Lettsom, September 28, 1787, in Rush, *Letters*, p. 441.

308 **"derived from a morbid state"**: Rush, *Diseases of the Mind*, p. 13.

308 **David Hartley**: Berrios, "Hartley's Views of Madness," pp. 105–106; BR to TJ, January 2, 1811, Rush, *Letters*, p. 1075.

309 **"full and tense"**: Ibid., p. 99.

309 **"The remedies on which"**: BR to John Coakley Lettsom, September 28, 1787, in Rush, *Letters*, p. 443.

Chapter 32

311 **The first draft**: "The Committee on Style and Arrangement," National Parks Service, https://www.nps.gov/inde/learn/historyculture/the-committee-of-style-and-arrangement.htm.

311 **It was published**: "Federal Constitution Adjourned," *Pennsylvania Packet*, September 18, 1787.

312 **nominated as a delegate**: Hawke, *Rush*, p. 348.

312 **"elegant and pathetic"**: McMaster and Stone, *Pennsylvania and Federal Constitution*, p. 149: "State Convention," *Pennsylvania Herald*, December 1, 1787.

313 **the city would vote**: "Philadelphia," *Independent Gazetteer*, November 8, 1787.

313 **"request the attendance"**: McMaster and Stone, *Pennsylvania and Federal Constitution*, p. 214. Much of the debate is from this source.

315 **"Doctor Puff"**: "Centinel, No. XIII," in McMaster and Stone, *Pennsylvania and Federal Constitution*, p. 642.

315 **"much afflicted"**: BR to Timothy Pickering, January 29, 1788, in Rush, *Letters*, p. 449.

315 **"[I] submitted to confirmation"**: Rush, *Autobiography*, p. 165.

316 **"It pleased God"**: BR to John Montgomery, April 9, 1788, in Rush, *Letters*, p. 455.

316 **"manumission**: Grubber Manumission, Philadelphia City Archive.

317 **"Billy my black boy"**: Rush, entry for June 23, 1788, Ledgerbook.

317 **"Federal Procession"**: Francis Hopkinson, "Federal Procession," *Pennsylvania Packet*, July 10, 1788.

318 **"Antifederal" spirituous**: BR to Elias Boudinot, July 9, 1788, in Rush, *Letters*, p. 470.

320 **"A Moral and Physical"**: Rush, *Enquiry into Effects of Spirituous Liquors*.

Chapter 33

321 **"My dear Mrs. Rush"**: BR to JA, July 2, 1788, Founders Online EA.

321 **"A multiplicity"**: JA to BR, December 2, 1788, ibid., EA.

323 **"most distinguished"**: Ramsay, *History of American Revolution*, 2, p. 320.

323 **"The History of our"**: JA to BR, April 4, 1790, Founders Online EA.

323 ***"I find you & I must"***: BR to JA, June 4, 1789, ibid., EA.

323 **"No! You and I will"**: JA to BR, June 9, 1789, ibid., EA.

324 **"His majesty, the President"**: JA to BR, July 24, 1789, ibid.

324 **"all Titles"**: BR to JA, June 4, 1789, ibid., EA.

324 **"I will take the familiar"**: BR to JA, July 5, 1789, ibid., EA.

324 **"In my notebook"**: BR to JA, April 13, 1790, ibid., EA.

324 **"still professed himself"**: Rush, *Autobiography*, p. 181.

325 **"My Friend Dr. Rush"**: JA to BR, April 18, 1790, Founders Online EA.

326 **"Sir, I learned"**: BR to JA, February 12, 1790, ibid., EA.

326 **"The charming Picture"**: JA to BR, February 17, 1790, ibid., EA.

327 **"I thank you for your"**: BR to JA, February 24, 1790, ibid., EA.

328 **"intended to have conclude[d]"**: BR to JA, April 13, 1790, ibid., EA.

328 **"In consequence of the"**: BR to JA, May 4, 1790, ibid., EA.

329 **"I imagined I was"**: BR to JA, March 23, 1805, ibid., EA.

330 **"a lofty scaffold"**: JA to BR, November 29, 1812, ibid., EA.

331 **"dead in a small hovel"**: Rush, *Autobiography*, pp. 180–83.

333 **"dragged in a few years"**: BR to JA, March 19, 1789, Founders Online EA.

Chapter 34

335 **"friends where you can visit"**: Mary Smith Cranch to AA, January 7, 1791, in *Adams Family Correspondence*, 9, pp. 173–74.

335 **"my intelligenser, dr. Rush"**: AA to Mary Smith Cranch, March 5, 1798, Founders Online.

336 **He was now teaching**: "University Organization After the 1791 Union," Penn University Archives & Records Center, http://www.archives.upenn.edu/histy/features/1700s/charter1791.html.

336 **Surgeons Hall**: "Penn's First Campus, 1749–1801," Penn University Archives & Records Center, http://www.archives.upenn.edu/histy/features/campuses/campus1.html.

336 **"Introductory Lecture to courses"**: BR to TJ, January 17, 1792, Founders Online.

336 **sugar maple trees**: BR to TJ, January 26, 1792, ibid. See also Rush, *Account of the Sugar Maple-Tree*.

337 **"the enlightened and humane"**: Brissot de Warville, *New Travels in the United States*, p. 118.

338 **young British physician**: "The original spin doctors—the meeting of perception and insanity," *Perception* 34, pp. 253–60.

338 **"patients afflicted by Madness"**: BR to Managers of Pennsylvania Hospital, November 11, 1789, in Rush, *Letters*, p. 528.

338 **oldest child, John**: BR to Walter Minto, April 20, 1792, ibid., p. 615.

338 **"I have discovered"**: BR to Enos Hitchcock, April 24, 1789, ibid., p. 511.

339 **Walter Minto**: "Minto, Walter," https://etcweb.Princeton.edu/CampusWWW/Companion/minto_walter.html.

339 **"charge of him and"**: BR to Walter Minto, March 24, 1792, in Rush, *Letters*, p. 612.

339 **"He is a lad of"**: BR to Walter Minto, April 20, 1792, ibid., p. 615.

340 **"public disgrace"**: BR to Walter Minto, September 18, 1792, in Rush, *Letters*, p. 622. See also BR to Walter Minto, May 9, 1792, ibid., p. 618.

341 **corner of Third and Walnut**: Private correspondence with J. M. Duffin (Senior Archivist, University of Pennsylvania Archives) based on his Mapping West Philadelphia website, www.archives.upenn.edu/WestPhila1777/, as well as city directories and insurance documents.

341 **"visionary"**: BR to JA, April 22, 1807, and, JA to BR, April 12, 1807, Founders Online EA.

342 **each share of which cost $25**: William Duer to Alexander Hamilton, August 16, 1791, ibid.

342 **"the bursting of the bubble"**: Rush, *Autobiography*, p. 204.

342 **oldest son, Philip**: BR to Alexander Hamilton, November 26, 1801, ibid.

343 **"Plan of a Peace-Office"**: Rush, *Essays*, p. 183.

346 **active in the Abolition Society**: Rush went on to lead the new American Convention of Abolition Societies—for which all the state abolition groups met biannually in Philadelphia, beginning in 1794. That same year, he quietly purchased tracts of land in south central Pennsylvania and tried to donate 5,200 acres to the PA Abolition Society to create a black farming settlement he hoped would be called "Benezet." The settlement never came to be, but long after his death, the donation was criticized by some historians who claimed he wanted to exile blacks from Philadelphia, for which there is no evidence.

Chapter 35

348 **"A malignant fever"**: BR to JSR, August 21, 1792, in Rush, *Letters*, p. 637.

348 **"beyond the reach"**: BR to JSR, August 21, 1792, ibid., p. 637.

349 **Marcus—who had been**: BR to JSR, October 14, 1783, ibid., p. 715.

349 **"The fever"**: BR to JSR, August 25, 1791, ibid., p. 640.

349 **seeing early cases**: Rush, *Account of Bilious Remitting Yellow Fever.*

350 **"flying from the city"**: BR to JSR, August 25, 1791, ibid., p. 640.

350 **"to put a stop to the tolling"**: *Proceedings of the College of Physicians*, p. 2.

350 **"unnecessary intercourse"**: Ibid.

350 **"too frequently upon handkerchiefs"**: Ibid.

350 **But since Shippen had**: Powell, *Bring Out Your Dead*, p. 84.

350 **"do good"**: BR to JSR, August 26, 1793, in Rush, *Letters*, p. 642.

351 **"I hope I shall do well"**: BR to JSR, August 25, 1793, ibid., p. 641.

351 **the boys had to leave**: BR to JSR, August 26, 1973, ibid., p. 642.

351 **one of the servants**: BR to JSR, August 29, 1793, ibid., p. 644.

351 **"For some days past"**: BR to JSR, August 27, 1793, in Rush, *Letters*, p. 643.

351 **"a man and his wife"**: Carey, *Short Account of Malignant Fever*, p. 35.

351 **"a solitary corpse"**: BR to JSR, September 1, 1793, in Rush, *Letters*, p. 646.

352 **"ineffectual to open"**: BR to Nicholas Belleville, September 3, 1793, ibid., p. 648.

352 **"chicken water"**: Ibid.

352 **"Adieu"**: BR to JSR, September 3, 1793, ibid., p. 649.

352 **"mercurial antidote"**: BR to JSR, September 5, 1793, ibid., p. 650.

352 **"new remedy"**: Ibid.

353 **John Mitchell**: John Mitchell, *An Account of the Yellow Fever*, p. 115.

354 **"mode of treating the disorder"**: Alexander Hamilton to College of Physicians, September 11, 1793, Founders Online.

354 **"I think it probable"**: BR to JSR, October 3, 1793.

355 **"As it is a time"**: Allen and Jones, "For Nursing of the Sick," *Dunlap's Daily Advertiser*, September 11, 1793.

355 **"It has pleased God to visit"**: BR to Absalom Jones and Richard Allen, September 1793, in Newman, *Freedom's Prophet*, p. 88.

356 **"late Doctor Lining"**: "For the American Daily Advertiser, from Benezet," *Dunlap's Daily Advertiser*, September 2, 1792, p. 2. For more on Dr. Lining, see McDonald Burbidge, "John Lining," http://www.clansinclairsc.org/brother_john_lining.htm.

356 **"I have bled twice"**: BR to College of Physicians, September 12, 1793, in Rush, *Letters*, p. 661.

356 **"Dr. Rush . . . hopes this information"**: Rush to His Fellow Citizens, "Treatment for Yellow Fever," *Federal Gazette*, September 12, 1793, ibid., p. 660.

356 **"Doctor Rush's success"**: Henry Knox to GW, September 15, 1793, Founders Online.

356 **"Everybody whose head aches"**: Henry Knox to GW, September 18, 1793, ibid.

357 **"After a restless night"**: BR to JSR, September 12, 1793, in Rush, *Letters*, p. 662.

357 **"My eyes are tinged"**: BR to JSR, September 13, 1793, ibid., p. 663.

357 **he had his first attack**: Ibid., p. 665n2.

357 **He had been living**: BR to Rachel Rush Montgomery, September 18, 1793, ibid., p. 666.

358 **"the French remedies"**: Rush, *An Account*, p. 302.

358 **"On our going into"**: Allen and Jones, *Proceedings of the Black People*, p. 18.

358 **"A white man threatened"**: Allen, *Life, Experience and Gospel Labors*.

358 **"among the late dead are"**: BR to JSR, September 18, 1793, in Rush, *Letters*, p. 669.

359 **"my dear and amiable pupil"**: BR to JSR, September 23, 1793, ibid., p. 676.

359 **"The Negros are everywhere"**: BR to JSR, September 25, 1793, ibid., p. 683.

359 **"overcome with fatigue"**: BR to JSR, September 26, 1793, ibid., pp. 684–85.

359 **"This infatuation with respect"**: BR to JSR, September 29, 1793, in Rush, *Letters*, p. 686.

Chapter 36

360 **"so much agitated"**: JSR to BR, September 22, 1793, in Rush, *Letters*, pp. 674–75.

360 **"I have endeavored to keep up my spirits"**: Julia Rush to BR, October 22, 1793, APS.

361 **"You write like a spectator"**: BR to JSR, September 30, 1793, ibid., p. 688.

362 **Rush's sister, Rebecca**: BR to JSR, October 1, 1793, ibid., p. 690.

362 **"I am denied the melancholy"**: JSR to BR, October 3, 1793, ibid., p. 701.

363 **"I cast a look"**: BR to JSR, October 2, 1793, ibid., p. 693.

363 **"I have no Papa"**: BR to JSR, October 8, 1793, ibid., p. 709.

363 **"Our son John you know"**: BR to JSR, October 10, 1793, ibid., p. 711.

363 **"attacked in the most violent"**: BR to JSR, November 8, 1793, ibid., p. 742.

364 **"I dreamed that I saw"**: BR to JSR, October 13, 1793, ibid., p. 714.

364 **"The disease continues to rage"**: BR to JSR, October 14, 1793, ibid., p. 715.

365 **thrilled at how nippy**: BR to JSR, October 21, 1793, ibid., p. 721.

365 **"revived the disease"**: BR to JSR, October 23, 1793, ibid., p. 723.

365 **"I shall probably require"**: BR to JSR, October 24, 1793, ibid., p. 724.

365 **"there is great sympathy"**: JSR to BR, October 11, 1793, APS.

366 **"When you have done"**: JSR to BR, October 24, 1793, ibid.

366 **"a prayer of the lowly"**: BR to JSR, October 9, 1793, in Rush, *Letters*, p. 708.

366 **"I find I am a perfect"**: BR to JSR, November 11, 1793, ibid., p. 745.

366 **"the printed directions"**: BR to JSR, October 29, 1793, ibid., p. 732.

367 **sent his apprentice**: BR to JSR, November 12, 1793, ibid., p. 745.

367 **baby Julia**: JSR to BR, October 29, 1793, APS.

367 **"most noted inhabitants"**: Carey, *Short Account of Malignant Fever*, p. 100.

368 **6 percent**: Gibson and Jung, Historical Census Statistics on Population Totals by Race, 1790 to 1990, p. 95.

368 **overcharged**: Carey, Short Account of Malignant Fever, pp. 77, 82.

369 **"We feel a great"**: Jones and Allen, *Narrative of Proceedings of Black People*, p. 17.

371 **"by the want of health"**: Rush, *Account of Bilious Remitting Yellow Fever*, preface.

Chapter 37

374 **Philippe Pinel**: Weiner, "Pinel's 'Memoir on Madness,'" p. 732.

375 **"restore alienated"**: Ibid., p. 730.

376 **"the blood of maniacs"**: Pinel, *Treatise on Insanity*, p. 151.

376 **William Tuke**: Bewley, *Madness to Mental Illness*, p. 5.

377 **heavily marked-up**: Carlson, *Rush's Lectures*, pp. 85–6.

377 **"acknowledged a belief"**: Rush, *Autobiography*, p. 231.

377 **preferred a quieter life**: Rush, *Letters*, p. 753n2.

379 **Mary Wollstonecraft**: Wigginton, "Late Night Vindication," p. 231.

379 **Tench Coxe**: Cooke, *Tench Coxe*, chap. 1.

379 **David Rittenhouse**: Rush, *Autobiography*, p. 234.

380 **"I declined the offer"**: Ibid.

380 **mother, Susanna**: Rush, *Autobiography*, p. 166.

380 **"retained the vigor"**: Ibid.

382 **"I have lately discharged"**: BR to John Redman Coxe, January 16, 1796, in Rush, *Letters*, p. 769.

382 **"my late success"**: BR to John Redman Coxe, April 24, 1796, ibid., p. 774.

382 **Dr. Francis Willis**: Pearce, "Role of Dr. Francis Willis," pp. 196–99.

382 **Calcutta**: BR to John Rush, May 25, 1796, in Rush, *Letters*, p. 776.

382 **"premature"**: BR to John Redman Coxe, May 25, 1796, ibid., p. 777.

383 **write his thesis**: Ambrose, "Plagiarism of Ideas," pp. 20–23.

383 **"almost hysterical"**: Caldwell, *Autobiography*, p. 245.

384 **"a man of immense"**: Rush, *Autobiography*, p. 236.

384 **"All is calm"**: BR to Samuel Bayard, September 22, 1796, in Rush, *Letters*, p. 780.

385 **"general suffrage"**: BR to Samuel Bayard, November 25, 1796, ibid., p. 782.

385 **"mournful occasion"**: Rush, "Eulogium upon Rittenhouse," p. 6.

386 **modern facility**: Morton and Woodbury, *History of Pennsylvania Hospital*, pp. 77–80.

386 **"Dr. Rush's Tongue"**: JA to AA, January 1, 1797, Founders Online.

387 **"The remorseless Dr. Rush"**: Cobbett, *Porcupine's Political Censor*, in *Porcupine's Works*, p. 362.

388 **"Is it probable"**: BR to Horatio Gates, August 25, 1797, in Rush, *Letters*, p. 788.

388 **planning to apprentice**: Rush, *Autobiography*, p. 369.

388 **why black people**: BR to TJ, February 4, 1797, in Rush, *Letters*, p. 785.

389 **"with humanity"**: BR to TJ, February 4, 1797, in Rush, *Letters*, p 785. This leprosy paper, a revision of one he delivered at the Abolition Society in 1792, became infamous in the twentieth century among academics who suggested that it informed or enabled physicians who had espoused racist medical ideas beginning in the 1830s. (One of the physicians was Rush's embittered former student Charles Caldwell, who had moved to Kentucky and began championing theories of racial inferiority.) I suspect Rush would have been shocked and saddened by the weaponizing of his ideas, and it's worth noting his whole quote to Jefferson about his intent in publishing the paper. He wrote, "The inferences from it will be in favor of treating them with humanity, and justice, and of keeping up the existing prejudices against matrimonial connextions with them." The latter point indicates that Rush was either against intermarriage or was not ready to attack prejudice against it. But overall, Rush was known

in his time as a champion of racial equality and abolition. In 1796, one racist newspaper reported incredulously that Rush had said in a public address that "the same *God* made *black men* as well as *white*! A thing too shocking to be believed by a *gentleman*!" For a balanced assessment of the impact of the leprosy paper, see the *Lancet* piece by medical historian William Bynum, July 27, 2002. "Rush's suggestion that black skin resulted from leprosy found few advocates," he wrote. "It remains one of the more bizarre attempts to account for human diversity while arguing for the ultimate brotherhood of mankind."

389 **"all the claims"**: Rush, "Observations Intended to Favour a Supposition," p. 295.

389 **"as Dr. Johnson said"**: Butterfield, "Rush as a Promoter," p. 34.

Chapter 38

390 **"was seized after a ride"**: BR to Horatio Gates, September 2, 1797, in Rush, *Letters*, p. 788.

390 **"Our combined exertions"**: BR to Ashbel Green, September 10, 1797, ibid., p. 789.

391 **"Rush behaves like"**: Myrsiades, *Medical Culture*, p. 98.

391 **"Mind is greatly clouded"**: Elias Boudinot to Timothy Pickering, September 4, 1797, in *Walter J. Husak Collection Auction Catalog*, p. 101.

391 **dozens of applications**: JA to BR, September 30, 1805, Founders Online EA.

392 **"celebrity of character"**: Oliver Wolcott, Jr., to JA, September 26, 1797, Founders Online EA.

392 **"on Account of ancient"**: JA to Oliver Wolcott, Jr., September 15, 1797, ibid., EA.

392 **"known, esteemed"**: JA to Timothy Pickering, September 18, 1797, ibid., EA.

392 **"lunatic system"**: *Gazette of the United States*, September 1797.

392 **"A Tavern Keeper"**: "A Tavern Keeper Shall Appear in Monday's Paper," *Porcupine's Gazette*, September 16, 1797.

392 **"The times are ominous"**: "Medical Puffing," *Porcupine's Gazette*, September 17, 1797; see also Carpenter, *Report of Action for Libel*.

393 **"villainous liquors"**: *Porcupine's Gazette*, September 22, 1797.

393 **"Doctor Sangrado"**: "Sangrado Practitioners," *Porcupine's Gazette*, September 21, 1797.

393 **"Those feeble attacks"**: "For the Gazette, by H.," *Gazette of the United States*, September 30, 1797.

394 **"an impudent puppy"**: Looney and Woodward, *Princetonians, 1791–1794*, p. 433.

394 **"If you think there"**: BR to John R. B. Rodgers, October 16, 1797, in Rush, *Letters*, p. 794.

394 **voted unanimously**: "Letter from the Faculty of Physic October 97, Recommending the election of Dr Rush to a medical professorship," Columbia College, October 19, 1797, Columbia University Rare Book & Manuscript Library.

394 **Hamilton was a prominent**: "Meeting of the Trustees of Columbia College," November 2, 1797, Columbia University Rare Book & Manuscript Library.

394 **be postponed**: BR to John R. B. Rodgers, November 6, 1797, in Rush, *Letters*, pp. 794–95.

395 **"whether the old leaven"**: Rush, *Letters*, p. 794n4.

395 **took the treasurer's job**: BR to Horatio Gates, November 30, 1797, in Rush, *Letters*, p. 796.

395 **"a few minutes"**: BR to to Ashton Alexander, February 20, 1797, in Rush, *Letters*, p. 796.

395 **"deplorable condition"**: JA to AA, March 22, 1797, Founders Online.

395 **"act towards him"**: BR to Ashton Alexander, February 20, 1798, Founders Online, in Rush, *Letters*, pp. 796–97.

396 **Timber and Slumb**: Ibid., p. 804n.

396 **brick dwelling**: BR to JSR, September 28, 1798, ibid., p. 808.

396 **"Sydenham Hut"**: BR to JSR, August 28, 1798, ibid., p. 804.

396 **surgeon's mate**: Sobocinski, "John Rush," p. 7.

397 **"Even the retirement"**: BR to JSR, August 29, 1798, in Rush, *Letters*, p. 804.

397 **Nearly 3,500**: Ellis, *A Melancholy Sense of Devastation*, p. 178.

397 **Lt. Archibald McElroy**: Carlson and Wollock, "Rush and Insane Son," p. 1321.

398 **"quitted physic"**: BR to John Montgomery, June 21, 1799, in Rush, *Letters*, p. 812.

398 **"Our eldest son"**: BR to AA, July 1, 1799, Founders Online.

398 **"venereal disease"**: Pennsylvania Hospital Manager's Notes, 1799.

398 **"This day died and"**: Rush, *Autobiography*, p. 246.

399 **"I have a view of the subject"**: TJ to BR, September 23, 1800, Founders Online.

399 **"keep religion and government"**: BR to TJ, October 6, 1800, ibid.

399 **"muskmelon seeds"**: Ibid.

400 **"cutt off in the flower"**: JA to TJ, March 24, 1801, Founders Online EA.

400 **"asylum for drunkards"**: Rush, *A Plan for an Asylum for Drunkards*, in Rush, *Autobiography*.

401 **"our friend"**: BR to AA, July 1, 1799, ibid.

401 **"your best friend"**: BR to AA, December 19, 1798, ibid.

401 **"*whisper* in your son's"**: BR to AA, July 18, 1799, ibid.

401 **Alien and Sedition Acts:** "The Alien and Sedition Acts," Avalon Project, http://avalon.law.yale.edu/subject_menus/alsedact.asp.

401 **hiding out in New York**: Myrsiades, *Medical Culture*, p. 4.

401 **"See Porcupine"**: "See Porcupine in Colors," HSP, https://discover.hsp.org/Record/dc-1379.

402 **Washington was seriously**: Markel, "December 14, 1799: The Excruciating Final Hours of President George Washington," *PBS NewsHour*, December 14, 2014.

402 **one paper could jam**: "General George Washington, Alexandria, December 16," *Philadelphia Gazette*, December 18, 1799.

403 **"white, trimmed"**: *Philadelphia Gazette*, December 19, 1799.

403 **mayor of Philadelphia**: *Gazette of the United States*, December 19, 1799.

403 **"first in war, first"**: Lee, "Funeral Oration."

403 **"sensible and moderate"**: Rush, *Autobiography*, p. 249.

403 **"unequivocal proof"**: GW to Archibald Blair, June 24, 1799, Founders Online.

Chapter 39

404 **"*the practice of Rush*"**: Cobbett, *Porcupine's Gazette*, January 13, 1800.

405 **"I affirm this John Rush"**: Cobbett, *The Rush Light*, February 13, 1800, p. 30.

405 **catch the next stage**: BR to Brockholst Livingston, March 5, 1800, in Rush, *Letters*, p. 816.

406 **"bludgeon cane"**: Looney and Woodward, *Princetonians, 1791–1794*, p. 434.

406 **"armed with a large iron"**: "John Stelle to the Public," *New York Commercial Advertiser*, March 11, 1800.

406 **"refused any fee"**: Myrsiades, *Medical Culture*, p. 207.

407 **"I cannot express to you"**: BR to AA, October 12, 1800, Founders Online EA.

408 **"I am sorry that"**: AA to BR, October 18, 1800, ibid., EA.

408 **"distressed family"**: BR to AA, October 17, 1800, ibid., EA.

408 **"It would be a great"**: TJ to BR, September 23, 1800, ibid.

409 **"Representative & elective"**: BR to TJ, October 6, 1800, ibid.

410 **she stopped in Philadelphia**: Rush, *Autobiography*, p. 254.

411 **"at our little farm"**: BR to AA, July 23, 1801, Founders Online EA.

411 **"will be read with pleasure"**: AA to BR, August 1801, ibid., EA.

413 **"I read the whole"**: Powell, *Richard Rush*, p. 7.

413 **"Johnson's writings"**: Ibid.

413 ***Port Folio***: Mott, *History of American Magazines*, p. 244.

413 **"You do not weep"**: BR to Alexander Hamilton, November 16, 1801, Founders Online.

413 **"I felt all the weight"**: Alexander Hamilton to BR, March 29, 1809, ibid.

414 **his lectures**: Rush, *Sixteen Introductory Lectures*.

414 **His hair braided**: Richmond Enquirer, "Biography of Dr. Rush," p. 279.

414 **"On the Connexion"**: Rush, *Sixteen Introductory Lectures*, p. 5.

415 **"On the duty and advantages"**: Ibid., p. 96.

415 **"the vices and virtues"**: Ibid., 122.

415 **"the duties of patients"**: Ibid., 320.

415 **"the construction and"**: Ibid., 182.

416 **"Dr. Rush remarked"**: Darlington, *Notes*, pp. 2–4.

417 **"a person whose business"**: Ibid., p. 22.

417 **"bound them over"**: Rush, *Autobiography*, p. 262.

417 **"has become a fashionable"**: Jacob Rush, *Charges and Extracts of Charges*, p. 150.

418 **"about 10 chosen"**: TJ to BR, February 28, 1803, Founders Online.

418 **"I shall expect to see"**: BR to TJ, March 12, 1803, ibid.

419 **"ever from love"**: Rush, *Autobiography*, pp. 265–67.

419 **prone to**: TJ to Paul Allen, August 13, 1813.

419 **"Rushes Pills"**: September 24, 1805, the Journals of the Lewis and Clark Expedition; Rush, *Autobiography*, p. 267n71.

419 **"Questions to Merryweather"**: Rush, *Autobiography*, p. 265.

420 **"Directions for Mr. Lewis"**: Ibid., p. 267.

420 **"His mission is truly"**: BR to TJ, June 11, 1803, Founders Online.

420 **"So anxious was he"**: Rush, *Autobiography*, p. 261.

420 **"The Causes of Sudden"**: John Rush, *The Causes of Sudden Death*, p. 3.

421 **"Elements of Life"**: John Rush, *Elements of Life*, p. 6.

422 **"reserve and throw away"**: Alexander Hamilton, "Statement on Impending Duel with Aaron Burr," June 28–July 10, 1804, Founders Online.

422 **"was learned, ingenious"**: Rush, *Autobiography*, p. 313.

Chapter 40

424 **"Mount Wollaston"**: JA to BR, February 6, 1805, Founders Online.

425 **"pass'd a couple"**: JQA to JA, November 3, 1804, ibid.

425 **"worth reading"**: JA to Thomas Boylston Adams, April 2, 1803, ibid.

425 **"There are Some Deleterious"**: JA to JQA, November 16, 1804, ibid.

426 **"My much respected &"**: BR to JA, February 19, 1805, ibid.

426 **"No civilized Society"**: JA to BR, February 27, 1805, ibid.

427 **"I hardly need to"**: BR to JA, June 29, 1805, ibid.

427 **"I cheerfully agree"**: JA to BR, July 7, 1805, ibid.

427 **"None of your letters"**: BR to JA, August 14, 1805, ibid.

427 **"deeply interest"**: Ibid.

427 **"the fireside"**: BR to JA, March 13, 1809, ibid.

427 **his 1790 dream**: BR to JA, March 23, 1805, ibid.

427 **"I admire the Brilliancy"**: JA to BR, April 11, 1805, ibid.

428 **"part of which"**: BR to JA, August 14, 1805, ibid.

429 **"I am extreamly Sorry"**: JA to BR, August 23, 1805, ibid.

429 **"I am pleased in reflecting"**: BR to JA, November 21, 1805, ibid.

430 **"There is Quackery"**: BR to JA, September 21, 1805, ibid.

430 **"both these certificates"**: BR to Secretary of the Navy, 39 Rush manuscripts 71, LCP.

430 **Within two weeks**: United States, *Register of Officer Personnel U.S. Navy*, p. 48.

430 **"Very contrary to my wishes"**: BR to JA, July 11, 1806, Founders Online.

430 **a skilled seaman**: Loomey and Woodward, *Princetonians, 1791–1794*, p. 435.

430 **before going to Edinburgh**: Rush, *Autobiography*, p. 280.

431 **"I entreat [my sons]"**: Ibid., p. 162.

431 **The duel took place**: Carlson and Wollock, "Rush and Insane Son," p. 1312.

431 **distinguished himself in battle**: "Turner Family Manuscript Archives," American History Live Salesroom Auction, June 12, 2015, https://auctions.bidsquare.com/view-auctions/catalog/id/663/lot/236969/cowans-auctions-turner-family-manuscript-archive.

432 **"kill or be killed"**: BR to JA, December 15, 1807, Founders Online.

432 **"some trifling argument"**: Ibid.

432 **"This morning at 10 o'clock"**: "Extract of a Letter from a Gentleman in New-Orleans, to His Friend in Washington, Dated October 1," *New York Weekly Museum*, November 14, 1807.

433 **concerned about John**: "Pennsylvania Hospital Managers' Notes, 1807," American Philosophical Society Archives, p. 58.

433 **"melancholy hallucinations"**: *The Life of Timothy Pickering*, vol. 4. p. 70.

433 **philanthropist Stephen Girard**: "Pennsylvania Hospital Managers' Notes, 1807," APS, 10.

434 **"gyrater"**: BR to Timothy Pickering, March 2, 1808, in Rush, *Letters*, p. 961.

434 **unlikely patient**: Rush, *Autobiography*, p. 322.

435 **"An event has occurred"**: Rush, *Close of a Lecture on the duties of patients to their physicians*. November 7, 1808. Found in Slack, *The American Orator*, p. 282.

435 **"Beg my father"**: John Rush to RR, June 25, 1808, in Looney and Woodward, *Princetonians, 1791–1794*, p. 436.

436 **"gunplay"**: Ibid.

436 **"attack of insanity"**: Carlson and Wollock, "Rush and Insane Son," p. 1315.

436 **"re-established"**: Ibid., p. 1314.

437 **"I will not pursue"**: Ibid., p. 1323.

437 **"settle your accounts"**: Carlson, p. 1314.

437 **"Our fellow student"**: Ibid., p. 1316.

438 **"My Eldest son John"**: BR to JA, July 26, 1809, Founders Online.

438 **"John's Misfortune"**: JA to BR, August 7, 1809, ibid.

438 **Charles's death from**: Kendall, "First Children Who Led Sad Lives," Smithsonian.com, February 11, 2016.

439 **"I have great pleasure"**: BR to JA, August 14, 1809, Founders Online.

439 **"I hope his gloom will wear off"**: JA to BR, August 31, 1809, ibid.

439 **a new edition**: Sydenham, *The Works of Thomas Sydenham, M.D.*

440 **turning into a proof sheet**: BR to JA, September 6, 1809, Founders Online.

Chapter 41

441 **"neither ancestors nor posterity"**: BR to JA, October 17, 1809, Founders Online EA.

443 **"A Dream again!"**: JA to BR, October 25, 1809, ibid., EA.

444 **a long holiday letter**: BR to James Rush, December 22, 1809, in Rush, *Letters*, p. 1029.

444 **"sufficient authority"**: Carlson and Wollock, "Rush and Insane Son," p. 1317.

444 **younger son Ben**: BR to James Rush, February 7, 1810, in Rush, *Letters*, p. 1035.

444 **"He arrived in Philadelphia"**: BR to JA, April 26, 1810, Founders Online.

445 **"much improved"**: BR to JA, April 26, 1810, Founders Online EA.

445 **"Could the advocates"**: Ibid.

445 **to remove a tumor**: BR to JA, September 20, 1811, ibid., EA.

446 **"The last time I saw him"**: JA to Joseph Delaplaine, December 17, 1815, ibid., EA.

447 **"The barber on combing"**: Samuel Coates, "Memorandum Book," p. 19, APS.

448 **"deranged at present"**: BR to James Rush, June 8, 1810, in Rush, *Letters*, p. 1052.

448 **Tranquilizer**: "Diseases of the Mind: Highlights of American Psychiatry through 1900," National Library of Medicine, https://www.nlm.nih.gov/hmd/diseases/index.html.

448 **"In this state they often"**: BR to John Redman Coxe, September 5, 1801, in Rush, *Letters*, p. 1810.

449 **Pinel's book had been translated**: Woods and Carlson, "Myth About Pinel," p. 32.

449 **"There is a great pleasure"**: BR to the Managers of the Pennsylvania Hospital, September 24, 1810, in Rush, *Letters*, p. 1063.

451 **"those states of the mind"**: Simon and Gold, *Textbook of Forensic Psychiatry*, p. 19.

451 **"Your and my Old friend"**: BR to TJ, January 2, 1811, Founders Online.

452 **"North and South poles"**: BR to JA, February 17, 1812, ibid., EA.

453 **"portraits of remarkable"**: TJ to BR, February 16, 1811, ibid.

453 **His son Richard and his wife**: *Letters*, 1081, n. 3 and 4.

453 **a collection of**: Rush, "Sixteen introductory lectures to courses of lectures upon the institutes and practice of medicine," Archive.Org, https://archive.org/details/2569048R.nlm.nih.gov).

454 **"Is it possible"**: *Sixteen Introductory Lectures*, p. 293.

455 **"the anguish of my Soul"**: Rush, *Autobiography*, p. 295.

455 **a large lump**: Frank Krystyniak, "Jim Olson's Essay on Abigail Adams."

455 **"Let there be no delay"**: BR to JA, September 20, 1811, Founders Online EA.

456 **"All my family rejoice"**: BR to JA, October 18, 1811, ibid., EA.

456 **"make the Excision of a"**: JA to BR, November 2, 1811, ibid.

456 **"going out in the dark"**: Ibid.

456 **leaving Philadelphia**: "*Richard Rush* (1817)," University of Virginia Miller Center, https://millercenter.org/president/monroe/essays/rush-1817-attorney-general.

456 **Comptroller**: Powell, *Richard Rush*, p. 19.

456 **"Shall I congratulate"**: JA to BR, December 4, 1811, Founders Online EA.

457 **"You have touched me"**: BR to JA, December 9, 1811, ibid., EA.

457 **"the ranks and privileges"**: Rush, *Letters*, p. 1109n2.

458 **"the unprincipled licenciousness"**: TJ to BR, December 5, 1811, Founders Online.

458 **"I exchange letters Once"**: BR to JA, December 16, 1811, ibid., EA.

459 **The next day Rush wrote to Jefferson**: BR to TJ, December 17, 1811, ibid.

459 **"I was never so much at a loss"**: JA to BR, December 25, 1811, ibid., EA.

460 **"Independently of his affection"**: BR to JA, December 26, 1811, Founders Online EA.

460 **"American manufacturers"**: JA to TJ, January 1, 1812, ibid., EA.

460 **When Jefferson wrote back**: TJ to JA, January 21, 1812, ibid., EA.

460 **"As it is thro'"**: TJ to BR, January 21, 1812, ibid.

461 **"My Dreamer! Your dream is"**: JA to BR, February 10, 1812, ibid., EA.

461 **"I rejoice in the correspondence"**: BR to JA, February 17, 1812, ibid.

462 **"In my Opinion"**: JA to BR, January 8, 1812, ibid., EA.

463 **"I did not require"**: BR to JA, February 12, 1812, ibid., EA.

464 **"two young girls"**: BR to JA, June 4, 1812, ibid., EA.

Chapter 42

465 **"the result of the reading"**: BR to TJ, April 26, 1812, Founders Online.

465 **Catherine, was pregnant**: Powell, *Richard Rush*, p. 30.

465 **"a meagre village"**: RR to JA, September 5, 1814, ibid., EA.

465 **secretary**: Richard Rush's Proposal that Thomas Jefferson become Secretary of State, May 24, 1812, Founders Online.

466 **"When tossed upon"**: Rush, *Autobiography*, p. 299. The original poem is William Cowper, "To Mary," http://www.luminarium.org/eightlit/cowper/mary2.htm.

468 **"a few larger, Struggling"**: BR to JA, July 13, 1812, Founders Online EA.

468 **"In entering upon"**: Rush, *Medical Inquiries and Observations upon Diseases of the Mind*, p. 9.

468 **"the 'Common Science'"**: BR to JA, November 4, 1812, Founders Online EA.

468 **"hitherto been enveloped"**: Ibid.

471 **She had died in the hospital**: Rolph, "Strange Insanity of Hannah Lewis."

475 **"constitutional with him"**: JSR to AA, June 23, 1813, Founders Online EA.

475 **"fellow Citizens"**: BR to JA, December 14, 1812, ibid., EA.

476 **"Reproaches, vilifications"**: JA to BR, November 14, 1812, ibid., EA.

476 **"run mankind still deeper"**: JA to BR, November 29, ibid.

476 **"advertized as the most"**: JA to BR, December 8, 1812, ibid., EA.

477 **"so far outdreamed me"**: BR to JA, December 14, 1812, ibid., EA.

477 **"his labors and his advancing"**: JSR to AA, June 23, 1813, ibid., EA. Julia's description of Rush's last months and death come from this long letter.

479 **"immortal"**: BR to JA, April 10, 1813, ibid., EA.

479 **"superintend"**: "The frigate Adams," *The Columbian*, April 5, 1813.

479 **"feared he was getting"**: JSR to AA, June 23, 1813, ibid., EA.

Epilogue

483 **"tydings that rent"**: AA to JSR, April 24, 1813, Founders Online EA.

484 **"The citizens testified"**: *Democratic Press*, May 1, 1813.

484 **"I reached his disconsolate"**: Powell, *Richard Rush*, p. 43.

484 **"unusually large"**: College of Physicians, *Transactions*, Centenniel Volume, p. 139.

485 **"His death is a public"**: *Philadelphia Freeman's Journal*, April 20, 1813.

485 **"the excellent Dr. Rush"**: *Poulson's Daily Advertiser*, May 1, 1813.

485 **"Another of our friends"**: TJ to JA, May 27, 1813, Founders Online.

485 **"I lament with you"**: JA to TJ, June 11, 1813, ibid., EA.

485 **"You know much"**: JA to Benjamin Waterhouse, May 9, 1813, Founders Online EA.

485 **"Dr Rush was a greater"**: JA to RR, July 22, 1816, ibid., EA.

486 **official period**: David Ramsay, *Eulogium upon Benjamin Rush*.

487 **handful**: Philip Physick to James Madison, April 21, 1813, Founders Online.

487 **to ask if he could have**: TJ to RR, May 31, 1813, ibid.

488 **"to the afflictions"**: TJ to BR, April 21, 1803, ibid.

488 **the doctor had burned**: RR to TJ, June 27, 1813, ibid.

488 **corruptions of organized religion**: JA to TJ, August 9, 1813, ibid.

488 **"I wish it may Stimulate You"**: Ibid.

488 **"often have I heard"**: RR to TJ, August 12, 1813, ibid.

489 **"it is my wish"**: Rush, *Autobiography*, p. 23. See the introduction to *Autobiography* for discussion of manuscripts.

489 **"I rejoice that Dr Rush"**: JA to John Fothergill Waterhouse, August 5, 1813, Founders Online EA.

490 **escaped on horseback**: Powell, *Richard Rush*, pp. 60–65.

490 **"I know not how"**: JA to James Mease, August 24, 1816, Founders Online EA.

492 **huge banquet**: Nicholas Wainwright, "The Diary of Samuel Breck, 1814–1822," p. 506.

492 **"sat down, about 6 o'clock**: *Boston Traveler*, July 29, 1825.

492 **"To the memory of Benjamin"**: *Statesman*, August 29, 1825.

493 **"These gentlemen sunk into"**: BR to JA, October 17, 1809, Founders Online.

493 **"Thomas Jefferson survives"**: McCullough, *John Adams*, pp. 647–49.

493 **"North and South poles"**: BR to JA, February 17, 1812, Founders Online EA.

493 **"Who could have supposed"**: *Niles Register* 30, July 22, 1826, pp. 370–71.

494 **"in a trice"**: Gross, *Autobiography*, p. 378.

494 **"seemed to have read"**: Wilson, "Acting of Forrest," pp. 483–91.

Afterword

497 **Rush's most controversial writings**: The saga of what happened to Rush's writing after he died is best summed up in the preface to Rush, *Autobiography*, pp. 1–10; the best analysis of what happened to his legacy appears in Butterfield, "The Reputation of Benjamin Rush."

498 **retrieve the massive**: The best explanation of Richard's role in the Smithson Trust case is in Powell, *Richard Rush*, p. 236–43; and on the Smithsonian site https://siarchives.si.edu/collections/siris_sic_9923 https://www.si.edu/about/history.

500 **burned much of**: Powell, *Richard Rush*, p. 178.

500 **"Rush left letters"**: Weir, "Commemorative Address," *Centennial Anniversary of the Institution of the College of Physicians in Philadelphia*, p. 16n.

503 **hired a Manhattan auction house:** "The Alexander Biddle Papers" Parke-Bernet Galleries 1943, 3 vols. The hard-to-find catalogues from this auction are a great Rush resource, not only because many of the items in them have never been seen again, but because it's a reminder of how many historical letters and documents were held by the Rush family for so many years during which histories were being written without them.

509 **six of the papers:** "Special Issue: The Republics of Benjamin Rush," *Early American Studies* 15, no. 2 (Spring 2017).

BIBLIOGRAPHY

Writings of Benjamin Rush

"An Account of the Late Dr. Hugh Martin's Cancer Powder, with Brief Observations on Cancers." *Transactions of the American Philosophical Society* 2 (1786).

"An Account of the Life and Character of Mrs. Elizabeth Ferguson." *Port Folio* 1 (1809): 520–27.

An Account of the Bilious Remitting Yellow Fever, As It Appeared In the City of Philadelphia, in the Year 1793. Philadelphia: Thomas Dobson, 1794.

An Account of the Sugar Maple-Tree, of the United States. Philadelphia: Aitken, 1791.

An Address to the Inhabitants of the British Settlements, on the Slavery of the Negroes in America. Philadelphia: John Dunlap, 1773.

The Autobiography of Benjamin Rush: His "Travels Through Life" Together with His Commonplace Book for 1789–1813. Edited by George W. Corner. Princeton: Princeton University Press, 1948.

Benjamin Rush's Lectures on the Mind. Edited, annotated, and introduced by Eric T. Carlson, Jeffrey L. Wollock and Patricia S. Noel. Philadelphia: American Philosophical Society, 1981.

Directions for Preserving the Health of Soldiers. Lancaster, PA: John Dunlap, 1778.

An Enquiry into the Effects of Public Punishments upon Criminals, and upon Society. Philadelphia: Joseph James, 1787.

An Enquiry into the Effects of Spirituous Liquors upon the Human Body. Philadelphia: Bradford, 1784.

"An Eulogium upon David Rittenhouse." Delivered to the American Philosophical Society on December 17, 1796, https://quod.lib.umich.edu/e/evans/N25938.0001.001/1:7.22?rgn=div2;view=fulltext.

Essays: Literary, Moral and Philosophical. Philadelphia: Bradford, 1798. https://quod.lib.umich.edu/e/evans/N25938.0001.001/1:7.20?rgn=div2;view=fulltext. Also, newer version edited by Michael Meranze, Union College Press, 1988.

"Excerpts from the Papers of Dr. Benjamin Rush." *Pennsylvania Magazine of History and Biography* 29, no. 1 (1905): 15–30.

"Historical Notes of Dr. Benjamin Rush, 1777." *Pennsylvania Magazine of History and Biography* 27, no. 2 (1903).

An Inquiry into the Influence of Physical Causes upon the Moral Faculty. Philadelphia: Haswell, Barrington and Haswell, 1839.

Letters of Benjamin Rush. Edited by Lyman H. Butterfield. 2 vols. Princeton: Princeton University Press, 1951.

The Life and Character of Christopher Ludwick. Philadelphia: Garden and Thompson, 1831.

Medical Inquiries and Observations, 5th ed. Philadelphia: M. Carey & Son, 1818.

Medical Inquiries and Observations, upon the Diseases of the Mind. Philadelphia: Kimber & Richardson, 1812.

My Dearest Julia: The Loveletters of Dr. Benjamin Rush to Julia Stockton. New York: Neale Watson Academic, 1979.

"Observations on the Means of Preserving the Health of Soldiers and Sailors." *Pennsylvania Packet*, April 22, 1777.

"Observations Intended to Favour a Supposition That the Black Color (As It Is Called) Of the Negroes Is Derived from the Leprosy." *Transactions of the American Philosophical Society* 4 (1799).

"On the Different Species of Manias." In Dagobert Runes, ed., *Selected Writings of Benjamin Rush.* New York: Philosophical Library, 1947.

An Oration . . . Containing, an Enquiry into the Natural History of Medicine Among the Indians in North-America . . . Philadelphia: Crukshank, 1774.

"Paradise of Negro-Slaves—A Dream." In Rush, *Essays: Literary, Moral and Philosophical.* Philadelphia: Bradford, 1798.

A Plan for the Establishment of Public Schools and the Diffusion of Knowledge in Pennsylvania. Philadelphia: Thomas Dobson, 1786.

Sermons to Gentlemen upon Temperance and Exercise. Philadelphia: John Dunlap, 1772.

Sixteen Introductory Lectures to Courses of Lectures upon the Institutes and Practice of Medicine. Philadelphia: Bradford and Inskeep, 1811.

Thoughts upon Female Education, July 28, 1787. Philadelphia: Prichard and Hall, 1787, http://greenfield.brynmawr.edu/items/show/2828.

Two Essays on the Mind: An Enquiry into the Influence of Physical Causes Upon the Moral Faculty and on the Influence of Physical Causes in Promoting an Increase of the Strength and Activity of the Intellectual Faculties of Man. Introduction by Eric T. Carlson. New York: Brunner/Mazel, 1972.

Books

Adams Family. *Adams Family Correspondence*, vol. 9, *January 1790–December 1793*. Edited by Margaret A. Hogan et al. Cambridge, Mass: Harvard University Press: 1963.

Adams, John. *The Works of John Adams, Second President of the United States*. Edited by Charles Francis Adams. Boston: Little Brown, 1850–56.

Adams, John, and Benjamin Rush. *The Spur of Fame: Dialogues of John Adams and Benjamin Rush, 1805–1813*. Edited by Douglass Adair and John A. Schutz. San Marino, Calif.: Huntington Library, 1966.

Allen, Richard. *The Life, Experience and Gospel Labors of Rt. Rev. Richard Allen*. Philadelphia: Martin & Boden, 1833. Online at http://docsouth.unc.edu/neh/allen/allen.html.

American Philosophical Society. *Early Proceedings of the American Philosophical Society for the Promotion of Useful Knowledge . . .* Philadelphia: McCalla & Stavely, 1884.

An Account of the Philadelphia Dispensary: Instituted for the Medical Relief of the Poor, April 12, 1786. Philadelphia: Budd and Bartrom, 1802.

Anishanslin, Zara. *Portrait of a Woman in Silk: Hidden Histories of the British Atlantic World*. New Haven, CT: Yale University Press, 2016.

Barber, John, and Henry Howe. *Historical Collections of the State of New Jersey*. New York: S. Tuttle, 1844.

Bell, Richard. *We Shall Be No More: Suicide and Self-Government in the Newly United States*. Cambridge, MA: Harvard University Press, 2012.

Bell, Whitfield Jenks. *Patriot-Improvers: Biographical Sketches of Members of the American Philosophical Society*. Philadelphia: American Philosophical Society, 1997.

Bewley, Thomas. *Madness to Mental Illness. A History of the Royal College of Psychiatrists*.

Bill, Alfred Hoyt. *A House Called Morven: Its Role in American History, 1701–1954.* Edited by Constance M. Greiff. Princeton: Princeton University Press, 2015.

Binger, Carl. *Revolutionary Doctor: Benjamin Rush (1746–1813).* New York: W. W. Norton & Company, Inc., 1966.

Brissot de Warville, Jacques-Pierre. *New Travels in the United States of America.* Translated from the French. New York: Swords, 1792.

Brodsky, Alyn. *Benjamin Rush: Patriot and Physician.* New York: St. Martin's Press, 2004.

Bureau of Labor Statistics. *History of Wages in the United States from Colonial Times to 1928.* Washington, DC: Government Printing Office, 1934.

Burnett, Edmund Cody. *The Continental Congress.* New York: Macmillan, 1941.

Butterfield, Lyman H., ed. *John Witherspoon Comes to America: A Documentary Account Based Largely on New Materials.* Princeton: Princeton University Library, 1953.

Caldwell, Charles. *Autobiography.* Philadelphia: Lippincott, Grambo, 1855.

Calvert, Jane E. *The Complete Writings and Selected Correspondence of John Dickinson.* Newark: University of Delaware Press, 2019.

Carey, Mathew. *A Short Account of the Malignant Fever, Lately Prevalent in Philadelphia.* Philadelphia. Printed by the author, 1793.

Carlson, Eric. Untitled book on Benjamin Rush and 18th Century Medicine, unpublished, manuscript discovered in Carlson Papers, Oskar Diethelm Library, Weill Cornell Medical College.

Carpenter, T. *A Report of an Action for a Libel, Brought by Dr. BR Against William Cobbett.* Philadelphia: W. W. Woodward, 1800.

Cash, Caleb, and Samuel Kirke. *An Account of the Births and Burials in Christ-Church Parish, in Philadelphia: From December 24, 1750, to December 24, 1751.* Philadelphia, 1751.

Cobbett, William. *Observations on the Emigration of Dr. Joseph Priestley.* Philadelphia, 1794.

———. *Porcupine's Politcal Censor, for March 1797 . . .* Philadelphia, 1797.

College of Physicians of Philadelphia. *Transactions.* Philadelphia: College of Physicians of Philadelphia.

Cooke, Jacob E. *Tench Coxe and the Early Republic.* Omohundro Institute and University of North Carolina Press, 2011.

Corner, Betsy Copping. *William Shippen, Jr.: Pioneer in American Medical Education.* Philadelphia: American Philosophical Society, 1951.

Cutler, Manasseh. *Life, Journals and Correspondence of Rev. Manasseh Cutler, LL.D.* Edited by William Parker Cutler and Julia Perkins Cutler. Cincinnati: Clarke & Co., 1888.

D'Elia, Donald J. *Benjamin Rush, Philosopher of the American Revolution.* Philadelphia: American Philosophical Society, 1974.

Darlington, William. *Heads of the Practice of the Physicians of the Pennsylvania Hospital During the Winter of the Year 1802–3.* Devon, Pennsylvania: Anro Press, 1973.

Daughan, George. *The Shining Sea: David Porter and the Epic Voyage of the U.S.S. Essex during the War of 1812.* New York: Basic Books, 2013.

Davies, Samuel. *Sermons on Important Subjects.* New York: Robert Carter, 1845.

———. *Religion and Public Spirit: A Valedictory Address . . .* (1860), https://quod.lib.umich.edu/e/evans/N07144.0001.001/1:4?rgn=div1;view=fulltext.

Ducellier, Michelle A. *La Société de Bienfaisance de Philadelphia.* Philadelphia: Historical Society of Pennsylvania, 1997, http://www2.hsp.org/collections/Balch%20manuscript_guide/html/french_benevolent_society.html.

Duncan, Louis C. *Medical Men in the American Revolution, 1775–1783.* Carlisle Barracks, Pa.: Medical Field Service School, 1931.

Ellet, Elizabeth. *The Women of the American Revolution.* New York: Baker and Scribner, 1850.

Fischer, David Hackett. *Washington's Crossing.* Oxford: Oxford University Press, 2004.

Flexner, James Thomas. *Doctors on Horseback: Pioneers of American Medicine.* New York: Fordham University Press, 1937.

Fox, Claire Gilbride. *Lancet & Pen: A Biography of Benjamin Rush, M.D.* unpublished, 1993, only known copy deposited by family of the late author in library of College of Physicians, WZ 100 B952F 1993.

Garvan, Anthony N. B., et al. *Mutual Assurance Company for Insuring Houses from Loss by Fire, Philadelphia. The Architectural Surveys: 1784–1794.* Philadelphia: Mutual Assurance Co., 1976.

Gibson, Campbell, and Kay Jung. *Historical Census Statistics on Population Totals by Race, 1790 to 1990, and by Hispanic Origin, 1970 to 1990, for Large Cities and Other Urban Places in the United States by Population.* U.S. Census Bureau, Working Paper no. 76.

Gibson, James E. *Dr. Bodo Otto and the Medical Background of the American Revolution.* Springfield, IL: Charles C. Thomas, 1937.

Goldsmith, Oliver. *The Hermit: A Ballad*. Philadelphia: Lippincott, 1886.

Good, Harry G. *Benjamin Rush and His Services to American Education*. Berne, IN: Witness Press, 1918.

Goodman, Nathan G. *Benjamin Rush: Physician and Citizen, 1746–1813*. Philadelphia: University of Pennsylvania Press, 1934.

Green, Ashbel. *The Life*. New York: Carter and Bros, 1849.

Gross, Samuel D., ed. *Lives of Eminent American Physicians and Surgeons of the Nineteenth Century*. Philadelphia: Lindsay & Blakiston, 1861.

———. *Autobiography of Samuel D. Gross, M.D.* Philadelphia: G. Barrie, 1887.

Hawke, David Freeman. *Benjamin Rush: Revolutionary Gadfly*. Indianapolis: Bobbs-Merrill, 1971.

———. *Paine*. New York: Harper & Row, 1974.

Hazard, Samuel. *Hazard's Register of Pennsylvania*. Philadelphia, 1831–35.

Henretta, James, Rebecca Edwards, and Robert Self. *America: A Concise History*. New York: Macmillan, 2012.

Isaacson, Walter. *Benjamin Franklin: An American Life*. New York: Simon & Schuster, 2004.

Jackson, Samuel. *Introductory lecture to the course of the institutes of medicine*. Philadelphia: T. K. and P. G. Collins, 1855.

Jefferson, Thomas. *Correspondence, 1792–1793*. vol. 7 of *The Works of Thomas Jefferson*. Edited by Paul L. Ford. New York: Cosimo, 2010.

Johnson, George. *History of Cecil County, Maryland, and the Early Settlements . . .* Elkton, Md.: Printed for the author, 1881.

Johnson, John W., ed. *Historic U.S. Court Cases: An Encyclopedia*. 2 vols. London: Routledge, 2001.

Jones, Absalom, and Richard Allen. *A Narrative of the Proceedings of the Black People, During the Late Awful Calamity in Philadelphia, in the Year 1793*. Philadelphia: William W. Woodward, 1794.

Journals of the Continental Congress, 1774–1798. Edited by Worthington C. Ford et al. Washington, DC: Government Printing Office, 1904–37.

King, E. F. *Ten Thousand Wonderful Things*. London, New York: G. Routledge and Sons, 1860.

Kloos, John M., Jr. *A Sense of Deity: The Republican Spirituality of Dr. Benjamin Rush*. Brooklyn, NY: Carlson Publishing Inc., 1991.

Labaree, Benjamin. *Catalyst for Revolution: The Boston Tea Party, 1773*. Boston: Commonwealth of Massachusetts Bicentennial Publication, 1973.

Leitch, Alexander. *A Princeton Companion*. Princeton: Princeton University Press, 1978, http://etcweb.Princeton.edu/CampusWWW/Companion/commencement.html.

Linn, John B., and William H. Egle, eds. *Pennsylvania Archives* 38, 2nd ser. Harrisburg: Lane Hart, 1879, https://archive.org/details/pennsylvaniaarch38penn.

Looney, J. Jefferson, and Ruth L. Woodward. *Princetonians, 1791–1794: A Biographical Dictionary*. Princeton: Princeton University Press, 2014.

Macpherson, John. *Macpherson's Letters, &c*. Philadelphia: William Evitt, 1770.

———. *A Pennsylvania Sailor's Letters, Alias The Farmer's Fall*. Philadelphia: Robert Bell, 1771.

Marshall, Christopher. *Passages from the Diary of Christopher Marshall*. Philadelphia: Hazar and Mitchell, 1839.

Mason, Susanna Hopkins. *Selections from the Letters and Manuscripts of the Late Susanna Mason*. Philadelphia: Rackliff & Jones, 1836.

Maurice de Saxe, Marshal Herman. *Reveries on the Art of War*. London, 1757.

McCullough, David. *1776*. New York: Simon & Schuster, 2005.

———. *John Adams*. New York: Simon & Schuster, 2001.

McGuire, Thomas. *The Battle of Paoli*. Mechanicsburg, PA: Stackpole Books, 2000.

———. *The Philadelphia Campaign, Volume One: Brandywine and the Fall of Philadelphia*. Mechanicsburg, PA: Stackpole Books, 2006.

———. *The Philadelphia Campaign, Volume Two: Germantown and the Roads to Valley Forge*. Mechanicsburg, PA: Stackpole Books, 2006.

McLachlan, James. *Princetonians, 1748–1768: A Biographical Dictionary*. Princeton University Press, 1976.

McMaster, John Bach, and Frederick Stone, eds. *Pennsylvania and the Federal Constitution, 1787–1788*. Philadelphia: Historical Society of Pennsylvania, 1888.

Merriam, Cyrus L. *Captain John Macpherson of Philadelphia, His Wife, Mary Ann MacNeal, and their Descendants*. Brattleboro, VT: Griswold, 1966.

Morgan, John. *The Journal of Dr. John Morgan of Philadelphia: from the City of Rome to the City of London, 1764*. Philadelphia: J. B. Lippincott, 1907.

Morris, Robert. *The Confidential Correspondence of Robert Morris*. Philadelphia: S.V. Henkels, 1917.

Morton, Thomas G., and Frank Woodbury. *The History of Pennsylvania Hospital, 1751–1895*. Philadelphia: Times Printing House, 1895.

Mott, Frank Luther. *A History of American Magazines*. Cambridge, Mass.: Harvard University Press, 1930.

Murphy, Jim. *An American Plague: The True and Terrifying Story of the Yellow Fever Epidemic of 1792*. Boston: Houghton Mifflin Harcourt, 2014.

Myrsiades, Linda S. *Medical Culture in Revolutionary America: Feuds, Duels and a Court-martial*. Cranbury, NJ: Associated University Presses, 2009.

Nash, Gary B. *Forging Freedom: The Formation of Philadelphia's Black Community, 1720–1840*. Cambridge, Mass.: Harvard University Press, 1988.

Nelson, Craig. *Thomas Paine: Enlightenment, Revolution, and the Birth of Modern Nations*. New York: Viking Press, 2006.

Newman, Richard. *Freedom's Prophet: Bishop Richard Allen, the AME Church, and the Black Founding Fathers*. New York: NYU Press, 2009.

Nisbet, Richard, and John Sparhawk. *Slavery Not Forbidden by Scripture*. Philadelphia: Sparhawk, 1773.

Norris, George Washington. *The Early History of Medicine in Philadelphia*. Philadelphia: Collins Printing House, 1886.

Ousterhout, Anne M. *The Most Learned Woman in America: A Life of Elizabeth Graeme Fergusson*. University Park: Pennsylvania State University Press, 2004.

Patton, Kenneth. *U.S. Naval Hospitals Historical Survey*, 1974.

Peale, Charles Willson. *Autobiography*, vol. 5 of *The Selected Papers of Charles Willson Peale and His Family*. Edited by Lillian Miller et al. New Haven, CT: Yale University Press, 2000.

Philadelphia: History of Its Growth. Philadelphia: Town Printing, 1904.

Pickering, Octavius. *The Life of Timothy Pickering*. 4 vols. Boston: Little, Brown, 1863–73.

Pinel, Philippe. *A Treatise on Insanity*. London: Cadell & Davies, 1806.

Powell, J. H. *Richard Rush, Republican Diplomat, 1780–1859*. Philadelphia: University of Pennsylvania Press, 1942.

———. *Bring Out Your Dead: The Great Plague of Yellow Fever in Philadelphia in 1793*. Philadelphia: University of Pennsylvania Press, 1993.

Powers, John C. *Inventing Chemistry: Herman Boerhaave and the Reform of the Chemical Arts*. Chicago: University of Chicago Press, 2012.

Ramsay, David. *A Eulogium upon Benjamin Rush, Delivered to the Circular Church of Charles on June 10, 1813*. Philadelphia: Brandford and Inskeep, 1813.

———. *The History of the American Revolution.* 2 vols. Trenton, N.J.: James J. Wilson, 1811.

Richard Rush, Republican Diplomat, 1780–1859. Philadelphia: University of Pennsylvania Press, 1942.

Rush, Benjamin, et al. *Old Family Letters, Copied from the Originals for Alexander Biddle.* Philadelphia: Lippincott, 1892.

Rush, John. *An Inaugural Essay on the Causes of Sudden Death.* Philadelphia: Thomas and George Palmer, 1804.

———. *Elements of Life, or the Laws of Vital Matter.* Philadelphia: Thomas and George Palmer, 1804.

Ryerson, Richard Alan. *The Revolution Is Now Begun: The Radical Committees of Philadelphia, 1765–1776.* Philadelphia: University of Pennsylvania Press, 1978.

Scharf, John Thomas, and Thompson Westcott. *History of Philadelphia, 1609–1884.* Philadelphia: Everts, 1884.

Sellers, Charles Coleman. *Dickinson College: A History.* Middletown, CT: Wesleyan University Press, 1973.

Simon, Robert I., and Liza H. Gold. *Textbook of Forensic Psychiatry.* New York: American Psychiatric Publishing, 2004.

Slack, Joshua P., ed. *The American Orator,* 2d ed. Trenton, NJ: Fenton, 1815.

Smith, Billy G., and J. Worth Estes. *A Melancholy Scene of Devastation: The Public Response to the 1793 Philadelphia Yellow Fever Epidemic.* Canton, Mass.: Science History Publications, 1997.

Smith, Billy G., *Ship of Death: A Voyage That Changed the Atlantic World.* New Haven, CT: Yale University Press, 2013.

Smith, Billy Gordon. *Life in Early Philadelphia: Documents from the Revolutionary and Early National Periods.* University Park: Pennsylvania State University Press, 1995.

Stockton, Annis Boudinot. *Only for the Eye of a Friend: The Poems of Annis Boudinot Stockton.* Edited by Carla Mulford. Charlottesville: University Press of Virginia, 1995.

Sydenham, Thomas. *The Works of Thomas Sydenham, M.D., on Acute and Chronic Diseases.* Edited by Benjamin Rush. Philadelphia: Benjamin & Thomas Kite, 1809.

Thomson, John. *An Account of the Life, Lectures and Writings of William Cullen, M.D.* Edinburgh, Scotland: W. Blackwood & Son, 1859.

Townsend, Joseph. *The Battle of Brandywine.* New York: The New York Times, 1969.

United States. *Register of Officer Personnel United States Navy and Marine Corps and Ships Data, 1801–1807.* Washington, DC: Government Printing Office, 1945, p. 48.

Van Doren, Carl. *Benjamin Franklin.* New York: Viking, 1938.

Washington, George. *The Writings of George Washington from the Original Manuscript Sources, 1745–1799.* Edited by David M. Mattesole and John C. Fitzpatrick. Washington, DC: Government Printing Office, 1931–44.

Watson, J. F. *Annals of Philadelphia, and Pennsylvania, in the Olden Time.* 2 vols. Philadelphia: E. S. Stuart, 1899.

Wharton, T. I. *A Memoir of William Rawle, LL.D.* Philadelphia, 1840.

Williams, William H. *America's First Hospital: The Pennsylvania Hospital, 1751–1841.* Wayne, PA: Haverford House, 1976.

Wulf, Karin. *Not All Wives: Women of Colonial Philadelphia.* Ithaca, NY: Cornell University Press, 2000.

Periodicals and Websites

Adams, John. "Diary." Massachusetts Historical Society, https://www.masshist.org/digitaladams/archive/diary/.

Allen, Erin. "Mathew Carey (1760–1839), Philadelphia Publisher and Provocateur." *Library of Congress Blog,* September 19, 2014, https://blogs.loc.gov/loc/2014/09/mathew-carey-1760-1839-philadelphia-publisher-and-provocateur/.

Allen, Richard, and Absalom Jones. "For the Nursing of the Sick and the Burial of the Dead." *Dunlap's Daily Advertiser,* September 11, 1793.

Ambrose, Charles T. "Plagiarism of Ideas. Benjamin Rush and Charles Caldwell—A Student-Mentor Dispute." *Microbiology, Immunology, and Molecular Genetics* (Winter 2014).

Berrios, G. E., "Hartley's Views of Madness," *History of Psychiatry 2015,* Vol. 26, pp. 105–16.

Bevan, Edith Rossiter. "The Continental Congress in Baltimore, Dec. 20, 1776, to Feb. 27, 1777." *Maryland Historical Magazine* 42 (1947): 21–28.

Blanco, R. L. "The Diary of Jonathan Potts: A Quaker Medical Student in Edinburgh (1766–67)." *Transactions and Studies of the College of Physicians of Philadelphia* 44, no. 3, (1977): 119–30.

Bleakley, A. "Force and Presence in the World of Medicine." *Healthcare* 5, no. 3 (2017): 1–8.

Butterfield, L. H. "The American Interests of the Firm of E. and C. Dilly, with Their Letters to Benjamin Rush, 1770–1795." *Papers of the Bibliographical Society of America* 45, no. 4 (1951): 283–332.

———. "Benjamin Rush and the Beginning of John and Mary's College over Susquehanna." *Journal of the History of Medicine and Allied Sciences* 3, no. 2 (1948): 30.

———. "Benjamin Rush as a Promoter of Useful Knowledge." *Proceedings of the American Philosophical Society* 92, no. 1 (1948): 34.

———. "Love and Valor; or Benjamin Rush and the Leslies of Edinburgh." *Princeton University Library Chronicle* 9 (1947–48): 1–12.

———. "The Reputation of Benjamin Rush." *Pennsylvania History* 17, no. 1 (1950): 4.

Calvert, Jane E. "Myth-Making and Myth-Breaking in the Historiography on John Dickinson." *Journal of the Early Republic* 34, no. 3 (2014): 467–80.

Carlson, E. T., and Jeffrey Wollock. "Benjamin Rush and His Insane Son." *Bulletin of the New York Academy of Medicine* 51, no. 11 (1975): 1312–30.

Cobbett, William. "*Porcupine's Gazette*, no. 779." *Porcupine's Gazette*, January 13, 1800.

Cook, Harold J. "Sydenham, Thomas." *Oxford Dictionary of National Biography*. Oxford: Oxford University Press, 2004.

DePalma, Ralph G. "Bloodletting: Past and Present." *Journal of the American College of Surgeons* 205, no. 1 (2007): 132–44.

Eve, Sarah, and Eva Eve Jones. "Extracts from the Journal of Miss Sarah Eve." *Pennsylvania Magazine of History and Biography* 5, no. 1 (1881): 26.

Finkelstein, David. "A Feverish Journey to United States Mint Treasurer," *The Numismatist*, February 2014, p. 37–44.

Fortune, Brandon Brame. "'Studious Men are Always Painted in Gowns': Charles Willson Peale's *Benjamin Rush* and the Question of Banyans in Eighteenth-Century Anglo-American Portraiture." *Dress* 29, no. 1 (2002): pp. 27–40.

Friis, Herman R. "A Series of Population Maps of the Colonies and the United States, 1625–1790." *Geographical Review* 30, no. 3 (1940): 463–70.

Gibson, J. E. "Benjamin Rush's Apprenticed Students." *Transactions and Studies of the College of Physicians of Philadelphia* 14, no. 3 (1946): 127–32.

Greenstone, Gerry. "The History of Bloodletting." *British Columbia Medical Journal* 52, no. 1 (2010): 12–14.

Hattem, Michael D. "When Benjamin Franklin Came Home: A Look at the Media Coverage of His Return." *Readex Report* 9, no. 1 (2014), http://www.readex.com/readex-report/when-benjamin-franklin-came-home-look-media-coverage-his-return.

Huntington, Tom. "Franklin's Last Home." *American Heritage* 57, no. 2 (2006): 49–52.

Johnson, Ann K. "Book Publishing and Publishers." *Encyclopedia of Greater Philadelphia*, http://philadelphiaencyclopedia.org/archive/book-publishing-and-publishers/.

Johnston, Christopher. "Hall Family of Calvert County." *Maryland Historical Magazine* 8 (1913): 291–301.

Krystyniak, Frank. "Jim Olson's Essay on Abigail Adams." Sam Houston State University, http://www.shsu.edu/~pin_www/T@S/2002/NabbyAdamsEssay.html.

Lee, Henry. "A Funeral Oration on the Death of George Washington." December 26, 1799, https://quod.lib.umich.edu/e/evans/N28374.0001.001?rgn=main;view=fulltext.

Louis, Elan D. "William Shippen's Unsuccessful Attempt to Establish the First 'School for Physick' in the American Colonies in 1762." *Journal of the History of Medicine and Allied Sciences* 44, no. 2 (1989): 218–39.

Louis-Courvoisier, Micheline and Philip Rieder. "Enlightened Physicians: Setting Out on an Elite Academic Career in the Second Half of the Eighteenth Century." *Bulletin of the History of Medicine* 84, no. 4 (2010): 578–606.

Maxey, David. "A Portrait of Elizabeth Willing Powel (1743–1830)." *Transactions of the American Philosophical Society* 96, no. 4 (2006).

Miles, Wyndham. "Benjamin Rush, Chemist." *Chymia* 4 (1953): iv–77.

Mintz, Steven. "The Constitution and Slavery." Gilder Lehrman Institute of American History, https://www.gilderlehrman.org/content/historical-context-constitution-and-slavery.

Musto, D. F. "Benjamin Rush's Medical Thesis, 'On the Digestion of Food in the Stomach.'" Edinburgh, 1768." *Transactions and Studies of the College of Physicians of Philadelphia* 33, no. 2 (1965): 121–38.

Nash, Gary B. "Slaves and Slaveowners in Colonial Philadelphia." *William and Mary Quarterly* 30, no. 2 (1973): 223–56.

Olton, Charles. "Philadelphia's First Environmental Crisis." *Pennsylvania Magazine of History and Biography* 98, no. 1 (1974): 90–100.

Owen, Alfred. "Jacques Barbeu-Dubourg, a French Disciple of Benjamin Franklin." *Proceedings of the American Philosophical Society* 95, no. 4 (1951): 331–92.

Owen, William O. "The Legislative and Administrative History of the Medical Department of the United States Army During the Revolutionary Period." *Annals of Medical History* 1 (Fall 1917).

Pearce, John M. S. "The Role of Dr. Francis Willis in the Madness of George III." *European Neurology* 78 (2017): 196–99.

Potter, Leslie. "Benjamin Rush and His Forgotten Country Estate." May 12, 2009.

Powell, J. H. "Speech of John Dickinson Opposing the Declaration of Independence 1 July, 1776." *Pennsylvania Magazine of History and Biography* 65, no. 4 (1941): 458–68.

Radbill, Samuel X. "Medicine in 1776: Colonial and Revolutionary Medicine in Philadelphia." *Transactions and Studies of the College of Physicians of Philadelphia* 44, no. 2 (1976): 1–8.

Roach, Hannah Bender. "Benjamin Franklin Slept Here," *Pennsylvania Magazine of History and Biography* 84, no. 2 (1960): 127–74.

Rolph, Daniel. "The Fort That Saved America." Historical Society of Pennsylvania, November 11, 2012, https://hsp.org/blogs/history-hits/the-fort-that-saved-america.

———. "The Strange Insanity of Hannah Lewis, in 18th-century Philadelphia." November 11, 2011, HSP, http://danielrolph.com/2011/11/the-strange-insanity-of-hannah-lewis-in-18th-century-philadelphia.

Slotten, Martha C. "Elizabeth Graeme Ferguson: A Poet in 'The Athens of North America.'" *Pennsylvania Magazine of History and Biography* 108, no. 3 (1984): 259–88 and n4.

Sobocinski, André B. "From the Book of Surgeons: John Rush, Surgeon, U.S. Navy." *Grog Ration* 5, no. 1 (2010): 5–9.

Stockton, Annis Boudinot. "Addressed to Col. Schuyler on His Return to Jersey After Two Years Captivity in Canada." *New York Mercury*, January 9, 1758.

Stone, Frederick D. "How The Landing of Tea Was Opposed in Philadelphia by Colonel William Bradford." *Pennsylvania Magazine of History and Biography* 15 (1891): 385–93.

Stryker, William S. *The Battles of Trenton and Princeton*. Boston: Houghton Mifflin, 1898.

Tarkington, Booth. "Young Literary Princeton Fifty Years Ago." *Princeton University Library Chronicle* 7, no. 1 (1945): pp. 1–5.

Tennent, Gilbert. "The Danger of an Unconverted Ministry" (1740). *Association of Religious Data Archives*, http://www.thearda.com/timeline/events/event_231.asp.

Vinson, Michael. "The Society for Political Inquiries: The Limits of Republican Discourse in Philadelphia on the Eve of the Constitutional Convention." *Pennsylvania Magazine of History and Biography* 113, no. 2 (1989): pp. 185–205.

Wade, Nicholas J. "The Original Spin Doctors—The Meeting of Perception and Insanity." *Perception* 34 (2005): 253–60.

Walter J. Husak Collection Auction Catalog, no. 406. Heritage Capital Corporation, 2008.

Weiner, Dora B. "Philippe Pinel's 'Memoir on Madness' of December 11, 1794: A Fundamental Text of Modern Psychiatry." *American Journal of Psychiatry* 149, no. 6 (1992): 725–32.

Wigginton, Caroline. "A Late Night Vindication: Annis Boudinot Stockton's Reading of Mary Wollstonecraft's A Vindication of the Rights of Woman." *Legacy* 25, no. 2 (2008): 225–38.

Wilson, Garff B. "The Acting of Edwin Forrest." *Quarterly Journal of Speech* 36, no. 4 (1950): 483–91.

Woods, Evelyn, and Eric T. Carlson. "A Myth About Pinel." *Mental Hospitals*, October 1960.

Woods, John A. "The Correspondence of Benjamin Rush and Granville Sharp 1773–1809." *Journal of American Studies* 1, no. 1 (1967): 1–38.

ILLUSTRATION CREDITS

3: Miniature by Dora Curtis (after Robert Edge Pine) Courtesy R.W. Norton Art Foundation; 16: Courtesy of Stockton Rush; 19: "A east prospect of the city of Philadelphia" by George Heap, Courtesy of the Library of Congress; 20: Van Pelt Library; 23: By Charles Walker Lind, courtesy of Princeton University Art Museum; 25: By James Massalon, courtesy of Princeton University Art Museum; 27: (left) Courtesy of Stockton Rush, (right) by John Wollaston, courtesy of Princeton University Art Museum; 31: (left) From the Collections of the University of Pennsylvania Archives, (right) Archives and Special Collections at Dickinson College; 38: By James Peale, after Gilbert Stuart. Courtesy of Independence National Historical Park; 41: From the Collections of the University of Pennsylvania Archives; 49: Royal College of Physicians of Edinburgh; 54: By Charles Willson Peale, courtesy of Independence National Historical Park; 61: Courtesy of The Lewis Walpole Library, Yale University; 65: (both) Courtesy of the American Philosophical Society; 76: (left) Courtesy of Philadelphia Museum of Art, Bequest of Mellicent Story Garland, 1963, (right) by Charles Willson Peale, courtesy of Independence National Historical Park; 86: Courtesy of the Library Company of Philadelphia; 90: Courtesy of the Boston Public Library; 100: (left) By Bass Otis, after Charles Willson Peale, courtesy of Independence National Historical Park, (right) courtesy of the Library Company of Philadelphia; 101: courtesy of Philadelphia Museum of Art, 125th Anniversary Acquisition. 103: Courtesy of the Library of Congress; 108: By Charles Willson Peale, courtesy of Independence National Historical Park; 111: By Charles Willson Peale, courtesy of Metropolitan Museum of Art; 117: Attributed to Bass Otis, after Thomas Thompson from the William Sharp engraving after a painting by George Romney, courtesy of Independence National Historical Park; 121: (left) by Charles Willson Peale, courtesy of Independence National Historical Park. (right): unidentified artist, after Thomas Sully, courtesy of Independence National Historical Park; 146: By Charles Willson Peale, courtesy of Winterthur Museum, Gift of Mrs. Julia B. Henry, 1960; 163: Courtesy of Architect of the Capitol; 164: Courtesy of National Archives; 165: Courtesy of the Library Company of Philadelphia; 168: Courtesy of the Library of Congress; 175: By Charles Willson Peale, courtesy of Philadelphia Museum of Art, Purchased for the Cadwalader Collection with funds contributed by the Mabel Pew Myrin Trust and the gift of an anonymous donor, 1983; 176: (both) By Charles Willson Peale, courtesy of the American Philosophical Society; 178: By Charles Willson Peale, courtesy of Independence National Historical Park; 181: Courtesy of the Metropolitan Museum of Art, Gift of John Stewart Kennedy; 187: (both) Courtesy of owner, David Schwartz; 189: (top) Courtesy of Yale University Art Gallery, (bottom) courtesy of the Princeton University Art Museum, commissioned by the Trustees; 209: Courtesy of the Library of Congress; 213: Courtesy of the Delaware Public Archives; 219: Courtesy of the Wellcome Trust; 231: Courtesy of the New York Public Library, Miriam and Ira D. Wallach Division of Art, Prints and Photographs: Print Collection; 261: Courtesy of Winterthur Museum, Gift of Mrs. Julia B. Henry, 1959; 264: (both) Courtesy of Pennsylvania Hospital Historic Collections, Philadelphia; 273: Van Pelt Library; 284: Courtesy of the Library Company of Philadelphia; 298: (left) Courtesy of the New York Public Library, Miriam and Ira D. Wallach Division of Art, Prints and Photographs: Print Collection, (right) courtesy of the Library Company of Philadelphia; 307: By Charles Willson Peale, courtesy of Independence National Historical Park; 310: By Thomas Sully, courtesy of Pennsylvania Hospital Historic Collections, Philadelphia; 320: Courtesy of the Library Company of Philadelphia; 341: Courtesy of the Library of Congress; 368: Courtesy of the New York Public Library, Miriam and Ira D. Wallach Division of Art, Prints and Photographs: Print Collection; 371: (both) Courtesy of the Library Company of Philadelphia; 372: Courtesy of the Archives and Special Collections at Dickinson College; 375: Courtesy of the Wellcome Trust; 386: Courtesy of the Library of Congress; 387: Courtesy of the Wellcome Trust; 405: Courtesy of the Library Company of Philadelphia; 428: (clockwise from upper left) By Charles Balthazar Julien Févret de Saint-Mémin, National Portrait Gallery, Smithsonian Institution; gift of Mr. and Mrs. Paul Mellon; by James Akin, courtesy of the Library of Congress, and by William Haines, both courtesy of National Portrait Gallery, Smithsonian Institution; 431: Courtesy of the Library Company of Philadelphia; 446: By permission of Lockwood Rush; 448: Courtesy of the American Philosophical Society; 475: (both) Courtesy of the Boston Public Library; 486: (clockwise from upper left) Courtesy of the American Philosophical Society; courtesy of National Portrait Gallery, Smithsonian Institution; Courtesy of the Library Company of Philadelphia; courtesy of Archives and Special Collections at Dickinson College; 497: Courtesy of Stockton Rush; 498: Courtesy of Library Company of Philadelphia; 502: Collection of the author; 510: Dickinson College/ Carl Socolow

ACKNOWLEDGMENTS

I am deeply grateful for the assistance of what I consider the "five families" of Benjamin Rush–related research: the Library Company of Philadelphia, the Historical Society of Pennsylvania, the American Philosophical Society, the College of Physicians, and the Rosenbach Library. All are within twenty blocks of where Rush lived, and are lucky to have immensely knowledgeable, dedicated staff. I am also indebted to several Philadelphia institutions that, despite having less Rush material, have staffs that care about him—and about making sure historians get things right, in particular Independence National Historical Park, the University Archives and Records Center at Penn, and the Pennsylvania Hospital Historical Collections. Thanks especially to Steve Smith at the Historical Society of Philadelphia; Charlie Griefenstein and Michael Miller at the American Philosophical Society; Karie Diethorn and Coxey Toogood at Independence National Historical Park; Jim Duffin and Mark Lloyd at the Penn Archives; Elizabeth Fuller at the Rosenbach; Stacey Peeples at Pennsylvania Hospital; Penn research librarian Holly Mengel, and independent researcher Leslie Potter.

The Library Company of Philadelphia went through a number of changes during this book, so I thank, in chronological order: John van Horn, director when this book started; Richard Newman, who during his tenure was generous enough to run seminars for me and my researchers, notably on African American churches, slavery (with visiting scholar Nicholas Wood from Yale), and mental illness care (with Newman's wife, Dr. Lisa Hermsen, a mental health historian); and most recently, Michael Barsanti, along with the rest of the devoted staff, especially James Green and Ann McShane.

Thanks to Benjamin Rush's kind descendants Lockwood Rush and Stockton Rush for allowing me to use paintings from their family collections and helping us get images (also thanks to Beth Allan, curator at Morven Museum).

It was my great fortune, in the late winter of 2013, to receive a last-minute invitation to write a paper and present at the "Republics of Benjamin Rush" conference at Dickinson, with the encouragement of University of Pennsylvania historian Daniel Richter and Dickinson historian Christopher Bilodeau. I was also lucky to be placed on a panel with Martha King, senior editor of the Thomas Jefferson Papers at Princeton, and William Ferraro, managing editor of the Papers of George Washington at the University of Virginia. Both have been enormously helpful, willing to answer, or at least consider, any question I've had, no matter how ridiculous. They also connected me with their colleagues in other such projects.

The most helpful of these was the terrific Sara Georgini, the series editor of the John Adams Papers at the Massachusetts Historical Society, who was very generous with her time and internal database. (The staff at Mass Historical was also terrific.) I got energetic assistance from Jane Calvert, the director of the John Dickinson Writings Project at the University of Kentucky, and I had an illuminating talk with Ellen Cohn, the editor of the Benjamin Franklin Papers at Yale.

I was fortunate to access the contagious Rush enthusiasm of Andre Sobocinski, a historian at Navy Bureau of Medicine, who helped navigate military and Washington, D.C., sources. Mental health special collections librarian Marisa Shaari at Weill-Cornell Medical Center Oskar Diethelm Library made it possible for me to spend a lot of quality time with the Carlson papers; thanks also to the director of the History of Psychiatry branch Dr. George Makari.

At crucial points in the research for this book, I was led in the right direction by wonderful medical historians, including Charles Rosenberg, Andrew Scull, and Nancy Tomes. And when I first started exploring the mental health of Rush's son, John—as well as that of Dr. Rush himself—I was fortunate to have the advice of the former chair of Penn's psychiatry department, Dr. Peter Whybrow, now the director of the Semel Institute for Neuroscience and Human Behavior at UCLA, who encouraged my interest in exploring Rush's most frenzied and dark periods as possible indicators of his own manic-depressive illness. He also informed my ideas about where bloodletting might fit into the history of psychiatric care, as a crude early method of breaking psychosis. (I met Peter through my friendship with Dr. Kay Redfield Jamison who, along with her late husband, Dr. Richard Wyatt, taught me so much about the medicine and politics of mental health, and how to narrate diseases of the brain.)

I have also, over the years, enjoyed impassioned discussions about Rush and the history of psychiatry with Dr. Jeffrey Lieberman, chair of the psychiatry department at Columbia and the former president of the American Psychiatric Association. I was doing some teaching in Jeff's department and some editorial consulting for him when the APA started talking about dropping Rush's face from its logo. I begged him (and others at the association) not to do it, and argued they should instead double down on the doctor's mental health legacy. I failed to save Rush's face—and will treasure my old APA convention bags featuring him—but I hope this book makes mental health professionals worldwide better understand Rush's contribution, and his importance as a medical role model. There is a reason both AMA and APA give annual Benjamin Rush Awards for public service.

I've been fortunate to get to know a lot of national figures in mental health and addiction because of the inspirational years I spent writing a book with Congressman Patrick Kennedy, who I am proud to call a friend and colleague.

A lot of Philadelphia area physicians and mental health professionals were very encouraging about this project, including Dr. Sandy Bloom and Ruth Ann Ryan (lifelong friends I made covering my first mental health story in 1984) and Joe Pyle at the Scattergood Foundation (which supports the WHYY Behavioral Health Journalism workshops I run). Our personal physician, Bradley Fenton, loaned me his copy of a first edition of Rush's *Medical Inquiries and Observations*, just so I could have it sitting near my desk while writing.

Thanks for so many kindnesses, personal and professional, to Jim Graham and Chris Meck at Graham Studios/Power Plant Productions—including Jim schlepping deep into the suburbs to photograph the Rush portrait on the cover, and taking my author photo.

I am deeply indebted to two departments at the University of Pennsylvania, which helped nurture this project in so many ways. One is the Center for Programs in Contemporary Writing, where I am a lecturer; there I am eternally grateful to Al Filreis, Julia Bloch, Mingo Reynolds, and Greg Djanikian, as well as to the staffs at CPCW and Kelly Writers House, who allowed me and several waves of independent study students to explore not only themes and characters for this book but also unique ways of researching and writing narrative history. I am also grateful to the History and Sociology of Science Department, where my colleague and friend David Barnes has helped me work with some of his very best students.

The process for researching this book began with a class of nine students who met once a week at Writers House during the 2013–14 academic year. They became the original Rushistas, of which there have been many since, and I wish I had taped their conversations because they were hilarious and always challenging; they also wrote some really smart papers. The original group included Brenda Wang, David Poplar, Alina Grabowski, Naomi Shavin, Katelyn Behrman, Zoe Kirsch, DJ Wendler, and Debbie Chiang, and they were led by Amanda Mauri—who became my de facto teaching assistant, and then my full-time researcher after graduating, overseeing the early research on this project. I then started working with smaller student groups, including Lily Young (who did great research on the Macpherson case), Laine Higgins, Casey Quackenbush, Aaron Mandelbaum, Mel Bavaria, and Rive Cadwallader.

Most of the writing over the last year and a half was done with the help of a really smart and supportive trio: Rebecca Heilweil (who started as a first semester freshman, is still with us as a graduating senior, and can do anything—including the massive job of overseeing the fact-checking), Julie Levitan (who did insightful research on so many of the characters), and Amanda Rota (who researched medicine by post, and handled all the visuals for the book). They all consistently went above and beyond the call of duty during the challenging final months of putting Benny to bed—and it has been my "peculiar happiness" to work with them. Thanks also for very helpful manuscript feedback from Rachel Bridges, Kieona Cook, and especially Samuel Byers, and to our selfless editorial friend and volunteer researcher Heather Paxton in Kansas City.

It is impossible to write a book like this without relying on the kindness of databases and websites. Thank goodness the National Archives created Founders Online; it is so useful and user-friendly that I only wish there was a Rush papers project to be part of it. We also relied on JSTOR, America's Historical Newspapers, the NIH's National Library of Medicine, the Library of Congress's American Memory project, Early American Imprints, archive.com, and the massive historic writings databases at the University of Michigan School of Medicine.

Thanks to the large community of journalists and authors I am fortunate to have as friends and colleagues and FB lifelines, including too many people to mention at Columbia University Graduate School of Journalism, the diasporas of *Philadelphia* magazine, *Vanity Fair*, *GQ*, *Glamour*, and the survivors of my magazine writing workshop. And thanks to the amazing, supportive folks who befriended us through my last book, on Fred Harvey, including the Harvey family (especially Daggett, Helen, Kay, Stewart, Natalie, Charlie, Steve, and Noel), Fran Levine, Jenny Kimball, Allan Affeldt, Tina Mion, Meredith Davidson, Katrina Parks, Steve Wimmer, and a small nation of Fredheads—as well as Jon Eig, the only author I'd ever swap proposals with.

This is my first book for Crown, my new home at Penguin Random House, where I am deeply appreciative of the support of publisher Molly Stern. This project was brought to the house and brainstormed with editor Vanessa Mobley, and was inherited and shepherded by Domenica Alioto. But *Rush* has had only one editor at Crown—and that is dynamo Meghan Houser, who worked astonishingly hard to provide in-depth and challenging editing, the kind we are told editors don't do anymore. They do. She does. (Thanks also to Crown's Rachel Rokicki, Sarah Breivogel, Courtney Snyder, Kathleen Quinlan, and Wade Lucas.)

This book was my first project with agent David Black. He has been remarkable, encouraging, incisive, and occasionally bitch-slapping (but in a good way), through challenging times both professional and personal. I am so fortunate to have him as an agent and a friend.

We have lost too many family members and close friends during this book—all of whom reasonably expected to be alive to read it, and I still can't believe they won't be. (My mom, on her deathbed, was still saying "when are you going to finish that book already?")

I ache from missing them but still take strength and love from them. They are (in the order in which we lost them over the course of eighteen harsh months): my aunt Barbara Fried Schultz; my father-in-law Dr. Edward Ayres; my wife's closest friend, Robert Goldstein; my mother, Estelle Caplan Fried; my uncle Stephen Schultz; my aunt Phylis Caplan; and my mom's best friend, Betty Silverman. May their memories be for a blessing.

My siblings, nieces, nephews, and cousins have saved us during this process, and I am so grateful to have my Fried, Schultz, Ayres, Caplan, Price, Mitchell, Creamer, Kozitzky, and Alberts relatives in my life. And thank god for our friends, especially the Last Supper Club, and my half-court hoops buddies.

Finally, thanks to my wife, author Diane Ayres, for everything she does as the love of my life and the editor of my dreams. I hope she forgives me for all the work time she has missed on her own excellent books to help me bring Benny to life. For so many things that challenge so many kinds of health in our lives, Diane is always the antidote.

INDEX

ABOUT THE AUTHOR

STEPHEN FRIED is an award-winning journalist and a *New York Times* bestselling author, who teaches at Columbia University in the School of Journalism and the Department of Psychiatry, and at the University of Pennsylvania.

He is the author of the acclaimed biographies *Appetite for America: Fred Harvey and the Business of Civilizing the Wild West—One Meal at a Time*, which was adapted into a PBS documentary, and *Thing of Beauty: The Tragedy of Supermodel Gia*, which inspired the Emmy-winning film *Gia* and introduced the word "fashionista" to the English language. He is the coauthor, with Congressman Patrick Kennedy, of *A Common Struggle: A Personal Journey Through the Past and Future of Mental Illness and Addiction*, and his other books include *Bitter Pills: Inside the Hazardous World of Legal Drugs*, *The New Rabbi*, and *Husbandry*.

A two-time winner of the National Magazine Award, he has written frequently for *Vanity Fair*, *GQ*, *The Washington Post Magazine*, *Smithsonian*, *Rolling Stone*, *Glamour*, and *Philadelphia* magazine.

Fried and his wife, author Diane Ayres, live in Philadelphia, just a few blocks from where Dr. Benjamin Rush lived and the nation was born.

ABOUT THE TYPE

This book was set in Caslon, a typeface first designed in 1722 by William Caslon (1692–1766). Its widespread use by most English printers in the early eighteenth century soon supplanted the Dutch typefaces that had formerly prevailed. The roman is considered a "workhorse" typeface due to its pleasant, open appearance, while the italic is exceedingly decorative.

By *New York Times* bestselling author

Stephen Fried

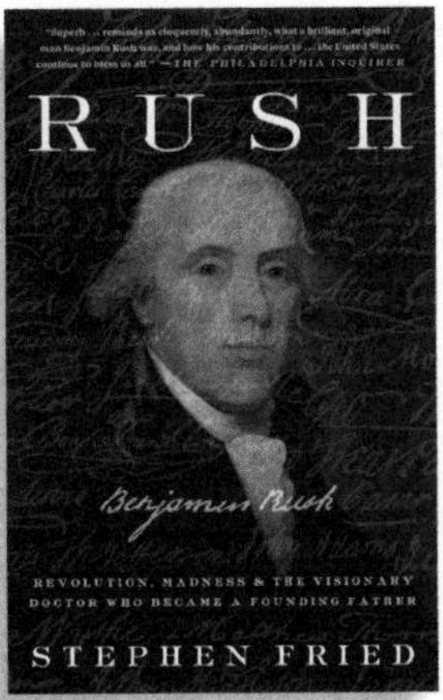

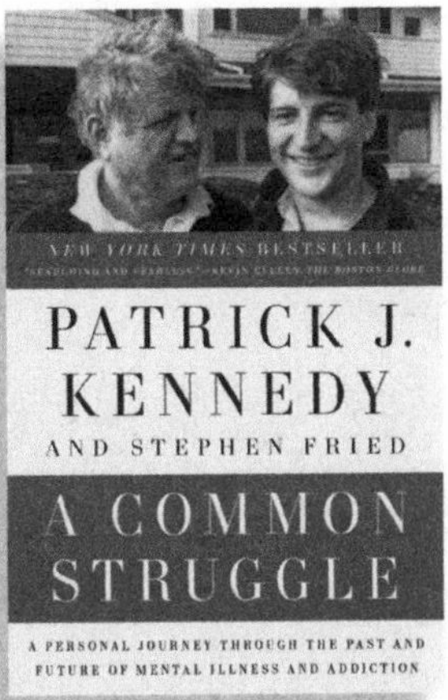

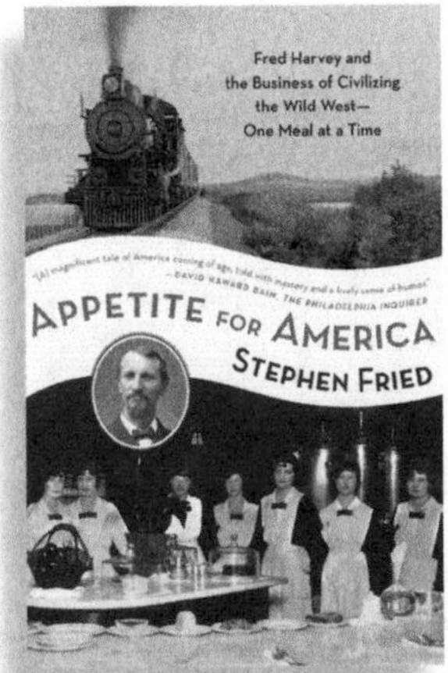

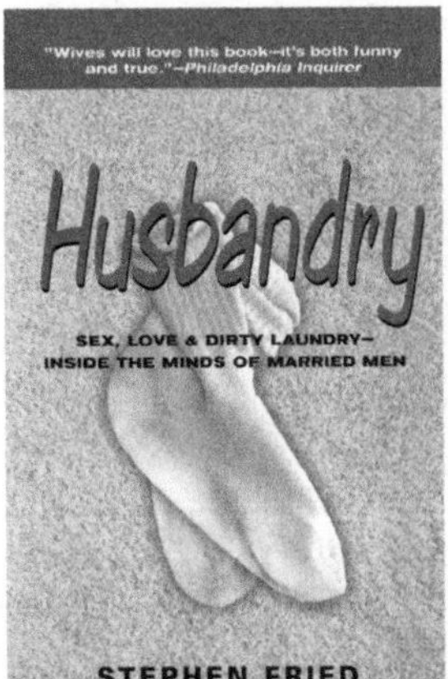

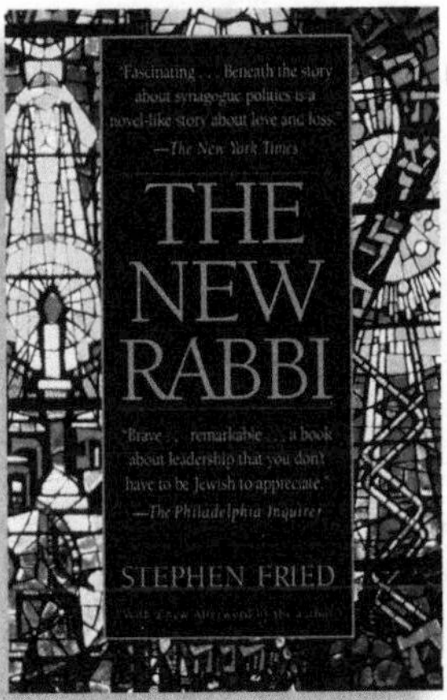

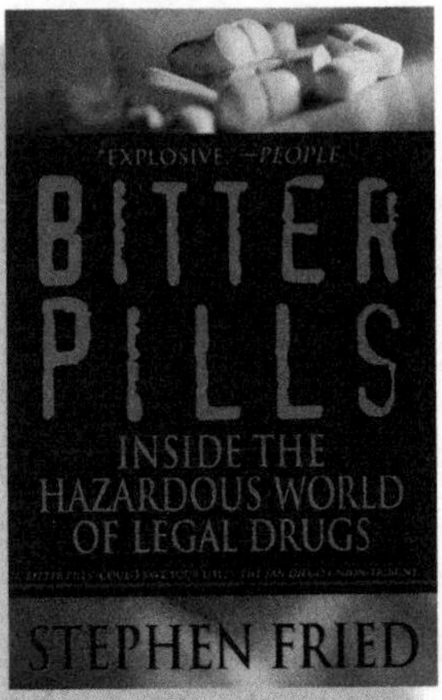

Available wherever books are sold

B\D\W\Y | blue rider press | BANTAM